BISHOPS AT LARGE

BISHOPS AT LARGE

by

PETER F. ANSON

with an introduction by

THE REV. HENRY ST. JOHN, M.A., O.P.

"Likewise Bishops, being principal pastors,
are either at large or else with restraint; at large,
when the subject of their regiment is indefinite
and not tied to a certain place. Bishops with
restraint are they whose regiment over the
church is contained within some definite
local compass, beyond which compass
their jurisdiction reacheth not."

—*Hooker, Ecclesiastical Polity, Bk. VIII, Sect. II*

the apocryphile press
BERKELEY, CA
www.apocryphile.org

apocryphile press
BERKELEY, CA

Apocryphile Press
1700 Shattuck Ave #81
Berkeley, CA 94709
www.apocryphile.org

First published in London, England by Faber and Faber, 1964.
First US edition published by October House, 1965.
Copyright 1964 by Peter F. Anson.
First Apocryphile edition, 2006.

Printed in the United States of America

Paperback edition: ISBN 0-9771461-8-9
Hardcover edition: ISBN 0-9771461-9-7

ADDENDA AND CORRIGENDA

pp. 239, 240, 241. for 'Orthodox Patriarch of Antioch', read 'Syrian Jacobite'.

p. 248   The North American bishops of Dr. Boltwood's organisation are now different from those given in para. 2.

pp. 248, 250, 498. In July 1964 Mar Georgius revived the American Patriarchate of the Catholicate of the West, formerly held by Ortega-Maxey and Wadle under the title of Malaga, with the nomination of Dr. E. N. Enochs as Patriarch of Los Angeles.

p. 256 1. 11. For 1940 read 1930.

p. 264 1. 6. For Free Protestant Episcopal Church of England read Evangelical Church of England.

p. 314 1. 20. Mgr Erni denies that he gave Mar Johannes Maria a third consecration on May 2, 1957.

p. 321 1. 2 from foot. After World War II Bishop Giebner became a Roman Catholic. He was re-ordained *sub conditione* with special permission to retain his wife and is still working as a priest in the diocese of Paderborn.

p. 380 n. 1, p. 485 n. 1 and caption to upper illustration facing page 520. Bishop Pitt-Kethley denies that he was ever British representative of the Universal Life Foundation.

p. 385 para. 2. Bishop Turner denies that he urged his Primate to adopt the style of Patriarch, or that Bishop Regnier encouraged it.

p. 385 n. 1. Bishop Turner also denies that the Order of Christian Unity was founded after he broke off relations with Archbishop Ignatius Carolus.

p. 389 n. 2. Dr. Cato-Symonds has ceased to be a member of the Hierarchy of the Old Holy Catholic Church.

p. 390.   In December 1963 Dr. Bruce broke off relations with the Old Holy Catholic Church and resumed the rank of a simple presbyter. It is understood that he has since been reconciled with the Old Roman Catholic Church (English Rite).

p. 391.   Bishop Erni has consecrated (or re-consecrated) Enos and Canivet. Other men, mostly French ex-Catholic priests, have been raised to the episcopate for the work of the Ecumenical League.

p. 419 n. 3. Bishop Mickiewicz died in 1923, not 1925.

p. 420.   Add n. Brown is said to have consecrated on January 1, 1927, W. D. Ortega-Maxey, subsequently re-consecrated by Brothers, March 24, 1927, and by Newman (Mar Georgius), June 6, 1946.

5

Addenda and Corrigenda

p. 438.   It appears that various men were reincardinated by Marchenna into the Old Roman Catholic Church in 1962 but later renounced their affiliations and are each operating independently. The 1964 *Yearbook of American Churches* gives the following for the North American Catholic Church: Archbishop E. A. Rogers (Primate Metropolitan); Archbishop J. H. Rogers; Bishop George Koerner; and Bishop Joseph Kelly.

p. 444.   Facing illustration.
          For Prince of Saxe-Noricum read Duke.

p. 467.   Mar Marcus Valerius died March 29, 1964.

pp. 486–7. Mgr Glenn denies that he was a member of the Old Catholic Orthodox Church, Superior of a Society of layfolk or *founder* of the Catholic Episcopal Church.

pp. 502–538. The information given about miscellaneous churches in the U.S.A. and Canada should be checked with the 1964 *Yearbook of American Churches*, although the editor stresses that 'ordinarily . . . it is not possible to verify the information by consulting published sources or other means.' The documentation for the American Churches is often confusing and contradictory and it is impossible to guarantee accuracy.

p. 504 1. 4 from foot. Read Parsell for Persell.

p. 507 para. 2. Allen Grover was not raised to the hierarchy of the American Orthodox Church until November 14, 1937.

p. 518 n. 1. Bishop Feldmann is still alive. He returned to Poland and re-joined the Mariavites of Plock.

pp. 534–5. It appears that the Brazilian Church is now linked with similar bodies in the Argentine, Bolivia, Chile, Panama, Paraguay, Peru, Uruguay and Venezuela. The 'Senior-Bishop' is Antidio J. Vargas (Santa Catarina, Brazil), who claims about sixteen bishops under his jurisdiction in South America. Bishop Ferraz was reconciled with the Holy See in 1960, when his episcopal orders were recognised as valid. He is attached to the diocese of Sao Paolo.

p. 541 n. 2. Reference should be made to Michel Bellin, formerly a priest of the Sacred Heart (Saint-Quentin). He claims that in 1950 he was mystically consecrated at Sorrento, by the Holy Trinity, SS. Peter and Paul, and the Archangel Michael. It was revealed to him that he was the 'Elect of Heaven' and 'Supreme Pontiff of Divine Love'. With his 'vatican' in Lorraine, Pope Clement XV has followers in France, Belgium and Canada. He is strongly opposed to the Liturgical Movement and at the 1963 'Council of Lyons' (where he was assisted by his 'College of Cardinals') decided to permit the ordination of women.

To
THE REV. HENRY R. T. BRANDRETH, O.G.S.
without whose help it
would have been impossible to write
this book

CONTENTS

Contents

Contents

Contents

12

ILLUSTRATIONS

13

Illustrations

INTRODUCTION

HENRY ST JOHN, O.P.

In *Bishops at Large* Mr Peter Anson has carried out a detailed and thorough exploration of some little-known by-paths in nineteenth and twentieth century ecclesiastical life. He is not an absolute pioneer in this work; others have preceded him and given him assistance, to whom he makes due acknowledgment of debt and tribute of gratitude in his Foreword. The work he has himself put into his explorations, however, is tremendous, and its result is the setting out of the story he has to tell with a completeness never before achieved.

The story is one of the strangest and most fantastic religious movements to be found in the whole range of what may be described, in general terms, as the erratic 'goings on' of the ecclesiastical underworld. The use of the word underworld in this context must be taken as connoting ecclesiastical eccentricity rather than roguery or crime, though neither of the latter is wholly absent from its records. The story is closely though not exclusively connected with movements of a 'Catholic' type mainly deriving from dissatisfied and unstable elements in Catholicism or Anglo-Catholicism. They stand as a rule for 'Catholicism' without the Pope, but their preoccupation, amounting to obsession, is the recovery of Christian unity by the widespread, and, in effect, indiscriminate propagation of 'valid' episcopacy and priesthood.

In almost every case the leaders of these multiple movements have been at pains to obtain episcopal consecration, from sources often remote and seldom wholly unquestionable, which they hoped would be indisputable. Having obtained episcopal character they proceeded to found a 'Church' based upon it, and their own particular version of what true Catholic orthodoxy is. In this way, so the visionary hope takes shape in the minds of these dreamers, *their* Church will become the centre and foundation upon which the unity of Christ's Church could be re-built.

15

Introduction

Unfortunately, nearly every Church so founded in the past hundred years has proved to be fissiparous, splitting by mutual excommunication or repudiation into new Churches, multiplying in number as they become reduced in membership. In all this there is a queer mixture of the irrepressible, the ridiculous and the pathetic; naïve goodness and sincere idealism, unconscious vanity and, at times, conscious roguery: its promoters frequently unstable to a degree, eccentric in some cases to the point of craziness, moving in a dream-world of unreality. A marked characteristic of this dream-world is a *folie de grandeur* of high-sounding titles and more than extravagant pretensions; these generally in inverse ratio to the number of their adherents and the size of the conventicles in which they worship and still worship, with elaborate ritual and ceremonial.

There is considerable irony in the historical fact that had St Cyprian's common sense and logical view that heretical baptism was wholly invalid won its way in the mind of the Church, bishops at large would have been impossible; no one would have believed in their orders but themselves, and excommunication would have rendered orders immediately invalid, with the problem of knowing where authority lay as the only way of settling the problem of validity. St Cyprian held that it was obvious that a sacrament apart from the authority and communion of the Catholic Church was *ipso facto* invalid and must be repeated. He was opposed in this by the contemporary Bishop of Rome, Pope Stephen, who believed in the contrary view as an apostolic tradition handed down in his see. This view became an insight in the mind of the Church and and grew in influence till it possessed the whole of the West. In the East the Cyprianic view held its grounds and survived until modern times, though it has now virtually disappeared. Nowadays, the Orthodox do not re-baptise or re-ordain; their acceptance of heretical or schismatic baptism and orders, if validly performed, is covered by the theory of 'economy'.

Today we see more clearly the leading of the Holy Spirit in the Church's farseeing but apparently illogical insight, God wills all men to be saved and come to a knowledge of the truth. The sacrament of baptism is the sacrament which gives entrance to the Church, and the Church is the sole ark of salvation to all. The saving sacrament then must be made as available as it can possibly be. The same insight, under the direction of the Holy Spirit, has led to the development of the doctrine of baptism by desire both

Introduction

explicit and implicit. It is of course unfortunate that a view of sacramental validity that confers so wide-embracing a benefit beyond the visible limits of the Body of Christ on earth should also be open to the abuse of treating valid orders and sacraments as the sole mark of the true Church, whatever the aberrations and eccentricities of those who possess them may be. But the ways of God are not always as neatly logical as the human mind would like to make them.

It may well be asked whether the disentangling of the story of these intricate 'goings on' that Mr Anson has accomplished with such skill and labour is worth the trouble taken over it. For some perhaps his book would prove a boring recital of unfamiliar and puzzling complications. But for those who are deeply concerned for Christian unity, and as deeply interested in the complex psychological factors, our own and other people's, which lie behind the theological divergences of divided Christians; for those too who realize the necessity of tackling eirenically the problems of authority, which are responsible for these divergences in belief, there can be much food for thought. Mr Anson's story shows us a *reductio ad absurdum* of the divinely ordained hierarchical structure of the Church constituted by apostolic succession, when divorced from almost every consideration but a mechanical conception of validity.

The obsession of the 'bishops at large' and their followers with the validity of orders has brought them to the belief that such validity is the sole hall-mark of the nature of the Church and its authority. *Ubi ordines validi, ibi ecclesia* is the principle upon which they all of them consistently act with a determined conviction. The result of this action is that they are in effect reduced to saying 'Get valid orders and you can choose what you believe'. They are unaware that they are saying this, and consequently lay great stress on the supreme importance of an orthodoxy, which turns out to be no more than their own particular and sometimes variable 'doxy'.

What they have forgotten in their often wild and eccentric way is that even a valid apostolic succession is of small value unless it is possessed by a Believing Community that is a visible organic society, divinely preserved from the loss of its structural unity. This unity preserves and is preserved by its *sensus fidelium* and by the teaching authority of its united episcopate. This is the essential nature of the Church as taught by the Eastern Orthodox Church

17

and the Roman Catholic Church in common, in accordance with historic tradition from the earliest times.

It is true, of course, that East and West are divided on the question of the place of the Papacy within the universal episcopate, but that is a domestic problem, concerned only with the full nature of apostolic succession as Christ ordained it. For the Eastern Orthodox and the Roman Catholic Church, organic unity and the indivisibility of the episcopate are essential. For both, schism cannot be within the Church, it is necessarily a cutting off from the Church, which leaves the Church undivided because indivisible. Only a Church of this nature can speak with a single voice concerning its own nature and authority and can claim infallibility for its own united teaching. This both Eastern Orthodox and Roman Catholic Churches, alone amongst the Churches of Christendom, do. The Churches sprung from the Reformation all hold the Church Christ founded to be a divided entity. Until its divided parts come together into a single organic entity it can have no single authoritative voice to speak to the world or to witness to the nature of its own constitution and teaching authority.

This is the crux of the problem of Christian unity. The ultimate alternatives in its solution are, either that the Church of Christ is an organic structural unity, kept so under God by its full possession of apostolic succession, or that the Scriptures, apart from the Church, are supreme, and the Church is the gathered community of those whose faith is drawn direct from the written Word, without the *necessity* of human intermediary. In the first alternative, the episcopate, as a function of the Believing Community, decisively interprets the inspired Scriptures, which are its possession in Christ; this is the work of the continuous witness of Tradition, embodying, by the Holy Spirit, the mind of Christ. In the second alternative, where there is no authoritative episcopate, individual faith is in the last resort alone authoritative within the believing community and alone interprets God's Word to men. This is the Catholic-Protestant dialectic, which Christendom must resolve if unity is to be achieved.

For other Churches, such as those forming the Utrecht Union of Old Catholics, the Churches of the Anglican Communion, and the Scandinavian Churches, each in its present state is a divided entity, so the authoritative functioning of their respective episcopates as a teaching *magisterium* in the manner of Rome and the Eastern Churches, is not possible. Still less is this possible in some other

Introduction

Lutheran Churches and certain Methodist bodies in North America which, although having bishops, do not claim apostolic succession in the traditional sense.

If Mr Anson's book succeeds, as it should if read with understanding, in directing its readers to this crucial issue in the problem of Christian unity by its *reductio ad absurdum* of the position of bishops at large, if it points to the fundamental reason why they are at large, it will prove of considerable value in the elucidation of the fundamentals of the ecumenical dialogue, and will be yet another sign-post on the road to unity.

FOREWORD

The byways of religion began to arouse my curiosity more than half a century ago. Even in my prep school days I was swopping sects with a boy who shared this hobby, which in my case was combined with collecting butterflies, theatre programmes, the names of railway engines, the movements of the squadrons of the Royal Navy, and those of theatrical touring companies. The child is the father of the man, and as I have nearly reached my second childhood, this book may well be the disastrous effect of a bug which got into my system in the reign of Queen Victoria.

As time rolled on I continued to be interested in obscure religious bodies, in spite of the fact that at the age of twenty-four I joined the least obscure of all churches—one whose membership on earth is estimated at 500,000,000. The smaller the sect, the greater the fascination, and what wonderful names I added to my collection. Living for more than a quarter of a century in a fishing port on the north-east coast of Scotland, where Papists were few and far between, I had every opportunity to investigate Jehovah's Witnesses, the Plymouth Brethren (Open and Close), the Disciples of Christ, not to mention the different species of Presbyterians to be found in the remoter parts of Scotland.

But I had never thought of compiling a catalogue, so to say, of the innumerable bodies, all claiming to be catholic and apostolic, boasting that their bishops and priests have valid orders, which have sprung up like mushrooms both in Europe and North America since the eighteen-sixties, until Mr Charles Monteith of Faber and Faber (at the suggestion of Mr Arthur Calder-Marshall) asked in the spring of 1961 if I would care to do so. My immediate reaction was to wonder if it would be possible to lay my hands on enough material about these organizations to make a readable book.

The first person to be consulted was obviously the Rev. Henry R. T. Brandreth, author of *Episcopi Vagantes and the Anglican*

Church, and Chaplain of St Georges, Paris. This was the only comprehensive source of reference, but it was long since out of date
and out of print. A revised edition was published in the autumn of
1961. He replied that he would be delighted to help me to clothe
the dry bones of his little book with flesh and blood, but explained
that the material he was willing to place at my disposal was so vast
that it would be impossible to forward it from France to Scotland.
He invited me to stay with him in Paris, so that I could work on
the spot.

When I arrived there I was confronted by such a pile of books,
pamphlets, brochures, leaflets, and files of letters, that I hardly
knew where to start. My host had been collecting all this data for
more than a quarter of a century. I returned home with half a
dozen notebooks filled with scribblings, doubtful if I should ever
be able to reduce them into some kind of order. Since then Fr
Brandreth has taken endless trouble to verify countless details and
dates. Having completed the original draft, I returned to Paris to
prune and polish the typescript.

The least I can do to express my thanks to my host and willing
collaborator is to dedicate this book to him, for without his help
during the past two years it would have been almost impossible to
write it.

The second and equally generous collaborator to be thanked is
the Rev. Alban Cockerham, a priest of the Liberal Catholic Church.
His knowledge of all the religious bodies mentioned in these pages
is encyclopedic. It was seldom that I asked a question that he
failed to answer, and invariably in much greater detail than I expected. He lent me much rare material, also some of the photographs which have been reproduced among the illustrations.

I was lucky enough to be introduced to Frederic Adams,
D.Litt., who gave me first-hand reminiscences of Archbishop
A. H. Mathew, and many more of the leading personalities of the
ecclesiastical borderland of the past fifty years, with whom he had
been personally acquainted at one time or another. Both Fr Alban
Cockerham and Dr Adams corrected every chapter before the final
revision was made, and saved me from making many false or
misleading statements.

Also deserving of special thanks is Mar Georgius, Patriarch of
Glastonbury and Catholicos of the West, who found time to put
the finest of combs through every line, and to add many valuable
footnotes. Not content with this, His Beatitude presented me with

Foreword

an almost complete set of his numerous publications, the titles of which are given in the bibliography. He also lent me most of the photographs of prelates which certainly add to the interest of this volume. His courtesy in this respect is remarkable, because in his position he might have been expected to complain about my treatment of the subject—and especially of himself in chapter ten.

I am specially grateful to Archbishop Wilfrid A. Barrington-Evans and Bishop Geoffrey P. T. Paget King. Each of them, representing two tiny rival branches of the Old Roman Catholic Church in England, with diametrically opposite points of view, criticized what I had written about them, with the utmost courtesy and friendliness, going to no end of trouble to ensure accuracy of detail in many controversial points. Meeting Mgr Gerard G. Shelley, Archbishop of Caer-Glow, at a luncheon party in Paris, also helped me to understand better the stormy history of the many churches claiming the Mathew succession.

Another rich and unsuspected source of material was placed at my disposal by Frederick Brittain, Litt.D., M.A., Fellow Praelector of Jesus College, Cambridge. Here I found a collection of letters to and from Archbishop A. H. Mathew, some of which throw new light on this enigmatic prelate, whose fantastic career is recorded in chapter six. Thanks to the Rt Rev. Mgr Joseph A. Marx, P.A., Vicar-General of the Diocese of Green Bay, Wisconsin, the chapter devoted to Joseph René Vilatte contains details of his escapades which have never been revealed so far. Then I must not forget my debt of gratitude to the Rev. Godfrey Anstruther, O.P., who must have spent many hours examining Roman archives before he laid his hands on the hitherto unpublished facts about the earlier years of Julius Ferrette, the 'Bishop of Iona'.

I also owe much to the Rev. J. G. Gerard C. Irvine, M.A., Vicar of St Cuthbert's, Philbeach Gardens, for his painstaking revision of the typescript. A second and more drastic pruning and polishing was made by Dom Sylvester Houédard, O.S.B., of Prinknash Abbey. His rare knowledge of the byways of church history led to the discovery of many wrong dates and tiny details.

A final revision was undertaken by Mr Allan W. Campbell, M.A., LL.B., who saved me from more than one appalling mistake, thanks to his familiarity with legal terminology and the subject-matter.

Among others who have supplied information are: H.S.B. Mar Joannes Maria Van Assendelft-Altland; Most Rev. Mar Marcus

Foreword

Valerius; Most Rev. Archbishop Ignatius Carolus; Rt Rev. Bishop R. Dominic Bruce; Rt Rev. Bishop Julien Erni; Rt Rev. Bishop Francis E. Glenn; Rt Rev. Dr W. B. Crow, Ph.D., D.Sc.; Rt Rev. C. Cato-Symonds, D.D.; Rt Rev. Mgr Ivan de la Thibauderie; Very Rev. W. H. de Voil, M.A., Ph.D.; Very Rev. Provost G. J. C. Douglas, M.A.; Rev. Canon Edward Every, B.A.; Rev. A. St Denis Fry; Rev. René Caflisch; Rev. G. B. Chambers; Rev. Marion A. Habig, O.F.M.; Rev. W. Walton T. Hannah, M.A.; Rev. Pedro Rivera, S.J.; Rev. L. H. M. Smith; Rev. F. T. W. Smith; Rev. J. Colin Stephenson, M.A., M.B.E.; Rev. Odo J. Zimmerman, O.S.B.; Higoumen Barnabas; Mr Donald Attwater; Mr A. Calder-Marshall, B.A., F.R.S.L.; Mr J. Mark M. Dalby; Mr N. A. M. Francis; Mr James B. Gillespie; Mr William W. Kenawell; Mr Archdale A. King; Mr Kenneth Leech; Mr John Pinnington; Mr L. C. Shepperd; Mr J. M. D. Smith; Mr W. J. Whalen; Mr Michael Windeatt; Mr Cecil Woolf, and Miss Mary A. Ever—to mention only some of my correspondents during the past two years.

The subject-matter of this book is schism; a noun derived from the Greek *skhisma*, meaning a rent or split. It deals in particular with rents or tears made in the garment of the Bride of Christ during the past hundred years, all of which resemble each other more or less, having been made for the most part by men who became dissatisfied with this or that form of organized Christianity, resulting in deliberate and formal separation from the unity of the Church, or from bodies which were already in schism. In the language of theology and canon law, schism is the rupture of ecclesiastical union and unity, i.e. the act by which one of the faithful severs as far as is in him lies the ties which bind him to the Church, and make him a member of the mystical body of Christ, or the state of dissociation or separation which is the result of that act. Human nature being what it is, schisms have been a persistent feature in the history of the Christian Church from the fourth century, but almost all the earlier ones were for dogmatic reasons, just as were those of the sixteenth century under the leadership of the Protestant reformers. Few of the bodies dealt with in these pages were the outcome of theological scruples; almost all arose because the founders found fault with the particular organization to which they belonged and wanted to remedy the situation. The only way open to them was to set up a rival church.

This book should be read purely as an historical study. I have

24

Foreword

tried to refrain from passing judgment on any of the founders of splinter churches or their followers, for it would be presumptuous for me, as a Catholic layman, to express personal opinions on actions which it is difficult for me to appreciate or to understand. Assumptions and values are outside my province. My object has been to record facts, and let the reader form his or her opinion from them. Accordingly, some readers may feel that these autocephalous churches (as they now prefer to call themselves) are edifying examples of true Christian liberty; others that they are merely symptoms of tragic revolt against authority, and a warning to those who are tempted to follow in the footsteps of these free-lance ecclesiastics.

The reader will find that the establishment of most of the nearly 150 new churches with which I deal has been hailed by publicity, suggesting that at long last the panacea had been discovered to cure all diseases in corrupt Christendom. Here was THE church for which mankind had been waiting for centuries. In some cases, as will be seen, the churches never got farther than the architect's plans, sections, and elevations; existing only in the vivid imagination of their respective progenitors and a handful of disciples. In other instances the walls arose, but the foundations gave way, and the flimsy superstructure collapsed like a castle made of a pack of cards. Again and again one is reminded of what Lewis Carroll wrote:

Humpty Dumpty sat on a wall,
Humpty Dumpty had a great fall;
All the king's horses and all the king's men
Couldn't put Humpty Dumpty together again.

Indeed, so many of these so-called autocephalous churches of the past hundred years belong to the world of *Alice in Wonderland* or *Alice Through the Looking Glass*—hence their fascination to the student of the byways of ecclesiastical history. 'Curiouser and curiouser!' cried Alice. Again and again we come across founders, of whom it could be said:

Tweedledum and Tweedledee
Agreed to have a battle;
For Tweedledum said Tweedledee
Had spoiled his nice new rattle.

I fear that some of my readers as they skim through the stories of these dissident bodies, which in some cases are stranger than fiction, may be tempted to say:

> *Twinkle, twinkle, little bat!*
> *How I wonder what you're at!*
> *Up above the world you fly!*
> *Like a teatray in the sky.*

They will meet a long procession of founders and disciples from the eighteen-sixties onwards all crying out: 'Will you, won't you, will you, won't you, will you join the dance?'

But to be serious: quite a number of the founders of these auto-cephalous churches really *did* believe that the end justified the means when they set up schismatic bodies. One and all discovered what they felt were more than adequate reasons for adding to the confusion of Christendom. They may have been right, or they may have been wrong; it is for the reader, not the author, to give a final judgment in any instance. 'And so, methinks, it is here; to expatiate, to digress, to indulge curiosity on every point, is for the historian.'[1]

Four of the founders of the groups of churches dealt with in these pages were lapsed Roman Catholics: Julius Ferrette, Joseph J. Overbeck, Joseph René Vilatte, and Arnold Harris Mathew. Each felt that he had found sufficient reasons for defying the canon law of the Latin Church which states that if one, after the reception of baptism, while retaining the name of Christian, refuses submission to the Supreme Pontiff or rejects communion with the members of the Church subject to the latter, he is a schismatic.[2] Each of these men was prepared to face the ecclesiastical penalty known as excommunication, which excluded them from the communion of the faithful, and imposed on them other deprivations and disabilities, involving the loss of all ordinary jurisdiction and incapacity to receive any ecclesiastical benefices or dignities whatsoever. They knew that to communicate *in sacris* with schismatics, e.g. to receive the sacraments at the hands of their ministers, to assist at services in their places of worship, is strictly forbidden to the faithful.

Other founders were disgruntled Anglicans, who were so sure that they were in the right and that the bishops were in the wrong that they had the courage to defy the *Constitutions and Canons*

[1] II Machabees 2, 31.
[2] Canon 1325.

26

Foreword

Ecclesiastical passed by the Convocations of Canterbury and York in 1604 and 1605, one of which stated:

'Whosoever shall hereafter separate themselves from the Communion of Saints, as it is approved by the Apostles' Rules, in the Church of England, and combine themselves together in a new brotherhood, accounting the Christians, who are conformable to the doctrine, government, rites, and ceremonies of the Church of England, to be profane, and unmeet for them to join with in Christian profession; let them be excommunicated *ipso facto*, and not restored, but by the Archbishop, after their repentance, and public revocation of such their wicked errors.'[1]

In North America some of the progenitors of these dissident bodies have been members of one or other of the Eastern Churches. They, too, were prepared to face excommunication *ipso facto* for schism, together with penalties similar to those incurred by Roman Catholics and Anglicans. Nearly all the founders of little autocephalous and often heretical churches on the continent of Europe have been lapsed Roman Catholics. A few of them in England have previously belonged to some nonconformist body, who, feeling the need for more ceremonial in public worship, did not see their way to enter into communion with either Canterbury, Rome, or any of the Eastern Churches. The only thing to do was to found a new church.

It will be noticed that hardly any of these founders have heard a clear call to revive primitive Christianity like the great sixteenth-century reformers, e.g. Calvin, Luther and Zwingli; or their fore-runners, Wycliffe, Waldo and Huss. In most cases they have been quite content with the later developments of ecclesiastical polity, ritual and ceremonial. They have not been satisfied with being simple superintendents or overseers of their flocks, which, after all, is the meaning of the Greek word *episcopos*. In almost every instance they have taken over the late medieval or post-Tridentine conception of prelacy—lock, stock and barrel. This, of course, has involved wearing vestments and other regalia in the Baroque, Gothic Revival, or Oriental fashions. They have loved devising elaborate names for their churches, and in some cases have changed them frequently. Quite often, so great was the urge to stress that they were major prelates, that they have given themselves impressive ecclesiastical titles, either eastern or western—Catholicos, Hierarch, Mar, Metropolitan, Monsignor, Pontifex, Primate,

[1] *Canon IX*, Authors of Schism in the Church of England censured.

27

Patriarch, and so on. The imitation of Christ has moved some of the more ambitious to procure splendid patents of nobility, usually foreign. This has enabled their followers to address them as Count, Marquis, Duke, Prince, and even Imperator.[1] University degrees have been acquired from obscure sources; the more degrees the better for a Metropolitan, Primate, or Patriarch. One or two, having rejected papal infallibility, have claimed to be infallible when speaking *ex cathedra*; excommunicating those with whom they disagreed on the least provocation. The display of splendour by many of the prelates mentioned in this book certainly adds to their interest, and none of my readers will feel that they lack colour and glamour, even if in some cases the gilt soon wore off the gingerbread.

It would have saved some of these priest founders of autocephalous churches so much worry had they found reasons for availing themselves of the powers now granted to priests of the Latin Rite to confer the sacrament of Confirmation. Again they might well have gone even further and agreed with certain modern theologians that in exceptional circumstances the Pope can give faculties to presbyters to ordain deacons and priests. Such being the case, granted that they were certain of the validity of their orders as a priest, they might have argued that there was no necessity for them to receive episcopal consecration.[2]

Schisms are easily made, but very difficult to heal. It will be seen how few of the bodies dealt with in these pages have been reconciled with any of the historic churches of the East or the West. There are, however, some rare instances of priests who have repented of schism, and Thomas Merton recalls one whom he met at the Cistercian Abbey of Gethsemani about 1941, and writes:

'The poor man, for some reason, had not lived as a good priest. In the end, his mistake had caught up with him. He had come into contact with some schismatics, in a sect known as "the Old Catholics", and these people persuaded him to leave the Church and come over to them. And when he did so, they made him an

---

[1] Some of these prelates remind one of His Serene Highness Gregor I, Sovereign Prince of the Independent State of Poyais, Grand Master of the Order of the Knights of the Green Cross, Cazique of the Poyer Nation, who appeared in England in the reign of William IV, and established his legation in London. His kingdom proved to be a deserted and pestilential swamp on the coast of Nicaragua.

[2] cf. H. Lennerz, S.J., *De Sacramento Ordinis* (Pontificio Universitas Gregoriana, Rome, 1953), p. 144. 'Et sic melius videtur concludere: Summi Pontifices hanc facultatem contulerunt simplicibus sacerdotibus; ergo hoc potuerunt; ergo ex concessione Summi Pontifici presbyter potest esse minister ordinationi diaconatus et presbyteratus.'

archbishop. I suppose he enjoyed the dignity and the novelty of it for a while; but the whole thing was obviously silly. So he gave it up and came back. And now here he was in the monastery, serving Mass every morning for a young Trappist priest who scarcely had the oils of his ordination dry on his hands.'[1]

Before getting on with the story it may be worth explaining that almost all the sects about which I have written have been connected either directly or indirectly with previous rents in the garment of the Bride of Christ. In some instances they are their by-products.

First came the schism of Utrecht in 1702, completed in 1713, when the majority of the Dutch bishops and clergy refused to accept the bull *Unigenitus* condemning Jansenism. The final break with the Holy See took place in 1724. A series of small schisms broke the unity of the Church in France later on; the first caused by the Civil Constitution of the clergy in 1790, followed by the so-called *Petite Église* formed in 1801 by groups who were dissatisfied with the Concordat drawn up between Pius VII and Napoleon Bonaparte, then First Consul, which led to the formal restoration of the Catholic Church in France after the Revolution. The last priest of the *Petite Église* died in 1847, but the schism still lingers on. In 1831 another schismatic body was founded by the abbé Chatel, but it was formally suppressed by the Government eleven years later.

Similar splits occurred in Germany after 1844, their two chief leaders being Johannes Ronge and John Czerski, both of them Catholic priests. The bodies they formed, never very numerous, soon declined, yet in a way they helped to create a mentality which made it easy for many more priests in Germany and Switzerland to throw off the yoke of the Holy See after the definition of the doctrine of papal infallibility by the First Vatican Council in 1870. Such was the origin of the Old Catholic Churches on the continent of Europe, which today claim a membership of 600,000 in the Netherlands, Germany, Switzerland, Austria, Czechoslovakia, Croatia, and Poland. They have given rise to several more schismatic bodies in the course of the present century.

But very few of the bodies dealt with in these pages have the right to call themselves 'Old Catholic', since only two or three of them are in communion with the Utrecht Union of Old Catholics, which has been in full communion with the Church of England

[1] *Elected Silence* (1949), p. 277.

Foreword

since 1931, and has been formally accepted since then by other parts of the Anglican Communion.[1] The former make up a sort of undefined no-man's-land of Christendom. Many of the little bodies lead a lonely existence, and are apparently quite satisfied with their isolation. Others dream of achieving eventual reunion with either the Western Patriarchate or one of the Eastern Churches not in communion with Rome, but are very far from achieving it. Taken as a whole, it is a dark, mysterious, shadowy, and unsubstantial world, often formed of 'such stuff as dreams are made on'—even the 'baseless fabric of a vision'. No matter: very often dreams and visions are more exciting than achievements; and if this book has any interest, it is because it deals more with reveries than with actions—golden dreams of the past, the present, and the future.[2]

Lastly I must warn readers of this book that by the time it is in their hands, there is no certainty that the information about the present state of any of the autocephalous churches dealt with will be correct. For it would be true enough to say of some of them (in the words of St Paul to the Ephesians) that they are 'like storm-tossed sailors, driven before the wind of each new doctrine that human subtlety, human skill in fabricating lies, may propound'. Stability has never been characteristic of bishops at large, or of the churches they have founded.

PETER F. ANSON.

Ferryden, Montrose, Angus.
May 1961–November 1963.

---

[1] *Holland* (12,000), Archdiocese of Utrecht, Dioceses of Haarlem and Dventer; *Austria* (40,000), one bishop; *Czechoslovakia* (5,000), Provisional Administrator; *Germany* (40,000), two bishops; *Poland* one bishop; *Switzerland* (28,000), one bishop; *Yugoslavia*, one bishop; *Polish National Catholic Church of America* (275,000) Prime-Bishop, and four other bishops. Also in full communion with the Protestant Episcopal Church in the U.S.A. are the *Philippine Independent Church* (2,500,000); the *Spanish Reformed Church* (800); and the *Lusitanian Church* (Portugal) (1,200). then the Polish, Philippine, Spanish and Portuguese Churches are described in chapter XI.

[2] None of the churches in this book appear among 'Other Religious Denominations' in *Whitaker's Almanack*. To show how little either the prelates or their places of worship count numerically in the religious life of London—or in any city of the world for that matter—it is worth mentioning that the long and comprehensive list printed in *The Post Office London Directory* includes only two of those mentioned in this book: the Liberal Catholic Cathedral, Caledonian Road, and St Andrew's Collegiate Church (Free Protestant Episcopal), South Tottenham. A possible reason why none of these 'autocephalous churches' represented in the London area advertise their Sunday services in *The Times* (along with Anglicans, Roman Catholics, Christian Scientists, and miscellaneous Protestant bodies) may be that their pro-cathedrals or churches are merely rooms in private houses. It is true that few churches of the Latin rite trouble to advertise in *The Times*.

CHAPTER I

Jules Ferrette, Mar Julius, Bishop of Iona, and alleged Patriarchal Legate of the Syrian Jacobite Church for Western Europe

A friendly intercourse between Anglicans and members of the Eastern Churches had continued at intervals from early in the seventeenth century. It started with the visit paid to Alexandria in 1610 by George Sandys, son of Edwin Sandys, who was Archbishop of York from 1577 to 1588. On his return home he reported that Cyril Lucar, the future Patriarch of Constantinople, had said that the differences between English and Greek churchmen were 'all but shells', and had assured his guest that the two bodies might easily be united. This oriental ecclesiastic can have known little, however, about the post-Reformation *Ecclesia Anglicana*, but a Greek Orthodox church was opened in London in 1677, and there was talk of founding a college at Oxford for students of the Eastern Churches. Between 1701 and 1725 several Levantine bishops and archimandrites turned up in England, usually in need of money. It was seldom that they were not hospitably entertained and given generous financial assistance. In 1716 the Nonjurors began a series of long-drawn-out negotiations to link up themselves with some of the Eastern Patriarchates, including that of Moscow. These ecumenical projects were finally defeated by Dr Wake, Archbishop of Canterbury, who warned the Orthodox Patriarch of Jerusalem to beware of the Nonjurors, as being both schismatic churchmen and disloyal citizens—a danger to both the established Church and the State.

John Wesley, who had failed to get any Anglican bishops to ordain any of his Methodist preachers, managed in 1763 to persuade Erasmus, Bishop of Arcadias in Crete (then being a refugee in England), to bestow the diaconate and priesthood on two men. He also seems to have asked Erasmus to raise one or both of them to the episcopate, but 'the Greek told them that it was contrary to the rule of his church for *one* bishop to make another'. On November 19, 1764, the Bishop of Arcadias ordained William Crabb subdeacon and deacon at the chapel in Wells Street, London, and made him a priest five days later.[1]

About 1840 as an indirect result of the Tractarian movement there was a renewal of intercourse between Anglicans and Eastern Christians. William Palmer (1811–79), then a deacon and Fellow of Magdalen College, Oxford, paid the first of two visits to Russia, armed with letters of recommendation from the President of his college, Dr Martin J. Routh. Palmer's object was to explore the possibilities of intercommunion between the English and Orthodox Churches. He was disappointed that the Russian bishops refused to admit him to the sacraments. Some time after the Gorham Judgment of 1851, which suggested that the Church of England believed no longer in the doctrine of baptismal regeneration, a small group of the clergy and laity composed a Memorial addressed to the Holy Synod of the Russian Church and had it privately printed. The purpose of this document was to petition some of the Orthodox Churches to provide a spiritual home for such Anglicans as, having come to believe that their own Church was, after all, merely a Protestant sect, were unable to accept the papal claims. Dr J. M. Neale, the first part of whose *History of the Holy Eastern Church* (devoted to the Patriarchate of Antioch) had appeared in 1847, refused to have anything to do with this project. There was a scheme to establish in Edinburgh a Scoto-Orthodox chapel to be served by a priest from Moscow, but nothing came of this either.

The hope that the Church of England might be linked up some day with the Eastern and Western Patriarchates was revived in 1857 by a handful of devout High Churchmen, who, believing that prayer could still move mountains, established the Association for the Promotion of the Unity of Christendom. Six years later came the formation of the Eastern Church Association, largely through the efforts of Dr Neale. It received the blessing of at least one Oriental prelate, the Archbishop of Belgrade and Metropolitan of Serbia. It was also in 1863 that the Lower House of the Canterbury Convocation appointed a committee to communicate with the General Convention of the Protestant Episcopal Church in the U.S.A. as to intercommunion with the Russian and Greek Churches. Shortly after this it was suggested that overtures should

[1] cf. L. Tyerman, *Life and Times of Rev. J. Wesley* (1890), vol. II, pp. 486–7.

be extended to the other Eastern Churches. This was done early in 1866.

Towards the end of the summer of that same year, two years after the papal condemnation of the Association for the Promotion of the Unity of Christendom, some of its Anglican members began to have renewed hopes of a not far distant reunion with at least one of the historic Eastern Churches. For a Frenchman calling himself 'Bishop of Iona' had appeared in England, claiming that he had been consecrated by a bishop of the Syrian Jacobite Church. We do not know how much of the story he told his Anglican friends, but here is a summary of his career.[1]

Jules Ferrette appears to have been born in France of Protestant parentage. In his youth he was received into the Catholic Church, and in 1851 he entered the novitiate of the newly erected French Province of the Friars Preachers at Flavigny, of which Père Lacordaire was Provincial. Ferrette was given the religious name of Raymond. After his profession the following year he was sent to Paris and later to Grenoble for his studies in philosophy and theology. By 1854 he was in Rome, living with the Italian Dominicans at S. Maria sopra Minerva. On June 10 he received the first minor orders in the Lateran Basilica. Another Dominican student was ordained with him—Tommaso Maria Zigliara, who was created cardinal in 1879. But the observances at the Minerva were not austere enough to satisfy Frère Raymond. He obtained permission to move to S. Sabina on the Aventine where a community of ultra-strict observance *à la française* was being run by Père Jandel, who in 1850 had been made Vicar-General of the Order by Pius IX *ad bene placitum*, and who was to be elected General in 1855. S. Sabina harboured erudites but also produced prigs.

Having been given the second minor orders, and ordained subdeacon on December 23, 1854, and deacon on April 7, 1855, Frère Raymond was raised to the priesthood by Cardinal Patrizi on June 2 that same year. The ceremony took place in the Lateran Basilica. Père Raymond's first Mass was served by his fellow Dominican ordinand, Edward Howard, later Cardinal. Père Jandel then ordered Raymond to join the Dominican Mission of Mesopotamia and Kurdistan, which was founded in 1750 by the Italian friars, and which passed to the Province of France in 1856. Père

---

[1] All the facts about Ferrette's career as a Dominican have been confirmed recently by the researches of the Rev. Godfrey Anstruther, O.P., of the Instituto Storico Dominicano, in Roman archives.

Raymond sailed from Città Vecchia to Beirut on September 6, 1855, bound for Mosul on the banks of the Tigris.

A proof of this convert Dominican's eccentricity and permanent urge of edifying his brethren is found in one of his letters, where he glories in having worn 'the holy habit' among Moslems and in Jerusalem, against the advice given him before leaving Rome. By March 1856 he was quarrelling with a certain Père Mousaz. On June 17 he wrote to Père Jandel that he had given up his belief in the Catholic religion, and no longer regarded himself a member of the Order. He wrote without any bitterness, but giving the usual Protestant objections to the contrast between the corruptions of Rome and the pure Gospel religion, and saying in a vague way that a man must follow his own conscience. What was unusual was the speed with which he apostatized within a year of his ordination: the process of disillusionment commonly takes longer.

Ten years later, when obliged to answer charges made against him in England, he wrote:

'I left the Church of Rome honourably, without losing the affection and esteem of any of those who had been my brethren. I left it because my theology was radically at variance with that of the Church of Rome, but without any special reference to the reunion of Christendom, which, I confess, I have been always anxious to promote.'

In another letter to Père Jandel, Ferrette (now calling himself 'Ministère [sic] du Saint Evangile') explained that Protestantism is to Catholicism what the observance of the Dominican rule at S. Sabina is to that at the Minerva. His former brethren informed the Minister-General that after he joined them at Mosul his teaching soon became Calvinistic. In their opinion he had been much too friendly with the French Consul (himself a lapsed Catholic), and also with the staff of a Bible Society. It appears that while still wearing the Dominican habit he had written to the Anglican Bishop Gobat in Jerusalem, asking his spiritual advice. This former interdenominational pastor had been very kind, but did not encourage him to join the Church of England.[1]

On June 22, 1856, Ferrette left Mosul for Baghdad, having said that he was going to India as a Protestant missionary. He changed his mind, however, and turned his steps westward. On arriving at Damascus he offered his services to the Irish Presbyterian Mission.

[1] The joint Anglo-Prussian bishopric in Jerusalem had been set up in 1841. Gobat was nominated by the King of Prussia as the second bishop in 1846, and before his consecration by Dr Howley, Archbishop of Canterbury, was ordained priest by Dr Blomfield, Bishop of London, being already a deacon.

Jules Ferrette

After 1857 his name disappears from Dominican archives, and for the next nine years we have only his own statements to rely on, and do not know how long he stayed with the Presbyterians.[1] But he related that at the request of Lord Dufferin he had given gratuitous services to the British Government in the interests of the poor Christians of Mount Lebanon in 1860, and that they were political in form only.[2] He explained that his selection could not have been determined by his knowledge of Syriac, as that language is not spoken in Syria, and added that this mission of charity had never given a new direction to his thoughts, nor made him neglect his duties as a Minister of the Gospel. In 1865 he published an Arabic Liturgy, and had become friendly with Mar Bedros, Bishop of Emesa (Homs), of the Syrian Jacobite Church.[3]

According to a fascinating story, which was first told nearly eighty years later, for which no documentary evidence has been produced so far as is known, Mar Bedros had obtained the sanction of the Patriarch Mar Ignatius Jacobus II to initiate a sort of Re-union Movement, and, because Mar Bedros was unable to leave his diocese, he was looking for a likely person to direct this movement in Europe.[4] It is asserted that Mar Bedros had 'tested out many ecclesiastics of different bodies who had occasion to visit him, and that ultimately in 1865, found the right man in the person of the Rev. Julius Ferrette.'[5]

[1] The *Journal Asiatique*, published by the Société Asiatique of Paris, included in its issue of December 1859 a paper entitled, Méthode simplifiée pour imprimer l'arabe avec les points voyelles, by Le Révérend Jules Ferrette, missionaire à Damas. He appears in the list of the subscribing members of the Société for 1860, 'mission-aire protestant à Damas,' but seems to have dropped out soon.

[2] For Lord Dufferin's Lebanon Mission of 1860-1, see Harold Nicolson, *Helen's Tower* (1937), pp. 126-31.

[3] 'Jacobite' is the name by which a number of Monophysite Churches, including the Syrian Church, are commonly called. The name is derived from Jacob Baradaeus, Bishop of Edessa (541-78), who saved the Monophysite heretics from the extinction which threatened them through persecution. They were accused of so identifying the two natures of Christ so as to obliterate the real distinction between the divine and the human.

[4] Largely because five Jacobite bishops had abjured heresy and schism between 1820 and 1850, resulting in most of their flocks around Damascus and in the southern Lebanon following them into communion with the Holy See, there still remained a bitter anti-papalist attitude among the bishops who continued loyal to Monophysitism. This makes it easy to understand why Mar Bedros should have welcomed a lapsed Catholic of the Latin rite, and an ex-Dominican friar. Since about 1840 the Jacobites had been on friendly terms with Anglican clergymen, including Mr G. P. Badger, the author of *The Nestorians and their Rituals* (1852), and Mr J. W. Etheridge, who visited the Jacobites about 1840. His book *The Syrian Churches* appeared in 1846. Later on American Congregationalists and Presbyterians tried to convert the Jacobites to Protestantism.

[5] Mar Georgius, *The Man from Antioch* (Glastonbury, 1959), p. 2. For details of Mar Georgius's career (Hugh George de Willmott Newman), see pp. 443-501.

Jules Ferrette

It is further alleged that, having discussed the introduction of Eastern Christianity into Western Europe (without reference to Monophysitism), Mar Bedros managed to persuade Ferrette to take the leading part in it. Then, so we are told, with the sanction of the Jacobite Patriarch of Antioch, the Bishop of Emesa (Homs) raised the French 'Minister of the Gospel' to the episcopate on June 2, 1866 (Old Style); and that the function took place at Homs, in the presence of many witnesses. An instrument of consecration, written by the consecrator himself, sealed with his seal, and verified by Mr E. T. Rogers, British Consul at Damascus, is said to have been presented to Ferrette, who was given the title of 'Mar Julius, Bishop of Iona'. Finally, Mgr Ferrette was 'dispatched as Patriarchal Legate for Western Europe, with authority to erect indigenous Orthodox Churches, under an autonomous Patriarchate of their own, and not in any way subject to Antioch'.[1]

This colourful episode cannot be ignored, because on its veracity rest many of the claims of the schismatic churches dealt with in these pages. Even in the last few years several founders of new bodies have claimed apostolic succession from the Bishop of Iona. It may be pointed out that no patriarch has ever had authority to erect 'autonomous patriarchates', and it is doubtful whether any has ever even claimed the right. In the Orthodox discipline an autocephalous church may be raised to patriarchal status by the Oecumenical Patriarch with the approval of the other Patriarchates.[2] None of the lesser Eastern Churches has ever made such claims. However frail and erratic Ignatius Peter III ('Peter the Humble') may have become, he was perfectly competent in 1866, when he was still Bishop of Emesa. It is also significant that when he visited England in 1874 there was no meeting between him and a British Patriarch. Moreover, it is hard to see how the cause of Christian Reunion was served by the Antiochene Patriarch erecting a diocese of his Monophysite Church in the Hebrides of all places. Did Ferrette choose Iona as his see out of respect for his Irish Presbyterian benefactors at Damascus? His theological opinions were always so elusive and *sui generis* that it is quite possible that

[1] ibid., p. 3.
[2] In the early Church, three sees only—Antioch, Alexandria, and Rome—were patriarchates. Byzantium and Jerusalem were added to the three earlier patriarchal sees in the fifth century. In more recent times the heads of several autocephalous Eastern Orthodox Churches—Russia, Yugoslavia, Rumania, etc., have acquired the patriarchal title. The heads of certain Eastern Churches in communion with the Holy See, also certain Latin archbishops (viz. Venice, Goa, Lisbon) are patriarchs.

Jules Ferrette

he regarded St Columba as an embryo Calvinist, and would probably have agreed with Sir George MacLeod and his Iona Community in holding that the Celtic Church in many ways displayed close parallels with the Russian or Eastern Church, as opposed to the Western or Roman Church, even that it was founded directly by Eastern missionaries.[1]

The Bishop of Iona made good speed on his eirenic journey from Syria to Britain. According to his own story, as soon as he arrived in London he went to the British Museum, where two scholars, Professors Charles Rieu and William Wright, translated his Syrian instrument of consecration into English. It seems that he had copies printed for distribution among his Anglican friends and benefactors. What is curious, however, is that he did not call on these two witnesses when he was forced to defend himself after being charged as an impostor. Throughout the subsequent controversy nobody ever testified to having seen the original Syriac document, which would have been more convincing than any printed translation.

Almost any alien, provided that he speaks broken English, grows a beard, and calls himself an abuna, apocrisarius, archimandrite, chorepiscopos, exarch, katolikos, mafrain, metran, pappas, rasophor, starets, synkellos, hieromonk, vartapet—or any other Oriental ecclesiastical title—invariably finds a warm welcome in England. He is usually taken on his face value—sometimes even by Nonconformists—and if down and out, he is clothed, fed, and given alms. Julius Ferrette was no exception. Among the High Church clergymen who hastened to offer hospitality to the Bishop of Iona was the Rev. George Nugée, Secretary of the A.P.U.C. This wealthy son of a fashionable Bond Street tailor and hatter loved entertaining celebrities. A year earlier, in the summer of 1865, the dusky Queen Emma, widow of King Kamahamcha of the Sandwich Islands, together with her maids of honour, had been his guests at the Manor House, Wymering, Hampshire. A prelate who claimed to have been consecrated by a metropolitan in a city on the Orontes was worthy of even more lavish luncheons than those Nugée gave to the young officers of the Portsmouth garrison

---

[1] See *The Abbey Services of the Iona Community* (Glasgow, n.d.), p. 20. Such opinions should be compared with, e.g., L. Gougaud, *Christianity in Celtic Lands* (1932); N. K. Chadwick, *The Age of Saints in the Early Celtic Church* (1961); *Studies in Early British History* (1954); and *Studies in the Early British Church* (1958); M. Deanesly, *The Pre-Conquest Church in England* (1961); and H. Williams, *Christianity in Early Britain* (1912).

on most Sundays. So Mar Julius, Bishop of Iona (as he signed letters) was received as his exalted status demanded. Rather than risk any trouble with Dr Sumner, Bishop of Winchester, Nugée did not invite this *episcopos* of the Antiochene rite to pontificate in the parish church, and Mar Julius had to be content with a choir-stall at the 'High Celebration', where his presence doubtless must have thrilled the handful of young men who formed the nucleus of the revived 'Order of St Augustine', of which the bachelor vicar was the Father Superior.

It is recorded that Mar Julius also took part in functions at ritualistic churches in London, including the recently opened, and already notorious, St Michael's, Shoreditch, where the altar was lit up with no less than fifty wax candles, besides two large candelabra, in addition to two rows of tapers on the rood screen. Vested, he made a striking figure, walking in processions, amid the banners, lights, and incense; providing just a useful symbol of catholicity and orthodoxy for display in the eighteen-sixties, when the ritualistic clergy were smarting from censures in several episcopal charges.

The advanced Anglo-Catholics could now feel that they were supported by the Patriarch of the God-protected City of Antioch and of all the Domain of the Apostolic Throne (the official title given to the head of the Jacobites) in the person of his alleged Legate. But some of the High Church clergy must have been disconcerted at the somewhat heterodox opinions expressed by the Bishop of Iona, who wrote to Fr Nugée on August 18, 1866:

'I want men tried in the ministry to advise me, and concert with me the means of rendering to so many disorganized Christian communities in the West, valid Sacraments and an undoubted Apostolic Succession, so that their Bishops, Archbishops, and Patriarchs may one day sit as equals with their brethren of the Eastern and Latin Church in the Oecumenical Council which will pronounce the end of the Schism. . . . They will not be asked to submit to any other Faith but that which the Holy Spirit teaches us in the Scriptures, for which the Martyrs have died, which the Oecumenical Councils have sanctioned. . . . They shall never be asked by me to hate or despise the Mother Church by which they have been prepared for the service of the Holy Catholic Apostolic and Orthodox Church of the West.'[1]

We can well believe that he was suspected of heresy if his letter

[1] *The Church Monitor*, October 1866, p. 109.

Jules Ferrette

to *The Church Times* of December 16, 1866, represented his considered position:

'I never lost all faith in episcopacy. Had I done so, I could have joined the Presbyterians, whose constitution is Episcopal after the model laid down in the Epistles of St Ignatius of Antioch, and whose standards require apostolic succession as a condition of the validity of the Sacraments, even of Baptism. Presbyterians hold the three orders of Bishops, Priests, and Deacons, and they are called Presbyterians, not because they deny Episcopacy, but because their first bishops were ordained by Roman presbyters, as was the case with the Church of England. Had I remained in communion with the Presbyterians, it was my intention to use my influence with some Eastern Prelates in order to restore the true succession among Presbyterians, after which they might have communicated it to the Church of England and to other Protestant Churches.' He also stated that the Greek Patriarch Hierotheas had written appreciatively with his own hand and seal, an *exposé* of the doctrine of the Orthodox Faith; an English translation of which was to appear shortly with his 'own humble approval'.

An Eastern bishop who ventured to call the Church of England a 'Protestant Church', and who equated it with Presbyterianism, was not likely to be universally welcomed, but his heterodoxy may not have been disclosed before the meeting held in London in October 1866, at which the Bishop of Iona outlined the Holy Catholic Apostolic Church of the West, which he hoped to form with the help of Anglicans, Presbyterians, and other Protestant bodies. *The Church Monitor* reported the proceedings and said:

'This prelate, who received the grace of the priesthood from a Roman Cardinal, and the gift of the episcopate from an Oecumenical Metropolitan of the Holy Eastern Church, has been appointed Bishop of an island ecclesiastical district, where the Light of the Gospel once shone brightly. It is his Lordship's intention, so we are informed, to forward the great undertaking of promoting intercommunion between East and West. Thus a work will be attempted which others ought long ago to have performed.'

Mar Julius I was kept busy during those first months in England. On September 30, 1866, he had published by J. Parker of London and Oxford a book entitled *The Euchologion, or The Eastern Liturgy adapted for Use in the West*.[1] In the preface he wrote that the rite

---

[1] Mr Gladstone's copy of this now rare book is preserved at St Deinol's Library, Hawarden.

was arranged so that 'in this matter an Orthodox Christian, an Anglican, a Roman Catholic, or a Protestant, will be enabled to join in all the services of the Church without having to utter a single word which their consciences perplexed by the omission of anything which any of them would deem necessary to the validity of an ordinance'. Prefixed to the *Euchologion* was a Pastoral Letter, in which this Syrian-Jacobite Bishop declared that he was prepared 'to give Holy Orders to pious and learned men, who, being duly elected, will declare themselves willing to conform to this liturgy'.

On September 30, 1866, Mar Julius celebrated his new vernacular rite for the first time in the Chapel of St Augustine's Home, Montpelier, Bristol. It was reported in the *Bristol Daily Post* (October 1, 1866) that 'he wore over his cassock of crimson silk, an elaborately embroidered alb of white silk, and a chasuble of gold-coloured silk, with a large Greek cross on the back and other enrichments, and also a pallium of white silk'. Many tapers twinkled on the gradines of the altar, and the chapel was filled with the fragrant fumes of incense. Assisting His Lordship were the Rev. Father Ouseley and Brothers Cyprian and Alban.[1]

The same newspaper informed its readers that

'The Right Reverend Archbishop is stated to have been associated with various Christian movements in the Holy Land, and he was also named to us as an ecclesiastic of much learning and piety. He speaks English very fluently, although, of course, with a marked foreign accent.'

After his visit to Bristol, the Bishop made a pilgrimage to some of the famous shrines of the Ancient British Church, including Glastonbury and Caerleon-on-Usk. So impressed was Dr F. G. Lee, the vicar of All Saints', Lambeth, by the personality of Mar Julius, so convinced by his credentials, that he asked him to contribute to the *Essays on the Reunion of Christendom*, by members of the Roman Catholic, Eastern and Anglican Communions, which he was editing.[2] On being informed of this, Dr Pusey flatly refused to write the Introduction. He explained that he could not, in any way, connect himself with Mr Julius Ferrette; and that he did

---

[1] cf. Mar Georgius, op. cit., p. 6. These Gothic Revival vestments were hardly in keeping with the Antiochene rite, and it is a pity that Mar Julius did not wear a *phaino*—a chasuble resembling a cope without hood or orphreys—together with all the other picturesque insignia of a Syrian prelate of this Eastern rite, instead of the 'gold silk garment with the large Greek Cross'.
[2] See p. 61.

Jules Ferrette

not know why he was said to be an ex-Dominican. Pusey wrote: 'They say all sort of things and (you hear probably and I suppose do not believe), of his connecting himself with American missionaries in the East, being dissatisfied with them, and seeking consecration from the Jacobites, of whom I see that he says that now (in the East I suppose he means, for the Egyptians certainly had not, lately) they have laid aside their heresy. I hope it may be so, but they have not purged themselves; and it would be for them to purge themselves with the Great Church and reunite with them. But he leaves his consecration (as far as I know) unattested and unexplained. From the way in which he speaks of Baptism by sprinkling one would suppose that he had been re-baptized; from the way in which he speaks of the double Procession, one would think that he had renounced it. But then, again, it is not the way of the Easterns to consecrate bishops *in partibus*, nor is it satisfactory to us to have a Greek or Jacobite See of Iona created, any more than a R.C. Bishopric at Westminster. There seems to me a *prima facie* improbability that he was consecrated Bishop of Iona. Then too, the way he writes of the Roman Church is exasperating, and we could not go along with him. His attack on Rome goes through our sides. I had a letter of introduction to him as a Mr Julius Ferrette, saying nothing of his episcopate. . . . Let one say what one will, one is responsible for the society which one keeps, for one need not keep it. And I feel that I must keep clear of Mr J.F.'[1]

The result of this intervention was that Dr Lee decided that it was wiser not to include Ferrette's contribution to the *Essays*.

Mar Georgius tells us, though without giving any documentary evidence, that in the autumn of 1866 Mar Julius went to Scotland, where he met both Episcopalian clergymen and Presbyterian ministers. We are informed that he thus acquired a fair knowledge of Presbyterian polity, and 'readily perceived that, in spite of its lack of Apostolic Succession, it bore witness in a very real sense to the Apostolic model of Church organization described in the Epistle of St Ignatius of Antioch'.[2] According to Mar Georgius, the Bishop of Iona was taken to see the Catholic Apostolic Church in Edinburgh, where, so it is related, he 'found the Ignatian model in actual operation, for there the Angel of the Church, who was a consecrated Bishop of that rite, was in evidence with his Priest, Elders, and Deacons. It was this type of episcopate which Mar

[1] H. R. T. Brandreth, *Dr Lee of Lambeth* (1951), p. 111.
[2] op. cit., p. 6.

41

Julius sought to restore.' Dr Pusey's suspicions would have been confirmed had he been told that Mr Julius Ferrette was flirting with both Irvingites and Presbyterians in Scotland.[1]

It may well be that (as Mar Georgius relates) Mar Julius made a pilgrimage to Iona. In 1866 this must have been quite an achievement, because the railway to Oban was not opened for another fourteen years. He is said to have contacted 'The Ancient Mystic Order of Culdees', which 'by the time of Mar Julius numbered a mere handful, and these were received into union with the See of Iona, after they had first admitted him into the Order, and elected and appointed him High Pontiff thereof'.[2] It would be interesting to find out anything about this Ancient Mystic Order of which otherwise nothing whatever is known, though Culdees are said to have continued on Bardsey Island, North Wales, till the Reformation.

After this Visitation of his Diocese, Mar Julius appears to have made his way to Norfolk, where he stayed with Dr J. T. Seccombe at Terrington St Clement, near King's Lynn, and perhaps raised his host to minor and major orders, including the episcopate.[3] In 1867 Simpkin Marshall published Seccombe's translation of *The Great Catechism of the Eastern Orthodox Church*, also of *The Holy Canons of the Syrian Oecumenical Synods*, which contained the words: 'printed by the authority of the Bishop of Iona'.[4]

Meanwhile more people were becoming suspicious of this freelance prelate. Among them was Malcolm MacColl, who attacked him in a *Guardian* article which was reprinted in *The Church Times*. Ferrette answered it, and maintained that sixty-three of the statements were 'pure invention', and only five true. He ended his defence as follows:

'I cannot afford to read, much less refute, all the falsehoods which are published concerning me. As I have selected Mr MacColl out of many and quite at random, he will not make the mistake of believing that what I have now to say applies to him in particular.

'I have seen more lying during the last three months than during

---

[1] It is not known if either Dr John Cook, Moderator of the General Assembly of the Church of Scotland that year, or Dr Charles Terrot, then Bishop of Edinburgh, entertained the alleged Legate for Western Europe of the Patriarchate of Antioch. It is improbable that Mgr John Strain, Bishop of Abila *in partibus*, and Vicar Apostolic of the Eastern District of Scotland, was among his hosts.

[2] ibid., p. 7.

[3] See ff. 75.

[4] See pp. 63, 83 for further details of Seccombe.

the whole of my previous life; and I am sorry to say that almost the whole of this appeared in the columns of one of the leading journals of the Church of England, the *Guardian*. In presence of such an immoral state of things, I withdraw the offer that I made of validating the orders of any deacon or priest of the Church of England who might apply to me.'[1]

Having thus washed his hands of the Church of England, Ferrette seems to have 'gone underground' for the next three years. How he managed to support himself, and where he found a refuge does not appear to be known. Could it have been with 'The Ancient Mystic Order of Culdees' in Scotland, whose members may have remained loyal to their 'High Pontiff'?[2] There is a legend that he formed small groups up and down Britain as the nucleus of a Holy Catholic Apostolic Church of the West, which he hoped would spread all over Europe sooner or later.

But there was at least one clergyman of the Church of England who accepted the validity of his episcopate, and never questioned his claims—the Rev. Richard Williams Morgan. He was born in 1815 at Llanfor Vicarage, Bala, being the son of the Rev. Richard Morgan, and his wife, Anna Margaretta, daughter of the Rev. J. Williams. He seems to have inherited Welsh Nationalism, Jacobitism, and Nonjuring interests from his ancestors on both sides. Ordained deacon in 1841 and priest in 1842 by Dr Connop Thirlwall, Bishop of St Davids, Morgan became curate of Mochavc, Montgomeryshire. From 1843 to 1853 he was perpetual curate of Tregynon in the Diocese of St Asaph. His nationalist outlook is proved by his request made in 1858 to Dr Sumner, Archbishop of Canterbury, to remove Dr Vowler Short, Bishop of St Asaph, on account of his ignorance of Welsh.[3] By this time Morgan had developed into a fervent Welsh Nationalist. He was a tireless but uncritical research worker, ready to believe anything that took his fancy, and indifferent to the lack of documentary evidence.[4] Like his

[1] *The Church Times*, December 15, 1866.
[2] It could be that this had something to do with R.T.N. Sprot of Culdees Castle, near Muthill, Perthshire. Sprot was an enthusiastic Episcopalian who collected ecclesiastics much as Lord Halifax did a bit later, and it is quite likely that he entertained Ferrette. The Order of Culdees may have been a secret group of Episcopalians or it may have been a leg-pull. In any case there was a Culdee community at Muthill as late as 1236. How much did Ferrette know of Britain and how well did he know English? His newspaper letters may have been written or translated for him.
[3] The *Dictionary of Welsh Biography* says: 'Short had school books prepared in which Welsh and English lessons were printed on opposite pages, though he himself was a monoglot Englishman.' He resigned in 1872, and died two years later.
[4] Fervent Legitimist and Jacobite views are not uncommon among the subjects of this book; viz. Mgr Williams, Archbishop of Caer-Glow; Archbishop R. C. Jackson,

Jules Ferrette

friend John Williams (Ab Ithel), he accepted the Druidic Order as the forerunner of Christianity, the Trojan discovery of Britain, and many other legends. He himself was a Bard of the Gorsedd, with the title of Môr Merion, and he took part in the 1858 Eisteddfod, which was run by the Welsh clergy, including Ab Ithel, and where all the major prizes went to the latter's family. In 1857 Môr Merion re-issued the first part of his monumental work entitled *The British Kymrig*, which was a history of Britain from before the Flood to A.D. 700. Sixty years later it attracted the attention of the British Israelites, who were instrumental in bringing out a new edition in 1922. It was in keeping with his credulous mentality that he should have believed that the British are descended from the lost Ten Tribes of Israel. Another book he wrote was *St Paul in Britain*, dedicated to Dr Thirlwall, Bishop of St Davids, who was probably the only English bishop in Wales ever to learn Welsh.

In 1858 Morgan left Wales and moved to the parish of Yeddingham in Yorkshire. Then comes a long gap in his record until 1870, where this stormy petrel found himself in 1870 as curate of Marholm, a village about four miles north-west of Peterborough, where he remained until 1874.

According to Mar Georgius, who unfortunately does not give us any sources, Morgan was already in touch with Ferrette, seeing 'clearly that any scheme for restoring the pre-Augustinian tradition in Britain must form part of a greater whole, namely, the establishment of a world-wide Orthodox movement, which, united in faith, hope, and love, would form a nucleus of the future Reunion of Christendom in God's good time, and in God's own way.'[1]

There can be no doubt that Mar Julius found a kindred spirit in this erratic, unstable, hot-headed Welsh clergyman. Mar Georgius (who regards himself as the canonical successor of Mar Julius) goes on to tell us that the commission given by Mar Bedros, Metropolitan of Homs, with the apparent sanction of the Patriarch of Antioch—
'whether by design or accident, one cannot say, extended over the whole Celtic lands of Western Europe; and so, completely accorded with the Pan-Celtic ideals of Mr Morgan. They were both, further-

---

of the Order of Corporate Reunion; and Mar Georgius, Patriarch of Glastonbury and Catholicos of the West. Similar views were held by the late Dr Adrian Fortescue but they are rare among British clerics of the Latin rite today.

[1] *The Man from Antioch*, p. 8.

44

more, agreed upon the question that the autocephalous patriarchate, which Ferrette had been authorized to establish, should be a British patriarchate, and not located in one of the continental countries, although it would naturally have jurisdiction there also. And now comes a proof of the astounding humility and sincerity of Mar Julius. He could easily, and probably with the consent of his old friend Peter the Humble, by this time Mar Ignatius III, Patriarch of Antioch, have made Iona the seat of the Patriarchate, and thus himself have been the first British Patriarch. No doubt many would have done this, but Mar Julius regarded himself purely as the Legate of the Apostolic See of Antioch, commissioned to find the right men to whom to pass on the Patriarchal authority, and so, he selected the Rev. Richard Williams Morgan.'[1]

Mar Georgius never quotes any letters or other documents to support his inspiring opinions about the origins of the so-called 'British Patriarchate', and it is difficult not to feel that he has rushed to a hasty conclusion. No matter, it is probable that some time in 1874, either at Marholm, or at Mapledurham, Oxfordshire, where Morgan was then staying, and taking occasional clerical duties, Mar Julius conditionally baptized, confirmed, ordained, and consecrated this enterprising Anglican clergyman. He is said to have given him the title and style of 'Mar Pelagius I, Hierarch of Caerleon-on-Usk, giving him jurisdiction over Great Britain, Ireland, and Western Europe, as the first Patriarch of a restored Ancient British Church'.

Was it due to Morgan's desire to emulate the early British heretic that made him choose Pelagius for his patriarchal name?[2] No doubt Caerleon was selected for his see because of his detestation of everything English. Unfortunately Glastonbury, the obvious see to revive, lay within the hated realm of England. Still Caerleon had compensations, claiming to be sanctified by the blood of the fourth-century ancient British martyrs Julius and Aaron.[3]

Mar Julius now fades out of the picture. Eventually he made his

[1] ibid., p. 10.
[2] But in fairness, the name Pelagius is supposed to be a graecized form of the Welsh 'Morgan' ('sea-begotten').
[3] In 1937, Mar Frederic, Primate of the Orthodox-Keltic Church of the British Commonwealth of Nations, consecrated Dorian Herbert as Bishop of Carleon in the so-called Free Orthodox-Catholic (or Jesuene) Church. Some years later Herbert claimed that he had revived the Ancient British Church, as the founder of a 'Holy Grail Christian Crusade against Brutality to Animals and all Wild Creatures', functioning under the spiritual patronage of King Arthur and his Knights. (See pp. 292–297.)

way across the Atlantic, and is said to have settled at Cambridge, Massachusetts. It is not known if he ordained any priests or consecrated any bishops during the years spent in North America. Finally he returned to Europe and settled first at Lausanne and later at Geneva, where in 1903 he published *Les Rites Essentiels du Christianisme*, and died shortly after this, without having been reconciled with the Roman Church.

The first Patriarch of the revived Ancient British Church did not feel obliged to sever his relations with the Church of England. He had no scruples about successively accepting the stipends paid him as curate of Stapleton, Shropshire, and Offord d'Arcy, Huntingdonshire (1883–6). There is a legend that His Sacred Beatitude, being anxious to carry on the succession obtained from the Syrian Jacobite Church, consecrated a certain Charles Isaac Stevens as his perpetual coadjutor with right of succession. His two assistants are said to have included Dr F. G. Lee, the Bishop of Dorchester in the Order of Corporate Reunion.

This ceremony is believed to have taken place some time in 1879, though it is not clear that there is any evidence for this year. Neither the exact date or the locality has ever been given, and no documents recording it have ever been produced. We have no knowledge of what rite was used. Stevens himself is a unsubstantial figure. Little has been discovered about his early life. There is a tale that he belonged to the Reformed Episcopal Church in the United States, and had been a member of an Order of Druids,[1] but this is only hearsay. As will be related in chapter seven, there is a tradition that in 1890 he laid hands on Leon Chechemian, the former Catholic Armenian *vartapet*, who joined the Church of Ireland, and then became one of the founders of the Free Protestant Episcopal Church of England.[2] If this is true, then what was the reason for Chechemian consecrating (or re-consecrating) Stevens at Hackney in 1898 ? This ceremony was recalled by the late Bishop William Hall, whose memories of the alleged second Patriarch of the Ancient British Church suggest that he was unfitted by nature as well as by education to perform any clerical duties.[3] Stevens is said to have assumed the title of Mar Theophilus, presumably in honour of the second century Bishop of Antioch of that name. He died in 1916.

[1] For the Reformed Episcopal Church, see p. 219, note 2.
[2] See p. 220.
[3] See p. 223.

Jules Ferrette

Mar Georgius relates that Mar Pelagius retired in 1888, after many years of roaming, and that he moved to the Isle of Thanet, where he became a lonely missionary among the folk whose ancestors had been, he would have maintained, perverted to Romanism by papal emissaries after 597. Making his head-quarters at Broadstairs, he conducted services in the patriarchal oratory. We are told that he maintained friendly relations with Dr Lee and with other members of the Order of Corporate Reunion, presumably in the hope of making them realize the futility of trying to set up a Uniate Church in England.[1] He ended his erratic career at Pevensey, Sussex, where he died on August 22, 1889.

Such is the fantastic yet tragic story of Julius Ferrette and his colleague. The former's ideals were definitely of the stuff that dreams are made of, and so were those of the Anglican curate he is said to have consecrated as the first Patriarch of a revived Britonic Church. Yet even today there are many prelates all over the world who claim that their apostolic succession is derived from Mar Julius I, Bishop of Iona, through Mar Pelagius I, Hierarch of Caerleon-on-Usk. Such faith—some people might call it credulity —is indeed 'that which gives substance to our hopes, which convinces us of things we cannot see'.[2]

[1] See chapter three.
[2] Hebrews xi, 1.

CHAPTER II

Dr J. Joseph Overbeck
and his Western Orthodox Catholic Church,
and the Archimandrite Timotheos Hatherly
and his Autocephalous Eastern Church

Not long after Mar Julius I, Bishop of Iona, decided to break off relations with Anglicans, on the grounds that they were untrustworthy liars, renewed interest in the Eastern Churches was aroused in England by another lapsed Roman Catholic priest—Dr J. Joseph Overbeck. Born in Germany in 1821, he became a professor of Syriac at the University of Bonn after his ordination to the secular priesthood. At the age of thirty-three he seceded to the Lutheran Church and took a wife.

There was nothing remarkable in this secession, because there had been a small though militant cis-alpine movement among the German bishops and other clergy since the latter part of the eighteenth century. Two of its earlier leaders were Benedikt Maria von Werkmeister (1745–1823) and Johann Michael von Sailer (1751–1832). About 1845 a schismatic German Catholic Church came into being, largely through the efforts of two suspended priests, Johannes Ronge and Johann Czerski. Before long, however, this small body abandoned almost every distinctive Catholic dogma, and evolved into a Protestant-Rationalist organization.[1] By way of protest against the latitudinarianism of the Ronge-Czerski schismatics, another ex-Catholic priest, Dr Pribil of Berlin, founded what he called the 'Protestant Catholic Church'.

In 1864 Pius IX issued the encyclical *Quanta Cura*, with a list of eighty condemned propositions attached, known as 'The Syllabus of Errors'. This papal manifesto caused indignation among liberal-minded scholars, and it also led to friction between the German bishops and the Government. By the time it appeared

---

[1] Almost exactly the same thing happened with the schismatic *Église catholique française*, founded by Mgr Chatel in 1831, which was officially suppressed by Louis-Philippe in 1842. (See p. 301.)

Overbeck was in England, having received a grant from the Prussian State to pursue patristic studies at Oxford. In 1865 he published an incomplete edition of the writings of St Ephrem Syrus.

One day it occurred to him that the Latin Patriarchate had been in schism ever since the twelfth century, and that the Eastern Orthodox Church was the sole heiress of Catholic truth and life.[1] Accordingly he lost no time in going to London, where he was received into the Russian Church by the embassy chaplain, Eugène Popoff.[2] But he was not allowed to exercise his priesthood in the Orthodox Church, because he had contracted matrimony after receiving major orders, albeit in the Latin Rite. Several times he asked for faculties, but his request was always refused. Thus he had no choice but to remain a layman, and from 1867 to 1878 he is said to have earned his living by teaching languages at the Royal Military Academy, Woolwich, though there is no record of him there.

Meanwhile his fertile imagination began to evolve a wonderful scheme for the Reunion of Christendom, which can be summed up in the words of a writer to *The Tablet* many years later.

'Were we of the West to submit to Orientalism? By no means. We were Westerns, and Westerns we should remain, since in God's providence the Western Church was framed on the Western mind and stamped with divine approval. In a slightly modified form the logic seems strangely familiar. Overbeck and his henchmen saw their way out of the impasse. All they had to do was to become Easterns without ceasing to be Westerns. They would join the Eastern Church and at the same time revive the Western. To initiate this tiny revolution which was to convulse the whole of the West, Anglicans included, Overbeck and his friends would seek reconciliation with any Eastern Church, that of Servia would serve the purpose, and they would humbly sue for absolution for the sin of schism. But preference would be shown to Russia, as the Church closest to the West.'[3]

The immediate result of this vision was that in 1869 Overbeck drew up *A Petition to the Most Holy Governing Synod of the Russian Church*. He obtained 122 signatures in its support, and the docu-

---

[1] cf. *The Orthodox Catholic Review*, vol. III, n. 1.

[2] Popoff was a friend of Dr J. M. Neale. cf. A. G. Lough, *The Influence of John Mason Neale* (1962), pp. 124, 127–8.

[3] George Cormack, 'The Western Orthodox Church', in *The Tablet*, January 16, 1909.

ment was forwarded to Moscow. The Holy Synod then appointed a Committee of seven to consider and report on the Petition. Overbeck seems to have been one of the seven. Eventually the Russian ecclesiastics gave their cordial approval to the scheme which, at least on paper, was plausible.

After the Vatican Council of 1870, and the formation of Old Catholic Churches in Germany and Switzerland, Overbeck was optimistic that many priests and layfolk would be eager to join his Western Orthodox Catholic Church. He had met Alexander Lycurgos, Archbishop of Syros and Tenos, who visited England in 1869–70, to consecrate the new Greek church at Liverpool. This Eastern prelate was given the honorary degree of D.D. at Oxford, and was present at the consecrations of two Anglican bishops. Disappointingly Lycurgos showed no interest whatever in the creation of a Western Orthodox Church; and, even worse, expressed it as his opinion that the Church of England was 'a sound Catholic Church, very like our own'; and that the two Churches would soon be united by friendly discussion.

Though the general principle of Overbeck's new Church had been accepted at Moscow, much still had to be discussed, including its liturgy. The Committee charged Overbeck to revise the Roman Mass, and purge it of all heterodoxy. This work kept him busy for about nine months, at the end of which he submitted his draft in Latin. It was finally approved by the Holy Synod as the authoritative rite for Western Orthodoxy. At the same time Overbeck composed what he called a *Libellus invitatorius ad Clerum Laicosque Romano-Catholicos*, which was published at Halle in 1871. This took the form of an appeal to Roman Catholic priests and layfolk to abjure schism and be reunited with what he regarded as the only true Catholic and Orthodox Church.

The Latin text of the new rite, entitled *Liturgia Missae Orthodoxo-Catholicae Occidentalis*, together with an English translation, appeared as a pamphlet in 1871. It was virtually the same as the 1570 Roman rite of St Pius V, except for a few details, one of which was a brief epiklesis containing the words, 'transubstantiating them by Thy Holy Spirit'. The only definitely new Oriental features were the words 'Agios o Théos' after the *Gloria in Excelsis* ('in remembrance of our union with the Orthodox Church'); and the giving of Communion under both species with a spoon.

Overbeck's visions widened. He saw the newly formed Old

Catholic Churches coming under the jurisdiction of the Eastern Patriarchates now that they had cast off the yoke of Rome. The persecution of the Anglican Ritualist clergy led him to believe that there would soon be a flourishing branch of the Western Orthodox Catholic Church in England. His confidence was increased by the apparent sympathy shown towards his scheme by the Oecumenical Patriarch.[1] He found time while teaching languages at Woolwich to write a book entitled *Die Wiedervereinigung der morgen-und abend-ländischen Kirchen* which appeared at Halle in 1873. Meanwhile he had found a strong supporter in Count Dmitry A. Tolstoy, Chief Procurator of the Holy Synod of the Russian Orthodox Church, who was ever ready to sponsor any movement exposing the political influence of the Papacy.[2]

Some of Overbeck's disciples, like himself, joined the Russian Church, while others entered the Greek Orthodox Church. Those living in London appear to have met from time to time for prayer and discussion. So far as is known, none of them became priests. Among High Church Anglicans who corresponded with Overbeck was Fr Nugée who, as related in the previous chapter, had been one of the first to sponsor Julius Ferrette, Bishop of Iona, and his dream of the 'Holy Catholic Apostolic and Orthodox Church of the West'. Once again Nugée clutched at a straw. But Overbeck can have had very little use for the Order of Corporate Reunion, because its promoters wished for reunion with Rome. He had nothing but contempt for Anglicans who remained in communion with Canterbury. On one occasion he remarked: 'We doubt whether the Establishment may even be called a church.' His ultimate aim, although he disclaimed any wish to form a new sect, seems to have been to set up in England a new National Church neither Anglican, Roman, nor Eastern, for he said: 'As soon as our Western Church has a hierarchy of three Bishops, she is fully entitled to national independence.'[3]

Between 1867 and 1885 he continued to leave no stone unturned in trying to win supporters for his Church, mainly through *The Orthodox Catholic Review*. He never lost hope of this international dream-church becoming a reality, and in 1881 visited the

---

[1] During all this Ambrose Phillipps de Lisle (a Roman Catholic) and certain High Church Anglican clergy and laity were preparing a scheme to form a Uniate Church in England, which in 1877 materialized as the Order of Corporate Reunion. (See chapter three.)
[2] An English translation of Tolstoy's *Romanism in Russia*, with a preface by Dr Robert Eden, Bishop of Moray and Ross, was published in 1874.
[3] cf. George Cormack in *The Tablet*, January 16, 1909.

Phanar and arranged for a committee to be set up to examine his project.[1]

The Patriarch of Constantinople, Joachim III, was sympathetic but non-committal. As to a few narrow-minded Anglicans, they regarded this proposed new Church as 'a schismatic proceeding, and a mere copying of the uncatholic and uncanonical aggressions of the Church of Rome'. Some went so far as to denounce it as a pseudo-Oriental nonconformist sect, which threatened 'to proselytize within the jurisdiction of the Anglican Episcopate'. Persons who held the Three Branch Theory of the Church found no room for a fourth Branch.

It appears that the idea of an Orthodox Western Catholic Church was finally rejected by the Holy Synod of Moscow in 1884, on the advice of Eugène Smirnoff, the new Russian Embassy chaplain in London.[2] Overbeck's importance lies historically in the effect he had on a few Eastern Orthodox theologians, who felt that the Old Catholics had been lost to Orthodoxy through mismanagement. He had tried and failed to push the Eastern Churches into a policy of proselytism in Western Europe.

A more logical attempt to infiltrate Orthodoxy into England was made by Stephen Georgeson Hatherly, who was Overbeck's contemporary. This single-minded mid-Victorian Englishman seems to have been as much drawn to everything Grecian as Lord Byron before him, with the result that, after displaying real tenacity of purpose and bulldog courage, he finally managed to acquire the status of Proto-Presbyter of the Patriarchal Oecumenical Throne in the Greek Orthodox Church. As a youth he was drawn by the Scriptural superiority of the Churches of Smyrna and Philadelphia over the Church of Rome, as indicated in the first chapters of the Apocalypse of Blessed John the Apostle. When the Beloved Disciple fell into a trance on the Isle of Patmos, he received no message to send to the Church of Rome, only to the seven Churches in Asia. Hatherly's studies convinced him that Christianity, from its beginning, was regarded by the world as 'a Hellenistic thing', and so it ought to be, even in the nineteenth century.[3]

[1] The Phanar is the expression used for the Patriarch of Constantinople and his curia, from the quarter of the city in which they have their offices.

[2] cf. George Florovsky in S. C. Neill and R. Rouse (ed.), *History of the Ecumenical Movement* (1954), pp. 205–7.

[3] cf. *A Lecture delivered in the Greek Syllogus, Manchester*, October 2nd (14th), 1874. (Cardiff, 1877) pp. 4–5.

Dr Pusey tried in a letter dated May 24, 1853, to persuade him to take Holy Orders in the Church of England, but to no purpose. Three years later, the year before the foundation of the Association for the Promotion of the Unity of Christendom, Hatherly was received into the Greek Orthodox Church in London. At that date all the Greek-speaking Orthodox Churches re-baptized all converts from either the Latin or Protestant bodies, holding the opinion that only baptism by immersion was valid. Remembering the Gorham Judgment of March 1850, that declared that the rejection of the doctrine of baptismal regeneration is 'not contrary or repugnant to the declared doctrine of the Church of England as by law established'—a decision that helped to drive H. E. Manning, R. I. Wilberforce, and other Tractarian Anglicans over to Rome—Hatherly must have been thankful to have escaped from heresy. Some time after this he left England for Turkey.

When news was received that he was planning to be ordained in the Greek Orthodox Church, several persons tried hard to prevent what they thought would be a blow to their hope of friendly relations between the Anglican and Eastern Churches. Among them were the Bishops of Carlisle, Ely, and Winchester. First of all the Eastern Church Association protested; Dr John Jackson, who had become Bishop of London in 1869, addressed a vigorous note to the Turkish Ambassador, pointing out the 'difficult complications' and 'serious consequences' predicted if this Englishman's ordination were not prevented. The Ambassador wrote to Aáli Pasha, the Grand Vizier, who, however, did not share Bishop Jackson's fears. After this Rev. William Denton sent telegrams to the Serbian Agent at Constantinople to use his influence; and Dr Wilberforce, Bishop of Oxford, convinced that everything was all right, wrote to congratulate the All-Holy Oecumenical Patriarch, thanking him for refusing to ordain this renegade Anglican, and 'thus preventing schism'.[1] Nevertheless Hatherly's ordination to the priesthood took place in Constantinople about 1870, in spite of the opposition resulting from the pro-Latin instincts of many distinguished Anglican bishops, clergy, and layfolk.

Having become a Greek *pappas*, Hatherly left Turkey for Russia, just too soon, however, to witness Moslems venerating the

---

[1] cf. ibid., p. 3, note 1. The Rev. William Denton, M.A. (vicar of St Bartholomew's, Cripplegate, from 1850 until his death in 1888), took a keen interest in the Eastern Churches. In 1862 he published *Servia and the Servians*, and in 1883 *The Ancient Church of Egypt*. Fr Ignatius was his curate for a short time in 1755.

'Honourable Belt' of the Holy Theotokos, brought in a three-mile long procession from Mount Athos to abate—successfully too— an epidemic of cholera. Then he returned to England with the name of Timotheos, and the rank of Proto-Presbyter of the Patriarchal Oecumenical Throne, and settled at Wolverhampton, where he opened a Greek Orthodox Chapel. Among his little flock were two laymen named Robertson and Shann, both of whom helped him to prepare a vernacular version of the Liturgy of St John Chrysostom.[1] But any missionary effort in Britain was banned by the Oecumenical Patriarch, who forbade the Proto-Presbyter Timotheos 'to proselytize a single member of the Anglican Church'. Very likely Archbishop Lycurgos had advised him that it was wiser to keep on the right side of the authorities of the Church of England.

So Hatherly had to limit his apostolate to aliens, and on December 18, 1873, he was mainly responsible for the opening of a Greek Seamen's Church at Cardiff.[2] His microscopic Anglo-Oriental body was still functioning in the spring of 1877, when the Rev. T. W. Mossman, vicar of West Torrington, Lincolnshire (not yet the Order of Corporate Reunion 'Bishop of Selby'), wrote to Dr F. G. Lee, asking:

'Can you put me into communication with the promoters of the Autocephalous Eastern Church in communion with the Churches of the East? Is not Mr John Baxter of Dorlaston and a Mr Hathaway [*sic*] of Wolverhampton, or somewhere in that neighbourhood among them?'[3]

Unlike Overbeck, Hatherly did not indulge in publicity, and his little body, which was in communion with the Greek Orthodox Church, remained very much of an underground movement. It has been said that a Greek bishop once ordained several deacons and priests; and it is possible that these ordinations were performed by Archbishop Lycurgos when he was travelling around England. If so, they were kept secret, since Lycurgos was a politician and diplomat, and did not want to imbroil himself with the Anglican authorities. Both in 1873 and 1874 the Proto-Presbyter

---

[1] G. V. Shann lived at Kidderminster. Among his publications were a translation of *The All Night Vigil* (1877); and *Euchology, A Manual of Prayers of the Holy Orthodox Church* (1891). Advertised for publication in May 1877 was *The Office for the Lord's Day*. Shann also contributed to Overbeck's *Orthodox Catholic Review*.

[2] On March 4, 1877, he attended the opening of another Church for Greek seafarers at Bristol, which was furnished with the assistance of the captain and crew of the brig *Thessalia*. Both these churches were entirely dependent on voluntary offerings.

[3] cf. H. R. T. Brandreth, *Dr Lee of Lambeth*, p. 119.

Timotheos lectured 'from the ambon' in the Greek Syllogus at Manchester; the second discourse being entitled *Ancient and Modern Trends of God's Providential Hand in the History of the Orthodox Church*. He stated, among other facts, how comforted he felt when he read in *The Church Times*, in a letter from Colonel Kiréeff, the words: 'We Easterns could not and would not enter into any bargain with the Old Catholics. We hope there will be no need of "shrewd diplomacy". We hope to find brethren in the West, but we do not purchase allies. As for our "iron conservatism", I hope we will deserve the accusation. We must, and I hope we will, "conserve" the truth which we have inherited from the undivided Church.' The Manchester Greek community was told that, in God's providence, the Eastern Orthodox Church might yet overthrow the Church of Rome, counting her children 'from the shores of the Adriatic to the bays of the Eastern ocean on the coast of America, from the icefields which grind against the Solovetsky Monastery on its savage islet in the North to the heart of the Arabian and Egyptian deserts, on the verge of which stands the Lavra of Sinai'.[1] Notwithstanding his poor material position as compared with an Anglican clergyman, this Englishman chose to become a priest of the Greek Church, and gloried in being able to proclaim in Manchester that there could be no true Christianity that had not a Hellenic or Greek aspect.

Some time after he had delivered this lecture he had the happiness to celebrate the Divine Mysteries in the Church of St George at Smyrna, where, in the presence of at least 2,000 persons, many of whom were English-speaking, he spoke to the congregation, reminding them of the sacredness of this spot, mentioned in the Book of the Apocalypse. The Angel or Metropolitan Bishop of Smyrna, knowing his wish to visit Philadelphia, which even the Turks called 'The City of God', gave him a Letter of Introduction to his brother Angel of Philadelphia, but the fears of the captain of the steamer in which the pilgrimage would have been made obliged the English Proto-Presbyter to cancel the expedition, much to his sorrow.

It is not certain how long it was after his return to England that Hatherly closed his chapel at Wolverhampton, and contented himself by ministering to Greek seafarers at Bristol and Cardiff.[2]

[1] ibid., p. 18.
[2] In 1882, when he was Archpriest of the Greek Orthodox Church at Bristol, he produced a fourth edition (with tunes) of Dr J. M. Neale's *Hymns of the Eastern Church* (1862).

It is related that he joined the Russian Church before his death. His actual relationship in England with the Patriarchal Oecumenical Throne was always somewhat nebulous, and his brave effort to plant a pure and primitive form of Oriental Christianity in England died with him.[1]

[1] About ninety years after Hatherly introduced the Byzantine Rite into Wolverhampton it was revived there by a priest of the Apostolic Exarchate for Ukrainians in England and Wales. Little could Hatherly have guessed that the sixth successor of Cardinal Manning as Archbishop of Westminster would also hold the title of Apostolic Exarch for the Ukrainians, with ten churches in England and Wales, and a pro-cathedral in Saffron Hill, London, E.C.1. Eastern Churches are now fairly numerous in Britain. In London alone there is a Greek Archbishop in Bayswater, and two Russian churches (a Cathedral at the former All Saints, Ennismore Gardens, acknowledging the U.S.S.R., and 'The Russian Church in Exile' off Gloucester Road); not to mention Armenian, Serbian, and Cypriot churches, and a White Russian (Byelorussian) Catholic Mission at North Finchley. There is even a Russian Orthodox monastery in Essex, in communion with Moscow. We have indeed become more Oriental-minded than when J. Joseph Overbeck and S. G. Hatherly dreamed of planting autocephalous Eastern Churches in England.

CHAPTER III

Ambrose Phillipps de Lisle
and the Order of Corporate Reunion

The two previous chapters dealt with projects to unite the Churches, and with schemes to form autocephalous Eastern Church of England with one or other of the Eastern Churches in Western Europe, founded with the express object of breaking the power of the Papacy. Now we turn to another plan which aimed at corporate reunion between the Church of England and the Holy See, by means of a Uniate Church, similar to those Eastern Churches which are in communion with Rome.

The vision of an English Uniate Church was first seen by Ambrose Lisle March-Phillipps (1809–78). Born of Anglican parents, his father being a wealthy Leicestershire squire, owning the estates of Garendon Park and Grace-Dieu Manor, Ambrose was received into the Roman Church at the age of fifteen. A few years before his death, he wrote to his fellow convert, the Rev. William R. Brownlow, who became Bishop of Clifton in 1894, that there had been three great objects to which he felt drawn after his conversion. The first was to restore the contemplative form of monastic life in England; the second to restore the primitive ecclesiastical chant; and the third (to quote his own words)—
'the restoration of the Anglican Church to Catholic Unity, and thus to reunite England to the See of St Peter as St Edward the Confessor foretold that the *Green* Tree of England, which was to be "severed from the original stock for the *space of three furlongs* (three centuries) should again return there without the help of any man's hand and flourish exceedingly". God knows how I have laboured for all these three objects, and how I continue to labour for the last of them.'[1]

This was a fair summary of the writer's life-work. As a boy he once saw a bright light in the sky and heard a voice saying,

[1] E. S. Purcell, *Life and Letters of Ambrose Phillipps de Lisle* (1900), vol. I, p. 349.

'Mahomet is anti-Christ, for he denieth the Father and the Son'. Phillipps does not seem to have had any dealings with Islam, but he went on having visions all his life. For more than half a century he laboured to reunite the Provinces of Canterbury and York with the Patriarchate of Rome. He was always a romantic. His methods of seeking to achieve reunion were true to his character. This can be seen from his correspondence with John Rouse Bloxam (1807– 91), a Fellow of Magdalen College, Oxford—a friend of most of the leaders of the Tractarian movement, and 'the father or grand-father of all ritualistics', as Lord Blachford put it.[1] The first letter, written in 1841, explained at great length that Phillipps regarded the Church of England as the true Catholic Church of the nation, even if no longer in communion with the Holy See. He was also 'disposed to admit the genuineness of Anglican orders', and told Bloxam that, as a priest of this true Catholic Church, he 'offered the immaculate lamb in the Most Holy Eucharist' every time he administered the Lord's Supper or Holy Communion according to the Book of Common Prayer.[2]

He went on to tell Bloxam that once the true Catholic Church in this kingdom had regained her liberty and independence from State tyranny, and was reunited with the Holy See, he had visions of 'the Service of God according to the holy Sarum rite' being 'celebrated in all Cathedrals, Collegiate and Conventual Churches in the Latin tongue'. He hoped that 'Vespers might be sung in English, and those portions of the Mass, which the Sarum rite prescribes to be said in a loud voice, might also be celebrated in English, whilst the Canon being said in a low voice by the Priest alone would continue in Latin'. The clergy would give up the recitation of Mattins and Evensong, and adopt the Sarum Breviary in Latin. Where there was 'a sufficient number to celebrate the Canonical Hours they would sing them in Latin using the holy ceremonies and the vestments'. The optimistic young convert was certain that 'the Holy See would give every *facility* for the restora-tion of the Catholick Unity in England. Thus the present Bishops and Priests might retain their wives, and even certain relaxations of the ancient Canons might be permitted in future for the Angli-can Clergy, if they desired it before God'.[3]

[1] Many of the letters were printed by R. D. Middleton in *Newman and Bloxam, An Oxford Friendship* (Oxford, 1947).
[2] Few of Phillipps's fellow Catholics would have endorsed this opinion, though it was not until 1896 that Leo XIII in his encyclical *Apostolicae Curae* formally condemned Anglican orders as invalid through defect of both form and intention.
[3] ibid., pp. 105–6.

The Right Rev. F. G. Lee, D.C.L., D.D., Bishop of Dorchester, Order of Corporate Reunion, vicar of All Saints', Lambeth, 1867–1899.

Phillipps was confident that Gregory XVI would 'sanction the suppression of the direct invocation of saints in the public liturgy', and understand that there must be restraint in 'the use of pictures and images' so far as England was concerned. He just could not 'conceive that there need be the slightest difficulty upon this head'. Moreover—and this was very important—he was sure that 'the great body of the Aristocracy would follow the movement of the Clergy' in the Romeward direction. If negotiations could be started at once, 'the public mind would soon be prepared'. It would be easy to convince the young Queen Victoria and the Prince Consort 'of the propriety of supporting such a glorious measure with the whole force of the State'. Should the Dissenters, the Orangemen, or the Evangelical party in the Established Church protest, or even 'proceed to open rebellion, they would be crushed immediately'. Last, but not least, it was certain that the Lower Orders would welcome 'the restoration of the old quadripartite division of Church property'.

These opinions were expressed only twelve years after the passing of the Catholic Relief Act, 1829, and shortly after the storm provoked by the publication of Tract 90. This thirty-two-year-old Leicestershire squire was clearly out of sympathy with the 'Establishment' of his day. He was, nevertheless, active and prominent in an equally real world which was in touch, as Victorian England generally was not, with the European Christian and Catholic tradition. He had a large family and he and his wife entertained lavishly at Grace-Dieu Manor. The house-parties often included Anglican clergymen and laymen of a temper congenial to their host. As the twentieth-century ecumenical movement has found, hospitality in a strange but friendly setting is a powerful solvent of ecclesiastical differences. The Anglican guests who assisted at the inspiring religious functions carried out in William Railton's Gothic Revival domestic chapel (enlarged and richly furnished by A. W. Pugin in 1848) must sometimes have found it difficult to remember that in the eyes of the Holy See they themselves were schismatics, if not heretics. Newman was characteristically wary. He was more than once invited to stay at Grace-Dieu, but he never went there until after his conversion in 1845, feeling that it was for bishops to take the initiative in reunion and that anyway Rome lacked the note of sanctity.[1]

As far back as 1841 the visionary squire of Grace-Dieu and

[1] See letter to Bloxam, quoted by Middleton, pp. 121-4.

Garendon had planned the formation of a Uniate Church in England; in a letter to Bloxam he said: 'It is no new thing for Catholicks of various rites to dwell together in the same country, each being governed even by Bishops in ordinary'.[1] It was on September 29, 1850, that Pius IX restored the Catholic hierarchy in England by Letters Apostolic (*Universalis Ecclesiae*), with the Metropolitan See at Westminster, and at first twelve Suffragan Sees. Phillipps rejoiced that the Roman authorities had not named any of the new dioceses after the medieval sees. He felt this was a proof that the Pope shared his opinion that the Established Church was the true and canonical Church of the nation. Now one could say that there were Catholics of both the English and Latin rites, each with its own bishops. Sooner or later Queen Victoria and the bishops nominated by her would realize 'it is their right and safe course to unite themselves to a foreign rite, and to the Mother Church of Christendom, and to the immediate pastoral care of Peter'. Everything would work out all right in the long run. All that was needed now was a crusade of prayer.

In the spring of 1857 Phillipps published his eirenic pamphlet *On the future Unity of Christendom*, conveying the impression that before very long both the Eastern Churches and the Anglican Communion would be reunited with the Western Patriarchate. In July he had a meeting in London with Bishop Forbes of Brechin, Mr F. G. Lee, and George F. Boyle (afterwards Earl of Glasgow).[2]

The purpose of this gathering was to discuss how Catholics of the English and Latin rites could unite together in prayer. On September 8, 1857, the feast of the Nativity of the Blessed Virgin

[1] Middleton, op. cit., p. 105.

[2] Alexander Penrose Forbes (1817–75), often known as the 'Scottish Pusey', came under the influence of the Oxford Movement in 1840. He was elected Bishop of Brechin in 1847, and for the rest of his life devoted himself to the pastoral work of his bishopric in accordance with scholarship, and working for the reunion of Christendom. His defence of the doctrine of the Real Presence in 1857 led to his censure by the Scottish college of bishops in 1860.

Frederick George Lee (1832–1902) was ordained priest in the Church of England in 1854. Appointed rector of St John's, Aberdeen, in 1859, he was forced to leave the city in 1864 owing to his bishop's objections to the ritual and ceremonial in the new Church of St Mary, Carden Place, 'the tartan kirk', built at his own financial risk. He became vicar of All Saints', Lambeth, in 1867, and remained in charge of the parish until he retired in 1899. He was received into the Roman Church shortly before his death. (See p. 82.) He was the author of many books dealing with theology, church history, occult phenomena, and ceremonial.

George Frederick Boyle, born in 1825, became 6th Earl of Glasgow in 1869. In his younger days he was one of the leading lay supporters of the Tractarian movement in Scotland, the founder of the College of the Holy Spirit, Cumbrae, and a generous benefactor to any cause which he hoped would promote Catholic principles.

Mary, an organization known as the Association for the Promotion of the Unity of Christendom was founded. Its object was defined as 'united prayer that visible unity may be restored to Christendom'. Although there were four Roman Catholics among the founders,[1] and it received the blessing of Cardinal Wiseman, many priests, including Manning, regarded it with suspicion, if not alarm.[2] It was Manning who persuaded the Catholic hierarchy in England to take action, with the result that a papal rescript, dated September 16, 1864, condemned the Association. The English bishops were ordered to take immediate steps to prevent the faithful having any further part in its activities.

Phillipps, who had adopted the name of de Lisle in 1863, as the representative of that ancient family, was not downhearted. Contemplating the Church of England from Grace-Dieu Manor of Garendon Park, his 'mind soared over the separation between Rome and Canterbury like a skylark over a hedge'—as was said of the second Viscount Halifax.[3] He rejoiced at the rapid progress of the Catholic Movement, and would point to the fact that his prophecy of 1841 had come true, vernacular versions of the Sarum Missal were being used in a few parish churches, if not yet in any cathedrals.[4] Vestments were being worn, and even incense burned in two or three places. Even more encouraging, perhaps, was the report of the foundation of a Congregation of the Venerable Bede —an esoteric body whose members were said to be working underground for the reunion of *Ecclesia Anglicana* with both the Western and Eastern Patriarchates.[5]

De Lisle's visions found expression in the chapter he contributed to *Essays on the Re-Union of Christendom*, published in 1867.[6] He painted a glowing picture of the Catholic worship now found in more and more Anglican churches—'restored in all their ancient grandeur. The sweet perfume of holy incense is again inhaled in our ancient temples, the names of Mary and the Saints are again

---

[1] Rev. William Lockhart, Inst. Ch.; Rev. Henry Collins (a Cistercian monk of Mount St Bernard Abbey); H. N. Oxenham; and Ambrose March-Phillipps.

[2] cf. Sir Shane Leslie, *H. E. Manning, His Life and Labours* (1921), p. 176.

[3] G. L. Prestige, *Life of Charles Gore* (1935), p. 341.

[4] This was untrue: no Anglo-Catholic clergymen at that date had begun to use vernacular versions of either the Roman or Sarum Missals. All they did was to insert the Gelasian Canon into the B.C.P. rite, plus 'Sarum' ceremonial.

[5] cf. J. Embry, *The Catholic Movement and the Society of the Holy Cross* (1931), p. 140.

[6] The book was dedicated to Francis Joseph I, Emperor of Austria; Alexander Nicolaewitch, Emperor of Russia; and Albert Edward, Prince of Wales; as being the leading laymen of the Roman Catholic, Eastern, and Anglican Communions.

honoured and invoked, and men are once more called to the practice of sanctity, and the imitation of the Saints', and 'the people are once more summoned to the Tribunal of Penance, and Catholic morality is again inculcated in pulpits that used to utter only the errors of Calvin or Luther'.[1] The second spring had been succeeded by high summer, and the fields were ripe for the harvest. 'Those pulpits that heretofore resounded with blasphemous denunciations of the Real Presence and scoffings at transubstantiation, now pour forth orthodox and devotional vindications of Christ's Presence in the Sacrament of the altar, and of the priceless value of that clean oblation, which the prophet Malachi had foretold should everywhere be offered among the converted Gentiles from the rising to the setting of the sun.'[2]

Any foreign ecclesiastic reading de Lisle's flamboyant phraseology might have inferred that Dr Longley, Archbishop of Canterbury, Dr Thomson, Archbishop of York, and the rest of the Church of England hierarchy were accustomed to pontificate at High Mass and Vespers in their respective cathedrals, vested in chasubles or copes, with mitres and croziers. De Lisle carefully avoided any reference to the persecution of the so-called 'Puseyite' clergymen, which would have suggested that the minds of the authorities in the Church of England were not quite so Catholic as the worship he described.

He was appointed High Sheriff of the county of Leicester in 1868, and chose Dr F. G. Lee as his chaplain, but Canon D. J. Vaughan, vicar of St Martin's, Leicester, refused to allow this notorious 'ritualist' to preach the assize sermon before the judges. The squire of Grace-Dieu also took on the spiritual responsibilities of godfather to Lee's second son, Ambrose de Lisle, when the child was baptized in the Church of England.

De Lisle invited some of his Anglo-Catholic friends to stay with him shortly after the publication of the *Essays*, some of which were quite as pro-Roman as his own contribution. Between them they drew up the tentative project for the Uniate Church. Communion under both kinds would be allowed, and even married bishops would be tolerated. On the other hand, it would be better if men already ordained were forbidden to take wives. Lastly, to ensure absolute validity of orders, it would be advisable in the first instance for deacons, priests and bishops to be re-ordained

[1] p. 262.
[2] ibid.

Ambrose Phillipps de Lisle

sub conditione by prelates of the Latin rite with powers delegated for that purpose by the Holy See.[1] The Uniate Church, which was planned at Grace-Dieu Manor, for the intentions of which many Masses were offered in its magnificent chapel, and in the unfinished church at Mount St Bernard's Abbey, would have a vernacular liturgy, based on the Book of Common Prayer. The promoters decided that 'such additions would only be made as would validate ordination services of bishops, priests, and deacons; and make orthodox and perfect the celebration of the Holy Eucharist'.[2]

Among those whom de Lisle invited to draw up a scheme for this Uniate Church was Dr John Thomas Seccombe, who stayed at Mount St Bernard's Abbey in his youth (though it is not certain that he was ever in communion with Rome), and later on is said to have joined one of the Eastern Churches, just as S. G. Hatherly did in 1856.[3] It was early in 1877 that Seccombe wrote to Dr Lee, saying:

[1] cf. Purcell, op. cit., vol. II, p. 19.

[2] By this time Mr Charles Walker of Brighton was busy correcting the proofs of a liturgy of this type, which was published in 1868 with the title of *Services of the Church, with rubrical directions according to the Use of the Illustrious Church of Sarum*. The Rev. John Purchas had already paved the way for this book by his *Directorium Anglicanum*, the first edition of which appeared in 1858. Its purpose was to 'accommodate the rubrics of The Book of Common Prayer to the ceremonial of the Mass in the Sarum Missal'. Dr F. G. Lee edited a revised edition published in 1865, which was somewhat 'higher' in tone. Even bolder, the Rev. Orby Shipley was working on *The Ritual of the Altar*, in which he would show how to celebrate the Communion service so that it would look very little different to the *Ordo Missae* as revised by St Pius V in 1570. The laity, too, were being well grounded in Catholic ceremonial, thanks to Mr Walker's little volume, *The Ritual Reason Why*, and, after 1874, *The People's Mass Book*.

Since 1858 it had been possible for Anglican clergy and laity to make use of a somewhat bowdlerized vernacular version of the *Horae Diurnae*, entitled *The Day Hours of the Church of England*. This book was the thin end of the wedge to *The Day Office of the Church*, which was an unexpurgated translation of a Mechlin edition of the *Horae Diurnae Breviarii Romani*. These were far from being all the vernacular diurnals on the market by the late eighteen-sixties. After 1870 a clergyman could substitute the recitation of Mattins as printed in the B.C.P. by buying the three volumes of *The Night Hours of the Church*, published by Dr Neale's Sisterhood of St Margaret, East Grinstead. All these liturgical books, and many more, were quite enough to make de Lisle believe that the prophecy of St Edward the Confessor, that 'the Green Tree of England' would be re-united with the See of Peter after three centuries, was about to be fulfilled.

[3] See p. 53. References to Seccombe's associations with Julius Ferrette, Bishop of Iona, will be found on p. 42. He was born in 1835. The official Medical Register 1877 gives Seccombe's qualifications as: Mem. Coll. Surg. Eng. 1858; Lic.Soc. Apoth. London 1859; M.D. Univ. St Andrews 1862. Between 1859 and 1864 he had a practice in Millwall on the Isle of Dogs, where he acted as Medical Officer to the South District Poplar Union, Public Vaccinator, and Surgeon to the Royal Liver Friendly Society. Then he moved to Terrington St Clements, King's Lynn, Norfolk, where he was Medical Officer to the 4th and 5th Districts Wisbech Union, and Surgeon to the Oddfellows, Tradesmen Friendly, Old Benefit, Wesleyan, and Independent Benefit Societies. His wide range of interests are indicated by one work listed in the British Museum catalogue: *Science, Theism and Revelation, considered in relation to Mr Mill's essay on Nature, Religion and Atheism* (1875). He died in 1895.

'I have been working hard at the scheme, not without result, as I will show you when we meet. There is nothing like having a definite course chalked out, for when the time of action comes it often happens that mistakes are made by want of consideration. But whatever is done, I hope the Establishment may remain for many years—even though we may not share the advantages of it.'[1]

At least a rough draft of this 'scheme' had been prepared some time before this, for it was early in 1876 that it was disclosed in a pamphlet by 'Presbyter Anglicanus'.[2] It took the form of an open letter addressed to Cardinal Manning.

De Lisle distributed copies among his friends, and on January 12, 1876, he wrote to Manning:

'I hear from various quarters—all more or less good and reliable sources—the actual number of whom Presbyter Anglicanus as the deputed mouthpiece variously estimated as from 500 to 1,000 of the clergy and from 50,000 to 100,000 of the laity. Be this as it may, if the snowball is favoured by the Holy See, it will gather round it even millions—all who care for Christianity in our very dear old England!—and of one thing I am perfectly certain, that WE with our *countless encumbrances* and our *frightful burden of abuses from one end of the Earth to the other*, shall never win England or any other nation again, but shall continue to lose every day more and more of the few that remain to us. But behold the Lord sends us an offer of new Life, which may be the germ of moral regeneration for the whole earth under the fostering care of the Holy See.'[3]

At this time de Lisle was in one of his most apocalyptic moods. A week later he addressed another letter to Manning, warning him of the 'avalanche' which he saw sweeping down in the near future over Westminster and the whole of Britain. He wrote:

'Will it be a snowball gathering in size as it rolls down, or will it evaporate in a cloud of vapour? This under God rests with you. If you give it a valiant support the movement will embrace all who are needed, from the Prince who is destined to rule us to the peasant who waits upon the landlords of England.'[4]

At that moment the Prince of Wales was touring around India, and it is difficult to believe that he would have been much inclined to give his support to a movement which had for its object to

[1] Brandreth, op. cit., p. 120.
[2] The author was Edmund Huff, but Dr Lee had a good deal to do with it.
[3] Purcell, op. cit., vol. II, p. 23.
[4] ibid., p. 25.

bring the Established Church under the control of the Papacy. As to the average village yokel, he had an ingrained fear and hatred of everything associated with popery. De Lisle also tried to win the support of Newman, but his reply, dated January 19, 1876, was very critical, even if sympathetic.[1]

Feeling, perhaps, that he had been too hard on de Lisle, Newman wrote again on January 27, saying:

'Nothing will rejoice me more than to find that the Holy See considers it safe and promising to sanction some such plans as the Pamphlet suggests. I give my best prayers, such as they are, that some measure of drawing to us so many good people, who are now shivering at our gates, may be discovered.'

Most Catholics were alarmed by the scheme proposed in the pamphlet, and it was attacked in *The Tablet*, Dr Littledale denounced it as a dastardly intrigue with Rome, and the majority of High Anglicans were hostile. Abuse was showered on 'Presbyter Anglicanus', who was suspected of being the vicar of All Saints', Lambeth. Dr Lee defended the pamphlet in several letters printed in *The Tablet*, stating that he had received assurances of sympathy which more than out-balanced the abuse of opponents. He explained that the scheme suggested was in no way a plot against the Established Church of England. A correspondent described him in the *Guardian* as 'a cheat, a swindler, a traitor, and a fool'. On April 19, 1876, 'Presbyter Anglicanus' (the Rev. Edmund Huff, rector of Little Cawthorpe, Lincs., 1853–91, and author of *First Principles of the Laws of England*) wrote:

'It remains to be seen whether any of the Anglican clergy will avail themselves of the opportunity which now seems offered to them of approaching collectively the Holy See, and submitting their difficulties to its consideration—thus opposing a united front to the growing forces of irreligion and unbelief.'

Things could not have been worse so far as the High Church Anglican clergymen were concerned. In February 1876 the Rev. C. J. Ridsdale, vicar of Folkestone, was tried by Lord Penzance at Lambeth Palace for illegal ceremonial with a verdict for the plaintiffs. In July the Rev. Arthur Tooth, of St James's, Hatcham, and the Rev. T. Pelham Dale, of St Vedast's in the City of London, were both summoned to appear before the courts. The former was committed to Horsemonger Gaol, and the latter confined in Holloway Prison. These cases were only the start of prosecutions

[1] ibid., p 26. The letter is given *in extenso*.

for what was maintained to be illegal ceremonial. There was sufficient excuse for Anglo-Catholics to seek any means of gaining their freedom from the trammels of the Establishment, no matter what means they employed: to the papalist minority it was evident that the Gordian knot must be cut and cut quickly.

The amiable de Lisle was moving heaven and earth to assist this minority, and he had the support of his domestic chaplain, Fr Cesario Tondini di Quarenghi, an Italian Barnabite, who was a priest of large ideas and extremely liberal views.[1] De Lisle wrote about him to Gladstone, saying: 'He is profiting, I think, by what he observes every day in the development of sound and charitable feeling between the members of our respective Communions.'[2] Fr Henry Collins, and other Cistercian monks at Mount St Bernard's Abbey, also encouraged their founder in his scheme for a Uniate Church in England. So de Lisle went on oiling the wheels at Rome; informing cardinals and monsignori that the persecuted Anglican clergymen deserved every possible sympathy and encouragement, not only for their own sake, but for that of the Catholic world at large. Fr Tondini petitioned Pius IX to bless an Association of Prayers for the Return of the separated Churches of the East, especially the Graeco-Russian Church, to Catholic Unity. At the end of the petition Tondini had inserted the request that papal approval might be 'extended so as to include in its intentions, not only the non-Catholics of the East, but also all Christians now separated from the centre of unity, and more especially the Anglicans, and others of these Kingdoms'.

The Pope returned the document, with the words: '*Benedicat et exaudiat vos Deus*', and dated May 13, 1877.[3] De Lisle immediately informed Gladstone of this glorious news, saying: 'The Pope has now committed himself over head and ears to the two points for which I have always agitated through good report and evil report. The first is for the Principle of Corporate Reunion. The second is for the special Prayers for the Reunion of the Graeco-Russian Church with our Latin Church.'[4]

Fr J. H. Crehan, S.J., commenting upon the above in an article published in *The Month* (June 1953), wrote: 'What de Lisle obtained from Pius IX, then in the last year of his life, will

[1] The Barnabites (Clerks Regular of St Paul) were founded in 1530 by St Antonio Maria Zaccaria.
[2] Purcell, op. cit., vol. II, p. 97.
[3] cf. *The Tablet*, June 16, 1877.
[4] Purcell, op. cit., vol. II, p. 175. Reading the petition carefully, it is impossible to discover any reference to 'Corporate Reunion'.

probably never be known, but if one supposed that the Pope had given de Lisle some verbal warrant for going ahead with his plans, it would explain something of what followed in the episode of the clandestine consecrations. It hardly needs saying that to de Lisle corporate reunion meant the creation of a Uniate Church in England with orders derived in the first instance from Latin prelates.'[1]

It is unlikely that it will ever be discovered what went on behind the scenes during the winter and spring of 1876–7, because in after years Dr Lee took care to destroy all evidence. Others involved in the project of a Uniate Church also felt it safer to burn the relevant letters and documents. The Rev. H. R. T. Brandreth, after thorough research, found little new material to give the readers of his *Dr Lee of Lambeth: A Chapter in Parenthesis in the History of the Oxford Movement*. It is possible, however, considering Fr Nugée's previous contacts as Secretary of the A.P.U.C. with Cardinal Patrizi and his knowledge of the workings of the Roman Curia, that it was he who negotiated with certain important ecclesiastics. Correspondence may have been carried on between the Vatican and St Austin's Priory in the New Kent Road, Nugée's 'monkery of rich men'—a most unconventional sort of community. It is suggested that 'Cardinal Mai, whose name was constantly whispered as being concerned in the conspiracy, did persuade the Pope to turn a pontifical "blind eye" to the proceedings until it should be seen how the venture would fare. This would account for some later curious facts.'[2] A more curious fact still is that Cardinal Mai died in 1854.

Whether the scheme was being planned in the slums of Lambeth or in the slums of Walworth, preparations went forward. Encouraged by what they regarded as papal approval and urged on by de Lisle from his mansion on Charnwood Forest, the promoters of the Uniate Church decided to hold a 'Synod' early in July 1877. They informed de Lisle, who replied:

'I hail the meeting of the first Synod of the new Ecclesiastical organization as one of the most important steps that has been taken since the era of the Reformation. I shall commend it to the prayers of our chaplain in the celebration of the most Holy Mysteries in our chapel tomorrow, and most heartily do I pray that God will pour out His Blessing upon the Synod, and guide it by His Holy and

[1] op. cit., p. 355.
[2] Brandreth, op. cit., p. 125.

67

Life-giving Spirit, so that it may become a great instrument towards promoting the Reunion of Christendom, and thus paving the way for the full development of the Kingdom of Jesus Christ over the whole world. The hearts of all good men seem now more and more turned towards Rome, and the healing of our deplorable divisions; but we have all sinned and we must all humble ourselves before God, and implore His mercy and assistance. The Holy Sacrifice will also be celebrated for this intention tomorrow in the Church of St Bernard's Abbey.'[1]

The Synod duly took place, and on July 7, 1877, *The Tablet* reprinted a notice which had appeared in the *Morning Post* the previous Thursday, headed 'The Order of Corporate Reunion'. It said that—

'The first synod of this new organization—regarding which such varied rumours and reports have been current for some months past—was held in London on Tuesday and Wednesday, the 3rd and 4th of this month. The proceedings, which, so we are informed, were conducted with all the order and gravity common to solemn synods, was opened by Mass of the Holy Ghost, according to the Sarum Rite, followed by prayers and intercessions given in Gavantus. The work undertaken by the promoters was carried on and completed in perfect unanimity. We understand that a formal pastoral of the rector and provincials will be issued early in September.'[2]

Further hints of this development were given by Dr Lee in a letter printed in the *Morning Post* on July 14, 1877. He stressed the major evils of the Established Church as it then existed, and in the final paragraph indicated what he and his colleagues had been devising in shadow of Lambeth Palace, saying:

'Absolutely denouncing all lawlessness, with sacramental basis on which no dark shadow of doubt can henceforth ever fall, and with dogmatic principles accepted by both East and West, we bind ourselves together anew under godly obedience and discipline for necessary self-defence, for co-operation, and for promoting the grand and most necessary work of Corporate Reunion, the highest and greatest need of our time. . . . Even the lower animals, when attacked, have the instinct to herd together for self-defence. We shall do no more, but we shall do no less.'

[1] *The Reunion Magazine*, vol. I (1877), p. 355.
[2] Bartolommeo Gavanti (1569–1638), a Barnabite liturgical scholar, was the author of *Thesaurus sacrorum rituum, Seu Commentaria in rubricas Missalis et Breviarii Romani* (Rome, 1628).

Ambrose Phillipps de Lisle

This letter evoked a sympathetic reply from the Irish poet, Aubrey de Vere (1814–1902), whom Lee had taken into his confidence. Like de Lisle, he had never lost his affection for the Church of England after he entered the Church of Rome in 1851 as the result of the Gorham Judgment.[1]

The Rector and Provincials of this new organization were now ready for their subversive activities. At the same time that William Booth and the inner circle of the Christian Mission in East London were drawing up a rough draft of the organization which a year later would be given the name of The Salvation Army, they were preparing a preliminary version of a Pastoral Letter, which was dated the Feast of the Assumption, August 15, 1877. Later on printed copies of this manifesto were sent to the Pope, and to all 'Catholic Bishops', which presumably meant those in communion with the Holy See. Copies were also posted to the leading newspapers in Britain, so that the general public should be made aware of this 'grand and most necessary work of Corporate Reunion' which had been launched. It started as follows:

Pro Deo, pro ecclesiâ, pro patriâ.

In the Sacred Name of the Most Holy, Undivided and Adorable Trinity, Father Son and Holy Ghost. Amen.

Thomas, by the Favour of GOD, RECTOR, of the ORDER OF CORPORATE REUNION, and *PRO-PROVINCIAL OF CANTERBURY*; *Joseph*, by the Favour of GOD, *PROVINCIAL OF YORK*, in the Kingdom of England; and *Laurence*, by the Favour of GOD, *PROVINCIAL OF CAERLEON*, in the Principality of Wales, with the Provosts and Members of the Synod of the Order, to the Faithful in JESUS CHRIST, whom these Presents may concern, Health and Benediction in the LORD GOD Everlasting.

EVERY faithful Christian must surely be distressed and bewildered at the spectacle afforded by the evil state into which the National Church of England has been brought by departure from ancient principles and by recent events. A long course of change, usurpation, and revolution has removed all her old land-marks. The evil is continually working; no man being able to foresee whereunto it will grow, or what will be the end thereof. Two things are

---

[1] The full text of his long letter will be found in Brandreth's *Dr Lee of Lambeth*, pp. 122–4.

certain, however: on the one hand, that all semblance of independent existence and corporate action has departed from the Established Church, so that she is given up, as it were, bound hand and foot, and blindfolded into the toils of her enemies; while, on the other hand, these enemies are waiting to rob her of her privileges and possessions, and are even now debating how to divide the spoil.

The very long Pastoral continued with a summary of the history of the pre- and post-Reformation *Ecclesia Anglicana*, now utterly dependent on the State. The writers stressed that the bishops had yielded up all canonical authority and jurisdiction in the spiritual order, since they were merely State officials. The Provincials of Canterbury, York, and Caerleon stated that they were engaged in securing 'three distinct and independent lines of new episcopal succession, so as to labour corporately, and on no sandy foundation, for the healing of the breach that has been made'. By the Favour of God they intended to make full use of their authority, and defy the Anglican bishops who had appealed unto Caesar. 'Under the patronage and protection of the Blessed Virgin Mary, Mother of God, the Holy Apostles Peter and Paul, St Gregory the Great, and St Augustine of Canterbury', these three prelates bound themselves together with other members of the Order to contend against the grave and complicated evils which threatened to overwhelm them. They based their dogmatic position upon the Decrees of the Council of Trent and of the Synod of Bethlehem.

It would take up too much space to give a full summary of the rest of this manifesto, which ended with the following words:

'As regards the chief aim of this new Order—Corporate Reunion —it is needful to remark finally, that, while We have to deplore the divisions existing amongst the churches, We cannot unchurch any having a true succession. Therefore, We pray for all, We remove all stumbling-blocks in the way of union amongst the baptized, whom We hail and regard as brethren, while, on disputed points of Church opinion not yet defined by lawful Authority. We appeal to a free General Council, with earnest prayers to God for its speedy assembly and guidance by the Holy Ghost. Amen.'[1]

To appreciate the full flavour of this ambitious pronouncement, and to understand how remote it was from reality, it must be considered in relation to contemporary events and the setting in which

[1] The full text of the Pastoral was reprinted in *The Tablet*, January 23, 1909.

Ambrose Phillipps de Lisle

it was composed. On January 1, 1877, Queen Victoria had been proclaimed Empress of India with much magnificence at Delhi, Calcutta, Madras and Bombay. Russia was at war against Turkey; *Our Boys* had not ended its run of 1,350 nights at the Vaudeville Theatre; and William Booth was planning in Whitechapel the reorganization of his Christian Mission as The Salvation Army for the revival of religion among the very lowest classes.

The Pro-Provincial of Canterbury and the Provincials of York and Caerleon drew up their joint Pastoral in a vicarage located in York Street, just off Lower Marsh, Lambeth, so called because the ground lay low, and was damp and soggy. Lower Marsh—the 'Petticoat Lane' of South London—was a sort of rag fair, filled with costers' stalls and barrows, lit up by hissing naphtha lamps after dark. No respectable lady wearing the still fashionable bustle, and quite unable to run because of the tightness of her skirt, dared to walk along Lower Marsh at night. Most of the parishioners of All Saints' were hawkers, small tradespeople, day labourers and mechanics. Few of them ever crossed the threshold of the church. Their poverty was appalling. The back windows of the vicarage looked on to a huddle of mean streets and alleys which had been one of London's most notorious red-light districts for about twenty years. There were at least a dozen gin-palaces, and many more beer shops within a few yards of All Saints'. The Provincials, Provosts and Members of the Order, when gathering for their secret deliberations, had to penetrate these labyrinths of crime, lust and poverty. Within earshot of the vicarage study the trains rumbled on the long brick viaduct between Waterloo and Vauxhall stations. On a hot summer evening, with the window open, the composition of this Pastoral Letter must have been disturbed by the cries of verminous, often bandy-kneed and bow-legged children; or the shouts of youths playing pitch and toss on the pavement of York Street—very likely ogling a gin-sodden female in bedraggled finery as she slipped into the shadows of the dark archway beneath the railway, safe from scrutiny by the police.

Less than half a mile away was Lambeth Palace, secluded in its walled park, one of the official residences of the Archbishop of Canterbury. The time was not yet ripe, however, for a Jesuit Cardinal to lunch there, or for the Primate of All England to call on the Pope, or envisage reunion with Rome on any terms.

The Pastoral was finally read on the steps of St Paul's Cathedral soon after sunrise on the morning of September 8, 1877, but without

71

reference to the Dean and Chapter or to the Bishop of London, Dr Jackson, who was a pious but tolerant Evangelical.

On September 16 *The Tablet* devoted a long article to this extraordinary document, which was entitled 'An Ecclesia in Imperio'. It began:

'We have been looking out since the spring for a phenomenon about which divers dark and mysterious hints have been privately dropped from time to time. It has at length burst upon an astonished world. This phenomenon is nothing less than a kind of Ritualistic crypto-hierarchy.

'On Saturday last, being "the Feast of the Nativity of Our Lady St Mary, the Blessed Mother of God, in the year of Our Lord, and of the World's Redemption, One Thousand, Eight Hundred and Seventy-seven, was drawn up, approved, ratified, and solemnly promulgated in the divinely protected City of London"—a phrase which gives a quite deliciously Oriental flavour to the proceeding— a kind of Bull, Brief, or Encyclical to all "the Faithful whom these Presents concern". It may be naturally asked by whom it is issued. We regret that here the information becomes somewhat defective. The surnames which appear on the face of the document are "Irons", as the delineator and engraver of the somewhat ambitious decoration prefixed to it, and the original of which is apparently intended to be worn round the neck of somebody, and that of "Adrian de Helte", Notary Apostolic, which testifies that on the 15th August this is a true copy of an instrument which we are informed was drawn up on the 8th of September.

'We regret to be unable to inform our readers who these gentlemen are. We do not for a moment suppose that the first name has anything to do with that of a well-known Anglican clergyman.[1] Of the second we know nothing whatsoever. . . . Now for the object of all this solemn fooling—for without wishing to speak harshly, or even unsympathetically, we can call it nothing else. Its authors have opened their eyes to the fact that, as all the authorities of their communion being against them, they are somewhat in the position of rebels. Therefore, by way of mending matters, they have resolved to invent amateur superiors of their own kidney. Nor is it even a pretended Religious Order which the Superiors are to govern. It is rather "a Church within a Church", to which anybody is admitted who can prove that he is baptized, or will submit to

[1] William Josiah Irons (1812–83), at that date a Prebendary of St Paul's Cathedral; still remembered a the author of snumerous popular hymns.

conditional baptism, unless he be "a presbyter" who has been twice married, a divorced person or a deceased wife's sister, a Freemason, or a member of a similar secret society.'[1]

This long article in a leading Roman Catholic weekly must have made de Lisle extremely indignant, but it showed how the Uniate Church for which he had been praying and working since 1841 was regarded by most of his co-religionists. The comments of the Anglican press were even more abusive. If de Lisle were in the secret, he kept to himself the identity of the 'Rector', and 'Provincials' of the new Order, not even revealing them to de Vere, with whom he exchanged several long letters in the autumn of 1877.[2]

With the appearance in the autumn of 1877 of the first number of *The Reunion Magazine*, edited by Dr Lee, the British public was able to understand that the O.C.R. was utterly disloyal to the Church of England, at least as understood by Queen Victoria and all her bishops. For 'Laurentius, Provincial of Caerleon' wrote that—

'It is quite true that we (O.C.R.) do not assume an attitude of independence towards the Holy See. We frankly acknowledge that, in the Providence of God, the Roman Pontiff is the first Bishop of the Church and, therefore ITS VISIBLE HEAD ON EARTH. We do not believe that either the Emperor of Russia or the Queen of England is the head of the Church. As the Church must have some executive head, and as there is no other competitor, we believe the Pope to be that head. But he is more than this, for he is our Patriarch as well. So that we admit his claim to the veneration and LOYALTY of all baptized men, and in a special degree of all Western Christians, and in these capacities we prayed for him in our Constituent Synod.'

After such a pro-papal pronouncement it was not surprising that many Roman Catholics began to look at the O.C.R. more favourably. Indeed, the Jesuit-edited *Civilità Cattolica* went so far as to publish a letter from its English correspondent in the issue for April 20, 1878, in which he wrote:

'The Order of Corporate Reunion actively pursues its labours, and its officers have sent forth a Pastoral Letter containing an exposition of its views and end. It is known that several Anglican ministers in connection with this Society have induced a Greek

---

[1] It was not until the Deceased Wife's Sister's Marriage Act, 1907, that the marriage of a widower with his wife's sister or of a widow with her husband's brother was made legal in Britain.

[2] See Purcell, op. cit., vol. II, p. 28.

Bishop—whose name, however, it has not as yet been possible to ascertain—to ordain them under certain conditions, in order that the doubt to which Anglican orders are subject may not be alleged as a reason for taking exception to the validity of their operations. The three leading officers of the Order have received Episcopal consecration from the same quarter—a quarter which, according to what is said, is of such a character as to completely exclude any question as to the validity of the Orders so conferred, when once the time shall come for submitting the matter for examination by the Holy See. So soon as a sufficient number of the Anglican clergy shall have in this way removed the difficulty which arises from their ordination, the Order hopes to be able to present its petition for Corporate Reunion with the Catholic Church, signed by a number of members so imposing as to render it impossible for the Holy See not to recognize the gravity and importance of the movement.'[1]

Had de Lisle survived this letter, he would have felt that he could almost chant his *Nunc dimittis*, and that his lifelong vision of the reunion of the Anglican and Roman Churches was very nearly a *fait accompli*. But on March 5, three weeks before this issue of the *Civiltà Cattolica* was published in Rome, he died a holy death at Garendon Park.

Very different from the line taken by the Roman Jesuits was that of the anti-papal section of the Anglo-Catholic party. They regarded the Order as utterly beyond contempt, as a new nonconformist sect, set up to defy the true Catholic Church of England. But there was nothing they could do, except to shower abuse, because so far nobody had managed to discover the identity of the mysterious Thomas, Joseph, and Laurence, the Rector and two Provincials of the Order. The secret was well kept.

It was not until December 18, 1878, that *The Church Review*, thanks to the investigations of the Rev. W. Allen Whitworth (then vicar of St John the Evangelist, Hammersmith, and later vicar of All Saints', Margaret Street), disclosed that it was fairly clear, but not absolutely certain, that 'Thomas' was the notorious Rev. F. G. Lee, vicar of All Saints', Lambeth, and that he and his two colleagues (whoever they were) had been consecrated secretly by Roman, Greek, and Armenian bishops.[2]

Mr Whitworth's letter was answered in a pamphlet, entitled *Is the Order of Corporate Reunion Schismatical?* The author was a Mr

[1] op. cit., vol. VI, p. 248.
[2] op. cit., p. 623.

Ambrose Phillipps de Lisle

William Grant, who claimed to be the Registrar of the Order. He corrected certain statements, but did not deny the charge that Dr Lee and his two associates had been consecrated in an irregular manner.

The mystery remained, and it was not until the spring of 1879 that a writer in *The Whitehall Review* said that he was certain that the Rector Provincial was Dr Lee, and the Provincial of York—the Rev. T. W. Mossman.[1] But he concluded wrongly that Bishop Laurence of Caerleon must be the Rev. Joseph Leycester Lyne, otherwise Fr Ignatius of Llanthony.[2] Eventually it was discovered that the third prelate is believed to have been the Norfolk physician and magistrate, John T. Seccombe. (See pp. 42, 63, n.3.)

The reason for selecting these titles is not clear. A diocese of Dorchester in Oxfordshire had been set up in 635 by St Oswald, King of Northumberland, and Cynegils, King of the West Saxons, with St Birinus as its first bishop. The see existed until about 1086 when it was transferred to Lincoln. Selby Abbey, in the West Riding of Yorkshire, founded by William the Conqueror about 1069, was never the seat of a bishopric in pre-Reformation times. The choice of Caerleon in Monmouthshire as the third see suggests that the Order of Corporate Reunion did not recognize the Rev. R. W. Morgan as first Patriarch of a 'revived' Ancient British Church, for he is said to have assumed this title in 1874.[3]

Hartwell de la Garde Grissell, the accomplished papal chamberlain, who collected books, bindings, birds' eggs, brass-rubbings, coins, relics, and much else, recorded in after years that Bishop Lee, who was staying with him in Oxford at the time, enthroned himself in Dorchester Abbey. They made the nine miles' pilgrimage on

---

[1] Thomas Wimberley Mossman (1826–85), ordained priest of the Church of England in 1850, served several curacies, before he was appointed rector of East Torrington and vicar of West Torrington, near Wragby, Lincolnshire, in 1859, where he spent the rest of his life. In 1866 he founded the Brotherhood of the Holy Redeemer for poor ordinands, later moved to Newcastle-upon-Tyne, because Dr Jackson, Bishop of Lincoln, objected to its 'Romish' character. Mossman's contribution to the 1867 *Essays on the Reunion of Christendom* was entitled 'Ritualism in its Relation to Reunion'. He was reconciled with the Roman Church by Cardinal Manning shortly before his death. (See p. 83.)

[2] Joseph Leycester Lyne (1837–1908) was ordained an Anglican deacon in 1860, but no Anglican bishop was prepared to raise him to the priesthood. In 1863, calling himself 'Ignatius of Jesus O.S.B.', he announced that he had revived the Order of St Benedict in communion with Canterbury. After moving his few monks from Claydon (Suffolk) successively to Norwich and to Laleham-on-Thames, he retired in 1869 to the Black Mountains of South Wales, where he erected the never-completed Llanthony Abbey. For his ordination by Joseph René Villate ('Mar Timotheos') see p. 115.

[3] See p. 45.

75

foot very early one morning, and Grissell witnessed the enthronement. There is no evidence, however, that Bishop Mossman ever
did the same at Selby Abbey. The late Prebendary H. F. S.
Mackay, vicar of All Saints', Margaret Street, used to tell a story
that when as a boy he was staying at St Davids, one morning he
found three strange clergymen in the choir of the cathedral. Two of
them were 'conducting a sort of service' over the third, who was
sitting in the bishop's throne. He inclined to think in after years
that he had assisted at the enthronement of Dr Seccombe as Bishop
of Caerleon.[1]

The mystery of the consecrations of Lee and Mossman has never
been solved. All that is fairly certain is that during the summer of
1877 they made a brief trip to Italy, apparently accompanied by
Seccombe, and stayed at Venice. This is how the Rev. H. R. T.
Brandreth sums up the various legends in his *Dr Lee of Lambeth*:

'Near that place (Venice), probably at Murano, Lee, Mossman,
and Seccombe were conditionally re-baptized and confirmed, made
deacon, ordained priest, and consecrated bishop by a mysterious
triumvirate of prelates, the identity of whom has never been
divulged, but who were popularly supposed to have been a Greek,
a Copt, and either a Roman or an Old Catholic. All evidence was
destroyed during Lee's lifetime and thus we are left to build our
theories on circumstantial evidence. It is just possible that the
generally accepted story is true, and certainly the O.C.R. bishops
allowed it to circulate, and no other version of the episode was
accepted by, or current among, responsible people during Lee's
lifetime.

'Certain facts are beyond dispute: namely, that a consecration
did take place in the summer of 1877; that it took place in Italy;
that the bishops consecrated were Lee and Mossman; that the consecrating prelates had Orders accepted as valid at Rome; It is
probable that the prelates were in communion with Rome. The
remainder of the story is open to question. Seccombe was almost
certainly a bishop before 1877, though he was probably given conditional re-consecration by Lee and Mossman on their return from
Italy. A picturesque addition to the story is that it took place on the
high seas, but, that too, is probably not true. The whole business
was so shrouded in secrecy that it is probably impossible

---

[1] cf. Brandreth, op. cit., pp. 141–2. The see of Caerleon was transferred to St
Davids about the time of the Saxon invasion of South Wales, is said to have been,
though modern scholars hold that Caerleon as a see was invented by Geoffrey of
Monmouth (*c.* 1100–1154).

today to arrive with any certainty at the facts of the case. . . .'[1]

Then there is another legend that the prime mover in these clandestine consecrations was Mgr di Calabania, Archbishop of Milan, and that at least one of them was performed by one of his suffragan bishops according to the Ambrosian rite.[2]

But there are yet more stories, and one of them told by the late Dr George C. Williamson, Litt. D., who had been a member of the O.C.R. in his youth, that one of the consecrations took place in Umbria, and the other at or near Venice, probably by some prelate connected with the Armenian Uniate monastery on the Island of San Lazzaro. The name of the Bishop of Murano was also mentioned in connection with the affair, but although Murano—an island in the Venetian lagoons—still has its ancient cathedral, many centuries have passed since it had a bishop, so this suggestion can be dismissed.

Fr Crehan, S.J., inclined to think that the consecrations did actually take place 'on the high seas', or at any rate on tidal waters outside the territorial limits of a diocese (presuming that these are three miles offshore like normal fishing limits), and pointed out:

'If the Pope had given de Lisle a general sanction to go ahead with his scheme, it is quite possible that he did not contemplate the actual steps which Lee and Mossman then took, and that he had not armed them with the canonical dispensations that would have saved them the embarrassment of a day at sea voyaging from Chioggia on the Venetian lagoon or rolling gently in the Pass of Malamocco.'[3]

After Dr Lee had published an article entitled 'The Order of Corporate Reunion' in *The Nineteenth Century*, November 1881, he was attacked again by both Anglicans and Roman Catholics, though some of the latter defended him. A writer in *The Tablet* (December 8, 1881) summed up what most people now felt about the whole business; that it was 'an *ignis fatuus* that has already lured on too

---

[1] op. cit., p. 124.
[2] Fr Crehan, S.J., in an article entitled 'Black Market in Episcopal Orders', which appeared in *The Month* (June 1953), stated that successive researches in the Curia and Archiepiscopal Archives have revealed no traces of consecrations either at the approximate date, or three years before and after the summer of 1877. In the same article he put forward the opinion that the consecrator could have been Mgr J. B. Gigli, O.S.F., who was Bishop of Muro-Lucano in South Italy from 1832 until he retired in 1859. There is no record of what happened to him after this. The story, however, rests merely on the discovery of a small phial labelled 'Holy Chrism supplied by the Right Rev. J. B. Gigli, Bishop of Chardica, and conveyed to the Right Rev. F. G. Lee, D.C.L., November 15, 1877. J. T. Seccombe'. It is not certain if this Franciscan prelate was still alive in 1877, but if so, he may have been responsible for the consecration of Dr Lee somewhere in Italy.
[3] 'Black Market in Episcopal Orders', in *The Month*, June 1953, p. 357.

many souls who had reached the threshold of the Fold, but who remain to die outside—How sad to have to say of such amiable men, Their last state is likely to prove worse than the first'.

The English Church Union, a society formed in 1859 to defend and further the spread of High Church principles among Anglicans, formally expelled Dr Lee from its ranks. The Society of the Holy Cross, composed of Anglo-Catholic priests, removed the name of Bishop Mossman from the Roll of Brethren, issuing a report 'warning Catholics not to be associated with the O.C.R., lest they should be involved in the guilt of schism and probably of sacrilege'.[1]

Taken all round the O.C.R. proved to be little more than a damp squib that did not explode. So few people joined the Order after 1879 that a certain Mr Umfneville, who had been appointed its 'Official Badge Maker', found a large number of badges left on his hands. To recover the cost he brought an action against Lee. Judgment was given in his favour, but on Lee's appeal it was reversed. Although Freemasons and members of other similar secret societies could not be enrolled in the O.C.R., nothing could have been more surreptitious than the manner in which its affairs were conducted. All those who were deemed worthy for initiation had to swear that they would never divulge anything about it, or even reveal the names of other members. Like the Seal of the Confessional, this obligation covered direct and indirect revelation, e.g. unguarded statements from which matters heard in the confessional could be deduced or recognized. How seriously the O.C.R. members regarded their oaths is proved by the fact that none of those who survived the disappearance of the Order in the eighteen-nineties appear to have made public its secrets, not even those who eventually submitted to the Roman Church.

Only four numbers of *The Reunion Magazine* appeared, and it ceased publication in 1879. How many persons were given conditional baptism is not known. Neither has it been recorded what were the number of confirmations imparted by the one or other of the three original bishops. The estimated figures of men ordained or given conditional re-ordination vary from fifty to eight hundred. Not all those who were given the tonsure and minor orders reached the priesthood. Some appear to have got no further than the sub-diaconate. There they were left high and dry, probably to their stupefaction and bewilderment. It is said that in certain cases laymen who had received the priesthood from O.C.R. bishops were

[1] J. Embry, *The Catholic Movement and the S.S.C.* (1931), p. 24.

recommended to go through the formality of Anglican ordination in the Scottish Episcopal Church.[1]

Since All Saints', Lambeth, was repudiated by the Anglo-Catholic organizations, most of the advanced clergy would discourage their flocks from attending services there, and in the confessional they would doubtless treat this as an act of schism. Nevertheless there were some who could not resist the temptation. They would be rewarded by the sight of the vicar in the purple-edged cassock, purple zuchetto, black chimere and episcopal rochet, which made up his costume at Mattins and Evensong. On greater festivals he might even be found wearing a mitre, a late tenth century episcopal headgear which most bishops of the Established Church still kept for their spoons and carriages, and which was not resumed by a Bishop of London until Mandell Creighton's appointment in 1897.

Apart from an increasingly scanty attendance of parishioners the bulk of the congregations was probably made up of the members of such subterranean organizations as the Order of the Holy Redeemer. This Order was remarkably similar to the Order of Corporate Reunion. It was started about 1890, and it made All Saints' the centre of its activities, which indicates that it was sponsored by Bishop Lee. In a letter written by a certain 'Brother John', dated in 1890, his correspondent is asked, 'Shall I have the pleasure of seeing you at All Saints', Lambeth, on Wednesday night, or shall I send you tickets? I can get you a seat in the choir or in the Lady Chapel with the Order.'[2]

This Order had an inner circle called the Brotherhood of the Holy Cross (B.H.C.), made up of young men studying for holy orders. In 1891 the Secretary-General of the Brotherhood wrote in his monthly letter that 'postulants' must make and sign a 'Declaration of Faith'. Its third clause consisted of the words: 'The position of the Bishop of Rome is that of "Archbishop of all the Churches", i.e. Chief Bishop (and consequently Pastor and Teacher) of the Church.' The *Barnet Times*, May 8, 1892, printed a letter, signed 'James, O.H.R.', in which he stated that he believed that 'no man is justified in staying within the Church of England, save when he feels the vocation of God to assist in restoring her to her lost place, in humble, implicit, and unquestioning submission to the See of

---

[1] cf. Letter in *The Tablet*, February 6, 1909.

[2] Walter Walsh, *The Secret History of the Oxford Movement* (6th ed., 1899), p. 237. It is possible that the mysterious 'Order' was a revival of the Brotherhood of the Holy Redeemer, founded by Mossman in 1866.

Peter, and to the authority of our Holy Father the Pope, which is the object of the Order of the Holy Redeemer'. In the following year it was announced that the Order had branches both at home and overseas. *The Manual* indicated that the inner circle was bound by rules of secrecy quite as rigid as those imposed by the O.C.R.

It appears that most of the ordinations and other ceremonies were carried out behind locked doors, either in the private oratory of All Saints' vicarage or until 1892 in the more spacious and stately setting of the Italian Baroque chapel of St Austin's Priory, Walworth, situated between the Elephant and Castle and the Bricklayers' Arms. It is said that a vernacular version of the Sarum Pontifical was used, and that Mass was celebrated according to the same rite. The young men who were ordained in this clandestine manner had the satisfaction of reflecting that their orders were unquestionably valid.[1] It is true that they were irregular, but jurisdiction was not a matter with which they were much concerned. As to the laying on of hands by Dr Thorold, who had taken over South London in 1877 as part of the diocese of Rochester, or by any other bishops of the Established Church, the O.C.R. prelates regarded this as little or nothing but a civil ceremony required to obtain a benefice after valid ordination by one of themselves. In 1889 or perhaps earlier the Bishop of Dorchester re-ordained *sub conditione* the Rev. David Lloyd-Thomas, rector of Grainsby, near Grimsby, and Local Secretary of the A.P.U.C. for the diocese of Lincoln. On July 1 of that year this clergyman preached at All Saints a special sermon on Corporate Reunion to celebrate the twelfth anniversary of the foundation of the O.C.R. He was received into the Roman Church early in 1897. On March 27 that same year *The Tablet* printed a statement that Leo XIII had decided that he need only be re-ordained conditionally.[2]

The Bishop of Dorchester—recalled in his later years as 'an old Oxford don planted in a London slum, somewhat crusty, but by no means rusty, very learned, very antique in his ideas, even in his choice of words'—lingered on in Lambeth forgotten by most of his surviving contemporaries. He was a militant Tory, who venerated

[1] There is a story that Archbishop Temple, who lived at Lambeth Palace at intervals between 1896 and 1902, once remarked to a friend: 'If you want an undoubted bishop, he lives just over my garden wall, Lee, the vicar of All Saints', practically all the strands of apostolic succession meet and unite in him.'

[2] See also *The Church Review*, April, 1, 8 and 29, 1897. W. Gordon Gorman, *Converts to Rome* (1910 ed.), makes no reference to Lloyd-Thomas being re-ordained, after his submission to Rome, and records of the fact that he had a wife and family who submitted at the same time. The Roman ruling must have been purely theoretical.

Ambrose Phillipps de Lisle

Disraeli and hated Gladstone. He believed strongly in class distinctions, and was quite sure that God had not made all men equal. Moreover, he was also an ardent Jacobite and a Legitimist. A visitor who called at the vicarage towards the close of the nineties related:

'As I sat and listened, I felt myself gliding back two or three centuries. The quaint phrases introduced into his conversation from Elizabethan times, the references to the Bishop of Rome as the undisputed head of Christendom, even the environment of the man, the old-fashioned furniture, made the outside din and tumult seem far away. I forgot that hansom-cabs were skimming along the wood-paved streets, that the hoky-poky man was at the street corner surrounded by a group of Board-school children, that the various editions of the half-penny dailies were succeeding one another with strange rapidity, to the yells of the newsboys, "Extra Speshul", "All the winners", "'Orrible double murder and suicide", etc. The Doctor transferred me to other times. . . .'[1]

Leading what was virtually the life of a hermit, buried in his books, the Pro-Provincial of Canterbury went on dreaming as he had always done. There is evidence that in 1892 he was still prepared to 'validate' orders or to confer them on young men before they underwent what they regarded as the legal formality of the laying on of hands by an Anglican bishop.[2] It had made no difference to the Bishop of Dorchester that there had been four Archbishops of Canterbury at Lambeth Palace since he was presented with the living of All Saints in 1867—Dr Longley, Dr Tait, Dr Benson, and Dr Temple—for all left him in peace.

Many more furtive functions must have taken place in the vicarage oratory, or maybe even in the spacious galleried neo-Norman 'pro-cathedral' off Lower Marsh between 1877 and 1899, when the church was demolished by the South Western Railway Company, which had acquired the property for extensions to Waterloo Station. The aged vicar was then forced into an unwilling and unwanted retirement.[3]

[1] M. Hay, *Ten Years in South London*, pp. 9–18, quoted in Brandreth, *Dr Lee of Lambeth*, p. 62.
[2] Among the latter was a young American, Frederick Joseph Kinsman, who wrote that he was thinking of getting ordained by Bishop Lee. He became Bishop of Delaware in 1908, but was reconciled with Rome in 1919, and died in 1944. (See J. A. Douglas in his preface to Brandreth's *Episcopi Vagantes*, 1st ed. only, 1947.)
[3] After the demolition of the chapel of St Austin's Priory, Walworth, its furnishings were handed over to the Nugée family. Some years later a Miss Nugée offered them to Dr Creighton, who was Bishop of London from 1897 to 1901, on condition that they were not broken up but kept together in one church. Some valuable furniture found a home in St Nicholas's, Blackwall, including the Renaissance screen; the residue was taken by Fr Dolling for St Saviour's, Poplar.

81

Ambrose Phillipps de Lisle

Shortly before his death on December 23, 1902, Bishop Lee was at long last received into full communion with the Holy See by Fr Kenelm Digby Best, a priest of the London Oratory. His body was taken to St George's Cathedral, Southwark, for a solemn Requiem Mass. He was buried beside his wife at Brookwood Cemetery, Woking, Surrey.[1]

Like the Bishop of Dorchester, the Bishop of Selby was left undisturbed in his parish. But he did not neglect to use the episcopal powers imparted to him by an unknown prelate in Italy. On November 12, 1881, he raised to the priesthood John Elphinstone Robertson, having previously given him minor orders, the subdiaconate and diaconate. Presumably the ceremonies took place at West Torrington, Lincolnshire, a small hamlet at the back of beyond where secrecy would hardly have been necessary. This cleric managed to officiate in several Anglican parishes until the vicar of Parkstone, Dorset, discovered the irregular source of his orders, and exposed him in *The Church Times*. The English Church Union thereupon demanded that Dr Christopher Wordsworth, Bishop of Lincoln, should inhibit this bogus bishop (for so they regarded him), but this fatherly prelate merely issued a warning and took no further action. However, a year or two later Bishop Mossman ordained Hugh Percy Armelle (*alias* Green) in the parish church of West Torrington, which still retains its Tractarian atmosphere.[2] This ceremony did arouse Dr Wordsworth to action, but 'having given charitable consideration to the age, learning, and moral character of Dr Mossman, and his long connection with the Diocese of Lincoln, has come to the conclusion that he may, without impropriety or injury to the Church, refrain under the circumstances from passing upon his offence, grave though it be, any more severe sentence than that of admonition, has pronounced such sentence accordingly, and warning him to abstain from any repetition of it, under pain of the law, and contempt thereof.'[3]

The Bishop of Selby, now aged fifty-seven, wrote to Cardinal Manning on December 14, 1883:

'I am walking on a path which is as sharp as a razor's edge. But I also feel that so far I am upheld by the prayers of our Immaculate

---

[1] Mrs Lee had made her submission to the Roman Church in 1881. It was decided that her confirmation by the Bishop of Selby was valid, and that she need not be reconfirmed even conditionally.

[2] Bishop Mossman erected the reredos in memory of his wife.

[3] Brandreth, op. cit., p. 134.

Mother. I know not how to express my gratitude to the Holy Father for sending me his special blessing.'[1]

Rather later Mossman wrote again to Manning, saying:

'I must in my character of a Catholic Bishop, by which I mean as possessing true episcopal orders, make to you as Head of the Catholic Church in this land an unrestricted and unconditional submission as to the exercise of the episcopal office for the time to come. The extent of what I have done in the way of Orders you know. With regard to the Sacrament of Confirmation, it has been my chief pleasure. If you tell me to discontinue this, I will, of course, do so.'[2]

Before long he became too frail even to administer Confirmation, using the oil of chrism, blessed by himself in secret. Hearing that he was not likely to live much longer, the Cardinal hurried to Lincoln, drove to West Torrington, received him into the Roman Church, and gave him the Last Sacraments. Dr Mossman died on July 6, 1885, and was buried in the churchyard of this hamlet, where his tombstone is near the south porch.

Very little has been recorded about the ecclesiastical activities of Dr Seccombe, reputed Bishop of Caerleon. Unlike the other two prelates of the O.C.R., he never made his peace with the Holy See. From 1875 he had been one of the churchwardens in his Norfolk parish, and he seems speedily to have subsided into ordinary Anglicanism. He was buried with Anglican rites after his death in 1895, when his second wife, to whom he was married in 1873, discovered to her surprise that he was a bishop.

Within two years of Bishop Lee's death a prelate calling himself 'Mar Stevens Ruby' was said to be running the O.C.R. in a hole and corner manner. On February 19, 1905, the archbishops and bishops of an apparently new organization known as The Society for the Restoration of Apostolic Unity issued their first and, so far as is known, their only Pastoral Letter. The identity of the three prelates who signed their names as 'Vergilius, Archbishop of Whitby; Cuthbert, Bishop of Lindesfarne; and Thomas, Bishop of Dorchester,' has never been revealed, but it is possible, however, that 'Cuthbert' was William Whitebrook, and 'Thomas' certainly Henry B. Ventham.[3]

---

[1] Sir Shane Leslie, *Henry Edward Manning*, p. 179. The papal blessing probably resulted from Manning having forwarded to Rome a copy of Mossman's *Latin Letter to His Holiness Pope Leo XIII, Successor of St Peter and Primate of the Catholic Church.*
[2] ibid.
[3] See pp. 271–274.

Ambrose Phillipps de Lisle

There was at least one man who survived Bishop Lee, and who claimed to be a true O.C.R. bishop. This was J. C. Whitebrook, whose brother William Whitebrook, was consecrated by Bishop Miraglia-Gulotti (of the Vilatte succession) on December 27, 1908, and who may have received a previous consecration.[1]

Arnold Harris Mathew, of whom more later, shortly after his consecration at Utrecht in 1908 as regionary Old Catholic Bishop for England, stated that he had revived the Order of Corporate Reunion.[2] This was not strictly correct, because his organization had no direct continuity with the original O.C.R. The prime mover in this later scheme was Francis Herbert Bacon, an Anglican whom Mathew had raised to the episcopate on January 7, 1911, as titular Bishop of Durham.[3] The issue for June 19, 1912 of *The Torch* (one of Mathew's several short-lived periodicals) featured a whole-page advertisement for 'The Revived Order of Corporate Reunion', of which Archbishop Mathew was the 'Honorary Prelate', and contained the following intimation.

'Since the extinction of the O.C.R. by the death of its three Bishops, the Rt Rev. Fredk. George Lee, of All Saints', Lambeth, the Rt Rev. Thomas W. Mossman, of Torrington, and the Rt Rev. Dr Seccombe, who were all of them consecrated to the Episcopate by the Most Eminent Lord Cardinal Archbishop of Milan in his domestic chapel, no definite step has been taken in the direction of Corporate Reunion with the Holy See. The letter of "Sacerdos Hibernicus" in *The Torch Monthly Review* of May 15th, created a profound interest, and brought together a body of persons who decided to revive the O.C.R.

'Facing the facts that the Roman Church has repeatedly denied the validity of Anglican Orders, and that the Ordinations of the Church of England are not recognized by any church claiming to be Catholic, the promoters of the Revived Order felt that all doubt must be set at rest so far as the Orders of its clerical members were concerned, and they appealed to Archbishop Mathew of the Old Roman Catholic Church, asking if he would accept the position of Honorary Prelate of the Order, and in that capacity give conditional ordination to such members as had received Anglican

[1] See p. 273. Between November 29, 1908, and March 6, 1909, *The Tablet* printed numerous letters dealing with the O.C.R., including several from the Whitebrook brothers. Eventually the editor wrote: 'As the correspondence seems to lead nowhere it may now cease.' This was true, because the writers were either obviously afraid of disclosing facts which they knew, or were simply fishing for information.
[2] See p. 186, n.1.
[3] See p. 182.

Ambrose Phillipps de Lisle

Ordination. His Grace has replied expressing his willingness . . .
and to conditionally ordain such members as are Clergy of the
Established Church and who, having received conditional Baptism
and the Sacrament of Confirmation, sign a Profession of the
Catholic Faith.

*The Archbishop stipulated that it must be made perfectly clear to all
concerned, that his services, in connection with this delicate and
important matter will be given on the express condition that no fee or
reward of any description shall be offered to or will be accepted by
him.*

The Order has now started on its way and seeks to enrol members.
Mere Ritualists are not invited, but earnest-minded Catholics who
sincerely desire to help forward the work of Corporate Reunion
with the Holy See will be cordially welcomed.'

The Titular Bishop of Durham was kept quite busy, giving conditional baptism, confirmation and re-ordination to Anglican
clergymen, usually in his domestic oratory at 33 Esmond Road,
Bedford Park, Chiswick. Their names have never been revealed,
because the revived O.C.R. was as clandestine in its proceedings as
was the original Order.

When Archbishop Mathew published in 1914 *The Catholic
Church of England, its Constitution, Faith, Episcopal Succession, etc.*,
he inserted several regulations to be observed by clerical members
of the O.C.R. For instance, the conditionally re-ordained priests
had to celebrate Mass daily, and to use the *Missale Romanum*, either
in Latin or in the vernacular, 'in place of the mutilated rite
sacrilegiously introduced by Cranmer and the Tudor "reformers" of
the Anglican Church. Where the Missal cannot be used in public
Masses, the defects in the Communion rite of the Book of Common
Prayer must be made good by the use of approved liturgical books'.
Among those recommended was *The Anglican Missal*, published by
the Society of SS. Peter and Paul, founded in 1911. It is not known
how many rectors, vicars, and curates of the Established Church,
having become members of the O.C.R., were re-ordained *sub
conditione* by either Archbishop Mathew or by Bishop Bacon, but it
has been estimated at between two and three hundred, though a
hundred would be nearer the mark. Sometimes the secret was
revealed to the elect, and it was an immense satisfaction to know
that one was receiving valid absolution from such priests, and

assisting at valid Masses said by them, so that there was no need to 'go over to Rome'.

It is possible that an elderly bachelor named Richard C. Jackson succeeded Bacon as head of the Order even before the latter was reconciled with the Church of England.[1] Some letters, dated July 1919, have come to light which are signed 'Richard, Abp. of the O.C.R.'[2] He is one of the most intriguing figures in the ecclesiastical underworld of the past hundred years. Born in 1851, he claimed descent from John of Norfolk, the younger brother and heir apparent of Roger Earl of Norfolk in the reign of Edward I.[3] It is related that at the age of twelve he could recite by heart the whole of the Psalter and much of Dante's *Inferno*. Among his tutors as a boy was Dr J. M. Neale. At Oxford he was introduced to Walter Pater in the spring of 1877. So impressed was the latter by this undergraduate's knowledge of poetry, painting, sculpture, music, and much else, that he decided to write a book about him. Such was the origin of *Marius the Epicurean*, first published in 1885. This typical young aesthete of the early Oscar Wilde era had been in close touch with the Order of Corporate Reunion from its foundation in 1877, and was one of its original members. In 1875 he collaborated with Fr Nugée in preparing a breviary for the use of the Order of St Augustine. After he came down from Oxford he joined this community in the slums of Walworth, best described as a residential club for religious eccentrics, and which was a hotbed of so-called 'Romanism'. Jackson adopted the monastic name of 'Brother à Becket'.[4]

After Fr Nugée's death in 1892 and the dispersal of his 'canons irregular', Brother à Becket retired to Thetford Manor, a large semi-detached house in Camberwell. His wealth, tastes, and temperament were indicated by three 'saloons' (as he called them) —'The Gold Room', 'The White King's Drawing Room', and 'The Salon di Dante'—all overcrowded with reputedly valuable

---

[1] See p. 325. Richard C. Jackson has sometimes been confused with Richard B. Jackson, who, as 'Br Illtyd', had been a monk at Llanthony after the death of Fr Ignatius, and who tested his vocation for a time with the Anglican Benedictines on Caldey Island. He rejoined the community after it was reconciled with the Roman Church, but left in 1921. He became a farmer and was associated with Bishop Stannard and his Catholic Christian Church. This Jackson was killed in 1927.

[2] Some of Jackson's signatures are 'Archprelate of the O.C.R.'

[3] cf. Thomas Wright, *The Life of Walter Pater* (2 vols., 1907), vol. ii, p. 20.

[4] There were many little Anglo-Catholic brotherhoods scattered around the poorer districts of London during the eighteen-eighties and nineties, none of which have survived, except the Benedictine one, founded on the Isle of Dogs in 1896, today represented by the Roman Catholic community at Prinknash Abbey.

paintings, sculptures, rare books, *objets d'art*, and miscellaneous bibelots, in the manner of the time. The bachelor establishment included a richly furnished private oratory.

By whom, when, and where Jackson was ordained priest and consecrated bishop is not known. It is possible that he was raised to the episcopate by the gentleman who called himself 'Apostolic Vicar of the Independent Church of Southern Switzerland', and 'Bishop of Santa Croce in Sicily'; otherwise Edward Rufane Benedict Donkin, who also claimed for himself the rank of Count.[1] Alternately the consecrator may have been either William or J. C. Whitebrook.[2]

Between 1918 and 1920 Jackson, then nearly seventy, attended High Mass at the Anglican Church of St John the Divine, Kennington, on the greater festivals. He was a gaunt and elderly figure, clad in frock coat, and shabby top-hat. He displayed a purple stock, a very large pectoral cross, and a jewelled ring. Rather less prelatical was the drooping grey moustache, retained, perhaps, in memory of Walter Pater. As the sacred ministers, the choir men and boys passed up the centre aisle of George E. Street's Gothic Revival Church, the Archbishop always turned to the priest, deacon, and subdeacon, and with arm slightly raised imparted his blessing. He spoke to nobody, and after the service returned to Thetford Manor, where it was said he lived an eremitical existence.[3]

Richard C. Jackson was eminently fitted to carry on the torch lit by Dr F. G. Lee and Ambrose Phillipps de Lisle. The latter would have found this second generation Archbishop of the Order of Corporate Reunion a kindred spirit in more ways than one. Jackson died in 1937, aged eighty-six.

Soon after the death of Archbishop Mathew in 1919, some of the Anglican priests whom he had conditionally re-ordained and raised to the episcopate managed to get hold of his Register, and carefully erased their names from its pages.[4] At the same time they went on trying to propagate the revived O.C.R. with great

[1] See pp. 141, 142.
[2] See p. 273. Mar Georgius thinks that Jackson may have been raised to the episcopate by Bishop Stevens of the Free Protestant Episcopal Church of England, who is also credited with the title of 2nd Patriarch of the Ancient British Church. (See pp. 46, 221.) About 1915 this aged prelate lived in Camberwell, and on at least two occasions visited the Catholic Apostolic (Irvingite) Church, accompanied by a man similar to the description of Jackson. Perhaps Donkin was the co-consecrator?
[3] These facts are taken from a letter to the Rev. H. R. T. Brandreth from the Rev. J. N. Menin, who was curate of St John the Divine, Kennington, from 1918 to 1920.
[4] See p. 215.

zeal.[1] One of these prelates—probably Bishop Bacon, who acted as Coadjutor to Mgr Williams of the Old Roman Catholic Church from January 17 to October 1, 1920—wrote to a certain 'Father', in a letter dated January 22, 1920, who had already arranged for a conditional re-ordination, and said: 'Why will you not receive the Episcopate at the same time?' The names of four bishops were mentioned in the letter, with a hint that Order could find room for yet another. This same prelate wrote to the same correspondent a fortnight later:

'The Archbishop of Canterbury and Bishops know nothing about the O.C.R., but are always trying to find out, but now that poor old A.H.M. [Mathew] is no more, they will find out still less. I would strongly advise W. not to receive the Priesthood with any idea that it will help him in the *Ecclesia Anglicana*, for it will not. It will make him an undoubted priest and this should be worth much, and all, but it would be better for him to seek ordination in the Anglican Church as a simple candidate (not mentioning the O.C.R.), and look upon the Ceremony as a Ratification of his Baptismal Vows, or something of that sort.'[2]

During the early nineteen-twenties, with their succession of Anglo-Catholic Congresses and Priests' Convention, the craze for baroque and rococo furnishings and decorations in churches went hand in hand with the urge among the more extreme clergy to get their orders 'put right', especially those who were praying and working for reunion with Rome. They wanted to ensure that the Masses they celebrated were 'valid', and a handful had no scruples about going through a conditional re-ordination, which they understood would cost them nothing.[3]

[1] Letters have been preserved which show how these bishops left no stone unturned in their efforts to persuade Anglo-Catholic clergymen to take the chance of getting their orders 'validated'. Most of them are marked 'confidential', and often initials only are given of the persons mentioned.

[2] It is probable that the 'W' mentioned in this letter was William Geoffrey Warwick, who received all minor orders and the subdiaconate from Archbishop Mathew, and whom Bishop Bacon ordained priest on July 14, 1920. It could be that he was also raised to the episcopate. Warwick was re-ordained for the Diocese of London in 1923-4, and after a varied clerical career, became rector of St George's, Bloomsbury, London, in 1939. By 1948 he was Vice-President and Chairman of the Society for Improving the Condition of the Working Classes. He died on November 19, 1955.

[3] The Rev. R. L. Langford-James, a well-known ultramontane-minded priest, now dead, told the story of how a certain O.C.R. bishop in the early 1920s did his best to get him to go into 'retreat' at his country rectory, there to have his orders validated, and then episcopally supplemented. No fee was demanded, of course, but various documents would have to be made out, signed, and sealed. The total cost, including board and lodging, for the lot would have been about £400. Thinking the matter over, the cleric felt that £400 was cheap for what was offered; but, on second thoughts,

Ambrose Phillipps de Lisle

One letter of this period mentions Fr Kilburn, of St Saviour's, Hoxton, as a likely candidate, for he was already saying Mass in Latin.[1] Of another Anglo-Catholic incumbent it was said: 'He wants to throw in his lot with us. He has money, and is apparently prepared to plank down some at once in order to get the O.C.R. going. . . . I think things are working up.'

Another letter makes it fairly certain that Noel Lambert (Vicar of St Gabriel, South Bromley, from 1916 to 1935) was an O.C.R. bishop.[2] It is possible that Allen Hay (vicar of South Mymms, near Barnet, from 1898 until his death) was raised to the episcopate by Archbishop Mathew.[3] But there were other Anglican priests who took good care that their secret re-ordinations or consecrations were kept dark.[4] In one letter written by an Anglican cleric in the nineteen-twenties, he refers to the Church of England as 'Old Mother Damnable', which had long become a classic phrase not to say a *cliché*. This correspondence, and also the memories of persons who were associated with what might be called 'The Back to Baroque Movement', fostered by the Society of SS. Peter and Paul, suggests that the more lawless Papalist clergymen only regarded the Established Church as a source of secure income, and were ready to work for it merely for the sake of the assured position it would give them. Their superstitious belief in the 'magic' of apostolic succession was very little different from that held by the members of the Theosophical Society, who at the same time were being raised to the priesthood or episcopate in the Liberal Catholic Church.[5]

Judging from the letters preserved, this clandestine, cloak-and-dagger way of obtaining guaranteed 'valid' orders by what were called 'bedroom ordinations', went on for several years. But the O.C.R. bishops and clergy were never united among themselves, and it would be uncharitable to quote some of the remarks they

---

he wrote that he would like to ask one other question: how much *more* would he have to pay later by way of blackmail? That query was never answered.

[1] Before long, however, he 'went over to Rome', and having been re-ordained by a bishop in communion with the Holy See, instead of an O.C.R. prelate, became a priest of the London Oratory. (For Fr Kilburn, see S. C. Carpenter, *Bishop Winnington-Ingram* (1948) pp. 140–47.)

[2] See pp. 178, 182.

[3] See pp. 193, 214.

[4] Between 1916 and 1935, when Lambert was vicar of St Gabriel, South Bromley, this church, hidden away in the slums between East India Dock and Bow Roads, became notorious as a hot-bed of underground episcopal activities. Bishop Bacon acted as Lambert's curate from 1920 to 1927.

[5] See p. 195.

made about each other, even if most of them are now dead.

Thus Bernard Mary Williams, who in 1919 succeeded Mathew as Metropolitan of the 'Western Uniate Church' (otherwise the Old Roman Catholic Church-Pro-Uniate Rite), was dismissed by one of the O.C.R. prelates as 'useless, erratic, and self-willed'. This is not surprising, because he had written in his first Pastoral (1920):

'I believe it to be fairly well known that I have never been in sympathy with the Order, and that I have never ordained one of its members. I propose to refuse Holy Orders on the lines of the Order of Corporate Reunion, while recognizing that I have a duty to those ordained by my predecessor.'[1]

There is evidence that the Order may still be alive, to judge from a printed leaflet issued by 'The Most Reverend Adrianus, O.C.R.', which appeared in 1958. This elusive prelate, having given a brief history of the Corporate Reunion Movement, went on to say:

'After the death of Bishop Jackson . . . the Order became disorganized, although the original line of Apostolic Succession was maintained. By 1957 there were only two members of the Executive Chapter alive, but they were inactive. They were deeply concerned with the future of the Order, and in April 1957 the present writer was approached and asked to undertake the revival of the Order. He accepted the task of perpetuating the testimony of the O.C.R. in the modern world, and immediately formed an interim Executive Chapter.

'The original objects of the O.C.R. remain as heretofore. Only bona-fide members of the Established Church of England are admitted as members, and all postulants are required to sign a Declaration of Faith. All Clergy and Laity who feel interested in the Order are invited to communicate with the address below. All correspondence is treated in strict confidence. BM/HGBX, London, W.C.1.'

So it could be that at this very moment there are cryptic prelates at large in Britain, seeking out Anglican clergymen for conditional re-ordination or tempting them with an offer of the episcopate. Little did young Ambrose March-Phillipps suspect in 1841 that the Uniate Church he had already begun to dream of would evolve after a hundred and twenty years into this sort of business.

[1] See p. 326.

CHAPTER IV

Joseph René Vilatte, Mar Timotheos, Old Catholic Archbishop of North America, and First Primate of the American Catholic Church

Joseph René Vilatte, like Julius Ferrette and Joseph J. Overbeck, was a lapsed Catholic of the Latin rite. As the direct or indirect progenitor of more than twenty schismatic churches, whose history is recorded in chapter eight, his adventures in the ecclesiastical underworld are worth relating in some detail.

He was born in Paris, the son of a butcher, on January 24, 1854. His parents belonged to the region of La Maine in north-west France, and adhered to the moribund *Petite Église*.[1] His mother died soon after his birth, and Joseph's boyhood and early youth were spent in an orphanage at Paris under the charge of the Brothers of the Christian Schools. The sons of St John Baptist de la Salle saw to it that he was re-baptized conditionally, and that he was confirmed at Notre Dame Cathedral, Paris, in 1867. During the latter part of the Franco-Prussian War he enlisted in the *Garde National*. After the siege of Paris and the horrors of the Commune, he decided to leave France for Canada, having been attracted by the appeals for settlers in rural districts. Soon after landing on Canadian soil Vilatte found that a teacher was needed for a school near Ottawa at some distance from the nearest Catholic church. He acted as catechist, and on Sundays when there was no chance of getting to Mass conducted services. A certain priest seems to have been impressed by this pious young Frenchman, and taught him Latin. After two years, having received his calling-up papers for military service, Vilatte returned to France. On arriving at Paris, he was told that seven years in the army would be required. To quote his own words: 'The spirit of liberty which I had imbibed in America, together with the memories of the horrors of the Franco-

[1] See p. 299. As the last priest of this sect died in 1847, the baby boy was probably baptized by a layman.

91

Prussian War, made me determined to leave my native land rather than re-enter the army. I went therefore to Belgium, and after a few months entered the Community of the Christian Brothers, a lay teaching Order at Namur.'[1] Whether as a conscientious objector or a simple deserter, he was in danger of arrest and imprisonment, just as the future curé d'Ars, St John Baptist Vianney, had been about sixty years before this, when he evaded military service.

Vilatte did not find his vocation with this religious institute, but left Belgium in 1876, feeling that he was called to the secular priesthood, and sailed for Canada. His next step was to offer his services to Mgr Fabre, Bishop of Montreal, who sent him to the College of Saint-Laurent, conducted by the Holy Cross Fathers, where he studied for three years. Vilatte relates that 'the teaching of the seminary was so rabidly Romanist that all other beliefs were condemned as heresies, which brought eternal damnation to all that accepted them. During my second vacation I learned that a famous French priest, Father Chiniquy, who was devoting his life to preaching against Roman error, announced in Montreal a series of sermons. . . . I attended with great fear several of them and returned to the seminary with my mind much disturbed'.[2]

What happened next is not quite clear, for Vilatte's memories vary in certain details from those of other people, who in after years did their best to blacken his character. According to his own story he left the Seminary, and sought the advice of a French Protestant pastor in Montreal, a professor at McGill University (founded in 1821), who helped him to continue his studies there for two years.[3] On the other hand McGill has no record of Vilatte

---

[1] *My Relations with the Protestant Episcopal Church* (edited by Mar Georgius, Glastonbury, 1960, p. 4). This interesting autobiography covers Vilatte's career as far as his consecration as a bishop in 1892, and contains the full text of numerous letters which are quoted in this chapter. It appears to have been written about 1910, but remained unpublished until thirty years after his death.

[2] ibid., p. 4. Pastor Chiniquy (1809–99) had been twice suspended by two different bishops before he left the Church and became a militant Protestant. Among his books were *The Priest, the Woman and the Confessional*, and *Fifty Years in the Church of Rome*. They had an enormous circulation at one time.

[3] Bishop Grafton of Fond du Lac, who later on must have gone to infinite trouble to investigate Vilatte's past history, tells us that after he returned to Canada in 1876, in addition to being a student at the College of Saint-Laurent at Montreal (1876–9), he also passed in and out of the Congregation of the Holy Cross, the Dominicans, Friars Minor, Brothers of the Sacred Heart, Brothers of St. Vincent de Paul, and the Alexian Brothers. It is more than likely that he was the guest of these religious institutes at one time or another, but one ventures to think that the canonical conditions normally imposed would have made it invalid, if not impossible, for him to be admitted to their respective novitiates all within four years. Bishop Grafton also tells us that Vilatte worked with the Congregationalists in Brooklyn, with the Presbyterians in Montreal, and that during the same period he was reconciled with the Roman Church more than

Joseph René Vilatte, Mar
Timotheos, Archbishop-
Metropolitan of the Old
Catholic Church of America,
Doctor Christiantissimus,
First Primate of the American
Catholic Church, etc., etc.
This photograph, taken at
Chicago in 1917, shows Mar
Timotheos in Eastern vest-
ments at the ordination of
Fr Peshkoff, a Russian priest
(left). On the right is a
Polish priest, Fr Francis
Kanski, raised to the epis-
copate secretly in 1925.

Arnold Harris Mathew,
Count Povoleri di Vicenza,
de jure Earl of Llandaff,
Regionary Old Catholic
Bishop for England, Arch-
bishop of London, and
Metropolitan successively
of the English Catholic
Church, Western Orthodox
Catholic Church in Great
Britain and Ireland, Anglo-
Catholic Church, Catholic
Church (Latin and Orthodox
United), Ancient Catholic
Church, Old Roman
Catholic Church, and
Western Catholic Uniate
Church, etc. etc.

as a student. During this period he was much troubled by religious doubts. He relates that he 'saw plainly that while on the one hand Romanism had added much error and corruption to the primitive faith, Protestantism had not only taken away Roman errors, but also a part of the primitive deposit of faith'.[1] In an effort to obtain peace of mind about 1882 he abandoned his studies at McGill University and, having been reconciled with the Roman Church, retired to the house of the Clerics of St Viator, at Bourbonnais, Illinois.[2] After about six months, still in a very unsettled state, he met Pastor Chiniquy again, and discussed his spiritual problems with this apostate priest. The advice given was that Vilatte should not return to Bourbonnais but should go to Green Bay, Wisconsin, where there awaited him a wonderful field of apostolate among the Belgian settlers, who, so it appeared, were ripe for conversion to Protestantism, for they were drifting from Romanism into spiritism and infidelity.

Chiniquy also advised Vilatte to write to Hyacinthe Loyson (1827–1912), who had been a Discalced Carmelite friar and a famous preacher until he was excommunicated in 1869. After he married an American widow three years later he formed a sect known as the Gallican Catholic Church.[3]

So it was in March 1884, with the blessing of the two unfrocked priests of the Latin rite, that Vilatte, still a layman, went northwards from Illinois to Wisconsin. He regarded himself as a free-lance Presbyterian missionary. The city of Green Bay (incorporated in 1854) had developed from a fur-trading settlement started in 1745, and it was the oldest French-Canadian settlement in Wisconsin. Vilatte's flock had their widely scattered homes on the peninsula between Lake Michigan and the 120 miles long inlet of Green Bay, the city of which name lies at the southern end of the inlet. The first group of Belgians had arrived in this district in 1853. So numerous were Catholics in the northern part of Wisconsin by 1868 that a new Diocese of Green Bay was formed from the territory of the Diocese of Milwaukee. By the time that Vilatte arrived on the scene many Belgians had ceased to practise their

---

once. Still, he was so astute and ingenuous all his life, that it may well be that the tale of his spiritual odyssey is true.

[1] ibid., p. 4.

[2] A community of teaching priests and brothers, founded in 1835 by the Rev. Louis-Joseph Querbes in the Archdiocese of Lyons, which soon made foundations in Canada, and later in the U.S.A.

[3] See p. 304.

religion, some having become Spiritualists. At Duval forty families of lapsed Catholics had opened a schismatic place of worship. Vilatte hoped to turn these people into Presbyterians. Before long, so he expected, Mgr Krautbauer, who had been appointed second Bishop of Green Bay in 1873, would find his flock reduced yet more in numbers. This prelate died on December 17, 1885, and was succeeded by Mgr Katzer, with whom Vilatte was later to have dealings.

Throughout his long life Vilatte was always interested more in ecclesiastical politics than in the dogmatic or spiritual aspects of religion. He never had the slightest scruples about changing his allegiance from one denomination according to the circumstances in which he found himself at the moment. The basic trouble was that he had no private income on which to fall back. Beggars can't be choosers, and this son of a French butcher was a hard-headed realist when it came to money, never a dreamer of dreams or a romantic visionary, like Julius Ferrette. He was always an opportunist, but never to any purpose. Unfortunately none of the horses he backed proved winners.

After about a year trying to convert the Belgians on the peninsula north of the city of Green Bay, he saw that it was not going to profit him to remain a Presbyterian missionary. On the advice of Hyacinthe Loyson, with whom he had kept in touch, he approached Dr John Henry Hobart Brown, Episcopalian Bishop of Fond du Lac. The lay missionary pointed out to the Bishop that in the north-east part of his diocese there were many hundreds of Belgian and French settlers who had already lapsed from communion with Rome, and that the rest were dissatisfied with a Church ruled over by an Italian pope. Here indeed was a God-given opportunity to organize 'a purified Catholic Church which would present the Gospel to the people as did the primitive Church, and exercise authority according to the spirit of free America'.[1] Vilatte suggested that the Presbyterian mission should be taken over by the Diocese of Fond du Lac as an Old Catholic outpost.

Bishop Brown, who was a broad-minded High Churchman, replied that he had already heard of Vilatte's mission work, and that he would be glad to help the movement. He explained that this would promote good relations between the Protestant Episcopal and the Old Catholic Churches, which in Europe were doing so much to break down the power of the papacy. Loyson had already

[1] ibid., p. 5.

Joseph René Vilatte

written to Vilatte, asking him to come to Paris, so that they could discuss the possibility of getting him ordained priest by Bishop Herzog at Berne.[1] This would be the first step towards setting up an Old Catholic Church in North America. Vilatte had replied that he did not want to abandon his little flock. He probably lacked the money to travel to Europe.

The next step taken by Bishop Brown was to inform Vilatte that he must be examined by two of the professors at Nashotah on his theological knowledge.[2] The result was satisfactory, and Dr Brown wrote that he would consult some of his fellow bishops regarding Loyson's advice that Vilatte should be ordained by Herzog.[3]

Word came on May 27, 1885, that these bishops had decided that this was the wisest course to follow; but Vilatte was then told that the Standing Committee of the Fond du Lac Diocese was convinced that 'the Anglican succession of Apostolic authority' was 'preferable to that of the Old Catholics'. Therefore it would be better for him to be raised to the priesthood by Dr Brown. This would stress 'the sufficiency' of Anglican ordinations in the U.S.A., and also 'save time and expense'. Lastly, it would help towards 'the knitting of a closer unity with the diocese from the beginning of the movement'.[4]

On the receipt of this letter Vilatte went to Fond du Lac, and told the Bishop that he did not want to accept Anglican orders, because this would prevent his mission work securing the support of the people. He insisted that testimonials should be given him to present to Bishop Herzog, and the following letter was written:

My dear Brother,

Permit me to introduce to your confidence and esteem the bearer of this letter, Mr René Vilatte, a candidate for Holy Orders

[1] Consecrated in 1876 by Josef H. Reinkens, Old Catholic Bishop of Bonn, as first bishop of the Christian Catholic Church of Switzerland.
[2] Nashotah in Wisconsin was where the first attempt had been made to establish a male religious community in the American Episcopal Church. Founded in 1840, the quasi-monastic character of the life gradually faded out, and eventually it evolved into a moderate High Church seminary. After 1890 Nashotah became a stronghold of the Catholic party, thanks to Fr Grafton, formerly a member of the Society of St John the Evangelist, being elected Bishop of Fond du Lac.
[3] Herzog was not allowed by the Swiss Government to perform episcopal acts outside Switzerland, but he ordained for the Gallican Church in France some men who were sent him by Loyson. He died in 1924.
[4] ibid., p. 7. Every bishop of the Protestant Episcopal Church in the U.S.A. has a 'Standing Committee' which he is bound to consult before taking action in important matters. It is supposed to be in keeping with the democratic ideals of the American political system.

in the diocese of Fond du Lac. Mr Vilatte is placed in peculiar circumstances. Educated for the priesthood of the Roman Catholic Church, he found himself unable to receive the recent Vatican Decrees, and for a short time associated himself with the Presbyterian communion, but, at last, by the mercy of God, was led into contact with this branch of the One, Holy, Catholic and Apostolic Church. He resided for a while at Green Bay, a city of this diocese. In the neighbourhood of this place there are settled about 30,000 Belgians. Of these a large number, probably 8,000, are believed to be inclined to the principles of a pure and primitive Catholicism. Several delegations of these Belgians have waited on Mr Vilatte, and besought him to become their priest. Mr Vilatte's character for piety, sobriety, purity, intelligence and prudence has been attested to the satisfaction of the authorities of this diocese. Our canons, however, require a longer probation as a Candidate than the exigency of the circumstances will bear. At the suggestion of Père Hyacinthe [Loyson] approved by the Bishop of Connecticut and other Bishops, and by the Faculty of Nashotah Seminary, and by me, Mr Vilatte approaches you, requesting you to ordain him to the priesthood, as speedily as you can find possible that he may enter upon the great work to which he seems specially summoned. It has been expedient to us to send him to you that he may learn personally something of the aims and spirit of the great movement of which you are a recognized leader and to be fitted to co-operate with you in some degree in this country. Mr Vilatte's pecuniary means are limited and he desires to be absent from this diocese as short a time as possible. I ask you to ordain him to the priesthood and attest his character, briefly but sufficiently, by saying that I am willing to ordain him, if it should not seem expedient to you so to do.

> Truly and lovingly your brother and servant,
> in the Holy Church of our Lord,
> J. H. HOBART BROWN,
> Bishop of Fond du Lac.[1]

Armed with this letter, Vilatte arranged to return to Green Bay, confident that the road at last was clear, and so he planned to sail for Europe. But the Bishop accompanied him to the railroad depot, and before the train started, said: 'I will ordain you priest to-morrow, if you will be satisfied with your ordination and rest here.'

[1] ibid., p. 7.

To this Vilatte replied: 'No! Old Catholic I am—Old Catholic I will be.' Then came an assurance from the Bishop—that he would never be subject to the Standing Committee of the Diocese. Even this did not satisfy Vilatte, who, wasting no more time, was off to Switzerland as soon as he raised the money for the trip.

He was ordained deacon and priest at Berne by Bishop Herzog on June 6 and 7, 1885. According to his own statement, he did not take the usual oath of canonical obedience to a diocesan bishop, but Bishop Grafton, writing nearly twenty years after the event, said that he took a canonical oath of obedience to the Bishop of Fond du Lac.[1] If Vilatte's statement was true, then his ecclesiastical status remained undefined; in fact, the only episcopal superiors who could claim any sort of canonical authority over him were Bishop Herzog and Bishop Brown, for the Archbishop of Utrecht does not stand in any metropolitan relationship to the other Old Catholic Churches. This was to be the cause of much trouble in the near future.

On his return to Wisconsin, Fr Vilatte opened a mission church for the Belgians at Little Sturgeon (Gardner). He dedicated it to the Precious Blood in order to stress that communion was given under both species. His first parish was located between two Roman Catholic churches. It appears that the House of Bishops of the Episcopal Church granted him permission to use the French version of the Swiss Christian Catholic liturgy, issued by Bishop Herzog in 1880.[2] The chapel was built with money given by Episcopalians, and the priest in charge was paid a salary from the same source. Dr Brown gave his *imprimatur* to a *Catéchisme Catholique* compiled by Vilatte, which rejected the doctrines of the Immaculate Conception and Papal Infallibility, and laid down that the Sacrament of Penance was not obligatory. Later on an Old Catholic mission of the Blessed Sacrament was opened in the city of Green Bay.[3]

All went well for the next three years. In September 1887 the Fond du Lac diocesan magazine referred to Vilatte as 'the young pioneer priest of the Old Catholic work in America, tall, with a

[1] cf. *A Journey Godward* (Milwaukee, 1910), p. 170.

[2] *Liturgie et Cantiques en usage dans l'Eglise Catholique Chrétienne de la Suisse*. A revised version of this French rite appeared in 1910. The Canon differs considerably from the Roman one, also the Office of Baptism. It contains a short form of Vespers, and it seems that this book was influenced by the Book of Common Prayer used by American Episcopalians.

[3] In 1961 there were thirteen Roman Catholic parishes in the city of Green Bay, and where Vilatte's chapel stood there is now a Franciscan friary. The original Old Catholic church, still called 'The Blessed Sacrament', is listed in the *Episcopal Church Annual* among Episcopalian churches without qualification.

winsome countenance and enthusiastic manner, a model of a priest and pastor. A young man of energy and dignity, culture and education, he has sacrificed his life to the cause of Old Catholic reform. We pray God to open the hearts and hands of Churchmen all over the land to the aid of his noble work'. By this time the cultured young pioneer priest felt he needed an assistant to enable him to win over more Papists to a purer and more primitive form of Catholicism. Mr Gauthier, whom he chose, had like himself been converted to Protestantism, as a Catholic schoolmaster, and had been sent by Dr Brown to Switzerland, where Bishop Herzog raised him to the diaconate and priesthood. On his return to the United States, Fr Gauthier was put in charge of the Old Catholic Church of the Blessed Sacrament at Green Bay. Vilatte now had three parishes under his control—Little Sturgeon, Green Bay, and Dyckesville.

Bishop Brown died on May 2, 1888, and was, on November 13, succeeded as Bishop of Fond du Lac by Charles Chapman Grafton, who had been one of the first members of the Society of St John the Evangelist ('The Cowley Fathers'), founded at Oxford in 1866. Grafton was a somewhat rigid High Churchman, who had imbibed much of the austere spirituality of the founder of his community, the Rev. R. M. Benson. His social background had always been that of what used to be called a 'gentleman', and he had lived mainly among pious and eminently respectable people. For this reason he did not at first suspect that behind the winsome countenance of the young priest of his diocese who appeared to be labouring so heroically to convert Roman Catholics to Old Catholicism was the brain of 'a mere adventurer' (as he put it twenty-one months later). It can be understood that the apostolate to which Vilatte was devoting himself made a special appeal to Grafton, who had a lifelong fear and detestation of the growing power of the papacy, and did everything possible to combat it.

Realizing, however, that the Old Catholic missions, of which it seems he thoroughly approved, were virtually a free-lance affair, Bishop Grafton managed to persuade Vilatte to transfer them legally to the Trustees of the Diocese of Fond du Lac, to be held in trust for Old Catholicism. In return for this the Trustees agreed to pay stipends to the priests and finance their work. So far as Vilatte himself was concerned, this soon proved to be a fatal error.

Yet judging from the tone of the pamphlet he published in July 1889, and entitled *A Sketch of the Belief of the Old Catholics*, Vilatte was still quite convinced that he had a vocation to be an Old Catholic mission-priest in the United States. He explained to his readers that it was sufficient to demonstrate that Old Catholics 'are as removed from Protestantism on the one hand as they are from Romanism on the other; in a word, that they are Catholics without any other qualification'. He played on American feelings— as he often did in after years—by stressing that 'the government of the Church ought to be democratic', unlike that of the Roman Church. He pointed out that 'Old Catholics recognize that religious orders are a source of strength and benediction not to be neglected', and as proof of this he had founded what was actually the first Old Catholic religious community in the world—the 'Monastery of the Precious Blood' at Dyckesville, Kewaunee Co., Wisconsin. Unfortunately he tells us nothing about this institute, but he added the letters 'S.P.B.' to his name, as did the other two members.

When Mgr Heykamp, Old Catholic Archbishop of Utrecht, heard of what was going on in Wisconsin, he wrote to Vilatte on September 19, 1889, urging him to break off all relations with the Protestant Episcopal Church. Since the second conference held at Bonn in 1875, the Dutch Old Catholics had been polite but distant towards Anglicans, whose orders they did not then recognize as valid.[1] On October 8, 1889, Mgr Diependaal, Bishop of Deventer, wrote a strongly worded letter, implying that the Old Catholic hierarchy in the Netherlands regarded Fr Vilatte, S.P.B., as one of their priests, and the recognized leader of the Old Catholic movement in North America.

The following April, Vilatte told Grafton about the correspondence with the Church of Utrecht, and suggested that he be raised to the episcopate. The Bishop of Fond du Lac hardly knew what to do, but he wrote to Archbishop Heykamp; 'It would be open to you to proceed to consecrate him and send him to America as *episcopus regionarius*. He explained that there might be considerable opposition if Vilatte were to be made an 'Abbot-Bishop [of the Society of the Precious Blood] and given the rank of suffragan to the Bishop of Fond du Lac'; adding that in this case he might 'be forced to leave his present position and begin work elsewhere. He would also be cut off from all financial support of every kind, as it is only through his connection with us and by reason of our commendation that he has been hitherto sustained. It would be very

[1] An enquiry was held in 1894—two years before *Apostolicae Curae*—and the Dutch Old Catholic bishops adjudged Anglican orders invalid.

hard upon the people to lose the pastor to whom they are attached'. Grafton then offered to transfer Vilatte to the jurisdiction of either Heykamp or Herzog, but hinted that this would involve losing financial help from Episcopalian sources.

It is clear that Grafton was now trying to rid himself of this difficult French priest who showed no signs of settling down as one of the clergy of the Fond du Lac diocese. On August 8, 1890, he wrote to Archbishop Vladimir, the Russian Orthodox Bishop of the Aleutian Islands and Alaska, who resided at San Francisco, and said: 'Mr Vilatte, who has had a strange history, has shown little steadfastness of purpose, except in trying to push himself into prominence'. Having given the Archbishop (unsuccessfully, as it happened) a brief summary of all the worst aspects of Vilatte's career, he ended his letter with the words: 'It is a sad pity that a man who, if he applied himself steadfastly to his work, might be a useful priest, shows so many qualities of a mere adventurer.'[1]

Thus, after twenty-one months the former Cowley Father summed up Vilatte's character. He was then aged thirty-five and extremely good-looking, with an irresistible charm of manner, and at least a veneer of piety. It is not surprising that Grafton was fascinated by his personality and accepted him at his face value, but now he was on the warpath, and in September 1890 he circulated a warning which was printed in all the newspapers of the Episcopal Church. Readers were asked not to send any more contributions to the Old Catholic mission of Dyckesville. The Bishop stated that the Rev. R. Vilatte had 'been, during the past year, seeking to obtain the Episcopate at the hands of the Church in Holland. Failing this he applied to Bishop Vladimir, asking to be admitted into the Orthodox Eastern Church. Lately I discovered that he was making proposals to the Roman Catholic Bishop at Green Bay, with a view to return to Rome'.[2]

This last accusation was true, for on August 15, 1890, Vilatte had written to Mgr Katzer, Bishop of Green Bay, saying: 'Being finally determined not to agree with the 39 Articles of the Episcopal Church, I insist on what I have already published in the English papers. We are accordingly determined never to become Protestants, and would prefer to see our people under the rule of Rome, rather than to see them turn Protestant, no matter of what form or colour.'[3]

[1] ibid., p. 34.
[2] ibid., p. 35.
[3] ibid., p. 33.

Joseph René Vilatte

But the Bishop of Green Bay was too cautious to open his arms wide to this lapsed Catholic. All he could suggest was that the first step would be for Vilatte to retract publicly, and then retire to a religious house under probation. After this it would rest with the Holy See to judge whether the orders conferred by Bishop Herzog were valid, and to prescribe what further theological studies were necessary. Whether it would be prudent for him to remain at Dyckesville, or even in the Diocese of Green Bay, could be settled later. Vilatte answered the letter at once in a non-committal manner, and nothing materialized. He had no intention of doing penance.

Meanwhile, over in Europe, Archbishop Heykamp, and some of his clergy, had been urging Vilatte to cast aside the Episcopalian yoke, and to free himself of all pretence of being under the jurisdiction of the Bishop of Fond du Lac. They assured him that there would be little difficulty in arranging for his episcopal consecration. Early in September 1890, Bishop Grafton, accompanied by several of his clergy, visited the parish of Duval. The local ordinary was both surprised and indignant when the pastor informed him that there were no candidates for confirmation, because the Old Catholic bishops of Holland had forbidden him to accept any sacraments from a Protestant prelate. Nevertheless Grafton insisted on addressing the congregation, stressing that he was their true Bishop, and reminding them of all the financial help they had received from him. The same scenes were repeated the following day at Fr Gauthier's church at Little Sturgeon, where once again the Bishop was told that he could not confer the sacrament of confirmation.[1]

Shortly after this stormy Visitation, Grafton wrote to Vilatte, insisting that he should give up his work and hand over the properties to the diocesan authorities, including all house furniture, altar vessels, and vestments. He ended his long letter with the words: 'A clergyman, entrusted as you are, by me, over the people at Dyckesville, is bound to instil into them love and loyalty to me and to the Church which I represent. If he cannot, then he is bound to go, and in the meantime say nothing that would unsettle them or lead them to Rome or away from their allegiance to me.'[2]

On September 19, Vilatte informed Grafton that he felt it his

---

[1] Vilatte had so little faith in the validity of Grafton's orders that he took care to procure from Holland the holy oils he required for use at baptisms.
[2] ibid., p. 37.

duty to sever his connection with the Episcopal Church. The Bishop replied that in order to effect this canonically it would be necessary for Vilatte to state in writing that he had renounced the ministry of the said Church to the Bishop of which he had made his oath of canonical obedience when he was ordained. It is probable that Grafton made an error in stating that Vilatte had taken an oath of obedience to his predecessor when Bishop Herzog raised him to the priesthood in Switzerland.

As a proof that he no longer accepted the jurisdiction of the Bishop of Fond du Lac, Vilatte opened a new mission station near Green Bay. On hearing of this the Bishop inhibited him until he had obtained authorization. On October 30 he informed this now free-lance priest that Bishop Herzog had written that 'there was no necessity or even possibility of giving a Bishop to the Old Catholics in the United States'. Grafton commented that 'the Old Catholics of Europe have no right to interfere over here. If the Bishop of Rome has not, certainly the Archbishop of Utrecht has not'.[1] Grafton appears to have believed firmly that the Protestant Episcopal Church was the only true Catholic Church in North America, and that it had exclusive territorial jurisdiction. At that date he could not even find room for 'The Three Branch Theory' of the Catholic Church, and he regarded the Roman Catholic hierarchy in the United States as schismatics, and probably as heretics. After the Old Catholic Congress held at Cologne in September 1890, the bishops had decided that it was inexpedient to carry out the consecration of Vilatte as their only official representative in the United States. It was not until 1897 that they appointed Stanislas Kozlowski as the first Old Catholic bishop for North America, with a roving commission over groups of scattered Poles.[2]

Realizing that he had been rejected by both the Episcopalians and the Old Catholics, Vilatte appealed to Bishop Vladimir for the second time. The latter replied that he would communicate at once with the Holy Synod of Moscow, and if no answer was received after a reasonable time, he would re-ordain him *sub conditione*, and

[1] ibid., p. 42.

[2] See pp. 415, 417, 524, 525. In his latter years Grafton's conception of Catholicity grew much broader, and he was prepared to accept practically all religious bodies which could prove a valid apostolic succession. There were, so he maintained, various branches of the Church, united to Christ, and having His life flowing, as it were, in their veins, from one body in His sight. (cf. *A Journey Godward*, p. 245.) From 1909 until his death in 1912 the Bishop held the status of Titular Abbot of an Old Catholic Benedictine monastery at Fond du Lac. (See p. 416.)

receive him as a priest of the Russian Orthodox Diocese of the Aleutian Islands and Alaska.

Matters dragged on until February 20, 1891, when Grafton informed Vilatte that he had been 'removed from the mission station of St Mary's, Dyckesville'. Vladimir, on hearing of this, assured Vilatte of his support, and urged him to 'fight against impostors who change the authority of the Oecumenical Councils on the authority of private opinions, and because sectarians and nihilists inside of Christendom, because they annihilate the one true only Catholic Orthodox Church'. Moreover, he promised to write a pastoral to the Old Catholics, defending Vilatte's 'Christian piety'.

On March 11, 1891, the Bishop of the Aleutian Islands and Alaska dispatched from San Francisco an impressively worded letter addressed to 'The Pious Old Catholic Parishioners and Trustees of the Church at Dyckesville', in which he said that it was 'a great joy' for them 'to be a branch of the great body of Jesus Christ, and members of the Church of Jerusalem, Antioch, Alexandria, and Constantinople, where are the seats and cathedrals of Patriarchs and Holy Synods of the Oecumenical Orthodox Church'. It would be 'a great honour to have their pious disposition to be brave soldiers of Christ'. Bishop Vladimir also asked God to help them 'to defend Christian truth against the errors of Papist and Protestant sectarians', who 'do not belong to the true Catholic Church of Christ and must disappear in time, like many other heresies'. He prayed fervently that they would defend with all their might 'the worthy and pious superior' of their mission 'against the persecution and encroachments of Anglican Protestants', who could not be regarded as their 'true brothers in Christ, because of heresies and lack of Apostolic succession'.[1]

It would be interesting to know what were the reactions of the simple and uneducated French and Belgian settlers in the north of Wisconsin to this Pastoral Letter from a Russian Orthodox Bishop nearly two thousand miles away on the coast of California. Few of them could have understood a word of it.

Bishop Grafton naturally was furious. He lost no time in writing to Vilatte that if he were an honest man he must do one of three things: '(1) Return to a loving and loyal obedience to him; (2) take a letter of transfer to the Archbishop of Utrecht, or to Bishop Vladimir; or (3) leave the country.' On April 13, 1891, he

---

[1] ibid., pp. 47–48.

suspended him for a period of six months from all priestly ministrations of all kinds whatsoever. Vilatte merely replied that he did not recognize Grafton's authority, and that he refused to leave the mission. On May 9, Bishop Vladimir issued an official document in which he stated:

'By the Grace of God, and the Authority bestowed on me by the Apostolic Succession, I, VLADIMIR, Bishop of the Orthodox Catholic Church, announce to all clergymen of different Christian denominations and to all Old Catholics that The Reverend Joseph René Vilatte, Superior of the Old Catholic Parish of Dyckesville, Wisconsin, is now a true Old Catholic Orthodox Christian, under the patronage of our Church, and no Bishop or Priest of any denomination has the right to interdict him or to suspend his religious duties, except the Holy Synod of the Russian Church, and myself. Any action contrary to this declaration, is null and void on the basis of liberty of conscience and the laws of this country.'[1]

From the worldly point of view it was tragic that Vladimir did not manage to control Vilatte. Had it been possible to raise him to the episcopate, his exceptional gifts might have proved extremely valuable to what at that date was perhaps the most Erastian Christian body in the world. Had he found his way to Russia, he might even have rivalled Gregory Efimovitch Rasputin as a sinister influence on Church and State. For if necessary he, too, could surround himself with an air of mysticism, and some people were unable to resist his plausible personality. Both Rasputin and Vilatte were of peasant origin.

Vladimir's assumption of jurisdiction over the length and breadth of the United States may have alarmed Grafton, even making him fear that the Ober-Prokuror of the Holy Synod might yet prove a greater menace to freedom in the Diocese of Fond du Lac than either the Bishop of Rome or the Archbishop of Utrecht. But there was little he could do about it, except to publish further warnings, describing him as a swindler who kept bad company, and whose associates, some of whom he mentioned by name, were his equals in crime and debauchery, which was the first mention of this sort of thing.

It was one of these men referred to by Grafton—a certain Harding, formerly a member of the Oblates of Mary Immaculate,

---

[1] ibid., p. 50. The Russian Orthodox Church established its first mission on what is now United States territory in 1794, when a band of monks settled in Alaska. A see with its seat at Sitka was erected in 1840, transferred to San Francisco in 1872.

Joseph René Vilatte

and a missionary in India, but who had ceased to be a practising Catholic—who inspired Vilatte to pursue a line of action which might prove more to his advantage than remaining under the protection of the Russian Bishop of the Aleutian Islands and Alaska.

The story told was as follows: In 1888 about 5,000 Catholics of the Latin rite in Ceylon and South India had formed a schismatic body, known as The Independent Catholic Church of Ceylon, Goa, and India. The reasons for this break with the papacy were political rather than religious. From the sixteenth century there had existed a concordat between the Holy See and the King of Portugal which allowed the latter to nominate bishops to the dioceses of the Latin rite in India, as well as in all other countries which had formerly been Portuguese colonies. This arrangement was known as the *Patronado* (patronage). By the second half of the nineteenth century it had become obvious that it was high time for the Patronado to be abolished. On January 2, 1887, Leo XIII set up a new Latin hierarchy for India and Ceylon, with the bishops (except in the province of Goa) directly dependent on the Congregation of Propaganda. This change aroused considerable indignation, because there still existed a strong sentimental link between Indian Catholics and Portugal. Many native priests were indignant at being transferred to the jurisdiction of French or Italian bishops. Thus came into being what was called the 'Patronado Association'. Its leaders petitioned King Luis I of Portugal to use his influence at Rome to have the royal patronage restored. On February 10, 1888, a Goan priest who had been a Brahmin, Antonio Francisco-Xavier Alvarez, was elected by the Association as first bishop of a schismatic church. He applied to Mar Dionysios V, Jacobite Metropolitan of Malankara since 1876, to consecrate him, but with no result. His appeal to Mar Ignatius Peter III, Jacobite Patriarch of Antioch, was more successful.[1]

Realizing that there was no further hope of being raised to the episcopate by any of the Old Catholic bishops in Europe, and possibly doubtful of the prospects of preferment in communion with the Patriarchate of Moscow, since he had no further word of this from Vladimir, Vilatte decided to write to Alvarez—who now styled himself 'Mar Julius I' and Metropolitan of the Independent Catholic Church of Ceylon, Goa, and India—asking if he would be

[1] It was this same prelate who as Bishop of Emesa (Homs) had raised Julius Ferrette to the episcopate as Bishop of Iona in 1866. (See pp. 35–37.)

willing to consecrate him. The answer, to the request, dated May 10, 1891, was so expressed as to make Vilatte feel that, at long last, he had found a prelate after his own heart, and a kindred spirit. Alvarez wrote:

'We from the bottom of our hearts thank God that He has mercifully shown us the way out of the slavery of Rome; and we rejoice to see a large number of Christians making heroic efforts in the same direction as ourselves in the New World. And we feel confident that the good God will deign to mercifully help these holy endeavours. . . . If the necessary arrangements could be made we would overlook the hardships connected with the voyage and go across the seas to confer the episcopate on such a worthy minister of God as yourself, particularly as Dr Lisboa Pinto urges us in the strongest terms to forget everything and think of America. . .'[1]

Vilatte replied that it would be better if he went to Ceylon, which would save Alvarez the hardships of going to North America. It is more than likely that he did not want this Brahmin prelate to discover that there were actually very few Christians in the United States who were desperate to free themselves from 'the slavery of Rome'. In a second letter Alvarez said he would be delighted to welcome the 'worthy minister of God' from Wisconsin.

No time was wasted. Vilatte placed his Old Catholic missions under the care of a certain Brother Augustine (apparently the same person as Harding), and explained to his flock the reasons for making the long voyage to the Far East. They were as follows: (1) Because the Old Catholics in America were forbidden by the Archbishop and Bishops in Holland to present their candidates to Anglican Bishops for confirmation, or to use holy oils blessed by them; (2) the fear that in the case of his death, his people would be without pastoral care, in which case he would be responsible should they be compelled to submit to Roman Catholic bishops; (3) the long silence of the Holy Synod of Moscow, and the apparent indifference of the Orthodox Church towards the Old Catholic Movement in North America; (4) the expressed Orthodoxy of the Independent Catholic Church of Ceylon, together with the urgent invitation to go there and receive the Apostolic Succession.[2]

[1] ibid., pp. 50–51. Lisboa Pinto, a medical practitioner, was the leading layman in the Patronado Defence Association, and also in the newly formed schismatic church.
[2] ibid., p. 32.

Joseph René Vilatte

There is a story that before leaving Green Bay, Vilatte held a Synod at which he was elected bishop, and begged to obtain an indisputable episcopal consecration as soon as possible. Bishop Grafton's version of this legend was slightly different, for he told a story that Vilatte 'carried around a paper amongst the few, poor ignorant people under his charge, which he demanded they should sign. Most of them complied, some of them little children. There was only one clergyman's name on this petition, and that, according to the statement of the clergyman so named, was forged'. This accusation may or may not be true, but Vilatte recorded that the poor people around Dyckesville donated $225 towards the expenses of his voyage to Ceylon. For the sake of economy he had to travel third class on the steamer. He sailed from New York on July 15, 1891, and was away from North America for over a year.

It was not until May 29, 1892, that Mar Julius felt justified in raising this free-lance French priest, now an American citizen, to the episcopate. For he took the precaution to consult the Patriarch Ignatius Peter III of Antioch. There was a long delay before his reply reached Ceylon.[1] The ceremony finally took place in the former Portuguese Catholic Church of Our Lady of Good Death, Colombo, which the schismatics had managed to retain. Mar Julius was assisted by his own consecrator, Mar Paul Athanasius, Bishop of Kottayam, and Mar George Gregorius, Bishop of Niranam. The Roman Pontifical was used.

In the alleged Bull of His Holiness Peter III, signed and sealed from the Patriarchal Palace at the Monastery of Sapran at Mardin on the borders of Syria and Kurdistan on December 29, 1891, the consecration of Joseph René Vilatte was granted for 'the Arch-Episcopal dignity, Archbishop Metropolitan, in the name of Mar Timotheos, for the Church of the Mother of God in Dyckesville, Wisconsin, United States, and the Churches of the Archdiocese of America, viz. the Churches adhering to the Orthodox Faith'.

On May 30, 1892, so it is related, an Agreement was drawn up between Alvarez and Vilatte, in which the latter acknowledged the Confession of Faith, the Canons and Rules of the Syrian Jacobite

---

[1] Writing to Fr Ignatius of Llanthony on November 21, 1898, Mar Julius said: 'We may, in this connection, inform you that just about the time of Mgr Vilatte's arrival in Ceylon we received a telegraphic message from Bishop Grafton asking us not to consecrate Mgr Vilatte. On enquiry from parties disinterested, and facts patent to us, we found to our full satisfaction that Bishop Grafton was only trying to pay off a private grudge. . . . We need hardly declare that both the Eastern and the Old Catholics will ridicule the idea of a Protestant Bishop endeavouring to become a Pope of an Old Catholic Archbishop'.

Church, and rejected all the doctrines which are declared heretical by the said Church. He promised that he would be subject and obedient to the Patriarch, and to his successors in the Apostolic See of Antioch. In return for this he would receive from the Antiochene Patriarchate the necessary supply of 'Mooran' (holy oil) which the Patriarch alone is allowed to consecrate. Vilatte also promised to remit to Antioch the annual collection of Peter's Pence. Finally, he acknowledged that if he ever severed himself from communion with the Monophysite Churches of the Antiochene Rite, or deviated from their Canons and Rules, he would be subject to dismissal from the dignity of Metropolitan. Mar Julius is said to have presented Mar Timotheos with a certificate of consecration, dated June 5, 1892, which conferred upon him the title of 'Archbishop of the Old Catholic Church of America', together with 'the power to consecrate churches, chancels, cemeteries, etc., and to perform all functions appertaining to Metropolitan rank'. The witnesses to this document were alleged to have been the U.S.A. Consul for Ceylon, and Dr Lisboa Pinto.

It has been suggested that Alvarez and Vilatte composed between them the wording of the Bull, and sent it to the venerable Patriarch, being fairly certain that he would sign it without asking any awkward questions about the antecedents of a priest in North America, who had been ordained by an Old Catholic bishop in Switzerland, and who had tried unsuccessfully to be raised to the Old Catholic episcopate. On the other hand, we have to remember that it was this same 'Peter the Humble', who when Bishop of Emesa (Homs) consecrated the former French Dominican, Julius Ferrette, and so it is said, sent him to Western Europe as Patriarchal Legate.[1] The two stories are consistent. The second is a sequel to the first.[2]

The newly consecrated Old Catholic Archbishop of North America felt it would be worth while to break the return journey to the United States in Holland, where, so he related in after years, he was received by the Old Catholic clergy, and stayed with the parish priest at Delft. There is also the tale that this priest and Bishop Diependaal of Deventer gave him the money for his first

---

[1] See p. 36.

[2] So far as is known no bishops of the Vilatte succession have ever produced the original Syriac document when challenged to do so. All that has been shown is a translation of the Bull of Ignatius Peter III, authorizing Vilatte's consecration, likewise copies of the certificates of his consecration by Alvarez. (cf. Brandreth, *Episcopi Vagantes and the Anglican Church*, 2nd ed., 1961, pp. 50–52.)

crozier, which was bought at Antwerp before sailing. We are told Vilatte visited his *alma mater*, the College of Saint-Laurent at Montreal, where he tried to impress the Holy Cross Fathers and the students by displaying his ring and pectoral cross. Having reached Green Bay, he found awaiting him notice of the threatened deposition which had been pronounced by Bishop Grafton in his Cathedral Church of St Paul, Fond du Lac, on March 21, 1891. This stated:

'In virtue of the authority left by Our Lord Jesus Christ to his Church of binding and of loosing and of putting away every brother that walketh disorderly, we do HEREBY DEPRIVE the said René Vilatte of all privileges and powers of the ministry of the Church and DEPOSE him from his office as Priest. . . . And we call upon all the faithful to keep themselves from any ministrations at his hands, and we do erase and blot out his name from the Register of the Clergy of this Church, in token that if he repent not and amend, God will blot out his name from the Book of Life.'

The Old Catholic Archbishop of North America also found awaiting his return to Wisconsin a Report issued by the House of Bishops at the General Convention of the Protestant Episcopal Church, presided over by Dr Doane, Bishop of Albany, which read:

'It appears that the bishops from whom M. Vilatte claims to have received consecration belong to a body which is separated from Catholic Christendom because of its non-acceptance of the dogmatic decrees of the Council of Chalcedon as to our Blessed Lord's Person:

'These bishops had no jurisdiction or right to ordain a bishop for any part of the diocese under the charge of the Bishop of Fond du Lac:

'M. Vilatte was never elected by any duly accredited Synod.

'It appears that M. Vilatte, in seeking the Episcopate, made statements not warranted by the facts of the case, and seemed willing to join with any body, Old Catholic, Greek, Roman, or Syrian, which would confer it upon him.

'More than two months before the time of his so-called consecration, he was deposed from the sacred ministry. In view of these facts we propose the following resolutions:

'*Resolved.* That, in the opinion of this House, the whole proceedings in connection with the so-called consecration of J. René Vilatte were null and void, and that this Church does not recognize that any Episcopal character was thereby conferred.

Joseph René Vilatte

'*Resolved*. That a statement of the above-recited facts be sent to the Archbishop of Utrecht, to the Old Catholics of Germany and Switzerland, and to the Metropolitans and Primates of the Anglican Communion.'

There is a story that when the Archbishop of North America visited the College of Saint-Laurent on his arrival in Canada from Ceylon, he remarked with a smile: '*Life is but a farce!*' After all, what right had these prelates, whose first bishop was consecrated in 1784 by bishops of the Episcopal Church in Scotland, to pass judgment on an archbishop whose consecration had taken place with the express permission of the 126th successor of St Peter as first Patriarch of Antioch?

By way of defiance one of the first things Vilatte did was to raise the wooden chapel of St Louis at Green Bay to the status of a pro-cathedral. He had two other little chapels under his jurisdiction: St Joseph's, Walhain, and St Mary's, Duval. It is recalled that he used to wear a Roman purple cassock in the streets, so as to make people realize that he was an archbishop. He started to publish a short-lived little monthly magazine, *The Old Catholic*, but it does not seem to have resulted in many converts.

To counteract proselytism, Mgr Mesmer, who had succeeded Mgr Katzer as Catholic Bishop of Green Bay on the latter's translation to the archiepiscopal see of Milwaukee on January 30, 1891, asked the Premonstratensian Canons if they could spare a few Flemish and French-speaking priests to work among the Belgians. One priest, Fr Pennings, and a lay-brother from Holland, came at once, and more sons of St Norbert followed them across the Atlantic. The former became some years later the first Premonstratensian abbot in the U.S.A.

At no time did Vilatte ever have a large following in Wisconsin. He claimed that they numbered between six and eight thousand, but even five hundred would seem to have been an exaggerated statement. In a grandiose and pretentious way he simply included all the Belgian settlers whom he hoped to win over to Old Catholicism, and even multiplied their numbers. He had to do this in order to make a big show in the Eastern States, where he canvassed among rich Episcopalians, trying unsuccessfully to raise money to build churches which could never be built, or to get clothes for free distribution among the poor. It was only among the small rabid element that he found followers. There were many staunch Catholics who refused to have anything to do with him, even when offered presents and 'free' religious services. In some places the 'Archbishop of North America' was driven away by the Belgians. But whenever he heard of dissatisfaction about church regulations, and so on, he was sure to turn up, organizing meetings, urging the people to throw off the yoke of Rome. In spite of all this propaganda, Vilatte did not even manage to make ends meet, and he was obliged to flee from one place to another to avoid creditors, who were on his track.[1] He was not invited to say prayers at the solemn opening of The World's Columbian Exposition in Chicago on May 1, 1893, as was Mgr Ireland, Roman Catholic Archbishop of St Paul; neither did he take an official part in 'The World's Parliament of Religions' which was a side-show at this mammoth affair.

Finding himself at the end of his tether less than two years after being consecrated, Vilatte decided that the best thing he could do was to be reconciled with the Roman Church. On March 26, 1894, Archbishop Satolli, the first Apostolic Delegate to the U.S.A., informed Mgr Messmer that Vilatte wished to submit to the Holy See. About three weeks later Vilatte wrote to the Bishop of Green Bay that he was already preparing his people for reconciliation with Rome. Further correspondence took place between Satolli, Messmer, and Vilatte. All looked hopeful, but behind the scenes the 'Archbishop of North America' was watching which way the wind was blowing, not wishing to commit himself, before he was sure it would pay him to become once again 'a slave of the Vatican'.

He could not decide whether to trust his luck to the Pope or to the Jacobite Patriarch of Antioch, but in August 1894 matters had got as far as the Apostolic Delegate advising Bishop Messmer to finance Vilatte's journey to Rome, because he could not afford the cost himself. No doubt Propaganda would refund the money. But the Roman authorities appeared to be in no hurry, and merely enquired about Vilatte's manner of ordaining priests, and other details of no immediate importance.

Matters dragged on like this for nearly four years. In February 1898 the Apostolic Delegate wrote to the Bishop of Green Bay that Vilatte was now quite ready to recant his errors and submit to Holy Mother Church as a layman. These two prelates, however, did not fully fathom the man they were dealing with. In the interval

---

[1] The above facts, and much that follows, have been supplied by the Rt Rev. Mgr Joseph A. Marx, Vicar-General of the Diocese of Green Bay, who, in the course of his long life has made exhaustive research into Vilatte's career in Wisconsin.

Joseph René Vilatte

Vilatte had published a prayer book and catechism for his Old Catholics. He had also announced the foundation of a sort of religious order—'The Knights of the Crown of Thorns'—which would have a monastery at Green Bay, as soon as he could find the money to build it.[1]

In spite of the offer of a journey to Rome, at the expense of either the Diocese of Green Bay or the Congregation of Propaganda, Vilatte continued to waver. Eventually Mgr Messmer realized that there was no hope of a sincere conversion, and wrote to Mgr Satolli: 'For the present he has an asylum among the schismatic Poles, who will pay him court until he will be infatuated and foolish enough to consecrate one of them for the episcopate. Then they will cast him out, and being in such an extremity, he will probably have one more recourse to the Catholic Church, asking for money and pardon. But will it be sincere?' This is exactly what happened, but not until about six years later, and even then the terms offered by Rome did not satisfy Vilatte.

After the Old Catholic Archbishop of North America left Wisconsin, some of his former followers joined a spiritist movement. A few returned to communion with the Holy See, and the rest submitted to the jurisdiction of the Bishop of Fond du Lac and ended their days as Episcopalians. As to his priests, Fr Gauthier appears to have been good and sincere, but his successor named Mouthy is said to have been a scamp and a drunkard, who married a girl and subsequently divorced her, and ended up as a Theosophist. Then came a priest, who called himself Lopez or Lops. Having failed to support himself as a doctor and a conjurer, he moved East, and took charge of a schismatic Italian congregation. Lops is said to have been the last priest of the Vilatte Old Catholic movement in and around Green Bay. Today it is almost forgotten, except among very old people.

Having failed to show to many Belgians the way out of the slavery of Rome, and apparently utterly indifferent to his obligations towards the Syro-Jacobite Patriarchate, Vilatte turned his attention to a much larger body of people, optimistic of gaining support from them. These were the now widely-spread Polish Catholics. There had been a fairly steady immigration of Poles into the U.S.A. since about 1830, and the first Polish priest arrived

---

[1] It appears that after his consecration in Ceylon, Vilatte was made Grand Prior of the Order of the Crown of Thorns. It was said at the time that the Jewel of this Order carried with it the honorary title of 'Doctor Christianissimus', and that the Jacobite Patriarch of Antioch was the Patron.

in 1851. More and more Poles crossed the Atlantic in the hope of making their fortunes in the New World after the war of 1863. A large number moved on to the Middle West, having heard that there was plenty of work to be had in Chicago and other big cities. After 1873 began a series of difficulties between the Polish priests, and the American Catholic bishops. So fused were religion and nationalism with the Poles that most of them were determined not to be integrated with other Catholics. They wanted a Church of their own, and to the extremists communion with Rome was almost a matter of indifference. Towards the close of the century schismatic Polish congregations existed in Baltimore, Buffalo, Chicago, Cleveland, New York, Toledo, and elsewhere. The chief leader of the schismatics was Antoni Kozlowski, who procured episcopal consecration from the Dutch Old Catholics on November 17, 1897.[1]

It appears that Vilatte's first direct service to the disgruntled Poles was in 1894, when a certain Fr Kolaszewski invited him to dedicate a church at Cleveland. Shortly after Kozlowski's consecration, Vilatte was approached by Stephen Kaminski, pastor of the Church of the Holy Mother of the Rosary, Buffalo, New York. This priest had failed to persuade the Old Catholic Archbishop of Utrecht to raise him to the episcopate. There is a story that he offered Vilatte $2,500 cash and $2,500 in notes, to be secured by mortgage on church property, if he would make him a bishop. Notices were sent out stating that both Cardinal Gibbons, Archbishop of Baltimore, and Archbishop Martinelli, the Apostolic Delegate, would assist at the ceremony. It is hardly necessary to add that neither of these prelates put in an appearance.

With characteristic bravado, Vilatte arrived in Buffalo, and on March 21, 1898, consecrated Kaminski in his own church, giving him the title of 'Assistant Bishop'.[2] Kaminski—alas!—had no opportunity to make himself useful to his consecrator; with creditors on his track he fled to Canada and thence to Europe. He was excommunicated by the Holy See, and abandoned by Vilatte.[3] The latter felt it safer to lie low until the storm had blown over, and he decided to have no more dealings with the Poles for the time being. His escapade in Buffalo had attracted too much undesirable publicity.

[1] See pp. 415, 524, 525.
[2] The consecration was reported in detail by both the *Buffalo Enquirer* and *Courier and Herald*.
[3] Bishop Kaminski returned to the U.S.A. later on, and remained in charge of his schismatic parish until he died in 1911.

Joseph René Vilatte

But it would have been unlike Vilatte not to have found another opening for his talents as an ecclesiastical adventurer, and he did so quickly. During the years 1890–1, when he had been trying to find a bishop to consecrate him, he had heard of, and possibly met, Fr Ignatius of Jesus, O.S.B., who was recuperating in North America, preaching and giving missions to raise money for his monastery at Llanthony in the Black Mountains of South Wales.[1] During his tour he had been publicized as 'The Evangelist Monk of the British Church', or 'The Druid of the Welsh Church', and he had informed Press reporters that he belonged to an elusive Ancient British Church, which was 'the oldest in the world after Antioch and Jerusalem'.[2]

The reason why Vilatte felt it might be to his advantage to link up with Fr Ignatius remains uncertain, but here is the most probable explanation. Having heard of Ignatius's obsession with the heresies of Dr Fremantle, the Dean of Ripon, and other Anglican clerics in high places, he was prepared to gamble on this eccentric monk supporting him in setting up an Old Catholic Church in Britain, of which he would become the Primate and Metropolitan. It has also been suggested that Vilatte had been told that Ignatius was wealthy and his Abbey richly endowed; also that this missionary monk seldom failed to rake in money by his eloquent preaching. The first step to laying his hands on the money would be to get Ignatius under his influence by raising him to the priesthood. After this the rest would be easy. As Mr Arthur Calder-Marshall points out: 'With an opportunist psychopath, such as Vilatte was, there is nothing inconsistent between these two possibly complementary courses of action.'[3]

We do not know when Vilatte sailed for England, but he turned up in London within three months of his consecration of Kaminski at Buffalo. He laid his plans carefully, and managed to persuade Dr F. G. Lee, the O.C.R. Bishop of Dorchester, upon whom he called, to give him a letter of introduction to Ignatius.[4] Not satisfied with this, he dispatched a telegram, signed MAR TIMO-THEOS, announcing that he would visit Llanthony within a few days. Unfortunately the Abbot, who had taken the title of Dewi-Honddu ('David of the Honddhu'), when he was initiated into the

---

[1] For details of Fr Ignatius's career see p. 75, n. 2.
[2] It is not certain if Fr Ignatius meant by this term the Ancient British Church, said to have been revived by the Rev. R. W. Morgan in 1874. (See pp. 45, 217, 219.)
[3] *The Enthusiast* (1962), p. 258.
[4] See p. 75.

Joseph René Vilatte

Gorsedd of the Bards of Wales by the Archdruid Clwydfordd in 1889, was away at the National Eisteddfod. His handful of monks had no idea who was the sender of the telegram, until they read Dr Lee's letter, vouching for the claims of this prelate, and hinting that it might be to their advantage to entertain him. No bishop—far less an archbishop—had ever deigned to stay at Llanthony since the monastery was founded in 1870, so one can picture the excitement.

Mar Timotheos arrived in the Black Mountains on July 18, and Dewi-Honddu—Fr Ignatius—was now back to welcome him. He had brought, not only his archiepiscopal regalia, but also what are described as 'most interesting Syriac documents with their authorized English translations, with the seals and signatures of the ecclesiastical and civil authorities concerned'.[1] His Grace explained that he was in a hurry, on his way to Russia at the special invitation of the Holy Synod of Moscow; but if 'The Reverend Father', or any of his monks would care to avail themselves of this unique opportunity to receive absolutely 'valid' holy orders, he would be delighted to supply them, there and then.

The rest of the story is best told in the words of Father Iltud Mary of the Epiphany, Monk, O.S.B., as he signed his name to a newspaper article.

'After the Old Catholic Archbishop's arrival at Llanthony there went up to God a ceaseless stream of prayer from 5 a.m. to 5 p.m., besides the midnight services, daily, that God's will might be done at the present crisis in our history that our Lord Jesus might be glorified. The Archbishop daily pleaded the Eucharistic Memorial for the illumination of the Divine Paraclete. Our Superior presented three objections to the Archbishop.

'1st. He could not follow the Old Catholics in their excessive rancour against the Church of Rome. The Church of Rome was a bulwark of Orthodoxy and Bible defence, and contained countless saints of God.

'2nd. He could never be other than a faithful son to the Church of Britain, and must use the "*Filioque*" until the National Church permitted its erasure from the Creed.

'3rd. Was not the Syrian Patriarch and his Church Monophysite ?'[2]

[1] cf. ibid., p. 253.
[2] *The Recent Ordinations of Father Ignatius at Llanthony Abbey* (reprinted from the *Hereford Times*) (Llanthony Abbey, Abergavenny, 1898), pp. 9–10.

Joseph René Vilatte

Mar Timotheos managed to convince Fr Ignatius that he need not worry about such trivial details, and Fr Iltud continues:

'We were satisfied. The ordinations were arranged to commence the next day.

'A monk who has been in our Monastery for some years [apparently Dom Iltud Mary himself], and is noted for his gravity, piety, and holiness of life, was to receive the five minor Orders the following day, Monday, July 25th. On Tuesday he was to be ordained deacon. The Reverend Father's Diaconate from the English Church being fully acknowledged, he and the other monk would receive the Priesthood on the Wednesday.[1] The Latin rite was used. To us it did not seem half so satisfactory as our own Prayer Book rite. The word "priest" was not even used, and at the laying-on of hands not a word was said. However, the validity of the rite is questioned by none, though that of the English ordinal is; and we are, of course, satisfied. We may question whether in future we in the Monastery may choose the rite as well as "choose the Bishop". We were too grateful to our dear Archbishop, however, to question or choose anything, for he won all our hearts by his humility and gentle courtesy.'

Vilatte was kept busy during those last three days at Llanthony. He also 'confirmed a boy, lately converted by the Grace of God'. He consecrated veils for the Nuns, gave every one separately his solemn Benediction, and consecrated the holy oils. But this was not enough to pay for the generous hospitality: His Grace had failed to persuade Bertie Cannell, the ex-Brother Gildas, who had returned to the monastery for a holiday, to accept all minor and major orders up to the priesthood. This unfrocked monk saw much of the Archbishop, because both found smoking necessary, and Fr Ignatius held the opinion that God would have provided man with a chimney if he had intended him to smoke tobacco. So Mar Timotheos and young Cannell had to creep out on to the mountain-side, and on one of these walks the former turned to his companion, and said: 'I make Father Ignatius a priest tomorrow, and I make *you a priest* too!'[2] Baron Rudolph de Bertouch, the son of Ignatius's first biographer, who met Vilatte, and who at that date was a somewhat worldly-minded Roman Catholic sixteen-year-old youth, whose only attraction to the monks was that they provided

---

[1] Some years later this monk, having returned to the world, was re-ordained by Dr Winnington Ingram, Bishop of London.

[2] Calder-Marshall, op. cit., p. 256. In 1939 Cannell published entertaining reminiscences of Llanthony and Fr Ignatius in *From Monk to Busman*.

him with shooting and fishing, recalls that he was also urged to accept the priesthood.

Before leaving Llanthony, Mar Timotheos blessed Ignatius as abbot, according to the *Pontificale Romanum*. It was hinted afterwards that he was paid for his services to the community, but as Mr Calder-Marshall remarks: 'Such an idea, in the terms of a crude bribe, is unthinkable; but it is probable that out of the love of Jesus Christ Father Ignatius pressed on Lord Timotheos some of the Abbey funds to defray his expenses. The amount cannot have been very much. In a few weeks Vilatte, who according to Bishop Grafton was a drunkard and so had more than normally heavy expenses, was broke.'[1]

All that was gained by these highly irregular ordinations was that Abbot Ignatius and his monks became schismatics in the eyes of Anglo-Catholics, instead of holy eccentrics who deserved pity and even admiration. Llanthony cut itself off from all relations with what the Reverend Father—both a 'British Israelite' and a firm believer in the so-called 'Flat Earth Theory'—used to refer to as 'our dear old Church' and her 'Apostate Bishops'.

News of these ordinations in South Wales reached the ears of Bishop Grafton in Wisconsin. He felt obliged to write a very long letter to *The Church Times* which was printed in part, with the comment: 'The whole is very melancholy reading, and we can well understand that nothing but a stern sense of duty would have induced the Bishop of Fond du Lac to write in such uncompromising terms.' Among other statements made was the following:

'I was obliged in the year 1892 to degrade René Vilatte from the priesthood and excommunicate him from the church.

'I have discovered that he was morally rotten; a swindling adventurer belonging to the same criminal class as your noted Tichborne claimant. He was reported to me for drunkenness, swindling, obtaining money under false pretences and other crimes, and as a notorious liar.

'The man has somewhat exceptional gifts as an impostor. He has the power of endurance of a Catiline, the audacity of a Jeremy Diddler, and the morals of a Tichborne. He can preach and pray with great fervour, and is wont when discovered to say with French loftiness that he forgives all his enemies.

'He has been surrounded by and had for his tools a small body of men, mostly ex-Romans, whose equals in crime and debauchery

[1] ibid., p. 259.

117

Joseph René Vilatte

are rarely found. His late secretary is now in a State prison. Another, who called himself amongst his many noms-de-plume, Brother William, and from whose writings most of the material in the articles of your Llanthony correspondent was derived, is now the inmate of an insane asylum, brought there by brutish and sottish drunkenness. Another co-worker, whom he ordained priest under the title of Father Basil, is a renegade from England, having formerly been connected with the Reformed Episcopal Church, and who fled to America, being accused as his Bishop wrote me, of criminal conduct with boys. His name is George Reader, and the authorities of Scotland Yard wrote concerning him, that, while they did not give information to private parties, they would do so to the chief of the police in any of our cities. Of another of his chief advisers, who has now given up the practical exercise of his ministry, I have written proof that he is an adulterer.

'I know of no clergyman or layman in my Diocese who has any other opinion of Vilatte but that his proper place is in the penitentiary. He belongs to the low class of criminal governed by inordinate ambition and insatiate greed for money and power. He has no religious principles, as is seen from the course of his life.'

Bishop Grafton then went on to give a detailed summary of Vilatte's career, including all his early migrations from one religious denomination to another, mentioning nearly twenty Roman Catholic communities in which he had been a postulant or novice. The effect of this article on readers of *The Church Times* was to make them feel that poor old Fr Ignatius had been fooled by this unscrupulous Franco-American prelate. But he was far from being the first person who had been captivated by what Father Iltud Mary calls 'our dear Archbishop's humility and gentle courtesy'. Many hearts had been won—and lost—by the way in which Mar Timotheos could, on occasion, 'preach and pray with great fervour'. But long before Bishop Grafton had exposed him he had left England for the Continent.

It is improbable that he ever got as far as Russia, which he stated was his destination when he disappeared from South Wales in the last week of July 1898. The next country in which he appeared was Italy. By the end of January 1899 most Catholic newspapers in Europe and North America had reported that Vilatte was seeking reconciliation with the Holy See of Rome, instead of union with the Holy Synod of Moscow. On February 2, Fr David Fleming, Definitor General of the Friars Minor, and

118

Joseph René Vilatte

Consultor of the Congregation of the Holy Office, issued a statement to the effect that Joseph René Vilatte had expressed his most sincere and heartfelt regret for having taught many errors and for having attacked and misrepresented the holy Roman Catholic Church; that he withdrew any such teaching, and regretted that he had obtained Holy Orders in an unlawful and irregular way; and that he had illicitly and sacrilegiously conferred upon others various orders. This penitent cleric called upon all those with whom he had co-operated in the past, especially those whom he had raised to the priesthood, to submit themselves unreservedly and unconditionally to the authority of the Vicar of Christ. On May 25, Bishop Zardetti wrote to Mgr Messmer that Fr David Fleming had the case well in hand.

Then came reports from Rome that Vilatte had not yet made his formal abjuration, or been reconciled with the Church. It was explained that he was awaiting the result of the Process before the Holy Office. As soon as a decision had been reached about the validity of his Orders, he would be received back into communion with the Holy See. Meanwhile the Holy Office had received an eight-page digest from the Bishop of Green Bay in which he laid stress on Vilatte's insincerity in the past; suggesting that he merely wanted the Roman authorities to say that his orders were valid, so that he might go to England and 'validate' the Orders of Anglican clergymen. Mgr Messmer disclosed that Vilatte had admitted to him personally that he had never been in good faith. Mgr Katzer, now Archbishop of Milwaukee, with whom Vilatte had been in contact many years before, also advised the Holy Office to delay passing judgment on his orders in order to test his sincerity.

It is not known how long the irregularly consecrated, but apparently penitent Archbishop remained in Rome, presumably at the expense of the ecclesiastical authorities, but early in 1900 it was reported that he was in France. His hosts were the Benedictine monks of the Abbey of St Martin de Ligugé, near Poitiers. He appears to have told them that he wanted to make a careful study of ordinations in the Syro-Malabar Church, so that he could convince the Holy Office of the validity of his episcopate.

One day Joris Karl Huysmans, the French novelist, who had been converted to a living Christian faith by a visit to the Trappist monastery of Igny, paid a visit to Ligugé. He was accompanied by a young friend of the Prior, Dom Chamard, by name Aubault de la

Joseph René Vilatte

Haute-Chambre. They encountered Vilatte at dinner in the refectory. Aubault recalled in after years that he was 'a clean-shaven, coarse-skinned giant of Herculean stature, who looked like an American athlete, and whose thighs were encased in pale green trousers'. Great was the astonishment of these two guests when one of the monks confided that this apparition was none other than Mgr Vilatte, 'the Old Catholic Archbishop of Babylon'. After tracing Vilatte's subsequent relations with the Catholic Church, Aubault concluded briefly but charitably: 'He is dead now; may he rest in peace, for his Havanas were excellent.'[1]

But the 'Old Catholic Archbishop of Babylon' was not merely enjoying the hospitality of the Benedictines, browsing in their library, and smoking cigars. He had been up to mischief as usual. On April 17, 1900, Cardinal Richard, Archbishop of Paris, circulated a warning among his clergy to be on their guard against priests who produced *celebrets* signed by Vilatte. On June 13 that same year the Roman authorities issued a decree of major excommunication against 'two priests', Paolo Miraglia-Gulotti and Joseph René Vilatte. On May 6 the latter had consecrated the former as Old Catholic Bishop for Italy, with the title of Bishop of Piacenza.[2] Thus came into being the 'Italian National Episcopal Church'. Bishop Gulotti soon found that the majority of Italians were quite content to be members of an international church. By May 1908 he was over in North America, working with Vilatte.[3]

Having gained nothing by wandering for two years around Europe, except, presumably, free board and lodging, Mar Timotheos decided to seek refuge in Canada, as he had done on several previous occasions. Early in 1901 he retired to St Joseph's Island, at the north end of Lake Huron, and this remained his headquarters for the next two years. Some of the half-breed Indians on the island were so overawed by his Roman purple cassock and archiepiscopal insignia, which he displayed on every possible occasion, that they

[1] Robert Baldrick, *The Life of J. K. Huysmans* (Oxford, 1955), p. 283—quoting from A. de la Haute-Chambre, *J. K. Huysmans, souvenirs* (Paris, 1942), pp. 16–17.
[2] This city had been a suffragan see of Bologna since 1582, and later directly subject to the Holy See.
[3] See p. 125. The first attempt to set up a 'national' Catholic Church in Italy was at Verona about 1850. After the Vatican Council of 1870 a Neapolitan priest, Domenico di Panelli, tried without success to form a sort of Old Catholic sect. He called himself Archbishop of Lydda. Rather more successful was the 'Chiesa Cattolica Nazionale d'Italia' founded in 1882 by Count Enrico di Campello, formerly a canon of the Vatican Basilica. It was supported by German and Swiss Old Catholics, the Evangelical party in the Church of England, and several American Protestant Episcopal bishops. This national church never had more than a small number of adherents. Campello died, reconciled with the Roman Church, in 1903.

120

Joseph René Vilatte

started to attend his chapel. This displeased the local Jesuit priest, whom Vilatte denounced more than once, for disrespect towards a prelate. 'The Old Catholic Archbishop of North America'—as he still called himself—must often have been very bored and lonely on his island in Ontario. Yet though he was right at the back of beyond he still kept a close watch on international affairs, ecclesiastical as well as political.

It looks as if he still had hopes of persuading Fr Ignatius of Llanthony to become the first archbishop of an autocephalous Old Catholic British Church, and letting him perform the consecration. This project had been in the air since November 1898. Ignatius wrote to an archbishop (apparently Alvarez in Ceylon) on October 9, 1900, suggesting that the Jacobite Patriarch of Antioch might allow the consecration of a bishop for Llanthony Abbey, and 'thus preserve for us the true priesthood for all time to come'. He feared that before long it would be impossible for any 'Catholic Christians to remain in Communion with the British Church'.[1] But it is not certain just how far Vilatte was mixed up with this project.

Nevertheless, apparently regarding the whole world as his province, and possibly to defy Mar Jacobus, Bishop of Mercia and Middlesex (Vernon Herford), who since his consecration in South India in December 1902 had been able to supply Syro-Chaldean (Nestorian) orders at Oxford, Mar Timotheos turned up again in South Wales in the summer of 1903. On June 14 he raised to the episcopate the Rev. Henry M. Marsh-Edwards, with the title of Bishop of Caerleon. The Syrian-Malabar line of succession was handed on in a room over a shop at Barry Dock. This ex-Anglican clergyman had been deprived of his living in the Diocese of Southwell on charges of immorality.[2] The following morning the Old Catholic Archbishop of North America, assisted by the Bishop of Caerleon, consecrated a young man named Henry Bernard Ventham, on whom he seems to have already conferred priest's orders. Ventham assumed the title of Bishop of Dorchester.[3] It is probable that more priests were ordained that summer, both in England

---

[1] cf. Donald Attwater, *Fr Ignatius of Llanthony* (1931), p. 160, note 1. Vilatte could have found good reasons for persuading Ignatius to become the episcopal head of the loyal remnant of the Ancient British Church, alleged to have been revived by Mar Pelagius Morgan in 1874. For in 1897 the apostate Armenian Uniate *vartapet*, Leon Chechemian, had managed to get constituted an amalgamation of the Ancient British Church, Nazarene Episcopal Ecclesia, and the Free Protestant Church of England, which was given the title of 'The Free Protestant Episcopal Church of England'. Chechemian was elected the first Archbishop in 1898.

[2] See pp. 269–271.
[3] See pp. 271–273.

and on the Continent, but documentary proof is lacking.[1]

It is hard to know how far Vilatte was ever sincere in what he did and what he said. For instance, what was at the back of his mind on June 20, 1905, when he wrote to the Jacobite Metropolitan of Malabar, telling him of ceaseless persecution he had to endure from both Episcopalians and Roman Catholics in America, yet boasting that he had managed to pervert at least 500,000 Papists? He added: 'I very sorrowfully confess that I had returned to the abominable heresy of Rome six years ago. It did not take me more than six months to see the abomination and desolation of that schismatical and heretical Roman Church. I immediately took my stand before God, rose and worked against the lie of Rome, in favour of our Holy Orthodox Faith.'[2]

A series of conflicts between the Church and State in France, arising from the anti-clerical legislation of Waldeck-Rousseau and Combes, gave Vilatte the idea that it might be to his advantage to return to his native country. This he did in the summer of 1906. The previous December a separation bill had become law, proclaiming that the Republic did not recognize any form of religion. It appears that Vilatte was already on friendly terms with Aristide Briand, who had been appointed Minister of Education in 1903, and probably thought that this astute politician would be able to make use of his services. There were rumours of the setting up of a National Church on Gallican lines. The State now had the power to sequester property administered by church councils, and pass it over to welfare and charitable institutions under the control of local authorities.

Vilatte, soon after his arrival in Paris, took advantage of this new law, and managed to obtain possession of the Barnabite church in the Rue Legendre, which he reopened for Old Catholic services. He contributed articles to a review of Gallican tendencies, called *L'église catholique française*. One of his former priests in Wisconsin, a certain Florent, who had also returned to France, wrote for *La Libre Parole*. Debts accumulated, however, and on March 2, 1907, the police in Paris took away the archiepiscopal mitres and crozier for default in payment. It looks as if Vilatte managed to retrieve his

---

[1] In one of his articles attacking Vilatte, Bishop Grafton quotes the fees he charged for ordaining a priest and consecrating a bishop, but does not give the sources on which he based this accusation of simony, which may well have been true.

[2] This statement referred to his toying with the idea of submitting to the Holy See in 1898–9, and his subsequent ordination of priests and consecration of bishops—none of them exactly for the 'Holy Orthodox Faith'.

regalia before June 21, when he ordained priest, Louis-Marie-Francois Giraud, formerly a Trappist monk of Fontgombauld, but who had since made a name for himself as a magician, and who was associated with the prelates and priests of the Universal Gnostic Church.[1] Shortly after this a notice was issued by Cardinal Richard, warning the faithful against apostate priests who were celebrating Mass under cover of a religious association directed by 'a pseudo-American bishop'. The Cardinal stated that 'this plot hatched in the silence characteristic of masonry will not succeed. Catholics will not let themselves be deceived. Clemenceau and Briand may rob us of our churches, but not of our consciences'. Vilatte was then excommunicated by the Archbishop of Paris for a second time. Realizing perhaps that his National Church was a failure, Mar Timotheos tried to join the Rumanian Orthodox Church as a simple priest, but its clergy in Paris were not interested in him. The only result of all this plotting and scheming was to launch a schismatic and heretical church sect, which in the past half-century has split up into several tiny splinter churches, with impressive titles.[2]

In the end, having seen that there was no chance of earning a living by his wits in France, and having bungled everything as badly as he had done with the Belgians and Poles in the United States, he again crossed the Atlantic.[3]

Chicago became the headquarters of the now free-lance Archbishop, who by this time had severed all associations with the Independent Catholic Church of Goa and Ceylon, the Syro-Jacobite Patriarchate of Antioch, as well as with the Old Catholic Churches in Europe. The consecration of Francis Hodur at Utrecht by three Dutch Old Catholic Bishops on September 29, 1907, followed by the organization of the Polish National Catholic Church in America, had been the final blow to his hopes of using these schismatics from the Roman Church for his own ends.[4] He moved around the country, and more than once found reasons to cross the border into Canada. It appears to have been at Winnipeg in 1909 that he ordained two monks from Llanthony Abbey—Dom Asaph Harris and Dom Gildas Taylor. The former returned to his Welsh monastery

---

[1] See pp. 306–310.

[2] See pp. 310–318.

[3] It is probable that in 1907 he consecrated Carmel Henry Carfora as Old Catholic Bishop for France or Italy. In any case, seeing that prospects were not hopeful in Europe, Carfora migrated to the U.S.A., where in 1916 he was re-consecrated by de Landas Berghes of the Mathew succession (see pp. 427, 428). But there is no documentary evidence of Carfora's previous consecration.

[4] See pp. 523–527.

Joseph René Vilatte

as Superior; the latter went to Mexico, where for some years he worked with schismatic clergy who were being sponsored by Vilatte as the nucleus of a national church.[1]

It was at Chicago a year or two after this that Mar Timotheos raised to the priesthood Dom Francis Brothers, Prior of St Dunstan's Abbey, Waukegan, Illinois. This was an Old Catholic fraternity, legally incorporated at Fond du Lac in 1909 by Bishop Grafton as 'The American Congregation of the Order of St Benedict', and of which he acted as Titular Abbot until his death in 1912.[2] But Mar Timotheos and the future Metropolitan of the so-called Old Catholic Church in America soon parted company; and in May 1915, the former was protesting against the activities of 'an Italian ex-Roman priest who is masquerading as one of our bishops'. This was probably Miraglia Gulotti, who, having had no luck as Bishop of Piacenza, had migrated to New York. Or it may have been Carfora, who seems to have been associated with Vilatte in France.[3]

Vilatte probably realized that it was useless trying his luck again in Europe, since most of the countries where he might have found friends and benefactors had been at war since August 1914. The only thing he could do was to devise some organization in the United States, of which he would be the head. By 1915 the former Old Catholic Archbishop of North America had launched a new schismatic body which he called 'The American Catholic Church'. During that same year he received a distinguished convert into this organization, whose grandiose title could only have deceived the very simple-minded. This was the Rev. Frederic Ebenezer Lloyd, whose career had been almost as adventurous as his own. Ordained priest of the Church of England by Dr Mackarness, Bishop of Oxford, for some years he worked as a missionary in Newfoundland, but his record there was not altogether satisfactory. For more reasons than one Mr Lloyd felt it better to move to the United States, where he was elected before long to a bishopric in the Protestant Episcopal Church. Investigations were made into his antecedents, with the result that he was degraded from the Anglican priesthood on January 16, 1907. The House of Bishops washed their hands of this clergyman, so he 'went over to Rome'. There

---

[1] Both monks joined the Benedictines of Caldey later on, but neither before nor after the community had been reconciled with the Roman Church in 1913 did they make use of their alleged Syrian-Malabar orders. Both are now dead.

[2] See p. 416. In 1911 it was formally united with a remnant of Kowlowski's Polish Old Catholic Church, then under the jurisdiction of Mgr J. F. Tichy. After his resignation in 1912, Prior Francis was elected as his episcopal successor. (See pp. 417, 418.)

[3] See p. 123, n.3.

were, however, no prospects of the priesthood, because he had been twice married.[1] After two years in communion with the Holy See as a layman, he returned to the Episcopalian fold, and was allowed to resume his ministerial functions. But as there was little chance of preferment, it is easy to understand why he found convincing reasons to join the newly founded American Catholic Church. Not only was Lloyd a man of great charm, endowed with good looks, but he had ample private means, thanks to his second wife.[2] It is not surprising therefore that Vilatte welcomed Mr and Mrs Lloyd with open arms.

A fortnight after Mgr Mundelein, Auxiliary Bishop of Brooklyn, had been translated to the archiepiscopal see of Chicago, another ceremony took place in this same city, reported as follows in *The American Catholic Quarterly*:

'By far the most important event in the Ecclesiastical history of the United States of America was celebrated on Wednesday, December 19th, 1915, when the Rev Frederick E. J. Lloyd, Doctor of Divinity, was Consecrated as first Bishop of the American Catholic Church, in St David's Chapel, 536 East Thirty-sixth Street, Chicago, Illinois. A day of rare, though wintry, loveliness, added to the interest of the occasion.

'The Consecration service began at 10.30, and continued about the space of two hours. The chapel was filled with worshippers, who were largely personal friends of Dr Lloyd. The entire Pontifical service was celebrated according to the Latin Rite, though, of course, in English. The Consecrator was the Most Rev. Archbishop Joseph René Vilatte, Primate and Metropolitan, and the Assisting Bishop, the Rt Rev. Paul Miraglia [Gulotti] of New York.'[3]

At the conclusion of this long function, Mar Timotheos addressed the newly consecrated prelate, saying:

'It needs no prophet to foretell for you and the American Catholic Church a great future in the Providence of God. The need for a Church both American and Catholic, and free from paparchy and all foreign denomination, has been felt for many years by Christians of all the denominations. May your zeal and apostolic ministry be crowned with success.'

[1] His second wife was born Philena R. Peabody. They seem to have been a devoted couple.

[2] Her ancestor, George Peabody (1795–1869), was an American merchant who had made a fortune in England. He left £500,000 to relieve the condition of the London poor, and also gave large sums for educational purposes in the U.S.A.

[3] It will be noticed that Miraglia-Gulotti had now been translated to New York from the titular see of Piacenza, Italy. (See p. 120.)

Joseph René Vilatte

By the time that the U.S.A. had joined forces with the Allies in April, 1917, Vilatte had already begun to fade out of the picture. He had reached the age of sixty-one in 1914, and his dynamic energy was already diminishing. At a Synod held in Chicago on April 10, 1920, three months after the Peace Treaty had been ratified in Paris, he offered to retire, and nominated Lloyd as his successor as Primate and Metropolitan of the American Catholic Church. The clergy present granted Vilatte the honorary title of Exarch.[1] He lived in retirement at 4427 North Mulligan Avenue, Chicago, and does not seem to have performed any more episcopal functions until September 22, 1921, when he helped to launch the African Orthodox Church, by consecrating in the Church of Our Lady of Good Death, Chicago, a negro from Antigua, George Alexander McGuire, as the first bishop of yet another new sect.[2]

It may be assumed that the funds at the disposal of the American Catholic Church (even with a generous donation from Mrs Lloyd), were not sufficient to allow the Exarch an adequate old-age pension. Not long after his consecration of McGuire, Vilatte decided to return to his native France. It is possible that he hoped that Mgr Giraud, the faith-healer and occultist (now known as Archbishop of Almyra and Patriarch of the *Église Catholique Française*), or Mgr Bricaud (alias Tau Jean II, or 'Joanny Bricaud'), the Gnostic writer on black and white magic, would befriend him as the virtual founder of their sects.[3] We cannot say what were his motives, but on June 1, 1925, Mar Timotheos made a formal declaration before Mgr Ceretti, Apostolic Nuncio at Paris, regretting and repenting having received Holy Orders and having conferred them on others contrary to the teaching and laws of the Holy Roman Church in which he hoped, by the grace of God, soon to be received. He asked pardon of God, for the scandal he had given, and promised to repair it by the example of his life, inviting all those who had followed his errors to imitate his example.

A week later *La Croix* and other newspapers announced that Mgr Vilatte, with an American boy-servant, was staying with the Cistercian monks of the Common Observance at the Abbey of Pont-Colbert, near Versailles. There were rumours that it was at the request of Pius XI that the Prior had offered the ex-Archbishop of

[1] Normally the primate of an independent church, between a patriarch and an archbishop, also a title of honour in the Eastern Churches.
[2] See pp. 264–269.
[3] See pp. 308–309.

the American Catholic Church an eventide home. Another bit of gossip was that the Pope had granted him a pension of 22,000 francs annually in recognition of his episcopal status.

On June 23, 1925, the *Bayerischer Kürier* published a statement, at the orders of the Swiss Christian Catholic Church, to the effect that Vilatte had never been a priest of this body or of any other genuine Old Catholic Church. Mgr Ceretti felt it worth while to reply to this newspaper as follows:

'Mgr Vilatte received the Minor Orders and the Order of Subdeacon on June 5th, 1885, the Order of Deacon on June 6th of the same year, and on the following day, i.e. June 7th, 1885, the Ordination to the Priesthood. All these Orders were conferred on him by Mgr Herzog (Old Catholic Bishop) in the Old Catholic Church at Berne. This is proved by documents bearing the seal and signature of Mgr Herzog.

'Concerning his Episcopal Consecration, it took place on May 29th, 1892. Mgr Vilatte was consecrated by three Jacobite Bishops in the Cathedral of Archbishop Alvarez (Julius First), i.e. in the Church of our Lady of Good Death in Colombo (Ceylon). Mgr Vilatte is likewise in possession of the consecration deed in question bearing the signatures of the three above-mentioned bishops and of the American Consul, who was present at the ceremony. So much for explanation, should you deem it appropriate for your use.'

This letter from the Apostolic Nuncio at Paris was printed in the *Bayerischer Kürier* on July 11, 1925. Vilatte must have been pleased that he had managed to convince Mgr Ceretti of the facts of his priesthood and episcopate, even if both were irregular.

For the next three and a half years he led a quiet and secluded life in a cottage within the monastery grounds, waited on by his boy-servant. Out of politeness he was addressed as 'Monseigneur', or referred to as 'Sa Grandeur'. His ordinary costume was a soutane, though without any episcopal insignia. Stories went around Paris that Pius XI had been prepared to allow Vilatte's reordination to the priesthood *sub conditione*, but that he had refused the papal offer, being convinced that he was a bishop as well as a priest. The aged prelate usually attended the daily conventual Mass, sitting in a remote corner of the chapel; receiving Holy Communion only on Sundays. No formal pronouncement on the validity of his orders was ever made by the Roman authorities.

Growing impatient of being treated as a layman, he managed to procure a chalice and vestments, and started to celebrate Mass in his cottage. According to the late Mgr Chaptal, Auxiliary Bishop of Paris, he got hold of a mitre and crozier (if he had not brought them with him from Chicago), and, presumably having consecrated the holy oils, gave minor and major orders up to the priesthood to one of the Cistercian novices. Not satisfied with this escapade, Mar Timotheos raised him to the episcopate. It appears that the ridiculous affair was kept quiet, but if true it is surprising that the Prior of Pont-Colbert did not order 'Sa Grandeur' to vacate his cottage and clear off the premises, there and then. Mgr Chaptal also relates that Cardinal Merry del Val had already decided that Vilatte had so 'commercialized'. ordinations and consecrations that he himself did not regard them as valid.[1]

The end came suddenly. Mar Timotheos died of heart failure on July 8, 1929. He was buried (not in episcopal vestments) in the cemetery at Versailles. One of the bishops he had consecrated and two priests he had ordained were among the mourners.[2] A requiem Mass was celebrated as for a layman in the monastery chapel. Shortly after the funeral both his American servant and his private papers vanished.

Such was the harlequinade to the pantomime in which this buccaneer ecclesiastical adventurer played the principal boy with a very odd cosmopolitan supporting chorus. If ever there was a bishop at large, it was this son of a Parisian butcher. The trouble was that he was born at least a hundred years too late; he was a flashy and baroque period-piece that did not fit into a Gothic Revival setting. By the time he appeared on the stage most religious denominations had become too respectable to be able to make use of his undoubted talents. Had he lived in seventeenth- or eighteenth-century France, he might easily have risen to be a Gallicanizing archbishop or even a cardinal; holding many rich benefices, plotting and scheming on the back stairs of the palaces of the Tuileries and Versailles, and a *persona grata*, if not with the Bourbon Kings, at least with their mistresses.

Yet when recalling the kaleidoscopic career of this utterly unstable Frenchman, it is as well to remember that 'the kingdom of heaven is like a net that was cast into the sea, and enclosed fish of every kind at once'. Peter the Fisherman *did* manage to get this

[1] Mgr Chaptal's revelations about these ordinations and consecration of the novice at Pont-Colbert Abbey were given in a letter to the Rev. H. R. T. Brandreth.
[2] Between 1898 and 1929 Vilatte consecrated at least seven bishops in North America and Europe. There is no saying how many priests he ordained.

very odd fish entangled in the meshes of his net before he died, and that is something for which we can be thankful. Yet at the same time, it is difficult to forget the remark made shortly after his consecration in Ceylon—'*Life is but a farce!*' Was his final 'conversion' really sincere? The answer is not ours to give.

CHAPTER V

Ulric Vernon Herford, Mar Jacobus, Bishop of Mercia and Middlesex; Administrator of the Metropolitan See of India, Ceylon, Milapur etc, of the Syro-Chaldean Church and of the Patriarchate of Babylon and the East; Founder of the Evangelical Catholic Communion

Utterly different in character and origins from Joseph René Vilatte was another independent bishop more or less his contemporary—Ulric Vernon Herford (1866–1938). Most of his wide circle of friends of many religious denominations or of none regarded him as an eccentric visionary, but few seem to have questioned his sincerity. He is remembered, not only for his inchoate learning and personal charm, but also for his fidelity to his convictions.

Born at Manchester of a distinguished Unitarian family, Ulric's father, W. H. Herford, was a pioneer of modern education. His cousin, Professor C. H. Herford, obtained international fame in the field of English literature. Ulric, having been educated at Owens College, Manchester (then a constituent college of the University), obtained there the degree of B.A. in 1889, and an Associateship the following year. From 1889 to 1891 he was a student at Manchester College, Oxford (Unitarian), whence he moved to St Stephen's House, presumably having become an Anglican and with Anglican orders in view. About 1892, however, he received a presbyterian form of ordination, and became minister of the Unitarian Chapel at King's Lynn. Then followed another spell at Manchester College, Oxford, and the charge of a Unitarian chapel at Whitchurch, Shropshire. He returned to Oxford in 1897 as minister of a congregation connected with Manchester College, the status of which was 'Free Protestant'.

The following year Herford built a new red brick chapel in Percy Street, off the Iffley Road, on the eastern side of Magdalen

130

The Right Rev. Ulric Vernon Herford, Mar Jacobus, Bishop of Mercia and Middlesex, Administrator of the Metropolitan See of India, Ceylon, Milapur, etc., of the Syro-Chaldean Church, and of Patriarchate of Babylon and the East; Founder of the Evangelical Catholic Communion.

The Right Rev. Rudolph Francis Edward St Patrick Alphonsus Ghislain de Gramont Hamilton de Lorraine-Brabant, Prince de Landas Berghes et de Rache et Duc de St Winock.

Ulric Vernon Herford

Bridge, not far from the 'Cowley Fathers' Church of St John the Evangelist. He called it 'The Church of the Divine Love'. The adjacent house became known as 'The Monastery', for it was occupied by a few young men who led a quasi-Franciscan life. He composed a Rule for this 'Order of the Christian Faith'. In February 1900, there appeared the first issue of a monthly paper, entitled *The Christian Churchman*. Herford's dream by this time was a united Christendom, in which, so we are told, 'the best and most precious elements of East and West, of Catholic and Protestant, should be gathered together in one Evangelical Catholic Communion. It was to be a long and lonely voyage, lasting to the end of his life, with little outward encouragement, and many disappointments. But it can truly be said that he never swerved from his course'.[1]

Having lived in Oxford on and off for more than ten years, Herford had acquired a fairly comprehensive knowledge of all aspects of Anglicanism. None of them appeared to offer just what he was seeking by way of a historic Church. Neither the austere Evangelicalism in a much restored medieval Gothic setting at St Aldate's, nor the ornate Anglo-Catholicism in the Byzantinesque basilica of St Barnabas, which at that date represented the two extremes, made sufficient appeal. It is easy to understand that he turned aside from what the Jesuits had to offer him in the floridly furnished St Aloysius's; and it was not until 1921 that Oxford saw the return of the Dominicans, whose spirituality and presentation of Catholic worship might have attracted him more.[2]

One day it dawned on him that he must look further east than the Cowley Fathers' church round the corner from Percy Street. By the autumn of 1901 he was certain that he must make a pilgrimage to Persia, for he was now convinced that the Nestorian Church was 'the purest and most primitive Branch of the Holy Catholic and Apostolic Church'. Herford was far from being the first English Protestant who had made this discovery. In 1842 Mr George Badger, Chaplain of the East India Company, visited Mesopotamia. Ten years later he published a two-volume book entitled *The Nestorians and their Rituals*, which was edited by Dr J. M. Neale. This led to missionaries being sent out to these 'Protestants of the East', who had no crucifixes, images or pictures

---

[1] George F. Tull, *Vernon Herford, Apostle of Unity* (Bradford, 1958), p. 14.
[2] Soon after the Capuchin Franciscans settled in at Greyfriars, Iffley Road, in 1911, Herford appears to have called on Fr Cuthbert, their first Superior.

of saints in their churches, who abjured the Mother of God, and abhorred the Pope.[1]

The idea at the time was that the Nestorians must be very much the same as Low Church Anglicans—Catholic in the primitive sense, but not Roman. All they needed was spiritual and material assistance from sound Protestants. In 1868, their Patriarch, Mar Shimun, and his clergy appealed to Dr Tait, Archbishop of Canterbury, to befriend them. But it was not until 1886 that Tait's successor, Dr Benson, helped to found the so-called 'Archbishop's' Mission to the Assyrian Christians, on High Church lines. It was possible for Herford to have read all about this 'purest and most primitive branch of the Holy Catholic and Apostolic Church' in Maclean and Browne's *The Katholicos of the East and His People,* first published in 1892.

But for some reason or another this Liberal Christian minister at Oxford did not take the direct and obvious route to his spiritual goal. Instead of getting in touch with the Anglican missionaries, who would have been able to introduce him to 'The Reverend and Honoured Father of Fathers and Great Shepherd, the Katholikos and Patriarch of the East'—the full title of the ecclesiastical and civil head of the Nestorian Church and people—Herford wrote to Mar Basilius Soares, Bishop of Trichur, a town on the Malabar Coast of South India, who was the head of a small body, whose original members had been Catholics of the Syro-Chaldean rite, who had defied the authority of the Holy See in the eighteen-sixties, and lapsed into schism. Mar Basilius called himself 'Metropolitan of the Syro-Chaldean Church in India, Ceylon, Socotra, and Messina'. His flock numbered no more than 8,000, if that; and their associations with the Nestorian Church were less than forty years old; Herford, throughout his life, was basically a simple soul, so kind-hearted, that he was an easy victim to beggars, hawkers, and other importunate persons; in this case he must have accepted this South Indian prelate on his nomenclature, without investigating his antecedents, since it would have been difficult to lay hands on any information at Oxford; few people at that date were even aware of the existence of this tiny sect.

Mar Basilius, otherwise Luis Mariano Soares (or Suarez), seems to have been a typical specimen of those South Indian Christians who are never so happy as when excommunicating each

[1] The Nestorians in the past so emphasized the distinction between the divine and human natures in Christ as to produce two Christs instead of one.

other and forming splinter-churches.[1] He was a Euro-Indian of Portuguese-Brahmin descent. He threw off the yoke of Rome in his youth, and was ordained priest by another lapsed Catholic, none other than Julius Alvarez, Metropolitan of the Independent Catholic Church of Goa and Ceylon, the consecrator of Joseph René Vilatte.[2] In 1899 Soares persuaded a certain Mar Antonios Abd-Ishu, who since about 1876, had been head of yet another schismatic sect, known as the Mellusians, to raise him to the episcopate. The Mellusians had their centre at Trichur in the northern part of the Travancore-Cochin State. Their history is confusing, and hard to condense, but briefly it is as follows. The founders were Syro-Malabar priests in communion with Rome, among whom was Antony Thondanatta, who in 1862 managed to receive consecration by the Nestorian Patriarch, Simon XVII Abraham, and thereafter styled himself Mar Antonios Abd-Ishu, Metropolitan of India. It appears that about three years later he was reconciled with the Holy See, but fell into schism again about 1876, when he assumed the headship of the Mellusians. He died in 1900, and was succeeded by Mar Basilius, i.e. Soares.

Herford wrote to this prelate on February 27, 1902, and said: 'I should be very glad to be of any service to you in England if we could establish ecclesiastical relations as I have a small independent monastic Church and many friends, and some fellow Presbyters who I think would be in sympathy with your Church.'[3]

Mar Basilius replied on March 25:

'I would be extremely pleased to accept your sincere request to establish ecclesiastical relations in amalgamating your pure and progressive work to our Church in all extensions.'

It must be admitted that Herford's picture of his so-called 'independent monastic Church' at Oxford was almost as far removed from the truth as was Vilatte's account of his Old Catholic Church in Wisconsin when he wrote to Alvarez in 1891.[4] But the difference was that Herford was absolutely sincere, whereas Vilatte was probably well aware that he was conveying a false impression to the head of the Independent Catholic Church of Goa

---

[1] Early in the present century there were at least eight Christian bodies on the Malabar Coast, all claiming succession from one or other of the Eastern patriarchates, and all quarrelling with each other. In addition to these, there were rival groups of Protestant missionaries. The Church of South India was not founded until 1947. (cf. Adrian Fortescue, *The Lesser Eastern Churches* (1913), pp. 374–5.)

[2] See pp. 107–108.

[3] Tull, op. cit., p. 19.

[4] See p. 105.

and Ceylon. The result was the same: each schismatic archbishop in the Far East was eager to have his sect brought into ecclesiastical relations with what he supposed must be a wealthy and powerful ally against papal pretensions and the machinations of Rome.

So the presbyter in Percy Street, Oxford, wrote back that he would be proud to entertain His Excellency if he could spare the time to come to England to consecrate him and another presbyter. Herford visualized that the roughly fifty or so members of his congregation, and the few members of 'The Order of the Christian Faith', who formed its 'monastic' section, would become a sort of English branch under the title of 'The Evangelical Catholic Church' of what he called 'The Church Universal'. He offered to pay part or the whole of travelling expenses, not only of the Metropolitan, but also those of another bishop to be co-consecrator. He reminded Mar Basilius that he 'would be able to see at least some portions of the Coronation Pageant of King Edward VII, which takes place in June'; adding: 'Our Churches are all independent and ours is quite under my power'. He hinted to his correspondent that if he raised him to the episcopate: 'I think we should soon have . . . a strongly organized Church which would help towards uniting all Christians in one. There are four of us here, and I hope to have more before long. We have many friends, and some of them are very influential. . .'[1]

On May 27, Mar Basilius wrote that he feared it would involve too great an expense to bring himself and another bishop to England, and to entertain them, and suggested that it would be cheaper if he were accompanied merely by his private secretary. Although the Coronation festivities of Edward VII greatly tempted him, he regretted that his 'responsible office' prevented any 'sudden move to a foreign country' until before November or December the following year. Herford replied that the thought had occurred to him that perhaps it would be better for himself and his fellow-presbyter to come out to India for their consecration. He asked Mar Basilius if his Church had its succession of bishops from the Nestorian Church in Asia Minor, which suggests that he had not troubled to investigate its brief history. The Metropolitan was asked to send 'a plan of the succession of bishops as far back as convenient'. As there had been only two bishops since the said Church came into existence, this request was easily met with. After the exchange of more letters, Herford sailed alone in the German

[1] ibid., p. 19.

Ulric Vernon Herford

liner, *Barbarossa*, bound for Ceylon, leaving England in October 1902. He landed at Colombo on November 15, and two days later crossed the straits to India.

It is to be presumed that this Unitarian minister ('in irregular Presbyterian orders for ten years', as he stated) had received Christian baptism, but his biographer does not mention it. Herford must have been in a frantic hurry to get the jobs done as quickly as possible, because he remained in south India no longer than a fortnight.[1] He was hurried through the ordinations as deacon and priest in two days. The ceremonies took place in the Church of Our Lady of the Seven Sorrows at Dindigul, on November 21 and 23. After this he and Mar Basilius moved to Palithamen in the Madura District, where on St Andrew's Day, November 30, this episcopal consecration was carried out in the Church of the Epiphany. Hereford was given the name, title, and style of 'Mar Jacobus, Bishop of Mercia and Middlesex (including the county of London)', with apparently full jurisdiction over Great Britain and Ireland.

Judging from the diary kept by Herford during the fourteen days spent in south India, he seems to have been rather surprised to find that these Nestorians were not quite the simple Bible Christians he had been led to believe. He describes their strange, almost barbaric, ritual and ceremonial—how 'gorgeous state umbrellas were held over the heads' of himself and his consecrator as they walked in procession round the village. There were 'curious heart-shaped standards surmounted by small crosses, and small scarlet flags which men bore in front. Seven horns were blown on each side in front, and numerous drums, and exactly the same (so far as I could perceive) notes were played and cry raised at the heathen funeral procession. In fact there was a triumphantly joyous din! Petards were fired off several times during the day'. He gives details of the as yet unfamiliar vestments which he had to put on before his consecration; and how crowds of men, women, and children came up, knelt, and kissed his ring, after he had been solemnly enthroned as Lord Bishop of Mercia and Middlesex. He ends his long account of these functions with the words:

---

[1] Had he managed to spare the time to investigate the other Christian Churches in Malabar, it is probable that he would have found the much Protestantized 'Mar Thomas Christians', or the Church of Anjur, a small body in communion with them, more sympathetic. Or again, the 'Church of England Syrians', who were in communion with Low Church Anglican missionaries, might have proved closer to the ideal of Herford's purest and most primitive Catholic and Apostolic Church.

Ulric Vernon Herford

'I felt sorry to leave them, as I had got quite fond of them . . . Of course, they must be in a childish condition, as shown by their tolerance of the "Xmas tree" tinsel decoration of the Church, but they seem to have many childlike virtues too. My ring and staff are the present of Mar Basilius. The silver ring is made by the village goldsmith, and the crozier carved out of wood by the village carpenter.'[1]

Although we have what appears to be Herford's own account of his ordinations and consecration, there have been, and still are, certain people bold enough to maintain that he was a complete impostor from start to finish! Their suspicions are due to the fact that the documents he produced in support of his claims are in his own handwriting, and sealed with an English rubber stamp. At the bottom are some signatures, with that of 'Mar Basilius' in red ink.[2]

It is related that Herford admitted to the late Sir James Marchant, K.B.E., that at least part of these documents was written by himself, and that he had signed the name of Mar Basilius in two of them. The probable explanation of this irregularity is that Soares had little or no education; in fact Herford remarked in his Diary that 'Mar Basilius seems very glad to make use of my small store of theological knowledge'.[3] As Fr Brandreth points out, this 'would, perhaps, also account for the fact that the forms of ordination and consecration mentioned thereon bear striking resemblance to those of the Anglican Book of Common Prayer, which one would not suppose would be familiar to a Brahmin Nestorian in southern India'.[4]

In after years it greatly distressed Herford when anybody ventured to cast doubts on the validity of his orders. He was very worried in 1909 that the Dutch Old Catholics refused to recognize his letters of consecration. Eventually he managed to procure a Statutory Declaration, dated November 26, 1919, in which Mr Stanier Walter, then Mayor of Oxford, vouched for the genuineness of certain documents and papers entrusted to him by the

---

[1] Mar Georgius (edited by), *A Voyage into the Orient, being Extracts from the Diary of the Rt. Rev. Vernon Herford* (Antwerp, 1954), p. 18.
[2] A photograph of the alleged Instrument of Consecration of Ulric Vernon Herford is reproduced facing page 92 of Brandreth's *Episcopi Vagantes and the Anglican Church* (2nd ed., 1961). It might fairly be said that similar jiggery-pokery with documents has not been unknown in the Roman Catholic Church; perhaps not in connotation with consecrations!
[3] Mar Georgius, op. cit., p. 18.
[4] op. cit., p. 92.

Ulric Vernon Herford

Bishop of Mercia and Middlesex, relating to his ordination, consecration, etc. But one cannot help wondering on what grounds the Mayor felt able to swear on so technical a matter. Last, but not least, the extraordinary thing is that this former Unitarian, 'Liberal Christian', or 'Free Protestant' minister, who was such a Modernist and so heterodox in most of his theological opinions, should have had such a superstitious belief in the 'magic' of apostolic succession.[1]

The newly consecrated Bishop of Mercia and Middlesex boarded the ss. *Gera* at Colombo on December 7, 1902, and landed at Southampton on New Year's Day. Not long after he returned to Oxford he wrote to His Beatitude Mar Shimun, Patriarch of Seleucia-Ctesephon and Catholicos of the East, informing him that he was now a bishop of the Chaldean Patriarchate, and explaining to him:

'I believe that our Syro-Chaldean Church is the purest and most primitive Branch of the Holy Catholic and Apostolic Church, and historically represents the *Evangelical Catholic Church* which I believe it is the purpose of Almighty God to make the centre of reconciliation and harmony to unite in one Fold, under the One Shepherd, our Lord Jesus Christ, the sadly sundered parts of Christendom, Eastern and Western, Catholic and Protestant. . . . I offer to you the loyal homage of myself and all the faithful under my jurisdiction in England, and our affectionate expression of reverence and respect. We shall ever consider ourselves in communion with your Beatitude unless you were to compel us to leave that communion—as I am sure that you would never willingly do— by imposing upon us conditions that our consciences and the authority of Holy Scripture would not allow us to bear.

'I am happy to be able to tell your Beatitude that several Churches in Ceylon will probably be in communion with your Church very soon and will, by placing themselves under my jurisdiction in this way join your Beatitude's Patriarchate.'[2]

It appears that Mar Basilius, in addition to consecrating Herford as Bishop for the United Kingdom of Great Britain and Ireland, had granted him an undefined status as British Administrator of the

---

[1] In this respect he resembled not only the Gnostic bishops of the Gallican Church in France, who claimed the Syro-Antiochene succession through Vilatte (see pp. 307, 308), but also the Theosophical prelates of the Liberal Catholic Church, who boasted of their Roman Catholic succession derived from the Church of Utrecht, via Mathew (see pp. 342–366).

[2] Tull, op. cit., p. 25.

Ulric Vernon Herford

Syro-Chaldean Metropolitan See in India. Even if the expected influx of a large number of Christians in Ceylon into the Patriarchate of Babylon did not materialize, nevertheless Mar Jacobus could now regard himself as taking precedence as a prelate over Dr Francis Paget, who succeeded Dr William Stubbs in 1901, for the Bishop of Oxford could not claim to be in communion with any of the historic Eastern Churches, as the Bishop of Mercia and Middlesex believed he was.[1]

Having settled down in Oxford again, Herford took his episcopal obligations very seriously. He started to collect money for the relief of his fellow Nestorians in South India. He bought candlesticks and other church furnishings for them, and arranged for a supply of Bibles to be sent to Mar Basilius from the British and Foreign Bible Society at Madras. We are told that 'Bishop Herford's concern for the Indian Christians and for their Assyrian parent Church was to be like a thread running through the embroidery of his life'.[2]

Mar Basilius died during a cholera epidemic in July 1903. In December that same year Mar Jacobus, now regarding himself as the Father in God of this handful of Nestorians in South India, wrote a very long pastoral letter, addressed to his 'beloved fellow-workers and children in the Lord', consoling with them at the loss of their Metropolitan, and giving them words of encouragement, lest they were tempted to return to communion with Rome. He begged them to honour the memory of their deceased Archbishop by 'clinging loyally to our holy evangelical Catholic Church' into which he had gathered them, so that they might find a clearer light from heaven upon their souls and minds, and be freed from the errors and false doctrine which had been taught them by the priests who were under the domination of the Vatican. 'Let no faint-heartedness, weakness or fear tempt you to desert our holy Church, or betray our cause', was his clarion call from Oxford; 'Do not like Judas, sell your Lord'. Moreover, instead of worshipping God in a language which they could not understand, his beloved children

---

[1] It is related that when people asked Herford in what part of Britain Mercia was situated, he would explain that this was the old diocese founded by St Chad in the seventh century, in which were included both Oxford and Birmingham, and much of the Midlands, right up to Northumbria. He would remark: 'Now it is all divided up by the Anglicans, and I look upon myself as an *episcopus in partibus infidelium*. That gives me the right to confirm and ordain in my old diocese until there is reunion.' (W. Rowland Jones, *Diary of a Misfit Priest* (1960), p. 95). On December 11, 1903, Herford by deed poll assumed the style of 'Ulric Vernon Herford, Mar Jacobus, Bishop of Mercia'.

[2] Tull, op. cit., p. 26.

Ulric Vernon Herford

would be glad to know that before long he would be able to give them a new Service Book in English and Tamil. Not only would it contain 'the most beautiful parts of the Latin Mass, which it will resemble, and of our ancient Syro-Chaldean and Malabar liturgies', but it would 'as far as possible, contain all the most beautiful parts from all the ancient liturgies of Greece, Egypt, Spain, England, and other parts of the Christian world'. The Evangelical Catholics of the Nestorian Church in South India would be able to boast that their new Service Book is 'more truly Christian and more really Catholic than any other Liturgy in the world'.[1] Mar Jacobus recommended that 'images of Saints should be removed from the altars of our Churches and be placed at the *sides* of the Churches', and felt that 'it would be well if no figure but that of our Saviour be placed on any altar'.[2]

Mar Jacobus felt that his South Indian flock needed a resident bishop, for he could hardly look after it properly more than five thousand miles away in Percy Street, Oxford. Had any of his presbyters shown signs of the qualifications for a bishop as laid down by St Paul in the third chapter of his first Epistle to Timothy, no doubt he would have been raised to the episcopate, and sent out to Trichur. It was in the autumn of 1904 that Herford thought he had come across the right man. He had read the story entitled *Hadrian the Seventh*, whose title page proclaimed the author to be 'Fr Rolfe'. There were other people who had felt called to write to this unknown cleric (as he appeared to be), expressing admiration for this narrative of a rejected student for the priesthood, who was elected Pope, and finally martyred. Realizing, no doubt, that much of the earlier part of the book was autobiographical, and feeling sorry for Frederick William Serafino Austin Lewis Mary Rolfe, otherwise known as Baron Corvo, Mar Jacobus decided to make him a generous offer. On receipt of a letter from this bishop in Oxford, Corvo wrote to G. T. Maquy on December 8, 1904:

'I shall have a rare tale to tell you in my next; for the perusal of *Hadrian* has induced a certain Syro-Chaldean prelate precipitously to offer me a bishopric over 25,000 Christians and 20 churches! I fancy the man's a fraud, and a schismatic, and that what he wants is

[1] The fact that this small group of nominal Nestorians used the *Missale Romanum* instead of, e.g., the editions of the *Liturgy of the holy Apostles Addai and Mari* (similar to the Byzantine *euchologion*), published by the Anglican missionaries at Urmi (Persia) in 1890 and 1892, suggests that there could have been very little Syro-Chaldean about them except in name, and umbrellas, flags, standards, flags, fireworks, and vestments.

[2] A feature of authentic Nestorian worship is that their churches contain no pictures or other images. A plain cross is used instead of a crucifix, even on the altar.

139

an Apostate. But we shall see. I'm making a few enquiries.'[1]

Having made enquiries Corvo wrote again to this same correspondent a week later:

'Bishop of Sodom and Gomorrah in *partibus* is excellent. But how frightful! I thought all those people were ritualists, or jesuits, or wesleyans. Vernon Herford, it appears, was introduced to H by Richard Whiteing of *The Yellow Van*, a fine talker whom I respect. If V.H. is a friend of his, I shall only tell him of my opinion and for ever after hold my peace. If not, I'll ask Barnard and Taylor (who are conducting my case against the Chartered Co's expert) whether it is desirable to send V.H.'s papers to Labouchere [of *Truth*]. You understand that, being in shady circumstances myself, I'm not anxious to pop into publicity unnecessarily . . . Of course I said from the first that a man who offered me a bishopric must be a fraud. What I felt was that there was 9/10 of a chance of his being a fraud and 1/10 of his being an ambassador from the divine ones inhabiting olympian mansions. That's all.'

The last letter from the author of *Hadrian the Seventh*, relative to Herford, quoted in this essay contains the words:

'. . . I've written to V.H. asking him straight whether he's in communion with the Roman See; and for the cause or reason for his application to me. We shall see what he says. Meanwhile, I'd be glad to hear how the imbroglio strikes you.'

Corvo showed more common sense when dealing with this affair than on many other occasions in his strange career. Very wisely he declined to be consecrated as a neo-Nestorian bishop for South India, and continued his literary work, which, at that moment, was profitable.

Mar Jacobus, having failed to find the right man to raise to the episcopate for the benefit of his overseas flock, set to work on a liturgy for his small following at home. The *Holy Sacrifice and Communion of the Lord's Supper or Eucharist* was published in 1905. The book contained musical settings for this new and novel rite, also a lengthy version of Vespers, based on the Order for Evensong in the Book of Common Prayer. No doubt because the Nestorian books are in a bewildering state of confusion, Mar Jacobus did not feel bound to adhere closely to the Chaldean rite, which, incidentally, does not contain the words of institution in its Canon.[2]

---

[1] Brocard Sewell, O. Carm, 'The Clerk without a Benefice', in *Corvo, 1860–1960*, ed. by Cecil Woolf and Brocard Sewell (1961), p. 40.

[2] The Anglican editions have interpolated the narrative of the Lord's Supper containing the words, on the theory that they had dropped out through a misapplication of the *disciplina arcani*.

Ulric Vernon Herford

He continued to be more than hopeful of a great future for his Evangelical Catholic Church which he said was in communion with the Patriarch and Katholikos of the East, and tried to infiltrate it on the continent of Europe as an alternative to Roman Catholicism. This brought him into touch with Hyacinthe Loyson, the ex-French Carmelite, then living with his wife at Geneva.[1] There is a story that Herford and Madame Loyson tried and failed to prevent Miraglia Gulotti (of the Vilatte succession) from consecrating the magician and occultist, Jules Houssaye, as first Metropolitan of the Gallican Church.[2] It is possible that by the early autumn of 1904 Bishop Herford had found and consecrated a coadjutor to assist him with his world-wide apostolate, if what Madame Loyson wrote on October 14, 1904 is true:

'If you or your coadjutor returns to India and would go by the Manayime Maritime line, I can, I think, get you reduced fares.'[3]

Before the Corvo incident just mentioned, there was a suspicious character hanging around Oxford, who usually called himself 'Apostolic Vicar of the Independent Catholic Church of Southern Switzerland', and who gave his name as Count Edward Rufane Benedict Donkin.[4] Very little is known for certain about his past, and it is difficult to distinguish between what is truth and what fiction in stories told about him. One tale is that Donkin had been a Benedictine monk in the United States, and that in the summer of 1899, having broken away from the Catholic Church, he was sent to Mexico at the expense of some American Protestants to congratulate Mgr Eduardo Sanchez Camacho on his brave efforts to form a National Church, and to assure him of their support. This prelate had been Bishop of Tamaulipas since 1880, but he had been forced to resign his see in 1896, when he retired into private life. After this he started to publish articles defamatory of Mgr Alarcon, Archbishop of Mexico. A second tale is that Donkin used to say that at some time or other he had been ordained priest by Vilatte, and that on November 30, 1902, he had been raised to the episcopate by a Syro-Chaldean bishop in South India. Later on he produced papers giving the witnesses of his consecration or re-consecration by Mgr Sanchez Camacho in the Chapel of Amadeus of Savoy, at Naples. What was missing, however, was the papal

[1] See pp. 304, 305.
[2] See pp. 306, 308.
[3] cf. Mar Georgius, op. cit., p. 4. It is possible that this 'coadjutor' referred to Corvo, and that Herford never suspected that he would decline the offer of a bishopric.
[4] See p. 87.

Ulric Vernon Herford

mandate authorizing this consecration for an autocephalous church. There is yet another strange story that Bishop Donkin preached in the Cathedral of Notre Dame, Paris, before he returned to England from Switzerland to meet the charges of fraudulent dealings made against him.

How this ubiquitous adventurer managed to get on suitable terms with Mar Jacobus, and persuaded him to undergo a second consecration from his hands is unknown but it is believed the secret consecration took place in August 1904. All Herford's biographer can say is that, 'he had no doubts whatsoever about his consecration by Mar Basilius', for which reason this re-consecration must have been accepted 'from some honest personal motive'.[1]

What we do know is that the Titular Bishop of Santa Croce in Sicily (as Donkin also styled himself) was 'a somewhat troublous and disruptive influence at Percy Street'; and that Herford 'naturally felt rather sensitive' about this secret consecration; 'and never alluded to the matter after'. Donkin remained at Oxford for some time, but we are told that Herford only 'occasionally came into contact with him on personal affairs'.[2] This is not surprising, because on June 27, 1905, Madame Loyson, who had known Donkin in Switzerland, wrote:

'More than we can tell we are sorrowful—Père Hyacinthe and I—that you were induced to receive re-consecration from *anyone*, and especially from such a villain, as this throws doubt on your first consecration! The consequence is disastrous . . . In the name of Père Hyacinthe, and my own, I express our most Christian sympathy—praying God to lead you where men mislead, and to help you to go forward doing a good work.'

It is improbable that Mar Jacobus felt it necessary to obtain a special dispensation from the Patriarch of Seleucia-Ctesiphon (Babylon) before he married Miss Alice M. Skerritt, of Hove, on the feast of St Antony the Abbot, January 17, 1907. This wealthy lady was some years his senior. Although she was never received into the Nestorian Church, and remained in communion with Canterbury throughout her life, she shared her episcopal husband's enthusiasm for animal welfare, and became joint-secretary of the Oxford Anti-Vivisection Society. The Herfords had no children, but always maintained a large family of cats.[3]

---

[1] Tull., op. cit, p. 37.
[2] ibid., pp. 37–88.
[3] The Bishop of Mercia may have recalled that it was only comparatively recently that the Nestorian Church had enforced celibacy on its higher clergy. The priests and

Ulric Vernon Herford

For the next twenty years the Bishop of Mercia and his wife led very busy lives. There were few societies in Oxford which they did not join if they felt it would benefit animals or human beings in one way or another. The Bishop himself became a familiar figure at conferences all over Britain, especially those of an ecumenical character. The Herfords eventually bought a house at 137 Banbury Road, Summertown, North Oxford. On Sundays the Bishop pontificated in the Evangelical Catholic Church of the Divine Love, over Magdalen Bridge. The services included 'The Divine Liturgy (Eucharist)' at 11 a.m. and Vespers at 6.30 p.m. There was at least one mid-week Benediction of the Blessed Sacrament, for the Mercian version of the Syro-Chaldean rite, like the Malabarese rite, had had interpolated many Western elements. Guilds of St Joseph and the Good Shepherd are said to have had a large membership. The British Administrator of the Nestorian Church in India, Ceylon, Socotra, and Messina went around Oxford on his pedal bicycle—always busy with baptisms, confirmation classes, choir-practices, visiting the sick, and hearing confessions. He seems to have made a fair number of converts, but does not appear to have compelled them to profess their belief in the Nestorian doctrine that there are two persons as well as two natures in Christ. So far as can be gathered, he himself remained a nebulous Unitarian. Those whose memories of Oxford go back half a century will recall the entertainment provided by this odd but lovable bishop, with a humble little 'pro-cathedral' off the Iffley Road, and how inquisitive Anglo-Catholic undergraduates sometimes attended the services there, though warned by the Cowley Fathers that by so doing they were guilty of schism.

In fact, Herford's churchmanship was nothing if not comprehensive. He was keenly interested in the English extension of Old Catholicism, and was on friendly terms with both Archbishop Mathew and Mgr Beale—one of the two Roman Catholic priests who were consecrated by Mathew in June 1910. This excommunicated Protonotary-Apostolic spent a few days with the Herfords that year. They also knew Mgr Scott-Hall, titular Bishop of Winchester, who had been raised to the episcopate by Mathew,

---

lower clergy may not only be married, but may marry wives in succession, and can do so after ordination. During the Middle Ages there was such strong prejudice against celibacy among the Christians of Mesopotamia and Persia that monastic life disappeared after the fourteenth century. (cf. Adrian Fortescue, *The Lesser Eastern Churches*, pp. 134–5.)

Ulric Vernon Herford

and who was their neighbour in north Oxford, with a little schismatic chapel in a street near the railway station.[1] On June 15, 1909, the Bishop of Mercia cycled from Brighton to Storrington (nineteen miles each way) so that he could assist at the funeral of George Tyrrell, the excommunicated Jesuit. By this time he appears to have been in frequent contact with Baron von Hügel and other leading Modernists in England.

The Evangelical Catholic Church, the name by which Herford's sect was generally known, obtained some publicity in April 1913, when Mar Jacobus marched through the streets of Oxford, vested in the robes of a prelate of the Latin rite, which he favoured to those of the Syro-Chaldean rite. He wanted to show his sympathy with the tramway employees who were on strike. It was about this time that he encouraged R. J. Campbell, Minister of the City Temple, to form an Order of Nonconformist 'Pioneer Preachers'. It was also in 1913 that the Herfords moved to 'Elmswood', Lathbury Road, north Oxford. The Church of the Divine Love was sold, and a new chapel opened in Howard Street. A domestic oratory, alongside 'Elmswood', was open to the public. It was furnished with western style pipe organ, and two eastern style ikons of the Prophet Elias and St Gregory Thaumaturgus, neither of whom was Nestorian. It was typical of Herford's eclectic Unitarianism that he should adorn his private chapel with an ikon of this third-century Greek Church Father, who was the author of a Trinitarian exposition of belief. However, this inconsistency was not noticed by the average worshipper, and these oriental decorative features helped to remind people that this modest place of worship claimed to be under the somewhat remote jurisdiction of the Syro-Chaldean Patriarch of Babylon, and was not in communion with the Diocese of Oxford.[2]

During the First World War the Bishop of Mercia was an ardent pacifist, supporting conscientious objectors, and quite prepared to go to prison himself if needs be. On May 15, 1915, he celebrated for the first time his vernacular version of the fourth-

---

[1] See pp. 182, 201.
[2] By the winter of 1915 Bishop Herford had three places of worship under his auspices in or around Oxford: his private chapel at 128 Woodstock Road, a new public chapel at 91 Howard Street, and another at Cowley. In December that year he reopened an Institute in Charles Street, used for social work. We are told that the Evangelical Catholic Boys' Club was 'rather a trial to the Bishop's patience'; also that 'if his enthusiasm for Temperance seems to us a little old-fashioned, we should remember that conditions were different and the unhappy results of immoderate drinking more serious'. (Tull, op. cit., p. 50.)

century Egyptian liturgy of St Serapion, Bishop of Thmuis in the Nile Delta.[1]

Another important landmark in the career of Mar Jacobus was recorded in November 1916, when he conditionally baptized and confirmed William Edwin Orchard, the Congregationalist minister, who, between 1914 and 1932, rose to national fame at the King's Weigh House, London. Orchard was ordained priest by Herford in 1916, being anxious to 'possess authority to celebrate the Eucharist as a propitiatory sacrifice', while still continuing his Free Church ministry.[2] But as he explained in his autobiography of religious development written after he was received into the Roman Church in 1932: 'it was soon made obvious, however, that this step was taken without sufficient enquiry into the issues involved, or with adequate consideration of the consequences; and it proved a cause of much unhappiness and misunderstanding.'[3]

Mar Jacobus had been drawn to this West End Congregationalist conventicle, not only because of its exotic ritualism, but by reason of it being a pacifist outpost during World War One. Its red banner, inscribed 'For Faith, Justice, and Peace' was raised in Trafalgar Square at Christmas 1916. The congregation of this unconventional place of worship in the heart of Mayfair, included almost every variety of reduced Christianity, embracing some whose leanings were towards Theosophy or Spiritism. The Bahai Movement, founded by Bahau'llah in Persia, which evolved from Babism, and which taught world-brotherhood on a spiritual basis, had been allowed to meet on the premises. In a room at the top of the building there were actually discovered small pylons, and a chest containing enigmatic objects, which, it could only be concluded, had been used for the worship of Osiris, the best beloved God, or some other resurrected esoteric Egyptian deity.[4]

Also associated with this legally Congregationalist chapel, was the so-called 'Society of Free Catholics'. Most of its members were Free Church ministers, who were striving to transform Nonconformist religion into something closer to Catholicism in faith and worship. The President was the Rev. J. M. Lloyd Thomas, a Unitarian minister at the old Meeting House, Birmingham,

[1] Bishop John Wordsworth had already issued an English edition of this rite, entitled *Bishop Serapion's Prayer Book*, published by S.P.C.K. in 1899, in the Early Church Classics series.
[2] He removed the modest communion table and replaced it by a high altar, with traditional Catholic furnishings.
[3] *From Faith to Faith* (1933), p. 131.
[4] cf. ibid., p. 118.

Ulric Vernon Herford

'an elaborate and expensive structure on which the Chamberlain family had lavished their ample funds'.[1] He is remembered as 'a personality of considerable force whose courage and energy were united with gifts of far vision and great practical statesmanship'.[2] Under the joint control of Dr Orchard and Mr Lloyd Thomas, the Society increased its influence, Bishop Herford did all in his power to encourage these liturgical pioneers, placing at their disposal his somewhat inchoate knowledge of Christian worship. A magazine, *The Free Catholic*, propagated the objects of the Society, which was finally dissolved in 1928.[3]

Thanks to Dr Orchard's persuasive powers as a preacher, it did not take long to convert the King's Weigh House congregation to the substance of Catholic ceremonies. Within a few years they had got used to altar lights, vestments, incense, reservation in an aumbry, Mass celebrated according to various rites, and Benediction at least every Sunday evening. Eventually Mar Jacobus supplied the King's Weigh House with a second priest and three deacons, who, like Dr Orchard, were convinced that they had obtained valid orders. With a staff of five clerics it was possible to provide a dignified High Mass, on Sundays and feast days in the elliptical auditorium of Sir Alfred Waterhouse's neo-Byzantine-Romanesque chapel, to which Sir John Burnet had added a chancel about 1901. The worshippers included lapsed Anglicans, dissatisfied Methodists, and even a few disaffected Roman Catholics. Dr Orchard maintained that he could 'feel' the presence of the Blessed Sacrament in any church, and was surprised when people suggested that this might be a merely subjective emotionalism. This did not matter, however, because neither the nearby Anglo-Catholic Grosvenor Chapel, nor the Jesuits at Farm Street Church, could rival the King's Weigh House in ritual and ceremonial. Its ministers liked to boast that, thanks to the Bishop of Mercia, both the Roman and Eastern Churches recognized the validity of the Masses they celebrated, even if the source of the orders obtained was, admittedly, somewhat irregular.

How these deacons and priests managed to obtain their 'valid orders' from Mar Jacobus has been described by the Rev. W. Rowland Jones, in his *Diary of a Misfit Priest*. He had received

---

[1] Conrad Noel, *Autobiography* (1945), p. 117.
[2] W. G. Peck, *From Chaos to Catholicism* (1920), p. 179.
[3] It was revived later on by Mar Frederic Harrington, who styled himself 'Primate of the Orthodox-Keltic Church of the British Commonwealth of Nations'. (see pp. 279–282.)

Ulric Vernon Herford

Anglican orders from Dr Hensley Henson, Bishop of Durham, and after holding curacies in four parishes, was invited by Dr Orchard to join the staff of the King's Weigh House. He did so with the cordial blessing of Dr Winnington Ingram, Bishop of London. But Dr Orchard explained to his new curate that it would be necessary for him to be re-ordained by a *real* bishop before he could say Mass. The simplest way to rectify what was lacking was to go to Oxford, where the British Administrator of the Metropolitan See of India, Ceylon, Mylapore, Socotra, and Messina would do the job without any fuss or bother.[1]

Mar Jacobus in his reply to Mr Jones's letter said: 'Look out for my purple stock. Everybody on the station at Oxford knows me, so if you do not see me ask a porter'. The Bishop was at the station all right, and the purple stock made a bright patch of colour, but what were even more noticeable were the 'musty green overcoat, and a huge string bag dangling from his episcopal arm'.[2] His Lordship excused himself from accompanying the ordinand to his home, explaining that Mrs Herford had asked him to buy a few things for tea, and hurried off on his bicycle. It took some time for Mr Jones to find his way to 'Elmswood', which he tells us was 'bedraggled, overgrown, and neglected', with the name 'scratched on the rickety gate'. Inside there were cats everywhere; on every chair and on every delectable spot.

There was a vegetarian supper, and a frugal breakfast the following morning. Mar Jacobus told Mr Jones that he had to be very careful as to whom he gave 'valid orders' because many men sought them from 'private and bad motives'. The Bishop then conducted the ordinand to the little sacristy of the domestic oratory. Here was 'a mass of multi-coloured vestments', and 'layer after layer of white linen', not to mention 'many varieties of stoles and folded chasubles, which needed pins as well'. Before vesting Mar Jacobus shouted to his wife to bring more safety pins. The ceremony started by His Lordship pulling a small lever attached to the wall, 'which set something like the melodious

---

[1] Among the curious clerics alleged to have been ordained by Herford was the late Rev. Alphonsus Joseph-Mary Augustus Montague Summers, M.A., F.R.S.L.; regarded as an authority on black and white magic, and the Restoration dramatists. His recreations were listed in *Who's Who* as 'travel; staying in unknown monasteries and villages in Italy; pilgrimages to famous shrines; the investigation of occult phenomena; ghost stories; talking to intelligent dogs, that is, all dogs; research in hagiology, liturgies, mysticism, the older English drama; late Latin literature'. *Montague Summers, A. Memoir* by Joseph Jerome is now in the press.

[2] op. cit., (1960), p. 92.

chimes of Bruges reechoing through the chapel and the house'.[1]

Mrs Herford had already advised Mr Jones that, like herself, he ought to stick to the dear old Church of England, where there was 'at least no arguing, no fuss, and no silly business', and where she 'got a bit of peace'. First came the ceremonies of baptism and confirmation with the holy oils smeared on generously. Before the ordinations started Mrs Herford had to be summoned as witness, because a certain Free Methodist deacon had failed to turn up, as he had promised to do. She sat at the back of the oratory and filled in the time by knitting.

Addressing her episcopal husband, she said: 'Do make it short, dear: I've got to get to the baker's early or I shall miss those lovely cakes'. But Mar Jacobus had no intention of curtailing the rite just for the sake of an extra good tea. Mr Jones continues: 'Mrs Herford was asked if she knew me, if she could vouch for my purity of character, if she had examined me in the Latin tongue, and if she had examined me in the certitude of my faith, and to all the questions she gave a vigorous affirmative. Altogether I had been in her presence not more than an hour, and she had never once called me by my right name. Still—it was to be a valid ordination!

' "Can I go now?", came the piteous voice of the episcopal spouse.

'The stentorian "Yes" from the Bishop revealed his pent-up disturbance and set free his faithful wife who had readily sworn her soul away on my behalf.'[2]

This long and elaborate series of ceremonies which took over two hours may have been typical of the clandestine ordinations carried out by the Bishop of Mercia. For which reason one cannot help feeling that his biographer was understating the case when he wrote:

'It is generally admitted by those who knew Bishop Herford that he was well-liked, sincere and good-hearted and undoubtedly well versed in his conviction and Faith. At the same time he struck some people as a very eccentric man, though not unkindly or spitefully so. In this respect he rather reminds one of St Philip Neri, who was also considered eccentric by the people of his day. The foolishness of the Saints often conceals spiritual wisdom and deep humility within.'[3]

[1] ibid., p. 97.
[2] ibid., p. 98.
[3] Tull, op. cit., p. 67.

Ulric Vernon Herford

It is a matter of opinion whether Mar Jacobus can be bracketed with the sixteenth-century saint who founded the Oratorians, granted that both of them were not afraid of defying conventions if they felt it would promote the greater glory of God. One of Herford's odd ideas was that the reunion of Christendom could be achieved quite easily through 'universally valid Orders'. All that was required was for every priest or minister of every Christian denomination—Catholic, Orthodox, and Protestant—to undergo a *second* form of ordination, accepted as 'valid' by all of them. This done, then the rest would follow as a matter of course. As Mr Rowland Jones points out: 'Herford's idea was brilliant, but it is clearly the *reductio ad absurdum* about the validity of Orders. Reunion is never likely to come about in that way'.[1]

Believing that 'he stood in the unique position of a Catholic prelate whose Catholicity was not bounded by denominationalism, but that he belonged to the whole Church of Christ, totally', Herford compiled a new service book for his world-wide flock in 1920. Entitled *The Lord's Supper or Mass*, this liturgical manual was re-issued in 1933–4.

His energy never flagged, so we find him attending Free Church Conferences in London; pontificating at High Mass in the King's Weigh House; sitting in choir, robed in Roman episcopal vestments at a celebration of the Byzantine rite in the Russian Church in Buckingham Palace Road; discussing international affairs with Bishop Eulogios Georgievsky, whom the Patriarch Tikhon of Moscow had appointed to be his representative for Western Europe; taking part in a Labour Day Demonstration in Hyde Park; then, more than once, calling on the Friars Minor at Forest Gate, E.7. Next comes word of him taking a black and white kitten, 'Freddie', to join 'Peter' and 'Patrick', already important cat members of the episcopal family at north Oxford. He writes of rushing off to confer with the Duchess of Hamilton, who, like himself, devoted herself to animal welfare. In fact, the Bishop of Mercia was here, there, and everywhere, constantly travelling between Oxford and London. On one of his trips to Town, he took the opportunity to have a serious talk with Mar Timotheos Abimelech, the Mellusian Bishop of Trichur, about the proposed removal of the Indo-Assyrian Christians to Australia.

In 1924 Mar Jacobus recruited Dr Percy Dearmer, who at that

---

[1] *Diary of a Misfit Priest*, p. 152. The number of priests ordained by Herford has been estimated between 40 and 200.

date was helping Miss Maud Royden with her interdenominational services at a refurnished and beautified Congregationalist
Chapel (known as 'The Guildhouse') in Eccleston Square, to assist
him with compiling a vernacular Breviary, which was never
published.

So far as is known, it was on February 28, 1919, that the Bishop
of Mercia performed his only consecration. That day he raised to
the episcopate one of his priests, who was a B.Litt. (Oxon) and
Barrister-at-law, William Stanley Macbean Knight.[1] This learned
and versatile prelate was given the title of 'Mar Paulus, Bishop of
Kent'. He later became Secretary of Spa Fields Chapel, Clerken-
well, London, founded in 1779, belonging to the Countess of
Huntingdon's Connexion.[2] Here he introduced ritualistic services
in emulation of those provided in the West End at the King's
Weigh House. It was on October 18, 1930 that Mar Paulus, without Herford's authority, consecrated a fellow barrister, who was
also a medical practitioner, Dr Hedley Coward Bartlett (of Pembridge Castle, Monmouth). He gave him the name and style of
'Mar Hedley, Bishop of Siluria'.[3] This action greatly distressed Mar
Jacobus, who three years before had expelled the Bishop of Kent
from the Evangelical Catholic Communion, degrading him from
episcopal status in April 1927.[4]

But soon after this painful exercise of jurisdiction, the Bishop of
Mercia had the consolation of consecrating a new high altar at the
King's Weigh House on Palm Sunday, 1927, when he used what
was described as 'a reduced version' of the Roman rite. This cere-

---

[1] Born in 1869, Knight became a solicitor in 1893; was called to the Bar, Inner
Temple, 1899; and Tutor, New College, Oxford, 1920. He was a member of the
London County Council and Vice-Chairman Local Government Committee, 1907–10;
Alderman and Chairman of Parliamentary Committee of St Pancras Borough Council,
1906–17; prospective Parliamentary Conservative candidate for Poplar until 1909; in
1910 left the Conservative and Municipal Reform parties, becoming Chairman Liberal
Association, East St Pancras, resigning 1916. He was also a member of the Central
Unemployed Body for London, 1908–10; and formerly a Vice-President of the Council
of Tariff Reform League. His wide interests included Grotius, and he was elected
Corresponding Member, Netherlands *Vereeningen voor de uitgave van Grotius*. In 1931
he was awarded the de Jong van Beek Prize of the Royal Academy of Science of
Amsterdam. His publications deal with many subjects (see *Who's Who*, 1940). He died
March 21, 1950.

[2] In the *Congregational Year Book* 1927, W. S. M. Knight, B.Litt, is described as
'Secretary' of the Chapel. It is probable that, being a barrister, he did not want to
reveal that he was in holy orders.

[3] For further details of Mar Hedley's episcopal activities, see pp. 453, 456, n.1, 459,
n.1, 496. He became one of the hierarchy of the Patriarchate of Glastonbury, in which
the Diocese of Siluria embraced the Principality of Wales and the County of Monmouth.

[4] It is not clear how long McBean Knight was connected with this chapel, which
drops out of the *Congregational Year Book* after 1932.

Ulric Vernon Herford

mony was followed by a Low Mass—not pontifical, so we are told. Having returned to Oxford, he celebrated his vernacular version of the Liturgy of St Serapion in the episcopal oratory on Maundy Thursday. For the consecration of the holy oils he used a translation of the *Pontificale Romanum*. It would have been more consistent with the Serapion rite, a local variant of the fourth-century Alexandrine liturgy, if he had used the Holy Week ceremonial of the Coptic Church instead. As it appears that chrism is never used at Coptic ordinations, and as the sick are anointed with oil from a lamp which had burned before a holy picture, Herford could have found adequate reasons for not blessing oils on Maundy Thursday, when celebrating an Egyptian liturgy. One cannot help wondering why he bothered to bless any oils, considering that the Nestorians dropped the sacrament of Confirmation long ago. It appears that they have never annointed the sick and dying with holy oils. Again, it would have been reasonable enough, even if he had been consecrated by a bishop of the Syro-Chaldean rite, to have worn the vestments of an Egyptian prelate to go with the Alexandrian rite. For some reason or another, Mar Jacobus alternated a plain vestment of Gothic Revival style with a paenula, but never the 'decadent (so-called) Latin-shaped chasuble'.[1]

Herford's adaptation of what appears to be only a revision of an older form of Egyptian eucharistic rite was also used by priests of the Evangelical Catholic mission at Stapenhill, near Burton-on-Trent, over which he kept a fatherly eye in his status of Bishop of Mercia. No doubt it helped them to believe the ancient legend that a colony of Copts settled in Ireland, and that possibly some of them found their way to Glastonbury.[2] In virtue of his jurisdiction covering the whole of Great Britain and Ireland, granted him by Mar Basilius at his consecration, Mar Jacobus had no scruples about allowing his clergy to engage in mission work beyond the original boundaries of Mercia—even on the north coast of Cornubia (Cornwall), where a chapel was opened at Portreath, near Redruth, for the benefit of the descendants of the ancient Cimbri.[3]

A second edition of the Liturgy of St Serapion was published in March 1927. His biographer writes:

[1] Tull, op. cit., p. 87.

[2] cf. Ledwich, *Antiquities of Ireland* (2nd ed.), pp. 88–89; Warren, *Liturgy and Ritual of the Celtic Church*, p. 56.

[3] The Ancient British Church, as revived by Mar Pelagius in 1874, does not appear to have gained even a foothold in Cornwall; perhaps because of the new 'Italian Mission' launched by Pius IX in 1850, when he erected a Diocese of Plymouth; also because Methodism had become strongly entrenched during the eighteenth century.

151

Ulric Vernon Herford

'In that eventuality, this Liturgy, lost for so long, is not foreign to our shores and its restoration in this country becomes all the more significant. How far Bishop Herford and his contemporaries were aware of this, we do not know.'[1]

Mrs Herford died on March 13, 1928. The Bishop sent an urgent message to Mr Rowland Jones to preside over the cremation at Golders Green. The latter tells us that at the end of the service, arranged by the Bishop, after the body slipped silently into the flames, it only remained for him to give a blessing, which he did 'in the name of the Father, and of the Son, and of the Holy Ghost'. Mr Jones adds: 'It was an angry Bishop who was to remain in my memory as the last vision of true Validity:

'You spoilt everything, Rowland, by that final blessing. You know very well I am a Unitarian!'[2]

The memory of this lady who loved cats was kept alive in the episcopal oratory at Oxford by the following epitaph: 'Most loyal and loving Wife, fearless advocate of all God's dumb and defenceless creatures. O Lord thou preservest man and beast.' The following year her widowed husband felt that when he celebrated the Liturgy of St Serapion it would be more correct and 'more expressive of the mind of the East Syrian rite' to substitute genuflections by profound bows. The Herfords had been such an inseparable pair for twenty years that it is not surprising that Mar Jacobus was stunned by her death, nevertheless he never ceased from his multiform activities on behalf of man and beast. In July 1929 he moved from his palace to the Manor House, Rodbourne Cheney, near Swindon, which remained his base for over a year. He was constantly travelling around England, and made a visitation of his Evangelical Catholic flock at Portreath, where he confirmed seven youths and two girls. Alarming reports had reached him about his spiritual children in South India. He decided to send his Vicar-General, Fr James York Batley, to investigate the situation of the Nestorian community, and he remained on the Malabar coast nearly two years. His first Report on the remnant of Mar Basilius's Church must have saddened Mr Jacobus, for he read that owing to ceaseless proselytism by the Jesuits in the Madura and Tinnevelly districts, many of the faithful had been unable to resist Roman aggression. But there was still hope, so the Vicar-General felt, for missionary work in keeping with the ideals of the

[1] ibid., p. 88.
[2] *Diary of a Misfit Priest*, p. 118.

Evangelical Catholic Communion around Maraman, where the Papist infiltration had not been so intensive.[1]

Still dreaming of the eventual reunion of Christendom, the Bishop of Mercia set to work on a *Catechism of Evangelical Catholic Doctrine* 'for Christians who refuse to recognize any real division in the One great Church of Jesus Christ', which appeared in January 1931. It consisted of 173 Questions and Answers, divided into sections. For the benefit of persons who could not in conscience accept any of the historic Christian Creeds, he composed a new one, entirely in the words of Holy Scripture.

Another book he edited was *A Collection of Prayers for the Welfare and Protection of Animals*, eventually published in 1934. Possibly because St Francis of Assisi has been accepted as the heavenly intercessor for all God's dumb creatures, and an example for Christian Pacifists to emulate, Herford began to dream of reviving the Order of the Christian Faith, which he had founded in Percy Street, Oxford, when he was still a free-lance Unitarian minister. He got so far as to issue an invitation to young men, unmarried and without entanglements, wishing to become postulants, to apply to him for further information about the Order.[2] A seventy-five acre property near Berkhampstead was acquired for the Friary. The Bishop visualized a community of Christian pacifists, observing one of the Rules of St Francis. There was little or no response to the appeal for vocations. It seemed that few youths felt the call to become Evangelical Catholic Friars Minor, much to the would-be founder's disappointment.

Christian Unity, World Peace, and Animal Welfare remained the absorbing interests for the rest of his life. His ecumenical outlook was shown when he celebrated his Liturgy of St Serapion, in 1932 in St Columba's Presbyterian Church, Oxford, and in 1933 in the Chapel of Balliol College, with the permission of the Master, Dr A. D. Lindsay. It was in 1932 that Dr Orchard's long ministry at the King's Weigh House came to an end with his reception into the Church of Rome.[3] It must have pleased Bishop Herford when on July 12, a resolution was passed stating that this Congregational

---

[1] Within the past thirty years this neo-Nestorian sect in South India appears to have dwindled even more, and it is not certain how many adherents it can claim today.

[2] Herford could truly be described as an *'anima naturaliter Franciscana'*. His biographer writes: 'Practical Christianity expressed in the exercise of works of mercy never came hard to him. On several occasions we know that Irish tramps came into the Chapel for Mass on Sunday and were given a good meal in the kitchen afterwards and sometimes they received clothing also.' (Tull, op. cit., p. 106.)

[3] He died in 1957, having been conditionally ordained priest of the Latin rite.

Ulric Vernon Herford

Chapel was 'an Evangelical Free Church, Catholic in Faith and Practice, standing for the Reunion of Christendom, Social Justice, and International Peace'. Thanks to himself, its Ministers were able to offer a choice of 'Catholic Sacraments'(derived from the Indian Nestorians), or of 'the Sacraments familiar to the Evangelical Free Churches', which did not require an apostolic succession for their validity. If this much frequented Congregational chapel in the West End of London could refuse to recognize any real division in the One Church of Jesus Christ, there was no reason why its policy should not be followed in other parts of the Christian world, and so spread the ideals of Mar Jacobus's Evangelical Catholic Communion. Herford's brain never stopped working. He went on dreaming of new societies which could be formed to promote the countless good causes he was so eager to promote.

On the feast of the Assumption of Our Lady, 1938, when he was too exhausted to give Benediction, Fr W. E. Jeffrey, a minister at the King's Weigh House, who was his guest at Oxford, performed the rite instead, in spite of the fact that the Blessed Sacrament is not reserved in Nestorian churches, and consequently, all extraliturgical devotions are unknown. It was also typical of Herford's liturgical comprehensiveness that he should have adopted the feast of the Assumption in his Evangelical Catholic Church. Although the Nestorians observe a fast of St Mary from August 1 to August 15, they do not keep the feast as the Falling Asleep of the *Mother of God*, as is done in other Eastern Churches. One fears that Herford was never an orthodox Syro-Chaldean, otherwise he would have joined with them in proclaiming: 'Woe and woe again to all that say that God died . . . who say that Mary is the Mother of God . . . who do not confess in Christ two natures, two persons (*hypostases*), and one *parsupa* of filiation. . . .'[1]

Ulric Vernon Herford died suddenly that same night. His body, clothed in episcopal vestments of Western shape, with mitre and crozier, was laid to rest in Wolvercote Cemetery, Oxford, after a service in the domestic oratory. The funeral arrangements were directed by Ramban Thoma, a Syrian hieromonk, who happened to be staying with the Cowley Fathers, but he found it impossible to ensure that the corpse of Mar Jacobus was put in a sitting position as is the normal Eastern custom for bishops. Among old friends at

[1] cf. Archdale A. King, *The Rites of Eastern Christendom* (Rome, 1948), vol. II, p. 313, n.198.

Ulric Vernon Herford

the graveside was Sir Michael E. Sadler, then Vice-Chancellor of the University of Oxford. After 'Elmwood' had been sold, and the little chapel dismantled, the ashes of Mrs Herford were removed from the aumbry, finding a last resting place beside her husband's body.

From the human point of view, one must regard as failure the life of this Unitarian minister who was consecrated by a neo-Nestorian bishop in South India, and who firmly believed that the reunion of Christendom could be brought about by a system of 'universally valid orders'—better still, refusing to recognize any real division in the Universal Church of Jesus Christ. His Evangelical Catholic Communion still exists, but it has proved to be ineffectual, so far, as the means for linking up all and sundry persons who call themselves Christians.[1]

[1] The surviving remnant is now ruled over by Antony, Titular Bishop of Nazareth, head of the Orthodox Catholic Church, with his residence in Bournemouth. (See p. 202.) A rival body with similar aims, founded in recent years, is Bishop Erni's Ecumenical League for Christian Unity, with its headquarters at Aire/Geneva. (See pp. 519, 520.) After Herford's death, Mar Paulus, Bishop of Kent (McBean Knight), who had been degraded by his consecrator from episcopal status in 1927, felt he had the authority to vest in Mar Hedley, Bishop of Siluria (Bartlett), the Metropolitan See of India, Ceylon, Mylapore, Socotra, and Messina, which the latter ruled over from Pembridge Castle, Monmouthshire, until his death in June 1956, when the Far Eastern jurisdiction passed to Mar Georgius, Patriarch of Glastonbury. (See p. 496.)

CHAPTER VI

Arnold Harris Mathew, Count Povoleri di Vicenza,
De Jure Earl of Landaff,
Regionary Old Catholic Bishop for England,
Archbishop of London, and Metropolitan successively
of the English Catholic Church,
Western Orthodox Catholic Church in Great Britain
and Ireland, Anglo-Catholic Church,
Catholic Church (Latin and Orthodox United),
Ancient Catholic Church, Old Roman Catholic Church,
and Western Catholic Uniate Church, etc. etc.

'BEHOLD A GREAT HIGH PRIEST WHO IN HIS DAYS PLEASED GOD AND WAS FOUND JUST.' Such was the epitaph inscribed on his tomb by the few friends left to the individual whose erratic career is dealt with in this chapter. It is a matter of opinion whether these words, taken from the Short Chapter at Lauds and Vespers in the Office of the Confessor and Bishop in the Roman Breviary, can be used truthfully of this priest of the Latin rite, who, having taken a wife, was raised to the episcopate in a schismatic church, from which he broke away, and then became the head of a small sect, the title of which he changed at least seven times before his death. Today there are about twenty religious bodies whose bishops and priests claim that their orders are derived from him. His spiritual children are scattered over the world. Some of them could hardly be called either catholic or orthodox.

Arnold Harris Matthews—to give him the surname by which he was known until the age of forty-two—was born at Montpellier, Hérault, France, on August 6, 1852.[1] His father, Major Henry Octerlony Matthews, is said to have regarded himself as the *de*

---

[1] This makes him two years older than Joseph René Vilatte, who was born in 1854; and fourteen years older than Ulric Vernon Herford, born in 1866.

Arnold Harris Mathew

jure third Earl of Landaff of Thomastown, Co. Tipperary, of the Peerage of Ireland.[1]

The title had been considered extinct since 1833, and there is no evidence that the Major ever tried to claim it.[2]

Arnold Harris was baptized with Catholic rites in France, but two years later, to satisfy his mother's scruples, he was conditionally re-baptized by an Anglican clergyman. He was educated at Cheltenham College, and afterwards at Bonn and Stuttgart. Many years later he wrote that he hardly understood the differences between the services at St Gregory's Roman Catholic Church, Cheltenham, and those at St Mary's, Prestbury, which were Anglo-Catholic. He attended both without distinction, and went on oscillating between Rome and Canterbury for the rest of his life.[3]

Feeling called to the Anglican ministry in 1874, Matthews joined the small but select group of young gentlemen (as an Exhibitioner of the Foundation) of the College of the Holy Spirit, situated on the Island of Greater Cumbrae in the Firth of Clyde. The tone of the services held in the adjacent miniature Gothic Revival Cathedral, designed by William Butterfield in 1849, was not perhaps quite so Catholic as intended by the pious founder, George Frederick Boyle, who became sixth Earl of Glasgow in 1869.[4] Dr Alexander Ewing, Bishop of Argyll and the Isles, a narrow-minded Broad Churchman, took good care that the students were not influenced by advanced ceremonial or anything suggestive of 'popery'. It may well have been due to this uncongenial atmosphere that Matthews soon made up his mind to 'go over to Rome'. His reconciliation with the Latin Church took place at Belmont

---

[1] There are three Thomastowns in Ireland—in the counties of Kildare, Tipperary, and Kilkenny. The English *Mathews* changed the spelling of the name to *Matthews* about 1800.

[2] A claim to the title could have been based on the story that Francis, 1st Earl of Landaff, had an elder son, Arnold Nesbet Mathew, by Elishe (or Ellis) Smythe, born in Paris at the house of her sister, the Vicomtesse de Rohan-Chabot, in 1765. This son was supposed to have died in 1783, but was said to be alive in India (a Major in the Royal Bengal Artillery). He was believed to have married, in 1806, Elizabeta, daughter and heiress of the Marchese Domenico Povoleri di Nogarote, Vicenza e Verona. This Arnold Nesbet Mathew (whose surname had been changed to Matthews, because he had been brought up by his father's uncle, Joseph Matthews, solicitor, of Woodend House, Croomhill, Gloucester) was the father of the said Henry Octerlony Matthews. The Irish property was left by Lady Elizabeth Mathew, sister of the 2nd Earl, who died suddenly at Dublin in 1833, to the Vicomte de Rohan-Chabot, but the legality of the devise was publicly questioned at the time. (cf. *Debrett's Peerage*, 1912, 'Landaff, Earldom of (Mathew)'; and *The Complete Peerage* (revised ed., vol VII, 1902), 'Landaff and Landaff of Thomastown'.)

[3] cf. *An Episcopal Odyssey* (Kingsdown, Deal, 1915), p. 13.

[4] See p. 60, n.2.

157

Cathedral Priory, near Hereford, where a Benedictine priest gave him a second conditional baptism. In January 1876 he was admitted to St Peter's Seminary, Partickhill, Glasgow. Having been hurried through his philosophical and theological studies in about eighteen months, he was ordained priest on June 24, 1877. The ceremony was performed by Mgr Eyre, Titular Archbishop of Anazarba, who, so it appears, had obtained for this brilliant young student a Roman degree of Doctor of Divinity, which was conferred by Pius IX.[1]

Dr Matthews spent only ten months as curate of St Andrew's, Glasgow. He soon found that it was not his vocation to be a secular priest in Scotland. By June 1878 he had become 'Brother Jerome', having entered the Dominican novitiate at Woodchester Priory, near Stroud, Gloucestershire. He made his simple profession on June 5, 1879, but was dispensed from these vows before the end of that year. The reason appears to have been thought that he had discovered immoral behaviour between two of his brethren. This was not the only occasion when a similar moral shock caused him to make a sudden decision to break off relations with individuals.

Reverting to the status of a secular priest, Dr Matthews found a refuge in the Diocese of Hexham and Newcastle, where Bishop Chadwick put him in charge of a new mission at Dunston-on-Tyne. Starting work in these depressing surroundings in February 1880, he built, partly at his own expense, a school-chapel and furnished it himself. Something went wrong, even before the opening of the chapel, for early in 1881, he moved to the Diocese of Plymouth, Bishop William Vaughan appointed him a curate at the Cathedral, and he made a name for himself as a preacher. His extraordinary power over wild animals was talked about. To the end of his days, he was far more at ease with God's dumb creatures than with human beings.

One day Dom Adam Hamilton, O.S.B., called at Bishop's House in Cecil Street. He was then trying to find a home for the monks of Pierre-qui-Vire, who, having been driven out of France, were staying in Ireland. This Benedictine of Ramsgate Abbey recalled in after years that it was Dr Matthews who suggested Buckfast Abbey, of which he had never heard, informing him that the property was for sale. Fr Hamilton wrote:

---

[1] Since 1869 this English prelate had been Administrator of the Western District of Scotland. On the restoration of the Scottish Catholic hierarchy early in 1878, Mgr Eyre became the first Archbishop of Glasgow.

Arnold Harris Mathew

'Our Lady never forgets anything. It is in part due to this unhappy priest that her shrine by the Dart has been so splendidly restored. She will surely have remembered this good deed at the passing of that very erratic personality.'[1]

It began to look as if Dr Matthews was incapable of taking root in any diocese, for after less than three years at Plymouth he moved to Nottingham in 1884. The choice of this particular diocese is not surprising because Bishop Bagshawe was always ready to welcome almost any clerical rolling stone, with the result that his diocese had become known as the *refugium peccatorum*. This kind-hearted prelate found him a curacy at Worksop. The following year he packed up again and migrated to the Diocese of Clifton, where Bishop Clifford entrusted him with the mission of Trowbridge, Wiltshire. In 1888 this same Bishop appointed him missionary-rector of St Mary's, Bath, a new church opened in 1881, to relieve the Benedictines of Downside, who served St John's, the older parish.

Many stories have been handed down both of the zeal and the eccentricities shown by Dr Matthews. Thus there is a legend that one Sunday he took a tiger-cub (some say a monkey) from Wombwell's Menagerie into the pulpit. Considering his life-long love of animals—including anthropoid apes—there is no particular reason to doubt the truth of this tale.

Once again, however, trouble was brewing. During a holiday in France he made friends with Hyacinthe Loyson and his wife.[2]

The result of this contact with this world-famous apostate Carmelite, may have helped to plant the seeds of doubt in the too receptive brain of Jerome Matthews.[3] According to his own statement, however, what troubled him most was a chance conversation in a train with a Unitarian; even more so, the discovery that his predecessor at St Mary's had been suspended for immorality. In any case matters soon reached a crisis. In July 1889 the parishioners received printed postcards informing them that Fr Matthews was unable to minister to them any longer as a Catholic priest. The reasons given were that he had ceased to believe in the fundamental doctrines of Christianity, and had repudiated the papal claims.[4]

[1] *Buckfast Abbey Chronicle*, Spring Quarter, 1942, pp. 14–15.
[2] See pp. 93, 142, 304, 305. Loyson influenced not only Vilatte and Herford, but also Matthews, and, for that matter, other lapsed Catholics.
[3] Since his dispensation from simple vows as a Friar Preacher he had used his religious name in preference to his Christian names.
[4] He stated in 1913 that the wording of this postcard had been compiled by R. R. Suffield (a former Catholic priest), and subsequently repudiated by himself. He explained that the only thing about which he was doubtful was papal infallibility. (cf. *The Times Law Reports*, May 2, 1913, p. 471.)

Arnold Harris Mathew

On July 13, 1889, *The Inquirer* (then the leading Unitarian newspaper) published a long notice rejoicing in the conversion of such a distinguished Roman Catholic priest. There were quotations from some of his reasons for ceasing to believe in orthodox Christianity, with promises of 'a brotherly reception into the Unitarian fraternity'. The editor wrote:

'Mr Matthews (like Mr Addis) finds in Unitarianism the expression of his religious convictions, and it is pleasant to think that his high abilities as a preacher will in future be exercised, not to advance the Papal Church, for which he has rendered such conspicuous service and made considerable pecuniary sacrifices, but be enlisted on the side of Liberal Christianity.'

The following week Mr Matthews wrote in the same newspaper:

'Sir,—Permit me to tender to you my most sincere thanks for your truly kind and sympathetic notice relating to my recent secession. I must ask your permission to express my deep sense of gratitude to Mr Suffield not only for his, I fear, too flattering expressions in his letter of last week, but also for the consolation he has afforded me at this most trying epoch of my life. Only those who, like myself, have experienced the anguish involved by such a step, can in any way understand one's bitter sufferings. It is for this reason, Sir, that I find your own generous expressions of such great comfort.'[1]

Mr Matthews spent about the same time with the Unitarian community as with the Friars Preachers. It did not take him much more than twelve months—if that—to regain his belief in most Christian doctrines. He was now *ipso facto* suspended from the Catholic priesthood, though he used to boast that no *formal* suspension had ever been issued. By way of experiment, encouraged by Mr Gladstone and his cousin Lady Suffield (lady of the bedchamber to the Princess of Wales), he decided to offer his services to the Church of England. But he was never formally received into communion with Canterbury, because he refused to sign *A Form of Renunciation of Roman Doctrine*, demanded by Dr Benson, then Primate of All England.

---

[1] *The Inquirer*, July 17, 1889. Both Addis and Suffield were ex-Catholic priests who became Unitarians. Addis is remembered as joint-author with Thomas Arnold of *A Catholic Dictionary*, first published in 1883, with the approval of Cardinals Manning and Newman. Brought up as a Presbyterian, he joined the Church of Rome, was ordained priest, and became an Oratorian. Having lost his faith, he drifted from vague agnosticism to Unitarianism, and lectured at Manchester College, Oxford. At the age of seventy he found his way into the Church of England, and Canon Hensley Henson nominated him as vicar of All Saints', Knightsbridge.

Arnold Harris Mathew

Dr Temple, Bishop of London, must have formed a high opinion of this convert from Romanism and Unitarianism, now aged thirty-eight, for he gave him informal permission to officiate at what was regarded as 'beyond question, the most remarkable, striking, sumptuous, and abnormal church built in London for the Anglo-Catholic Communion since All Saints', Margaret Street'.[1] This was John Dando Sedding's Holy Trinity, Sloane Street. Its consecration on the Tuesday in Rogation Week, 1890, coincided more or less with the publication of Oscar Wilde's *The Picture of Dorian Gray* on June 20 that same year; and it was not long before both the church and the novel were alike being extolled as unique works of art or denounced as dangerous to faith and morals. Mr Matthews performed several marriages in this *fin-de-siècle* Chelsea church, but their validity was subsequently contested in the House of Commons, because he had never been formally licensed as curate.

It was quite in keeping with the honorary curate's unstable temperament as well as with the mixture of French Flamboyant Gothic, English Perpendicular, and Italian Renaissance architectural styles used by Sedding for this church, that Matthews should decide to change his name for something more exotic—almost evocative of the grey pastel-paper with white back and tiny gold marigolds, which Charles Ricketts had designed for the cover of *Dorian Gray*.[2] In October 1890—two months after the death of Cardinal Newman—Arnold Jerome Matthews adopted by deed poll the names of Arnoldo Girolomo Povoleri, which made more appeal to the aesthetic instinct, although the motive was said to be respect for his distinguished North Italian grandmother—the daughter of the Marchese Domenico Povoleri di Vicenza, Verona, e Nogarote.[3]

Meanwhile Count Povoleri had fallen in love, unable to resist the charms of a Miss Margaret Duncan, the fifth daughter of

[1] T. Francis Bumpus, *London Churches Ancient and Modern* (n.d.), 2nd series, p. 367.
[2] cf. *The Letters of Oscar Wilde*, ed. by Rupert Hart-Davis (1962), p. 276.
[3] It is a curious coincidence that it was also in 1890 that Frederick William Rolfe assumed the Italian title of 'Baron Corvo', thanks to having been 'adopted' by the Duchess Caroline Sforza-Caesarini (daughter of Viscount Tamworth), after he had been dismissed from the Scots College, Rome. (cf. Sylvester Houédard, O.S.B., 'A Request for Rolfe' in *Corvo 1860–1960* (Aylesford, 1961), p. 142; and A. J. A. Symons, *The Quest for Corvo* (Penguin ed., 1934), pp. 65, 302). In Britain it is no offence to assume a bogus title. 'No legal action can be taken unless it can be proved that the imposter has induced someone to part with money, or goods, or to grant him credit by reason of his supposed title, for although in the eyes of the law it can be an offence to obtain money or credit under false pretences, it is not an offence to contract a marriage under an assumed title (except as regards making any false statement to the Registrar)'. (Cyril Hankinson, *My Forty Years with Debrett*, (1963), p. 159).

Arnold Harris Mathew

Henry Duncan, Esq., of Toronto, Canada. It was not long before they were engaged. On February 22, 1892, the Rector of Holy Trinity, the Rev. Robert Eyton (who also held the office of Sub-Almoner to Queen Victoria and had previously been curate-in-charge at St Mary's, Graham Street) performed the marriage of his self-unfrocked priest-curate with this lady.[1] It had to be a quiet wedding because Society was still in deep mourning for the young Duke of Clarence, whose lamented death on January 20 had aroused the loyalty and sympathy of Her Majesty's subjects in every part of the Empire.

It can well be believed that the fashionable and emancipated congregation of this West End church—already famous by the rejection of almost every hitherto accepted Victorian convention in architecture and decoration—got a thrill. They could now say that, like Mrs Erlynne in Oscar Wilde's much discussed play, *Lady Windermere's Fan* (produced at St James's Theatre two nights before this wedding), the bridegroom had had the courage to 'sin' for the sake of love.

On the other hand, the priests and congregation of St Mary's, Cadogan Street, round the corner, must have regarded Arnoldo Girolomo Povoleri and Margaret Duncan as another Martin Luther and Catherine von Bora—a couple living in legal concubinage. No matter: the Italian *contessa* (as she could now call herself) seems to have found the ideal husband for the moment. Even if the title brought in neither money nor estates, it helped her to hold her own as a Chelsea *chatelaine*.

Major Matthews died in 1894, whereupon his son and heir decided that it would benefit him to take his place in the British peerage as well as in the Venetian *nobilità*. Having consulted Sir Albert Woods, Garter King of Arms, the Rev. Count Povoleri put forward the claim to be the fourth Earl of Landaff of Thomastown, County Tipperary. This added to the *éclat* of Holy Trinity, Sloane Street, now able to proclaim that its Honorary Curate was a *de jure* Irish Earl as well as an Italian Count, for the Rector merely belonged to an ancient Shropshire county family.[2] This rise in social status led no doubt to Lord and Lady Landaff receiving more invitations to luncheon and dinner parties—even dances. Unfortu-

[1] In *The Times* notice (January 24, 1892) the bridegroom was described as 'The Rev. Count Povoleri', but his name was misspelled 'Sovoleri'.
[2] The Rev. Robert Eyton (1845–1908) was the second son of the Rev. R. W. Eyton, Rector of Ryton, Salop. Ordained in 1870, and having served several curacies, he was appointed Rector of Upper Chelsea in 1884, and made Prebendary of St Paul's the following year.

nately this happy situation did not last long. In 1895 Prebendary Eyton, who held a definite place in the Victorian Establishment, was appointed Rector of St Margaret's and Canon of Westminster. He was succeeded at Holy Trinity by the Rev. R. H. (afterwards Canon) Gamble, who retained the Rev. Lord Landaff as his honorary curate, and is said to have spoken well of him. Mathew kept in contact with Eyton at Westminster, but when the 'crash' came in 1899, and the Canon was obliged to flee the country to avoid exposure for alleged homosexual offences, and Eyton's name was 'mud' at Holy Trinity. Mathew feared that he might be tarred with the same brush. He cast the dust of Chelsea off his feet, ended his associations with the Church of England, and reverted to lay status. His next adventure, so it appears, was helping to establish a Zoological Gardens at Brighton. Sad to say the company went bankrupt. In 1898 the *de jure* Earl had to appear in court in a case involving embezzlement, tried before Mr Justice Phillimore. It was made clear, however, that he himself was entirely innocent.

Meanwhile he had regained his faith, and once more firmly believed all that the Holy Catholic, Apostolic Roman Church believes and teaches, and rejected and condemned whatever she rejects and condemns. So far as Mathew's peace of mind was concerned, this was awkward, because now he had to face the fact that he had incurred the penalty of excommunication by presuming to contract what, in the eyes of the Church, was merely a civil marriage thus, putting himself in the category of moral cases reserved to the Holy See. No priest in any part of the world, on his own authority, could give him absolution; nor could the sinner receive holy communion, far less start celebrating Mass again, as he longed to do.

A son and heir, Francis Arnold Dominic Leo, was born on August 31, 1900, and given the style of Viscount Mathew.[1] Three years later, on June 16, 1903, his father wrote to Pius X, hoping to get the Anglican marriage regularized, but the Roman authorities refused to dispense him from the vow of celibacy, and 'Lady Landaff' showed no desire to retire to a convent. The only thing to do under the circumstances was to lead the life of a suspended priest, and to try to support his family as best he could.[2]

---

[1] A daughter, Margherita Francesca, was born in 1895, and a second daughter, Mary Teresa Gertrude, in 1907.

[2] Although it hardly seemed relevant, Mathew quoted in support of his request the famous case of John Butler, the Catholic Bishop of Cork, who resigned his see in 1786,

Arnold Harris Mathew

Having failed to benefit financially from the Brighton Zoo, the *de jure* Earl of Landaff turned to literary work as a means of earning his living; and it must be admitted that from the human point of view he found his true vocation. For about ten years he managed to settle down as a Catholic lay author—the longest period in his life that he was content with any particular form of activity. Seldom a year passed without the publication of a book, in addition to pamphlets and articles. Their subjects ranged from anthropology to zoology, though the seamier sides of church history were most in evidence. His main literary output covered the years between 1898 and 1912. He had a ready pen, a facile style, a vivid imagination, and an encyclopedic if somewhat chaotic knowledge.[1] His life-long lack of logic, and inability to see how he appeared to other people is nowhere more evident than in his entry for *The Catholic Who's Who* (1906) which starts off:

'MATHEW, Arnold Harris (de jure 4th Earl of Landaff as great-grandson of Francis Matthew, 1st Earl)'

He mentions his marriage to Margaret Duncan, and gives the titles of several books he had edited, translated, or written, but there is no reference to his being a priest of the Catholic and Roman Church, or to his children. One wonders if Sir Francis Burnand, Editor of this source of reference, or the publishers, Burns & Oates, were aware of the unrecorded details of the *de jure* Earl's career. Still, they may have felt that the past had better be forgotten, for there was no doubt about his present loyalty to the Holy See. He had just written in the preface to a collection of essays, entitled *Ecclesia, the Church of Christ* (also published by Burns & Oates):

'Sects may come and sects may go, but the Church is eternal, because she is divine and consequently one and indivisible; holy,

---

on succeeding to the title of 12th Baron Dunboyne. He was then aged seventy, and his appeal was turned down by the Holy See, so he became a Protestant and married. He died in 1800, having been reconciled with the Roman Church, and devised the Dunboyne estates to Maynooth College.

[1] Among his books were the following: *Christianity or Agnosticism* (1898), *A Guide to Bruges* (1903), *The Conversion of Sir Tobie Mathew* (1905), *The Beginnings of the Temporal Sovereignty of the Popes* (1905), *The Catholic Scholar's Introduction to English Literature, Faith and Scripture, The Life of Lady Abbess Knatchbull, The Life and Times of Lucrezia Borgia, The Life and Times of Caesar Borgia, The Life and Times of Pope Alexander VI* (1912), *The Napoleon of the Church—The Life of Hildebrand* (1910), *The Adventures and Tragic End of Dixon Smithson, A History of France* (2 vols.), *A History of French Literature, The Tragedy of Francesca di Rimini and Paolo di Pallo, The Diary of John Burchard* (3 vols., 1911). All his books published after 1908, when he became an Old Catholic bishop, deal mainly with the corruptions of the medieval papacy.

Arnold Harris Mathew

Catholic, both in time and extent, apostolic and Petrine, that is papal.'[1]

For some years past the Landaffs had been the owners of a modest estate at Chelsfield, and could regard themselves among the lesser landed gentry of Kent. On Sundays and Holydays of Obligation the *de jure* Earl assisted at Mass as one of the congregation at the nearest place of worship, at that date the Chapel of St Joseph's and St Anne's Orphanage at Orpington, which was open to the public. The Countess, who never became a Catholic, attended an Anglican church.

On May 7, 1907, a *nihil obstat* and *imprimi potest* were given by the Westminster archdiocesan censors to A. H. Matthew's authorized translation of Mgr Duchesne's *The Churches Separated from Rome*. Its title page stated that the translator was '*De jure* Earl of Landaff, of Thomastown, Co. Tipperary'.

Some sort of brainstorm must have taken place shortly after the proofs of this book had been corrected, and from which Mathew never recovered, for on August 12 he wrote to Dr Davidson, Archbishop of Canterbury:

'The Papacy, instead of being the "visible centre of unity", I regard as the centre and origin of ecclesiastical discord and disunion, the fomenter of schisms, and the seat of ecclesiastical despotism and tyranny.'

It is possible that this moral somersault was the result of frequent correspondence with George Tyrrell, who finally severed his association with the Society of Jesus in 1907. He and Mathew had been collaborating on the third edition of Dr H. C. Lea's *History of Sacerdotal Celibacy in the Christian Church*, which appeared that same year. In these two volumes will be found stories of all the scandalous excesses which have been charged against a celibate priesthood since the beginning of the Middle Ages. Taken as a whole, they could be more than enough to turn any simple-minded and uncritical reader against the Papacy. What must be remembered is that Mathew throughout his life made sudden decisions for reasons which most of his friends found utterly unconvincing. At least four of these major decisions were due to the supposed discovery of sexual immorality among clerics.

For the second time, apparently on the advice of the now excommunicated Tyrrell, Mathew sought preferment in the Church

---

[1] Other contributors to *Ecclesia* included Dom John Chapman, O.S.B., Fr Benedict Zimmerman, O.C.D., and the Rev. Robert Hugh Benson.

of England.[1] Dr Harmer, Bishop of Rochester, in whose diocese Chelsfield was situated, regretted that he did not see his way to find him a cure of souls. Dr Davidson, Archbishop of Canterbury, with characteristic caution, demanded a period of probation before he could recommend this married Roman Catholic priest for an incumbency.[2]

The Rev. Lord Landaff was not discouraged by the archiepiscopal rebuff. He explained that he preferred to abandon the idea of returning to the Anglican fold meantime. Dr Davidson accepted this statement, but replied that it did not preclude him from re-opening the question should he so desire.[3] But Matthew's ever fertile brain had now thought of another way by which he could resume his clerical status, and start celebrating Mass again. About the middle of September 1907 he wrote the first of many letters to Edward Herzog, the Christian Catholic Bishop in Switzerland, who replied on the 21st of that month:

'Unfortunately we have not at present proofs that Catholics in England are disposed to reject the jurisdiction of the Roman Curia, but if Old Catholic associations were formed, if such associations were constituted an ecclesiastical union, represented by a Synod, and if this Synod recognized the principles we profess, proceeded to elect a bishop, I should be very happy to participate in the consecration of this bishop. But I do not believe that it is allowed to start the work of which you speak by the consecration of a bishop. We do not wish to create bishops *"in partibus"*. This is the reply I have always given when Anglican priests put themselves forward.'[4]

This and the following letters suggest that Mathew wanted to form an Old Catholic Church in England, but it is not clear if he pictured himself as its first bishop. The correspondence continued for the next six months, with letters almost every week. Some of them refer to persons in England who were in favour of launching an Old Catholic movement. Rather later Mathew started to write to Bishop Van Thiel of Haarlem, whose replies were more cautious in tone than those of Herzog.[5]

---

[1] Two letters of protest to *The Times* of September 30 and October 1, 1907, after the publication of Pius X's encyclical '*Pascendi*', condemning Modernism, led to Tyrrell's minor excommunication.

[2] Mathew appears to have informed the Anglican bishops that he had never been formally suspended by the Roman Catholic authorities.

[3] cf. G. K. A. Bell, *Randall Davidson* (1938), p. 1016.

[4] Letter in possession of Dr F. Brittain, of Jesus College, Cambridge.

[5] These letters are also in the possession of Dr F. Brittain.

Arnold Harris Mathew

It is more than likely that Mathew argued that many would be eager to join an English branch of the Old Catholic Church, a few of whom might be Modernists, who wanted to be Catholics, but could not accept the rigidity of Rome in regard to theological speculation; but the greater number would be extreme Anglo-Catholics, who feared the Report of the Ritual Commission, set up in 1904 to examine evidence relating to alleged illegal ritual and ceremonial. Were the State to make it impossible for them to lead what they called 'a Catholic life' in communion with Canterbury and York, the only alternative would be to form an independent Catholic Church in communion with Utrecht. Mathew argued that although some of these priests among this group might be able to accept the papal claims; yet if they had wives, they would have to be content with the status of laymen. The Old Catholic Church he visualized would not enforce clerical celibacy.

A hint of his negotiations with the continental Old Catholics was given by Mathew in the letter he wrote to Dr Davidson on December 1907, in which he said:

'I think that a way to serve the Church of England as *une église amie* may be open to me, which will also, I hope, help forward the movement of Re-Union of those Churches which reject the modern Papal pretensions. I have been approached within the past few days by several Roman Catholics who wish to embrace the tenets of the Old Catholic Communities of Germany and Switzerland and have implored me to assist them. If this can be done in harmony and friendship with the Established Church I think a sphere of very useful labour is thus unexpectedly presenting itself, one also which it may be my duty to enter upon. Should this prove to be so the enquiries which have been made will have been very advantageous to our movement. I have long thought that if it were possible for a Bishop of the Church of England to accept the services of an Old Catholic Coadjutor, or Assistant, who could take part in Ordinations, the Roman Catholic and Orthodox objections to Anglican Orders would be effectually silenced without any sacrifice of principle whatsoever. Such an arrangement might be difficult. I do not know.'[1]

The truth is that Mathew was now being used as the tool of a small group of disgruntled Roman Catholics who had for their leader a priest named Richard O'Halloran. In 1895 Cardinal Vaughan had put him in charge of a new mission at Ealing.

[1] ibid., p. 1017.

O'Halloran had purchased the property on which a temporary church and presbytery had been built, and it was held by trustees. There was an understanding that, in due course, a transfer would be made to the archdiocesan authorities. Six years later the Cardinal announced that he had decided to hand over the mission to the Benedictines of Downside, having had much trouble with this irresponsible Irish priest. O'Halloran was furious and refused to depart. Since the title deeds of the church in Mattock Lane were in his name he could not be evicted by the civil authorities, with the result that His Eminence was powerless. The majority of the congregation remained loyal to their former priest, and continued to worship in his church, thus causing a schism at Ealing. By way of defying the Downside monks who by this time had built the first part of a church in Blakesley Avenue, O'Halloran got busy with forming a rival Benedictine community, with the help of an ecclesiastical adventurer named Henry Bernard Ventham, who took the religious name of Columba Mary, and who had already been ordained priest, probably by Vilatte.[1] But within a few months this pseudo-Old Catholic community was disbanded after running into debt.

In the first decade of this century the Modernist movement had led a number of priests to revolt against what they regarded as the obscurantism and tyranny of Rome. As far back as 1903 O'Halloran felt he had sufficient following to ask Bishop Herzog to send a bishop to England to confirm about twenty ex-Roman Catholic candidates from his now schismatic congregation at Ealing. Herzog, however, took the precaution of consulting Dr John Wordsworth, Bishop of Salisbury, who passed on the letter to the Archbishop of Canterbury. Dr Davidson, advised caution, not wishing to get the wrong side either of the Old Catholic Bishops or of Mgr Bourne, who had been translated from Southwark to Westminster in September 1903, following the death of Cardinal Vaughan.

There were two other already excommunicated priests of the Latin rite in touch with Mathew at this time—Herbert Ignatius Beale and Arthur William Howarth, both formerly of the Diocese of Nottingham. Beale had managed to obtain the rank of Protonotary-Apostolic, and Howarth that of Domestic Prelate to Leo XIII. Their diocesan, Mgr Bagshawe, who had once taken the extreme step of excommunicating the members of the Prim-

[1] See p. 121.

Arnold Harris Mathew

rose League, had been forced to resign in 1901, with the title of Bishop of Hupaepa *in partibus*. His infirmities made him quite incapable of looking after the diocese. He was succeeded by Mgr Robert Brindle, who, after a distinguished career as an army chaplain, had been consecrated in 1899 as Auxiliary for Westminster. There was a general clear-up of the *'refugium peccatorum'*. The new Bishop, whose ideas of discipline were military, accused both Beale and Howarth of misuse of mass-stipends, and other irregularities. The former maintained that Bishop Bagshawe knew of and tolerated their activities; as he had been almost senile for many years this is quite possible. The two Monsignori then began a press campaign, with a series of inflammatory letters. The result was that Cardinal Vaughan demanded to see their briefs. They refused to hand them over, proclaiming far and wide that they regarded any penalties inflicted on them without trial as null and void. Mgr Beale retired from the parish of St Edward's, Nottingham, of which he had been the incumbent since 1896, and before long opened a quasi-Old Catholic chapel at Gunnersbury, W.3., where for several years he defied the authority of Archbishop Bourne. Here he was in close and frequent contact with O'Halloran at Ealing. Howarth continued to protest that he was innocent and remained at Corby, near Grantham, to which mission he had been appointed in 1905. Since such was the type of Roman Catholic flotsam and jetsam Mathew offered to the Primate of All England as the nucleus of *'une église amie'*, it is not surprising that the latter showed little enthusiasm. Practically all the priests had a grievance of some sort, and whatever attraction there may have been to Old Catholicism, it was more negative than positive.

Mathew himself had too much kindness, sympathy, and generosity, to suspect anybody's motives. Meanwhile he was keeping up a frequent correspondence with Old Catholics in Holland and Switzerland, and by December 30, 1907 he felt able to inform Archbishop Davidson's chaplain:

'In view of the difficulty of arrangements for entering the Ministry of the Church of England, I have at length definitely decided to abandon the idea and to throw in my lot with the Old Catholics. We shall open a Mission in this country for the benefit of those Roman Catholics who are unable to continue conscientious adhesion to the Vatican, and this we shall do in a spirit of perfect and cordial amity for the Church of England and in no spirit of aggression, still less of proselytism . . . I am now in correspondence with the Archbishop of Utrecht, who will formally authorize the formation of a branch of the Church in Great Britain on the lines I have indicated.'[1]

Mathew must have been rather disappointed when he received the Archbishop's reply, dated January 10, 1908. His Grace explained that although he was 'at all times glad to learn of any movement in the Church of Rome in the direction of sounder principles of doctrine and usage', he could hardly be expected to look favourably upon the establishment in England of another body claiming to be 'the true representative of the Catholic Church as it comes down to us from the past', because he regarded the body of which he was the canonical head as the true *Ecclesia Anglicana catholica*. He could see no reasons for the formation of 'another society claiming that position, even though it does so in a less exclusive and arrogant spirit than that which finds its centre and expression in the Vatican'.[2]

O'Halloran on his part was determined to get this English branch of the Old Catholic Church set up as soon as possible. His next step was to arrange a meeting for February 18, 1908. Mathew was not present at this meeting, but was informed afterwards that seventeen priests and sixteen laymen had elected him unanimously as first Regionary Old Catholic Bishop in Great Britain. At first he flatly refused to accept the office, but eventually he agreed to do so. O'Halloran composed a letter, dated March 13, signed by three clerics and three laymen, requesting Mgr Gerardus Gul, Old Catholic Archbishop of Utrecht, to consecrate this *ipso facto* excommunicated priest of the Latin rite who had been elected to the episcopate. It appears that this letter and other documents were forwarded to Bishop Herzog at Berne and Bishop Demmel at Bonn, for on March 22 the latter wrote to Mathew:

'I have doubts if the proposal to hold the consecration on April 8 will be adopted in Holland. I know that the Rev. O'H—— has received a somewhat unsympathetic impression from the Bishop of Haarlem; but it seems to me that it was always a mistake on the part of Monsieur O'H not to allow him to come to Ealing. I have tried to find a reason for this refusal to the Bishop; but I am not convinced that the latter is altogether satisfied.'

There can be little doubt that O'Halloran did not want Bishop

[1] ibid., p. 1018.
[2] ibid., p. 1018.

Van Thiel to discover how small a following Mathew had in England, and tried to keep him out of the way. Herzog advised Mathew to invite Van Thiel to stay with him at Chelsfield, adding: 'He would come at his expense; the Bishop of Haarlem is not poor. A personal talk with him would help to shorten the discussions in the episcopal conference.'

Herzog wrote on March 27, that Van Thiel had been in touch with him, and was satisfied with what he had heard of events in England, and saying: 'Do not believe that the situation would be improved if O'Halloran wished to cut himself off from you.'[1]

Two days later Herzog wrote that he had been informed that the Dutch bishops had met at Haarlem on the 26th. After a long discussion they had agreed to hold the consecration at Rotterdam on April 22. Meanwhile Mathew had posted lithographed cards to his friends informing them that he would be raised to the episcopate on April 8. While he was making preparations to go to Holland, a letter arrived from Herzog with the embarrassing question: '*Étes vous marié?*' No mention had been made of a 'Lady Landaff', and the Dutch bishops were horrified when they discovered that the bishop-elect had a wife and three children. Although clerical celibacy had been abolished by the Swiss Old Catholics in 1875, and in Germany two years later, it remained obligatory in Holland until 1922. As a matter of courtesy, Mathew informed Archbishop Davidson of the forthcoming consecration, but the latter made no comments.

Having heard of the forthcoming consecration, Dr John Wordsworth, Bishop of Salisbury, composed a strongly worded protest to his friend Bishop Van Thiel, in which he said: 'You can judge for yourselves whether a man with this history is likely to become a strong leader in a difficult and anomalous position'. The Dutch hierarchy, however, ignored this letter, possibly because at that date they did not recognize 'John Sarum', or any of the Anglican episcopate as true Catholic bishops.[2]

---

[1] Letters in possession of Dr F. Brittain.

[2] It was not until 1932, after a conference held at Bonn, following the seventh Lambeth Conference of 1930, that the Church of England and the Old Catholic Churches of Holland, Germany, and Switzerland were united in full communion. Each body agreed to recognize the catholicity and independence of the other, and maintain its own; also to admit members of the other communions to participate in the sacraments; though not requiring from either communion the acceptance of all doctrinal opinions, sacramental devotion, or liturgical practice characteristic of the other, but implying that each believes the other to hold all the essentials of the Catholic Faith. (cf. C. B. Moss, *The Old Catholic Movement* (1948), p. 347.) By 1936 most of the overseas provinces of the Anglican Communion were in communion with the continental Old Catholic Churches.

Arnold Harris Mathew

After serious discussion as to whether a Catholic priest who had contracted after ordination what in the eyes of the Church was merely a civil marriage could be raised to the episcopate, the Dutch hierarchy felt that in this case the end justified the means, and decided to make an exception to the thousand years rule of the Latin and Eastern Churches, even if from their point of view the bishop-elect was living in concubinage. Mathew was informed that everything had been arranged satisfactorily, and bidden to come to Holland. On the morning of April 28, 1908, Archbishop Gul, assisted by the Bishop of Haarlem, Deventer, and Berne, consecrated the Rev. Count Povoleri di Vicenza, *de jure* Earl of Landaff.[1] The ceremony took place before the Baroque high altar of the Old Catholic Cathedral of St Gertrude, Utrecht, which in recent years has been turned into an Old Catholic Museum. The Countess of Landaff was not among the congregation.[2]

The *historic* continuity of the apostolic succession thus imparted cannot be questioned. It can be traced back in an unbroken line to the nephew of Urban VIII, Cardinal Antonio Barberini the Younger. From 1657 until his death in 1671 he was Archbishop of Rheims, who in 1667 consecrated as his coadjutor Charles-Maurice Le Tellier. In 1670, by the orders of Clement X, Le Tellier raised to the episcopate Jacques-Bénigne Bossuet. He in his turn, as Bishop of Meaux, consecrated Mgr de Matignon in 1693. The succession was passed on by him to Dominique-Marie Varlet in 1719, and next to Peter John Meindaerts in 1739.[3] This last-named was the first Vicar-Apostolic of Utrecht not recognized by the Holy See, a schismatic Church having come into existence. Gerardus Gul was the eighth Old Catholic Archbishop in the Netherlands, and from him the Antonio Barberini succession was passed on to Arnold Harris Mathew.

The Anglican bishops may have had sufficient reason to protest at this consecration from the point of view of jurisdiction. Yet they could not deny the validity of either Mathew's priesthood or his

---

[1] A penalty of suspension reserved to the Holy See is incurred by those who presume to receive orders from one who, through declaratory or condemnatory sentence, is excommunicated, suspended, or interdicted, or from a notorious apostate, heretic, or schismatic (*suspension a divinis*). (cf. Canon 2372.)

[2] For photographs of this impressive function, at which all the prelates wore gorgeous vestments of baroque or rococo shape, see illustrations facing pages 4 and 16 of A. H. Mathew's *What are we to think of Anglican Ordinations?* (1910).

[3] Varlet, as Bishop of Babylon *in partibus* (already out of communion with the Holy See because of his alleged Jansenist opinions), consecrated three Archbishops of Utrecht before raising Meindaerts to the episcopate, all of whom died. He also consecrated Jansenist Bishops of Haarlem and Deventer before his death in 1742.

episcopate, for both were derived from unquestioned Roman Catholic sources. In 1908 the Church of Rome herself accepted the validity of orders conferred by the Church of Utrecht, which had been in a state of schism for nearly two hundred years.

The consecration was reported in both the *Church Times* and *The Guardian*. The latter journal also contained a letter from the Rev. George Angus, the Roman Catholic priest at St Andrews, Fife, which was reprinted in *The Tablet* for May 16. He wrote:

'I read an account of the consecration of the Rev. A. H. Mathew by the Dutch Old Catholic Bishops with some curiosity, for the following reasons. I possess a book entitled *Ecclesia*, consisting of a planned series of writers, seven in number, all of whom are in communion with Rome. The volume is edited by Arnold Harris Mathew, who dates from Chelsfield, Kent, and himself contributes two papers, also a Preface. There is an Appendix by the Rev. Spencer Jones, reproduced from an American periodical. The date is 1906.

'Is this recently consecrated Old Catholic Bishop for England the same clergyman who edited *Ecclesia* (also, presumably, for England) only two years ago, and who was then, so far as can be judged from the book a Christian in obedience to the See of Rome? If so, the conversion, or transition from Rome to Utrecht seems somewhat sudden, and perhaps I may be forgiven for asking the above question.'

The Tablet reprinted another letter to *The Guardian*, signed 'Incredulous', which read:

'Your Old Catholic correspondent announces the consecration of Mr Mathew as first Old Catholic Bishop for England. Who is this Mr Mathew? Is he really "an Old Catholic Bishop, or what is he?" He himself tells us that he is a lineal relative of Sir Toby Mathew, who was a grandson of Bishop Barlow, who consecrated Parker, the first Protestant Archbishop of Canterbury. . . . On close examination we find that Mr Mathew is not unlike his relative Sir Toby. He was Protestant or Catholic, priest or layman, Jesuit or secular— all things in all circumstances to gain his objects. And at this moment we cannot discover whether Mr Mathew is Roman or Anglican, or Old Catholic or Agnostic, or Jesuit or secular priest, or what he is. Is he a Bishop? And if he is a Bishop, of what denomination? And where are his disciples? Scientists and Modernists (like our friend Fr Tyrrell) must recognize in him the "unknown species" whose evolution cannot be classified. Perhaps it is because he has so many spots or shades of all religions that *The Mirror* announces his consecration as the unification of all jarring Christian sects, and himself as the healer of divided Christendom.

'It is stated that he has already a following of seventeen ex-Roman Catholic priests and eight fully-organised parishes in Ealing, Bromley, Orpington, Brighton, Birmingham, Hull, Nottingham, and Chelsfield. But no human eye can see these men in the flesh. We are told that they are there, that they exist; but no man on earth can find them. Doubtless Mr Mathew has studied magic, and he has the power, like Simon of old, to do many marvellous things in proof of his Apostolic election and mission. Faith is the belief in things unseen; but it requires a very strong faith indeed to believe that Mr Mathew has, or ever had, seventeen ex-Roman priests and eight congregations in these towns, and no one but Mr Mathew can see them. I am like St Thomas, I believe what I see, and I undertake to give £10 to each of these ex-Roman Catholic priests, if Mr Mathew will produce them, and thus pay the penalty of my incredulity.'

'Mr Mathew' did not accept the challenge made by 'Incredulous' who was thus saved from having to hand over the sum of £170 for the benefit of the Old Catholic Church. On May 23, 'Harmatopegus' informed readers of *The Tablet* that 'The *Catholic Who's Who and Year Book* 1908 recognises Mr A. H. Mathew as a Catholic author and married man. It is to be presumed that Mrs Mathew is dead; for the Jansenists of Holland exact celibacy in their clergy. But even so, if the 'Old Catholic' correspondent of *The Guardian* is not the victim of a hoax, is it not a great slur on the "seventeen ex-Roman Catholic priests" who are said to obey him as a bishop, that they were forced to elect a layman, if they did so elect him, to be consecrated *per saltum* their first bishop? And if they did not elect him, on whose recommendation did the Jansenist Archbishop of Utrecht act?'

On his return to England from the Netherlands, Bishop Mathew got a nasty shock when he discovered that practically everything told him by O'Halloran was untrue.[1]

He had been convinced by the latter that there was a large body

---

[1] An article appeared in the *Internationale Kirchliche Zeitschrift* at Berne (July-September 1915) which gave a detailed account of how O'Halloran deceived Herzog when negotiating with Utrecht. It looks as if the document produced, with the names of parishes, clergymen, and trustees of congregations who wished to place themselves under an Old Catholic bishop, was based more on this Irish priest's vivid imagination than on actual facts. It is improbable that there were sixteen lay and seventeen clerical members who elected Mathew as their bishop on February 18, 1908.

Arnold Harris Mathew

of both Anglo-Catholics and cisalpine Roman Catholics in England
waiting impatiently to be united on the basis of an Old Catholic
Church. The original source of this supposition seems to have been
an article by the Rev. Arthur Galton in the *Fortnightly Review* for
September 1902. This ex-Catholic priest, who had joined the
ministry of the Church of England, had implied that there were at
least 250 of his former brethren wanting to break away from the
tyranny of the Vatican, and become the nucleus of a purified, non-
papal Catholic Church, similar to those existing already in Holland,
Germany, and Switzerland. But in fact Mathew's friends proved to
be a mere handful, very far from the numbers promised by their
flights of fancy.

Immediately after discovering the true facts, Mathew wrote to
Archbishop Gul, telling him that both of them had been deceived by
O'Halloran. He offered to resign, but the Dutch bishops refused to
consider the idea. It has been said that O'Halloran then demanded
that Mathew should raise him to the episcopate, but to no avail. As
far as he himself was concerned, every effort made by the excommunicated priest at Ealing to get even with Cardinal Vaughan and
his successor Archbishop Bourne by setting up a schismatic church
in England came to nothing.

On April 11, 1908, Tyrrell wrote to Mathew, congratulating
him on his consecration, and saying:

'Though I am miles from Jansenism I have the greatest respect
for the plucky little Utrecht community. But I thought that Utrecht
would faint at the idea of a wedded bishop. Perhaps they are not
immoveable in that matter. Naturally I look forward to you making
a thorn in the side of the Papists, and this you can do far better with
the authority of the Alt-Kath body behind you. I think you must use
your pen in the cause a good deal, and translate the Alt-Kath
literature for the benefit of the Anglicans from whom you are likely
to draw recruits . . .'[1]

Feeling that he had to accept facts as they were, and make the
best of a bad job, Mathew wrote a letter to *The Guardian*, which
was printed on May 27, 1908:

'I now wish to say that having received this important office and
mission, notwithstanding my express desire that another whom I
believed to be more competent and more worthy to undertake both,
should be chosen in my place, it appears to be my duty to use every
possible endeavour that my ministry may be of service in the

[1] Maude Petre, *Life of Fr Tyrrell* (1912), vol. II, p. 379.

interests and welfare of mankind. I therefore earnestly beg for the cordial co-operation of all sincere Christians, in order that, in spite of my numerous shortcomings and my unworthiness, I may succeed in some degree in the accomplishment of the Divine purposes, particularly by seeking to bring about a better and more charitable understanding between some of the many contending denominations into which the Christian people in this country have, unfortunately, become divided.'

This same newspaper in its issue of June 3 published a letter from Bishop Van Thiel, who then acted as secretary to the Old Catholic bishops of Holland, Germany, and Switzerland, expressing the wish that Bishop Mathew would 'receive the cordial support of the British people and Church in the trying circumstances in which he has been placed'. This was a polite way of stating that he had been consecrated under false pretences, though not of his making.

The Lambeth Conference which took place that summer felt very differently. A resolution was passed deprecating 'the setting up of a new organised body in regions where a Church with apostolic ministry and Catholic doctrine offers religious privileges without the imposition of uncatholic terms of communion, more especially in cases where no difficulty of language or nationality exists'. The Anglican bishops stressed that there were no genuine Old Catholics in England, for which reason no good could be expected from setting up a second schismatic body in this country, the first having been established by Pius IX in 1850. Oddly enough the Roman Catholic Hierarchy of England and Wales did not feel it worth while to make any official pronouncement about the new church brought into being by one of its lapsed priests. The Bishops just ignored the whole business as beneath contempt. After all had not Mathew himself written: 'Sects may come and sects may go, but the Church is eternal?' So far as his own sect was concerned, his prophecy would come true.

George Tyrrell, however, did not believe this, and kept on encouraging Mathew. On July 25, 1908 he pointed out the advantages of what he called the 'primitive "household" church and priesthood', and hoped that his friend 'might inaugurate a new and important era in Church history' by confining his clergy to men who earned their living in secular professions. 'Cut off the pecuniary advantage, and you cut off the rest of sacerdotalism, and all the doctrinal and other corruptions it entails.'[1]

[1] ibid., p. 380.

Arnold Harris Mathew

Mathew, for his part, grateful for the support of this celebrated ex-Jesuit, publicized that he was prepared to provide a refuge for discontented Roman Catholic priests and layfolk, and to give them a spiritual home. In spite of the lack of official recognition by the Church of England, he gave lectures in favour of Anglican ordinations; and joined the Society of St Willibrord on its foundation in the autumn of 1908. Its object was to bring about closer relations between the Anglican and Old Catholic communions. Two years later, however, he resigned his membership in a hurry, reports having reached him of the gravely immoral life of its founder and secretary whose sudden death in Tottenham Court Road certainly prevented his arrest and imprisonment.

Tyrrell, writing on February 17, 1909, told the editor of *The Guardian* that, much to his regret, the Old Catholic body in England 'seemed to be on its last legs'. From his point of view this was a tragedy because he had hoped that the Anglo-Dutch *entente* 'would erect a lightning conductor between the Spencer-Jones Ultramontanes, to rob them and their Roman abettors of some of their favourite traps for the ignorant'.[1] Now it appeared that 'for lack of two-pence worth of patience and latitude' the scheme would be wrecked. It was sad to think that 'fundamental positions and principles' would have to 'give way to a purely ecclesiastical law fabricated for a condition of things that has wholly passed away'.[2]

Who's Who for 1909 contained the entry: '*Right Rev. Arnold Harris Matthew—see Earl of Landaff*', and gave more hitherto unpublished facts concerning his ancestry and career. The public were informed that 'Lord Landaff is *de jure* right heir to Admiral Thomas Matthews of Llandaff Court, who died in 1751, leaving extensive estates in three counties, which he bequeathed under a trust "to last 500 years" to his right heirs of the land'. His Lordship claimed also to be 'a lineal descendant of Sir David Mathew of Llandaff, standard-bearer to Edward IV, 1461'. Moreover he was 'a believer in the Baconian authorship of Shakespeare; originated the idea of keeping wild animals in captivity without the employment of cages in zoological gardens, the plan having been sin

---

[1] He was referring indirectly to *The Lamp*, a magazine started in 1903 in the U.S.A. by Fr Paul James Francis, who founded the Society of the Atonement at Graymoor, New York, in 1898. The Rev. Spencer-Jones, rector of Moreton-in-the-Marsh, Gloucestershire, collaborated with him with *The Prince of the Apostles*, published in 1904. On October 30, 1909, this small American Episcopalian community of Brothers and Sisters made its submission to the Roman Church; Mr Jones, however, died an Anglican.

[2] ibid., p. 385.

adopted in Germany with great success; and has successively acclimatized anthropoid apes in this country'. His recreations were stated to be 'field natural history, archeology, and literature'.[1]

In August 1909 he arranged with the Anglo-Catholic firm of Cope and Fenwick to produce an Old *Catholic Missal and Ritual,* adapted from the Roman Rite as used by the Dutch Old Catholics. Printed in the series of 'Christian Liturgies', it carried the imprimatur of Archbishop Gul of Utrecht. Mathew ordered this book to be used in the chapels and oratories under his jurisdiction.

In the meantime 'Lord and Lady Landaff' had moved from Chelsfield, Kent, to 151 Fellowes Road, South Hampstead. One of the rooms of their house was furnished as an oratory, in which, on February 9, 1909, the Bishop performed the first of his episcopal functions, when he ordained deacon and priest, the Rev. W. Noel Lambert, then Minister of an independent Congregational Chapel in River Street, Islington. Dr Winnington Ingram, Bishop of London, had been duly notified of this irregular ordination within his diocese. Lambert placed his chapel at Mathew's disposal, and four months later it was consecrated as a pro-cathedral, dedicated to St Willibrord.[2] Lambert himself was appointed Rector, and several priests were ordained there, among whom was James Columba McFall, whom Mathew raised to the episcopate as Old Catholic Bishop for Ireland in 1916.[3]

Until September 1909 Mathew's only first-hand knowledge of continental Old Catholicism had been gained during his brief visit to Holland for his consecration.[4] A journey to Vienna to take part in the eighth International Old Catholic Congress led to the discovery that the majority of the bishops and clergy were far more Protestant in their outlook than he had suspected. It is related that he warned some of the Dutch delegates that 'if they allowed themselves to be overwhelmed by the "Old Catholics", and walked in their ways, the Church of Utrecht would become the Protestant Modernist sect it soon afterwards became'.[5] There is a story that

---

[1] The famous Mappin Terraces in the Zoological Gardens, London, appear to be Mathew's lasting memorial.

[2] Lambert appears to have been baptized a Catholic. He was a precursor of Dr Orchard in teaching 'high' sacramental doctrine to his Islington flock. For further details of his career, see pp. 182, 210, n.3, 273, 325.

[3] See pp. 280, 304-342, 444, 445

[4] It is possible, however, that he may have met German Old Catholics when he was a student at Bonn and Stuttgart, which was about the same time that they broke away from Rome.

[5] This statement was hardly correct, and the Church of Utrecht today would strongly object to this designation.

Arnold Harris Mathew

about this time a union was formed between Mathew and some of the followers of Bishop Anton Kozlowski, who died on January 14, 1907. Since his consecration at Berne in 1897 this prelate had held a roving commission over groups of Polish Old Catholics in the United States, given him by Mgr Gul, Archbishop of Utrecht. But if this union did take place, it did not continue for long.[1]

On his return from Austria, Mathew felt himself even more isolated, because, in addition to having lost his confidence in most continental Old Catholics, he had developed grave doubts about the validity of Anglican ordinations, as a result of a closer study of sixteenth-century history. He now agreed with Leo XIII that the intention of the Anglican Church as expressed in the ordination rite is defective because the acts and words explicitly conferring the power for priests to offer sacrifices, were omitted by the Reformers. In March 1910 he delivered a lecture at Carshalton, where he stated that many Anglican priests had asked for conditional re-ordination, but that he was reluctant to oblige them.[2] This lecture was printed as a pamphlet, entitled *Are Anglican Orders Valid?* It led to a reply from Bishop Van Thiel, who explained that Mathew's opinion did not represent those of any of the Old Catholic bishops on the continent. He was in communion with them, but in all other respects they regarded him as a free-lance prelate, representing himself and his clergy only. Most of his former friends were deserting him one by one. After the publication of Tyrrell's posthumous work, *Christianity at the Cross Roads*, in 1909, Mathew must have realized that if this ex-Jesuit were still alive their relationship could not have remained unchanged since the author questioned whether Christianity was the final religion, and not merely the germ of a universal religion which would eventually evolve.

About the time of the publication of Tyrrell's book Mathew assisted Archbishop Gul, Bishop Van Thiel, and Bishop Demmel at the consecration in Utrecht on October 5, 1909, of Jean Marie Kowalski as first bishop of the Polish Mariavite Church, probably unaware of the very strange doctrines and customs encouraged in this schismatic sect, founded in 1906.[3]

Determined to assert himself at home, on April 22, 1910 he provided his little pro-cathedral in Islington with a Dean and

[1] See pp. 113, 415, 524, 525
[2] There is evidence that he did re-ordain a fair number of Anglican clergymen from about 1910 onwards.
[3] See pp. 516-523

179

Arnold Harris Mathew

Chapter. No other Old Catholic cathedral in the world had a chapter, except Utrecht. Lace rochets and black mozettas (with scarlet hoods) were bought for F. H. Bacon, C. F. Hinton, J. McFall, and J. S. Seaton, who were installed as canons, under W. N. Lambert as Dean. The Bishop was presented with a ring, and Bacon was given the rank of Archdeacon.[1]

After the installation of the Chapter, Mathew raised himself to the status of Metropolitan, and adopted the title of 'Old Catholic Archbishop of London'. Always a loyal monarchist, he was looking forward to a royal command to attend a levée at Buckingham Palace, but the death of Edward VII on May 6 prevented this. Four days later *The Islington Gazette* printed the archiepiscopal statement: 'His Majesty had been made aware of our Movement, and expressed his interest in it.'[2]

On June 13, at Corby, Lincolnshire, the Archbishop consecrated the two excommunicated Roman Catholic priests already mentioned—Mgr Beale and Mgr Howarth. The former proclaimed that episcopal status would be a useful weapon in his fight with the Roman authorities. He then went off to Caldey Island, where he was entertained by the Anglican Benedictines. Had he thoughts of persuading Abbot Aelred Carlyle to have his orders rectified, or even to throw off the yoke of Canterbury, and have his monks received into the Old Catholic Church?[3]

The Old Catholic Archbishop of London defended his consecration of these two excommunicated monsignori with the explanation that it was vitally important to secure the Old Catholic Church in England against the loss of Apostolic Succession. The Dutch Old Catholics regarded this plea as nonsense, and were extremely

---

[1] Mathew had to borrow the sum of £105 to pay for the canonical regalia, vestments, etc., but his chief benefactor had to admit when cross-questioned by F. E. Smith, K.C., during the *Mathew v. The Times Publishing Co. Ltd.* case, in April 1913, that he had not then succeeded in getting back his money. It has been said that at least part of the money was lent by the overgenerous Vernon Herford, who was on friendly terms with Mathew about this time.

[2] cf. Mar Georgius, *In the Shadow of Utrecht* (1954), p. 8.

[3] As rector of St Edward's Catholic Church, Nottingham, Beale had been on very friendly terms with these monks when they were living at Painsthorpe in Yorkshire. About 1905 he had bought expensive sets of vestments made by one of the community, and had been a benefactor in a variety of small ways from time to time. So far as is known, Beale never performed any episcopal functions. Later on he was reconciled with the Roman Church, but eventually deserted it for the Church of England. His last years were spent as rector of All Saints', Great Sutton, Essex. The patron of the living was W. N. Lambert, the first priest ordained by Mathew, but who abandoned the Old Catholic Church for the Church of England within a year or two. (See p. 182.)

Howarth lived in retirement at Bishop's Manor, Corby, Grantham, until his death in 1942, and apparently never exercised the episcopate obtained from Mathew.

indignant when they heard of the affair. An article appeared in their official organ, *De Oud-Katoliek* on December 1, 1910, in which it was made clear that their English colleague had broken the Declaration of Utrecht, drawn up by the five Old Catholic bishops on September 24, 1889. It was pointed out that he had done so in four different ways in raising Howarth and Beale to the episcopate: (1) by failing to inform his fellow bishops; (2) by performing the consecration secretly; (3) without assistants; and (4) because the two priests were still technically subject to the Holy See.

Having read this article, Mathew sat down and composed what he called a 'Declaration of Autonomy and Independence', washing his hands of the Dutch Old Catholics, and making it quite clear that he was not going to be subject to them any longer. His detailed defence of his action was based on seven points, most of them concerned with the increase of Protestant abuses among his co-religionists on the continent. For instance; they had granted permission to Anglican priests (whose orders he had now ceased to recognize as valid) to celebrate the Communion services in Old Catholic churches, and they admitted Anglican lay-folk to the sacraments. He also expressed strong disapproval of the new vernacular revision of the Dutch liturgy.

There were times when the *de jure* fourth Earl of Landaff was unable to see the obvious facts of life until they hit him in the face. Anybody but himself would have realized that what he maintained were recent Protestant abuses had existed among the continental Old Catholics for a long time. Although in his negotiations with Utrecht he had made good use of Bishop Herzog of Berne, who was a very 'broad churchman', he does not appear to have studied the 1880 liturgy of his Church (*Gebetbuch fuer die christkatholische Kirche in der Schweiz*). Had he done so, he would have discovered that it was far more Protestant in tone than the 1909 Dutch vernacular *Misboek*, which is a fairly conservative vernacular version of the Roman rite.

The 'Declaration of Autonomy and Independence' was printed in *The Guardian* on January 6, 1911. The Old Catholic Archbishop of London now found himself as the opposite number to the Cardinal Archbishop of Westminster, the Bishop of London, and indirectly to the Metropolitans of Canterbury and York. His jurisdiction covered the whole of Great Britain and Ireland, but his duties were not burdensome, for the only places of worship requiring his supervision were chapels at Chiswick, Croydon, Broadstairs, Belfast, and

Oxford, together with his tiny pro-cathedral in Islington. Most of these chapels were rooms in private houses. Two of his clergy soon abandoned him. One of these, C. W. Bollman, a former Lutheran pastor, whom he had ordained priest on September 19, 1910, and who had furnished a room in his house in Kensington as a public oratory, dedicated to St Boniface, went over to the Church of England. The other was an even graver blow: the Dean of his pro-cathedral, W. N. Lambert, got reconciled with Canterbury. Both these priests were the legal owners of two of the Archbishop's two places of worship in London, so all that he could do under the circumstances was to transfer the pro-cathedral to a room in his house in Fellowes Road, South Hampstead, and forget about the 'chapel of ease' in Kensington. But he used Archdeacon Bacon's private oratory at 33 Esmond Road, Bedford Park, for most pontifical functions.[1]

It is recalled by some of Mathew's surviving friends that after the birth of his second daughter in 1907, relations between him and his wife became strained. This is not surprising, because it must have been a disappointment to have changed the position of a noble lady and fashionable curate's wife for that of consort to a bishop regarded as bogus by her former friends in Chelsea. The Countess was often away, and her husband's clerical associates seldom met her.

Three weeks after the publication of the Declaration of Autonomy and Independence, proof was given that the Archbishop of London now regarded himself as subject to no higher authority. His handful of clergy elected four of their number and pressed for their immediate consecration. These were Francis Herbert Bacon, Cuthbert Francis Hinton, Frederick Clement Egerton, and William Scott-Hall. On January 7, 1911, without assistants, Mathew raised these four priests to the episcopate, with the titles of Bishops of Durham, Hereford, Norwich, and Winchester respectively. The independent branch of the Old Catholic Church in England could now boast of a hierarchy of seven. The 'sheep', which when rounded up numbered probably less than a hundred, were well supplied with 'shepherds'—roughly one shepherd for fourteen sheep. Feeling very optimistic about a glorious future for

---

[1] Both Bollman and Lambert were received into the Church of England. Dr Winnington-Ingram accepted their orders as valid, and allowed them to minister in the Diocese of London. Bollman conducted services in St Mary's, Charing Cross Road, and became the only representative of genuine Old Catholicism in England. For Lambert's subsequent career, see pp. 273, 325.

his Church, Mathew wrote to Cardinal Merry del Val four days later, informing him that he soon hoped to 'catholicize the Protestant and the unbelieving in the British Empire'. He begged His Eminence to obtain papal approval for the use of a vernacular version of the Roman rite in this small body out of communion now both with the Holy See and with the Church of Utrecht.

Having given the independent Old Catholic Church in Britain a hierarchy, the Metropolitan began to dream of spreading the religious life for men and women. On February 2, 1911, he inaugurated a Benedictine monastery at Barry, Glamorganshire, and installed a certain Dom Gilbert Vincent as Superior. Two or three novices were clothed, among them James Charles Thomas Ayliffe Williams. This young man had already tested his vocation with the Anglican Benedictines on Caldey Island, but after about six months realized that his health would not stand up to their then austere observances.[1] But this embryo abbey came to an end within a year of its foundation. The money promised for its endowment failed to materialize, and there was some scandal about the Father Superior, and about the person (or persons) who were to have provided the cash. Mathew also hoped to found a community of nuns, and had in mind as its nucleus two or three Sisters who had left the Anglican Benedictines at West Malling at the time of the election of Sister Mary Pauline Ewart of the Society of All Saints as second Abbess early in 1907.

Now that the *de jure* Earl of Landaff had cast himself adrift from the continental Old Catholics, he had to find a new name for his schismatic sect. The simplest thing was to call it 'The English Catholic Church'. The day after their consecration the Titular Bishops of Durham, Hereford, Norwich, and Winchester elected him 'Anglo-Catholic Archbishop of London', and duly notified the Holy See; as a result their consecrator was put under a major excommunication. This was reported in *The Times* on February 28, 1911. Mathew was furious, and wrote to Cardinal Merry del Val, protesting against this papal action. He also instructed his solicitor to issue a writ for libel against the Times Publishing Company Limited.

In spite of the fact that he and his associates had been anathematized and excommunicated in the papal decree of February 11, 1911, and the faithful warned against all contact with them,

---

[1] It was Williams who was consecrated in 1916 as coadjutor with right of succession to Mathew. (See p. 206.)

Mathew had the temerity that same day to write to Mgr John Cuthbert Hedley, O.S.B., Bishop of Newport and Menevia, with a proposal to set up a Uniate Church in Britain. He informed him that there were many discontented Anglo-Catholics waiting to join such a body. Having met with no encouragement in this quarter, he made a similar suggestion to Cardinal Merry del Val on May 14, and said:

'It would be very desirable that a Uniate body should be formed; and that it should be directly subject to the Holy See—at any rate for some time.'[1]

Strange to say, the then Papal Secretary of State did not agree with the 'Anglo-Catholic Archbishop of London', and no more was heard of the proposal.

Meanwhile the Church of Utrecht had published a devastating reply to the Declaration of Autonomy and Independence. As on so many occasions, Mathew contrived to defend himself. On February 17, 1911, he explained to readers of *The Guardian* that he had not broken away from this Church or from other continental Old Catholic bodies. All he had done was to emphasize his independent status in Britain. He managed to find what he felt were convincing reasons in favour of other actions criticized by the Dutch bishops. Another defence of his position and polity followed on April 28.[2] But there was no need for him to be depressed. A wealthy lady had offered to pay for the erection of a cathedral in London in which he would be able to pontificate in a manner befitting the 'Archbishop and Metropolitan of the English Catholic Church', the style which he gave himself in March 1911.

All this sort of thing sounds quite crazy today, but did not seem so early in 1912. Mathew knew that there were a number of extreme Anglo-Catholic incumbents whose churches were banned by their respective bishops, and who appeared to be quite content to remain in this state of spiritual isolation so long as they could say Mass in the vernacular with the ceremonial of the Latin rite. A few, however, did wake up to their illogical position, and it was in 1910 that took place what were known as the 'Brighton Troubles', with several priests in that town and many members of their congregations being reconciled with the Holy See. Their example was followed by about half a dozen clergymen, and many

---

[1] cf. Mar Georgius, *In the Shadow of Utrecht* (Antwerp, 1954), p. 14.

[2] When the Old Catholic hierarchy met in 1913 they issued a formal statement that Bishop Mathew had ceased to be an Old Catholic on December 29, 1910, and that after that date they recognized none of his episcopal actions.

more layfolk. But there were some ecclesiastical 'rebels' who did not see their way to accept the papal claims, and who disapproved of what they regarded as the obscurantist opinions of Pope Pius X. All they wanted was to lead a 'Catholic Life', and it really did not matter very much in the long run, who was their ecclesiastical major superior, because they had grown accustomed to doing without one for many years; treating their Anglican bishops merely as machines for conferring holy orders and administering the sacrament of confirmation. So there was a lot to be said in favour of accepting the jurisdiction of the self-styled Archbishop of London, and helping him to establish an 'English Catholic Church'. It began to look as if there might be a future for such a body. Moreover the Modernist element in the Church of England was becoming more and more a cause of alarm, but it did not reach a climax until the publication of the collection of essays entitled *Foundations* in 1912.

By this time the Archbishop was in close touch with a small circle in London whose members encouraged his dreams and visions, and gave him financial assistance. Among them were Madame Olga Novikoff, sister of General Alexander Kiréef, and the Baroness Nathalie d'Uxkull, both of them ardent Pan-Slavists. These two ladies were on friendly terms with almost all the leaders of movements on the Continent for setting up non-papal national churches, including the Committee of Liberal Catholics in Italy.[1] It was at their suggestion that 'Lord Landaff' wrote to the Holy Synod of Moscow, hopeful of the influence of General Kiréef with this erastian body, so that its members would agree to the affiliation of the English Catholic Church with the Russian Patriarchate. The reply received was not encouraging.

Accordingly the Baroness d'Uxkull and Madame Novikoff put their heads together, and recommended that it might be worth while to tackle Archbishop Gerasimos Messera of Beirut, who had been sent to Europe by the Orthodox Patriarch of Antioch to raise money. Doubtless these two ladies showed Mathew the article by Messera, published in the *Journal de Genève* on January 20, 1911, on the Reunion of Christendom. Some of the statements suggested

---

[1] The head of this organization was a Mgr Panelli, a lapsed Catholic who called himself Archbishop of Lydda, who managed to win the support of the Archimandrite Alexander, chaplain to the Russian anbassador in Rome. Panelli went to Russia, where he met General Kiréef, who was suspicious of his credentials. (cf. *Quelques Lettres du Général Alexandre Kiréef au Professeur Michaud sur l'Ancien-Catholicisme*. Ed. by Madame Olga Novikoff (Paris-Neuchatel, n.d.), pp. 26, 55.

that the Archbishop of Beirut was a very 'broad churchman', with a comprehensive eirenic outlook. It may be wondered if his Patriarch was aware of the opinions promulgated in Switzerland; for instance that—

'It must be clear to all that a renewal of unity between the Churches must have as its basis the complete preservation of all their respective rights and privileges . . . We publish this exhortation to the whole Christian world, in the hope of finding in the hearts of all believers an echo of sincere sympathy. In doing this we have fulfilled our fraternal duty, and have set aside all responsibility for the divisions among Christians.'[1]

Gerasimos Messera went to England during the summer of 1911. He met the Archbishop of Canterbury, but it seems that he did not receive much sympathy or the expected financial help. The Baroness d'Uxkull and Madame Novikoff took him under their wing, and arranged that he should be introduced to the Anglo-Catholic Archbishop of London.

The result was that on August 5, 1911, a conference took place at the Manor House Club, Bredon's Norton, Worcestershire, which was 'Lord and Lady Landaff's' country address. There were present Archbishops Mathew and Messera, Bishop Scott-Hall, Baroness d'Uxkull, Colonel Haggard, and Socrates Spiro Bey, a professor of Arabic at the University of Geneva. After a friendly discussion with his hosts, Messera agreed to receive the English Catholic Church into union with the Orthodox Patriarchate of Antioch, and Mathew took an oath of allegiance to the absent Patriarch. A document was drawn up in Arabic, and translated into English by Socrates Bey. It is hard to believe that an Orthodox Patriarch of Antioch would have been prepared to accept a married prelate into communion with his Church. 'Lady Landaff' did not take part in the conference, and it is probable that her existence behind the scenes was again kept dark, as at the time of her husband's consecration in 1908.

This unprecedented union of what was legally merely a small English nonconformist sect with one of the historic Eastern Churches was such an important event, that ten days later Bishop Bacon gave his *nihil obstat* and Archbishop Mathew his *imprimatur* to a pamphlet entitled *The Articles of Belief of the Old Catholics*

---

[1] A translation of this article appeared in Mathew's short-lived periodical, *The Torch*, on April 15, 1912. It was followed by other articles on the Eastern Orthodox and Uniate Churches, apparently written by Mathew himself.

Arnold Harris Mathew

in Great Britain and Ireland of the Western Orthodox Church.[1]
Not satisfied with having obtained an apparent union with the
Orthodox Patriarchate of Antioch, the Baroness d'Uxkull and
Madame Novikoff urged Mathew to approach the vigorous and
broad-minded Photios, Orthodox Patriarch of the Great City of
Alexandria and All Egypt. The result exceeded their expectations,
for on February 13–26, 1912, His Holiness wrote to the Archbishop and Metropolitan of the Western Orthodox Church,
accepting him and his flock into union with the Patriarchate of
Alexandria. He granted them permission to use the Latin rite
omitting the *Filioque* so long as the faithful in Great Britain
and Ireland recognized the canonical ordinances of the seven
Oecumenical Synods which form the basis of the Orthodox Faith.

As might be expected, the Primate of All England was surprised
and displeased when he heard of what had been going on behind his
back. It has been said that he dispatched Dr Winnington-Ingram to
Syria, and on March 23, 1913 a bargain was made that this so-
called Act of Union should be repudiated by the Orthodox
Patriarch of Antioch.[2] Nevertheless, according to Mathew's successor, Archbishop Williams:

'Whether the backsheesh, which seems to have been considerable, fell short of His Beatitude's expectations or not, we do not
know. What we do know with absolute certainty is that no repudiation of this Act of Union was ever made.'[3] Neither does it appear
that the Orthodox Patriarch of Alexandria ever formally repudiated
his pact before his death in 1925. But the English Catholic Church
did not retain the title of the Western Orthodox Church for long,
no more than a few months, as will be related.

On April 18, 1913, the case *Mathew v. The Times Publishing
Company (Limited)* came up before the King's Bench Division. It
concerned defamation—libel—and the translation of a papal bull
and its publication simply for the information of its readers, which
the defendants maintained was not a contravention of 13 Elizabeth;
for the words of this statute 'publish or . . . put in ure' means publishing so as to make the bull operative in this country. Mr Roskill,
K.C., and Mr Hugh Fraser appeared for the plaintiff; and Mr F. E.
Smith (later Lord Birkenhead) for the defendants. The reputedly

---

[1] This was the name given by J. Joseph Overbeck to the body he tried and failed to
erect between 1867 and 1885. (See pp. 49–52.)
[2] No mention of this mission is made in S. C. Carpenter, *Bishop Winnington-
Ingram* (1949).
[3] *Supplement to the Diocesan Chronicle*, May 1949, p. 4.

Arnold Harris Mathew

libellous article had been published in *The Times* on February 28, 1911. The defendants denied the meaning put by the plaintiff on the words complained of, and pleaded: (1) that they were true in substance and in fact; (2) that they were a fair comment on matters of public interest; and (3) that they were privileged.

The actual words which Mathew maintained amounted to libel were the translation of *nefario crimini* by 'wicked crime'. He insisted that the correct translation was 'impious fault'. This phrase occurred in the *Acta Apostolicae Sedis* of February 15, 1911, which contained the text of the excommunication of three Englishmen (Mathew, Beale, and Howarth), which, as stated in *The Times*, had been pronounced by Pope Pius X.[1]

Dated February 11, 1911, this papal decree warned the faithful against 'the pretensions and deceits' of the persons mentioned, whose consecration was declared to be unlawful, sacrilegious, and wholly contrary to the commands of the Holy See, and the sanction of the sacred canons. The persons themselves were 'excommunicated and anathematized together with all others who' to this *wicked crime* have given aid, counsel, or consent'. They were ordered to be 'cut off from the communion of the Church, and as utterly schismatic, to be avoided by all Catholics'.[2]

Cross examined by F. E. Smith, Mathew made sufficiently wild and irresponsible statements to convince those in court that he was a pitiful clerical megalomaniac, deserving of sympathy rather than abuse. Mr Justice Darling summed up and put the following questions to the jury: (1) Were the defendants actuated by malice in publishing the matter complained of?; (2) Are the words true in substance and in fact?; and (3) damages? As to the damages, no evidence had been given that the plaintiff had been shunned by anyone in consequence of the publication.

The jury answered the first question in the negative and the

---

[1] The document set forth that 'For some time past we have known that it has been to you a source of grievous scandal and of deepest sorrow of mind that the priest Herbert Ignatius Beale and Arthur William Howarth, of the clergy of the diocese of Nottingham, seeking the things which are their own, and not the things that are Jesus Christ's, and led away by their ambition, after several attempts to procure for themselves the rank of the Episcopate from men who are not Catholics have lately reached the pitch of audacity in which, having obtained the fulfilment of their wishes, they have arrogantly informed Us of their episcopal consecration. Nor was this information left without authentic testimony, for the person who was the chief author of this sacrilegious misdeed—a certain *pseudo* Bishop named Arnold Harris Mathew—was not ashamed to confirm the fact in letters, full of self-assumption, which he has addressed to Us. This person has, moreover, thought to bestow upon himself the title of Anglo-Catholic Archbishop of London'.

[2] *The Times Law Reports*, May 2, 1913.

Arnold Harris Mathew

second in the affirmative; adding that they deprecated the publication of the bulls of the Pope of Rome in England which affected the status of individuals. On the application of F. E. Smith, judgment was entered for the defendants, with costs.

So the poor Anglo-Catholic Archbishop of London had merely made himself the laughing stock of the British public, and he had to pay for his folly. Some of his statements during his cross-examination by F. E. Smith proved how utterly illogical and inconsistent he was. For instance, when he said: 'I consider myself to be within the Roman Catholic Church, and the same Church as that to which the Pope belongs, and I have always been of that opinion', he must have forgotten for the moment that since he cast aside his Catholic priesthood in 1889, he had been both a Unitarian and an Anglican, as well as an Old Catholic. Having taken such trouble to widen his schismatic status by obtaining union with the Orthodox Patriarchs of Antioch and Alexandria, it is hard to see how he could still regard himself as being in communion with the Patriarch of the West.

After April 1913 the *de jure* Earl of Landaff was treated lightly for the rest of his life, even by most of his followers, the majority of whom merely made use of his services for their own purposes; casting him aside when he had done the job wanted.

But he could still count on the loyalty of the Baroness d'Uxkull and Madame Novikoff. He was always sure of a welcome in the London salon presided over by the masterful and ever-scheming Belgian Baroness, whose advice he frequently sought. It was one or the other of these two ladies who introduced the Archbishop to a most distinguished Austrian nobleman—Rudolph Francis Edward St Patrick Alphonsus Ghislain de Gramont Hamilton de Lorraine-Brabant, Prince de Landas Berghes et de Rache, Duc de St Winock. It was well known that he was related to most of the European royal and noble families included in the *Almanach de Gotha*. It was not long before Count Povoleri di Vicenza, Nogarote e Verona, fourth Earl of Landaff of Thomastown, Co. Tipperary, became close friends with the Prince de Landas Berghes et de Rache, Duc de St Winock. They found they had many interests in common. The former had a passion for genealogies, and must have revelled in delving into the latter's long line of ancestors starting in the early Middle Ages among whom were Dukes of Lorraine and Brabant.[1]

---

[1] De Landas also claimed kinship with the 13th Duke of Hamilton and 10th of Brandon (Premier Peer of Scotland, Heir Male of the House of Douglas). Whether

Arnold Harris Mathew

The Prince, though brought up in communion with the Holy See, prided himself on being liberal-minded and did not agree with Pius X that Arnold Harris Mathew was only a 'pseudo Bishop', cut off from the communion of the Church, and utterly schismatic, who must be avoided by all the faithful. On the contrary, before very long he said that he would like to be received into Mathew's 'Catholic Church', optimistic that it had a great future ahead. Then, with hardly a moment's delay, the illustrious convert was given the four minor orders, subdiaconate and diaconate, and raised to the priesthood in Bishop Bacon's oratory on November 21, 1912.[1] Six weeks after *The Times* libel case, on the Feast of SS. Peter and Paul, June 29, 1913, Prince de Landas Berghes et de Rache, Duc de St Winock, was consecrated by the Most Rev. and Rt. Hon. Archbishop of London.

Some of those who recall this Austrian Prince-Bishop are of the opinion that, although he was indeed a fascinating, cosmopolitan, and cultured personality, he would have made trouble had he remained long in touch with Mathew. For one thing, it seems probable that he merely wanted to obtain the episcopate in order to set up a new anti-papal Church on the Continent, and felt that Mathew's aristocratic connections would be more useful to him than those of the Old Catholic Bishops in Holland, Germany and Switzerland. As to the prelates of the Vilatte succession in France at that date, none of them could be said 'to come out of the top drawer'; they were hardly the sort of men for a Prince-Bishop to consort with! Almost certainly if he had remained in Britain 'The Catholic Church' (as it had come to be—somewhat ambitiously— called) would have split into two groups: those who had a social background and those who had not. The Baroness d'Uxkull and her circle would definitely have sided with the Prince-Bishop, and 'Lord Landaff' would have been almost certain to have done the same. Later on a schism in the ranks did occur, but for very different reasons, as will be related.

Mathew's flock was so small at all times that his archiepiscopal duties, even with the distractions involved by being a husband and the father of three children, allowed him more than enough leisure

---

this link was found in the Duke's fairly recent collateral forebear, Princess Mary of Baden, or some more remote ancestor as far back as the twelfth century is not certain.

[1] Ordained the same day were James C. T. A. Williams (who took the religious name of Bernard Mary), and Frederic Adams, B.A. (now M.A. and D. Litt.); both were converts from Anglicanism.

to turn out books and pamphlets. In 1912 he launched *The Torch*, described as 'a Monthly Review advocating the Reconstruction of the Church of the West and Reunion with the Old Orthodox Church of the East', of which only three issues appeared. For the benefit of his Anglo-Catholic Church, the Metropolitan composed *A Catechism of Christian Doctrine*, printed and published at Bromley, Kent. *The Torch* had a short-lived successor in *The Union Review*, which was also edited by the versatile Archbishop. Another booklet was *The Ancient Catholic Church of Great Britain*, of which he claimed to be the canonical head. He changed the title of his sect far more frequently than he had changed his own name in the past, and it was often difficult to remember what it was called from month to month.[1]

On March 15, 1914, the first and only issue of *Le Réveil Catholique* was published in Paris. It contained a photograph with the caption: '*Sa Grandeur Monseigneur A. H. Mathieu, Archevêque de Londres, Comte de Landave, Métropolitain de la Grande Bretagne et d'Irlande, Evêque Provisoire de l'Église Catholique Française*'.[2] Readers were informed that Mgr Mathieu had agreed to consecrate a bishop for a new National Church in France. An appeal was made to all French people who wished to be good Christians and Catholics without being ultramontanes or enslaved by the Jesuits, to join this body. It offered many advantages; for instance, clerical celibacy would be abolished, as being dangerous and contrary to nature, although voluntary celibacy would be permitted to members or religious orders; the veneration of images would be discouraged, and public worship would be in the vernacular. Meanwhile the nascent Church was under the jurisdiction of a Vicar General. A small chapel, dedicated to Blessed Joan of Arc, had been opened in the Passage Elysée des Beaux Arts, Paris. It was expected that before long Mgr Mathieu would consecrate M. l'Abbé Demezières, or whatever other priest might be elected, as the first bishop of the Église Catholique Française.[3] But these dreams and visions faded

---

[1] The 1914 edition of *Who's Who* added a few more details about the Earl of Landaff, stating that 'he had introduced numerous insectivorous birds into the colony of New Zealand'. Added to his recreations were 'fishing and zoology', and by this time he had become a 'life member of the Clifton Zoological Society'.

[2] Subsequently Mathew asserted that the last designation had been printed without his knowledge, and that he had no intention of becoming the head of a schismatic body in France.

[3] This seems to have been planned as a rival body to the Gallican Church, at that date ruled over by the occultist and faith healer, Julius Hussay, who styled himself 'Metropolitain de l'Église catholique française', and who had been raised to the episcopate by Miraglia Gulotti (of the Vilatte succession) on June 21, 1911. Giraud, on

out after Germany declared war against France on August 3, 1914. Ascension Day, 1914, was celebrated by Archbishop Mathew with the publication at Bromley, Kent, of *The Catholic Church of England: Its Constitution, Faith, Episcopal Succession*, etc. It was typical of his pretentiousness to state that he had divided England into five ecclesiastical Districts: London, Northern, Eastern, Western, and Southern, with London as the Metropolitan See.[1] Scotland would soon be raised to a Vicariate-Apostolic.[2] Obsessed with the delusion of his own importance, he was planning an International Congress to be held in London, to which representatives of all the Catholic and Apostolic Churches in the world would be invited. Nothing like it had ever been thought of since the first Vatican Council of 1870, but that was on a very small scale compared to the Congress Mathew dreamed of. Then the Metropolitan got down to brass tacks, and ordered that his clergy were to use the Roman Missal, either in Latin or in English.[3]

The Most Rev. The Right Hon. Archbishop of London announced that he was prepared to re-ordain Anglican priests to ensure the validity of their orders.[4] He proclaimed that his little sect was really 'the "Old" Catholic Church of England', because it taught 'only the Faith of Old England, as it was taught when our fore-fathers all believed alike and worshipped together, and before any religious disputes, sects, and religious differences among Christians existed in this country'.[5] Having raised himself to the status of a Supreme Pontiff of a Universal Church, he felt it his duty to plant his new organization in many other countries, in each of which it would be autonomous. To stress its international importance he printed the full texts of Union with the Patriarchates of Antioch and Alexandria. On the last page of this booklet was a photograph of the proposed 'Cathedral of Our Lady of England', with an appeal for £175,000 to erect it in London.

July 21, 1913, consecrated Joanny Bricaud (an authority on black magic and satanism) as his coadjutor, so if the Mathew schismatic Church in France had ever materialized, it might have met with serious opposition, unless it had been integrated with the Gnostic bishops and priests. (See pp. 307, 308.)

[1] de Landas Berghes was nominated the first Vicar-Apostolic, because of his alleged kinship with the Duke of Hamilton.

[2] No doubt Mathew pictured himself as a twentieth-century Pope Innocent XI, who on January 30, 1688, created four Districts or Vicariates for England and Wales: the London, Midland, Northern, and Western. On July 3, 1840, Pope Gregory XVI increased the number of Vicariates to eight.

[3] Permission was granted for the adoption of certain Anglo-Catholic missals, including one published by the Society of SS. Peter and Paul in 1912.

[4] For details of Mathew's revived Order of Corporate Reunion, see pp. 84–90.

[5] op. cit., p. 26.

Arnold Harris Mathew

Intoxicated with all these beautiful dreams and visions, the Archbishop must have felt when he was celebrating Mass that Ascension Day that the words of the Offertory had indeed been fulfilled: 'God goes up, loud are the cries of victory; the Lord goes up, loudly the trumpets peal, alleluia'. Any student of nineteenth-century ecclesiastical architecture would have detected that the photograph of the London cathedral had been taken from a model of a building erected more than fifty years previously. Mathew revealed his inspiration in a letter to Allen Hay, Vicar of South Mymms, written in May, 1914. He said: 'I want a *granite* Cathedral, a replica of the Votiv Kirche at Vienna—a heaven-born design for a church, which lifts the soul as its spires point to celestial spheres.'[1] Presumably the money was not coming in as fast as was expected, for on June 14 he informed the same correspondent that it would be madness to erect a great cathedral without sufficient endowment to keep it in repair, and sufficiently staffed. He added: 'It is the ridiculous edifice at Westminster that causes anxiety. Those three large concrete domes *crack*. Fancy making such abominations!'[2]

For the next six weeks the Archbishop's dreams were mostly about the granite replica of the Vienna votive church which he was determined to erect in the heart of London. Unfortunately, however, on June 28 the Archduke Francis Ferdinand and his morganatic wife, the Princess of Hohenberg, were assassinated at Sarajevo, with the result that on July 28 Austria-Hungary declared war against Servia. On August 4, Britain was at war with Germany.

During that summer Mathew was not wholly pre-occupied with his cathedral. He had been approached by an Anglican clergyman, the Rev. Frederick Samuel Willoughby, M.A., who told him a tragic story of how he had been forced to resign the living of St John-the-Baptist, Stockton-on-Tees, because of Protestant persecution. Willoughby, ordained to the priesthood in 1888, was an extreme Anglo-Catholic, and had been the founder and first Principal of St Chad's Hostel, Hooton Pagnell, Yorkshire (1899–1906), where candidates for the Anglican ministry were trained on High Church lines. He had been the incumbent of this parish at Stockton since 1906. He explained to the Archbishop that certain of his flock had spread malicious gossip about his morals when he was

---

[1] The Votivkirche (1856–79) was designed by H. von Ferstel. It is a fanciful Gothic Revival composition with two lofty Western wedding-cake-like spires.
[2] Letters in possession of Dr F. Brittain.

away on holiday, and had informed Dr Moule, Bishop of Durham. His Lordship had not disclosed to Willoughby the nature of the serious charges made against him. After a private investigation the Vicar was asked to resign his benefice. He did so, for like Dr Moule, he did not want any further publicity, and eventually availed himself of the provisions of the Clerical Disabilities Relief Act 1870, on January 19, 1915. The result of this shock, so Willoughby told Mathew, was a complete loss of faith in Anglicanism.

Most of Mathew's friends appear to have agreed that he was genial, kindly, easily persuaded, scholarly, but utterly unbusinesslike. He was neither a good leader nor a capable administrator. He always *wanted* to do the right thing, but invariably he *did* the wrong one. On the other hand his integrity was seldom questioned. When dealing with this ex-parson he made one of the worst mistakes in his life.

The Archbishop accepted Willoughby's statements on their face-value, and immediately offered to find work for him in what had now been renamed 'The Ancient Catholic Church of England'. It is to be presumed that 'Landaff' did not read such popular weeklies as *John Bull*, which in its issue of June 20, 1914, stated that, because of the revolting facts revealed, this clergyman was utterly unfit to act as the shepherd of a Christian flock. Any bishop but Mathew would have thought twice before taking on a cleric of such nation-wide notoriety.

No time was wasted. Willoughby, having been baptized conditionally, confirmed and given minor orders, subdiaconate and diaconate, was raised to the priesthood. Shortly after this he was made a member of the Cathedral Chapter, and able to wear a lace rochet and a black mozetta with a scarlet hood.

In September 1914 Prince-Bishop de Landas Berghes et de Rache had left England for the United States, with the connivance of the Foreign Office. As an Austro-Hungarian subject it would have been necessary to intern him as an enemy alien. This might have been awkward because he was related to most of the royal families of Europe. So the Archbishop of London was left without a Coadjutor. The titular Bishops of Durham, Hereford, Norwich, and Winchester could not be relied on. Three of them had already broken away from the Ancient Catholic Church of England, and the fourth was in Canada.

On October 10, Mathew sent a printed letter to his clergy,

informing them that an election had taken place in which votes had been cast for nine priests. Canon Wedgwood had received six votes and Canon Willoughby ten. This gave the latter a clear majority, none of the others having obtained more than four votes each.

The consecration of the former Vicar of St John's, Stockton-on-Tees was carried out in the banqueting hall of the Bell Hotel, Bromley, Kent, on the feast of SS. Simon and Jude, October 28, 1914.[1] An altar and all the correct ornaments were hired from the firm of Jones and Willis. In an impressively worded Latin *instrumentum consecrationis* it was stated that the Most Illustrious and Most Reverend Count Landaff of Thomastown in Ireland had performed this solemn rite according to the *Pontificale Romanum*. The document was witnessed by six persons, including Canons Farrer and King, both of them members of the Theosophical Society and the Order of the Star in the East.[2] The new prelate was given the style of Titular Bishop of St Pancras.

All went well for a time, and the Archbishop felt he had found the ideal Coadjutor.[3] Willoughby's rapid promotion, however, disturbed some people, who thought that Mathew ought to have gone further into the *John Bull* allegations, and sought information from the Bishop of Durham before conferring any orders on this ex-Anglican incumbent with such a shady past.

There were other troubles brewing, but in the first months of World War One, the Ancient Catholic Archbishop of London seems to have been blissfully unconscious of them. For at least two years, perhaps longer, he had been in close touch with several leading Theosophists, apparently without investigating the orthodoxy of their beliefs. One of his priests, Fr Wedgwood, was already deeply implicated in the Theosophist movement. Mathew gave him permission to continue his active work for the Theosophical Society without compromising his position in the Church; and went so far as to use Wedgwood's private oratory for administering baptism, confirmation and minor orders on Willoughby.[4] It is hard to say

---

[1] Bishop Moule insisted that Willoughby should avail himself of the provisions of the Clerical Disabilities Relief Act, 1870, to avoid formal degradation.

[2] cf. Alban W. Cockerham, 'The Liberal Catholic Ministry II', in *The Liberal Catholic*, September 1957, pp. 267–8.

[3] Mathew and Willoughby were the joint authors of a tract entitled *The Conversion of Great Britain: What can the Ancient Catholic Church of England do?* The Bishop of St Pancras wrote another tract about the same time—*The Ancient Catholic Church of England: Her Authority, Her Mission, Her Work, Her Appeal.*

[4] cf. T. H. Redfern, 'Bishop Mathew and his Theosophical Clergy', in *The Liberal Catholic*, July 1956. Full details of Wedgwood's early career are given in chapter nine, pp. 344–346

just how far Mathew grasped the heterodox opinions of the majority of his priests. On the other hand, his elusive mind may have been attracted to Theosophy, just as it had been to Unitarianism a quarter of a century earlier.[1]

Dr F. Adams (one of Mathew's few surviving friends) is convinced that he never accepted the Theosophical doctrine that there are 'Masters', i.e. supermen who, instead of being released from the wheel of life and death after they become perfect, have elected to remain on this earth in order to help humanity in its struggle towards perfection. He certainly did not believe that the most exalted of these Masters—the Lord Maitreya—assumed the body of Jesus nearly two thousand years ago, and that in 1914 he was about to take the body of an Indian youth named Krishnamurti, who would be hailed as the twentieth-century Christ. Nevertheless, the Archbishop, if he read the newspapers, must surely have known that Krishna had been brought to England by Mrs Annie Besant in 1911, but he may have been too pre-occupied with his 'Declaration of Autonomy and Independence'. By 1914 this young Indian had had nearly three years of training at the expense of the Theosophical Society.[2]

That Mathew was taking a keen interest in Theosophy is proved by a letter, dated August 19, 1914, i.e. two months before Willoughby's election to the episcopate, which he wrote to Canon Reginald Farrer, who was an active member of the Society as well as a priest of the Ancient Catholic Church of England. He said:

'I so often have seen a sort of mental vision of Mrs Besant in the garb of an *abbess*! It is very curious, but I think something is working in her mind and that she is seeing more clearly the divinity of

[1] The Theosophical Society was founded in 1875 by Colonel H. S. Olcott and Madame H. P. Blavatsky. Its objects are : (1) to form a nucleus of the Universal Brotherhood of Humanity without distinction of race, creed, sex, caste, or colour; (2) to encourage the study of comparative religion, philosophy, and science; (3) to investigate unexplained laws of nature and powers latent in man.

[2] The future Messiah was born near Madras in 1895. It was in 1909 that C. W. Leadbetter (formerly an Anglican clergyman) decided that this youth must be trained as a new manifestation of the Lord Maitreya. The latter had been variously termed in history as Orpheus, Hermes Trismegistus, Vyasa, Krishna, Buddha, Zoroaster, and Jesus Christ. Among his 'Messengers' on earth had been Confucius, Lao-tze, Pythagoras, and Plato. In recent years they had included Master Koot-Hoomi and Madame Blavatsky. Mrs Besant and Mr Leadbetter secured the legal guardianship of Krishnamurti and his brother, and in 1910 Leadbetter published articles in *The Theosophist* giving the thirty previous incarnations of this Indian youth, ranging from 22,662 B.C. to A.D. 624. They appeared in book-form in 1913, entitled *Man, Whence, How, and Whither*, under the joint authorship of Besant and Leadbetter. So Mathew had no excuse for not informing himself of the beliefs now held by most of the priests of his Ancient Catholic Church of England, who, in spite of their cultus of the Lord Maitreya, were quite happy to say Mass according to the Roman rite.

the Catholic system and revelation, which is alone able to satisfy the soul's aspirations and longings. She would be another St Teresa or a St Catherine of Siena—and I have for some time—quite a year —felt that that is her destiny. But we shall see.'[1]

Other letters from Mathew have been preserved which prove conclusively that by the autumn of 1914 even his own family were growing alarmed by his consorting with these curious people for on December 15 he wrote to Canon Farrer:

'. . . My wife and her relations . . . are bitterly hostile to our movement *and* to Theosophy. They have heard of various members of the T.S. becoming associated with, and friendly to us, and of my going on a few occasions to 1 U.W. [Upper Woburn] Place. Their anger is not concealed'[2].

The truth is that Mathew had so many interests, and in the early spring of the following year, when most people were reading what the newspapers had to report about the British and French forces attacking the Turks in the Dardanelles, or rejoicing over the repulse of the Germans near Ypres, the Archbishop of London was devoting himself to careful observations on the flight of thrushes.[3]

He may well have been so pre-occupied with ornithology and ornithoscopy that he was blissfully indifferent, for the moment, to either theosophy or the irresponsible behaviour of two of his hierarchy, now roaming around North America. On December 2, 1914, Bishop Bacon had raised to the episcopate a certain Thomas J. Bensley. On January 12, 1915, Bishop de Landas Berghes et de Rache, whose titles and aristocratic manners may have assisted his acceptance in the Episcopal Church, assisted at the consecration of Hiram Richard Hulse as Bishop of Cuba. This missionary district had been erected in opposition to the metropolitan see of San Cristóbal de Habana, founded in 1787. So it was that, without his authority, Mathew's Old Catholic line of succession found its way into the Protestant Episcopal Church, giving a number of its clergy the belief that their orders were valid in the eyes of Rome.

In the spring of 1915 Mathew's vivid imagination ran riot again. On May 11, four days after the Cunard liner *Lusitania* had been torpedoed by a German submarine off Ireland, he wrote to the

---

[1] ibid., p. 82. For full details of this remarkable lady, see the well documented *The Last Four Lives of Annie Besant*, by A. H. Nethercot (1963), published too late for quotations from it in this book.

[2] ibid., p. 82.

[3] cf. the *Observer*, March 15, 1915.

Rev. J. V. Macmillan, Archbishop Davidson's chaplain, offering to reconsecrate Dr Winnington-Ingram, Bishop of London. That same day he proclaimed:

'The Catholic party in the Established religion of Queen Elizabeth will be invited to come into union with us . . . For this work we received our mission from the spiritual descendant of the British Apostle of the Netherlands, St Willibrord. We are both willing and hopeful that the work may be carried on in union with the Holy See. If His Holiness, Pope Benedict XV, who is a Pontiff of high intelligence and profound learning, anxious to keep abreast of the times, will deign to listen to us, and to assist us with his approval, His Holiness will have no reason to regret the confidence he may repose in us . . . In no other way can the British Empire be restored to Catholic Unity.'

But Benedict XV was too much occupied to consider the friendly advice given him by the Metropolitan of the Ancient Catholic Church of England, for on May 22 Italy declared war against Austria. By that date Mathew had suddenly changed the name of his sect to 'The Old Roman Catholic Church'.

As a change from war-news, *John Bull* devoted several pages to further revelations of Bishop Willoughby's morals, having managed to collect more scurrilous stories. This time Mathew did take notice. He ordered the Titular Bishop of St Pancras to attend a Synod on May 19, but the latter ignored the summons. His Metropolitan dismissed him from the Old Roman Catholic Church, and suspended him from the exercise of holy orders. Canon Williams's plea that the Coadjutor might be reduced to lay status was rejected. Willoughby, backed up by his wife, who appears to have believed in his innocence, wrote to Mathew, pointing out that if legal action were taken against him the results might be embarrassing for all concerned. It would certainly have been awkward for the Old Roman Catholic Archbishop of London if it had come out in court that he had raised a self-unfrocked Anglican parson to the episcopate without taking the trouble to investigate the report that he had been found guilty of homosexual offences.

On the same day that Mathew suspended the Bishop of St Pancras from holy orders and dismissed him from the Old Roman Catholic Church, *The Guardian* printed a letter from the Rev. J. V. Macmillan, Chaplain to the Primate of All England, and a memorandum thereon, with the caption 'An Episcopal Odyssey'. The letter, addressed to 'The Right Rev. Bishop Mathew' said:

Arnold Harris Mathew

'I am directed by the Archbishop of Canterbury to send to you, in accordance with an intimation already given to you by the Bishop of London, a reply to certain recent letters which you have addressed to His Grace and to the Bishop of London. If the Archbishop understands the purport of these letters aright, their suggestion is that you and those who are at present associated with you should be regarded as constituting or representing the Holy Catholic Church in this country, the Church of England remaining as a religious body as associated with the National life but with no claim to a regular or orthodox position in any ecclesiastical sense.

You further suggest that the Bishop of London should submit himself to you for re-ordination, in which case you would be prepared, as the Archbishop understands, to grant him some official recognition. The Archbishop of Canterbury feels that it is hardly possible to treat these letters seriously or to reply to them in terms which you would regard as more discourteous than the silence which you deprecate. But as you press for a reply, the Archbishop thinks it best that I should, on his behalf, enclose to you a memorandum recalling in bare outline some of the incidents of the last eight years. In view of the facts which are therein referred to, the Archbishop feels it to be impossible for him to enter with you into a discussion of the subjects raised, or to regard your letters on these public matters as bearing a confidential character. He is quite willing, therefore, that you should make this letter and the memorandum public if you desire to do so, and he reserves to himself a similar discretion.'

The Memorandum gave the essential facts of Mathew's spectacular career, from 'his preparation for the Anglican Ministry', his 'ordination to the Priesthood in the Church of Rome (1877), his marriage in 1892, his re-admission to the Church of England, and his temporary service, under the name of Count Povoleri, in a London Curacy, with the sanction of Bishop Temple'. Step by step the rest of his odyssey was followed. One paragraph read:

'After his complete breach with the Old Catholics of Holland in 1910, he describes himself as "Catholic Bishop", or, again as "Bishop in England and Ireland of the English Catholic Church", called a few weeks later "The Western Orthodox Catholic Church in Great Britain and Ireland". Shortly afterwards the title used is "Archbishop of London". In March 1911, the title is "Archbishop and Metropolitan of the English Catholic Church". This became "The Catholic Church in England, Latin Uniate Branch", and two

199

months later, "The Catholic Church in England, Latin and Orthodox United", under a leader described as "Archbishop of England", and subsequently as "Sa Grandeur Mgr. A. H. Mathieu, Archevêque de Londres, Comte de Landave, Métropolitain de la Grande-Bretagne et d'Irlande, Evêque provisoire de l'Église Catholique Française".'

After this exposure by the Archbishop of Canterbury, any other man but Mathew would have wanted to hide himself, until he had been forgotten. But the 'Comte de Landave, Métropolitain de la Grande Bretagne et d'Irlande'—head of 'The Catholic Church in England, Latin and Orthodox United'—felt the moment had now come for him to exercise what he believed to be his God-given authority as never before. At the suggestion of Canon Williams he composed a Pastoral Letter which was promulgated from St Willibrord's Oratory, 28 Red Lion Square, Bloomsbury (which had now replaced the ex-Congregational chapel in Islington as the pro-cathedral of the so often-renamed little sect), dated the Feast of the Transfiguration, August 6, 1915 (incidentally Mathew's 64th birthday), was ordered to be read in all churches at the principal Mass the following Sunday. The Metropolitan requested that each priest would, the following day, submit his assent to the orders contained in the said Pastoral.

In the strongest and most authoritative language he 'definitely and absolutely' forbade the reverend clergy and the faithful under his jurisdiction to join either the Theosophical Society or the Order of the Star in the East. If any priests or layfolk belonged to these organizations, they were to resign their membership at once. The Archbishop reminded them that 'it is not permitted to Catholics to accept such doctrines as the transmigration of souls, or reincarnation; neither may any Catholic admit the very painful and blasphemous assertion that our Divine Lord Jesus Christ, far from being that which the Nicene Creed describes Him to be, is simply the reincarnation of some other probably mythical personage'.

A proof that Mathew by this time was no more than a figurehead in the Old Roman Catholic Church is given by the fact that none of his clergy, with the exception of Canon Williams, felt obliged to obey his orders.[1] As to the laity, it is said that only two ladies resigned their membership of the Theosophical Society and

---

[1] The priests who refused to obey Mathew's orders were Wedgwood, King, Gauntlett, Farrer, and James. Later on Seaton, Dean of the Cathedral, threw in his lot with the schismatics, who called themselves 'The Old Catholic Church' until they adopted the title of 'The Liberal Catholic Church' in 1917. (See p. 350.)

the Order of the Star in the East as the result of the Pastoral. In quick succession both Canon Farrer and Canon Wedgwood wrote to the Archbishop, saying that he had broken faith with them, and that they must place their resignation in his hands. Neither of them were prepared to resign from these two organizations, or from any other movement in which they found spiritual truth. Canon Farrer demanded 'complete liberty of action' to form his own judgments as to what he should believe or disbelieve. He was not prepared to accept the Pastoral as an infallible *ex cathedra* statement, or to treat Mathew as if he were Pope.

The Archbishop's next step was to dissolve the Chapter on September 18, and although the London clergy continued to use the Oratory in Red Lion Square for their public services the ancient Catholic Church of England, the Old Roman Catholic Church, and all their predecessors, were reduced to a pile of heresy-haunted dust and rubble. The one-time Archbishop of London, Metropolitan of Great Britain and Ireland, in union with the Orthodox Patriarchates of Antioch and Alexandria, Count Povoleri di Vicenza, and fourth Earl of Landaff, now found ample reasons for regarding himself as an early twentieth-century Athanasius—a 'Father of Orthodoxy', 'Pillar of the Church', and 'Champion of Christ's Divinity'. Like the fourth-century Archbishop of Alexandria, he too had been forsaken by almost every one of his followers; priests and layfolk who had lapsed into heresy. Worse still, not one of the seven bishops he had consecrated in the past five years had remained loyal to him. He deplored the fact that he had raised to the episcopate those two excommunicated Roman Catholic priests, Beale and Howarth. He could hardly find words strong enough to describe that scoundrel Willoughby. Then there was Bacon who had retired into lay communion, and publicly announced his break with the Old Roman Catholic Church.[1] Egerton, formerly a schoolmaster, had been reconciled with the Church of Rome, and was now serving as a common soldier. There were rumours that Scott-Hall had also submitted to the Holy See. Hinton had vanished to North America, where he had joined the Protestant Episcopal Church. Last, but not least, there was Prince-Bishop de Landas Berghes et de Rache, of whom 'Lord Landaff' had had such high hopes. He had been forced to flee to the United States because he was an alien in danger of internment, and so long as the war lasted, he would have to remain on the other side of the Atlantic. Poor Mathew was

[1] See pp. 197, 325.

driven nearly to desperation when five weeks after his Pastoral had been issued on September 26, the unfrocked Bishop of St Pancras had the effrontery to consecrate two Theosophists, Bernard Gauntlett and Robert King.[1]

To add to his troubles the Countess was seeking a legal separation from her archiepiscopal spouse, and claiming the custody of their three children. He himself was reduced to dire poverty, because there were no ecclesiastical funds on which he could draw. To make matters worse, he had set aside his private income to his wife in return for a specified allowance, which she now refused to pay him. Unfortunately no legal deed had ever been signed and witnessed to support his claim.

Ethelbert Lodge, Bromley, Kent (rented from Bishop Bacon), which had been both the archiepiscopal curia and outer-suburban country estate of the Landaffs for several years, had to be given up. His Grace and his domestic chaplain, Canon Williams, retired to more modest quarters at 'The Brambles', Kingsdown, a small village a mile south of Walmer on the coast of Kent. Having little to occupy their time, they set to work on composing a reply to the Archbishop of Canterbury's letter and memorandum published in *The Guardian* the previous May. It took the form of an Open Letter, and was given the same title as that of the caption used by *The Guardian—An Episcopal Odyssey*.[2] The pamphlet was headed with the words: '*Ergo inimicus vobis factus sum verum dicens vobis*'. In the prefatory note Mathew explained: 'In order that it may be possible to form an opinion on the ingenuous implications in the article in question, and incidentally of the good taste displayed in these documents, and in their publication in the Press, I reproduce them *in extenso*.' *An Episcopal Odyssey* is a pathetic story from start to finish. It reveals the simplicity and naivety of its author, and how again and again he was fooled by those he trusted. The final paragraph reads:

'Our body is small and extremely poor. So poor, indeed, that its indigence defies description. My Clergy receive no remuneration or emoluments whatsoever, and work without hope, and, it would seem, without prospect of any earthly reward for their labours. There is not a man at present with me who has not jeopardized his all, and some of my clergy have made sacrifices which they would not allow me to mention, in order to carry on the work

[1] See p. 344.
[2] This pamphlet, privately printed at Kingsdown, near Deal, was sold for 4*d*.

which we honestly believe Almighty God has committed to us. As yet we see little result beyond failure and disappointment. The greatness of our work in the interests of Re-union is the measure of our trial, and, when we have proved ourselves more worthy, we may be blessed to the extent that our toil has not been wholly in vain. The Movement will go on in spite of all difficulties, and notwithstanding the persecution and scorn of our enemies, however severe it may be.'

During that autumn of 1915, when the Archbishop and his private secretary were living alone at 'The Brambles', the British and French forces were being gradually driven off the Gallipoli peninsula. Unless one is mistaken, the body, about which Mathew wrote with such pathos, then consisted of nobody but himself and his domestic chaplain, though there may have been a few layfolk who still remained loyal to their rejected Metropolitan. It is a pity that he did not give the actual numbers of those clergy who were said to be working without any remuneration, or hope of earthly reward.

On December 18, the 'Archbishop of the Old Roman Catholic Rite in Great Britain and Ireland, *de jure* 4th Earl of Landaff of Thomastown, Co. Tipperary' (as he is described on the cover and title page of *An Episcopal Odyssey*) appointed Canon Williams as 'Grand Vicar'; about a fortnight later a notice was sent out that 'the Rite' had been closed down.

On December 31 he added his signature to printed copies of *An Act of Submission to His Holiness Pope Benedict XV*, and posted them to his friends. This three-page leaflet starts with the words:

'Having spent two months, beginning from 18th October 1915, in almost uninterrupted solitude and retreat, in order that I might devote much prayer and study to a careful reconsideration of the position I was induced, in 1907, to adopt, in relation to a Movement which appeared likely to help forward the return of our Nation to the Faith of our Forefathers, it behoves me to inform my friends of the result of this period of serious contemplation.'

Having explained in detail how he had been brought back to a belief in the Primacy of the Roman Pontiff as the Successor of St Peter, and its fundamental importance, he went on:

'When a man perceives clearly that he has blundered, or been misled, it is his obvious duty, at no matter what sacrifice, to acknowledge the fact. This I am now doing, by offering my contrition, with humble, unconditional, and entire submission to His Holiness Pope Benedict XV.

'I have, therefore, sent my petition for absolution from censures and for restoration to the visible unity of the Church, to His Eminence Cardinal Merry del Val, Prefect of the Holy Office.'[1]

On January 8, 1916, the following notice appeared in *The Tablet*: 'The Rev. Arnold Harris Mathew, whose submission to the Holy See has already been announced, writes to us with regard to his position, as follows: "Although the Orders of the Dutch schismatical clergy were, down to 1910, undisputed in Rome, I make no claim to be regarded as a bishop, or to exercise episcopal functions, or to use any episcopal insignia. I desire to conform in everything to whatever may be the commands or wishes of the Holy See. Neither do I intend to claim even to exercise priestly functions, unless and until as I earnestly hope, this privilege may be permitted to me. *It is my firm resolve which nothing will ever alter*, to obey the commands of the Holy Father, whose word I am perfectly willing to await, and I shall do nothing whatsoever, either publicly or privately, in any ecclesiastical matters without the permission of Superiors".'

About the same time that this statement appeared in *The Tablet*, Canon Williams—still holding his status as 'Grand Vicar' and styling himself 'Administrator of the vacant see'—informed readers of *The Guardian* that the Old Catholic movement in Britain had been wound up.

Thirty-three years after this event, Archbishop Mathew's successor as Metropolitan explained that his reason for making his announcement was that the Theosophical clergy had seized the opportunity offered by Mathew's sudden and unexpected resignation, to claim that they themselves constituted the Old Roman Catholic Church. He stated that he himself was far from sure that his ecclesiastical superior would 'burn his boats', recalling how often in the past he had changed his mind at the last moment. He also suspected that Mathew would demand 'reasonable terms' before he made his submission to the Holy See, and that he was 'not nearly so sanguine as he was, as to the fulfilment of the conditions which he had been led to expect as almost certain to be granted'.[2]

---

[1] So sure was Mathew that he had 'come home' at long last that he went to the expense of having a small notice printed, stating that he had 'offered his unconditional, humble submission to the Sovereign Pontiff'. These slips were stuck on to the covers of copies of *An Episcopal Odyssey* sold between January 1 and March 13, 1916.
[2] cf. *Supplement to the Diocesan Chronicle*, May 1949, p. 6.

Arnold Harris Mathew

Evidently the terms proposed by Benedict XV, Cardinal Merry del Val—more likely Cardinal Bourne—were not considered 'reasonable'. The Archbishop, encouraged by his 'Grand Vicar', came to the conclusion that it was his duty to revive that moribund remnant of the Old Roman Catholic Church in Great Britain and Ireland, which had not been perverted by Theosophical heresies. On March 5, 1916, in order to prevent confusion with the schismatic clergy, he renamed his sect 'The Western Uniate Catholic Church'. By the first Sunday in Lent, 1916, he had resumed his purple cassock and archiepiscopal regalia. That *'firm resolve which nothing will ever alter'* had lasted no more than two months.

Even more incredible, considering all that he had said in the past about the invalidity of Anglican orders, and that more than once he had informed the Archbishop of Canterbury that the Church of England had no claim to be the Catholic Church in this country, and that its bishops were merely state officials, was his writing to Dr Davidson, to suggest that his little flock should become a sort of Anglican Uniate Church. With an equal lack of consistency, he made up his mind at the same time to raise Canon Williams to the episcopate. On March 25, a reply came from Dr Davidson, asking Mathew to visit him at Canterbury any day convenient to him for a friendly talk. To quote from what the bishop-elect wrote in after years:

'Both the Archbishop and I were very puzzled as to what could be behind this move. Previously Dr Davidson had circulated both here and in the United States of America a very damaging statement which he called a *Memorandum* which contained many false statements with regard to Archbishop Mathew. The latter requested me to prepare a reply to this Memorandum.[1] I did so, and copies were sent to the Holy Father, the King, many of the Cardinals, High Officers of State, a number of important Dignitaries in this country, and every Anglican Bishop throughout the world. Dr Davidson was taken by surprise. It was undoubtedly the greatest blow to his prestige he had ever received, and if Archbishop Mathew had not himself ruined its effect by his ill-timed and precipitate offer of submission to the Holy See, which had been urged upon him by certain Catholic ecclesiastics who themselves composed the terms on which his submission was

---

[1] It was Williams who actually wrote *An Episcopal Odyssey*, though published under Mathew's name.

offered, our freedom from further Anglican molestation would have been secured.'

Five days later Mathew wrote to his friend Allen Hay, the vicar of South Mymms, explaining what an advantage it would be for the Church of England to be in communion with the Western Uniate Catholic Church, just as he had formerly pointed out to Cardinal Merry del Val the benefits such a union would confer upon the Church of Rome. He said:

'I had given up all hope of that, when I made up my mind to offer to submit to Papa, but Papa's Merry deputy is a Spaniard, and appropriately, an Inquisitor, and I never liked the Inquisition or the Inquisitor in *any* shape.'

Hay was asked to 'besiege Heaven' that the meeting with the Archbishop of Canterbury would have the desired result—'All depends on that'.[1]

On the Feast of the Seven Sorrows of Our Lady, April 14, 1916, Archbishop Mathew raised to the episcopate Bernard Mary Williams as his perpetual coadjutor with right of succession. The ceremony took place in the private oratory at 'The Brambles', Kingsdown. The following morning the two prelates went to Canterbury, but the interview between the two Archbishops took place alone. For (to quote the words of the newly consecrated Coadjutor): 'Dr Davidson was well aware that he could not attain his object were I present'. Williams always seems to have had a tremendous idea of his influence in the affairs of the Old Roman Church.[2]

Davidson told Mathew, not mincing his words, that his 'relation successively to the Church of England, then to the Church of Rome, then to the Church of England again, then to the Old Catholics, then to the Eastern Church, then to the independent organization (under his headship), then to the Church of Rome again, and now to the Church of England again', gave 'a story of loyalties and disloyalties' which, in his opinion, was 'incompatible with any adequate sense of the responsibilities belonging to membership in an organized body which has Christ as its head'. The Primate of all England remarked that he could not 'in honesty refrain from pointing out' to Archbishop Mathew 'the position in which men' had been placed who had been ordained or consecrated by him

---

[1] Letter in possession of Dr F. Brittain.
[2] A detailed account of this interview, as recalled by Dr Davidson, will be found in G. K. A. Bell's *Randall Davidson* (1938), p. 1021.

'whether validly or invalidly'. What was their position now? He reminded Mathew that he had purported to consecrate at least eight bishops, and that he had ordained many more men to the priesthood. He could not understand why this utterly irresponsible prelate had now written to him stating that he had decided to 'terminate the organization', and asked: 'Is this a tolerable position to maintain?'

While the Archbishop of Canterbury was reprimanding the Metropolitan of the Western Uniate Catholic Church (Old Roman Catholic Rite) the newly consecrated Coadjutor was waiting impatiently in a Canterbury hotel. Thirty-three years afterwards he recalled that meeting:

'Archbishop Mathew should not have accepted a private verbal apology for such a world-wide injury, but such was his guilelessness, foolishness, if you will, that he did so, and agreed, at Dr Davidson's very earnest request, to arrest the further issue of our reply to his Memorandum, which had not at that time reached the hands of the general public.[1] Dr Davidson, and *not* Archbishop Mathew, then suggested as a *quid pro quo*, that a way should be found in which Archbishop Mathew and his Clergy should "cooperate"—that was the word used by Dr Davidson—with the Anglican Communion, with Archbishop Mathew in due course. Mrs Davidson sent a telephone message expressing her regret that she had been prevented from returning in time to preside at tea, as she had intended to do, and which I had impressed upon him the necessity of declining. Archbishop Mathew returned immediately to the hotel where I awaited him, and before all else a precise account of this important interview was written down for record, so that there might be no mistake with regard to any particular concerning it at any future time.'[2]

It is difficult not to be amused at the attitude of the Lord Archbishop of Caer-Glow—to give Williams the title he assumed in after years—and it is interesting to compare his account of that 'important interview' with Mathew's recollections of it, given in a letter to Allen Hay dated April 19, 1916, i.e. four days after it took place:

'I was never more agreeably surprised in my life than I was by my interview with the Archbishop. I have rarely met anyone who

[1] Apparently Williams had forgotten about that little slip pasted on to all copies sent out after Mathew had decided to get reconciled with the Roman Church.
[2] *Supplement to the Diocesan Chronicle*, p. 5.

received me with greater feelings of respect and reverence, and I feel that *doctrinally* he is on all essential points quite what one would wish, though he may not be *au fait* at matters of ceremonial, or attach much importance to externals. After all, such things are purely secondary, and if the *Faith* is right the rest is of *minor* consequence. He seemed to me to be very liberal minded, and what impressed me most of all was his *humility* which edified me extremely. I think him a really fine character, one who could not easily be replaced when he goes to his reward. For some strange reason the great historic throne in Canterbury Cathedral has been placed on the wrong side and in the wrong place. The Archbishop in a suitable mitre and on his throne in the right place would make a very imposing figure as the spiritual chief of the Church of England.'[1]

But Bishop Williams did not trust Archbishop Davidson, and after he and Archbishop Mathew got back to Kingsdown, he continued to stress that it was not safe to believe the Primate of All England, although from the point of view of doctrine he might be 'what one would wish'. Although he had never met the Primate, he was convinced that he was 'undoubtedly wholly insincere'; and that, in his opinion, there were 'a thousand reasons' against Old Roman Catholics (or Western Uniate Catholics) having anything to do with the Church of England. After all, how could Catholics consort with Protestants? What right had a *Protestant* Archbishop of Canterbury, whose orders were almost certainly invalid, to impose terms on a *Catholic* prelate who 'by the Grace of God' was 'Archbishop of the London District of the Old Roman Catholic Church and Metropolitan'? In the end, Mathew acted on the advice of his Coadjutor, and decided that the whole thing was preposterous. *Ecclesia Anglicana* was dismissed as beneath contempt.

The Western Catholic Uniate Church must be extended, and so, at Kingsdown on the Feast of the Visitation of Our Lady, July 1, 1916, James Columba McFall was consecrated as Bishop for Ireland.[2] Looking back on this incident in 1949, Williams wrote:

'In this unfortunate matter of providing a Bishop for work in Ireland, Archbishop Mathew was overborne. I would have prevented this had I known of the negotiations on time . . . but he had been persuaded that since this Bishop was required for Ireland,

---

[1] Letter in possession of Dr F. Brittain.
[2] McFall had been ordained priest by Mathew in 1910, and had received one vote at the episcopal election held in 1914, which resulted in Willoughby being consecrated as Bishop of St Pancras. For further details of his career, see pp. 340–342, 444, 445.

the matter need not be referred to me. Since our jurisdiction does not extend to Ireland the Irish bishop's consecration is irregular, and he is not recognized by this Rite.'[1]

What Mathew had written about the indigence of his clergy was certainly applicable to himself by the summer of 1916. He and his wife had now separated by mutual consent. For two years she had discontinued paying him his allowance. There seemed to be little or no hope that the *de jure* Earl of Landaff would ever obtain possession of the vast Irish estates of Thomastown, situated in the Golden Vale, with the River Suir flowing to the east. It was here that one of his wealthy eighteenth century ancestors had built a splendid mansion, in which he dispensed lavish hospitality to forty guests so long as they cared to stay with him. This manner of life would have just suited the Archbishop; even more so his wife. Not knowing what to do next, he toyed with the idea of retiring to a cave in the chalk cliffs near the South Foreland, to lead an eremitical life, and so prepare for death; celebrating Mass in solitude, and keeping body and soul alive on a few beans, a little oil, and water.[2]

At the same time, realizing that he had had no luck with the Archbishop of Canterbury, Mathew made a desperate appeal to the Bishop of Durham to give him a benefice; explaining that he was quite prepared to be re-ordained conditionally if this would make things easier. But Dr Moule—a devout Evangelical, who was first Principal of Ridley Hall, Cambridge—reminded the former Archbishop of London that he was validly ordained already, being in Roman Catholic orders.[3]

By this time Mathew seems to have grown aggressively anti-Roman and strongly pro Anglican, judging from the letter he wrote to Allen Hay on May 16, 1916.

'My one desire has all along been to try to do *something* for re-union. Rome slams her doors in my face and will listen to nothing but the most grovelling submission and subservience. . . . There should be a little public decency somewhere, and an act of union should be publicly made and signed by those who would, if allowed to do so, come with me. There might be several priests and one or two bishops.'[4]

[1] *Letter addressed to His Grace the Lord Archbishop of Canterbury*, October 27, 1947. Williams must have forgotten that: (1) he himself signed McFall's instrument of consecration; (2) Mathew first styled himself 'Metropolitan of Great Britain *and Ireland*' as far back as 1911.
[2] cf. Mar Georgius, op. cit., p. 25.
[3] From a letter in possession of Dr F. Brittain.
[4] ibid.

Arnold Harris Mathew

As might have been expected, nothing came of this dream to unite a handful of Anglican clergy and the Western Uniate Catholic Church.[1] On March 25, 1917, the indigent Archbishop, who had been forsaken by all but a very few friends, drew up a document, addressed to Bernard Mary Williams. Giving him the style of 'Old Catholic Bishop of the Western District', he wrote:

'In the event of my relinquishment of the charge communicated to me at my consecration at Utrecht on the 28th April, 1908, or in the event of my death, I wish that you may take the place in relation to the Movement which then will be vacated by me. The Register of Ordinations and any other papers, etc. there may be, which relate to the Movement, will be handed over to you.'[2]

The reference to his 'consecration at Utrecht', and 'the Movement', suggest that Mathew had suddenly put himself back (in imagination) to the status of Old Catholic Regionary Bishop for England. Bishop Williams managed to raise enough money to maintain his Metropolitan in reasonable comfort, though hardly what his exalted position demanded.[3]

New quarters were found for the Archbishop at Lees Cottage, Walmer, Kent. Once again he began to correspond with Dr Davidson, requesting permission to officiate in Anglican churches. The Primate refused to consider the idea, and told him, that if he were formally admitted to communion with Canterbury, he would have to be satisfied with the status of a layman. Mathew also appealed to the Bishop of London, and his letters were sent on to Archbishop Davidson. On September 12, 1917, the latter wrote to the former:

'The story has now become a pathetic one. It is pitiable to think of Bishop Mathew's desertion by the lady whom he wrote about as

---

[1] Mathew's authority was defied on October 3 and 4, 1916, when Bishop de Landas, on his own initiative, consecrated W. H. F. Brothers and Carmel H. Carfora. Before long these two prelates set up rival Old Catholic bodies in the U.S.A. (See pp. 413–439.)

[2] Mar Georgius, op. cit., p. 25.

[3] It is probable that on August 22, 1917, Mathew consecrated two Anglican incumbents—John Arnold Carter and William Noel Lambert—but no documentary evidence is forthcoming. Carter, who had also been one of Mathew's clergy and a member of his cathedral chapter, was re-ordained in the Church of England in 1920–1. Having served several curacies, he was appointed rector of Hampton Poyle in 1925. After holding many offices, including that of Examining Chaplain to the Bishop of Coventry (1946–51), he became vicar of Lillington, Warwickshire, since 1927, and retired on June 30, 1958.

Lambert's earlier career has been related on p. 178. When he joined the Church of England, Dr Winnington-Ingram appointed him as curate at St Saviour's, Poplar (1913–16), and without re-ordaining him *sub conditione*, as he did with apparently all other priests ordained by Mathew so that they should have civil law status. Later on Lambert became vicar of St Gabriel's, South Bromley (1916–35). He died in 1954, as rector of South Norwood, Middlesex.

Countess of Landaff, and whose picture he sent to us with pride. What is meant by her being able to claim the control of her children if she deserts her husband, I do not in the least understand. The pamphlet about his earldom, and the pictures of his countess, look strangely now. It is also pathetic that he should now find himself in financial straits, if that is indeed so. I fear that the fomenting of schisms, and the founding of Churches, have involved much expenditure on some one's part, both in East and West, and it is possible that this has hit him hard. I feel intensely sorry for him, foolish and harmful as his doings have been . . . Bishop Mathew is, to the best of my belief (though of course I speak without knowledge of what is said by his wife or anyone else against him), a virtuous old fellow, with a delightfully attractive manner, a fine appearance, a certain amount of ecclesiastical learning, and a strange lack of balance. His harmfulness has lain in the real lightness (strenuously as he denies it) with which he has played fast and loose with great questions of Church Order, and thus set going, in different ways and in different lands, schisms which it may take many years to heal. He has given to ecclesiastical adventurers less honest than himself, an example fraught with abundant peril None the less, I have a personal regard for him, and although he has only himself to thank for his present position, I should like to be able to help him, in some way which did not do harm to the Church wherein I am set to be a responsible custodian of what is right. I should certainly fail as such a custodian if I were to say now, what neither you nor any other Bishop whom I have met would wish me to say, that after all that has passed, we propose to recognize him as one who might rightly hold the trust of ministry in the Church of England.'[1]

Various people suggested suitable jobs for this venerable founder of churches. Some felt it would be safe enough to make him the chaplain to a hospital or home; others a secretary or librarian. But Dr Davidson was adamant that such posts would be dangerous, remarking that Mathew was 'not the sort of man to fit in appropriately to work of a secretarial sort'. As to placing him as 'a duly accredited priest of the Church of England in charge of the religious life of a public institution', Dr Davidson was certain that, so far as he could judge, it would be 'wholly wrong'.

Nevertheless Archbishop Mathew still had such a high opinion of himself, believing that he was in an utterly different category to

[1] Bell, op. cit., p. 1022.

other prelates of autocephalous churches in England, that he wrote
to his Coadjutor, Mgr Williams on November 17, 1917, grumbling
about the schismatic activities of Bishops Marsh-Edwards, Vernon
Herford, A. C. A. McLaglen, J. C. Whitebrook, James McFall,
and 'Stevens the Patriarch'; dismissing them with the words:
'*What* a crew!'[1] Moreover from the point of view of the Most
Rev. The Right Hon. Archbishop, none of these over-the-border
prelates were fit to consort socially with the direct descendant of
Gwaethvoed, a legendary chieftain of Gwent, the progenitor of
Mathew of Llandaff in the reign of Richard II, from whom sprung
the lines of Mathew of Annefield, Thurles and Thomastown in
Ireland, as well as those of Mathew of Castell-y-Mynach in
South Wales.

Had Mathew made another attempt to be reconciled with the
Church of Rome, it would have been more difficult to regularize his
position. The truth which he appears to have forgotten is that he
had been ordained for the Western District of Scotland in 1877,
and that he had been found guilty of many canonical crimes and
offences since he lapsed into Unitarianism in 1889. Most of the
censures and vindictive penalties (as they are termed in the *Codex
Juris Canonici*) that affected him were reserved to the Holy See.
The former Father Matthews had continued to break the laws of
the Catholic and Roman Church by taking a wife in 1892, and,
later on, getting himself raised to the episcopate in a schismatic
body. The one-time Anglican theological student and priest of the
Latin rite had indeed wrecked his life, though as Archbishop
Davidson remarked: 'He has only himself to thank for his present
position'.

Even if no Church wanted him as either a priest or a prelate
there were social functions to which he was welcomed because of
his alleged earldom. It must have given him great satisfaction to
be invited to a private reception held in Bayswater to honour the
ninety-second birthday of the Empress Eugénie. The *Indépendance
Belge* reported on May 10, 1919, that among those present were
'Monseigneur l'Archevêque Marquis de Povoleri, Comte de
Landaff', who was accompanied by his son 'Comte de Povoleri,
Vicomte Mathew', and his daughter 'Lady Margherita Mathew'.
Other distinguished royal and noble guests were 'la Princesse
Saliha d'Égypte; le Prince Konitza d'Albanie; la Princesse Paléo-
logue; Prince Paul Salvator de Pologne; la Princesse Alice Tyan;

---

[1] cf. Mar Georgius, *A Twig on the Tree of Life*, p. 14.

la Princesse Sophie Duleep Singh; le Prince Ferdinand Tyan; et la Princesse Carina Barclay de Tolly'. The one-time friend and consecrator of Rudolph Francis Edward St Patrick Alphonsus Ghislain de Gramont Hamilton de Lorraine-Brabant, Prince de Landas Berghes et de Rache, and Duc de St Winock, must have been in his element at that aristocratic *soirée*, hob-nobbing with the minor royalty of Europe. He must have been as happy as Frank Harris at the fabulous dinner party he arranged at Claridge's in 1891 for Princess Alice of Monaco, widow of the Duke de Richelieu, at which Oscar Wilde and George Moore enlivened the conversation. No doubt it recalled the far off days when, as the Rev. Count Povoleri, he had played the part of a curate at a fashionable West End Anglican church. The scene described is almost evocative of a Ronald Firbank novel, or an Edwardian ruritanian musical comedy at Daly's Theatre. What a marvellous drawing Aubrey Beardsley could have made of 'Monseigneur l'Archevêque Marquis de Povoleri, Comte de Landaff' in his cappa magna— worthy of those he did to illustrate *Mademoiselle de Maupin*.

Once again he had renewed his correspondence with Archbishop Davidson, and two months before the Bayswater party, the latter had reminded him in much the same words as on previous occasions:

'You have been in a very marked way, quite conscientiously and genuinely, a promoter of "Schism" in the true sense of that word. Your ecclesiastical position is different to what it has been, and you claim at my hands a recognition which would be met on your part by the kind of declaration of allegiance to Anglicanism which you desire to make. The question, however, is what line ought the Anglican Bishops to take towards one who during a considerable series of years set on foot and promoted what cannot, I think, be fairly regarded otherwise than a schismatic Church in England.'[1] Mathew could not or would not understand this point of view. He continued to build castles in the air, with cloud-capped towers, paranoiacally refusing to face up to reality. He seems to have felt that the Anglican bishops were persecuting him, whereas most of them hardly knew that he existed; or if they did, regarded him as a pathetic eccentric. In September 1919 he wrote to Dr Davidson, almost accusing him of libel and defamation of character saying:

'I have endured thirty years' persecution, at the hands of certain

[1] Letter in possession of Dr F. Brittain.

people, and at the close of life this assault comes as a blow from one whom I wished to look upon with respect if not as a friend.'[1]

By this time Allen Hay, Vicar of South Mymms, had provided him with a home in a cottage in the village.[2] Here the venerable white-haired prelate worshipped in the parish church, but only as one of the congregation. The ritual and ceremonial were more ornate than what he had ever managed to achieve in either of his little so-called 'pro-cathedrals'. But permission was never asked on his behalf from the Bishop of London for him to celebrate the Communion Service. The Vicar did enquire if the Bishop would allow the old man to sit in choir wearing his episcopal robes and insignia. There was no question of his pontificating.

Still regarding himself as an Honorary Prelate of the Order of Corporate Reunion, an office he had accepted in 1912, Mathew accepted it as his duty to validate the orders of any Anglican clergymen who sought him out in his retreat at South Mymms. These clandestine ceremonies conducted in the cottage included conditional baptism and confirmation. It was understood that no fee or reward of any description must be offered or would be accepted by the Archbishop for services rendered.[3] How many secret ordinations were performed during the summer and autumn of 1919 is not known, but letters prove that early in December a certain Anglican chaplain in the B.E.F. was able to sail for the Far East with the feeling that he was a 'real priest'. It is possible that Mathew performed another of these surreptitious ordinations on December 19. He died suddenly the following day, the Vigil of St Thomas, the doubting Apostle. Unlike Charles–Maurice de Talleyrand-Périgord, Bishop of Autun in 1838, the Most Rev. the Right Hon. Earl of Landaff had no Catholic niece at hand to call in a priest before his death, so he never got the chance to make a solemn declaration in which he openly disavowed 'the great errors which . . . had troubled and afflicted the Catholic, Apostolic and Roman Church, and in which he himself had had the misfortune to fall'. As a would-be member of the Established Church he was buried with Anglican rites near the south door of the village church. The wording on his tombstone is as follows:

[1] ibid.
[2] The wording in some of the many letters written to Hay suggests that Mathew may have 'validated' his orders, or even raised him to the episcopate, although there is no documentary evidence of his consecration. Hay is now dead.
[3] See p. 85.

Arnold Harris Mathew

Of your charity pray for the good estate of
ARNOLD HARRIS MATHEW, D.D.
Bishop of the Old Catholic Church
De Jure Earl of Landaff of Thomastown, Co. Tipperary
who entered into rest 20th December 1919
*"Behold a great priest who in his days
pleased God and was found just".*

As he died unshriven and unhouselled, it is somewhat doubtful
whether this epitaph can be correctly applied to such an erratic and
unfortunate individual. But it is not for us to judge him; only God
can judge the hearts of men. It is best to leave Arnold Harris
Mathew with the prayer: 'May he rest in peace'.[1]

Within a few hours of his death his Register was got hold of by
some interested parties (said to be Anglican clergymen) without
permission of Bishop Williams. This Register has been recovered,
and it contains several disguised erasures, but no ostensible references to the consecrations of Lambert and Carter.[2] A copy of the
Register, made by the Archbishop himself, was given to Williams
before the former's death; in this he states that he had performed
no consecrations than those indicated. Mathew's episcopal seal,
some documents and other papers also disappeared mysteriously.
Thus any document with his seal would not in itself be a proof of
consecration or ordination. Nevertheless there would seem to be
sufficient evidence that two or three Anglican clergymen did
receive the episcopate from his hands, though, for obvious reasons,
they kept it secret.[3]

---

[1] Mathew has another epitaph with a high-sounding Latin inscription in the half-
restored chapel at Buckden, Huntingdonshire, erected by his disciple, R. Edelston
Bartorde Montalbo, Envoy to Great Britain of the Republic of San Marino.

[2] See p. 210 n. 3.

[3] cf. H. R. T. Brandreth, *Episcopi Vagantes and the Anglican Church* (2nd ed., 1961),
p. 37, n. 5.

CHAPTER VII

CHURCHES CLAIMING THE FERRETTE
SUCCESSION

Ancient British Church,
United Armenian Catholic Church,
Free Protestant Episcopal Church of England,
Free Catholic Church, Apostolic Catholic Church,
English Orthodox Church,
English Episcopal Church,
South African Episcopal Church, Indian Orthodox Church,
Evangelical Church of England,
Western Orthodox Catholic Church, etc.

Whereas the Vilatte and Mathew streams are well authenticated and documented, the Ferrette succession is very weak in satisfactory proof of its relation to the bodies mentioned in this chapter. So far as can be discovered, no convincing evidence has ever been produced proving a clear link between these sects and Mar Julius, Bishop of Iona, and with the Jacobite Patriarch of Antioch.[1] On the other hand, it could be that still earth-bound spirits 'as yet unready for the Great Return' have delivered messages, just as they are alleged to have done to the psychic archeologist, Frederick Bligh Bond, that the Syrian and Celtic Churches really were quite closely connected.[2]

[1] There are persons who like to think that there was a pre-Ferrette succession, but the trouble is to run it to earth after the lapse of time. The theory is that it was either (1) some offshoot of the Nonjurors, which survived Bishop Charles Booth, a watchmaker in Manchester, who removed to Ireland, where he died in 1805, and who may have consecrated a successor; (2) Russian or Greek Orthodox lines perhaps connected in some way with J. J. Overbeck's activities. (See pp. 48–52.) There is also an unlikely story of an unidentified Scottish Episcopalian bishop sometime about 1866 who claimed to have received a valid succession. During the 1860s two gentlemen signed their letters + Oswin and + B.K., and J. T. Seccombe also prefixed a cross to his signature. But this does not imply that they claimed episcopal status, because Anglican monks and nuns have done the same, not to mention Augustus Welby Pugin.
[2] cf. *The Gate of Remembrance* (Oxford, 1921), p. 97; also pp. 422, 423 of this book.

Churches Claiming the Ferrette Succession

If, as did the credulous Fr Ignatius of Llanthony, one is prepared to accept the theory that the British people is ultimately descended from the ten Israelite tribes which were taken captive into Assyria in 722–721 B.C., and thereafter wholly disappeared from Hebrew history, then it is not so difficult to believe in the medieval legends of the Holy Grail. They relate how St Joseph of Arimathea found his way from Palestine to Britain, founded a church in the Vale of Avalon, where rites and ceremonies were performed like those of the Syro-Egyptian Church; St Joseph said to have been the emissary of St Mark the Evangelist. There could be a substance of truth in these legends, because serious historians are usually agreed that the Copts before the Moslem conquest of Egypt were great travellers; that a colony of them settled on the Isle of Lérins, whence some found their way to Ireland.[1] So it may be that the dormant consciousness of those who accept the Grail and similar legends has received messages by automatic writing or other similar psychic methods not approved by the Roman Church that an invisible and intangible Syro-Egyptian Church survived (like a Rip Van Winkle) in England for roughly eighteen hundred years, waiting until some magician's wand could awaken it again. No matter: it is safer not to accept these fascinating tales on their face-value. They *may* be true, but we cannot be *sure*.

So far as external and objective evidence is concerned, however, the story only begins with the arrival in England of Leon Chechemian in 1885. Previous to this everything is more or less a mirage. He claimed to have fled from Asia before the advancing wave of Turkish persecution, in which the Armenians were the chief victims. He was utterly destitute, and for between times, earned his living in a stable and within sandwich-boards. Appeals to both Dr Temple, Bishop of London, and to Dr Benson, Archbishop of Canterbury led to nothing, and this impoverished Armenian was driven to desperation.

Having had no luck with the Anglicans, Chechemian managed to find the money to pay his fare to Edinburgh, where he was welcomed with open arms by the Scottish Reformation Society, then, as now, constrained by motives of conscience to expose the evils of Romanism. He lived on the charity of some of its members, attended St Luke's Free Kirk, and improved his English by studying at New College, a Presbyterian theological establishment. He was given an enthusiastic reception at the Annual Meeting of this

[1] cf. F. E. Warren, *Liturgy and Ritual in the Celtic Church* (1881), p. 56.

Society on March 7, 1887, and was exhibited as an innocent Protestant victim of the sinister power of Romanism, and earnestly commended to the kindness of sincere Christians, for he had no other means of support. In April 1887, *The Bulwark*, the official organ of the Scottish Reformation Society, published the first of a series of articles in which Chechemian told the story of what he regarded as a miraculous conversion.[1]

He related that as a boy he had been forced to join the Armenian Uniate Church, and so fell into the clutches of the Scarlet Woman. Pious Presbyterians must have revelled in lurid revelations of clerical scandals which presented Popery as they had always supposed it to be. This spiritual Aeneid recorded how Chechemian had received all the minor and major orders within a week. After his ordination to the priesthood at Malatia in 1866, he was appointed to several parishes in Armenia. Had he not been a person of unusual ability, it is doubtful if he would have managed to acquire the rank of *vartapet* in 1878.[2] His memories contain stories of difficulties with bishops as well as of immorality among the priests. By 1881 Chechemian had escaped from Armenia and was in Constantinople. Here he tried to get financial help from the Anglican chaplain by expressing his detestation of Popery, while still celebrating the Armenian Liturgy in the Church of St John Chrysostom at Pera. After many adventures he managed to effect his escape from Turkey, and reached England, with little more than the clothes he wore. He complained bitterly of the 'cruel' way he was treated by both the Bishop of London and the Archbishop of Canterbury, explaining that this was 'because God made their hearts harder than stones'. He quoted a letter from Dr Temple, dated June 4, 1886, in which the Bishop pointed out that he had not invited this Armenian priest to London, and could not undertake to maintain him. So Chechemian said that 'the curse of Judas, which was given from God' had been inherited by these two Anglican bishops, also by Mr Curtis, the Church of England Chaplain at Constantinople. Nowhere in these memories did Chechemian claim to have been raised to the episcopate. He recorded how he was ordained a priest, and was made a *vartapet*, using the word

---

[1] Vol. XVI (Edinburgh, 1887).
[2] The office of *vartapet* is peculiar to the Armenian Church. It is conferred by a sort of ordination ceremony. *Vartapets* are celibate, like bishops, or widowed secular priests. They are given responsible posts, and are divided into minor and major classes. Their chief duties are preaching and teaching. A pastoral staff, known as a *gavazan*, is allowed them which is similar to a Byzantine bishop's crozier.

'doctor' as more intelligible to Scottish Presbyterian readers.[1]

After about two years in Scotland, the former Uniate ecclesiastic went over to Ireland where in May, 1889, he conducted services in Berry Street Church and St Enoch's Church, Belfast. A newspaper reported that 'Dr Chechemian enjoys the confidence of and is warmly recommended by the most eminent men in the Presbyterian Church of Scotland. But he is also well in favour with the Anglican Church, being permitted to preach in the Church of Ireland by permission of the Archbishops of Armagh and Dublin; and in the Church of England by the Archbishop of Canterbury and the Bishop of London, the latter recommending him as "a bishop of a church other than the established church".' This last statement suggests that Dr Temple was not aware of the precise status of a *vartapet*—or did Chechemain mislead him?

Shortly after this a pamphlet was published, entitled *An Eastern's Steps from Darkness to Light.* Chechemian's *apologia* greatly moved the fourth Baron Plunket, then Archbishop of Dublin. In 1890 he received the ex-Armenian Catholic priest into the Church of Ireland, and licensed him as a clergyman of the diocese.

Nevertheless there is a strange story, told by Mar Georgius and others for which no documentary evidence has been produced, so far as is known, that on August 15, 1890, Chechemian founded what he called 'The United Armenian Catholic Church in the British Isles', and constituted himself its first Primate.

About the same time the mysterious Mar Theophilus (Stevens) appeared out of the clouds; more correctly, from a back street in Hackney. What he had been doing, other than playing the organ, since his alleged consecration by Mar Pelagius (Morgan) in 1879, is uncertain, but fortunately he had a wife who was able to support him. There is a tale that some time in 1890, Stevens, assisted by Bishop A. S. Richardson, formerly of the Reformed Episcopal Church in the United States[2], laid hands on Chechemian. So

---

[1] But it is stated that in after years his episcopal seal bore the words: 'Consecrated a Bishop at Malatia, Asia Minor, 1879'.

[2] The Reformed Episcopal Church came into being in 1873, when Bishop George D. Cummins and a number of clergy and layfolk withdrew from the Protestant Episcopal Church by way of protest against the growth of Ritualism. Alfred A. Richardson was made a bishop at Philadelphia in 1879. Later on he was judged bankrupt and sought refuge in Britain, where a branch of the Reformed Episcopal Church had already been formed. An attempt to unite it with the Free Church of England, founded in 1844 by some evangelical clergy and laymen of the Established Church, who were opposed to the Tractarian movement, did not succeed, and it was not until 1927 that these two bodies, which upheld the Protestant and Evangelical forms of worship, were finally united, and given the official title of 'The Free Church of England'. Bishop Richardson,

far as is known no instrument of consecration has ever been produced. What appears to be a recent addition to the story handed down by prelates of the Ferrette sucession, is that Chechemian was given the title of Mar Leon, Archbishop of Selsey in the Ancient British Church. It is difficult not to suspect that the whole tale must be apocryphal. If this consecration was carried out *sub conditione*, as is usually stated, then it looks as if neither Stevens nor Richardson realized that a vartapet has no episcopal status—actually a doctor of divinity exercising the office of an archdeacon.[1] In any case they could only give to this Armenian, who had been ordained priest by a bishop in communion with the Holy See, such episcopal orders whose 'validity' would be questioned by many, since Richardson's orders derived from the Protestant Episcopal Church. There appears to be no documentary proof of either Morgan or Stevens's consecrations, and no clear knowledge of what rite was used—although there is a tale that the East Syrian rite was adopted for each ceremony. Thus Chechemian is the very narrow 'bottle-neck' through which the alleged Syro-Jacobite Ferrette succession has been transmitted to our day, and many would think the transmission of doubtful value. The Free Protestant Episcopal Church of England, of which Chechemian was the first Archbishop after its foundation in 1897, avoids the difficulty by stating incorrectly that 'on April 23, 1878, the Rev. Leon Chechemian was consecrated Bishop of Malatia (in the great Cathedral of Malatia) by the Archbishop Chorchorunian and received the titles Most Honourable Lord Doctor and Very Reverend'.[2] The mystery is increased

---

having performed a number of ordinations, and helped to consecrate Thomas Greenland at Christ Church, Carlton Hill, London, June 11, 1888, died at Boulogne-sur-Mer in 1907. The Free Church of England—not to be confused with either the Evangelical Church of England, Free Protestant Episcopal Church, or English Episcopal Church—now has about forty churches in Britain, the present Primus being Bishop Frank · Vaughan, D.D., consecrated in 1913. A revised edition of its own version of The Book of Common Prayer was published in 1956. (See *A History of the Free Church of England, otherwise called The Reformed Episcopal Church* (2nd ed., 1960.)

[1] Supporters of the Ferrette line of succession say that this ceremony took place in order to surmount the difficulty that an Armenian Uniate Bishop is merely an auxiliary and canonically debarred from exercising episcopal functions without the specific commission from his ecclesiastical superiors. But can one believe that two staunch Protestants like Stevens and Richardson would have bothered about details of Armenian Uniate Canon Law?

[2] Boltwood, *The Origin, Orders, Organisation, etc., of the Free Protestant Episcopal Church* (n.d.), p. 4. This same pamphlet states that the F.P.E.C. has orders 'derived from Armenian, Anglican, Roman, and Greek sources', but does not explain clearly what were the sources of the last three; except that 'the Bishops of the three amalgamating Churches had received prior consecrations, the orders of each being obtained from separate sources; all orders being merged into one in subsequent consecrations and ordinations'.

Churches Claiming the Ferrette Succession

by the entry in *Crockford's Clerical Directory* for 1893, which reads as follows:

'CHECKEMIAN, Leon.—University of Mount Lebanon. Hon. D.D. by Abp. of Malatia 1878. Deacon and Priest 1866 Malatia. Received into Church of Ireland 1890. General Licence Diocese of Dublin 4th November 1890. Formerly Priest at Besui 1866–68; Aintab 1868; Gurum 1868–77; Malatia 1868–77; Malatia 1878–81; Constantinople 1881–85. *18 Hume Street, Dublin.*'

As might be expected, there is no reference to his also holding the positions of Primate of the United Armenian Catholic Church, and Archbishop of Selsey in the Ancient British Church.

Both Stevens and Chechemian had some very curious friends in the ecclesiastical underworld of the early nineties. Among them was a pious cycle-dealer, named James Martin, D.D., LL.D. Not satisfied with any organized form of Protestantism, he had founded 'The Nazarene Episcopal Ecclesia', which may have been inspired by the early Christian Jewish group of this name. This tiny sect with a British Israelite ethos had its first headquarters in Flaxman Road, alongside Loughborough Junction Station on the old London–Chatham, and Dover Railway. In 1890 Mr Martin moved his disciples to Kent House Road, Sydenham, near the Crystal Palace, where he opened a seminary, known as 'Nazarene College'. It has been said that he had received a laying on of hands by Bishop Richardson of the Reformed Episcopal Church in the U.S.A.; also that later on he sometimes signed his letters 'Antipas, F.D.' (*Fidei Defensor*).[1] Little or nothing has been recorded of Chechemian's movements between 1890 and 1897, and it is uncertain how long his headquarters were in Dublin. It has been stated that it was in the latter year that he managed to get legally constituted what was called 'The Free Protestant Episcopal Church of England'.[2] This was an amalgamation of the Ancient British Church, the Nazarene Episcopal Ecclesia, and the Free Protestant Church of England.[3] It has been stated that sometime in 1897 Chechemian, now known to the initiated as Archbishop of Selsey, raised James

---

[1] Presumably the name was adopted out of devotion to the Antipas mentioned by St John (Apoc. II, 13), who was 'put to death in Satan's dwelling-place, your city' (Pergamos in Asia Minor).

[2] Reproduced on the cover of the official organ of this body, *The Intuitive Interpreter*, is 'The Archiepiscopal Seal of the Very Right Rev. Most Hon. Lord Leon Checkemian, D.D., LL.D.' On it we read: 'Consecrated a Bishop at Malatia, Asia Minor, 1878. Elected Archbishop of the F.P. Ep. Ch. of England, 1898.' The coat of arms includes a mitre, crown, and pallium, with the motto: 'Watch and Pray'.

[3] The last named was an offshoot of the Reformed Episcopal Church of America.

Martin to the episcopate, with the title of Archbishop of Caerleon-upon-Usk. We are also told that he reconsecrated Charles Stevens, at that time Chief Patriarch of the fabulous Church alleged to have been founded in A.D. 33 by Caractacus, King of the Silures (an ancient British tribe), about five centuries before St Augustine and his Italian missionaries drove this venerable Church underground.[1]

Far be it from us to deny the truth of these Celtic legends, for it may be that they were transmitted to the chronicler from 'beyond the veil'—like the messages from 'The Masters' received 'on the astral' by Bishops Wedgwood and Leadbeater of the Liberal Catholic Church.[2]

On Guy Fawkes Day 1897, the new Protestant sect, claiming early Celtic origins, was given another overseer in the person of Charles Albert McLaglen, with the title of Colonial Missionary Bishop for Cape Colony, and Bishop of Claremont. At the ceremony held in St Stephen's Church, East Ham, Chechemian was assisted by Martin, and by two other bishops upon whom he had recently laid hands—G. W. L. Maaers and F. Boucher.[3] The idea seems to have been that McLaglen should transplant this new form of legally constituted Protestantism in South Africa, and thus check the growth of ritualism and sacerdotalism in the South African Province of the Anglican Communion, but he never took possession of his see. The greater part of his long life was spent in East London, where he devoted himself to many kinds of charitable work among the poor and the outcast.[4]

In recent years certain writers, anxious to stress the Catholicity and Orthodoxy of the Ancient British Church have given McLaglen the title of 'Mar Andries' to keep up the Syro-Jacobite tradition of the Bishop of Iona. It is extremely doubtful, however, if the

[1] cf. C. D. Boltwood, *The Origin, Orders, Organisation, etc., of the Free Protestant Episcopal Church* (n.d.), p. 1. This pamphlet is largely a re-casting of 'Archdeacon' Ernest A. Asquith's brochure with the same title issued in 1917.

[2] See pp. 348, 360

[3] Both these 'overseers' were militant Protestants: Maaers was actually sent to Spain so that he could help Bishop Cabrera and the clergy of his Reformed Church in their crusade against Popery. Cabrera had been made a bishop by Plunket in 1894, and the Hibernian Church was giving active support to his efforts to counteract idolatry and supersitition among the Iberians.

[4] From his youth MacLaglen had worked with the London City Mission. Later on he helped to organize the Gordon Memorial Day Nursery for Little Children; the Shaftesbury Memorial Brigade for Homeless, Destitute, Deaf, Dumb, and Crippled Boys; the Denmark Street Free Soup Kitchen; and St Andrew's Mission. He carried on these Evangelical Protestant religious and social activities for more than half a century. (cf. Mar Georgius, *The Man from Antioch*, Glastonbury, 1952, p. 16.)

Churches Claiming the Ferrette Succession

Titular Bishop of Claremont took any interest in the Eastern Churches. It is a pity that the archives of the Ancient British Church (presumably now filed with those of the Nazarene Episcopal Ecclesia and the Free Protestant Church of England) cannot produce documentary evidence of Stevens, Chechemian, Martin and McLaglen using the titles of 'Mar Theophilus', 'Mar Leon', 'Mar Jacobus', and 'Mar Andries'. A photograph of these three bishops shows then robed in linen rochets with balloon-shaped sleeves, black scarves, and university hoods. Each carries a tasselled college cap or mortarboard. The only Oriental features are the bushy beards and flowing moustaches which all display.[1]

The more one reflects on the combination of rigid Protestantism with fascinating legends of the Ancient British Patriarchate and its affiliated organizations, autocephalous tropoi, etc., one cannot help suspecting that a later generation of chroniclers wanted them to be true, and accepted them as true. The wish was father to the thought.

Mar Theophilus, the second British Patriarch, helped to augment his income as organist at a chapel in Mare Street, Hackney. His wife contributed £200 a year towards the upkeep of this dissenting place of worship; an annuity which ceased at her death about 1900. According to the late Bishop William Hall, there is no reference to Mar Theophilus in the archives of the Free Protestant Episcopal Church before 1898. We are told that 'Stevens was grossly unfit for a minister, and was only good for a church organist, for he had a dreadful impediment in his speech that rendered him quite useless. He always used the Book of Common Prayer for making deacons, priests and bishops'. After his wife's death he found another pro-cathedral for the Ancient British Church in Speldhurst Road, South Hackney, just north of Victoria Park, known later on as 'The Church of Martin Luther'.[2] The second British Patriarch died in 1916, and was laid to rest by the future Bishop Hall in Norwood Cemetery. The ritual and ceremonial at the burial service were those of the Free Protestant Episcopal Church of England.

The pure Protestant character of the Chechemian line of apostolic succession was perpetuated by the third British Patriarch, Mar Jacobus I (Martin), who, on the Feast of St James of Compostella, July 25, 1915, priested William Hall in the corrugated iron

---

[1] Reproduced in *The Origin, Orders, Organisation, etc. of the Free Protestant Episcopal Church of England.*
[2] See p. 226.

chapel near Kent House Station, Penge, adjacent to Nazarene College. That same day were also ordained Messrs. Asquith, Harris and Surridge. Benjamin Charles Harris was hurriedly made a Bishop with only extemporary prayers; having been a priest for five minutes before he was raised to the episcopate. He was given the title of Bishop of Essex, though as Bishop Hall recalled in after years: 'he was only good enough for a Salvationist, and in some ways not good enough for that. His consecration was a farce'.[1]

Chechemian soon grew tired of playing the joint roles of Mar Leon and the first Archbishop of the Free Protestant Episcopal Church of England, combined with that of Primate of the United Armenian Catholic Church in the British Isles during interludes. He found them too exhausting, and after two years reverted to lay status. He migrated to Tunbridge Wells, where he ran a shop for the sale of beads and bijouterie. The former Catholic Armenian *vartapet* ended his days as a Baptist, and died a very old man in the nineteen-twenties.

The next man to be raised to the episcopate of the elusive Ancient British Church was Herbert James Monzani Heard, Headmaster of Raleigh College, Brixton, South London.[2] He had been ordained an Anglican deacon by Lord William Gascoyne Cecil, Bishop of Exeter from 1916 to 1936, but decided that the priesthood of a Church alleged to be the oldest in the world after Antioch and Jerusalem was preferable to that of the post-Reformation Church of England. Then followed a call from the Patriarch, Mar Andries (McLaglen), to proceed to the episcopate. It was on June 4, 1922 that the latter laid hands on Mr Heard. The simple ceremony took place in what was then called St Andrew's Church, Retreat Place, Hackney, where the Rev. William Hall conducted Sunday services for the benefit of persons in North-East London who found the neighbouring Anglican places of worship too ritualistic and Romish.

The consecrand was given the title of Bishop of Selsey.

This schoolmaster prelate—bearded like his consecrator—was

---

[1] Letter to the Rev. Alban Cockerham, dated March 24, 1956.
The *Fellowship of Independent Evangelical Churches* (1948) gives an idea of Harris' comprehensive churchmanship: 'Kings and Nazarene College, Church of England—Hackney and Sydenham, 1912–20; Congregational Church, Tunbridge Wells, 1920–27; Evangelical Free Church, Romford, 1927–29; East Barnet Baptist Church, 1929–34; Nonconformist Chaplain, Mental Hospital, Abbots Langley, 1936–.' The reference to the 'Church of England' should read 'Free Protestant Episcopal Church of England'.
[2] The 'Monzani' was added only towards the end of his life.

Churches Claiming the Ferrette Succession

aged sixty-five when he became the titular successor of St Wilfrid.
He is remembered as having 'the appearance of an old country
farmer, addicted to rough tweed suits—very bluff and hearty'.[1] It
was in favour of the Bishop of Selsey that Mar Andries resigned
the primacies of the Ancient British and United Armenian Catholic
Churches. Heard, however, felt unable to take on the additional
burden of ruling over the Free Protestant Episcopal Church of
England. His own flock in Sussex must at best have been infinitesimal, and it is probable that it existed mainly in his imagination, which was exceptionally vivid.

Behind Heard's beard, bluff and hearty manner, and usually well
tailored suits, lay an artistic and romantic temperament. His level
of churchmanship was neither high nor low, but rather infinitely
comprehensive. As will be seen, he found room for almost all
schools of thought. In his younger days, more than twenty years
before he became an Ancient British prelate, he was one of the
founders of the Imperial College of Music. It was in 1907 that he
formed an Order of St James, the membership of which was open to
all Christians. Having been initiated as 'Companions' or 'Knights',
its members promised to devote their lives to working among
men, women, and children of all denominations or none. The aims
of the Orders were 'organizing Religious, Business, and Social
Intercourse amongst people, irrespective of creed or dogma'. At
the 'monastery', located at 600 Green Lanes, Stoke Newington,
'The Rev. Brother James, O.S.J.' conducted correspondence
courses in Music, Arts, Science, Theology, and Commerce. He also
held 'professional examinations for Accountants, Herbalists,
Organists, Music Teachers, and Others'. Considering that the
Bishop of Selsey was obviously a man of many talents, it is rather
surprising that Mar Georgius should write that, 'being a schoolmaster, and not a man of business, nor yet an organizer, he did not
know which way to turn. It was almost inevitable that he would
make mistakes, and he did, in fact, make one or two very bad
blunders . . . He had never yearned to be a Bishop, but
having been chosen and consecrated to the charge, he did his
best to fulfil his obligations, leaving the result to the hand of
God'.[2]

Soon after Heard had declined to take on the charge of the Free
Protestant Episcopal Church a man was found who appeared to

[1] Mar Georgius, *Varied Reflections* (Antwerp, 1954).
[2] op. cit.

possess all the qualifications of a bishop as given by Paul the apostle in his first epistle to Timothy. This was the Rev. Mr Widdows, minister of the Church of Martin Luther in Speldhurst Road, South Hackney, formerly the pro-cathedral of the Ancient British Church, where Mar Theophilus used to pontificate according to the Book of Common Prayer. After a simple but no doubt reverent laying on of hands by Mar Andries (McLaglen), the new prelate was given the name and title of Ignatius, Bishop of Hackney. Unfortunately it was soon quickly discovered that the Metropolitan's past life had not been so blameless as had been supposed. The elders (quoting the words of Peter in Acts I, 20) said among themselves: 'Let his habitation be desolate, and his bishoprick let another take'.[1]

As a result of the exposure of Mr Widdows, the Bishop of Selsey became Primus of the Free Protestant Episcopal Church of England, though much against his wishes. After he gave up teaching at Brixton, the fifth British Patriarch, as a few of his followers called him, retired to Broadstairs, Kent, where he tried to revive the moribund remnant of Mar Pelagius's Britonnic Church, its members being a handful who disapproved of the Anglo-Catholic type of services in the neo-Norman parish church dedicated to the Holy Trinity. His Beatitude also rented a room at 271 Green Lanes, Palmers Green, N.13, as the offices of his Patriarchate.[2] For a time, at least, this address was also that of the curias of the Free Protestant Episcopal Church of England, and of the United Armenian Catholic Church in the British Isles. Towards the end of his life Patriarch Heard held the offices of Chancellor of the International Orthodox Catholic University, and of the Université Philotechnique Internationale.[3] Both these organizations had, in fact, much the same scope as his Order of St James, except that they granted degrees instead of diplomas.[4]

Andrew McLaglen died in 1930, and was buried in Kensington Cemetery, his coffin carried to the grave by his six sons. The service was strictly Protestant in character, and hardly in keeping

---

[1] According to *Truth Cautionary List* (1908), 'Ignatius, Bishop of Hackney' was 'a notorious scoundrel who has served two terms of penal servitude in this country on disgusting charges, but still fools silly Protestants at the Church of Martin Luther, South Hackney'. He was the author of a book entitled *Ex-Monk Widdows*, similar in character to the *Awful Disclosures of Maria Monk* (Montreal, 1835).

[2] See p. 240.

[3] See p. 493.

[4] It is hardly necessary to state that neither of these universities ever obtained official recognition. They were free-lance establishments with merely a paper existence.

with the deceased's status of Mar Andries, Patriarch of the Ancient British Church.

It was on Easter Monday, April 20, 1930, that the Bishop of Selsey performed his first consecration, when he raised to the episcopate a priest of the Church of England, Victor Alexander Palmer Hayman, giving him the title of Bishop of Waltham of the Free Catholic Church. The ceremony took place in St Alban's Mission Church, Leytonstone, E.10, of which Hayman was in charge; and in the presence of the churchwardens and the congregation. Considering that the new Bishop was a militant Anglo-Catholic it is surprising that he should have been willing to be consecrated by the Primus of the Free Protestant Episcopal Church of England, as well as Patriarch of the Ancient British Church, or that the latter should have been prepared to lay hands on him. Hayman withdrew from the Church of England a few days later. Dr Wilson, Bishop of Chelmsford, must have been glad to dispense with the services of this insubordinate cleric. Hayman's idea at the time was that the Free Catholic Church which he had founded should serve as a sort of independent Anglo-Catholic body of an extreme type. He visualized it as a refuge for priests who were being persecuted by their bishops, and found it impossible to hold and practise what they called 'The Full Faith' in communion with Canterbury. Those who recall Hayman maintain that he was a man of real ability, with a definite 'personality', well-read, and widely travelled.[1] Unfortunately he could not 'keep on the rails' when out of prison.

As the Bishop of Waltham had no cathedral, he had to make do with a small oratory at Forest Gate, E.7., which he dedicated to St Cyprian. Here on August 17, 1930, he ordained deacon and priest a certain George D. Figg, who, like his Bishop, had been an ardent Anglo-Catholic, working in several of the famous 'outposts of the faith' in London suburbs. Fr Figg's conception of 'Catholicity' was nothing if not 'Free', because after his ordination he appears to have ministered, not only in Hayman's little oratories, but also in certain Anglo-Catholic churches. On Easter Monday, 1944, he acted as deacon at the consecration of Mar Georgius by Mar Basilius Abdullah III.[2]

The subsequent career of Bishop Hayman was far from peaceful. For a time 'My Lord, Victor' held the position of Chaplain to Sir

[1] He was M.A. of Queens' College, Cambridge.
[2] See p. 450.

Churches Claiming the Ferrette Succession

Oswald Mosley's British Union of Fascists; in consequence of which he was detained in a concentration camp on the Isle of Man during the second World War. By 1946 his Free Catholic Church had become an 'autocephalous tropus' of the Catholicate of the West.[1] After his release he provided himself with a coadjutor in the person of Peter Ewart O'Dell Cheshire, who was consecrated, so it is said, on April 18, 1948.[2]

On May 18, 1949, the *Daily Mail* displayed a caption: 'Primate gets two-year sentence: clerical garb aided frauds'. The reporter stated that 'Victor Alexander Palmer-Hayman, aged 56, described as a clerk in holy orders with no fixed abode, who styled himself on his notepaper as the Most Rev. V. A. P. Hayman, D.D., Primate and Archbishop of Waltham in the Free Catholic Faith, was at Middlesex Sessions yesterday gaoled for two years on six charges of obtaining money by false pretences from a number of off-licence holders. . . . The prosecution stated that Hayman, wearing a clerical collar, obtained money for advertisements for the "Free Catholic" magazine, of which he was the general editor, when he well knew he was not in a financial position to produce the magazine'.

Sir John Cameron, prosecuting, forced the alleged Archbishop of Waltham to admit that his 'palace' was 'a basement room in a house at Kelross Road, Highbury, London, and in an alcove was an oratory which was for his own use'.[3] Hayman admitted that he had already been fined £20 at West Ham for 'obtaining money from off-licence holders on the representation that, as the son of a publican—he was stated to be the son of an Excise officer—he was able to get whisky'. It came out in the evidence that the Archbishop had been living by this and similar frauds for several years, 'relying on his clerical garb and plausible tongue', and also that he was living apart from his wife who was a nurse.

On the Primate's release from gaol, the Church Army, his College, and many old friends tried to help him. Money was found to

---

[1] See p. 456, n. 1. On June 22, 1948, Hayman assisted Mar Georgius at the reconsecration of Mar Timotheos, Metropolitan of Aquileia. (See p. 319.)

[2] Bishop Cheshire earned his living at Chatham, and sometime in 1950 he raised to the episcopate John Clarence Lockhart, who was one of Mar Georgius's priests. On April 20, 1952, Cheshire consecrated Brougham Claxton, whose few followers called themselves 'The English Rite'. Later on Claxton submitted to the jurisdiction of Bishop Paget King of the so-called 'Canonical Old Roman Catholic Church'. (See p. 339.) His orders were regarded as invalid, and he was re-ordained up to the priesthood.

[3] This was quite near Steenoven House, the present headquarters of the 'Canonical' Old Roman Catholic Church.

take him to Canada, or to any other part of the world, where he could make a fresh start in life, but he insisted on remaining in England. He was determined to revive his Free Catholic Church—or rather, to sponsor yet another schismatic sect. For on October 15, 1950, he re-consecrated George Forster as Bishop of Devonia in the Chapel of Our Lady, Battersea, S.W.11.[1] The new prelate was the founder of the so-called 'English Orthodox Church', and he assumed the style of Patriarch, with the title of 'The Most Rev. Mar David, F.I.C.I., C.S.C.N.'. The Patriarchate was set up at 170 Battersea Bridge Road, where was published for a time *The Orthodox Catholic News*.[2]

Having had nothing but bad luck for more than a quarter of a century with his Free Catholic Church, the Archbishop of Waltham still believed that it might have a glorious future. A number of young men must also have been convinced of this, otherwise they would not have accepted minor and major orders up to the priesthood at his hands. To ensure that the Church would continue after his death, on March 4, 1956, he consecrated Edgar Melville Barker as his Coadjutor, with the style of Bishop of Beulah.

The new prelate's career had included brief associations with several religious bodies at one time or another. In April 1947, styling himself 'presbyter and canon missioner' of 'The Christian Mission—The Devotion of the Wishing Well', he was acting as honorary curate at an Anglican church in West London. Seven months later, judging from a letter on the printed writing paper of The Christian Mission, complete with an impressive coat of arms, Canon Barker had been raised to the episcopate, for he signed himself '✠ Bishop John Barker'. It has been stated that he was consecrated on August 6, 1947 by Bishop Anthony Wilson (or King), then head of the Christian Mission at Leeds, who was understood to have been given some sort of Mariavite episcopal status.[3] Then on May 27, 1950, his signature 'John Barker (priest)' appears as '*Secretarius ad hoc*' of the Patriarch of Glastonbury and Catholicos of the West on the Instrument of re-Consecration of H. P. Nicholson, as Mar Joannes, titular Archbishop of Karim, Primate of the Ancient Catholic Church.[4] But Fr Barker's associations with 'The Miracle Cathedral' in Chelsea did not last long, because by 1951

[1] Cheshire had raised Forster to the episcopate on July 17, 1949.
[2] On January 30, 1952, the Free Catholic Church and the English Orthodox Church were united, retaining the former's title.
[3] See p. 522.
[4] See pp. 475, 476.

he had become the head of a short-lived Apostolic Catholic Church, with its headquarters at Queen's Park, London, N.W.6. Eventually he transferred himself to the Free Catholic Church, and was soon raised to the see of Beulah.

Determined to force people to take notice of the Free Catholic Church, the Archbishop of Waltham again solicited advertisements for its magazine, but this time in south London, where he was not so well known. The result was the same: he was arrested, tried, and committed to prison. By this time Barker had developed doubts about the validity of Hayman's orders, and is said to have informed one of the priests that he had better find another prelate to ordain him.[1] ✠ Victor Waltham's health broke down in H.M. Prison at Wandsworth, and he was moved to the nearby St John's Hospital, where he died on October 6, 1960. The Metropolitan-Primate's body was cremated at Streatham; the service being conducted by Archbishop Nicholson of Karim. Before Hayman's death he appointed Bishop Barker as his successor.

The second Archbishop of Waltham, not satisfied with being Primate of the Free Catholic Church, now claimed that he was the Administrator in England of the Old Roman Catholic Church, repudiating both Mgr Shelley, Archbishop of Caer-Glow, and Mgr Barrington-Evans, Archbishop of Verulam. The former's Vicar General, Bishop Paget King, issued a statement on this claim in which he said:

'Neither he [Barker] nor the prelates he claims to be in communion with in Germany and in America have any connection with the Old Roman Catholic Church, although some years ago the people he mentions in Germany did apply to be received into our Communion—an application which after due investigation, we had to reject . . . We solemnly affirm, therefore, that these men have no connection of any kind with the Old Roman Catholic Church in Great Britain.'

Archbishop Barker was not impressed, and on November 29, 1960, he summoned a High Synod of the Free Catholic Church, when it was decided to enter into an Instrument of Union with the branch of the Old Roman Catholic Church ruled over by Mgr Kelly of Niagara Falls, N.Y.[2] On December 11 that same year His Grace of Waltham was solemnly enthroned in the Ancient Catholic Cathedral, Stamford Hill, N.15, by Mar Joannes, Archbishop of

---

[1] It seems that Barker took the precaution to have a third consecration *sub conditione*.
[2] See p. 434.

Karim. He was given the official status of second Primate of the Free Catholic Church and Administrator for Great Britain of the Old Roman Catholic Church, no matter what protests might be made by ✠ Gerard Caer-Glow or ✠ Wilfrid Verulam. On July 14, 1962 these two bodies were legally incorporated as 'The Willibrord Association (Old Roman Catholic)'. On September 16, the Archbishop of Waltham, assisted by Mar Georgius, Patriarch of Glastonbury, and Mar Joannes, Archbishop of Karim, consecrated Joseph David Overs as his Bishop-Auxiliary. The function took place in the Ancient Catholic Cathedral.

The versatile Bishop Heard, in his status of fifth British Patriarch, re-consecrated *sub conditione* on Whit Sunday, 1938, Mar Frederick Harrington, founder of the Orthodox-Keltic Church of the British Commonwealth of Nations. The purpose was to unite in one person all the churches claiming the Ferrette and Vilatte lines of succession, said to number 20,000,000 of the faithful in every continent.[1] On May 16, 1939, Heard, acting as Primus of the Free Protestant Episcopal Church of England, laid his hands on William Hall at St Andrew's, Stonebridge Road, South Tottenham, appointing him Bishop of Middlesex and the Eastern Counties. This Evangelical prelate then earned his living as chaplain to Abney Park Cemetery, Stoke Newington. Later on he succeeded Heard as Primus of this body, which severed all associations with the Ancient British Church.

The Protestant character of the Chechemian succession, as derived from George David Cummins, first Presiding Bishop of the Reformed Episcopal Church in the U.S.A., was safeguarded by Benjamin Charles Harris. A quarter of a century after James Martin, founder of the Nazarene Episcopal Ecclesia, had charged him to feed the little Free Protestant Episcopal flock in the Diocese of Essex, he chose three godly and well-learned men to be ordained and consecrated Bishop, in the persons of Gordon Pinder, Charles Leslie Saul, and James Charles Ryan.

In 1922 a small group of earnest Protestants founded a new body which they called The Evangelical Church of England, with the object of starting parishes in districts without churches and also where the local Anglican place of worship was encouraging what they regarded as idolatry and superstition. The first bishops received a laying on of hands by presbyters in 1923. By descent they were from B. Price, as was a further bishop, W. Newton, in

[1] See p. 282.

231

1930. Six years later Newton laid hands on Gordon Pinder and Charles Saul; and on November 17, 1944 these two (with J. C. Ryan mentioned above, and who had also been consecrated previously by presbyters) received episcopal consecration from Bishop Harris at St Paul's Church, Outwood, near Radcliffe, Manchester.[1] At this time the sect had about seven churches, mostly in the north of England. Pinder and Saul soon parted company, the former continuing to rule over the Evangelical Church of England. He was assisted by a certain Paul Scott-Montague, who finding himself down and out, had tried unsuccessfully to get paid work with Bishop Saul. As there was nothing doing in the south of England, Scott-Montague was grateful to Pinder who had two or three stipendiary churches under his jurisdiction, when he offered him a job as paid secretary. Before long he was appointed Archdeacon, and under his influence Pinder's followers became more 'central' in their churchmanship.[2] The Archdeacon dressed the part to the full-gaitered, hat with a rosette, and nothing lacking to impress the general public. A correspondence between the Venerable Archdeacon of the Evangelical Church of England and Dr Rawlinson, Bishop of Derby, with the object of uniting this little sect with the Established Church, achieved nothing.[3]

After the failure of these negotiations Scott-Montague, still acting as Pinder's Archdeacon, was re-ordained conditionally by Mar Georgius, who appointed him Legate of the Glastonbury Patriarchate. In 1949 he was reconciled with the Roman Church by Dom Bede Griffiths, O.S.B., then Prior of Farnborough Abbey.[4] When Pinder died in 1951 there were two candidates to succeed him: John L. Baines and John Dugdale. The latter was elected, and in the absence of a bishop, received a laying on of hands by other presbyters.[5]

After Bishop Saul had broken off relations with Archbishop Pinder, he formed a rival sect to which he gave the name of 'The

[1] At that date it appears that Bishop Harris still held the official status of Nonconformist Chaplain to the Mental Hospital, Abbots Langley.

[2] Saul, who had been excommunicated by Pinder, founded the English Episcopal Church, with its headquarters at Acton, W.3. (See pp. 233, 234.)

[3] This correspondence was published under the title *Reunion* (n.d. or p.).

[4] Scott-Montague was the author of an article entitled 'The East-West Bridge Church', explaining the aims of the Catholicate of the West. It was published in *The Universe*, August 19, 1949, after his submission to the Holy See.

[5] Baines seceded from the Evangelical Church of England, and was consecrated independently by Hall in 1952 (see p. 244). The latter retired in 1955 and was succeeded by James Ormerod, who received episcopal consecration from Hall on July 24, 1959. The E.C. of E. is now limited to one church, St Aidan's, Preston, but there are quite a number of unattached congregations in Protestant Lancashire.

Churches Claiming the Ferrette Succession

English Episcopal Church', with its headquarters at 15 Newburgh Road, Acton, W.3, where he held services in an oratory dedicated to St Mark. He became friendly with Mar Georgius, Patriarch of Glastonbury, and on September 8, 1945, in the Cathedral Church of Christ the King, New Barnet, the latter, assisted by the Archbishop of Olivet (J. S. M. Ward), re-consecrated him *sub conditione*, with the title and status of Mar Leofric, Archbishop of Suthronia in the Eparchy of All the Britons.[1] On June 5, 1946, Mar David I, Patriarch of Malaga and Supreme Hierarch of the Catholicate of the West in the Americas (W. D. de Ortega Maxey) gave Saul a few more valuable lines of succession at St Mark's, Acton.[2] The followers of Mar Leofric were made yet more sure of the validity of his orders after Mar Timotheos (Stumpfl), Metropolitan of Aquileia, had imparted the Syrian-Gallican line on June 22, 1947.[3] On November 24, 1946, Mar Leofric had acted as proxy for Bishop Earl Anglin James, when the latter was enthroned *in absentia* in the Patriarchal Domestic Chapel of St Aristobulus, Kew, as 'His Eminence Mar Laurentius, Archbishop and Metropolitan of Acadia, and Exarch of the Catholicate of the West in the Canadas'.[4] Mar Leofric helped to re-consecrate several bishops of the Catholicate of the West during the two years that he was associated with Mar Georgius. But his churchmanship was just as broad as that of Bishop Heard, and he combined the part of Mar Leofric, Archbishop of Suthronia with that of Bishop of Hayes, his original title in the Evangelical Church of England. As such he performed several ordinations, including that of A. St Denis Fry, whom he raised to the diaconate in 1946 and the priesthood the following year, having accepted the Honorary Presidency of St Nicolas School, Clevedon, Somerset, where Mr Fry was a master.[5]

In spite of all the episcopal blood transfused by a host of prelatical donors, Bishop Saul was re-converted to the simple Protestant

---

[1] See p. 452.
[2] See p. 455.
[3] See p. 319.
[4] See p. 458.
[5] Fry was introduced to Saul by one of the latter's clergy, Dr Donald Omand, then Dean of the London College of Theology, who was ordained priest of the Church of England in 1955. The Clevedon School was under the jurisdiction of Dr Pinder, Archbishop of the Evangelical Church of England.

On June 24, 1950, A. St Denis Fry and Dr W. D. Terry, M.A., Litt. D. (Cantab.) were made prelates of the interdenominational Order of Christ our Most Holy Redeemer by Mar Benignus, titular Bishop of Mere (R. K. Hurgon, see p. 454), having received conditional baptism, confirmation, minor and major orders in the Ancient Catholic Cathedral of the Good Shepherd, Chelsea, lent by Archbishop Nicholson of Karim for this function.

faith of his youth, and cast off what he had come to regard as the mummery and superstition of the Catholicate of the West. In February 1948 he was advertised as presiding over a meeting of the National Union of Protestants, to attack the Church of England Canon Law revision; and Archdeacon Scott-Montague wrote to *The Church Times*, explaining that Saul was no longer a member of the Evangelical Church of England, which by this time was hoping to link up with the Established Church, and had grown more tolerant of high churchmanship. St Mark's, Acton, and other chapels under the jurisdiction of Bishop Saul became refuges for Evangelical-minded Anglicans who had been driven from their churches by sacerdotal or rationalistic teaching. The faith and worship of the English Episcopal Church fell into line with that of the Church of Ireland. The official liturgy is the 1662 *Book of Common Prayer*.

On January 8, 1950 Bishop Saul imposed hands on D. L. T. Tollenaar, originally a Liberal Catholic priest in Holland, who became known as 'Old Catholic Bishop of Arnhem'.[1] On June 4 that same year he raised to the episcopate the Rev. F. A. W. Rutherford, formerly an Anglican incumbent, as Bishop of the South African Episcopal Church. Bishop Rutherford stated in an official publication that his Church was 'not denominational but inspirational'; also 'that any visiting minister whose tradition is that of the simpler ways of reading the Holy Scripture and breaking the Bread in the unliturgical way is welcome to use the Holy Table of the South African Episcopal Church'.[2]

After Archbishop Pinder's death in 1951, Bishop Saul's English Episcopal Church became associated with Dr Bacon of Failsworth, Manchester, who had been consecrated as Bishop of Repton in 1943, by Dorian Herbert, Bishop of Caerleon, founder of the Jesuene or Free-Orthodox Catholic Church, which by 1957 had changed its name to 'Ancient British (Agnostic) Church'.[3] For nearly thirty years St Mark's, Acton, has been a Protestant oasis in a desert of Anglo and Roman Catholicism, proud to be regarded as

---

[1] See p. 401. It was Tollenaar who on August 5, 1951, consecrated Wilfrid A. Barrington-Evans as first Bishop of the Old Roman Catholic Church (English Rite). (See pp. 399–401.)
[2] cf. Brandreth, op. cit. (2nd ed., 1961), p. 85, n. 3.
[3] See p. 298.

the only evangelical church in the district, where, so it is said, the quiet reverent atmosphere and simple prayer-book services are much appreciated by an élite of Christians.[1] Spiritual healing is done and the former Mar Leofric, Archbishop of Suthronia (who has now ceased to style himself 'Right Rev.') writes in his *Parish News* (June 1962) that God is beckoning on the Acton congregation 'to a complete and full change of mind' in order that they may be 'the thought-changers of the world', so that they may 'rise in the spiritual life to the height of a spirit-filled experience'.[2]

James Charles Ryan, whose original name was Joseph K. Chengalvaroyan Pillai—the third man upon whom Bishop Harris laid hands in 1944—had made his first trial of the Christian religion with the South Indian United Church. Later on he was ordained by a former minister of the British Methodist Mission, and still later he founded an Evangelical Church of India. Within a year of being raised to the episcopate by the Bishop of Essex on the Evangelical Church of England, on August 25, 1945, he was reconsecrated *sub conditione* by Mar Georgius, Patriarch of Glastonbury, assisted by the titular Archbishop of Olivet (J. S. M. Ward) and the titular Bishop of St Marylebone (W. J. E. Jeffrey), when he was given the title and style of 'His Eminence Mar James, Archbishop of India, and Exarch of the Catholicate of the West in the Indies'. This stately function took place in the Cathedral of Christ the King, New Barnet. After a varied career in which he has played many parts Mar James, under the name of The Most Rev. K. Chengalvaroya Pillai acts as National Director of the Department of Interdenominational Relations in The American Holy Orthodox Catholic Apostolic Eastern Church (affiliated with the Orthodox Catholic Patriarchate of America); with his offices at The Chancery, 247 East 126th Street, New York 35.[3]

Bishop Heard had a wonderfully comprehensive conception of catholicity, and was so kind-hearted that he was always ready to impart either the Syrian-Antiochene or the Free Protestant Episcopal succession to almost anybody who asked for the one or the other of them. On March 18, 1939, he laid hands on William Hall, giving him the title of Bishop of Middlesex and the Eastern

---

[1] Newburgh Road, Acton, is now the headquarters, not only of the English Episcopal Church, but also of the Apostolic Exarchate for Ukrainians in England and Wales. The Most Rev. Eugene Augustine Hornyak, whose Exarch is the Archbishop of Westminster, has his curia at No. 14; Bishop Saul at No. 15.

[2] Another and more recent title of Bishop Saul's body is 'Church of England (Evangelical)'. It appears to be catering for West Indian immigrants.

[3] See p. 264.

Counties in the Free Protestant Episcopal Church of England.[1] On May 20, 1940, followed the much more ornate re-consecration *sub conditione* of James Dominic Mary O'Gavigan, who at that date styled himself Archbishop and Metropolitan of the English Branch of the American Orthodox Catholic Church.[2]

About three years later Mar Jacobus II became acquainted with Dr William Bernard Crow, M. Sc. (Wales); M. Sc., Ph. D., and D. Sc. (London). This distinguished biologist had been ordained priest in the Liberal Catholic Church in 1935. Archbishop Harrington, Primate of the Orthodox-Keltic Church of the British Commonwealth of Nations, had granted a charter to The Order of the Holy Wisdom, founded by Dr Crow to present what was called 'The Orthodox Catholic Faith' to persons of theosophical and occult leanings in their own 'language', and in such a way as to make manifest that the teachings, types, and symbols of the older non-Christian religions found their perfect fulfilment and consummation in the Person of Jesus Christ, and in His Church. This cabalistic Order had three sections: *The Ancient Orthodox Catholic Church*, devoted to purely religious activities; *The Universal Spiritual Kingdom*, covering noblesse and chivalric activities; and *The Universal Rite of Cosmic Architecture*, which dealt with quasi-masonic affairs. It was obvious that this triune organisation needed a bishop, so that it could function as an autocephalous Church. Dr Crow had hoped to be consecrated by ✠ 'Frederic, Mar et Met' (as Harrington usually signed his name), but he died on January 17, 1942.[3] It was typical of Mar Jacobus's indifference to denominational and dogmatic distinctions that he offered to raise the founder of the Order of the Holy Wisdom to the episcopate. The ceremony took place on Whit Sunday, June 13, 1943, in the consecrand's private oratory at 4 Broadmead Road, Woodford Green, Essex, where he resided with his wife and daughter. At that date the new prelate, who was given the name of 'Mar Bernard, Bishop of Santa Sophia', held the position of Senior Lecturer in Biology in the South-West Essex Technical College, Walthamstow, E.17.[4]

His entry in *Who's Who* (1940) takes up seventy-six lines. Born in 1895, he had been educated at the Coopers' Company School. For lack of space it is impossible to give a complete list of his

---

[1] Hall had been ordained deacon and priest by Stevens in 1913.
[2] See p. 293.
[3] See p. 280.
[4] On January 4, 1945, Mar Bernard procured the Old Catholic (Mathew) succession from Mar Theodorus, Bishop of Mercia (S.E.P. Needham). (See p. 374.)

numerous degrees (which include those of the London University, the University of Wales), or of the learned societies with which he was connected. His offices included being Vice-President of the National Association of Masso-Therapists, and membership of the International Phrenological and Psychological Institute. He was also a Doctor of Divinity of the International Orthodox Catholic University. His publications covered a wide range of subjects. In addition to numerous articles and reviews in biological, medical, and theosophical journals, he had published many books since 1926. Among their impressive titles are *The Human Body as a Colony of Animals*, *The Principles of Zodiacal and Planetary Physiology*, and *The Morphology of Dreams*.[1]

This versatile lecturer in Biology issued a leaflet on the 'Festival of the Holy Wisdom, Sun in Libra, 1943 A.D.' in which he set forth the nature and objects of an Order of the Holy Wisdom (*Ekklesia Agiae Sophiae*) which he had founded, and which was in communion with the Ancient Universal (Orthodox Catholic) Church. 'Those genuinely interested' were invited to become members, and read:

'The Order is not a Church, but an organisation within the Universal Church, which seeks to reproduce, as fully as possible within its own sphere, for the benefit of its members and humanity in general, the deep spiritual experience enshrined in ritual and symbols. It is particularly concerned with cosmic symbolism. It endeavours to teach the doctrines and practices of the Ancient Wisdom Religion, and to preserve such knowledge of value which has largely disappeared in the historical development of outer institutions.

Being absolutely universal (that is truly Orthodox and Catholic) it has access to the divine wisdom of Theosophy, embodied in the symbols of all nations. It utilizes the knowledge passed on in the great streams of sacred tradition, not excluding those of the Far East, the Brahminic-Yogic, the Ancient Egyptian, Zoroastrian-Magian, Kabalistic, Gnostic-Masonic, Gothic-Rosicrucian, Druidic-Bacchic, Chaldean, Buddhist-Lamaistic, and Islamic-Sufic. It has, however, no connection with any existing Masonic or Rosicrucian fraternity.'

This 'Ancient and Universal Rite of Cosmic Architecture,

---

[1] In the 1960 edition of *The Author's and Writer's Who's Who* the entry for 'Crow, William Bernard' gives the list of his publications, but contains no reference to his priesthood or patriarchal status.

Universal Spiritual Kingdom, and Institute of Cosmic Studies' had for its special object the establishment and maintenance of a planetary and zodiacal temple of the universal religion, where suitable candidates would be prepared and enrolled by the Bishop of Santa Sophia. For the time being, a room in a dwelling house, adorned with symbols of the planets, representing the Universe, would have to serve for the celebration of one or other of the Ancient Mysteries in their primitive form. Thanks to the guaranteed Syrian-Jacobite apostolic succession imparted to the episcopal celebrant, the faithful could now feel quite sure of their validity. It was explained, however, that 'whilst repudiating fortune-telling and similar superstitions it encourages the study of non deterministic astrology and dream interpretations, believing the same to be helpful to making in agreement with their use in Biblical days'. Seekers after Holy Wisdom were reminded that St Thomas Aquinas had written: 'The celestial bodies are the cause of all that takes place in this sub-lunar world. They influence human actions directly, but not every action caused by them is inevitable.' To be forewarned is to be forearmed.

In this esoteric Order there was a hierarchy of degrees of initiation 'derived from and analogous with that of the ancient mystery cults of the universal religion'. The Grand Master, by virtue of a charter granted by Mar Frederic, Archbishop of the Diocese of St George in England, and Primate of the Orthodox-Keltic Church of the British Commonwealth of Nations (of the Vilatte succession), was said to possess the authority necessary to maintain the status of the Order and its members, and to confer valid degrees of initiation.

In the summer and autumn of 1943 most people were taken up with the advance of the Allied Forces from Sicily into Italy, or the German retreat from Russia, or recovering from the Battle of Britain, and could not spare time to meditate on cosmic symbols. Few appear to have felt the urge to assist at the celebration of the Ancient Mysteries, when the Bishop of Santa Sophia used a home-made crozier, and two war-time thuribles, fashioned out of coffee-tins, painted gold.

By the autumn of 1943 Mar Jacobus II had reached the age of seventy-six, and, so we are told by Mar Georgius, realized that the time had come to make provision for the future of his British Patriarchate. He summoned a Synod of the Ancient British Church; and at this meeting on September 9, a revised Constitution was promulgated for the benefit of its few adherents, the number of which was never revealed. The venerable Patriarch had been greatly shocked by a Notice issued by Mar Ignatius Ephrem I on December 10, 1938, in which His Beatitude had proclaimed:

'to all whom it may concern that there are in the United States of America and in some countries of Europe, particularly in England, a number of schismatic bodies which have come into existence after direct expulsion from official Christian communities and have devised for themselves a common creed and a system of jurisdiction of their own invention.

To deceive Christians of the West being a chief objective of the schismatic bodies, they take advantage of their great distance from the East, and from time to time make public statements claiming without truth to derive their origin and apostolic succession from some Apostolic Church of the East, the attractive rites and ceremonies of which they adopt and with which they claim to have relationship.'

The Syrian Orthodox Patriarchate of Antioch and all the East had dared to denounce one of these bodies in particular:

'the so-called "One Holy Orthodox Catholic Church", as it describes itself, presided over, as it is claimed, by the so-called Frederic Harrington, "Metropolitan" in the city of London, of 324 Hornsey Road.'

This body, like others in America which were mentioned, claimed succession through Vilatte, and some of them had, so Ignatius Ephrem maintained, published statements which were untrue 'as to an alleged relation "in succession and ordination" to our Holy Apostolic Church and her forefathers'. For this reason he proclaimed:

'We find it necessary to announce to all whom it may concern that we deny any and every relation whatsoever with these schismatic bodies and repudiate them and their claims absolutely. Furthermore, our Church forbids any and every relationship and, above all, intercommunion with all and any of these schismatic sects and warns the public that their statements and pretensions as above are altogether without truth.'[1]

Frederic Mar et Met (otherwise Frederic Harrington of 324 Hornsey Road, London) had died on January 17, 1942, at the early age of fifty-two, after suffering great privations.[2] It is related that

[1] cf. Brandreth, *Episcopi Vagantes and the Anglican Church* (2nd ed., 1961), appendix A, pp. 118–19.
[2] See p. 282.

before Harrington's death Mar Jacobus II had promised that sooner or later Mar Ignatius I would get a nasty shock, which would have the effect of a knock-out blow at Homs on the Orontes where he resided. The time now seemed ripe to deliver it.

Accordingly on Sunday, October 17, 1943, that which was to become known to history as 'The Council of London' was held. While the Russians were bombing the Germans at Dnepropetrovsk and Dneprodserchink in the east central Ukraine, major and minor prelates of the Ancient British Church, British Orthodox Catholic Church, Apostolic Episcopal Church, Old Catholic Orthodox Church, Order of the Holy Wisdom, and Order of Antioch, made their way to 271 Green Lanes, Palmers Green, No. 13, part of which was rented as an office for the Ancient British Patriarchate. This was a pretty little semi-detached red brick house, designed in the most rococo phase of the 'naughty nineties' architecture, with high pitched gables, coy little bow-windows, and a riot of decorative trimmings in stone, wood, plaster, and half-timber.[1]

Mar Jacobus, whose memory was erratic, forgot about this gathering, and did not turn up until it was nearly over. The Council was not reported in *The Times*, or *The Tablet*. It was not mentioned by any newspaper even ecclesiastical, anywhere in the world, but its Acts, summarized as follows, were issued in a printed leaflet, which stated:

'(i) The Council embracing steadfastly the definitions of the Seven Oecumenical Councils and the Holy Apostolic Traditions repudiated the heresies of Monophysitism and Jansenism and all other heresies; (ii) that in view of Ignatius Ephrem I having disclaimed all connection with the above mentioned extensions of his patriarchate, lawfully made by his predecessor, the said Ignatius was no longer recognized as holding office, that in consequence of the Patriarchal Synod and many of the bishops in Syria and Malabar having adhered to the aforementioned the right to elect to the vacant see was declared to be vested in the Council; (iii) that in order to prevent confusion with the followers or the adherents of the aforesaid patriarch it was provided that the Church within the rightful Patriarchate of Antioch should no longer be called "the Syrian Orthodox" or "Jacobite" Church, but should be hereafter known as "The Ancient Orthodox Catholic Church" and by no other name; that the original jurisdiction of the Patriarchate

---

[1] The part-Patriarchate has now become the offices of a building firm, and lacks a plaque on its exterior, recording that the Council of London took place here in 1943.

should be remain as heretofore, but its extensions in the West were specifically recognized and confirmed in their rights; that the traditional name "Ignatius" in the official designation should be abandoned, and the name "Basilius" substituted therefor; that the full Patriarchal title should in future be as follows: "His Holiness Mohoran Mar Basilius *N.*, Sovereign Prince Patriarch of the God-protected city of Antioch and of all the Domain of the Apostolic Throne, both in the East and in the West"; (iv) Mar Bernard, Bishop of St Sophia (Grand Master of the Order of the Holy Wisdom) was elected to the vacant Patriarchal See of Antioch, under the title of Basilius Abdullah III, to whom all bishops dependant upon the See of Antioch were required to make their canonical submission within six months from the date of the Council, unless lawfully hindered; (v) the Council support all legitimate measures for Christian re-union and exhorted the faithful to pray for this end; (vi) the Council protested against resolutions 27 and 28 of the Lambeth Conference 1920, which it regarded as an unwarranted attack upon the validity of Episcopal Orders of many Catholic and Orthodox autocephalous Churches and a hindrance to the re-union of Christendom. These acts were duly signed and sealed by the authorized representatives of the aforementioned eccleciastical organisations.'

Considering that the Notice issued by the Syrian Orthodox Patriarchate of Antioch on December 10, 1938, had been directed specifically against 'all the sects claiming succession through Vilatte', and contained no reference to those claiming the Ferrette succession, it is difficult to understand why the Ancient British Patriarchate should have felt that the document was worth treating seriously; but this is how Mar Georgius has explained the Council of London with remarkable ingenuity.

'In 1943 a division took place among the Jacobites, those who adhered to Monophysitism continuing as the Syrian Orthodox Church under the Patriarch Ignatius Ephrem I, whilst another section at the Council of London repudiated Monophysitism and Jansenism and elected as Patriarch H. H. Basilius Abdullah III and adopted the title "The Ancient Orthodox Catholic Church".[1]

This was not a revolt against Ignatius Ephrem I, for he himself in 1938 had severed all connection with certain portions of his

---

[1] There is no reference to this schism in the section devoted to the Syrian Jacobite Church in Donald Attwater's *The Christian Churches of the East*, vol. II, *Churches not in Communion with Rome* (1961), pp. 204–10.

Patriarchate, which, being left in a position analogous to that visualized by Canons 37 and 39 of the Council of Trullo, A.D. 691, had no alternative but to elect a Patriarch, and at the same time took the opportunity of making their formal submission to the Seven Oecumenical Councils.[1]

By a deed of Declaration dated 23rd of March, 1944, the Ancient British Church and the British Orthodox Catholic Church, all previously referred to, united with the Old Catholic Orthodox Church. The latter body was derived from the Old Catholic Movement established in Britain in 1908 by the late Archbishop Arnold Harris Mathew, who had been received into union with the Greek Orthodox Patriarchs of Antioch and Alexandria in 1911 and 1912 respectively.[2] The United Church adopted the title "The Western Orthodox Catholic Church", and was constituted as the Catholicate of the West by the Patriarch Basilius Abdullah III, and thereupon became a fully autonomous and autocephalous member of the family of Orthodox Churches with full territorial jurisdiction in Britain and Western Europe.'[3]

This all sounds reasonable enough, but the fact remains that none of the dissident Churches of the East—Orthodox, Monophysite, or Nestorian—recognized 'The Western Orthodox Catholic Church' as 'a fully autonomous and autocephalous member' of their respective families, or admitted that it had 'full territorial jurisdiction' in any part of Europe. If the truth must be told, those so-called 'extensions' of the Antiochene Patriarchate in the West were a chimera, based on the tradition handed down from the eighteen-sixties that the apostate French Dominican, Julius Ferrette, having been consecrated Bishop of Iona by Mar Bedros, Bishop of Emesa (Homs), had been appointed by the Jacobite Patriarch as his Legate in Europe, with the specific purpose of erecting an autocephalous British Patriarchate.[4] To the objective observer, the so-called Council of London and its Acts are of the stuff that dreams are reminiscent of, an Arabian Nights tale. For

---

[1] There is no evidence that any Patriarch of Antioch had ever regarded any of these tiny schismatic bodies in England as 'portions' of his Patriarchate. As to the Canons of the Council of Trullo 691, they had little or no application to the situation in 1943. (cf. Brandreth, *Episcopi Vagantes and the Anglican Church* (2nd ed., 1961), p. 74, n. 2.)

[2] See p. 448, 449. As a matter of fact, the Old Catholic Orthodox Church was the sect founded in 1922 by the Lord Patriarch Banks after his consecration by Willoughby. (See p. 371.)

[3] *Catholicate of the West: Historical Notes concerning the Western Orthodox Catholic Church.* Orthodox Catholic Leaflets, no. 2. For the subsequent history of the Catholicate of the West, see chapter ten (pp. 443–501.)

[4] See pp. 36–47.

none of the prelates who took part in its brief session could claim jurisdiction over more than perhaps a dozen followers, and some of the Churches had only a paper existence. They did, on the other hand, take themselves quite seriously.

War-time travel restrictions made it impossible for the Mefrain, and the Bishops of Aleppo, Beirut-Damascus, Jerusalem, and Mosul (each holding the title of Metropolitan) to make their canonical submission to the new Patriarch within six months from the date of the Council. It is doubtful, however, if any of them felt called to repudiate Monophysitism or Jansenism; any more than the Malabar-Jacobite bishops in India, who remained loyal to Mar Ignatius Ephrem I. So Mrs Crow did not have to entertain these Oriental prelates as their status demanded in the new Antiochene patriarchate at Woodford Green. Neither did their presence add glamour to the celebration of the Ancient Mysteries in their pristine form carried out by the initiates of the *Ekklesia Agiae Sophiae* in their planetary and zodiacal temple of the Universal Religion.[1]

The venerable Mar Jacobus II is said to have been deeply impressed by the results of the Council of London. The moment had come when he could lay aside his many burdens. He was allowed to retain the see of Selsey, covering the county of Sussex, with the rank of Archbishop *ad personam*. He gave his consent to the election of Hugh George de Willmott Newman (titular Abbot Nullius of St Albans) as first Catholicos of the West, and in that status he was duly consecrated by Mar Basilius Abdullah III on Easter Monday, April 10, 1944.[2] Somewhat later Mar Jacobus II resigned his office as fifth Patriarch of the Ancient British Church in favour of de Willmott Newman, on whom he bestowed the rank of sixth Patriarch. The Brixton schoolmaster, Herbert James Heard, who had done some very curious things since he became a bishop in 1922, died at Tunbridge Wells on September 9, 1947, aged eighty.

William Hall, the Chaplain at Abney Park Cemetery, Stamford Hill, who succeeded Heard in 1939 as Bishop Primus of the Free Protestant Episcopal Church, took good care that it did not lack pastors. In June 1950, he raised to the episcopate one of Mar Georgius's former priests, John Beswarwick, who had made a name

---

[1] Mar Ignatius Ephrem I died in 1957, and was succeeded by Mar Jacob of Beirut, who became Mar Ignatius Jacob III, without reference to the claims of Mar Basilius Abdullah III. So the last-named was able to continue as Senior Lecturer in Biology at Leicester College (Technical and Commerce), and did not have to migrate to Homs in Syria.

[2] See pp. 448-451.

for himself as a faith-healer.[1] It is said that this latter prelate, who usually signed his name 'John of Petros', tried to emulate Mar Theophilus (Stevens) by reviving a form of Christian Druidism. Beswarwick is believed to have laid his hands on several bishops, including Eric Smith (1952), Jan Van Moll (1954), and George Haas (1956), but little is recorded of their episcopal activities.

Archbishop Hall, having lost his church at Retreat Place, Hackney, owing to site demolition, induced a patron to provide a deposit and a mortgage on a Methodist chapel in Stonebridge Road, South Tottenham, which became redundant in 1932, when the Wesleyan Methodists, Primitive Methodists, and United Methodists were amalgamated as 'The Methodist Church'. He re-opened it as St Andrew's Collegiate Church, which served as the pro-cathedral of the Free Protestant Episcopal Church, as well as the accommodation address of the Nazarene College, which had passed to each Bishop Primus since its foundation by James Martin in 1890. Also registered here under the Companies' Act was St Andrew's Correspondence College (Tottenham) Limited.

The Chechemian succession now passed on to a few more staunch Protestant-minded ministers. Among them were Charles Denis Boltwood, ordained priest in 1950, and raised to the episcopate on Palm Sunday, 1952; and John Leslie Baines, an Anglican clergyman, originally associated with Pinder's Evangelical Church of England, details of whose career in communion with Canterbury are still printed in *Crockford*.

Bishop Boltwood took over St Andrew's Collegiate Church from Archbishop Hall, thus relieving him of certain financial obligations. Before very long the former Methodist chapel became the headquarters of the British Synod of the Ecumenical Church Foundation, with Bishop Boltwood as its President. It was advertised as 'a specific Church, pertaining to the Christian Church throughout the world—Ecclesiastical, Evangelical, Apostolic, and Unsectarian'. Mrs Boltwood, M.A., D.D. was raised to the rank of Archdeaconess. She and her episcopal spouse were assisted in the Synod by an Archdeacon, Chaplain, four Deacons, and six Deaconesses. All the fourteen members of the Synod had one or more degrees conferred by the 'College of Science', founded in 1942. It is improbable that many of the inhabitants of South Tottenham were aware that the Ecumenical Church Foundation, located in a back street off Seven Sisters Road, 'enjoyed the chartered rights' of the

[1] See p. 474. He died on October 4, 1962, aged seventy-nine years.

Churches Claiming the Ferrette Succession

innumerable Academies and Colleges, both in Europe and America, even in more distant continents, with which it was said to be affiliated. Few realized that the President 'had been honoured with nobility titles, knighthoods of many ancient and Knight Templar Orders, and over one hundred academic awards, including Gold and Silver Medals, etc., for his writings in Theology, Philosophy, Literature, and in the Arts and Sciences in the fields of culture and art.'[1] Members of this Foundation had to subscribe to the Thirty-Nine Articles of the Anglican Book of Common Prayer as the substance of their belief; a proof of its sound Protestant basis. The head of the International Synod was Archbishop Earl Anglin James, D.D., LL.D., K.C.G.[2]

This illustrious Canadian Archbishop, who in the course of about twenty years has managed to collect more than a hundred and twenty honorary degrees, not to mention countless fellowships in fine arts, applied arts and music, has led an adventurous life. Born at Memphis, Tennessee, in 1901, his father was a racetrack groom. The James family moved to Canada, where, having tried hard for eight years to obtain a B.A. degree at the University of Toronto, young Earl Anglin gave himself his first degree in 1929 (a fellowship of music), and managed to get his photograph published in all the city newspapers. Two years later he incorporated a National College of Music, Art and Literature under provincial letters patent, and named himself its head. Between 1931 and about 1945 he seems to have prospered by granting diplomas, degrees, certificates and credentials of all sorts. In 1943 he told a newspaper reporter that he held the world's record for college degrees.

His ecclesiastical career was equally remarkable, for starting as a simple Anglican layman he acquired a Doctorate of Divinity, and soon rose to the rank of Old Roman Catholic Bishop of Toronto, having been consecrated by Archbishop Carfora on June 17, 1945.[3] Too busy with professorial and episcopal duties in Canada to travel to England, Bishop James was enthroned

---

[1] ibid. It is curious that Bishop Boltwood does not appear in either *The Author's and Writer's Who's Who*, or in *Kelly's Handbook of the Titled, Landed and Official Classes*. His writings are not included in the printed catalogues of either the British Museum, or the Library of Congress. The catalogue, now called the National Union Catalog, is kept up to date with monthly, quarterly and annual supplements.

[2] In November 1946 he had been solemnly enthroned (*in absentia*) by Mar Georgius, Patriarch of Glastonbury, as His Eminence Mar Laurentius, Archbishop and Metropolitan of Acadia, and Exarch of the Catholicate in the West in the Canadas. (See p. 458.)

[3] See p. 433.

Churches Claiming the Ferrette Succession

in absentia by Mar Georgius, Patriarch of Glastonbury, on November 24, 1946. The function took place in the patriarchal oratory at Kew, where James was given the style of 'His Eminence Mar Laurentius, Archbishop and Metropolitan of Acadia, and Exarch of the Catholicate of the West in the Canadas'.[1] His Eminence managed to find the time to combine his exarchal obligations between the Atlantic and the Pacific with those of Dean of St Andrew's Ecumenical Church Foundation and University College, London, England. Rather later he assumed the status of Dean of St Andrew's International Synod, which claimed twenty-seven agencies around the world. In 1950 the Archbishop and Metropolitan of Acadia consecrated Grant T. Billett as Patriarch of a free-lance Old Catholic Church in America, and so helped to pave the way for the foundation of several more sects with impressive titles.[2]

Even more incredible was the Archbishop's rise in the social sphere. Eventually he claimed among other ranks those of a General of the Legion of Honour, Foreign Minister of Togo, Duke of Scala, Prince of Palma, Prince of the Irish Principality of Thomond, and Sheriff of Chicago. More recently he took the title of 'His Excellency the Right Honorable Doctor Sir Earl Anglin James'. But he has not neglected his ecclesiastical duties, and he is now styled ' ✠ [1]Laurentius I, Founder EAJ Peace Missions, Archbishop-Primate'. This organization, so he states, was founded 'to perpetuate and Commemorate the Memory of Our Elmer Anglin James, the famous sportsman worthy of Merit and Honor, who gained Fame of Queen's Plate of England and Duke of York Stakes, being associated with Baron de Rothschild of France . . . etc.' With its headquarters at Miami, Florida, the EAJ Peace Missions are said to have, besides the Primate, an assistant archbishop, a bishop, a vicar-general, and even an aide-de-camp, in the person of the Rt. Hon. Count Dr Bruce Vickers. His Eminence still continues to award degrees and diplomas for almost every conceivable branch of knowledge from his National University College, 62 Wroxeter Street, Toronto. It has been reported that he maintains an Ambassador at Washington, D.C., but this has not been confirmed.[3]

With Archbishop Earl Anglin James in Canada as its supreme

[1] See p. 458.
[2] See p. 538, n. 2.
[3] Cf. Barbara Moon, 'The Prince of Degree Merchants', in *Maclean's Magazine* (Toronto, April 6, 1963).

head, St Andrew's Collegiate College could boast of an international group of eighteen patrons, each with impressive titles and degrees. Among them were Prince Amoroso d'Aragona, Ph.D., LL.D. (Academia 'Phoenix and Minerva'); Dr Salah-ad-Din, D.D., D.Sc., Ph.D. (Founder World Organiser of GRESCO, Australia); Dr Charles Lathrop Warn, D. Litt., Ph.D., LL.D. (G.M. of the Ancient Order of Ursus); and Professor Dr Eng. don Alberto R. Palumbo, Ph. D., LL.D. (Bibliotheca Partenopea, Italy).[1]

From the Mother House of this unsectarian organization in South Tottenham, the presbyters, deacons, and deaconesses appeared to carry on an intensive system of Spiritual Education, including a 'Dynamic Prayer Course', to help people to obtain that 'Dynamic Release' which brings and maintains Success and Prosperity. One of the leaflets issued proved how Prophecy was being fulfilled by the 'Spiritual Cataclysmic Movements in the Heavens and on the Earth Planet'. Archbishop Earl Anglin James, Bishop Boltwood, and his archdeaconess wife, felt that this noble work 'should be recognized as wholly Worthy and Beneficial to our Queen and to the Governments of the Commonwealth of Nations, *and to the people in very truth*'. It is sad to reflect that neither Her Majesty, nor any of the sovereign independent states of the British Commonwealth of Nations, took the Ecumenical Church Foundation under their patronage.

Meanwhile Bishop Boltwood had met Mar Georgius, and they decided that it would be to their mutual advantage to co-operate. For one thing; 'His Sacred Beatitude, the Patriarch of Glastonbury, Caertroia, and Mylapore; Successor of St Thomas; Apostolic Pontiff to Celtica and of the Indies; Prince Catholicos of the West, and of the United Orthodox Catholic Rite'—to give Mar Georgius his official style and titles—badly needed a building in which he could carry out pontifical functions, not yet having managed to raise the money to erect a cathedral at either Glastonbury or London, or in any other part of his world-wide spiritual dominions. So he was glad to have the free use of the former Methodist conventicle in South Tottenham. On July 6, 1956, the Prince Catholicos of the West re-consecrated the Bishop of the Free Protestant Episcopal Church of England, giving him the status of Titular Bishop of Thorney, also that of Auxiliary to his Beatitude north of the

---

[1] cf. *Prospectus of the Ecumenical Church Foundation*. Prince Amoroso d'Aragona was also associated with the Old Holy Catholic Church. (See p. 384.)

Thames.[1] The ceremony was performed according to a vernacular version of the *Pontificale Romanum*. The association of the Ecumenical Church Foundation with the Catholicate of the West was purely a marriage of convenience, and it is surprising that it managed to hold together for as long as four years.

In 1958 Bishop Boltwood made a tour of North America, where he laid his hands on several ministers, and made bishops of four of them—Emmet Neil Enochs (Missionary Bishop for California), Emanuel Samuel Yekorogha (Liberia), Charles Kennedy Samuel Stewart Moffat (Canada), and Benjamin Eckhart (U.S.A.). All these overseers were for Dr Boltwood's Protestant organization, from whose original title the words 'of England' were dropped, in view of its extensions overseas.

Archbishop Hall, so it is stated, 'passed into the higher life' on October 9, 1959, when Dr Boltwood succeeded him as Bishop-Primus of the Free Protestant Episcopal Church. It is possible that Hall had laid his hands some time before this on a minister named James A. Cunningham. Shortly before his passing on, Hall consecrated T. H. Davenport, who appears to have succeeded him for a while.[2]

About a year after the death of Bishop-Primus Hall, Dr Boltwood, who still held among his duties that of Protosynkellos of the Catholicate of the West, and Auxiliary to the Patriarchal Throne of Glastonbury, heard a clear call to revert to the elusive Protestantism of Chechemian, Martin, and McLaglen, which involved a break with Mar Georgius.[3]

Although free from state control, the Free Protestant Episcopal Church is so erastian in spirit that its Synod recommends that wherever possible the Liturgy issued by the authority of the reigning Sovereign of Great Britain, the Royal Family, and the country should be used. This must create tricky liturgical problems in the overseas dioceses. Again, it is curious that although this body is so uncompromisingly Protestant in all its doctrines and modes of worship, it should feel it worth while to stress that its orders are

[1] See p. 495.

[2] Cunningham's notepaper is headed 'Free Protestant Episcopal Church', and underneath this is printed 'Founded in U.S.A. in 1784 by Dr Samuel Seabury (First Bishop). Established in London at Hackney in 1897'. At the time of writing this Bishop's address is a caravan camp in Essex. His name does not appear in the list of bishops published at St Andrew's Collegiate Church.

[3] See p. 498. Judging from a photograph of Bishop-Primus Boltwood reproduced in a recent official brochure, this did not necessitate resuming the Low Church Anglican garb adopted by the three founders of the F.P.E.C.E., for he is depicted in a variant of the robes of a prelate of the Latin Rite, including a large tufted biretta.

derived from Armenian, Anglican, Roman, and Greek sources.[1] We are told that it 'condemns and rejects the following erroneous and strange doctrines as contrary to God's Word:

(1) That the Church of Christ exists only in one order or form of ecclesiastical polity.

(2) That the Christian ministers are 'priests' in another sense than that in which all believers are a 'royal priesthood'.

(3) The the Lord's Table is an altar on which the oblation of the Body and Blood of Christ is offered anew to the Father.

(4) That the presence of Christ in the Lord's Supper is a presence in the elements of Bread and Wine.

(5) That Regeneration is inseparably connected with Baptism.

(6) That the Laws of the Realm should punish Christian men with death.

(7) That it is lawful for Christian men to wear weapons, and serve in wars other than in aiding the wounded or in assisting in civil defence, such as First-Aid, Rescue and welfare and such-like services.'[2]

Bishop-Primus Boltwood opens his arms wide to any Evangelical sect, Christian groups, Missions, and similar organizations to enjoy the protection and privileges afforded by his headquarters in South Tottenham. Earnest young men and women are invited to seek admission to St Andrew's Collegiate College, to be trained by post as loyal Protestant Ministers, Preachers, and Evangelists.

The Head of the Church Council of the Free Protestant Episcopal Church is Bishop James B. Noble, Ph. D. (of the Church of St Joseph of Arimathea, Cilcain, Mold, Flintshire), raised to the episcopate in 1957.[3] A more recent episcopal member was the Right Rev. William C. Cato-Symonds, who became Titular Bishop of Elmham on April 15, 1962.[4] There are two Bishops with juris-

[1] The *Origin, Orders, Organisation, etc., of the Free Protestant Episcopal Church* (n.d.), p. 2.

[2] ibid., pp. 7–8. The first five of these principles are identical with those put forth by the Convocation of the Free Church of England, but this body takes no stand against capital punishment or military service.

[3] It appears from recent letter headings that Bishop Noble is now the Presiding Bishop of the Free Protestant Episcopal Church of England (described as 'a Universal Ecclesiastical and Episcopal Church'), and that he rules over it from his retreat in the heart of the Clwydian Mountains of North Wales.

[4] Having been ordained deacon and priest by the Bishop of Sodor and Man (1929–30), served several Anglican curacies, been Vicar of St Andrew, Whittlesey (Diocese of Ely) from 1940 to 1947, and a Chaplain to the Forces, Cato-Symonds resigned his orders in 1948. He is said to have been re-ordained by Mar Georgius, before he joined the F.P.E.C., and became a bishop. He has now become Coadjutor to Archbishop Ignatius Carolus of the Old Holy Catholic Church. (See p. 389.)

diction in Canada; the one at Brandon, Manitoba, the other at London, Ontario. In the U.S.A. Bishop Enochs rules over the faithful, from his headquarters at Los Angeles, California. Bishop Yekorogha keeps a watch over both Anglo and Roman Catholic aggression in Liberia and Nigeria. Bishop-Primus Boltwood has under his immediate jurisdiction a few lonely Protestant outposts in British Guiana and the West Indies. From his curia off Seven Sisters Road, London N.15 he does his best to 'maintain the principles of the Reformation, and to work for the unity of Christendom', certain that his organization 'is scriptural in its tenets, making the Word of God its sole rule of Faith and Practice; is liturgical in its worship, and holds the doctrines of grace substantially as they are set forth in the Thirty-Nine Articles of Religion'.

The autocephalous churches and their offshoots claiming the Syrian Jacobite succession from Mar Julius, Bishop of Iona, are impossible to card-index, so elusive and contradictory are their beliefs and practices. It is not surprising therefore that His Holiness Mar Ignatius Jacob III, the present Patriarch of the God-protected City of Antioch and of All the Domain of the Apostolic Throne, does not recognize any of them. Not only do these schismatic sects differ in doctrine and discipline from this ancient but now sadly reduced Monophysite Church of the Antiochene Rite, but certain facts have to be faced, which can be summed up as follows:

1. The Syrian Jacobite Church has never recognized the existence of a British Patriarchate claiming succession from Mar Bedros, Bishop of Emesa (Homs). In 1958 its Patriarch warned the public that the 'statements and pretensions [made by the heads of churches in England claiming this succession] are altogether without truth'.

2. There is no documentary evidence that Ferrette consecrated Morgan (Mar Pelagius), or that the latter raised to the episcopate Stevens (Mar Theophilus) as his Co-adjutor with the right of succession as British Patriarch.

3. It is practically certain that Chechemian (later known as Mar Leon) had never been a Catholic Armenian bishop; on the other hand it is probable that he was raised to the episcopate in 1890 by Stevens and Richardson, whose lines of succession are doubtful.

4. The only consecration of Stevens of which we have any

definite knowledge is the one which took place in 1898, and which was performed by Chechemian.

Such then are the very insecure foundations on which rest all the churches claiming their apostolic succession from the Syrian Jacobite Church through Mar Bedros and Ferrette.

CHAPTER VIII

CHURCHES OF THE VILATTE SUCCESSION

(A) American Catholic Church,
American Catholic Church (Western Orthodox),
American Episcopal Church,
American Catholic Church (Syro-Antiochean),
American Holy Orthodox Catholic Apostolic
Eastern Church, affiliated with the Holy Orthodox
Catholic Patriarchate of America:

(B) African Orthodox Church,
African Orthodox Church of New York
and Massachusetts, Afro-American Catholic Church,
African Greek Orthodox Church:

(C) Old Catholic Church, Catholic Christian Church,
Orthodox Catholic Church in England,
Autonomous African Universal Church,
Orthodox-Keltic Church
of the British Commonwealth of Nations,
Autonomous British Eastern Church
(Orthodox-Catholic Province of our Lady of England,
Devon and Cornwall),
Jesuene or Free Orthodox Catholic Church,
Holy Orthodox-Catholic Church of Great Britain:

(D) Eglise Catholique Française,
Eglise Orthodoxe Gallicane Autocéphale,
Eglise Primitive Catholique et Apostolique,
Eglise Catholique Apostolique Primitive d'Antioche

252

The Most Rev. Frederick
Ebenezer John Lloyd, Second
Primate of the American
Catholic Church. The photo-
graph was taken in 1932, the
year before his death.

The Most Rev. Mar Justinos
(Thiesen) of Cologne,
Patriarch of the Primitive
Church of Antioch, etc.

Churches of the Vilatte Succession

Orthodoxe et de Tradition Syro-Byzantine, Sainte Eglise Apostolique et Gallicane, Sainte Eglise Celtique en Bretagne, Sainte Eglise Apostolique, Communion Evangelica Catholica Eucharistica, Hochkirche in Osterreich, Indian National Church, etc.

Some twenty bodies in North America, Africa, and Europe claim the Vilatte succession—more so indirectly. Through him, they maintain, their orders are derived from the Jacobite Patriarchate of Antioch, by way of the Independent Catholic Church of Goa and Ceylon. In recent years, however, the Vilatte stream in some of these sects has been merged with those of the Chechemian, Mathew, and other lines, and they glory in their very mixed ancestry.

By 1917 people in North America who were not satisfied with either the Roman or the Protestant Episcopalian presentations of Catholicism could take their choice of three varieties of non-papal and non-anglican character: (1) *The American Catholic Church;* (2) *The Old Roman Catholic Church;* and (3) *The Catholic Church of North America.* The last two bodies had been formed by Bishops Carfora and Brothers of the Mathew succession. If you were a Slav, there was the Polish National Catholic Church. Besides the above mentioned bodies there was the Liberal Catholic Church with places of worship in many parts of the United States and Canada; and already a number of small bodies claiming Eastern origin, certain that their bishops and priests had valid orders. Throwing off the yoke of either Rome or Canterbury—or of any of the Eastern Patriarchates for that matter—had not helped to bring about the Unity of Christendom in North America.

A. THE VILATTE SUCCESSION IN NORTH AMERICA
The American Catholic Church

Although legally incorporated in 1915, during the height of the First World War, though the United States was still a neutral nation, this Church, with Mar Timotheos as its first Primate, did not make much progress until after 1920, when he was succeeded by Frederick Ebenezer Lloyd, D.D., D. Litt., Mus. Doc., who was active, astute and optimistic.[1] The moment was opportune, for the

[1] See p. 126.

country was beginning to experience a major boom. 'The post-war period, so full of restlessness, with its craze for entertainment and passion for frivolity, had already given birth to the Jazz Age. The flapper had arrived, a little tipsy, with short skirts and bobbed hair. It was a time for petting and necking; for flasks and roadside taverns; for movie "palaces" and automobiles . . . All America was stepping out on an emotional binge.'[1] Such was the background against which the American Catholic Church grew up. Lloyd was but one of many religious adventurers who were 'determined to lead the parade on a grand detour to Heaven'. Able to cut a figure in society, he had many more qualifications for becoming a star turn than his French predecessor, who never managed to convince people that he was a 'real gentleman'.

Within three years he gave his sect three bishops. The first of these was Carl Nybladh, an Episcopalian clergyman of Swedish extraction, who was consecrated at Chicago in 1921. A few of his flock followed him into communion with Lloyd, but most of them found their way back into the Episcopalian fold. The second was Samuel Gregory Lines, a former priest of the Protestant Episcopal Church. He was consecrated by Archbishop Lloyd on July 21, 1923, in the Armenian Church at Los Angeles, lent for the occasion; seven months after the solemn opening of Sister Aimee Semple McPherson's $1,500,000 Angelus Temple in the same city. Lines took the title of Bishop of the Province of the Pacific.[2] Not having managed to win over many Scandinavians by making Nybladh bishop, Lloyd consecrated on June 24, 1924, another ex-priest of the Protestant Episcopal Church, by name Axel Zacharias Fryxell.

In August 1925 Lloyd convened a Conference of Old Catholic bodies at Chicago. Before the delegates dispersed he managed to achieve an apparent union between his American Catholic Church and some of them. It was agreed to adopt a joint title of 'The Holy Catholic Church in America'. The object of this amalgamation was 'to make good children, good men, good women, and thus good citizens'. The 'Special Aim and Mission' of the Holy Catholic

---

[1] Carey McWilliams, 'Aimee Semple McPherson: Sunlight in My Soul', in *The Aspirin Age*, ed. by Isabel Leighton (1950) p. 60.

[2] With the *nihil obstat* of Lloyd, Lines published *The Liturgy according to the Use of the American Catholic Church (Western Orthodox) in the Province of the Pacific*. This new rite was authorized for use in California, Oregon, Wyoming, Washington, Arizona, Nevada, Utah, Colorado, Idaho, and Montana; until the adoption of a Missal by the entire American Catholic Church. Lines's *Liturgy* was based on the Roman Rite, but with interpolations suggesting Theosophical influence.

Church in America would be 'to offer itself as the only logical centre for the reunion of Christendom, according to the time-honoured maxim: In essentials unity, in non-essentials liberty, in all things charity'. Each unity of the body would retain its own particular title, e.g. American Catholic Church, Old Roman Catholic Church, and Polish Catholic Church.[1]

The conference resolved to publish a joint periodical, *The American Catholic.* The first issue (September, 1925) stressed that the way was now open 'to all non-papal Catholics to come into true unity with all who are of like purpose to themselves'. An invitation to join the ranks of the Holy Catholic Church in America was 'cordially given'. Prospective members were invited to write to either Archbishop Lloyd of the American Catholic Church, or to Archbishop Carfora of the Old Roman Catholic Church.[2] Everything looked marvellous on paper. Lists of the bishops and priests of both these sects were printed, with their addresses, conveying the impression of two widespread and powerful non-ultramontane churches, now in full communion with each other. But it soon became the exclusive organ of Lloyd's followers.

The American Catholic Church was boosted as 'an independent, self-governing body, yielding no allegiance or obedience to any foreign ruler, ecclesiastic or Church, but standing solidly for American ideals in institutions—free speech, free press, political and religious liberty for all, with interference from none, and complete separation of Church and State'. This manifesto was probably directed mainly to Archbishop Mundelein, who had been promoted to the see of Chicago in 1915, and created Cardinal Priest in March, 1924. But it is doubtful if many Roman Catholics in the State of Illinois felt it worth while to transfer their allegiance from this German prelate subject to an Italian pope to that of the English-born primate of the new independent Catholic church which repudiated all foreign rulers.

The state of theoretical national and ecclesiastical unity was of brief duration. Schisms and sub-schisms soon began to rend the garment of the Holy Catholic Church in America. Within a few years it became hard to tell to what body this or that congregation belonged. Nevertheless bishops and priests went on being added to the American Catholic Church by the energetic Primate or his

---

[1] The last-named was a handful of schismatic Poles under the leadership of Fr Boryszewski (see p. 259.)
[2] See p. 430.

suffragans. Daniel Cassell Hinton was consecrated by Lloyd on March 27, 1927, with the status of Coadjutor. Having no colour prejudices, Lloyd raised to the episcopate on June 1, 1927, a negro named Leopold Peterson, who composed a new Liturgy for the Church.[1]

Gregory Lines, Archbishop of the Pacific, was an unstable character, and twice lapsed into schism. On December 21, 1927, in order to defy the authority of Archbishop Lloyd, he consecrated a lapsed Roman Catholic priest, named Joseph A. Boyle, as his coadjutor in California. Then it was reported at Chicago that on August 30, 1940, Boyle—now known as Bishop Justin—had raised to the episcopate a member of the Theosophical Society, Lowell Paul Wadle.[2]

In February 1928 Archbishop Lloyd informed one of his friends that Mar Severus (later Ignatius Ephrem I, Jacobite Patriarch of Antioch), then acting as Legate of Mar Ignatius Elias III, had called on him at Chicago, with the express orders of His Beatitude. Lloyd said: 'he is a glorious person and altogether delightful', and intimated that they had conversed together on many important matters, including that of Vilatte's submission to the Holy See. What was most gratifying was the affirmation by this Syrian prelate that the clergy of the American Catholic Church were 'all true bishops and true priests'.

When Mar Severus got wind of the stories being spread by Lloyd, he denied the whole thing emphatically, and wrote in his quaint English:

'This liar man and of his followers, had wrote to His Holiness, our Patriarch, about that disguised persons, he charge me to make an enquiry. I was obliged to meet him [Lloyd] in a very simple way and investigate his quality in Chicago. I told him orally the falsification of the heretic Vilatte's papers and the invalidity of his acts, foolish and laughable consecrations and titles; that Vilatte himself, Frederick Lloyd, and all African and Negro branches of their heretic company.'[3]

Like a strayed sheep, the Archbishop of the Pacific found his way back into the American Catholic Church but he soon broke loose again. On December 16, 1933, he raised Howard E. Mather to the

---

[1] Other bishops consecrated by Lloyd or his suffragans were Casimir François Durand (September 16, 1926); Francis Kanski (1926); and Arthur Edward Leighton (Easter, 1927).

[2] See p. 536.

[3] From a letter in possession of the Rev. H. R. T. Brandreth.

episcopate, although he was only a Congregationalist minister.[1] The reason given for Lines's second lapse into schism was his annoyance that Hinton and not himself had been elected Primate on Lloyd's retirement in 1932.

Life was not altogether a bed of roses for Archbishop Lines, for there were so many varieties of Christianity in post First World War Southern California from which to take one's choice. They ranged from what Archbishop Cantwell and other prelates and priests yielding allegiance and obedience to an Italian Church had to offer, to the much more sensational home-made attractions at the Angelus Temple, Los Angeles, where from 1923 until 1944, when she 'stepped up to glory', Sister Aimee Semple McPherson magnetized millions by her sex appeal, dynamic preaching, and her chorus girls vested in virginal white, with grey-lined blue capes. There was really very little demand in a city with more than 200 registered religions for what Archbishop Lines could supply as a mixture of Catholicism and Theosophy. Not having the resources to erect a cathedral on the scale of the Angelus Temple, the Archbishop of the Pacific had to make do with a room in the Auditorium of the Philanthropy and Civics Club House for his pontifical functions. Notices informed the public that the Western Orthodox Church was 'Catholic but not Roman—American in being loyal to things that are really fundamental, liberal in all else'. Unlike the foreign ritual and ceremonial propagated by the Roman Catholic clergy of the Archdiocese of Los Angeles, in this hundred per cent American form of worship 'every article of apparel worn by the officiating ministers, and every word spoken, and act performed had Scriptural, Historic, Scientific, Mystical, Spiritual, and practical meaning'. It was claimed that the Sunday services made up 'a magnificent institution for the accomplishment of public worship'. Yet for some reason American Catholicism as presented by the schismatic Archbishop failed to make any wide appeal. It never dazzled the community, and faded out as new neo-theosophical bodies succeeded it, some of them off-shoots of the Liberal Catholic Church, others inspired by its teachings.

In Chicago, too, the situation was not altogether happy. The financial as well as the spiritual future of the American Catholic Church looked precarious. The stock market had been playing

[1] Some years later Mather was re-ordained deacon by Tyarks, the Caucasian bishop of the African Orthodox Church, and priested by Leighton of Fryxell's schism from the American Catholic Church. He took the title of 'Timothy, Archbishop and Exarch of the Order of Antioch', into which he had been received about 1925.

ducks and drakes since May 1929. Archbishop Lloyd began to think that it might be a wise precaution to transplant his body across the Atlantic and decided to summon a General Synod in September. Just a month before the final Wall Street crash on October 28, which ended the Coolidge-Hoover Prosperity era, the Archbishop, with Bishops Daniel C. Hinton, Gregory Lines (re-united for the time being), Francis Kanski, and Axel Fryxell as co-consecrators, raised John Churchill Sibley to the episcopate. The ceremony took place on Michaelmas Day in the chapel of the American Catholic Theological Seminary at Chicago, when the new prelate was given archiepiscopal dignity as Metropolitan for the British Empire, also that of Vicar General of the Order of Antioch in England.[1]

In spite of ceaseless dissensions within the ranks of his followers the Primate never lost hope of a great future for his Church. In the summer of 1929 he had issued the following message to *The American Churchman*:

'I have a work to do in America. By the help of God I am striving to do it, every day, every moment of every day. My all consuming purpose is to turn the hearts of my fellow countrymen to Christ in the church of His love; to show them their need of that ageless and unconquerable faith, and to establish the Catholic Church in and for America on a lasting foundation, without the guidance of any foreign earthly power, depending on the governance and the inspiration of the Divine Spirit. The American Catholic Church is a lamp of faith whose light will never be dimmed.'

Encouraged by his rich wife, née Philena R. Peabody, he continued to issue messages of hope for the near and distant future from his Consistory at 64 West Randolph Street, Chicago, proclaiming:

'The Church of the future in the United States will not be Protestant, because Protestantism is gradually falling to pieces, and its appeal is no longer that of true Christianity. It has been rendered nugatory by the violent and smashing incursions of politics.

---

[1] Sibley was born at Crewkerne, Somerset, in 1859. For some years he taught at Swansea Grammar School, and obtained the degree of Mus. Doc. in 1894. On April 23, 1924, Lloyd conditionally re-baptized and confirmed him in St Edythe's Chapel, London, and subsequently gave him minor and major orders up to the priesthood. For details of his later career, see pp. 276-278.

The Order of Antioch, founded by Lloyd, was open to any cleric with major orders who could prove to his own satisfaction continuity in one way or another with the Syrian Jacobite Church, even if its Patriarch did not recognize these claims.

Nor will the Church of the future be Protestant-Episcopalian (or as some of the members of the Protestant-Episcopalian Church call it, Anglo-Catholic), because it is part of the Anglican Communion.

Furthermore, the future Church of America will not be Roman Catholic, because that Communion is both Roman and Italian.

The Church of the future will be both Catholic and American.

May God speed the day.'

Lloyd's last consecration appears to have been that of Francis Ignatius Boryzsewski, a naturalized Polish priest, formerly one of Carfora's clergy, who had set up a little schismatic Polish Church of his own. The Metropolitan-Primate retired early in 1932, and died the following year, after a long, strenuous, and very varied career. He was survived by his wife.

Daniel C. Hinton, who succeeded Lloyd as Primate, to the indignation of Gregory Lines, may have felt that the problems waiting to be solved resembled those of Franklin D. Roosevelt, who succeeded Herbert C. Hoover as President of the United States in March 1933. Both the American Catholic Church and the American Nation needed a 'New Deal'. The loyal remnant of American Catholics in California, who had not followed Lines into schism for the second or third time, needed a shepherd of souls, so in August 1933 the Primate raised Percy Wise Clarkson to the episcopate for their benefit, no doubt having assured himself that the new prelate had adequate means of support, for the nation-wide depression was settling into a way of life, with more than 30,000,000 persons dependent on public and private charity. Bishop Clarkson opened a pro-cathedral at Laguna Beach, where he propagated not only American Catholicism, but also his own brand of Theosophy, which, so it is said, included numerology and other esoteric beliefs.

Another peculiar prelate was Francis Kanski, who as a priest had been a devoted friend to Vilatte. He had been secretly consecrated by Lloyd in 1926, at the time when President Calvin Coolidge, with whom economizing in every department had become a mania, was checking his wife's bills, lest she was spending too much money. On May 1, 1934—four weeks before the birth of the Dionne quintuplets at Callander, Ontario—Kanski consecrated a certain Denver Scott Swain, of McNabb, Illinois. Not satisfied with the validity of his orders, Swain had himself re-ordained up to the priesthood by Carfora in 1942, but he was suspended nine months later, because he had obtained his ordination through misrepresentation, and also because he attempted to seek re-consecration as a bishop in some other body. He then founded an independent sect which he called 'The American Episcopal Church', for which his over vivid imagination claimed a membership of 100,000. Swain must have had great powers of persuasion, because on January 17, 1947, he managed to get himself and his followers received into union with the Catholicate of the West in England, when Mar Georgius constituted his sect as an 'autocephalous affiliated Rite'.[1] It was unfortunate, however, that on November 1 that same year, *The American Lutheran* had the courage to denounce Archbishop Swain as a 'several times married ex-convict', with the alias of Denver Swari; and affirmed that he had been twice confined in Joliet Prison, Illinois, for a confidence game, to which he had pleaded guilty. Moreover, the Archbishop had succeeded in getting his name into *Who's Who in America*, where he stated that in 1936 he had been granted the degree of Doctor of Laws at the age of nineteen, the degree of Bachelor of Divinity (both from unlocated universities), and had been ordained priest and consecrated bishop in the Protestant Episcopal Church all in the one year. But the *American Lutheran* seemed to have found evidence that this distinguished ecclesiastic had actually spent that particular year as an inmate of a penitentiary; and had been obliged to return to prison in 1939. One of his statements which might well have been true was that he had received apostolic succession through seven or eight lines besides that of Vilatte, for lines of succession could be picked up with no fuss or bother during the nineteen-thirties, if one chose to look for them.

One of Vilatte's followers wrote about this time that he was 'the pioneer blazing the way for the (Old Catholic) movement to establish a Church in America which would be truly Catholic, without the errors of Rome, free and independent from every tie but those which are binding by the Decrees of the Ecumenical Councils of the Undivided Church of Christ'.[2] He might be better described as a comet against whose tail many innocent persons were singed, even after his death.

Archbishop Hinton's efforts to establish the American Catholic Church on a lasting foundation were a miserable failure. 'The Church of the Future', which his predecessor visualized so clearly,

---

[1] See p. 458.
[2] Bishop Daniel [Hinton], *Status of the American of the American Catholic Church* (n.d. or p.).

is now almost forgotten; the name of this once much advertised body has now disappeared from *The Yearbook of American Churches*.

On the other hand, Bishop Clarkson's Cathedral at Laguna Beach, California, dedicated to St Francis of Assisi, still appears to function under Archbishop Lowell P. Wadle, who was consecrated on August 30, 1930, by the former Roman Catholic priest, Bishop Justin Boyle.[1] It seems that Wadle became Co-adjutor to Bishop Clarkson in 1940. Two years after the latter's death, Wadle took over his flock, and described himself as 'Primate of the American Catholic (Vilatte Succession) Apostolic Church of Long Beach'. When Mar David I, (W. D. de Ortega Maxey), Patriarch of Malaga, Archbishop Primate of All the Iberians, and Supreme Hierarch of the Catholicate of the West in the Americas, resigned in 1951, to become pastor of the First Universalist Church of Los Angeles, he handed over his duties to Archbishop Wadle.[2]

There are a few more little bodies in the U.S.A. which claim the Vilatte Syro-Antioche succession, but in most cases it has been mixed with other streams. The following are among them:

(i) *American Catholic Church (Syro-Antiochean)*

This independent branch of the American Catholic Church, apparently formed by one of its bishops (possibly Cyril J. C. Sherwood), came into being some time after 1915, when Vilatte set up his American Catholic Church and consecrated Lloyd. Very little has been discovered of the history of this body, but according to the the *Yearbook of American Churches 1961* it claimed to have forty places of worship and an inclusive membership of 4,563 in 1958, with sixty-six ordained clergy having charges. The President of the Synod at the time of writing is Archbishop Herbert F. Wilkie, with his residence at 1811 North West Court, Miami 36, Florida. The Vice-President, Bishop Francis A. C. Dalrymple, has his headquarters at 264 Decatur Street, Brooklyn 33, N.Y.[3]

(ii) *Catholic Church of America*

By the time of the First World War it was estimated that nearly one-third of the Lithuanian nation had found its way to North

[1] See p. 256.
[2] See p. 489. Wadle has assisted at the consecration of several bishops of other lines of succession; including Odo A. Barry (Archbishop of the Canadian Catholic Church, 1946) (see p. 536), and Frank B. Robinson (Byzantine American Church, 1945) (see p. 513). It appears that his theology has always inclined towards Theosophy.
[3] This sect is not to be confused with the two divisions of the Syrian Orthodox Church in North America: (1) The Syrian Orthodox Church, with Archbishop Antony Bashir as its Metropolitan; and (2) the Syrian Orthodox Church of Antioch (Archdiocese of the U.S.A. and Canada), ruled over by Mar Athanasius Samuel.

America, and some of these emigrants—like the Poles—wanted to have 'national' or 'independent' parishes, refusing to be integrated with normal Catholic life. The Lithuanians hated the Poles because their nation had been subjected to them for many centuries. This added to the difficulties of the Roman Catholic bishops and clergy in the U.S.A. A Lithuanian National Catholic Church was organized at Scranton, Pennsylvania in 1914, with the help of Bishop Hodur, the founder of the Polish National Catholic Church of America. This body did not satisfy some people, among whom was a certain Stephen Geniotis, who, so it appears, was ordained priest by Bishop de Landas Berghas et de Rache in 1916, worked for a time under Carfora, and then drifted into the Vilatte-Lloyd American Catholic Church. It is possible that he was secretly raised to the episcopate by Lloyd. About 1930 he appeared on the scene as Bishop Geniotis of the Catholic Church in America, and claimed that he and his clergy had orders of Syrian origin, which suggests a Vilatte source. On the other hand, Geniotis claimed that he had been raised to the episcopate by de Landas. His activities roused Bishop Crummey of the Universal Episcopal Communion to issue a *Bulletin of Information upon the Ecclesiastical Status of one Stephen Geniotis, a suspended Priest of the North American Old Roman Catholic Church*, after which the Catholic Church of America disappeared. Considering that there are roughly 50,000,000 Catholics of the Latin Rite, and about 900,000 Eastern Rite Catholics in North America, the founder of this little sect must have had a tremendous sense of mission.

(iii) *American Catholic Church (Archdiocese of New York)*

This body is included among Old Catholic Churches in the *Year-book of American Churches*. The 1961 edition informs us that 'its orders come from the Syrian Church of Antioch, commonly called the Jacobite Apostolic Church', and that 'its doctrines are, with few exceptions, those held by the Old Catholic Church in Europe, but it is not in communion with that body'.[1] Its Primate, the Most Rev. James Francis Augustine Lashley, is a negro, and has his offices at 357 West 144th Street, New York 31. It has been stated that he was raised to the episcopate by Bishop William F. Tyarchs, who was deposed by the Patriarch McGuire of the African Orthodox Church in 1932.[2]

[1] op. cit., p. 83.
[2] In 1947 this little-known body claimed to have twenty churches and an inclusive membership of 8,435.

Churches of the Vilatte Succession

(iv) *American Holy Orthodox Catholic Apostolic Eastern Church, affiliated with the Orthodox Catholic Patriarchate of America*

The comprehensive, reunion-all-round title of this small body is quite in keeping with the best Vilatte tradition, suggesting that it is the greatest ecclesiastical show on earth. Its founder, Cyril John Clement Sherwood, was born at Golden, New York, in 1895. It seems that in his youth he was associated with Archbishop-Abbot Brothers (of the Mathew succession) and his quasi-Benedictine community.[1] About 1927 Sherwood went over to the American Catholic Church, and was ordained priest by Archbishop Lloyd. Then he moved to England, where he graduated at Lloyd's Inter-collegiate University, with the degree of B.D., granted him presumably by John Churchill Sibley, later Archbishop.[2] On May 18, 1930, he was raised to the episcopate of the African Orthodox Church by William F. Tyarks, who at that date styled himself Archbishop-Metropolitan. This Caucasian prelate used a vernacular version of the *Pontificale Romanum*, and the ceremony took place in St Peter's Chapel, 336 East 14th Street, New York City.[3] Two years later Sherwood was re-consecrated *sub conditione* by Archbishop McGuire, Patriarch of the African Orthodox Church.[4] Shortly after this he formed a new church of his own and gave it the name of the American Catholic Apostolic Eastern Church of New York. It claims to be 'one in Faith with the Church of Constantinople and with every other Orthodox Eastern Church of the same profession'. We are told that 'in 1935 a Provisional Synod was set up for the purpose of establishing an American Patriarchate. The Patriarchal Holy Synod was fully established in March 1951 in the City and State of New York'.[5] But Archbishop Sherwood is nothing if not ecumenic in outlook, for it is stated that he is also a member of the Joint Department of Stewardship and Benevolence of the National Council of Churches of Christ in the U.S.A., besides being a member of the Conclave of Bishops of the African Orthodox Church.[6]

The headquarters of the Archbishop President of the Holy Synod of the A.H.O.C.A.E.C. are at 247 East 126th Street, New York 35, where is published the official organ of this body, *The*

[1] See p. 413.
[2] See p. 277.
[3] cf. A. C. Terry-Thompson, *The History of the African Orthodox Church* (1956), p. 89.
[4] See p. 265.
[5] *Yearbook of American Churches 1961*, p. 43.
[6] Terry-Thompson, op. cit., p. 89.

263

Voice of the Community. At the head of its Department of Inter-denominational Relations is His Eminence The Most Rev. K. Chengalvaroya Pillai, otherwise James Charles Ryan, an Indian whose pilgrim's progress to the A.H.O.C.A.E.C. has been by way successively of the South India United Church, British Methodist Mission, Evangelical Church of India, the Free Protestant Episcopal Church of England, the Catholicate of the West, and the Indian Orthodox Church.[1] According to the latest statistics published, the total membership of this body was 3,500 in 1958, with 22 ordained clergy in charge of 27 places of worship.

(v) *The African Orthodox Church, African Orthodox Church of New York and Massachusetts, Afro-American Catholic Church, and The African Greek Orthodox Church.*

The largest spiritual family claiming Vilatte as its progenitor is the African Orthodox Church, now split up into several groups. It had originally come into being through Marcus Garvey, a Jamaican negro, who in 1914 founded the Universal Negro Improvement Association. He called himself 'Provisional President of Africa'. Not satisfied with organizing international conventions for Africans, he set about furthering the cause of black emancipation by the formation of independent negro churches.

A fair number of coloured folk in North America belonged to the Protestant Episcopal Church, and many had been admitted to its ministry, but none had ever been raised to the episcopate, because of their race and blood. Until comparatively recently no negro in communion with Rome was likely to find a bishop in the United States prepared to make him a priest, the colour prejudice was too strong.[2] Inevitably, in course of time, countless independent negro churches sprang up: most of them were of either Baptist or Methodist origin, and none had any pretensions to 'valid' orders until Vilatte came along.[3]

Having gained little or nothing, materially or spiritually from launching an Old Catholic Church for the Belgians, and encouraging the Poles in North America to set up a National Church, from trying to revive an Ancient British Church, from sponsoring a Gallican Church in France, from providing a bishop for the Italian

---

[1] See p. 235.
[2] As late as 1911 there were only five Catholic priests in the U.S.A. who were coloured men. (cf. *Catholic Encyclopedia*, Vol. XII, 'Race, Negro', p. 629.)
[3] The first independent negro church in the U.S.A. was founded in South Carolina in 1773–5.

African Orthodox Church
(Left to right) : Rt Rev. Hubert A. Rogers, D.D. (Auxiliary Bishop to the Primate, later Archbishop of New York) ; Rt Rev. Richard G. Robinson, D.D., B.D., I. Th. (Bishop of Philadelphia) ; Rt Rev. Robert A. Jackson, D.D., B.D. (Bishop of Miami) ; Most Rev. William E. Robertson, D.D., Ph.D., D.C. (Patriarch-Elect, Primate American Province, and Archbishop of New York) ; Most Rev. Edmund R. Bennett, D.D. (Bishop of Brooklyn) ; Most Rev. Clement J. C. Sherwood, D.D.

National Church, or from his own American Catholic Church, he decided to try his luck with the negroes. His consecration of George Alexander McGuire on September 18, 1921—the last he performed before he retired to France and was reconciled with the Holy See—was described as follows:

'What that historic event may yet mean for the African Race, only the march of the coming centuries may reveal . . . Out of that Episcopal consecration in the Church of Our Lady of Good Death has followed the consecration of two other bishops, and about thirty other members of the clergy. Over 100 persons have been confirmed, and fully 28 stations and congregations established in Canada, the United States, Cuba, and Trinidad. In that first consecration of a bishop was the germ of a Racial Church. No bishop, no church.'[1]

McGuire, formerly a Protestant Episcopal Church missionary in the West Indies, assumed the style of 'Patriarch Alexander of the African Orthodox Church of the World'. Between 1921 and 1928 this body increased its hierarchy by four more prelates, all consecrated by the negro Patriarch.[2] In March 1928, *The Negro Churchman* reported that 'history was made on February 12, when three Bishops of African descent consecrated a Caucasian as first Bishop of the American Catholic Orthodox Church. The World moves!' This alleged native of the country between the Caspian and the Black Seas was a William F. Tyarks, who a few months later raised to the episcopate, Clement J. C. Sherwood.[3] Thus came the first break in the ranks of the African Orthodox Church. Many more were to follow.

It was stated about this time that the Liturgy of the African Orthodox Church was 'a combination of Anglican, Roman, and in a few instances, Greek Orthodox formularies, prepared with the special purpose of making an appeal to Negro Episcopalians and Roman Catholics'. The Mass was the chief service; the Roman Pontifical was used for conferring minor and major orders; the Western shape of vestments was recommended; and the official hymnal was *Hymns Ancient and Modern*. The legal headquarters of the Church was at Miami, Florida, in which State membership

---

[1] *The Negro Churchman*, November 1924.
[2] William E. J. Robertson (November 18, 1923); Arthur S. Trotman (September 10, 1924); Reginald G. Barrow (September 8, 1925); and Daniel W. Alexander (September 11, 1927).
[3] Sherwood was the founder of the American Holy Orthodox Catholic Apostolic Eastern Church (see p. 263).

increased rapidly during the nineteen-twenties. The ritual and ceremonial, also the high-sounding nomenclature, made an instant appeal to the coloured people. This new religious body offered more than any other could, but above all, openings for leadership.

We are told that when McGuire returned to the United States from Antigua in 1921, 'the vision of liberty and independence took possession of him. So great was the desire for ecclesiastical freedom because of the limitations and injustices as well as insults, that he resolved to cast off for ever the yoke of white ecclesiastical dominance'.[1] The Patriarch's followers had the same visions of liberty and independence, but as time went on, some of them cast off not only the yoke of white but also of black ecclesiastical dominance.

A large schism occurred in 1938. McGuire had died four years before this, and without his powerful personality, the African Orthodox Church began to disintegrate. William E. J. Roberston had succeeded McGuire as Patriarch, with the title of James I, and headquarters at 122 West 129 Street, New York 27. He had a rival in Arthur S. Trotman, who had already joined a schismatic body under the leadership of Barrow, with the title of 'The African Orthodox Church of New York and Massachusetts'. McGuire had suspended Barrow, and now Barrow had to suspend Trotman, who thus became the Primate of a second rival sect. Then a third schism took place when Bishop Brooks, consecrated by Barrow, seceded from him and formed the Afro-American Catholic Church. The Trotman original secession Church has had three Primates, the present one being Archbishop Frederick A. Toote who was consecrated by Trotman on November 25, 1938.[2]

The parent body, however, has managed to carry on. It has found its way into the Bahamas, but does not seem to have made many converts in these islands. The Rev. Richard D. Siblis, a convert from Protestant Episcopalianism, was sent as a missionary to Cuba in 1924. On July 3, 1938, he was raised to the episcopate by the Patriarch William E. J. Robertson.

So far as numbers go, this negro Church has always been more

---

[1] A. C. Terry-Thompson, *History of the African Orthodox Church* (New York, 1956), p. 50.

[2] Word comes that the Trotman branch of the African Orthodox Church has heard the call to engage in mission work among white peoples. For this purpose a certain Brother Francis Anthony (Vogt) was consecrated at the Cathedral of the Good Shepherd, West 114th Street, New York City, on January 21, 1962, at the hands of Archbishop Gladstone St Clair Nurse, assisted by Bishops Noel K. Smith and G. Duncan Hinkson.

flourishing in North America than in Africa. But a definite effort to extend its influence overseas was made on September 11, 1927, when the Patriarch McGuire, assisted by Bishops Robertson and Trotman, consecrated Daniel W. Alexander at Boston, Massachusetts. The new prelate was of South African birth, with a coloured American father and a coloured mother from Durban. He took the title and style of His Eminence Daniel William, D.D., D.Chr., Archbishop and Primate, Province of South Africa. Having returned home he made his headquarters at Beaconsfield, a suburb of Kimberley, and dedicated his Pro-Cathedral to St Augustine of Hippo.

Living far away from him on the north side of Lake Victoria in east-central Africa, was a young native Christian, named Reuben Sabbanja Sabiminba Mukasa, who was employed as cook to an Anglican archdeacon. He had been brought up as a Low Church Anglican by the Church Missionary Society. From boyhood he had been drawn to everything Greek, and in after years he became known far and wide as Reuben Spartas. As early as 1935 he was corresponding with McGuire in North America. In one letter he told the Patriarch that he had 'vowed to go to hell, jail, or die for the redemption of Africa'.[1]

It was not long before Reuben Spartas broke away from the white controlled Church and joined the African Orthodox Church. When Bishop Alexander visited Buganda in 1931–2, he ordained this young convert as his Vicar Apostolic, and raised several native Christians to the diaconate. Schools were opened and converts multiplied, through the powerful personality of Spartas. In 1933 he wrote to Dr Lang, Archbishop of Canterbury, informing him that the Church of England had 'no Catholic Faith, Doctrine, and real Principles'. He also said: 'Inside Anglicanism I was speaking with the voice of an insolent child who presumes to teach his grandmother to suck eggs. As one of the leaders of an old and truer Church, I would, and do, speak with better authority on the question of reunion.'[2]

Spartas, however, wanted something more secure in the nature of a church than the one imported to Africa from America. He realized that its orthodoxy was merely superficial. He turned his eyes to the historic Eastern Churches, and began to dream of

[1] F. B. Welbourn, *East African Rebels, A Study of some Independent Churches* (1961). This book gives a detailed history of the African Orthodox Church, especially its development in Africa, and contains a full bibliography.
[2] ibid., p. 84.

uniting his followers with the Orthodox Patriarchate of Alexandria. With this end in view he wrote to Maletios Metaxakis, who had succeeded Photios as Patriarch of Alexandria in 1925, and received a most sympathetic reply. This was not surprising, for this ex-Patriarch of Constantinople was a cleric of very liberal views, filled with reforming zeal, and looked on with suspicion by his more conservative clergy. The moment came when Spartas and most of his followers in Buganda decided to secede from the jurisdiction of Bishop Alexander in the Cape Province of the Union of South Africa. It was in 1934 that they became an independent body, known as the African Greek Orthodox Church

From then onwards there was a closer contact between Buganda and Egypt. Formal recognition was given by the Patriarch of Alexandria to this new Church in 1946. The integration between the Central Africans and the Eastern Orthodox was completed on July 19, 1959, when the Patriarch appointed a Metropolitan for East Africa, and Spartas vowed obedience to him. The ritual and ceremonial of the African Greek Orthodox Church were brought into line with those of the Byzantine Churches. We are told that:

'It is part of the genius of Spartas that he has been able to translate into beautiful Luganda the Orthodox Liturgy of St John Chrysostom, and to attend a celebration of this liturgy is a moving experience. The Litany, forming such an important feature of the Greek Liturgy, fits easily into the natural rhythms of Luganda; the Greek music to which it is set, is more closely akin to the traditional Kiganda folk-song, with its leader and chorus . . . Spartas has had the courage to use such words as *kabona*—the old pagan word for priest, rejected by the Anglicans and Roman Catholics alike. . . . At a time when liturgical revision is in the air, it may be that Spartas has provided a pattern for which the whole Church in East Africa may well be grateful.'[1]

The African Greek Orthodox Church is no longer merely a local schism, but part of the Orthodox Patriarchate of Alexandria. Even though its churches are made of mud, they always contain an ikonostasis. So far it has very few priests, and without the help of the Greek community, which maintains schools, it would be in a serious financial position. The African Greek Orthodox Church was the first of all the schismatic sects mentioned in this book to be brought into communion with one of the ancient churches of Christendom.

[1] ibid., p. 101.

It is extraordinary that its remote progenitor was Joseph René Vilatte.

His Eminence Daniel William Alexander, Archbishop and Primate, now a very old man, still rules over several thousand persons in Uganda belonging to the original African Orthodox Church, with an even larger following in Kenya. His jurisdiction (on paper) is said to cover the whole of Africa, from Cape Town in the south to the borders of Abyssinia in the north.

The present Patriarch of the African Orthodox Church is Archbishop W. E. Robertson (James I). Archbishop R. G. Robinson is Primate of the Western Province in the U.S.A. They went to South Africa in June 1960, and in the Anglican Church of All Saints, Beaconsfield, Kimberley, assisted His Eminence Daniel William to consecrate Surgeon Lionel Motsepe and Ice Walter Mbina. The Roman Pontifical was used for the ceremony, which took place during a pontifical High Mass. In view of the negative decision about the validity of Vilatte's consecration by the bishops of the Protestant Episcopal Church, this function, held in a place of worship belonging to the Church of the Province of South Africa, has a historic significance. A former Anglican Archdeacon of Bloemfontein writes that the aged Archbishop and Primate is 'a man of very real and wide culture. I think that we have much to be thankful for in that he is exercising his ministry in so careful and responsible a manner, as it would be possible for him to flood the place with priests possessing orders which are possibly valid though irregular. . . . Alexander can command a very real respect'.[1]

(C) *The Vilatte Succession in England:* (i) *The Old Catholic Church.*

The alleged Syrian-Malabar succession was reintroduced into Britain by Mar Timotheos five years after his ordination of Fr Ignatius of Llanthony in 1898. In the summer of 1903 the Archbishop of North America turned up in South Wales, and on June 14, he raised Henry Marsh-Edwards to the episcopate, with the title of Bishop of Caerleon—in spite of the fact that the holder of this titular see, Mar Theophilus (Stevens), of the Ancient British Church was still alive.[2] The new prelate was an Anglican clergyman who had been deprived of the living of West Bridgford, Nottingham, and pronounced incapable of holding further preferment by the Consistory Court of the Diocese of Southwell on charges of immorality.

[1] Frank H. Hulme, *Blackwall to Bloemfontein* (Durban, 1950), pp. 327–8.
[2] See p. 223.

The ceremony took place at Barry Dock, near Cardiff, and an account of it appeared in the *Western Mail*. The beauty of the service was described, with reference to the sunlight streaming through stained-glass windows. Then it was discovered that the glass consisted of paper transparencies pasted over the windows of a room over a shop. The owner, a Protestant agitator, was a thorn in the flesh of the priest-in-charge of St Paul's, Barry. A photograph of the consecration was exhibited in a shop window at Cardiff, showing Vilatte and Marsh-Edwards, both in pontifical vestments, also two young men wearing albs, whom Vilatte had ordained priests at the same service. Following this appeared several letters from Marsh-Edwards in the *Western Mail*, describing himself as 'Bishop of Caerleon in the Orthodox Eastern Church'. How he arrived at this idea is difficult to understand, for neither the Syrian-Antiochene nor the Syro-Malabar Church is in communion with any of the Orthodox Eastern Churches.

This alleged Eastern prelate with a Welsh title then wrote to Dr Davidson, Archbishop of Canterbury, begging him to forget the past, and to allow him to be reinstated in the Church of England as a simple priest. This was the first of several such attempts made, for Marsh-Edwards had a wife and children to support, and was perennially hard up. When it became clear that he would receive no preferment from the Archbishop he turned to breeding goats.

An advertisement appeared in the *Farm and Garden* on November 13, 1909, which read:

'His Lordship the Bishop of Caerleon has a large stock of Nannies for sale, in milk and kid, very healthy and hardy. Apply Manager, Galatea, Chilworth, Surrey.'

These goats landed His Lordship in the bankruptcy court, and several people lost their money through finding themselves saddled with herds of aged and milkless nannies. So the Bishop of the 'Orthodox Eastern Church' and his family moved to Ringwood, Hants, where he opened a school, at which one of his sons acted as headmaster. Having tried and failed to link up with Arnold Harris Mathew's Old Catholic Church, he acquired a disused Baptist chapel in Ashley Road, Branksome, Bournemouth, which he renamed 'St Aidan's Old Catholic Church'. But the Marsh-Edwards mixture of Old Catholicism and Eastern Orthodoxy failed to catch on. It did not make any noticeable difference to the congregations at St Aldhelm's, Branksome, St Osmund's, Parkstone, or any of the Anglo-Catholic churches in Bournemouth. Once again the Bishop of Caerleon found himself in financial straits. His pro-cathedral was sold, and eventually turned into a cinema.[1]

Then to add to his worries, *Truth* started to ask awkward questions which were answered by the Rev. W. Gwyther, who had been a curate at Roath, Cardiff, at the time of Marsh-Edwards's consecration. Next it transpired that the Bishop had been negotiating with the Syrian-Jacobite Patriarch of Antioch; for in 1922 Mar Severus Barsanum, Archbishop of Homs, wrote to Canon J. A. Douglas, to enquire if a Bishop Marsh-Edwards, of Church Hatch, Ringwood, Hants, was known to the Archbishop of Canterbury.

Not long after this the Bishop of Caerleon applied for a chaplaincy at St Ninian's Episcopal Cathedral, Perth. He informed Provost Smythe that he was acting as suffragan for the Patriarch of Antioch, but did not specify whether it was the Orthodox, Uniate, or Monophysite one. Mr Gwyther (Dean of St Andrews from 1938 to 1940) was able to inform the Provost of what he knew of this mysterious prelate's career. A reply was sent that as the name of Marsh-Edwards did not appear in *Crockford* it was impossible for him to be given a licence in the Scottish Episcopal Church. The Bishop of Caerleon died many years ago, and his adventures are now almost forgotten.[2]

To return to Barry Dock and the year 1903, five months after the ninety-three-year-old Leo XIII had celebrated the twenty-fifth aniversary of his pontificate amid world-wide Catholic rejoicings.[3] On the morning of June 15, following the consecration of Marsh-Edwards the previous day, Vilatte assisted the latter to raise Henry Bernard Ventham to the episcopate; needless to add without reference to either Mgr John Cuthbert Hedley, O.S.B., Bishop of Newport and Menevia, or Dr Richard Lewis, Bishop of Llandaff. The new prelate took the title of Bishop of Dorchester, this see being vacant since the death of Dr F. G. Lee on December 23, 1902.[4] Ventham's career had been nothing if not adventurous. As a youth he had been a member of

---

[1] In 1918 a pamphlet entitled *Old Catholics and the Vicar of Branksome* was published. It consisted of letters between the Rev. Canon Douglas Maclean, who was in charge of All Saints' and St Aldhelm's, Branksome, and the Rev. P. J. O'Connell (Old Catholic), who wrote from St Aidan's, Ashley Road. The latter never disclosed to what group of Old Catholics he belonged, and most of the correspondence dealt with the validity or non-validity of Anglican orders.

[2] Most of these facts are taken from a letter from the Very Rev. W. Gwyther to the Rev. W. H. de Voil, September 30, 1937.

[3] He died on July 20, 1903.

[4] See p. 82.

the Order of Corporate Reunion and of Fr Nugee's Order of St Augustine in Walworth.[1] Then followed a close association with the Benedictine Oblates founded at Ealing by Benjamin Fearnley Carlyle, and after 1893 this 'very eccentric and extremely voluble young man' (as Abbot Carlyle recalled him in after years) was a frequent guest of the Anglican Benedictine nuns at Malling Abbey. Next we hear of him as a novice at Llanthony Abbey, but he does not appear to have remained long under the dictatorial jurisdiction of Fr Ignatius. Ventham—like Vilatte—was fundamentally an opportunist who never minded changing his religious allegiance according to the circumstances in which he found himself at the moment. He seems to have been plausible enough to combine the roles of an Anglican lay-reader in the Diocese of Bath and Wells with that of a Roman Catholic layman in other parts of England. About 1900 he was ordained priest, probably by Vilatte.

A year or so later, having adopted the religious name of Columba Mary, he tried to form an Old Catholic Benedictine community, with the support of Fr O'Halloran, the suspended Roman Catholic priest at Ealing.[2] Dom Columba Mary's first novice was a young lapsed Roman Catholic named Ambrose Thomas, who had been dismissed from the novitiate at Erdington Abbey, near Birmingham.[3] Ventham and Thomas furnished a monastic chapel, but there was no money to pay the bills sent in. A writ was served, whereupon Thomas sought sanctuary with the Anglican Benedictine Brothers on Caldey Island, and Ventham lay low. Br Aelred Carlyle (not yet an abbot) paid the debts, and advised the fugitive novice to get reconciled with the Church of Rome. He sailed away from Caldey on a ketch, bound for Bideford and Buckfast Abbey.[4]

What happened to the Bishop of Dorchester after this debacle is not certain. In any case he had gained nothing by becoming a prelate of a virtually non-existent church, except the fun of dressing up in pontifical vestments and celebrating Mass in whatever room in his lodgings that might be furnished as an episcopal oratory.

---

[1] See pp. 67, 80, 86.

[2] See pp. 167-70.

[3] Founded in 1876 by German Benedictines of the Beuron Congregation. The community was disbanded shortly before the First World War.

[4] Having failed to become either Catholic or Old Catholic monk, Thomas ended his days as an Anglican layman. He became a familiar figure at Thaxted, Essex, where he called himself the Marquis d'Oisey, claiming that he belonged to an ancient and noble family in Flanders. He designed ladies' dresses, and took a keen interest in folk-dancing as well as in most of the religious and social activities sponsored by the vicar, the Rev. Conrad Noel, grandson of the 2nd Earl of Gainsborough, well known for his support of Communism and services of an advanced 'English Use' type.

Churches of the Vilatte Succession

Sometime after 1908 he joined forces with Arnold Harris Mathew, following the latter's consecration as Regionary Old Catholic Bishop for Britain, and was re-ordained by him up to the priesthood. Not feeling drawn to link up with either the Liberal Catholic Church, Old Roman Catholic Church (Pro-Uniate Rite), Old Catholic Church in Ireland, Church Catholic, or Apostolic Service Church (all of which claimed the Mathew succession), or the Catholic Christian Church (of the Vilatte succession) ruled over by Bishop Stannard of Walsingham, Ventham decided in 1922 to be reconciled with the Church of England. After studying at King's College, London, he went through what he regarded as merely the legal formality of being made a deacon and priest by Dr Winnington-Ingram, Bishop of London. In 1924 he became curate to the Rev. W. Noel Lambert at St Gabriel's, South Bromley, who had been raised to the episcopate secretly by Mathew in 1917. The other curate was Francis Bacon, consecrated by Mathew as titular Bishop of Durham in 1911, but who had been received back into the Church of England in 1920.[1] From 1924 to 1926 this East London parish was unique in being staffed by three irregularly consecrated former Old Catholic prelates, and some very irregular things went on there, including clandestine ordinations, or 'validation' of Anglican orders by one or other of the three bishops.[2]

Thanks to Lambert's recommendation in 1927, the dowager Marchioness Townshend presented the former Bishop of Dorchester with the living of South Creake, Norfolk.[3] For the first time in his life Ventham was certain of an adequate income, a comfortable home, though he now had full pastoral responsibilities. He never forgot that he was a bishop, and it is well known that he used to consecrate the holy oils during Mass on Maundy Thursday, and he may well have performed other episcopal functions in secret from time to time. He regarded the Established Church of England with a cynical indifference, doubtful if many of its clergy had valid orders. The parish of South Creake in his eyes was a sort of ecclesiastical peculiar, of an East Anglian *petite église* of which he was the Primate. Those who met the hospitable Bishop of Dorchester in the thirties will recall his racy stories of the strange characters with whom he had consorted during his adventurous career—not always fit for pious ears. He died on January 14, 1944, having refused

[1] See pp. 182, 325.
[2] See pp. 89, 325.
[3] It was her husband, the 6th Marquess, who died in 1921, who presented the afterwards notorious Rev. Harold Davidson to the living of Stiffkey, Norfolk.

Anglican Last Sacraments. His ashes were buried beneath the altar in the north aisle of South Creake Church.[1]

Apparently on December 27, 1908, England was provided with a third Old Catholic bishop of the Vilatte succession in the person of William Whitebrook. His consecrator was the Italian prelate, Miraglia Gulotti, Bishop of Piacenza.[2] It is said that Whitebrook refused the titular see of Whitby which Gulotti offered him.[3] There is a legend that Whitebrook had received a previous consecration from Bishop McLaglen of the Free Protestant Episcopal Church of England, and that the ceremony took place in the Soup Kitchen, which was one of his many philanthropic activities in East London.[4]

As boys, both William and his brother, J. C. Whitebrook, had been acolytes at All Saints', Lambeth, and so had actually been brought up in the secret world of the Order of Corporate Reunion. It appears that some time before the latter end of the year 1905, Bishop Whitebrook had made his submission to the Holy See, because he befriended Benedict Donkin, who called himself 'Bishop of Santa Croce', and arranged for his reconciliation with the Roman Church before his death on March 7, 1906.[5] Whitebrook wrote of himself: 'I have been one of the outcasts of Israel. In order to come home, I have sacrificed everything possible for me to sacrifice, save my means of secular livelihood'.[6] He died in 1915.

[1] His lasting memorial is the restoration and refurnishing of this church, which gives the idea of what the interior may have looked like in the later Middle Ages.
[2] See p. 120.
[3] This Italian bishop stayed with Whitebrook until May 1909, when he left for the U.S.A. to join Vilatte.
[4] cf. Letter in *The Tablet*, February 13, 1909, p. 256.
[5] See p. 141. Mar Georgius, *A Voyage into the Orient* (1954), p. 5.
Donkin was tried at the Lewes Assizes in 1906, where Mr Justice Grantham told the Jury that he had been the victim of persecution rather than prosecution, with the result that they found him innocent on every count. Bishop William Whitebrook (see p. 83) took him off the streets, where it is said that his family had left him to perish from hunger, and nursed him night and day for three months. (cf. *The Tablet*, February 13, 1909.) Shortly before Donkin's death 'a priest of the Archdiocese of Westminster' reconciled him with the Roman Church. It has been said that this priest was Fr O'Halloran of Ealing, who was suspended at that time. In a case of *articulo mortis* he did not need to obtain faculties. Donkin related the facts of his consecration upon oath to 'the principal magistrate of Bexley Kent'. The date of his death is given as March 7, 1906, but it may have been in 1907. He was vested in 'a simple Benedictine habit', and buried in Bexley cemetery at the expense of Bishop Whitebrook. (cf. *The Tablet*, February 27, 1909.) These facts are confirmed in letters from the late J. C. Whitebrook, dated November, 1951.
[6] *The Tablet*, February 13, 1909, p. 255. A letter from a firm of solicitors in this same journal (March 13, 1909) stated: 'The deed attesting the valid consecration according to the Roman rite of our client, Bishop William Whitebrook is in the hands of the Catholic authorities of this country at Archbishop's House, Westminster.' There is little doubt that J. C. Whitebrook was also raised to the episcopate, and it is quite

Churches of the Vilatte Succession

(ii) The Catholic Christian Church

The original line of the Vilatte succession in England was continued by Bishop William Whitebrook when he consecrated Basil Maurice Stannard, giving him the title of Bishop of Walsingham.[1] The new prelate, who had been a monk at Llanthony in his youth, went on earning his living as managing clerk for a solicitor at Leicester for many years, though he served in the Army as a combatant during the First World War. In 1933 he founded the 'Catholic Christian Church'. That same year one of his priests, who had opened a chapel at Bournemouth, published a pamphlet entitled *A Statement of the Primary Doctrines and Principles of the Catholic Christian Church*. The first and only issue of *The Christian Catholic* appeared in the spring of 1934. In it the new sect is described as

'a body of Christians, which combines loyalty to the ancient Christian Faith and Practice of undivided Christendom with all that is best in the thought and experience of today. We aim at the combination of all that is Catholic with all that is really Evangelical. We are conservative, yet liberal, combining authority with ordered freedom, and tradition, with what is modern, remembering that what is modern today is part of the tradition of tomorrow.'

Readers of this lively but short-lived magazine were informed that the 'Catholic Church of Crotia' [*sic*] was now in full communion with the Catholic Christian Church, whose Secretariat was located at 151 Southcote Road, Bournemouth.[2] It was good to hear that the Catholic Croats had thrown off the yoke of Utrecht, because the Dutch Old Catholics had lapsed into communion with the Church of England, 'which is a mixture of Protestant, Modernist, and Catholic elements'. Before very long this new Free Catholic Church would be linked up with 'other Catholic bodies with undoubted Orders and undisputed orthodoxy in various parts of the world'. The faithful were reminded that 'the selling of soaps advertised by Messrs Greig & Co' was strongly recommended for raising funds for the Christian Catholic Church, 'especially for juvenile organizations.'

---

possible that his consecrator was Dr F. G. Lee, though he would never admit this. He died in 1961, having made his submission to the Roman Church many years before, and become a barrister.

[1] The date usually given is April 7, 1912, but as Whitebrook is supposed to have made his submission to the Roman Church before 1906, this is puzzling.

[2] The Catholic Church of Croatia mentioned, seems to have been the Kalogjera group of the Yugoslav Old Catholic Church, which was repudiated by the Dutch, German, and Swiss Old Catholic bishops in 1933. (See p. 537.)

Churches of the Vilatte Succession

Like so many other bodies in the Vilatte succession, this little sect failed to appeal to those who wanted to be both ancient and modern. The Bishop of Walsingham died at Leicester on May 9, 1953, after being received into the Catholic and Roman Church. He is remembered as 'learned, courteous, and in every way respectable, but he seemed quite content in the ultimate event to let his work die with him, when he died'.[1]

(iii) *The Orthodox Catholic Church in England*

After John Churchill Sibley returned to England in the autumn of 1929, following his consecration in Chicago as Metropolitan of the American Catholic Church for the British Empire, it was decided to give this European branch of Vilatte's organization the title of 'The Orthodox Catholic Church in England'.

Archbishop Lloyd had visited England in the summer of 1928, and, 'by the Christian brotherliness of the Rev. P. Meroujian Khosrov', he had admitted twelve members of the Anglican Church into the Order of Antioch; five priests, two deacons, two lectors, and three nuns. The function took place in the Armenian Church of St Sarkis in London.[2] The meetings of the Order continued to be held in this church until Canon J. A. Douglas told Fr Khosrov that the Syrian Orthodox Church (with which the Armenian Church was in communion) repudiated all the bishops and clergy of the Vilatte line of succession. By this time Sibley had gained the support of a fair number of Anglo-Catholic priests, and the members of at least one Anglican sisterhood.

It must be admitted that the Vicar-General of the Order of Antioch in England almost rivalled Vilatte as a religious confidence trickster. There was something vulpine about the features of the Archbishop-Metropolitan of the Orthodox Catholic Church. He had a close-trimmed beard, but his fierce white moustache was more reminiscent of 'Kaiser Bill'. It is recorded that he usually wore a black suit, black spats, a purple stock, and a wide-brimmed hat with a rosette. He was a familiar figure in Chelsea, 'making for the saloon bar of the Redcliffe Arms, Fulham Road, which he visited once a day'.[3] This designing prelate acquired the reputation of being very learned, and a keen musician. He was known affectionately to his followers as 'The Old Arch'. Quite a number of people who accepted him at his face-value, were convinced that he

---

[1] Mar Georgius, *Varied Reflections* (Antwerp, 1954).
[2] cf. *The American Churchman*, December 1928, p. 18.
[3] Mar Georgius, *Varied Reflections*.

was being maliciously attacked and maligned. After his death it was said that he had 'continued to carry forward the torch committed to his hands'.[1]

The Archbishop and his wife resided at 22 Ferndale Road, West Chelsea. Their 'palace' was also the headquarters of the nebulous organization known as 'The Intercollegiate University' said to have been founded in the United States in 1888, and which had been incorporated with the American Catholic Church. After he returned to Europe as British Metropolitan-Primate he issued a circular stating that this University offered 'exceptional advantages to earnest students through its varied carefully arranged courses of Study in Theology, Arts, Music, and Practical Business'. All degrees common to better known universities could be prepared for, and were conferred 'after thorough preparation'.[2] Once a year there was a religious service in the Anglican Church of St George's, Bloomsbury, beneath the statue of George I which surmounts the pyramidal spire. Afterwards honorary degrees were distributed, followed by a banquet, usually at the nearby Holborn Restaurant, with speeches about Liberal Culture. The reunion often ended appropriately with an entertainment by a professional conjuror.

Although Sibley himself was a conjuror in more ways than one, he was caught out on at least two occasions. On March 7, 1931, *John Bull* published an article in which he was called 'The Most Rev. Dr Bunkum', and described as 'a dealer in bogus degrees'. Another caption was worded: 'Sham Archbishop's Abbey Ramp.' It had been discovered that in 1929 Sibley had issued an appeal for £15,000 to restore Minster Abbey, Kent; more correctly the medieval manor house erected on the site of the Benedictine nunnery founded by King Egbert in 670. The idea was that Minster should become 'a National Centre of Christian Fellowship' under the direction of the Order of Antioch. It was claimed that arrangements had been made for the immediate dedication of the abbey, and that after a lapse of four centuries Mass would again be celebrated in the crypt beneath the ruined tower. The public were informed that the proprietor of a Margate cinema, who had bought the property, was running it as a show-place, and to add glamour,

[1] J. S. M. Ward, *The Orthodox Catholic Church in England* (New Barnet, n.d.), p. 37.
[2] This establishment was never granted recognition as one of the degree-giving universities in Great Britain. The archiepiscopal Chancellor never attempted to convince the University Grants Committee, appointed in 1919 by the Chancellor of the Exchequer, that his seat of learning was worthy of financial assistance in order to ensure that it was fully adequate for national needs.

had furnished a chapel, complete with altar.[1] Far from raising the £15,000 to purchase Minster Abbey, Sibley found that he had not enough money even to pay the printer's bill for the appeal issued.[2]

The second attack on the Archbishop-Metropolitan of the Orthodox Catholic Church in England was made in October 1935, when Sir Wyndham Childs, formerly of Scotland Yard, described him as 'one who made a fair revenue by the sale of worthless degrees'.

In December 1938 he was denounced as 'a notorious charlatan'. The previous May the headquarters of the Intercollegiate University had been transferred from Chelsea to Cromwell Road, South Kensington. At the annual banquet that year the Chancellor was thanked for his 'long and generous services to the cause of the University', and presented with a loving-cup.[3]

Archbishop Sibley died in December 1938, aged eighty. The habitués of the Redcliffe Arms saloon bar, Chelsea, missed his daily visits. The *Inter-Collegian* (July 1939), paying tribute to his memory, said: 'He was a man of strong and somewhat complex character, uniting something of a Richelieu with a marked kindliness and great personal charm.'

(iv) *The Autonomous African Universal Church and other unifications of West African Churches in Africa and Florida of the Orthodox Faith.*

The first consecration of a bishop performed by the Metropolitan of the Orthodox Catholic Church in England was that of Kwamin Nsetse Bresi-Ando (who sometimes used the name of Ebenezer Johnson Anderson), on March 6, 1935. Anderson, a West African native, was the registered proprietor of African Churches Stores Ltd, which had its headquarters at Accra, Gold Coast Colony (now Ghana). It advertised itself as 'importers of African produce and other commodities; exporters of European

---

[1] Bishop Harrington, the founder of the Orthodox-Keltic Church of the British Commonwealth of Nations (see pp. 280–282) was also mixed up with this scheme, (*John Bull*, October 12, 1931). The Bishop explained that Minster Abbey would become 'a centre where all Christian bishops—Eastern and Western—could meet, co-operate, and exchange opinions, preventing overlapping, hatreds, etc.'

[2] In 1937 Minster Abbey passed into the hands of Benedictine nuns from St Walburga's Abbey, Eichstatt, Bavaria, who now have a flourishing Catholic community there.

[3] About 1948 the Intercollegiate University, which had often been attacked in various newspapers, went out of business. Before it was disbanded its goodwill and the two chief officials were handed over to the so-called University of Sulgrave (see p. 374), and after the dissolution of that body, passed to the Western Orthodox University, chartered for that purpose by Mar Georgius. (See p. 457.)

Frederic (Frederick
·les Aloysius Har-
ton), Archbishop of
)iocese of St George
ngland, Primate of
)rthodox-Keltic
rch of the British
imonwealth of
.ons.

The Most Rev. Chur-
chill Sibley, Metro-
politan of the American
Catholic Church for
the British Empire
(Orthodox Catholic
Church in England),
Vicar General of the
Order of Antioch,
Chancellor of the Inter-
collegiate University.

and other foreign manufactures; gold and other mineral concession transactors'. Kwamin Nsetse Bresi-Ando claimed to be a tribal chief, and it was said that he had been a Methodist bishop for about fourteen years. Business having brought him to England, he was living at Hornsey, North London—a neighbourhood hardly in keeping with his illustrious rank. After his consecration Bresi-Ando assumed the title and style of Mar Kwamin, Primate of the Autonomous African Universal Church and other unifications of West African Churches in Africa and Florida of the Orthodox Faith. He had a very vivid pan-African imagination, for he informed *The Hornsey Journal* on September 13, 1935, that 'this Church is in full communion with the Abyssinian and Coptic Churches', but did not explain how or when this union had been brought about. He also stated that there were two Provinces of the Church in South America under his jurisdiction.

It is difficult to know just what confidence may be placed in the accuracy of Mar Kwamin's statements, for in this same article he said that 'The Orthodox Catholic Church in Africa, which is led by the Primate, consists of over 20,000,000 people'. There can be little doubt, however, that his followers did number several thousand, and that he had many church buildings, of which photographs are in existence. Later on he assumed the style of Prince-Patriarch of Apam, and managed to gain the support of several priests and bishops of the Chechemian and Vilatte successions in England. Eventually he returned to the Gold Coast, and sent shiploads of goods to Mar Frederic Harrington, whose story follows next, but it seems that they were never paid for. The Prince-Patriarch's religious opinions were said to have become more Protestant when he got back to Africa, after the *Ancient Christian Fellowship Review* (October 1946) referred to his work as 'The Bible Mission to Nigeria'; it seems, however, that this name properly refers to an organization founded by Mar Georgius to supply Bibles to Mar Kwamin's flock.

(v) *Orthodox-Keltic Church of the British Commonwealth of Nations.*

On Sunday, September 1, 1935, about a month before Mussolini invaded Abyssinia, and African affairs were getting priority in the newspapers, Mar Kwamin, en route for South America to hold visitations of his alleged flocks scattered over that vast continent, performed an exotic little function in his oratory of St Ignatius of

279

Antioch, 9 Matilda Street, Islington.[1] This was the consecration of Canon Frederick Charles Aloysius Harrington, who had been ordained priest of the Orthodox Catholic Church in England by Archbishop Sibley, and initiated by him into the Order of Antioch.[2] The new prelate took the title of Mar Frederic, Archbishop of the Diocese of St George in England, and adopted the curious form of signature: '✠ Frederic, Mar et Met'.[3]

The purpose of this consecration in a back street of Islington was to found the new sect which was called imposingly 'The Orthodox-Keltic Church of the British Commonwealth of Nations'.[4] For it had been revealed to the former director of the Harrington Standard Typewriter Co., that 'the Keltic Peoples are the Tribal Families of Spiritual Israel in Dispersion—the sons of Jacob by Sara'. He stated that the 'Keltic' peoples today 'are to be found in Ireland, Wales, Scottish Highlands, Britain (Cornwall, Devon, and Lancashire), Brittany (exiled Britons), Isle of Man, Iceland, Channel Islands, and several colonies in France, Luxembourg, Andorra, America, and Africa, each having their own Elect Prince or Tribal Head'.[5]

✠ Frederic, Mar et Met., fixed his headquarters at 324 Hornsey Road, London, N.7, where he was in close touch with Mar Kwamin. He pictured himself as the Supreme Pontiff of a new Universal Church composed of a 'unification of the Sons of Jacob by the Seed, and the Ex-Gentile Sons of Jacob by Adoption into One House (of Jacob), and One Spiritual Nation (Christian)', through Apostolic Succession, leading to what he called 'The Theandric Final Life'. Of this there are seven stages, which, so he admitted, have 'never been fully studied and defined by the Church'.

---

[1] This oratory was a converted workshop behind a dilapidated house. Matilda Street lies on the east of Caledonian Road, between Copenhagen Street and Richmond Avenue.

[2] At one time or another Harrington had been associated with several business ventures of dubious character, including the Harrington Standard Typewriter Company, which was liquidated with a total deficit of £30,000.

[3] According to *The Hornsey Journal* (September 13, 1935), Mar Frederic received letters or telegrams of congratulation from Prince Paul Salvator (of Poland); Prince-Abbot Esmonde of San Luigi (Africa); S. E. Mgr. Eftimios Archwichi, Greek Melkite Zahlé; (Republic of Lebanon); Most Rev. Mar Timotheos of the Holy Apostolic See of Aquilea (Austria); Count de Quesnel, Tournai (Belgium); Rev. Fr Francis (Putney); Rev. Fr Michael of the Order of Antioch; Rev. Fr Superior of the Order of Christ the King; Very Rev. Fr Alban, O.D.F.; Professor Crow (Head of Department of Biology at the Huddersfield Technical College, affiliated to Leeds University); Mr P. W. Donner, M.P., and others.

[4] The short title of this body was 'The British Orthodox Catholic Church'. Later it became one of the four original units of the Catholicate of the West. (See p. 240).

[5] The *Orthodox-Keltic Rite of the Ordination of Deacons and Priests, etc.* (1939).

Churches of the Vilatte Succession

The Archbishop of the Diocese of St George in England informed the public that the Orthodox-Keltic Church could trace its origins to St Mark and the Coptic Church, assisted by St Peter, St John, and St Paul, from Antioch. It was St Joseph of Arimathea who nominated and consecrated the first British Bishop, Aristobulus (father-in-law of St Peter the Apostle), as his Assistant at Glastonbury. Moreover the Keltic Church had been represented at the Apostolic Council of Jerusalem in A.D. 51. Thanks to Almighty God, it had been the privilege of ✠ Frederic Mar et Met to re-erect in North London this venerable Church, 'as the first stage towards the re-union of Mankind to God. The first and last are one in the same Body united'.

The most amazing revelations were granted to this long-bearded, oriental-looking prelate, either in his hole and corner Oratory in a back yard off Matilda Street, Kings Cross, or in Hornsey Road, where he resided. Day by day it became clearer how to plan a 'System' for his Holy Keltic Church; which would consist eventually of autocephalous English-speaking churches throughout the British Commonwealth of Nations, the United States of America, South Central, and Central East Africa. He pictured 'The Body Religious' made up of sixteen Patriarchs (including the Primate), fifteen Metropolitans, fourteen Archbishops, thirteen Bishops, twelve Chorepiscopi, eleven Archpriests (with an Abbot-Archbishop), and ten priests. There would also be a specified number of lesser dignitaries, ordained by the laying on of hands and represented in the governing body of this world-wide organization, including seven Monks and Hermits, six Nuns, and even a Matriarch. No Christian Church would be able to offer such rich and ornate ritual and ceremonial as this new one with its '*phanar*' or '*curia*' in Holloway, N.7.

One of the attractions would be a holy dance during the ordination of priests. It was stated that 'the Ordinands, bearing lighted candles, accompanied by their Sponsors, pass round the Altar three times in honour of the Holy Trinity, calling aloud each time *Alleluia*, which is repeated by the Sponsors'. Mar Frederic composed a *Divine Liturgy* for his new Church, which contained 'The Ancient Apostolic Rite, a Shorter Keltic-Syrian Rite, and Authorized Eastern Benediction Service, selected Antiphons, Hymns, etc, and a List of 250 Pre-Roman Keltic Saints'.[1]

A leaflet issued about this time contained the words: 'You are

---

[1] This Liturgy was never, in fact, printed, though advertised for sale at 21s.

invited to "come in". Do not remain "outside". Many Apostolic missionaries of both sexes are required immediately. Apply Director of Theological Studies, O.S.C.N., 273 Hornsey Road, N.7. So hasten the time of the Great Reunion in Christ, Our Lord. ✠ Frederic, *Mar et Met.*'[1]

On Whit Sunday, 1938, Mar Frederic was re-consecrated by Mar Jacobus II (Heard), with the object, so it was stated, of uniting in one person all the churches claiming the Vilatte and Ferrette lines of succession, a union which would link up at least 20,000,000 of the faithful in all parts of the world. This vision never materialized. Even the Holy Orthodox-Keltic Church itself, as a separate body, had a very brief existence. For on December 10, 1938, His Beatitude Mar Ignatius Ephrem 1, Syrian Jacobite Patriarch of Antioch issued the document mentioned already in which he denounced as bogus 'the so-called "One Holy Orthodox Catholic Church", as it describes itself, presided over, as it is claimed, by the so-called Frederic Harrington, "Metropolitan" in the city of London, of 324 Hornsey Road, and all the sects claiming through Vilatte . . . an alleged relation "in succession and ordination" as to our Holy Apostolic Church and her forefathers'.[2]

The following year, on September 3, 1939, Britain declared war on Germany. Mar Frederic packed up his pontificalia for the duration of hostilities, and as Mr Harrington found secular employment with the London County Council. This left him with little or no time to attend to the spiritual welfare of the widely scattered Keltic peoples. He died in poverty on January 17, 1942, having already commended the care of the Sons of Jacob by the Seed, and the ex-Gentile Sons by Adoption to the jurisdiction of Mar Jacobus II, hoping that he would manage to make them One Spiritual Nation, when world peace was restored.

(vi) *The Confraternity of the Kingdom of Christ, and the later history of the Orthodox Catholic Church in England.*

The northern suburbs of London were the scene of yet more apocalyptic omens and portents during the twenties and thirties. Early in October 1928 Mr John Sebastian Marlow Ward and his

---

[1] The O.S.C.N. was the Order of the Spiritual Christian Nation, which, after Mar Frederic's death, was carried on by Mar Jacobus (Heard), and by him passed on to Mar Georgius, who still operates it. (See p. 471.)
[2] The full text of this 'Notice from the Syrian Orthodox Patriarchate of Antioch and all the East' will be found in Appendix A, of H. R. T. Brandreth's *Episcopi Vagantes and the Anglican Church* (2nd ed. 1961), pp. 118–19.

wife, Jessie, who lived at Golders Green, began to have what they described as 'a series of remarkable spiritual experiences wherein they were warned that the end of this Age was approaching, that the Civilization of the West was doomed, and that before its final collapse, Christ would come in Judgment, not to destroy the physical world, but to end the Age and give a new Revelation which would serve as the spiritual foundation of the Age and Civilization to follow'.[1] Ward was born at Belize, British Honduras, in 1885, and was the son of the Rev. H. M. Ward, a former vicar of the one-time Anglo-Catholic stronghold, St Mary's, Charing Cross Road, London. He was educated at Merchant Taylors' School, and Trinity Hall, Cambridge (Scholar), and was the winner of the Latham Prize (1907), and took Second Class Honours in the History Tripos (1908). After being head of the Diocesan Boys' School, Rangoon, he became Director of the Intelligence Department of the Federation of British Industries, a post he held from 1918 to 1930.

In November 1928 Mr and Mrs Ward had a joint vision in which they were ordered to found a mixed community of men and women to prepare for the Second Coming of Christ. After yet more mystical experiences, 'having been for some time prepared for the ordeal', on May 13, 1929, they 'were led by the Angelic Guardian of the work into the presence of Christ the King, and by Him solemnly consecrated for the task and given the requisite authority to organize the work and to found the Abbey. In the language of those who have studied the mystical phenomena this experience would probably be described as one of the greater Initiations. At the same time the promise was made to them that Christ would ever guide them in their Mission'.[2]

Such was the story told by the Wards. It should be mentioned that he was regarded as one of the greatest living authorities on Freemasonry and Occultism. He claimed to hold the 33rd Degree of the Ancient and Accepted Rite (though more likely in the dubious 'Ancient and Primitive Rite of Yarker', or elsewhere), and had contributed the article on Freemasonry to the *Encyclopedia Britannica*.[3] His only rival in this sphere of esoteric knowledge was

---

[1] *The Confraternity of the Kingdom of Christ. What it stands for and how it came into existence* (n.p. or d.) p. 15.

[2] ibid., p. 16.

[3] Among the many books he had published were *Fairy Tales from Burma; Freemasonry and the Ancient Gods; Textile Fibres and Yarns of the British Empire: An Explanation of the Royal Arch Degree; The Hung Society of China* (2 vols); *The Moral*

Churches of the Vilatte Succession

Dr W. B. Crow, Bishop of Santa Sophia, and Grand Master of the Order of the Holy Wisdom.[1]

Ward appears to have believed that Freemasonry is not only the survivor, but also the guardian of the ancient mysteries of which the Christian sacraments are but one evolution. He wrote that these mysteries have passed through the ages

'via the Dionysian artificers, the actual builders of the Temple, who were, no doubt, influenced by Egyptian and other mysteries; but the main basis on which the system was built up was the primitive initiatory rites, which, with them as with the Egyptians and Mayas, developed into a mystery.'[2]

He accepted the idea of re-incarnation as an obvious article of faith; and he subscribed to the very ancient Gnostic idea of Christ being the offspring of God the Father (*yhwh*) and God the Mother (*Ruach Hagadosh*); and that the Holy Ghost is not the Third but the Second Person of the Holy Trinity, and is feminine, i.e. 'God the Mother'.

It was in January 1930 that Ward resigned the directorship of the Intelligence Department of the Federation of British Industries, so that he could devote himself exclusively to the pursuit of occult knowledge. The following month he and his wife announced that they had 'received instructions in the mystical state to go down to Birchington in Kent where they would find a building which would form the Chapel of the Confraternity. They went as instructed, and after many adventures, found a medieval tithe-barn, which was subsequently purchased and re-erected at Hadley Hall'.[3] Meanwhile, under supernatural guidance, they had bought this property at New Barnet. For they were eager to prepare a home where Christ would be sure of a welcome when he returned to earth to impart His new Revelation. By this time they were convinced that out of all the millions of the world's inhabitants they had been chosen as the twentieth century Holy Family.

The fifteenth-century half-timbered barn was transformed into a chapel. The interior was furnished with old oak carvings and sculptures, also pictures by Italian and Flemish old masters, ancient stained-glass windows, and many more costly decorations.

---

[1] *Teachings of Freemasonry; The Sign Language of the Mysteries* (2 vols); *Cotton and Wool*; *The Psychic Powers of Christ; The World before the Coming of Man; Can our Industrial System Survive?* and *Who was Hiram Abiff?* At one time Ward had been Master of the Industries Lodge, 4100 on the Register of the Grand Lodge of England. See pp. 236-238.

[2] *Freemasonry and the Ancient Gods*, p. 341.

[3] The *Confraternity of the Kingdom of Christ*, p. 17.

Churches of the Vilatte Succession

The first members of the community took possession of Hadley Hall on June 24, 1930, the Feast of St John the Baptist, and it was renamed 'The Abbey of Christ the King'.[1]

On February 14, 1931, Dr Michael Furse, Bishop of St Albans, dedicated the Chapel with Anglican rites, and expressed the hope that it would become, so to say, 'a lighthouse in the spiritual life of the district'. At the same time he appointed the vicar of the parish as chaplain to the community.[2]

The Confraternity of the Kingdom of Christ consisted of three Orders. The First Order was composed of men and women who took life-vows of obedience, poverty, and self-sacrifice after a novitiate normally lasting three years. There was no vow of celibacy, because married couples were admitted if they showed proofs of a true vocation. Neither did self-sacrifice for the male and female novices preclude marriage if it became clear that their mutual striving after perfection demanded more than a spiritual relationship. All property was handed over to the Abbey. No one was allowed to retain any personal possessions, and a new name was taken to stress a closer relationship with Christ the King. The members of the Confraternity ran a school—St Michael's College —in which the children were given a thorough grounding in the Christian religion as understood by the Wards. The Brothers and Sisters also tried in various ways to prepare New Barnet for the second coming of Christ.

It is not altogether surprising that neither Bishop Furse nor Bishop Frere, whose advice was sought, felt able to approve a Constitution for the Confraternity which was submitted to them. Towards the end of 1934, the former refused to renew the Chaplain's licence, being alarmed at what he heard was going on at the Abbey. The reasons he gave were that Ward had 'no authority to Minister the Word and yet had done so by opening the Abbey Church to outsiders'.[3] The Father Superior related later on that

[1] It was also in 1930 that the Olivetan Benedictine monks founded a Priory of Christ the King at Cockfosters, about two miles east of New Barnet, which was often confused with the Abbey of Christ the King. Unlike the latter, the former still flourishes.

[2] Bishop Furse stated in a letter to the Rev. H. R. T. Brandreth (August 14, 1939) that Ward and his wife had been commended to him by Canon Wigram, Secretary of the Archbishop's Assyrian Mission, and said: 'At their request I dedicated the chapel on the distinct understanding that it should be used only by members of the Community. The vicar of the parish celebrated there from time to time, and did what he could for them.'

[3] J. S. M. Ward, *The Orthodox Catholic Church in England* (n.d. or p.), p. 38. He tells us that the treatment given to the Abbey of Christ the King 'has striking analogies with the treatment of Fr Ignatius at Llanthony by the Anglican Church at an earlier date'.

as a result of this episcopal action he came to the conclusion that 'in the ecclesiastical sense the Anglican Church has no valid orders, and therefore no Priests and no Bishops, and that the gentleman who calls himself a Bishop is only a layman given the name of a Bishop by Act of Parliament, and appointed by the State like any other State Official'.[1]

So Ward and his wife turned to the Autonomous African Universal Church as a substitute for *Ecclesia Anglicana*. On September 12, 1935 he was ordained deacon and priest by its Primate, Mar Kwamin, who three days later raised him to the episcopate. On the 24th the newly consecrated prelate informed the Bishop of St Albans that he and his Confraternity had severed all relations with the Established Church.

After these ceremonies Bishop Ward discovered to his dismay that Mar Kwamin's *Instrumentum Consecrationis* had been withheld by Archbishop Sibley, who had found out that, in spite of an agreement, this West African bishop was operating in England.[2] This impelled Ward, on the advice of a certain Liberal Catholic priest, to make a personal call on Sibley in Chelsea, hoping to persuade him to provide the necessary evidence of Kwamin's consecration. But the Exarch of the Order of Antioch declined to produce the requisite document, and offered instead to re-ordain and re-consecrate Ward, who accepted the offer. Accordingly, Archbishop Sibley turned up at New Barnet on October 4, and the following morning re-baptized, confirmed and re-ordained Ward up to the priesthood. On October 6, a second consecration was performed by Sibley, who used a vernacular version of the *Pontificale Romanum*. He also ensured the validity of Mrs Ward's diaconate by re-ordaining her, and was gracious enough to grant her episcopal husband the degree of D.D. (Intercollegiate University).[3] At the same time the Abbey and Confraternity were re-registered as part of the Orthodox Catholic Church in England, which until then had got little further than its Metropolitan's writing paper, and had made no visible advance within the British Empire.

The tithe-barn chapel was presumably licensed for marriages;

---

[1] ibid., p. 38.
[2] A sworn statement is preserved by Mar Georgius in the archives of the Catholicate of the West.
[3] Among the witnesses of the instrument of consecration were several male and female members of the confraternity with such mystic names as Sister Via Crucis, Sister Filia Reginae, Filius Domini, and In Manibus Domini.

since, in December 1937, it witnessed the nuptials of Abbé Kaufmann and Emma Talbot-Ponsonby; a solemn pontifical function carried out by Archbishop Sibley, assisted by Bishop Ward. After Sibley's death in December 1938, Ward succeeded to the Primacy of the Orthodox Catholic Church in England.[1] This enabled him to regard himself as head of the alleged Antiochene succession in Europe, derived from Vilatte.

It is recalled that Archbishop Ward made a striking figure when he went shopping in New Barnet, wearing a scarlet cassock, cape and biretta.[2] Very often he was accompanied by his wife, whose costume was much more glamorous than what she might have worn had she been a member of the Anglican Deaconess Community of St Andrew, or of the Order of Deaconesses formally restored by the Convocation of Canterbury in 1923. Far more in keeping with her status of Reverend Mother of the mixed Confraternity was the picturesque white habit, coif, and veil, set off by a large gold pectoral cross suspended on a gold chain.[3] Their frequent companion on such walks was a certain Fra Filius Domini (in the world, Colin Mackenzie Chamberlain), who wore a brown quasi-Franciscan habit, although the male members of the Confraternity had been raised to the rank of Canons Regular.

About the same time that the Abbey of Christ the King ceased to be in communion with Canterbury, St Michael's College was closed. A Folk Park had been opened in the grounds; its purpose being to show the social life of England from prehistoric times down to the present day. Among the exhibits were the Magdalenian Man (*c.* 20,000 B.C.), numerous Roman relics, and Queen Victoria's brandy flasks.[4] It was advertised as 'the only open-air folk-park in the British Empire'. Schoolchildren were taken there in large parties, and 1*s.* 3*d.* was charged for admission.

---

[1] Sibley's office of Exarch of the Order of Antioch did not pass to Ward, but remained in abeyance until 1946. That year Timothy Howard Mather, who had been raised to the episcopate by Gregory Lines in 1933 during his second schism from the American Catholic Church (see p. 257), and who had acquired the status of Head of the Order in the U.S.A., appointed Mar Georgius as British Exarch.

[2] A friend, who was in close touch with Ward at this time, remembers him attending Masonic meetings in London, robed as a major prelate of the Latin rite; and that to see a collar and apron over a scarlet cassock, and a scarlet biretta hanging on a peg in the anteroom, added an unusual note of colour on such occasions.

[3] Reverend Mother seems to have acted as a Medium, receiving orders and messages from Saints and Angels. This enabled her to control the members of the Confraternity, including Reverend Father.

[4] cf. E. V. Lucas, 'An Educational Abbey' (A Wanderer's Note Book), in *The Sunday Times*, September 9, 1934; also *A Brief Guide to the Abbey Folk Park and Museum* (*1935*).

The Confraternity obtained unwelcome publicity in May 1945, when the Reverend Father Superior and Reverend Mother, together with four brown-robed Sisters, and four young Canons Regular—'in clerical collars and celestial crowns'—found themselves in the High Court of Justice. A Mr Stanley W. Lough had charged Ward and his wife with enticing his daughter, Dorothy Bartola (Sister Terese) into the Abbey at the age of sixteen, although parental consent had been given in writing during her novitiate. The case lasted from April 30 to May 18, 1945, because it concerned an affair for which no previous authority could be cited. The plaintiff claimed damages and injunction against the defendants on the ground that, by enticing away and harbouring his daughter, they had deprived him of her services. It came out in the evidence that Mr and Mrs Lough had never been allowed to see their daughter when she was living at the Abbey except in the presence of Reverend Father and Reverend Mother. Mr Justice Cassels in summing up remarked that the defendants struck him as serious-minded persons believing what they taught; that some people might think they were much misguided; 'but this is a land which tolerates many kinds of religious beliefs'; adding:

'I think there is some force in the suggestion that they are a couple suffering from a form of megalomania, taking delight in high-sounding titles. They seem to me to be playing at keeping a nunnery and indulging in make-belief, forming their own rules, and exacting vows of obedience from their little band of followers . . . The defendants may be attracted by some other form of religion. What is to become of Dorothy if the little community should fall to pieces one day, as it might do if the trustees have no more funds coming in? . . .'

The plaintiff was awarded £500 damages, but it was pointed out that such an award was a mere form, because the defendants had put it out of their power to possess so sordid a thing as money. An injunction was granted to forbid them from continuing to harbour Dorothy Bartola Lough.

On August 25, 1945, Ward underwent a third episcopal consecration, this time from Mar Georgius, Patriarch of Glastonbury and Catholicos of the West, who was assisted by the Archbishop of India (Ryan), and the titular Bishop of St Marylebone (Jeffrey). Ward was given the title of Mar John, Titular Archbishop of Olivet. The same day the Orthodox Catholic Church in England was received into full communion with the Catholicate of the West, and the name 'Georgius our Catholicos' added to the Canon of the Mass. The tithe-barn chapel had already been raised to cathedral status.[1]

The following year, on June 6, 1946, a very long and complicated ceremony took place at New Barnet: the consecration of Fra Filius Domini (Colin M. Chamberlain), also that of William D.de Ortega Maxey as Patriarch of Malaga, Apostolic Primate of All the Iberians, and Supreme Hierarch of the Catholicate of the West in the Americas.[2] The Archbishop of Olivet and the Patriarch of Glastonbury were assisted by four other prelates—the Archbishop of Suthronia, the Bishop of Verulam, the Bishop of Minster, and the Titular Mar of Mere. It is recorded that 'the venerable rite of the Holy Apostolic Church of Armenia (Oriental) and the rite of The Orthodox Catholic Church in England (Occidental) were both performed'.[3] It is hard to say how many different lines of succession were alleged to have been imparted by the six consecrating prelates. We are told that 'an observer, regarding the ancient fabric and furnishings, and the golden robes of the mitred prelates, not to mention the monastic garb of the community, might well have imagined himself back in the twelfth century . . . The service was sung throughout, and beautiful music composed by members of the community was used, accompanied by the inspiring notes of the Cathedral organ.' Alas! In spite of this perfection in ritual and ceremonial, Mar Georgius came to the conclusion not long after that poor Fra Filius Domini was not a validly consecrated bishop, and issued an official statement to this effect, adding that it was 'through no fault of his own', but of 'lack of unity of operation'. Considering the mixture of rites used, this is not surprising. It appears, however, that as the instrument of consecration had been signed by the six co-consecrators, the difficulty was not realized immediately.[4]

The Dorothy Lough case had made the Abbey of Christ the King well-known from one end of Britain to the other. Information about the life of this mixed community had been obtained for certain newspapers by very dubious methods. It is related that the case 'completely shattered the physique of the Reverend Father,

---

[1] For subsequent consecrations performed by Mar Georgius at the Cathedral of Christ the King, see pp. 465, 496.
[2] See pp. 454, 455.
[3] *Orthodox Catholic Review*, June 1946, p. 3.
[4] The Confraternity had left England before Mar Georgius could consult Archbishop Ward.

who was a very sensitive man'. His disciples were convinced that he had been subjected to diabolical persecution for fifteen years. The only thing to do was to find a new home for the Confraternity. On July 13, 1946—just a month after the above-mentioned consecration ceremony—Mar John, Archbishop of Olivet, Reverend Mother, and the more devoted of their disciples disappeared from New Barnet, without informing anybody but a few intimate friends. Those who were let into the secret swore not to divulge that by divine guidance a refuge had been found in Cyprus. Elaborate precautions were taken to get Sister Terese out of the country, and to prevent the whereabouts of the community from becoming known. It is said that the identity documents of another person were obtained for her; also that she travelled disguised, with her hair dyed, and under an assumed name. Before leaving England the Archbishop entrusted the clergy of the Orthodox Catholic Church to the patriarchal care of Mar Georgius.

On this Mediterranean island Mar John with Archbishop Makarios, head of the Enosis (union with Greece) movement as his opposite number, was able to take on the role of a twentieth-century Valentinus, the famous second century Gnostic teacher, who fled there from Rome after he had seceded from the Church, and initiated an élite, composed of 'pneumatics', into the mysteries of the *pleroma*, their redemption being effected by the aeon Christ. After three happy and peaceful years in Cyprus, the Archbishop was called to his eternal reward. It was stated in a letter that some of his disciples had a vision of him in the company of the Saints after he had joined 'the Astral Confraternity' in July 1949; and some even maintained that they had seen the marks of the Stigmata on his corpse, suggesting that he himself had been the *'alter Christus'*.

The former Fra Filius Domini, who had been given the title and style of 'Gregory, Titular Archbishop of Bethany', assumed the Primacy of the Orthodox Church in England, and ruled over it from his residence near Limasol, with 'His Blessedness the Archbishop of Constantia, New Justinianopolis and All Cyprus', the head of the Cypriot Church, as his neighbour at Nikosia. Later on the remnant of the Confraternity of the Kingdom of Christ, under the leadership of the widowed Reverend Mother, left Cyprus for Australia, where she still directs her faithful disciples on the road to heaven.

One of Archbishop Ward's priests, Fr William Martin Andrew,

and who had remained in England, met with the disapproval of Mar Georgius, with the result that he was suspended from the exercise of his priesthood. So Fr Andrew went to Cyprus, where in March 1951 he was raised to the episcopate by the titular Archbishop of Bethany, who gave him the name and style of 'Antony, titular Bishop of Nazareth'.[1] On his return to England he dedicated the Church of Christ the King, Osborne Road, Bournemouth, on June 23 that same year.

This episcopal action aroused the indignation of the Patriarch of Glastonbury, who summoned Bishop Antony to appear before the Supreme Ecclesiastical Tribune of the Catholicate of the West, sitting at 23 O'Neill House, Cochrane Street, St John's Wood, N.W.8, on August 5, 1951. He stated that 'not having been lawfully, canonically or validly consecrated', Fr Martin Andrew had not the right to exercise episcopal functions. 'If you fail to appear', so Mar Georgius wrote, 'you will be pronounced contumacious, and the same will be heard and decreed in your absence, and judgment given accordingly.' The same day the Patriarch wrote to each of the clergy of the Orthodox Catholic Church in England, stating that since the death of Archbishop Ward, he himself was the legal and canonical head of this Church, and summoned them to attend a Synod, to be held immediately prior to the Tribunal on the same day.

Both Synod and Tribunal took place on the day appointed. At the former the majority of the clergy declared that they regarded Bishop Antony, and not Mar Georgius, as their major ecclesiastical superior, but the Tribunal pronounced Antony deposed and excommunicate. Three weeks later Mar Georgius issued a Bull by which he expelled the Orthodox Catholic Church in England from the Catholicate of the West.[2]

Since being cast out of the Catholicate and the Apostolic Eparchy of all the Britons, the Orthodox Catholic Church in England, claiming an unbroken succession of bishops from St Peter

---

[1] Gregory, titular Archbishop of Bethany, may have forgotten that the Archbishop of Trani (Latin Rite) has also the title of Bishop of Nazareth, because the title of that see was transferred to Barletta, after the fall of Palestine in 1190, to which diocese Trani then belonged. Mgr Martin Andrew (now resident at 30 Richmond Road, Bournemouth, England) must not be confused with either Mgr Reginaldo Addasi O.P. (whose address is Arcivescovado, Trani, Bari, Italy) or with the present Eparch of Nazareth, of the Greek Orthodox Patriarchate of Jerusalem. Neither of the two last-named prelates has the privilege of being in communion with the Orthodox Catholic Church in England.

[2] cf. Information Bulletin, No. 14. *The Secession of the Orthodox Catholic Church in England from the Catholicate of the West* (Glastonbury, 1951).

the Apostle, has had its headquarters at Bournemouth. The Pro-Cathedral of the titular Bishop of Nazareth is hidden away off Osborne Road, Winton. It is a devotional little building, formerly a stable and later a carpenter's shop. The altar-piece is a memorial to Archbishops Ward and Sibley. The Liturgy used is stated to be based on that of 'the Holy Eastern Church of Syria' but 'with abridgments and other and concessions in Western environment'. Vestments of Eastern shape are worn, and the ancient ceremonial of the Antiochene Rite is the norm of its Bournemouth variant.

Within the last few years Bishop Antony has taken on the remnant of Bishop Vernon Herford's Evangelical Catholic Communion; since Bishop Jeffrey has been obliged to retire for reasons of health and age.[1]

(vii) *Orthodox-Catholic Province of Our Lady of England in Devon and Cornwall (Autonomous British Eastern Church).*

Shortly before Christmas 1935 a leaflet was printed with the title *An Orthodox-Catholic Consecration, For New Diocese on South Coast.* The first paragraph read:

'We are living in a wonderful age, besides progress generally, we often see History repeating itself . . . At the Dawn of a New Age, we again witness the missionary zeal of the Eastern Churches, this time to regain those lost to the Primitive Faith and Form. It was only in August last, after 38 years' negotiations, that an Autonomous British Eastern Church was made possible by the Consecration of a Bishop here according to Apostolic Rites. On the 16th November the new See of Our Lady of England and Devon and Cornwall was canonically erected and its First Bishop consecrated and installed by the Metropolitan Frederic of the Holy Orthodox-Catholic Church in Great Britain, who was assisted by visiting Orthodox Prelates in this country.'

It appears that neither Lord Rupert Ernest William Gascoyne Cecil, Bishop of Exeter, nor Dr Walter Howard Frere, Bishop of Truro, nor for that matter, Mgr John P. Barrett, Bishop of Plymouth, were invited to assist at the consecration of a bishop who

[1] See p. 155, n. 1. In communion with the Orthodox Catholic Church is the Society of St Antony in England, whose Leader is Fr E. Spicer, M.D., with a Mother House and Priory Church at 89 the Vale, Acton, W.3. Spiritual healing is carried on at a Naturo-pathic Clinic. St Michael's Retreat, Feltham, Middlesex, is described as a small international centre where students of all denominations are welcomed in the spirit of Christian unity and friendship. The Abbey Church of Christ the King, New Barnet, is still used for Orthodox Catholic worship, but the domestic quarters have been turned into an Artists' Colony.

proposed to work in their respective dioceses. The identity of these Orthodox prelates who were available in England in the autumn of 1935 was not revealed.[1] Whoever they were, they found their way to the tiny Oratory of St Ignatius of Antioch in Matilda Street, Islington, where the ceremony took place with what were called 'Apostolic Rites', and lasted nearly two hours. The first bishop of this 'Autonomous Eastern Church' set up in Devon and Cornwall was the Very Rev. James Dominic O'Gavigan, O.H.C., whose name suggests Irish Roman Catholic origins. We are told that 'according to the Orthodox-Catholic tradition' he adopted the ancient title of 'Mar', and chose as his episcopal name 'Jacobus' (after Mar Jacobus 'The Brother of our Lord'). Mar Jacobus, however, would no doubt be generally addressed by his friends as 'Bishop O'Gavigan'. Even more astonishing was the intimation that this Autonomous Eastern Church had similar ideals and objects as those of the Ancient Keltic Church. It was hard to believe that this new body was really 'in full intercommunion with most Churches in Europe, Asia, Africa, and America', and could not be 'regarded as sectarian in any worldly sense'. It was understood that the Founder had a financial interest in Church Farms Ltd. at Accra, of which Mar Kwamin Nsetse Bresi-Ando was the managing director. Mar Jacobus hoped that this West African archbishop would assist him with the foundation of an Orthodox-Catholic (British Eastern) University at Plymouth, which would impart degrees without the necessity of residence, but this seat of learning got no further than paper.

Not very long after his consecration Mar Jacobus repudiated the jurisdiction of Mar Frederic, and joined up with the several-times consecrated C. J. C. Sherwood, formerly a bishop of the African Orthodox Church, and founder of the American Catholic Apostolic Eastern Church of New York.[2] Thus re-consecrated by prelates of the Ferrette, Vilatte, and Mathew lines, O'Gavigan assumed the

---

[1] It looks as if O'Gavigan had received a previous consecration, for on April 17, 1934, he appealed in the *Somerset County Gazette* for funds to restore and refurnish Cannington Abbey, near Bridgwater. He stated that this pre-Reformation foundation had been acquired by 'the Western Province of the Holy Orthodox Church (Autocephalous)', and that the buildings would 'serve as a training college and monastic house for aspirants to the ministry or the religious life'. Donations were to be sent to 'The Most Rev. Mar Jacobus, D.D.' The buildings referred to were 'The Priory', occupied by Benedictine nuns until the dissolution in 1536, and again from 1807 to 1836. The last named belonged to the convent founded at Paris in 1652, and whose home for the past 127 years has been at Colwich Abbey, Staffordshire. O'Gavigan's monastic house never materialized.

[2] See p. 263.

title of 'Archbishop of the Orthodox-Catholic Province of Our Lady of England in Devon and Cornwall'.[1] He was killed on August 20, 1940, in an air-raid at Newton Abbot, Devon, during the second World War, and his 'Province' died with him.

(viii) *The Jesuene, or Free Orthodox-Catholic Church.*

On October 24, 1937, Mar Frederic, Primate of the Orthodox-Keltic Church of the British Commonwealth of Nations, consecrated Dorian Herbert as Bishop of Caerleon. This free-lance cleric had already founded a new sect known as either 'The Jesuene Church', or 'The Free Orthodox-Catholic Church'. But there is little or nothing Catholic or Orthodox in the ordinary sense about the beliefs held by its members. The founder proudly proclaimed that they were 'rationalistic in interpretation, unorthodox and heretical'. He stated: 'We base the unity of our organization upon the acceptance, as a true standard of human conduct, of the moral code and precepts laid down in the life and teaching of Jesus recorded in the Four Gospels. We do not profess any creed, nor do we regard "belief" as a criterion of membership of the Church. Our two-fold purpose, therefore, is to free Christian interpretation from intellectual bondage, and to abolish the commercialization of the Christian religion.'

The Bishop of Caerleon professed a great veneration for Father Ignatius of Llanthony, but it is permissible to think that the latter would have been horrified at some of his opinions. For ✠ Dorian had the courage to write: 'I have no hesitation in declaring myself to be a heretic.'

On August 1, 1943, he consecrated Frank David Bacon, of Manchester, as Bishop of Mercia for the Free Orthodox Catholic Church. Herbert, who, in spite of his heterodoxy, revelled in ritualism, used a vernacular version of the *Pontificale Romanum*. The ceremony took place in the 'Llanthony Chapel', Cae-Kenfy, Abergavenny, which served as the pro-cathedral, and which contained many relics of Fr Ignatius. The Bishop explained to the congregation that his Church made 'no distinction between those who profess to call themselves Christians'; stressing that an 'open welcome was given to all to participate at its altars'.[2] Not content

[1] It is understood that he assisted the Lord Patriarch Banks of East Molesey at the consecration of the Rev. S. E. P. Needham, Vicar of Farthinghoe, Northants, on May 28, 1940, when the latter took the title of 'Mar Theodorus, Bishop of Mercia'. (See p. 374.)

[2] 'A Picturesque Ceremony at Abergavenny: Consecration of a Bishop', reprinted from *The Abergavenny Chronicle* (n.d.) The Bishop of Mercia—later of Repton—was given a second consecration by Mar Georgius in 1946. In recent years Bishop Bacon

with inviting anybody to receive Communion, Herbert gave further proof of his broad-mindedness by extending a cordial invitation to ladies to minister at his altars. He published a pamphlet, entitled *Women Priesthood*, stating that he would be delighted to raise members of the female sex to holy orders, in this way emulating Michael Kowalski and other Polish Mariavite bishops, as well as setting an example for the Lutheran Churches of Denmark, Sweden and Norway to follow.[1]

In 1946 he wrote to a certain lady that he 'was prepared to confer Orders upon women of piety and reasonable education who may be wishful to serve the cause of Christ in that capacity', even if they could only exercise the office of priestess in their own private oratories for the benefit of their relations and friends. He explained: 'I do not impose any doctrinal limitations, but extend the widest possible freedom of interpretation. I do not ask for any recompense for my services as Bishop except for the actual cost of travel and lodging incurred when visiting to confer Orders.'

Possibly in order to guarantee that the orders he imparted to women were really 'valid', he took the precaution of being reconsecrated by Mar Georgius on December 3, 1944. The ceremony took place in the Oratory of SS. Cosmas and Damian, Lepton, Huddersfield. Thus inoculated with the spiritual blood-streams of alleged Syrian-Antiochene, Armenian-Uniate, and Order of Corporate Reunion lines of succession, the Bishop of Caerleon on the following day, consecrated an electrical engineer, named George Henry Brook, as Bishop of the Order of Rievaulx. He was known later as Mar Adrianus, Bishop of Deira in the Eparchy of All the Britons of the Catholicate of the West.[2]

The Order of Rievaulx was not, as might be supposed, a revival of the Cistercians, but a group of Tertiaries of both sexes, who observed a simple rule. In the summer of 1946 Mar Adrianus appointed Mar David I, Patriarch of Malaga, as Grand Master for

---

has acted as a Labour Party councillor at Failsworth, Manchester, besides engaging in educational work in connection with Huddersfield Technical College, so it is understood. He has published a small book on the Eastern Churches, entitled *Eastern Pilgrimage*.

[1] See p. 517.

[2] See p. 453. Deira was the ancient British Kingdom, extending from the Tees to the Humber. It has been said that Brook had previously been consecrated by Mar Jacobus O'Gavigan in 1940. On May 5, 1945, he was re-consecrated *sub conditione* by Mar Georgius, with whom he was associated at that time. He is now one of the fifteen members of the Sacred Synod of the *Église Catholique Apostolique Primitive d'Antioche Orthodoxe et de Tradition Syro-Byzantine*, of which Mar Joannes Maria Van Assendelft is the Prince-Patriarch. (See p. 314.)

the Americas. On August 18 the latter prelate solemnly installed Prioress Francine as head of the trans-Atlantic branch. The ceremony took place in the Patriarchal Chapel at Los Angeles, California.[1]

In the autumn of 1947 Bishop Herbert heard that at long last an attempt would be made shortly to revive monastic life at Llanthony Abbey, as it had been led in the time of Fr Ignatius. It must have rejoiced his heart to ordain deacon and priest William Albert Corke, who had received the four minor orders from Mar Georgius. Corke immediately assumed the rank of Abbot, and on January 1, 1948, he was raised to the episcopate by Bishop E. O. Cope, known as 'Ignatius, O.S.B.' of the new sect called 'The Free Anglo-Catholic Church'.[2]

In spite of his wide-ranging heterodoxy, Bishop Herbert had a profound belief in the magic of apostolic succession. By this time he had assumed the title of Mar Doreos, and he yearned to revive the long dormant Ancient British Church, regarding himself as the canonical successor of Mar Pelagius Morgan; ignoring the fact that this nebulous Church was already part of the Catholicate of the West.[3]

On August 11, 1953. Mar Doreos informed the *Bournemouth Daily Echo* that:

'The early British Church, which for the first 600 years of the Christian era was the only Christian Church throughout the whole of Britain, continued its independence until the eleventh century. When its Antiochene Apostolic succession was broken down and ended in favour of the Roman Catholic succession of Canterbury, it ceased to exist.'

The alleged canonical successor of St Joseph of Arimathea and St Aristobulus explained to the reporter that his revived Britonnic Church did not as yet possess any cathedrals; nor did he dwell in a palace like the prelates of the Established Church of England. His humble abode was at 197 Chepstow Road, Newport, Mon., fortunately within a mile or so of Caerleon, where there was a Roman Catholic church dedicated to the Ancient British martyrs, Julius

[1] cf. *Ancient Christian Fellowship* (Los Angeles), October-December, 1946. The so-called 'Ancient Christian Fellowship' became part of the Apostolic Episcopal Church under Mar John Emmanuel (see pp. 508-512), but it was also under the jurisdiction of Mar David I of the Catholicate of the West. (See pp. 455, 473.)

[2] For the brief history of 'The Order of Llanthony Brothers', see pp. 391-398,

[3] See pp. 240, 242, 447. He even went to the expense of having a leaflet printed showing how what he called 'The Holy Orthodox-Catholic Church of Great Britain' derived its apostolic succession from the Syrian Church of Antioch by various lines.

and Aaron. He was a widower, and had been a vegetarian for thirty-seven years; was a keen chess-player, and a Freemason. In this respect he followed in the footsteps of Mar John, Archbishop of Olivet. Music was his hobby, and he was a devotee of Beethoven and Handel. Another tremendous interest was work among the various groups of Moslems in Britain. His assistant was the Rt. Rev. Leonard M. Parsons, D.Sc. (Lond.), Ll.D., Bishop of Avalon, whom he had recently consecrated.

The greatest achievement of the revived Britonnic Church was the organization of a 'Holy Grail Christian Crusade against Brutality to Animals and all Wild Creatures'. This Order, so Mar Doreos explained, was widely scattered throughout England and Wales, and functioned under the spiritual patronage of King Arthur and his Knights. He said:

'We strive to emulate that wonderful chivalry in the spiritual sense of their great exploits against injustice. Hence our acceptance of the gin-trap challenge. We do our work on the rugged paths of the world. We attach importance, not to any person's profession of "belief" so much as to what he or she actually does to interpret the Holy Teaching of Jesus into actual good works.'

The Bishop informed the readers of this Bournemouth newspaper that Ancient British Church-folk had already distributed thousands of anti-gin-trap leaflets, and this apostolate had been so intense that the Knights of the Holy Grail were heavily in debt.

The Rt. Rev. Dorian Herbert, D.Th., Bishop of Caerleon, British Church, and Prior of The Order of The Holy Grail (as he was described), obtained further publicity in the summer of 1954. On July 20 he headed a 'Mercy Parade' through the main streets of Liverpool. Six feet tall, vested in the habit of the Order, with a white knotted Franciscan (or Ignatian?) cord round his waist, mitred, and armed with a crozier, he was not easily missed in the crowd. This Parade was a brave attempt made by the Knights of the Holy Grail to save three old police horses from being shot. The Bishop made a personal offer of £100 to the Lord Mayor and Corporation for his three brethren of the animal world, but with no effect; they were martyred. An S.O.S. for £1,000 followed to found a Chapel of Compassion at either Bristol, Birmingham, or Oxford. Such a shrine, he pointed out, would 'radiate the true Gospel of Christian Compassion towards our creature brethren amongst the peoples of other nations also'. Sad to say there was little response, which proved how few decent-minded people were left in Britain. The Bishop of Caerleon's twentieth-century Christian Crusade Against Brutality to Animals and all Wild Creatures was almost as much of a failure as the last Crusade against the Moslems undertaken by St Louis in 1270.

In 1949 the head of the Ancient British Church, whose attitude towards the disciples of the Prophet differed from those of the thirteenth-century King of France and Ambrose Phillipps de Lisle, took part in the first international conference of Moslems held in Great Britain as guest of His Eminence Sheikh Abdulla Ali El Hakimi, Head of the Moslem Community of the United Kingdom. Robed in cope and mitre, Bishop Dorian sent a greeting of goodwill to eleven Moslem nations throughout the world.

By Christmas 1957 Bishop Dorian's writing paper displayed the word 'Agnostic' after his name, which he explained as follows:

'The incorporation above of the definition "Agnostic" is to indicate that as Bishop of Caerleon, British Church, I desire to make it clear that I do not subscribe to modern interpretations of conventional Christianity. The original British Church, in company with the earliest other Christian churches, existed before the creeds and theological dogmas were formulated. . . . The Agnostic Christian is one who openly admits that he does not know, and rejects the fanciful notion that certain privileged ecclesiastical authoritarians, or any others, have any more real knowledge than he has. His christian fellowship is based upon loyalty to identity of purpose—and not upon fear, or the promise of reward here or hereafter. Real nobility of character is in doing good for its own sake.'

Whether Fr Ignatius, whose 'miraculous tabernacle' from the high altar of Llanthony Abbey is now enshrined in the Oratory of the Holy Grail at Newport, Mon., would approve of 'Agnostic Catholicism' as preached by Mar Doreos, Bishop of Caerleon, of the Central Province of the Holy Orthodox-Catholic Church of Great Britain and Ireland (otherwise The British Church), is somewhat doubtful.

(D) (i) *L'Église Catholique Française, l'Église orthodoxe gallicane autocéphale, and other Gnostic bodies in France directly or indirectly associated with Vilatte.*

Mar Timotheos was far from being the first person to form a heretical and schismatic church in France. Many predecessors had helped to prepare the ground for him in the past hundred years. He fits into a pattern, which cannot be understood without a knowledge of some of the strange organizations which sprang up underground after the French Revolution, and which offered a substitute for orthodox Catholicism.

To start with there was the Constitutional Church formed in 1790, when the National Assembly ordered the clergy to adhere to the Civil Constitution. Many of the 130 dioceses were suppressed by the Government and new ones erected. It was decreed that the bishops should be elected by local conventions of the clergy, and confirmed by the metropolitans, but without confirmation by the Holy See. All clergy were required to take an oath to maintain the Constitution, on pain of deprivation. Pius VI insisted that this legislation must be resisted. Only four bishops took the oath, and most of the rest went into exile, as did about 1,657 priests. Supported by the Government, the schismatic body gained adherents, and new bishops were consecrated. Several of them married. By 1795 the Constitutional Church had obtained comparative freedom of worship, on condition that Sunday was not observed, the *décadaire* or ten-day week having been substituted. Two of the chief leaders of the schism were the abbé Grégoire, who became Bishop of Blois, and the ex-Jesuit, M. J. Dufraisse, was who consecrated Archbishop of Bourges.[1] In 1801, Napoleon, as First Consul, concluded a Concordat with the Holy See, and twelve Constitutional bishops were allowed to retain their sees, having submitted to Pius VII.

But it was this Concordat that resulted in another schism, known as the *Petite Église*. It consisted of the French Catholics who refused to accept the agreement made between the Government and the Pope. These priests and layfolk remained loyal to a number of bishops, still in exile, who would not return to their dioceses when ordered to do so by the Pope. On the downfall of Napoleon in 1815, and the restoration of the Bourbon monarchy, most of the exiled bishops were reconciled with the Holy See. Three prelates: Mgr de Courcy, Bishop of La Rochelle; Mgr de Thémines, Bishop of Blois, and Mgr Seignelay de Colbert, Bishop of Rodez, refused to obey the instructions issued by Pius VII.[2]

---

[1] Cf. M. Vaussard, *Lettres à l'abbe Grégoire de l'ex-Jésuite M. J. Dufraisse* (Paris, 1962).

[2] The real name of the Bishop of Rodez was Traill, and he was a younger son of the laird of Castlehill in Caithness, Scotland. He was sent to France, where one of his uncles had been educated at the Scots College, Paris. After his ordination he was

Mgr de Thémines acted as Primate of the *Petite Église* until his death in 1829. He never consecrated a successor, and the last priest of this schismatic body, the abbé Ozouf, died in 1847. Its adherents were most numerous in Brittany, La Vendée, and around Lyons. Finding themselves with no priests they continued to worship together, and ensured that laymen baptized validly. About 1903 an effort was made to link up the remnant with the Old Catholic Church of Utrecht, but nothing came of it. It is estimated that there are still roughly 3,500 members of the *Petite Église* in France. They are known as *Louisets* in Brittany; *Filochois* at Toulouse; *Clémentins* in the Rouergue; *Illuminés* or Dissidents in Poitou and the Vendée; elsewhere as *Blancs, Burs, Fidèles* or *Elus*.[1]

The *Église Johannite des Chrétiens Primitifs* was a cryptic body which had its origins in the alleged associations of Freemasonry with the Knights Templars, the military order founded in 1118, but suppressed by Clement V in 1312 on charges of immorality, superstition and heresy. In 1704 the 'Little Resurrection of the Templars' took place, with a fictitious history and elaborate ceremonial. The members even tried to get the Order of Christ in Portugal—legitimate descendants of the Templars—to recognize them. Many Masons joined these revived Templars, and in time Masonic membership became a pre-requisite. This led to a sort of pseudo-Catholic religion being invented. The esoteric Church had a Patriarch and a Primate, both of whom were consecrated and enthroned with ornate ritual and ceremonial. The ordained priests were known as Doctors of the Law.

Among the fairly numerous Catholic ecclesiastics who were initiated into the revived Order of the Temple was Mgr Mauviel (1757–1814), consecrated at Paris in 1800 as Constitutional Bishop of Cayes in Haiti. Then there was also Bernard Fabré-Pelaprat (1777–1838), who had been ordained priest by the Bishop of Lot. In 1803 he was consecrated Pontiff of the Johannite Church of Primitive Christians by a dubious prelate named Arnal. On July 29, 1810, he was re-consecrated *sub conditione* by Mgr Mauviel, by this time Primate of the Johannite Church. Fabré-Pelaprat was a leading Mason by this date. He

---

appointed Vicar-General of Toulouse, and consecrated Bishop of Rodez in 1781. He never returned to France, and spent the latter part of his life either in London, or staying with wealthy kinsfolk in Scotland, most of whom were Presbyterians.

[1] cf. Ivan de la Thibauderie, *Églises et Évêques Catholiques non Romains* (Paris 1962), pp. 71–72. Vilatte's parents belonged to the *Petite Église*, and childhood memories may have influenced him in after years.

fabricated the so-called 'Charter of Transmission', if he did not inherit it from 1704, and fabricated relics. The sword of de Morlay (last Grand Master in 1314), some bones rescued from burning were discovered; also a spurious Gospel, known as *Levitikon*. So far as can be discovered this body was very much of a secret society, worshipping behind locked doors. Between 1810 and 1841 numerous bishops were consecrated, and even more priests, most of them lapsed Catholics, ordained for the celebration of occult rites. After 1860 little more was heard of the heretical and schismatical *Église Johannite des Chrétiens Primitifs*, the orders of whose clergy may have been valid, even if highly irregular.[1]

This twilight-church—very much of the catacombs—was perhaps the first of innumerable sects which have sprung up in France during the past century-and-a-half; all of them striving to revive some more or less forgotten heresy. Most people think of France as a Catholic country, but since the collapse of the Church at the Revolution, it has produced almost as many curious little sects as England has done in the same period, though none of them have increased and multiplied as has been the case with some of the Nonconformist bodies this side of the Channel.

In 1831—the same year that the abbé Lamennais issued in the last issue of *L'Avenir*, his 'Acte d'Union', in which he called for the union of all freedom-loving men, optimistic that Gregory XVI would put himself at the head of this crusade—another schismatic body was formed in France, known as the *Église Catholique Française*. Lamennais had already prophesied an impending revolution, and demanded the separation of the Church from the State, and it was Mgr Ferdinand Chatel (1795–1857), a convinced Gallican, who took a short cut to this end. In 1830 he lapsed into schism, and opened an independent chapel at Paris on February 20, 1831. Four months later he was initiated in the Order of the Knights Templar, and was raised to the episcopate by Mgr Machault, Primate of the esoteric Johannite Church. With the help of Mgr Poullard, who had been consecrated constitutional Bishop of Autun in 1801, Mgr Chatel formally erected his national Church in January 1833. Small groups were formed in Paris, Brussels, Nantes, and in parts of the Vendée, Haute-Vienne, and Hautes-Pyrénées. In 1837, Julien Le Rousseau, curé of the chapel at Nantes, was raised to the episcopate as Bishop for Belgium.

[1] cf. Ivan de la Thibauderie, *Églises et Évêques Catholiques non Romains* (Paris, 1962), pp. 39–48.

Mgr Chatel assumed the title of 'Bishop Primate of the Gauls', and drifted further and further into liberal Catholicism. Between 1842 and 1844, the ecclesiastical and civil authorities carried on an open warfare against this schismatic sect, which was eventually suppressed by Louis-Philippe. Its adherents lingered on in out-of-the-way places during the Second Empire, even after the death of the founder in 1857.[1]

A much more esoteric body was formed about the same time as Mgr Chatel's *Église Catholique Française*, and which was the prototype of others. The founder, Pierre-Eugène-Michel Vintras, was born at Bayeux in 1807, and at the age of twenty-four became the manager of a cardboard factory, where he found a kindred spirit in Ferdinand Geoffre, an adventurer who belonged to a mystic-magic circle. In August 1839, Vintras claimed to have had a vision in which Our Lady, St Joseph and the Angels bade him found an *Oeuvre de la Miséricorde*, to herald the coming of the Paraclete.[2] The movement was organized in 'sacred septenaries', and spread as rapidly as did the Catholic Apostolic (Irvingite) Church in England, and during the same period. Several priests became members of the *Oeuvre*; alleged miracles took place, one of them the apparition and disappearance of Bleeding Hosts at Mass and outside Mass celebrated in Vintras's cardboard factory at Tilly-sur-Seule (Calvados). He took 'the Archangel of All Seraphim' (called St Rathauël) as his Guardian. In 1841 the abbé Charuoz published the *Opuscule sur des communications annonçant l'Oeuvre de la Miséricorde et renovabis faciem terram*, of which 6,000 copies were printed. It was instantly condemned by the Archbishop of Bordeaux; and for some reason Vintras found himself in prison for six years. Protests were made by his disciples—who were nothing if not ultramontane—that only the Pope could condemn a movement of this sort. Gregory XVI actually did so in a Brief addressed to the Archbishop of Bordeaux in February 1844; whereupon a pamphlet

---

[1] cf. de la Thibauderie, op. cit., pp. 49–51.

[2] It was in 1836 that the Twelve Apostles of the Catholic Apostolic (Irvingite) Church in England addressed a memorandum to the civil and ecclesiastical rulers of Europe, warning them of the near approach of the Second Coming of Christ. Shortly after this they began their missionary journeys on the Continent and in North America. France was assigned to the Rev. H. Dalton, and this nation was supposed to represent Asher among the twelve tribes of Israel, symbolizing 'a yearning after fraternity'. It would be interesting to find out if Vintras's vision was associated with contacts with Irvingites. The Twelve Apostles were recalled to England in March 1839.

In 1928 Mr and Mrs J. S. M. Ward claimed to have had a similar vision to that granted to Vintras, bidding them to found a community to prepare for the fairly immediate return to earth of Christ the King. (See pp. 282, 283.)

was issued, protesting that he had no authority for his action without trial of four priests, including Père Lamarche, O.P., who had vouched for its orthodoxy. About 1844, Vintras—still in prison—founded the *Chevalerrie de Marie* for an élite of his followers. Two years later the abbé Charuoz became the head of the movement, and in 1848 he issued a pastoral letter denouncing a certain Gozzoli for the charges made against 'The Saints of Tilly'—another inner circle of the *Oeuvre*.

On regaining his freedom early in 1848, Vintras had a vision in the Renaissance Church of St Eustache, Paris, on Easter Day.[1] He proclaimed that the High Priest Christ had consecrated him *Pontife Adorateur*, *Pontife d'Amour*, and *Pontife Provincial*, and had shown him how to celebrate a new Liturgy. On May 10 Vintras began his sacerdotal ministry by saying this Mass in the vernacular. The consecration was done 'in union with Mary and Joseph'. During this Mass the Host is alleged to have been marked with a Bloody Heart. Soon after this the abbé Héry published a pamphlet to prove the validity of Vintras's orders. On May 20, Vintras consecrated seven *pontifes divins*—all of them Roman Catholic priests. Two days later they re-consecrated their consecrator *par réciprocure*. It was not surprising that the Provincial Synod of Rouen condemned this strange heretical movement, and excommunicated all who assisted at its liturgy. In 1851 Pius IX confirmed this condemnation in a Brief addressed to the Bishop of Nancy, three of whose priests had been consecrated *pontifes*.

By 1852 the *Oeuvre de la Miséricorde* had gained such notoriety all over France, that Louis-Napoléon, urged by the Bishop of Bayeux, ordered its dissolution. Vintras fled to Belgium; the abbés Maréchal, Héry, and Breton were arrested by the police and taken to Paris for trial by bishops. Héry and Breton managed to escape to England, where Vintras eventually joined them, as did the abbé Baillard, who had ruled over a group at Sion in Lorraine. The result of this dispersion was the formation of new groups in England, Italy, and Spain. In October 1859, an 'Eliate University' (*Université Éliaque*) was founded in England; and during the same year Vintras published *L'Evangile éternel*—in emulation of the Spiritual Franciscan, Gerard of Borgo San Donino, who in 1254 compiled excerpts from the writings of Joachim of Fiore (c. 1132–1202), which proclaimed an Eternal Gospel. Vintras was back again in France in 1863, when he consecrated many pontiffs, and in

[1] St Eustache witnessed the riotous 'Festival of Reason' in 1793.

1865 founded at Lyons *le sanctuaire intérieur du Carmel d'Elié*, which he visualized as the centre of his new religion. After a tour of Spain he founded the *Carmel blanc* at Florence, which was specially favoured with Bloody Hosts, disappearing wine, and other alleged miracles. He died at Lyons on December 7, 1875. His successor was the abbé Boullan, who assisted by the abbés Charuoz and Héry, transformed the *Église vintrasisanne* into a thoroughly occultist and spiritualist body.[1]

Hyacinthe Loyson (1827–1912) was mixed up with the fortunes of several schismatic bodies during the course of his long life.[2] Having been suspended from exercising his priesthood on a charge of indiscipline, in 1869 he broke away from the Order of Discalced Carmelites, in which he had achieved fame as a pulpit orator. Three years later he married an American lady in London, and became known as l'abbé Loyson. In 1873 he was put in charge of an Old Catholic church in Geneva. The conservative-minded Church of Utrecht, which did not abolish compulsory clerical celibacy until 1922, gave Loyson little encouragement, though Bishop Herzog of Berne was more sympathetic, especially after the Swiss Old Catholics abolished clerical celibacy in 1875.[3] The married abbé moved to Paris in 1879, where he opened a chapel. Dr Robert Eden, Bishop of Moray and Ross, and Primus of the Scottish Episcopal Church, and Dr Henry Cotterill, Bishop of Edinburgh, kept an informal oversight of what was called the Gallican Catholic Church.[4] In 1888 Dr Cleveland Coxe, Bishop of Western New York in the American Episcopal Church, took this French schismatic body under his patronage and helped to finance it. Loyson was never an organizer, and people were attracted to his chapel mainly by his gifts as a preacher. After his resignation in 1893, the Dutch Old Catholic bishops agreed to accept his few followers into

[1] cf. Maurice Barrès, *La colline inspirée* (novel based on Vintras), (Paris, 1913); E. Mangenot, *La colline inspirée . . . à propos d'un roman* (Paris, 1913); E. Mangenot, MSS on Vintras and Baillard in Library of Seminary at Nancy; J. Bricaud, *L'abbé Bouillan: sa vie*, seas doctrines, *et ses pratiques magiques* (1927); Maurice Garfon, Vintras: *hérésiaque et prophète* (Paris, 1928); E. Amann, *Vintras (Michel) D. Th. C. 15.3055* (Paris, 1948).

[2] See pp. 93, 142, 159.

[3] At one time Loyson tried to persuade Dr Tait, Archbishop of Canterbury, to raise him to the episcopate; apparently with the idea that he and his disciples might become a sort of French branch of the Church of England, until the schismatic sect had its own hierarchy and became sufficiently widespread to justify it being constituted an autocephalous church in communion with Canterbury and York.

[4] Bishop Eden revised its Liturgy, and inserted a clause in the Canon, accepting the Three Branch Theory of the Church, with prayers for the Pope, the Patriarch of Constantinople, and the Primate of All England.

communion.[1] In 1884 Loyson and his wife invited Vilatte to Paris, so that they could discuss the possibility of getting him ordained as an Old Catholic priest for service in the Protestant Episcopal Diocese of Fond du Lac.[2] In 1888 the ex-Catholic friar helped to plant the seeds of doubt in the mind of Fr Matthews, then priest in charge of St Mary's, Bath, which led to his becoming a Unitarian the following year.[3] During the first decade of the present century the Abbé and Madame Loyson, who were then living in Switzerland, were in close touch with both Bishop Vernon Herford of Mercia and Middlesex, and with Bishop Benedict Donkin of Santa Croce in Sicily.[4] In fact, there seem to have been very few bishops and clergy of the ecclesiastical borderland with whom the Loysons were not associated at one time or another.

The schismatic bodies mentioned so far defended their basic position on a certain group of religious opinions known as 'Gallicanism'. These opinions might be summed up as the belief that from as early as the fourth century the majority of French bishops and clergy had held the true doctrine of papal authority, and that from time to time they had set a splendid example to the rest of the Catholic Church by their defence against the insidious encroachments of Rome. In the seventeenth century what were called 'The Ancient Liberties of the Gallican Church' became a subject of controversy. The four Gallican Articles, drawn up by the French bishops, were condemned by Alexander VIII in 1690, and by Louis XIV three years later. After this Gallicanism went underground, but it continued to be taught in not a few seminaries throughout the eighteenth century, and lingered on among a handful of the clergy until living memory.

The anti-clerical government of the early nineteen hundreds was only too ready to encourage any project to set up a National Church in France independent of the Holy See. Nobody was more eager than Aristide Briand, the future Premier, who in 1903 began his long career as Minister of Education. He appears to have been on friendly terms with Archbishop Vilatte, who had already sown the seeds of a new schismatic body in France by ordaining two priests

[1] Since then there has usually been an Old Catholic priest in charge of a never very numerous flock in Paris. Today they are allowed to have Mass celebrated in the British Embassy Church in the Rue d'Auguesseau, because since 1932 the Church of England has been in full communion with the Old Catholic Churches of Holland, Germany, and Switzerland.
[2] See p. 93.
[3] See p. 159.
[4] See p. 142.

in Paris in 1898.[1] Two years later he decided to get reconciled with Rome, but, as related already, he changed his mind, and returned to North America.

He was back again in France early in 1907, and taking advantage of the law passed in 1901, he formed an *association culturelle catholique, apostolique et française*, which gave legal status to the small group of clergy and layfolk who regarded him as their leader. But Vilatte seldom remained long in any place, and having opened an Old Catholic chapel in Paris, and laid the spiritual foundations of a schismatic church, he left its organization to others.[2]

He was succeeded as Primate of this Gallican *Église catholique française* by Julius Houssaye (or Hussay), who on December 4, 1904, had been consecrated at Thiengen in Germany by Paolo Miraglia-Gulotti, Bishop of Piacenza.[3] Houssaye, formerly a Catholic priest, was an occultist and faith healer. Under the name of the 'Abbé Julio' he published several treatises on magic and symbolism.[4] Why this bearded, patriarchal-looking apostate priest should have believed that he was called to be a shepherd of souls is difficult to understand, but doubtless Miraglia-Gulotti did not bother to investigate his theological opinions. Certainly Houssaye himself believed that a bishop has greater powers as a 'dealer in magic and spells' than a mere priest.

Birds of a feather flock together; among those who chose this now famous necromancer as their spiritual director was an ex-Trappist monk of Fontgombault, Louis-Marie-François Giraud. Equally dissatisfied by the mortifications of the Cistercian life and the life of Catholic mysticism he left his monastery and joined the *Église catholique française* (otherwise the *Église Gallicane*). He was raised to the priesthood by Vilatte on June 21, 1907, but it was the Abbé Julio who decided that this convert had the vocation to be a bishop, not so much for pastoral work as for his rare gifts as a magician. On June 21, 1911, he raised Giraud

[1] See p. 120.
[2] See p. 120.
[3] See pp. 120, 125.
[4] The best known is *Le Livre des grands exorcismes et bénédictions, prières antiques, formules occultes, recettes spéciales et applications des Signes et Pentacles contenus dans les Grands Secrets Merveilleux, les Prières Liturgiques, le Livre des Exorcismes et les petits Secrets Merveilleux . . . Recueil rare et précieux ne devant être confié qu'aux personnes vertueuses, douées du don de faire le Bien et de combattre le Mal sous toutes ses formes.* The first edition, illustrated with many weird diagrams, appeared in 1908.

Another work by the Abbé Julio is a 532 pages volume called *Prières Liturgiques— assistance à la Messe:* in more ways than one this nightmare of a book on white magic (especially the magic of the Mass) is evocative of Leadbeater's *Science of the Sacraments*, published about twenty years later (see p. 358).

to the episcopate in the Old Catholic chapel at Aire, near Geneva.[1] Among the new prelate's most devoted disciples was a certain Madame Mathieu, much resorted to as a faith-healer. Her home was at Gazinet, a village near Bordeaux, on the road to Arcachon. By 1909 she had built a chapel in her garden, where apostate or suspended priests were welcome to celebrate Mass. She claimed to perform miracles by the laying on of hands. Here Mgr Giraud made his headquarters, because 'la bonne maman Mathieu', as the initiates called her—though others called her the 'sorceress'—was proud to give him free board and lodging.

The countryside around Gazinet became notorious as a little hot-bed of occultism and alleged witchcraft. It is curious that certain districts in almost every country have been the breeding grounds of heretics and schismatics more than others, and France is no exception.[2]

Some time during the year 1890 a certain Jules Doinel founded a Universal Gnostic Church in France, and assumed the rank of Patriarch. His object was to revive the mystical doctrines expounded by Origen (c. 185–c. 254) the Alexandrian Biblical critic, theologian and spiritual writer, which included the pre-existence of souls and metempsychosis, i.e. that souls migrate from one body into another until complete purification has been achieved. Doinel claimed that he had received a double spiritual consecration; the first by Jesus in person, the second during a spiritualist seance by two Bogomile bishops.[3] It is possible that Doinel derived many of his heretical doctrines from a later generation of Martinists who led an underground existence in France between 1860 and 1880, and who claimed links with the Knights Templars.[4] Some of them had been initiated into the Masonic Rites of Memphis-Mizraim, revived in 1839 by Marconis de Nègre, and said to have been brought to Europe by Ormus, an Egyptian priest in the first century A.D. Doinel, known as Tau Valentin II, consecrated three bishops, who took the name of Papus, Sédir, and Chamuel, forming the Sacred Synod of this Gnostic Church. The history of the French

---

[1] Aire-Geneva is now the headquarters of Bishop Julien Erni, President of the *Ligue oecuménique pour l'unité chrétienne*, of which Mgr Giraud was one of six co-founders in 1937. (See pp. 519, 520.)

[2] cf. H. Ch. Chéry, O.P., *L'Offensive des Sectes* (Paris, 1960). Most of the facts related in this section have been taken from this valuable source of reference.

[3] The Bogomiles were a tenth-century dualistic sect, which appeared in Bulgaria, and spread to Constantinople and Philippolis in Thrace which became its centre. They seem to have been an offshoot of the Catharists (cf. D. Obolensky, *The Bogomils*, 1948).

[4] See p. 300.

Churches of the Vilatte Succession

Gnostics is wrapped in mystery; many priests were ordained and bishops consecrated by esoteric rites. It is known that Mgr Houssaye (the abbé Julio) was a close friend of the symbolist poet, Fabre des Essarts, who had been made a Gnostic bishop (with the name of Tau Synesius) by Papus, Sédir, and Chamuel.[1]

Another Gnostic body was founded by Jean Bricaud, a typical specimen of the lapsed Catholics in France who drifted into magic, occultism and spiritism early in the present century. Born in 1881, he studied for the priesthood, but was so drawn to pseudo-mysticism that he ceased to practise his religion. By 1909 he had acquired the title of *Président de la Société occultiste mondiale,* as well as that of *Patriarche de l'Église gnostique universelle.* Subsequently he rose to be *Président du Suprême Conseil de l'Ordre Martiniste,* and *Grand Hiérophante du rite ancient and primitif de Memphis-Misraim.* He also held the office of *Recteur de la Rose Croix,* which shows that he was a Rosicrucian.

Bricaud became friendly with Mgr Giraud, who may have raised him to the priesthood in 1912. What is certain is that the ex-Trappist monk, consecrated the ex-seminarist on July 21, 1913, giving him the Gnostic name of Tau Jean II. The ceremony took place in the Gallican church at Saint-Amand, Roche-Savine.

Tau Jean II gathered round him near Lyons a group of fervent Gnostic clergy and layfolk, and on May 5, 1918, consecrated Victor Blanchard, under the name of Tau Targelius.[2] The Patriarch published several books on magic and satanism.[3] He 'passed on' in 1934, and was succeeded by Constant Chevillon, raised to the episcopate by Mgr Giraud on January 5, 1936, with the name of Tau Harmonius.[4] He was killed by German soldiers on March 22, 1944, after the Vichy government had suppressed the Gnostic Church.

[1] After the death of Tau Synesius, Chamuel (Tau Bardesanes), became head of this body. Many more bishops have been consecrated up to the present time, some of them not unknown in the world of art and letters.

[2] Claiming succession from Bricaud via Blanchard, between twelve and twenty Gnostic bishops were consecrated, apparently in France, between 1933 and 1960. They adopted the style of 'Tau', and were given an undefined jurisdiction over various provinces of France, Flanders, Etruria, Venetia, Lusitania, Brazil, Africa, etc.

[3] Joris Karl Huysmans took an interest in Tau Jean II at one time. cf. Ch. Guillemain, 'J. Bricaud (1881–1934), *Révelations de J. K. Huysmans, occultiste et magicien',* in *Bulletin de la Société J. K. Huysmans,* No. 37 (1959).

[4] Two lines of succession, derived respectively from Blanchard (Tau Targelius) and Chevillon (Tau Harmonius) have helped to spread the Gnostic Church from France to Portugal, Italy, Belgium, North Africa and South America. The names of most of the prelates have been kept secret, but all have been given the prefix 'Tau'.

For details of these French Gnostics, see Ivan de la Thibauderie, *Églises et Evêques Catholiques non Romains* (Paris, 1962), pp. 75–81.

Churches of the Vilatte Succession

Mgr Giraud and most of the priests and layfolk of the Gallican Church, even if not Gnostics themselves, were closely associated with them. Gnosticism was very much in the air fifty or sixty years ago. Even the Benedictine monks of Solesmes felt it worth their while to study what are known as the 'Magic Vowels' used in Gnostic rites and ceremonies. In 1901 they published a book entitled *Le chant gnostico-magique*. Attempts were being made in England to spread these ancient heresies, for instance by G. R. S. Mead in his *Fragments of a Faith Forgotten*. They fitted in quite easily with Theosophy and Rosicrucianism. J. I. Wedgwood, the future Bishop of the Liberal Catholic Church, was but one of many young Englishmen who dabbled in them.[1] All over France, especially in the south and west, little groups of neo-Gnostics flourished. Most of them had their own priests and bishops, for it was believed that the magical rites could only be effective with an apostolic succession guaranteed to be 'valid'.

The next bishop to be consecrated by Giraud for the Gallican Church was Pierre-Gaston Vigué. He had been ordained priest by Herzog, the Christian Catholic Bishop in Switzerland, and was raised to the episcopate on December 28, 1921. There was no danger of the Vilatte succession in France coming to an end, for on February 2, 1930, Giraud added to his hierarchy Bernard-Isidore Jalbert-Ville. This one-time seminarist, and secretary to Mgr Bocannia, Bishop of Narni in Umbria, having failed to find a bishop in communion with the Holy See to give him even the subdiaconate, had no difficulty in persuading the Patriarch of the Gallican Church to raise him to major orders up to the priesthood. The ordination took place at Bordeaux in 1928, after which Jalbert-Ville acted as curé of Gazinet. Some years after his consecration he was given the title of Bishop of Almyra, with the right of succession as Patriarch.

On October 7, 1935, His Beatitude, assisted by Vigué, raised Gérard-Marie-Edmond Lescouzères to the episcopate, with the title of Bishop of Salmas. This new prelate was of humble origin: he had been a travelling hosier before he was ordained by Giraud in 1928, and then appointed arch-priest of Saint-Louis-de-Gazinet. Shortly after this the Patriarch and the Arch-priest published a *Profession de foi de l'Église catholique, apostolique et gallicane*, which contained a preface by a Mgr Maxime Adrot of Paris, who called himself 'Prefect Apostolic'.

In 1937 Mgr Giraud, Mgr Vigué, and Mgr Lescouzères were

[1] See p. 345, n. 1.

among the clerics of various bodies who met at the *Institut Suisse des Frères*, otherwise the *Schweizerische Diakonieverein*, at Rusch-ilikon, when it was decided to form the *Ligue oecuménique pour l'unité Chrétienne*—'in the holy communion of the rediscovered Universal Church'. The scope of the League was so broad that it found room for almost anybody calling himself a Christian.[1]

Filled with zeal for promoting the Reunion of Christendom the three Gnostic prelates returned to France. All seems to have gone fairly well until the early nineteen-forties when there was a violent quarrel between the Patriarch and his coadjutor, Jalbert-Ville. Acting not at all in the spirit of the Ecumenical League for Christian Unity, Giraud deposed Jalbert-Ville 'for rebellion, insubordination, and acts of independence'. The excommunicated coadjutor retaliated by opening a chapel in a house at Bordeaux, where he ordained several priests. Unlike Lescouzères, he was a celibate, devout, so it seems, even if eccentric. He had private means, and had helped Giraud in many ways in the past.

Nevertheless the Patriarch, having perhaps cursed Jalbert-Ville with some of the occult formularies found in the Abbé Julio's *Livre des grands exorcismes et bénédictions*, chose Lescouzères as his coadjutor with right of succession, convinced that here was a virtuous person, endowed with gifts to do good and fight evil under all its forms.

Giraud, who had wandered into many strange spiritual paths since he cast off the Cistercian habit, died in 1950, and most of his clergy refused to accept Lescouzères as their next Patriarch. In defiance, he formed a rival sect to which he gave the name of *L'Église catholique apostolique et gallicane*. So, Jalbert-Ville became Patriarch after all, and he made his headquarters at Bordeaux. On July 24, 1951, he consecrated Louis-Jean-Marie Fournié as *Evêque de la Gaule narbonnaise*. On August 12 that same year Fournié raised an ex-Jesuit Jean-René Malvy to the episcopate. Meanwhile Jalbert-Ville had assumed the impressive titles of *Sa Béatitude, évêque titulaire d'Almyre par la bienveillance du saint-siège d'Antioche, Primat de l'Église catholique française et patriarche du saint-siège gallican—143e successeur de saint Pierre apôtre dans la lignée syro-jacobite*.[2] Towards the end of his life this irregular prelate made his

---

[1] See p. 519.

[2] There is no evidence forthcoming that the Syrian Jacobite Patriarchate recognized Jalbert-Ville's exalted status in France, any more than it did those of Mar Frederic and those other prelates in England, who also claimed that their orders were derived from Antioch.

peace with the Catholic and Roman Church before Mgr Richaud, Archbishop of Bordeaux, on March 19, 1955. He died on March 3, 1957.

After Jalbert-Ville's reconciliation with the Holy See, the *Église catholique française* took for its leaders Bishops Vigué and Fournié, also a certain Mgr Jean-Baptiste Brouillet (alias 'Père Jean Vindi'), who had been ordained priest by Giraud, and who had charge of two oratories at Bordeaux. There were other chapels hidden away at Toulouse, Angers, Lyon, Aix-en-Provence, and a few more around Bordeaux. This tiny sect could scarcely be regarded as more of a menace to the Catholic Church in France than were its counterparts to the Established Church in England. Still, there was always the hope of making a few converts, and propaganda was carried on by the bulletin *Le Catholique français*, edited by Père Patrick, who—like Hyacinthe Loyson—had been a Carmelite friar. Jalbert-Ville employed him as private secretary, and he liked to add the initials 'O.C.F.' to his name as a symbol that he belonged to a select order of 'Little French Carmelites,' whose members were said to live in stricter accordance with the spirit of Elias and the early hermits of Mount Carmel. It is possible, however, that they perpetuated something of the spirit of the 'Interior Sanctuary of the Carmel of Elias', founded at Lyons in 1856 by Vintras, the consecrator of so many 'pontifes divins'.[1]

Judging from their publicity, the major apostolate of the bishops and priests of the *Église catholique française* has almost invariably been directed to faith-healing and occultism. As twentieth-century Gnostics, they have tried to revive the ritual side of these early heretics, who practised peculiar forms of baptism and confirmation, and who had their own substitute for the Catholic celebration of the Holy Eucharist. Their modern successors in France, however, when celebrating Mass, appear to have been content with a vernacular version of the Roman rite. The ancient Gnostics, also Tibetan Buddhists, attached the utmost importance to the correct utterance of certain vowels, regarding each vowel as representing a musical note, one of the seven planets or archons, and the seven together as the Pleroma of the Universe. The Abbé Julio had initiated his disciples into the mysteries of cosmogenic speculations by means of geometrical diagrams and mathematical diagrams, guaranteed to develop the spiritual life. The teachings imparted by the first Primate of the Vilatte-founded Gallican Church were

[1] See p. 303.

regarded as divinely inspired by his followers. They were passed
on to a second generation of tiny groups who met for worship,
usually behind the locked doors of rooms in the back streets of
towns, or in remote country villages. It was the feeling of belonging to an esoteric little body that drew mystical-minded men—
even more so women—to the *Église catholique française*. They
were, and still are, convinced that it offers a much more uplifting
and soul-satisfying type of spirituality than that of the Roman
Church—more select, more exciting, and above all, different.
Nobody would venture to contradict this.[1]

On April 29, 1956, Vigué consecrated Ivan-Gabriel Drouet de
la Thibauderie, Comte d'Erlon, who assumed the title of 'Monseigneur Gabriel de Saint-Marie'. After Jalbert-Ville's death the
following year he took on the duties of Regent of the *Église
Catholique Française*, with his residence at 9 Rue du Général-
Gallieni, Romainville (Seine). Here he edited the monthly review,
L'Étincelle, said to have been founded by the abbé Julio in 1887.[2]

Meanwhile Lecouzères did everything possible to stress the
importance of his own rival church, and he assumed the impressive
titles of *Evêque de l'Église gallicane, secrétaire du Collège épiscopal
des Églises catholiques apostoliques orthodoxes d'Occident, membre
dirigéant de la Ligue oecuménique pour l'Unité Chrétienne'*.[3] He moved
his curia from Gazinet to the village of Monteil in the commune of
Pessac, where he opened a small oratory, dedicated to St Vincent-
de-Paul. His chapter consisted of two honorary canons, one of
whom, residing in Paris, acted as Prefect-Apostolic for the North
of France. On April 19, 1953, Mgr Lescouzères provided himself
with a coadjutor in the person of Bernard-Alexandre Ducasse-
Harispe, who had been ordained priest by Giraud. Another addition
to the hierarchy of the *Église orthodoxe gallicane autocéphale* was
made some time in 1956, when Lescouzères consecrated an ex-
Olivetan Benedictine, Gaston Seghers, who in 1953 had been
married in Brussels by Bishop Ducasse-Harispe. The latter prelate
assisted at the consecration and the new bishop took on the duties
of Vicar-Apostolic for Belgium.

Despite its liberal outlook, the propaganda of its bulletin *Le*

[1] cf. Robert P. Casey, 'Transient Cults', reprinted from *Psychiatry: Journal of the Biology of Interpersonal Relations*, November 1841.
[2] de la Thibauderie's book *Églises et Evêques Catholiques non Romains* (1962) is a valuable source of reference to most of the bodies dealt with in this section.
[3] This was the organization founded by Pastor Julien Erni, of Bienne, Switzerland, in 1937. (See pp. 519, 520.)

Gallican and its willingness to provide a refuge for dissatisfied Roman Catholic priests, the *Église catholique apostolique et gallicane* has not managed to win many adherents. So far as can be discovered, this little body consists of handfuls of persons at Lyons, Cannes, and a few other towns in France and Belgium. It is difficult to keep up-to-date with any of these schismatic bodies. They are always quarrelling among themselves, and forming yet more splinter-churches. Some of these obtain bishops from other lines of succession, or, having done so, get them re-consecrated anew to ensure a more 'valid' episcopal status. The allure of these tiny sects seems to be that they are *chic* and *distingué*, able to offer exclusive modes of spirituality and worship not found in France's *grand magazin écclésiastique*—the Catholic and Roman Church.

Yet another body of the Vilatte succession came into being on January 25, 1953, when Mar Justinos Thiesen, who then called himself Archbishop of the Old Roman Catholic Church in Germany, consecrated Jean-Marie Blom Van Assendelft-Altland at Cologne. The new prelate returned to France, soon broke off relations with his consecrator, and opened an independent Old Catholic chapel in Paris. One of his first episcopal acts was to re-consecrate on July 11, 1954, the one-time ex-Jesuit novice, Jean René Malvy, who had been raised to the episcopate by Mgr Fournié (*Evêque de la Gaule narbonnaise*) on August 8, 1951. Mgr Van Assendelft-Altland, assisted by Mgr Malvy, on February 20, 1955, consecrated a doctor of medicine, Charles Boromée, Comte d'Eschevannes and assumed the name as *archevêque titulaire d'Arles*—a gesture of defiance against Mgr Charles De Provenchères, the then Catholic Metropolitan of this fifth-century see.[1]

A month later Mgr Assendelft-Altland, who had now ceased to be associated with Mar Justinos, was in London, where on March 20, 1955, he was re-consecrated in the Cathedral of the Good Shepherd, Chelsea, by Mar Joannes (Nicholson), Archbishop of Karim, and Primate of the Ancient Catholic Church,[2] assisted by Mar Peter (Knill-Samuel), titular Bishop of Naim. Enriched with many more lines of apostolic succession, he assumed the style of Archbishop of the Ancient Catholic Church for France. In November that same year the Archbishop of Karim consecrated the chapel opened by Van Assendelft-Altland at Chelles (Seine-et-Marne).

---

[1] D'Eschevannes had been ordained by Lescousères, but had transferred his allegiance to Van Assendelft-Altland. By 1956 he had become Primate of the *Sainte Église catholique Gallicane autocéphale.*
[2] See p. 475.

Churches of the Vilatte Succession

By this time the *Église ancienne catholique* had fallen into line in more ways than one with Nicholson's independent body in Chelsea. Having gathered round him a group of ladies reputed to possess charismatic gifts, Van Assendelft-Altland formed them into a community of spiritual healers. They were vested in white habits, and known as *Religieuses dominicaines soignantes*. Their convent was at Boulogne-sur-Seine.

The following year this Flemish prelate managed to acquire the exalted status of His Sacred Beatitude Mar Joannes Maria, Prince Patriarch of the *Église Catholique Apostolique Primitive d'Antioche Orthodoxe et de Tradition Syro-Byzantine*. This enabled him to proclaim that he was the 147th successor of St Peter the Apostle as Bishop of Antioch.[1] On November 18, 1956, the Prince Patriarch consecrated and crowned at Rome, (though not in the Vatican Basilica where Charlemagne was crowned) His Imperial Majesty Marziano II Lavarello Lascaris, Basileus of Constantinople and of all the Christian Orient. This youth was believed to be the *de jure* 269th Roman Emperor; the successor of both Augustus and Constantine. At the same ceremony the Dowager Empress Olga was also crowned.[2] On May 2, 1957, the Prince-Patriarch received his third consecration from Mgr Erni.

Just how, when, and where this Antiochean Church of the Syro-Byzantine Tradition came into being is not certain. No matter, its growth has been phenomenal according to official statements. In 1957 it claimed Archbishops in Canada, Germany, West Africa, and Holland; a Patriarch in South Africa; a Missionary Bishop in America (with jurisdiction over the Gold Coast, Nigeria, Liberia, Trinidad, and British Guiana); a Primate with two Suffragan Bishops in England; an Archbishop-Patriarch with a Coadjutor in France; and Bishops in Italy, Ceylon, and Malaya. Fourteen of these prelates (all of them with the prefix 'Mar') now form the Sacred Synod of this apparently vast international body.[3] The

---

[1] He traced his line of succession from Mar Ignatius Peter III (see pp. 35, 36), via Vilatte, Mar Georgius, and Mar Johannes (Nicholson).

[2] cf. *Rituel du Sacre de sa Majesté Impériale Marziano II: Documento Ricordo della pubblica Cerimonia solennemente celebrata in Rome il 18 novembre 1956.* (Bologna, 1957.)

[3] H. S. B. Mar Joannes Patriarch (France), Mar Amandus (Czechoslovakia), Mar Athanasius (India), Mar Christopher (U.S.A.), Mar Eduardo (Mexico), Mar Franciscus (Canada), Mar James-Franciscus (South Africa), Mar José (Cuba), Mar Justinos (Germany), Mar Lukos (Ghana), Mar Nicolas (Nigeria), Mar Rupertus (England), Mar Stephanus (Austria), Mar Adrianus (Order of Apostolic Reunion), and Mar Gulielmus (Order of Christian Unity). We recognize a few old friends among the 'Mars', all of whom have belonged to less distinguished autocephalous churches in the past.

His Imperial Majesty
Marziano II Lavarello
Basileus of Constan-
tinople and of all the
Christian Orient,
crowned at Rome,
November 18, 1956,
by the Prince-Patriarch
Joannes Maria Van
Assendelft-Altland,
Primate of the Eglise
catholique apostolique
primitive d'Antioche
orthodoxe et de
tradition Syro-
Byzantine.

His Whiteness the Humble
Tugdual I (Jean-Pierre
Danyel), Archbishop of
Dol, Abbot of Saint-Dolay,
Kayermo and Keroussek,
Primate of the Holy Celtic
Church, President of the
Union of all the non-Roman
Christian and Apostolic
Churches. The titles of
'Whiteness' and 'Humble'
ire said to be of Druid
origin.

phanar of the Patriarchate is at 149 Rue de Bagnolet, Paris, 20e; the patriarchal pro-cathedral—Chapelle de Notre Dame de l'Unité —is a converted cellar at 36 Rue de Saintonge, Paris 3me, furnished in exquisite taste, so a recent visitor relates. The Divine Liturgy is celebrated here, and the young and handsome Prince-Patriarch (like the Archbishop of Karim) also conducts healing services with the laying on of hands, and anointing with oil. The 1956 Constitutions of the Franco-Byzantine church suggested that in doctrine, polity, ritual and ceremonial it had much in common with the Ancient Catholic Church of Chelsea and Clapton, out of which it evolved.[1]

The *Église Primitive Catholique et Apostolique* claimed a total membership of fifteen in 1959. It is ruled over at Paris by Mgr Marc-Marcel Laemner, a former Liberal Catholic priest, who was raised to the episcopate in 1937 by Giraud and Vigué. He is a practising physician, and holds his degrees from the Sorbonne.[2]

Almost as exclusive is the *Sainte Église apostolique*, which evolved out of the *Association culturelle archidiocésaine de Saint-Alix pour la France et Union française de l'Église gallicane, catholique et apostolique, tradition Bossuet.* Its founder, Mgr Roger Regnier, claims a Uniate Armenian succession. He is a militant Gallican, strongly opposed to everything ultramontane, and a firm believer in little independent churches—the more the better. It appears that his handful of priests specialize in faith healing and occultism, for strongly recommended to the faithful are the writings of the Abbé Julio (Mgr Houssaye), especially his *Livre des grands exorcismes et bénédictions, prières antiques, formules occultes,* etc.[3] The postal address of this mystic élite is BP 52, Colombes (Seine).

Last, but not least, there is the *Sainte Église celtique en Bretagne,* founded by Jean-Pierre (Clodoald) Danyel. Born of French parents on June 22, 1917, he was baptized in the Rumanian Orthodox Church. At the age of thirty-two he was re-baptized and confirmed in the Greek Orthodox Church at Paris. He felt called to found a French-speaking Byzantine Rite parish in France, and had a following of twelve persons, but no Rumanian, Russian, or Greek Orthodox bishop would consider raising him to the priesthood. On

---

[1] Early in 1959 the Prince-Patriarch consecrated Giovanni Taddei, a former Catholic priest. On July 30, 1961, the latter consecrated Alfonso Capaldo as bishop for the Argentine, and also Georges Chrétienne.

[2] Leamner was one of the six co-founders of the Ligue oecuménique pour l'Unité Chrétienne in 1937. (See p. 519.) He consecrated Charlos Bos as his coadjutor.

[3] See p. 306, n.4.

December 25, 1949, the Archimandrite Alexis Van der Mens-brugghe (formerly a Catholic Benedictine monk of the Belgian Congregation) admitted Danyel to the monastic state of the Ortho-dox Eastern Church. The French monk had no choice but to continue earning his living in the office of a paper-mill, though he managed to find time to recite daily the whole Byzantine Office. Early in 1951 he wrote to a Liberal Catholic priest in England: 'Where can I find a bishop whose orders are recognized by Roman Catholics and Orthodox, and who yet himself is neither, since neither Church understands the needs of today?' This priest referred him to Marc Fatome, the Mariavite Bishop for France.[1] An invitation to Nantes resulted, and on July 15, 1951, having passed a theological exam-ination and been given minor orders, subdiaconate and diaconate, Danyel was raised to the priesthood, and status of hieromonk. The Roman Rite in French was used for all the ceremonies.

Not without reason Père Danyel began to doubt if the orders he had received would be recognized by Roman Catholics and Eastern Orthodox theologians, so he applied to the newly consecrated Mgr Lutgen, Archbishop of Antwerp, Metropolitan of the *Église catholique du rite dominicain*, who consented to pass on the fifteen or more lines of apostolic succession received from Mar Georgius, Patriarch of Glastonbury and Catholicos of the West.[2] Having received all minor and major orders over again, Danyel was raised to the priesthood and made hieromonk for the second time on March 1, 1953, in Mgr Lutgen's Pro-Cathedral Chapel, 41 Rue James-Watt, Schaerbeik-Brussels.

By this time the hieromonk's interests had been diverted from Byzantium to Britanny, after brief interludes with the Mariavites and the Belgian Catholic Apostolic Church of the Dominican Rite. Taking the religious name of Tugdual, he retired to Morbihan, where at what he called the Abbaye de la Sainte Présence au Bois-Juhel, near Saint-Dolay, he began to lead an eremitical life in emulation of the ancient Celtic monks. He was now dreaming of reviving the Celtic Church which had existed in Brittany in olden times; very much as Richard William Morgan, Mar Pelagius, Hierarch of Caerleon-upon-Usk had done in the eighteen-seventies, when he tried to revive the so-called Ancient British Church.[3]

Breton Nationalism in recent years has led to some very strange

[1] See p. 518.
[2] See pp. 462, 497.
[3] See pp. 43–47.

activities, and it is not surprising that Tugdual the Hermit managed to collect disciples. On December 25, 1956, the General Chapter of the Order of St Columbanus, with the consent of the General Assembly of the Community of Brittany—whoever they were—elected Tugdual as first Bishop of this new (or revived) Celtic Church, in virtue of the Act of Nomination granted by the *Siège ecclésial oecuménique*.[1] The Bishop-elect, who had passed through successively the Rumanian Orthodox, Russian-Orthodox, Mariavite, and Belgian Dominican Rite Churches, looked around for a prelate to consecrate him, and eventually selected Mgr Ireneaus, Archbishop of Arles, who at that date was Primate of the so-called *Sainte Église catholique Gallicane autocéphale*—in private life Comte Charles Borromée d'Eschevannes.[2] The co-consecrators were equally illustrious: Mgr Comte Eugène de Batchinsky, titular Bishop of Berne and Geneva, Primate of the *Sainte Église Orthodoxe Ukrainienne conciliare autocéphale en exil*; and Mgr Julien Erni, titular Bishop of Bienne, Switzerland, whose status of Secretary-General of the *Siège ecclesial oecuménique* gave him an undefined jurisdiction over every continent.[3] On May 2, 1957, Erni re-consecrated d'Eschevannes, giving him a spiritual blood transfusion of more than a dozen lines of succession. Three days later an imposing pontifical function took place in the Pro-Cathedral Chapel of the Abbey-Nullius of Bois-Juhel, when Tugdual assumed the title of Bishop of Redon.

He went to the expense of having printed an eighteen-page brochure, giving the fullest possible details of the sixteen lines of apostolic succession believed to have been acquired:—Syro-Antiochene, Syro-Malabar, Syro-Gallican, Syro-Chaldean (Nestorian), Chaldean-Uniate, Coptic-Orthodox, Armenian-Uniate, Order of Corporate Reunion, Old Catholic, Mariavite, Non-juring, Anglican, Russian-Orthodox, Syro-Russian Orthodox, Greek-Melkite, and Liberal Catholic. He had lost nothing but gained much by the refusal of Eastern Orthodox bishops in France to ordain him to the priesthood.

[1] This mysterious body was part of the *Ligue oecuménique pour l'Unité chrétienne*, presided over by Bishop Julien Erni in Switzerland, who had now assumed the status of a Supreme Pontiff of a Universal Church.

[2] On May 25, 1958, Mgr d'Eschevannes consecrated Paul Cazenave as coadjutor bishop of the *Église Catholique Gallicane Autocéphale*; and on June 24, 1961, re-consecrated Jean Damage, who had been raised to the episcopate by Mgr Engel Plantagenet.

[3] De Batchinsky had been consecrated at Florence on May 7, 1955, by Mgr Nicolas Urbanovich, of Winnipeg, Canada, assisted by Mgr Fusi, the Mariavite Bishop for Italy (see p. 518).

Since his consecration the Bishop-Abbot appears to have continued to lead the life of a hermit in Brittany, praying for more vocations to his Order of St Columbanus, and convinced that his Holy Celtic Church is far more suited to the Breton temperament than the bureaucratic rigidity of Romanism. Visualizing suffragan bishops sooner or later, he raised himself to Metropolitan status on December 19, 1959, with the title and style of Tugdual I, Archbishop of Dol.[1] Prepared, if necessary, to face bitter persecution by the ultramontane bishops and clergy of the Dioceses of Rennes, Vannes, Saint-Brieux, Quimper, and Nantes, he is confident of an ultimate victory over the 'Italian Mission', and the reconversion of the Breton race to the church order of its ancestors. Like Mar Theophilus, the second Patriarch of the Ancient British Church, Tugdual I is trying to revive Druidic rites and customs, which have lain forgotten for many centuries, and of which the only thing known to historians is that they must have existed.[2] Time alone will show if Archbishop Tugdual I of Dol and his *Sainte Église Celtique* will prove more successful than Mar Frederic and his short-lived Orthodox-Keltic Church of the British Commonwealth of Nations.[3] Both bodies possess a certain affinity, and of all the countless sects claiming the Vilatte succession, they are perhaps the most bizarre.[4]

(ii) *Offshoots of the Vilatte succession in Germany, Austria, Switzerland, etc.*

As the progenitor of schismatic bodies, Vilatte is also represented in Germany, Austria, and Switzerland, where tiny groups of his spiritual offspring can be found if one cares to track them down.

The Vilatte succession in these countries started on December 28, 1921, when Mgr Giraud, Patriarch of the *Église catholique*

---

[1] See p. 46.

[2] On August 7, 1960, the Archbishop of Dol consecrated Yvon Laigle, with the style of Gall, Bishop of Aran; and on the same day ran also raised Michel Raoult to the episcopate, with the name of Iltud.

[3] See pp. 279-282.

[4] For Druidic reasons the Archbishop has now adopted the style of '*Sa Blancheur l'Humble Tugdual I*'. Among his other offices are those of Abbot of Saint-Dolay, Kayermo and Keroussek; and President of the Union of all Apostolic non-Roman Christian Churches. In 1962 Archbishop Ignatius Carolus, Primate of the Old Holy Catholic Church, awarded him the degree of Doctor of Divinity. 'His Whiteness' is trying to develop a devotion to what he calls the Celtic (invocation 'Hum . . . Hum' written OIV). His custom of performing the sacrament of Baptism on the seashore at midnight (*in naturalibus*) appears to have caused scandal in Brittany. The present membership of the Church consists of ten bishops and two or three layfolk. Quality counts more than quantity with the Celts.

française, raised to the episcopate Pierre Gaston Vigué, who had been ordained priest by Bishop Herzog, of the Swiss Christian Catholic Church.[1] Giraud provided another free-lance bishop for Switzerland and Germany by consecrating Armin Robert Geyer in August 1925, who passed on the succession to a certain Karl Eugen Herzog on June 24, 1929, as Bishop of a so-called Catholic Church of Germany.[2] He retired to Switzerland, with the title of 'Evêque-Doyen' until his death.

On June 3, 1924, Vigué consecrated Aloysius Stumpfl, whose priesthood is said to have come from Bishop Herford of Mercia and Middlesex. Stumpfl assumed the title of 'Mar Timotheos, Orthodox Missionbischof', with an undefined jurisdiction over Austria. Little is recorded of his activities during the next twenty years, but on June 1, 1947, he arrived in England as a destitute refugee. It was stated that 'the Regionary Bishop of Aquileia, who presides over the work of the Catholicate in Austria, has accepted an invitation to stay with His Beatitude the Catholicos in order to report on the work in Central Europe, and generally to confer with him and the other English bishops regarding the more technical points connected with the restoration of Orthodox Apostolic Catholicism'.[3] Mar Georgius and his wife gave him generous hospitality for several months.

On June 14 the Patriarch of Glastonbury re-ordained the Metropolitan of Aquileia up to the priesthood (*sub conditione*); and on the 22nd of the same month reconsecrated him 'by way of additional Commission'. Six days later Mar Timotheos reconsecrated Mar Leofric, Archbishop of Suthronia; who on July 14, re-consecrated Mar Georgius. Four days after this the Metropolitan of Aquileia took part in a Salvation Army service at Canterbury, where a collection (amounting to £3 3s) was taken up on behalf of his persecuted co-religionists. He travelled around England, explaining that he had ministered in Austria to Russians who were not in communion with the Patriarchate of Moscow. A fair number of Anglican incumbents as well as Nonconformist ministers, helped this supposed Orthodox prelate. It appears that on July 27 he was re-consecrated once again, this time by Bishop Stannard of the Catholic Christian Church.[4] But Mar Georgius

---

[1] See p. 95.
[2] Cf. K. E. Herzog, '*Woher die evangelish-katholish Successions weihen?*', in *Die ungeteilite Kirche*, October–November, 1935.
[3] *Orthodox Catholic Review*, June 1947, p. 22.
[4] See p. 275.

had begun to suspect this Austrian prelate, and on January 10, 1948, during the celebration of Pontifical High Mass in the Cathedral and Abbey Church of Christ the King, New Barnet, Herts, he solemnly excommunicated 'by bell, book and candle' 'His Grace Mar Timotheos, Metropolitan of Aquileia', 'for sacrilege, superstition, etc.'; together with two other bishops, three priests, and one exorcist.[1] Stumpfl, having returned to the continent, consecrated five more bishops, starting with Friedrich Wiechart on April 14, 1949, who assumed the title of 'Mar Ignatius'.[2] Three days later, assisted by Wiecheart, he raised to the episcopate Joseph Maria Thiessen, with the title of 'Mar Justinos'. Mar Timotheos died in 1951, without being reconciled with the Catholicate of the West.

Mar Justinos, who made his headquarters at Cologne, had large ideas of his own importance, apparently believing that his jurisdiction extended across the Atlantic. As will be related in detail in the next chapter, he issued a Bull on November 15, 1952, solemnly excommunicating several bishops of the Mathew succession in the United States.[3] The omnipotent Mar Justinos consecrated Peter Libertram Potargent on December 16, 1956, giving him the title of 'Mar Makarios'. Another addition to his loosely organized hierarchy was made on October 14, 1958, when he raised Manfred-Apollos Strenger-Wehrenpfennig to the episcopate, nominating him Bishop of the so-called 'Hochkirche in Osterreich'.

Mar Justinos has given another proof that he regards himself as the Supreme Pontiff of a Universal Church as well as 'Patriarch of the Primitive Church of Antioch', because it has been stated that on November 12, 1961, he consecrated at Munich a man named Joel S. Williams, at one time a licensed lay reader in the Anglican Diocese of Bombay. It is believed that Williams was ordained priest on January 23, 1955, and that he 'was elevated to Archpriesthood on March 6' the same year as Spiritual Head of the so-called 'Indian National Church'. We are told that then he 'was unanimously elected Bishop by all the Congregations, continued as

---

[1] See p. 463, n. 2.
[2] By a Rescript of the Holy Office, dated November 9, 1926 Joseph Thiesen, who had been raised to the priesthood by Mar Timotheos (Stumpfl), was reconciled with the Roman Church by the Archbishop of Cologne on November 18, 1926. His letters of orders from Mar Timotheos were endorsed by the Vicar-General of Cologne, under seal with a statement that he 'had received Holy Orders at the hands of a schismatic bishop'. Herr Thiesen was warned that an authorization to exercise the priesthood could not be given to him. Later on he fell into schism again.
[3] See p. 435, 436.

Bishop-Elect for about five years', before he went to Germany to be raised to the episcopate as Archbishop of Bombay and Primate of the Indian National Church.[1]

The French neo-Gnostic line of the Vilatte succession found its way into Germany by several more clandestine consecrations, partly because none of the genuine Old Catholic prelates were prepared to add to the number of bishops at large. On August 25, 1930, Mgr Vigué, who, since he ceased to be Coadjutor to Mgr Giraud had taken the title of Bishop-Consultor of the Syro-Jacobite episcopate in the West, with his headquarters in Switzerland, laid hands on a Lutheran pastor named Friedrich Heiler. His assistant was Gustavus Adolphus Glinz, consecrated the previous day. Heiler assumed the title of Bishop of the so-called *Communion Evangelica Catholica Evangelica*. Born in 1892, and brought up a Roman Catholic, he identified himself with Lutheranism by communicating at the hands of Archbishop Söderblom, at Uppsala in 1919. Greatly influenced by the mysticism of von Hügel, his theology developed on Catholic lines after 1922, when he was appointed professor of the Comparative History of Religions at the University of Marburg. As one of the leaders of the High Church movement in Germany, Heiler founded a Lutheran order of quasi-Franciscan Tertiaries. Feeling called to the episcopate he approached several Old Catholic bishops, but with no result, so he had to be satisfied with the Gallican stream of the syro-Jacobite succession.[2] He ordained several priests, who continued to minister as the pastors of Lutheran Churches. He became first President of the High Church Ecumenical Union of the Augsburg Confession in Germany, and he was also the co-founder of the Catholic Eucharistic Association of the Brotherhood of St John. In October 1940 he consecrated Martin Giebner. Dr Heiler belongs to another class from that of most of the bishops mentioned in this book. He is a world-famous

---

[1] Williams has managed to acquire some impressive ranks, titles and degrees; including Member of Royal Society of Teachers, England; Venerable Order of St Sebastian of Antioch, France; Grand Prior of India, Knight Commander, Grand Cross of Justice, Sovereign Hospitaler Order of Jerusalem; Doctor of Sacred Theology, St John's Seminary, U.S.A. Recently he sent out invitations to his consecration of a Mr John J. Levi as first Bishop of Delhi in the Indian National Church. The function was to take place in St Paul's, Bombay, an Anglican place of worship of which Williams managed to gain possession. For the past few years both Williams and J. C. Ryan (Joseph Chengalvaryan Pillai), Archbishop of the India Orthodox Church (see p. 235), have been operating in connection with the All-India Federation of National Churches, an anti-foreign missionary group of native churches in India.

[2] Cf. Heiler, F., 'The Historic Episcopate', in *The Living Church* (Milwaukee, April 4, 1931), pp. 789–91.

scholar and the author of several widely read books.[1] His chief work has always been to break down the barriers of ignorance and prejudice between Christian Churches—Catholic, Orthodox, and Protestant.

[1] They include *Der Katholismus* (1923), *Evangelische Katholizität* (1926), and *Das Gebet* (1932). In conjunction with Sigismund-Schultze, Heiler published in 1950 the first issue of the annual *Die Oekumenische Einheit*.

CHAPTER IX

CHURCHES OF THE MATHEW SUCCESSION

*Old Roman Catholic Church (Pro-Uniate Rite),
Canonical Old Roman Catholic Church in Communion
with the Primatial See of Caer-Glow,
Old Catholic Church in Ireland,
Old Catholic Orthodox Church,
English (Old Roman Catholic) Rite,
Liberal Catholic Church (and Two American Schisms),
The Church Catholic, Old Catholic Orthodox Church
(Apostolic Service Church),
Old Catholic Evangelical Church of God,
Old Holy Catholic Church (Church of the One Life),
Free Anglo-Catholic Church
and Order of Llanthony Brothers,
Old Roman Catholic Church (English Rite),
Old Catholic Church in America
(Catholic Church of North America,
or Orthodox Old Catholic Church in America),
Independent Episcopal Church
of the United States and Canada,
North American Old Roman Catholic Church,
Old Roman Catholic Church
in North America (Two Groups),
Diocese-Vicariate of Niagara Falls,
Mexican Old Roman Catholic Church,
Église Catholique Evangélique, etc*

Churches of the Mathew Succession

During the forty-three years of Arnold Harris Mathew's priesthood, and the twelve years of his episcopate, he changed his religious opinions so often and so suddenly, that it is never safe to attribute any convictions to him at any stage of his erratic career. It is improbable that this 'great priest who in in his days pleased God and was found just' (as he is described on his tombstone) wished that any of the sects of which he was the progenitor should remain as his lasting memorial. At the time of his death in 1919 there were scarcely half a dozen people left who recognized his jurisdiction as Archbishop of London and Metropolitan of his so frequently renamed Church. During the last two years of his life, so far as can be gathered from his letters, he left no stone unturned in attempting its reconciliation with the Church of England, although on what he considered to be reasonable terms. When he died in 1919 he was buried with Anglican rites by the vicar of South Mymms. Bishop Williams, who had been consecrated as his coadjutor with right of succession, was not informed of his death in time for him to be present at the funeral. Bishop Bacon, however, who had just returned from some years in Canada, was among the mourners.

After that burial service at South Mymms, four independent little bodies in Great Britain and Ireland, as well as two in North America, could claim Mathew as their direct or indirect founder, in the sense that they derived their orders from him.[1] Except for the Liberal Catholic Church which was growing rapidly and had bishops and priests in almost every continent, the other sects hardly counted numerically at all, and few people were aware of their existence.

(i) *Old Roman Catholic Church (Western Catholic Uniate Rite)*, *now known as either The Old Roman Catholic Church in Communion with the Primatial See of Caer-Glow, or The Canonical Old Roman Catholic Church, or The Old Roman Catholic (Pro-Uniate) Rite of Great Britain (America and Canada)*.

Having assumed the Primacy of the Western Catholic Uniate Rite (otherwise known as The Old Roman Catholic Church), Bishop Bernard Mary Williams held a Synod in the north of England on January 17, 1920. Feeling unable to shoulder the burden of duties which were virtually non-existent, and not being too

---

[1] Old Roman Catholic Church (Western Catholic Uniate Church), Old Catholic Church in Ireland, Liberal Catholic Church, The Church Catholic, Old Catholic Church in America), and North American Old Roman Catholic Church.

The Most Rev. Wilfrid
A. Barrington-Evans,
Archbishop of Verulam,
Primate of the Old
Roman Catholic Church
(English Rite).

The Most Rev. Bernard Mary
Williams, Primate of the
Western Catholic Uniate Rite,
later Archbishop of Caer-Glow,
and Metropolitan of the Old
Roman Catholic Church (Pro-
Uniate Rite).

robust in health, he begged to be given a Bishop-Auxiliary, since his theoretical status was now greater than that of the Cardinal Archbishop of Westminster—'*Coetus Episcopalis totius Angliae et Cambriae Praeses Perpetuus*'. At the same time he regarded himself as the opposite number of both the Primate of all England, the Archbishop of Canterbury, and the Primate of England, the Archbishop of York. Those present at the Synod elected Mgr Francis Bacon, titular Bishop of Durham, consecrated by Mathew in 1910, as Auxiliary with right of succession. He had recently returned from north America after four years' absence from England.[1]

This versatile but unstable prelate resigned his office on October 1 that same year, leaving Mgr Williams in sole charge of the Old Roman Catholic Church in Britain. The kind-hearted Dr Winnington Ingram, Bishop of London, welcomed the titular Bishop of Durham back into the Anglican fold, and immediately found him a congenial curacy at St Gabriel's, South Bromley, where the vicar was the Rev. W. N. Lambert, the one-time Dean of Mathew's Old Catholic Cathedral in Islington, of which Bacon had been one of the Chapter.[2] For the next seven years this East End church served as the headquarters of the revived Order of Corporate Reunion, where both the vicar and curate were available to validate the orders of Anglican clergymen who wanted to feel they were real priests in the eyes of Rome.[3]

The Lambeth Conference of 1920 had declared that, should any cleric ordained by the late Archbishop Mathew seek to minister in communion with Canterbury or York, he must be re-ordained *sub conditione*. Mgr Williams was shocked, and felt it his duty to point out that five of his predecessor's priests had been officiating in Anglican churches without having been re-ordained, and that one of them was the vicar of a London parish—meaning Lambert.[4]

The year 1920 saw the first of several Anglo-Catholic Congresses, and with them a rapid increase of baroque and rococo furnishings in Anglican Papalist churches, which in some instances included an urge on the part of the clergy to ensure that their orders were equally post-Tridentine. This involved getting them

---

[1] At that date Dr Hensley Henson was Bishop of Durham.
[2] See p. 180. It is probable that Lambert was raised to the episcopate by Mathew on August 22, 1917, a year after becoming vicar of St Gabriel's, South Bromley.
[3] See pp. 89, 273.
[4] This statement has been questioned. It is claimed that only two of Mathew's priests who joined the Church of England were re-ordained conditionally.

rectified in an irregular manner by some quasi-Old Catholic prelate. In consequence of this Mgr Williams issued a Pastoral Letter
in Advent 1920, addressed from 'The Edge', Stroud, Gloucestershire, stating that he himself had no intention of giving conditional
re-ordination to any more Anglican clergymen, such as Bishop
Bacon, following the policy of Mathew, was then doing with a
view to reviving the Order of Corporate Reunion.

The following year the Archbishop moved his Metropolitan
Curia to a bungalow called 'Madam's Wood', near Painswick, on
the western edge of the Cotswolds, where he spent the rest of his
life. The numbers of his flock were infinitesimal, and it would be
true enough to say that the Old Roman Catholic Church existed
more in his imagination than in reality. He had a tiny congregation at Bristol, and about this time he took under his wing two or
three ex-Anglican Benedictine nuns, formerly members of the
West Malling community, who called themselves 'Benedictines of
SS. Mary and Scholastica'.[1]

On April 11, 1922, the continental Old Catholic bishops issued
a joint statement to the effect that Mathew's consecration had been
secured by the production of false testimony, and that it would
never have taken place had the consecrators known that the conditions stated in the documents received by them were virtually
non-existent.[2] They stated that they had subsequently broken off
relations with Mathew, and that 'without entering on the question
whether an ordination obtained by sacrilegious fraud can be valid',
decided that they could have 'no ecclesiastical relations' with those
persons who claimed to have received orders at Mathew's hands.

Having little to do, except celebrate Mass and recite his Office
in the wooden oratory alongside his bungalow below Painswick
Beacon, the Metropolitan led an almost eremitical existence. He
filled in his days by writing very long letters to his friends, and
composed several pamphlets of a controversial nature. In 1924 he
published at Stroud *A Summary of the History, Faith, Discipline
and Aims of the Old Roman Catholic Church in Great Britain*.[3] This

---

[1] cf. P. F. Anson, *The Call of the Cloister* (1955), p. 428.
[2] See pp. 174, n.1, 176. This was what the Dutch bishops had said already in the
letter printed in *The Guardian*, June 3, 1908.
[3] It was in this pamphlet that Williams first stated that the Old Roman Catholic
Church owed its origins to St Egbert of Northumbria (*c.* 639–729); a monk of
Lindisfarne, who studied at Mellifont in Ireland. By his efforts monk missionaries
(Willibrord, etc.) were sent to Frisia. There is a legend that Egbert died at Iona, on
Easter Sunday, the first time that Mass was celebrated there according to the Roman
rite.

was followed by *The English Text of the Ordinary of the Mass*, translated for the benefit of the two or three priests who ministered in oratories under his jurisdiction, for there were no ecclesiastical buildings which could be called chapels, far less churches.

With that inconsistency which characterized him all his life, at Easter 1925 the Metropolitan issued a new Constitution which repudiated the whole historical and doctrinal position of Old Catholicism. It accepted the doctrines of Papal Infallibility, the Immaculate Conception, and the Decrees of the Council of Trent. What he was incapable of seeing was that, having made the Dogma of Papal Infallibility necessary for his salvation, he ought to have submitted to the Bishop of Clifton as the Pope's representative in Gloucestershire. What it amounted to was that Mgr Williams fell back upon the Protestant principle of private judgment. He put his Old Roman Catholic Church in much the same position as that of extreme Anglican Papalists. All that differentiated himself and his few clergy from those in communion with the Holy See was that they celebrated the Roman Rite in English instead of in Latin, and that the priests were not bound to celibacy.

The immediate result of this new Constitution was that a handful of layfolk, under the leadership of a lawyer named Charles David Evans, seceded from the Old Roman Catholic Church, and set up a new organization which they called 'The Old Catholic Orthodox Church'. They placed themselves under the remote jurisdiction of Mgr McFall, who regarded himself as Old Catholic Bishop for Ireland, and who was not recognized by Mgr Williams.[1] But McFall never ordained any priests for this tiny sect, so unless its members had recourse to free-lance clergy, they had to be satisfied with non-liturgical services. In the early nineteen-thirties, however, a Fr Francis Finch-Styles, a priest of the Vilatte-Lloyd American Catholic Church, came over to England and ministered to them.[2]

This schism in the ranks of the Old Roman Catholic Church (Pro-Uniate Rite) was not the only trial which the Metropolitan had to endure. His former Auxiliary had been presented with the living of All Saints, Mile End New Town, E.1 in 1927, after serving for seven years as curate of St Gabriel's, South Bromley.

---

[1] See p. 209.
[2] Fr Francis tried to form a 'Society of Old Catholic Apostles', and for a time said Mass on Sundays in a room at the Battersea Public Library. Unfortunately, however, his efforts to convert Clapham to so-called Old Catholic Orthodoxy were a failure, and he was denounced from the pulpit by the priests of the Roman Catholic Church of St Vincent de Paul, Altenburg Gardens.

No doubt feeling that his stipend needed augmenting, he started a mail-order chemist's business under the name of Howard Barron, with its office in Replingham Road, Southfields, S.W.18. Unfortunately the manageress was charged with selling drugs to women to procure abortions. The Anglican Vicar and titular Old Catholic Bishop of Durham, as legal proprietor, was sentenced at the Old Bailey on February 10, 1928, to eighteen months imprisonment. This widely publicized scandal greatly distressed Mgr Williams.

In December 1928 the Benedictines of Caldey Island moved to Prinknash Park, within less than a mile of the Metropolitan's bungalow. The occasional sight of these white-habited monks when out for a walk reminded him of the far off days when he had tested his vocation with this same community. There was, however, no direct contact between the Primate of the Old Roman Catholic Church (Pro-Uniate Rite) and his Roman Catholic monastic neighbours, although he himself was absolutely convinced that there was no difference in religion, since they both accepted the Decrees of the Council of Trent, and all subsequent papal dogmatic decisions. The only distinction was that he celebrated Mass in English and the monks were obliged to use the Latin tongue.

On the Feast of SS. Peter and Paul, 1930, Mgr Williams published a pamphlet entitled *A British Uniate Rite*, which was a reprint, with slight alterations, of one issued shortly after the death of Archbishop Mathew in 1919. It was described as 'Suggestions submitted . . . for the consideration of those who having been born in a country wrenched from Catholic Unity by the "Reformers", find themselves out of communion with the Holy See through no fault of their own and desire Corporate Reunion'. The author produced what he regarded as conclusive reasons 'Why Catholics should not remain in the Church of England', and gave an idea of the Uniate Church which he fully expected would soon materialize under his jurisdiction.

In October 1934 he summed up his ecclesiastical position as follows:

'I am under no illusions whatever as to the Roman Catholic Church, either with regard to its Divine or human sides. Generally speaking, Roman Catholics are the most un-Christlike of Christians, and it is this unhappy fact together with fear of Vatican politics, and not the Catholic Faith, which makes union between the Holy See and the people of this country impossible, except only by means of a Uniate Church. There are, alas, ten thousand sound reasons why the Anglican Communion can never serve as the base of a Uniate Church. On the other hand, "Thou art Peter, and upon this Rock I will build my Church" and "Other foundation can no man lay than is laid", so whether we like the human side of things or not, there is nothing else for it, if we would save our souls.'[1]

He informed the same correspondent that, from the very first, Dr Davidson, Archbishop of Canterbury, had made up his mind to destroy the Old Roman Catholic Church, and, so it was to be feared, had no scruples about the methods used. As to the episcopate of this body, Mgr Williams was afraid that he was the only legitimate and orthodox Bishop left. He added:

'If, before my death, we become convinced that it is the Divine Will to withdraw the means of building up a Uniate Church for England which the Good God has held out through this Movement to the people of this country, we shall, of course, submit to the Holy See the moment we become so convinced.'

Years passed, and the eremitical Archbishop of Caer-Glow remained very much in the background in his retreat on the Cotswolds.[2] Still dreaming of the expansion of his rite, in 1939 he published at Gloucester *The History and Purpose of the Old Roman Catholic (Pro-Uniate) Rite in Great Britain*, in which he tried to explain what to ordinary folk seemed a position of sitting on the fence. He wrote:

'We disclaim all pretensions to being in any sense "a Church". We are simply a Rite within the Catholic Church . . . The Pro-Uniate Rite is the lineal descendant of the ancient Church of Britain. Among her Saintly Founders she numbers St Egbert of Northumbria, who sent St Willibrord and his eleven companions to evangelise the Catti, Batavi, and Frisones. The Rite had survived in the Netherlands for thirteen hundred years, whence it had been re-introduced in England by Bishop Mathew in 1908. . . . That there is both necessity and room for a *British* Uniate Rite is only too clearly proved by the unhappy fact that notwithstanding the increase in the number of Christians, Religious Houses, and Clergy, the Latin Rite will *never* bring England back to the Faith and to Catholic Unity . . . It will never be more than tolerated in this country. It will never be liked, and the people will never take it to

---

[1] Letter to the Rev. W. H. de Voil.
[2] Caer-Glow is said to be a mountain in Wales with which Williams had some ancestral connection. It is also said to be the ancient name for Gloucester.

their hearts, and it will continue to repel the many who are attracted by the little they have somehow managed to learn of the true Faith.'

These statements imply that Mass was celebrated in Anglo-Saxon by the monks of Ripon in the seventh century; and that this vernacular liturgy was introduced into Frisia by St Willibrord about 678. The implication that this rite was adopted at Utrecht six years later when the see was founded, and somehow or other managed to survive until 1908, when Bishop Mathew brought it back to England, is a delightful fantasy. To Mgr Williams and his half a dozen priests it seemed true that they were the canonical successors in the twentieth century of Willibrord, Swithbert, the two Ewalds, Laurence and other Northumbrian monk-missionaries, and that they celebrated Mass according to the same rite as that used by them in Frisia, Westphalia, and the Rhineland—a rite far superior to the *Missale Romanum* of St Pius V, obligatory on all bishops and secular priests in Britain who are in communion with the Holy See. The Metropolitan continued in the same strain:

'The Pro-Uniate Rite has its roots deeply imbedded in our native land. It is not a modern importation, as are the non-Catholic religions, the progenitors of which arrived in this country in Tudor times. . . . It has never broken Catholic Unity, and therefore has not within it the seeds of disunion which must lead to the production and multiplication of sects. In this most important particular, the Old Roman Catholic (Pro-Uniate) Rite stands alone, and it is therefore the *only* means in this country (except the Latin Rite) which is capable of bringing about a real and lasting union among Christians. The *truth* of this fact is most clearly demonstrated by the tremendous opposition which the Pro-Uniate Rite has had to endure at the forces of disunion—the measure of persecution to which it has been subjected.'

It is difficult to grasp the workings of the Metropolitan mind, when he proceeded to forbid his clergy to use any liturgical books which did not contain the *nihil obstat* and *imprimatur* of a bishop in communion with the Holy See. English missals, rituals, breviaries, diurnals, etc., published by Anglo-Catholic firms were not allowed, however closely they conformed to Roman Catholic originals.

An enthusiastic defender of the Pro-Uniate Rite was found in the Rev. George Aubrey St John-Seally, who was ordained priest by Mgr Williams in 1940, and ministered in the oratory at Devonshire Lodge, 15 Marylebone Road, London, for four years. He expounded its virtues in a printed leaflet, and said: 'It offers freedom from Ultramontane and State domination, and international politics.' He stressed that, unlike the C. of E., the O.R.C.C. was 'entirely without "views", "schools of thought", "higher criticism", or "modernism", for it professes the Old Faith in its integrity and entirety'.

The controversy over the Church of South India, which had started in 1930, when the Lambeth Conference gave general encouragement to its projection, reached a peak when this new body was finally inaugurated in September 1947. It appears that Williams had been persuaded by at least one of his clergy that at long last many Anglo-Catholic priests and layfolk would realize that the only refuge for those who wished to keep their faith intact was the Pro-Uniate Rite. It is possible that the expected stampede of Anglicans into his fold at no distant date may have moved the Archbishop of Caer-Glow to ordain four more priests in the Marylebone oratory in 1947.[1]

One of them, Wilfrid Andrew Barrington-Evans, was the son of a Baptist deacon, his mother being an Anglican. Brought up in the Church of England, he became a devout church-worker, eventually holding licences as a Reader in the Dioceses of London, Oxford and Southwark. He married in 1922, and earned his living in a London bank. In January 1947 he informed Dr Wand, Bishop of London, and he and several friends had decided to secede from communion with Canterbury to that of Caer-Glow, and returned his Reader's licence. Two months later he was ordained deacon and priest by Archbishop Williams, and placed in charge of the Pro-Uniate Rite chapel in Marylebone. Not long after this he opened a chapel at West Drayton, Middlesex, where he resided with his wife and family; feeling that many persons would appreciate the Pro-Uniate Rite as an alternative to the Latin Rite, which had been celebrated in the Church of St Catherine the Martyr since it was dedicated by Cardinal Manning on September 30, 1869.

Fr Barrington-Evans founded and edited a *Diocesan Chronicle*, the first issue of which appeared in 1947. The following year a second Pro-Uniate place of worship was opened in West Kensington, removed the following May to a house in Park Crescent, Regent's Park, not far from the oratory at Devonshire House, which was closed down. There was, however, no noticeable decrease

---

[1] Wilfrid A. Barrington-Evans, James Ritchie-Long, Geoffrey P. T. Paget King, Arthur J. Mortimer, and Arthur J. Bennett.

in the congregations at All Saints', Margaret Street, St Cyprian's, Clarence Gate, St Mary Magdalene's, Munster Square, or at any of the other Anglo-Catholic churches in the neighbourhood, as the result of this Pro-Uniate invasion of Marylebone, led by the Archbishop of Caer-Glow and his little army. Neither did the Roman Catholic clergy at Our Lady of the Rosary, Marylebone Road, St James, Spanish Place, or St Charles's, Ogle Street, find that the faithful were being lured away from the Latin Rite by the attraction of a vernacular liturgy. It is impossible not to form the impression that the half-dozen or dozen priests under the jurisdiction of Mgr Williams were so taken up with debating among themselves that they had little time for pastoral work.[1]

The Metropolitan presided over a Synod which was held at West Drayton on October 20, 1947—exactly a month after the formation of the Church of South India. He expressed the hope that this reunion would mark the beginning of a new era for the Pro-Uniate Rite in Britain. Many alleged serious errors in H. R. T. Brandreth's recently published *Episcopi Vagantes and the Anglican Church* had been detected, and were discussed *in camera*. It was resolved to send to every bishop of the world-wide Anglican Communion an open letter addressed to Dr Fisher, the Primate of All England. This document was drawn up, and the hierarchies of the respective Provinces were politely requested to leave the Pro-Uniate Rite alone. The Archbishop and his clergy felt that the bitter persecution to which they had been subjected by the authorities of the Church of England, since the days of Dr Randall Davidson, must cease. A renewed pledge was given that there would be no more conditional re-ordinations of Anglican clergymen, however hard they might plead for the validation of their orders in the hope of feeling themselves at last 'real' priests. The next issue of the *Diocesan Chronicle* featured an urgent appeal for vocations to the priesthood. England, Wales, and Scotland were waiting to be converted to Pro-Uniatism: the harvest indeed was great, but the labourers few. Assurances were given that in the event of the death of Mgr Williams without consecrating a successor, consecration from an American source had been guaranteed.[2] The Metropolitan hinted that this might not be necessary,

[1] cf. 'The First Four Years', in *Onward!*, November 1962.
[2] This was James Christian Crummey, head of the Universal Christian Communion in the U.S.A., who had been consecrated by Carfora on March 19, 1931. (See p. 431.) It appears that Crummey had agreed to raise Fr Matthew Buckroyd to the episcopate, or any priest he might nominate. He was therefore given the rank of 'Grand Vicar' and the status of Canon about this time.

because a certain French coadjutor bishop, whose name could not be disclosed, had promised to supply the Pro-Uniate Rite with a bishop, so long as the consecration was kept secret.[1]

In some respects Archbishop Williams was quite as unpredictable as Arnold Harris Mathew. In inconsistency at least he perpetuated the Mathew Tradition for over thirty years. So far as can be made out, he virtually 'closed down' the Church in 1920, but 'reopened' it again four years later, when he completely broke with the continental Old Catholics by making Papal Infallibility an article of faith, and accepting the Decrees of the Council of Trent. This action on his part repudiated the Union of Utrecht. He ordained at least one priest in 1930, but four years later almost made up his mind to submit to the Holy See. After this he shut the doors again until the 'forties, when he had visions of spreading the Pro-Uniate Rite; sanguine that the Roman authorities would realize that the conversion of England could be achieved only by setting up a Uniate body with a vernacular liturgy.

The truth is that Williams was a hermit living in a dream-world, more at home in romance than in reality. Typically, he was an ardent Jacobite and a fervent believer in Legitimacy. In his domestic oratory he used to pray publicly every Sunday after Mass for 'Otto our Emperor and Rupert our King', holding Prince Rupprecht of Bavaria as the *jure divino* sovereign of Great Britain and Ireland. Every year on May 29 he used to pin oak leaves on his biretta, soutane, and chasuble to commemorate the restoration of the Stewart dynasty, but presumably not the restoration of the Church of England. It gave him immense satisfaction that through his mother he could claim descent from Malcolm III and St Margaret, Queen of Scotland; also less illustrious links with the Dukes of Buckingham in the seventeenth century. But his greatest pride was in having a maternal ancestor who was 'out for the King' in the '15, who lost everything for his loyalty, yet sent his son to the '45. The bones of this Jacobite forebear lay in the Well of the Dead on Culloden Moor. 'We have never compromised our loyalty,' Williams wrote to a fellow Jacobite on 'Oak Apple Day' 1942, 'we have never worshipped the rising, now setting sun. I do not recognize any law in this country passed since December 1688 as binding in the forum of conscience.'[2] He liked to boast that he must

[1] This French prelate is now dead. It seems that he was given misleading information about the history and the numerical extent of the O.R.C.C., and that when he was told the true facts he withdrew his offer.
[2] Letter for the Rev. W. H. de Voil.

have been alone in Britain when he celebrated a public Requiem Mass for 'His Sacred and Imperial Majesty The Emperor Francis Joseph' at the time of his death in 1916 during the First World War.

The Archbishop of Caer-Glow kept up a ceaseless correspondence with other Jacobites and Legitimists; and stated that he would have been only too glad if the Bavarian Prince could have driven the Hanoverian usurper off the throne of Britain.

'I never admit defeat,' he explained. 'Oh yes, it all looks impossible enough, but everything worth while has always been impossible, and it is so often the impossible that happens. The way to bring back the King is to make ourselves worthy of it, and God would do the rest. As things have been, and are, it is fitting that we should be misruled by servants.'[1] In fact the vegetarian, eremitical, Jacobite, Legitimist prelate was always sponsoring lost causes. At the same time he was utterly convinced that he was the innocent victim of ceaseless and sinister persecutions for his religious and political opinions.[2]

The situation went from bad to worse and the affairs of the Pro-Uniate Rite more and more chaotic. In November 1948 a Synod was held at the archiepiscopal bungalow, where the Metropolitan announced that he had decided to consecrate Canon Matthew, not with the right of succession, but merely 'to hold the episcopate'. Later he proposed that Fr Barrington-Evans should be made Archdeacon, announcing that he, and not Canon Matthew, would in the event of his death be responsible for the administration of the Rite, in the presumption that the clergy would elect a Bishop whom Canon Matthew would then consecrate. By the following March Mgr Williams had changed his mind again: Matthew was not to be raised to the episcopate, or Barrington-Evans appointed as Archdeacon. The priests hardly knew from day to day what new ideas would occur to the Archbishop of Caer-Glow.

Meanwhile he was writing a supplement to his *Diocesan Chronicle*, which appeared in May 1949. Most of its four pages were devoted to correcting errors said to have been discovered in the recently published book by Dr C. B. Moss, entitled *The Old*

---

[1] Letter dated May 29, 1948.

[2] He left instructions that his funeral pall was to be made up of the Papal Flag, the Imperial Austrian Flag ('because the Austrian Emperor as Holy Roman Emperor, stands next to the Holy Father as Christ's Vicar in Temporals'), the Jacobite Standard raised at Glenfinnan, and the Pro-Uniate Rite flag. (Letter to the Rev. W. H. de Voil, June 14, 1951.)

Catholic Movement. At the same time the Metropolitan took the chance to dismiss the Anglican Communion as 'the creation of the foreign Protestant Reformers under Elizabeth, her Minister Cecil, and his Church-despoiling friends. . . . Nothing, not even all the chasubles in the world can change the fact that the Anglican Communion is an essentially purely Protestant foundation. Secondly, from her foundation until now, she has suffered from a complete lack of Order of any sort or kind, as is proved by the writings of her founders who did not believe in the necessity of Ordination. . . . Thirdly, because of the rampant heresy within the Anglican Communion (even the Catholic-minded party is permeated with Modernism) which she is powerless to restrain or repress, even if her Authorities were inclined, or dared to attempt to do so. . . . Can the cause of God be served by such means? Could a Uniate Church be built upon such a foundation? Surely not?'

Having expressed his mind to Dr Woodward, the Bishop of Gloucester, the Archbishop of Caer-Glow tried to assure the newly appointed Bishop of Clifton, Mgr Joseph E. Rudderham (within whose diocese he resided), that the Pro-Uniate Rite accepted 'the one true faith of Jesus Christ precisely as it is defined by the Infallible Authority of the Holy See. We condemn every heresy, without exception, which the Holy See has condemned. We detest all schism, and in the words of Willibrord Van Os [Old Catholic Archbishop of Utrecht, 1814–25] we have never broken the sacred bond of Catholic Unity, or made common cause with any who having done so, remain in schism. Moreover, and this is a very important point, we have proved that the Rite is capable of stability. Since the defection of the ancient Church of Utrecht, this Rite remains the sole lineal descendant, representative and heir, indeed, all that remains of the Ancient British, Anglo-Saxon, and Medieval English Churches, and our roots have been embedded in our native soil from the earliest days of Christianity. It is not our purpose to provide a resting-place for disgruntled Latin Catholics whom we refuse to receive, or for Ritualists and cranks from elsewhere. Our Mission is to those who for one or other of many reasons remain uninfluenced by the Latin Rite. Our mission is that which no other religious organization is able to offer, namely, to provide all the advantages of a Uniate Rite, except as yet, our actual constitution as such by the Holy See.'

As to the Old Catholic Churches of Holland, Germany, Switzerland, Austria, Czechoslovakia, Yugoslavia, the Polish National

Catholic Church in America—and, in fact, every other schismatic body not in communion with the Holy See, claiming valid orders from the Ferrette, Vilatte, Mathew, Herford, or other lines of succession—they were dismissed with a stroke of the Metropolitan's pen. He was apparently incapable of realizing that if average Roman Catholics had even heard of his beloved Pro-Uniate Rite, they would certainly regard it as merely a tiny sect, founded by an apostate priest, who, having been married by an Anglican incumbent, was consecrated as bishop in a schismatic Church, from which he subsequently broke away, and died with a major excommunication from the Holy See still hanging over him.

While the 'Chard Chimes' at Prinknash Abbey down the road echoed through his bungalow windows night and day as a reminder that the Pro-Uniate Rite was still a long way from being recognized by the Holy See, the Archbishop of Caer-Glow went on seeing visions, planning and organizing, in his dream world. Early in 1950, for no apparent reason, he suddenly turned down a man who was due to be ordained subdeacon. Then he informed Fr Barrington-Evans that he was seriously considering 'closing down' the Rite for good and all. To add to his worries, two of his priests— G. A. St John-Seally, and G. P. T. Paget King—whom he had expelled and deposed from Orders on January 31, 1948, had set up a body of their own which they called 'The English (Old Roman Catholic) Rite'.[1]

Events on both sides of the Atlantic, together with the Archbishop's refusal in July 1950 to consider any arrangements to ensure the continuation of the Pro-Uniate Rite in the event of his death, led to much grumbling and discussion among his priests, as to what action they should take. However, a month later the Metropolitan appeared to be more optimistic of the future, and was prepared to talk about ordaining some more priests. Then without warning he announced that he would perform no further episcopal functions, and ordered his clergy to stop celebrating Mass, except privately for their own devotion. They felt that they could not obey him, and after an exchange of letters decided that the future of their pastoral work involved severance of all relations with the Metropolitan.

On September 22, 1950, a declaration was signed in London,

---

[1] These two priests had a chapel in London dedicated to the Blessed Sacrament and the Immaculate Heart of Mary, where, according to the Parish Magazine, all sorts of elaborate religious functions took place until about 1950.

repudiating the jurisdiction of the Archbishop of Caer-Glow, who found himself with only two priests—Canon Matthew and Fr Bennett—both of whom appear to have been in sympathy with the 'rebels' under the leadership of Fr Barrington-Evans, though declining to join them out of respect to the oaths of canonical obedience which they had taken to Mgr Williams.[1]

In a sense it was the story of Arnold Harris Mathew over again, for he, too, had been abandoned by all but one of his priests in 1915.[2] As to 'going over to Rome', this was out of the question. Writing to the Rev. W. H. de Voil on September 24, 1951, Mgr Williams explained:

'All the Popes since Pius IX have been Socialists, except Benedict XV, the only gentleman among them. I could never submit to a Socialist Pope, but if we had a sound Pope, and I could have been received on the terms of the Pacification of Clement IX, then I would have taken the course before now, but that remains the only course I could take. I cannot believe that Almighty God requires me to take an oath I well know to be false in order to save my soul. That is what the present position amounts to, and well the Authorities know it.'

Indeed it was a tragic situation. Not only did the Archbishop of Caer-Glow find it impossible to submit to the Patriarch of the West, for various reasons he did not see his way to submit to any of the Patriarchs of the dissident Eastern Churches—Orthodox, Nestorian, and Monophysite. He refused to consider seeking communion with the bishops of the Anglican Provinces of Canterbury and York. He regarded with horror all the archbishops and bishops of the Ferrette and Vilatte lines of succession who were functioning in England; they were dismissed as heretics as well as schismatics. Even greater was his detestation of his rivals in the Mathew line of succession, because none of them accepted his authority. Lastly he could not picture himself as a prelate of the Eparchy of All the Britons in the Catholicate of the West, paying allegiance to Mar Georgius, Patriarch of Glastonbury. The truth was that in the end he became convinced that he was the only real Catholic and Orthodox bishop in Britain.

Bernard Mary Williams died on June 9, 1952, after an illness lasting from the previous Easter. It is fairly certain that he wished his Pro-Uniate Rite to come to an end, and it is said that before his

[1] See p. 331.
[2] See p. 200.

death he wrote to the Archbishop of Canterbury and the Cardinal Archbishop of Westminster to this effect. He was buried in the churchyard at Fretherne, Gloucestershire, after a requiem Mass had been celebrated in the little wooden oratory at Madam's Wood.

None of the three priests who had remained loyal to Mgr Williams felt that they were justified in carrying out his last wishes by dissolving the Pro-Uniate Rite, and they continued to operate under the title of the Old Roman Catholic Church. To add to the complex situation, Mar Georgius, Patriarch of Glastonbury, claimed that if there was a legitimate successor to the Archbishop of Caer-Glow, it was himself, because his succession was derived from Archbishop Mathew by way of Archbishop de Ortega Maxey, Patriarch of Malaga, who derived his orders in one line from the Prince de Landas. None of the six other bishops previously consecrated by Mathew had left a succession, so, in the opinion of Mar Georgius, 'the jurisdiction was canonically vested in the senior line derived from the original repository of the jurisdiction'.[1] Neither the loyal remnant of three priests, nor Fr Barrington-Evans, the head of the schismatic body, were prepared to accept the somewhat complex arguments put forward by the Patriarch of Glastonbury.

Shortly before his death—but after the formation of the schismatic body—one of the two priests who had been deposed and excommunicated in 1948, Fr Paget King, was reconciled with his former Metropolitan, and was with him during the last illness. Some time after the funeral, arrangements were made for Paget King's consecration by a Bishop of the North American Old Roman Catholic Church—Gerard G. Shelley; but the negotiations broke down.[2] Eventually it was decided that as Bishop Shelley was likely to remain indefinitely in Europe, with his headquarters in Rome, where he was employed as a translator by UNESCO, the tiny remnant of the original Pro-Uniate Rite in Britain did not really need a resident bishop.[3] So it was that Mgr Shelley became the successor of Mgr Williams, and took the title of Archbishop of Caer-Glow.

It was quite in keeping with late medieval precedent that the Primate of this branch of the Old Roman Catholic Church should

[1] *In the Shadow of Utrecht* (Hove/Anvers, 1954), p. 33.
[2] Shelley had been ordained priest by Mathew in 1914. He went to America, where he is said to have been consecrated by W. F. Brothers on December 18, 1949, and then re-consecrated by R. A. Marchenna on March 25, 1950. (See p. 434.)
[3] Shelley was, in fact, elected by the clergy who had remained loyal to Williams at the time of his death. A photograph of the document is in the possession of the Rev. H. R. T. Brandreth.

reside several thousands of miles from Caer-Glow in Wales, with his headquarters outside the walls of Vatican City. Fr Paget King was appointed Vicar General, and the curial offices were established at Steenoven Mission House, 16 Aberdeen Road, Highbury, London, N.5.[1]

On August 12, 1957, the second Archbishop of Caer-Glow issued an Encyclical Letter from Rome addressed to the Bishops, Clergy, and Laity under his jurisdiction. He stated that in view of the many unauthorized persons still making claims to be Old Roman Catholic prelates, the only bishops he recognized were Richard A. Marchenna (U.S.A.), Zigismund Vipartas (U.S.A.), George T. Koerner (U.S.A.), Hans Heuer (otherwise known as 'Bishop Willibrord', resident in Germany), and José P. Ortiz (Mexico).

On Whit Sunday, 1960, Mgr Shelley, assisted by Bishop Willibrord, consecrated his Vicar General, Geoffrey P. T. Paget King, as Coadjutor Bishop for England of the Old Roman Catholic Church. The ceremony took place in the Chapel of St Thomas of Canterbury at Steenoven House—one of a long row of houses in a drab terrace, hidden away to the east side of Highbury Grove, a remote part of North London, now much favoured as a place of residence by members of the Victorian Society. At the time of writing the only other places of worship in Britain maintained by this small body are chapels at Brixton, London, S.W.2, and Tonbridge, Kent. There have been several defections among its few clergy, and vocations are badly needed. On February 23, 1962, by the unanimous decision of the Synod of the Primatical See of Caer-Glow, and with the approval and consent of the Episcopal Synod in the U.S.A., a revised edition of the Constitutions and Rules of what is called 'the whole canonical Old Roman Catholic Church in every country' was published. It is laid down that the only authorized liturgical books are those of the Latin Rite 'known as the Rituale Romanum, the Missale Romanum, and the Pontificale Romanum, in accurate and authorized translations, and in any Supplements to any of these or

[1] The name 'Steenoven' recalls Cornelius van Steenoven, the first Archbishop of Utrecht not in communion with Rome. He was consecrated in 1724 by Dominique-Marie Varlet, Bishop of Babylon *in partibus*, who had been a missionary in Persia, but was accused of Jansenism on his return to Europe. He retired to the Netherlands, where he consented to oblige the now schismatic Chapter of Utrecht by consecrating Steenoven. The following year Benedict XIII declared that Steenoven's election was null and void, and his consecration 'illicit and execrable'. In 1943 Shelley had founded in New York a 'Port Royal Society' to propagate the Jansenist traditions of this famous Cistercian abbey of nuns—a proof that he did not share the ultramontane opinions of Mgr Williams.

books which may at any time be authorized for use by Old Roman Catholics by the authority of the Primate'. It is also laid down that 'in conformity with the universal rule of the Catholic Church, no cleric having been ordained to the Subdiaconate may thereafter contract matrimony. In accordance with Eastern custom, married men may be ordained, subject always to the approval of the spouse. No man who has been married twice may be ordained. No married man may be elected to the Episcopate unless his wife has previously died'. These regulations on matrimony differentiate this body from almost all the others dealt with in this book. On January 1, 1963, Bishop Paget King, Coadjutor to the Primate, issued an official statement that Archbishop Marchenna and the Old Roman Catholic Church in North America had 'by its own free act and will separated itself from Communion with the canonical Old Roman Catholic Church'; explaining that all the Bishops, Clergy and Laity had 'returned to the irregular and uncanonical status in which they were from 1942 to 1957'.[1]

(ii) *Old Catholic Church in Ireland*

Archbishop Mathew's second spiritual child did not have a very long life, and never attracted much publicity, for it existed mainly in the Celtic imagination of its founder, James McFall.[2]

His conception of Catholicity was always nebulous and eclectic. From his youth his absorbing interest had been religious ceremonial. Early in 1905 he came over from Ireland, and stayed with the Anglican Benedictine monks at Painsthorpe in Yorkshire. On his return to Belfast, he wrote an article, printed in *The Catholic Times*, hardly able to find words in which to express his enthusiasm for 'the perfection of the singing, the splendour of the liturgical functions, and the magnificent vestments'.[3] By way of showing his admiration for these Church of England monks, the Irish Roman Catholic layman presented Abbot Aelred Carlyle with a wooden crozier and prayer desk, carved by himself.[4]

[1] The ethos of Steenoven Mission House in recent years has drifted far from the puritanical rigidity of Port Royal and the early eighteenth-century Jansenists. Animal Welfare, Bodybuilding, Music Circles, and Play Reading Groups, are among the many social activities sponsored at Highbury, bringing Old Roman Catholics in contact with others outside the fold of Caer-Glow, so that they can 'learn to relax and laugh together'. In addition to a magazine *One Faith*, there is published a quarterly *St Ambrose Bulletin* 'for the benefit of those interested in the study of liturgy and ways of worship'. Archbishop Shelley resigned the primacy in the autumn of 1963.

[2] He had been ordained priest by Mathew in 1910.

[3] cf. P. F. Anson, *Abbot Extraordinary* (1958), p. 84.

[4] They are still preserved at Prinknash Abbey, though only some of the younger generation of monks seem aware of their origin.

Five years later McFall, having seceded from communion with the Holy See, found himself a priest of the Old Roman Catholic Church. Six years after this he was in the happy state of not only selling mitres and other pontifical vestments, but of donning them himself. Shortly after his consecration he was solemnly excommunicated by Mathew.

There is a story that he refused to perform any episcopal acts in Ireland for many years owing to a promise made to Cardinal Logue, Archbishop of Armagh, and we are told that 'apparently the Cardinal did not mind much what James did as long as it was not within his jurisdiction, for all his activities were mainly in England, though he did once visit the Channel Islands. It must be admitted that he was a man of no great education, though in many ways knowledgeable, particularly in relation to pre-Reformation monastic matters'.[1]

As stated already, in April 1925 Bishop McFall found himself the nominal head of a schism from the Old Roman Catholic Church in England, which styled itself the Old Catholic Orthodox Church. Under the leadership of W. C. D. Evans, a number of lay people dissociated themselves from Mgr Williams when he became a militant Papalist.[2] Relations between McFall and Williams became even more strained after the latter proclaimed that he did not rule over 'a Church', and that his followers were merely 'a Rite within the Catholic Church'. The Archbishop of Caer-Glow always seems to have resented the presence of a more or less free-lance bishop in Ireland, whose instrument of consecration he had witnessed. As late as October 27, 1947, he felt it his duty to inform Dr Fisher, Archbishop of Canterbury, that McFall was not recognized by the Pro-Uniate Rite, since it had not been canonically erected in Ireland.

In the winter of 1933 Mgr McFall defied the authority of the Archbishop of Caer-Glow, the Bishop of Brentwood, and the Bishop of Chelmsford by performing another episcopal action within an area which each of them regarded as under his jurisdiction. On December 21 he consecrated the Rev. Thomas R. Coatbridge Williams, Ph. D., who had succeeded Bishop Beale as rector of Great Sutton, a village among the marshlands at the upper end of the River Roach in Essex.[3] It is possible that this consecration was

---

[1] Mar Georgius, *Varied Reflections* (Antwerp, 1954), p. 11.
[2] See p. 327.
[3] Williams had been a student at Lichfield Theological College in 1904. It is understood that on October 4, 1918, McFall had raised him to the priesthood at East Hagbourne, Berks, and in April 1921 given him the rank of Canon. In 1926–7, having been

connected in some way with the revived Order of Corporate Reunion, or with a wish to make sure of the maintenance of the Mathew line of succession. Although the ceremony is recorded as having taken place in public, it was not until January 1940 that Dr Wilson, Bishop of Chelmsford, admitted that he had heard of it.

The Regionary Bishop of the Old Catholic Church in Ireland, whose conception of jurisdiction was even more elusive than that of the bishops of the Celtic Church, made another trip to England in the autumn of 1938, when he gave minor and major orders up to the priesthood to Hugh George de Willmott Newman on October 23. No sooner had he returned to Belfast than he released the newly ordained priest from his jurisdiction, and forgot all about him.[1]

This happy-go-lucky Irish prelate died in 1960, still running a church furnishings shop in Belfast, under the name of his daughter, Miss Columba McFall. On more than one occasion when he was in Britain he enjoyed the hospitality of the now Roman Catholic Benedictine monks, first on Caldey Island, and later at Prinknash, whose ritual and ceremonial had so thrilled him when he was their guest at Painsthorpe in 1905. It has been said he used to proclaim that he was always a Roman Catholic, who happened only accidentally to be out of communion with the Holy See. This is precisely what Mathew had insisted on during his cross-examination by F. E. Smith.[2] Both prelates had a limitless capacity for self-defensive delusions.

(iii) *The Liberal Catholic Church*

By the summer of 1915 the majority of the clergy serving the Old Roman Catholic Church had become members of the Theosophical Society and the Order of the Star in the East. It gave them a shock when Archbishop Mathew ordered them to resign their membership of these organizations in his Pastoral Letter, promulgated on August 6 that year.[3] They had plenty of reasons to regard their Metropolitan as obscurantist, unenlightened, and behind the

---

reconciled with the Church of England, Williams was re-ordained for the Diocese of Chelmsford. Having served three curacies, the Rev. W. Noel Lambert (one of Mathew's bishops), presented him with the living of Great Sutton in 1929, where he remained until 1947. From 1947 to 1950 he was Rector of Walton-le-Wolds, and from 1950 to 1953 of Hopton Wafers, when he moved to Acton-Burnell in the Diocese of Hereford.

[1] For further details of de Willmott Newman—the future Mar Georgius, Patriarch of Glastonbury and Catholicos of the West, see chapter ten.

[2] See p. 189.

[3] See p. 200.

times. Even after nearly half a century no Anglican bishop has felt it necessary to denounce clergy tainted with the same heresies.

Mrs Besant wrote in October 1911 :

'Theosophy is spreading much among the clergy of the English Church and the ministers of the Nonconformist communities. Not only have we members of the Theosophical Society among the clergy, but there is an increasing number who welcome sermons on Theosophical teachings, and many more who themselves teach a mysticism undistinguishable from Theosophy.'[1]

This statement was perfectly true. For twelve years after the publication in 1899 of *Christian Mysticism* by William R. Inge, then Vicar of All Saints', Knightsbridge, there had been a spate of books on the spiritual life—not all of them orthodox—culminating with Evelyn Underhill's *Mysticism* and her *Path of Eternal Wisdom*, both published in 1911. It became fashionable to regard oneself both as a 'Mystic' and a 'Modernist', which often involved becoming a vegetarian as well. As alternatives, there were Mrs Mary Baker Eddy's so-called 'Christian Science', or the 'New Thought Movement', and Spiritualism—all of which offered a kind of religion less mundane than that supplied by conventional Anglicanism. Among the Church of England clergy who were openly expounding theosophical doctrines from their pulpits in the first decade of this century was the Rev. W. F. Geikie-Cobb, who at St Ethelburga's, Bishopsgate, in the heart of the City of London, combined them with the richest of Anglo-Catholic ceremonial, and at the same time defied the Bishop of London by remarrying divorced persons. He had previously been Assistant Secretary of the English Church Union.[2] Even the Benedictine library on Caldey Island accumulated at this period a large miscellaneous selection of books and pamphlets dealing with Theosophy, Rosicrucianism, Reincarnation and similar forms of non-Christian mysticism.[3]

The Rev. L. W. Fearn, a curate of St John's, Westminster, and Warden of the Church Mystical Union, attracted large congregations by his exposition of the teachings of the Rev. Holden E.

[1] *The Theophist*, October 1911, p. 17.
[2] Eventually he seceded from the Church of England in order to promote Freemasonry for Women.
[3] Robert Hugh Benson, writing in 1910, admitted that 'Theosophists are wonderfully alive to what may be called the more mysterious and spiritual elements in the Catholic Religion. . . . There are certain points of view that they understand far better than many uneducated Catholics; on the other hand, it is extremely rare to find among them a capacity for that simplicity and obedience and submission that is the foundation of the moral life of faith'. (*Non-Catholic Denominations*, p. 195.)

Churches of the Mathew Succession

Sampson, as set forth in his *Life of the Lord Jesus Christ, the Great Master of the Cross and Serpent*, and *Progressive Redemption*, both of which were based on Theosophy and accepted the doctrine of Reincarnation. The Rev. C. W. Scott-Moncrieff (father of the well-known Scottish Roman Catholic author) was an enthusiastic member of the Order of the Star in the East. Under the name of 'A Christian Theosophist' he tried to be an early twentieth-century John the Baptist, preparing the way for the advent of Krishnamurti as the re-incarnation of Christ. Many other Anglican clergymen had absorbed the pseudo-mysticism propagated by Mrs Besant and leading members of the Theosophical Society, without actually joining it, so it really was a little hard that Archbishop Mathew should take such a strong line when the Bishops of the Church of England were lying low.[1]

The half-dozen priests of the Old Roman Catholic Church lost no time in rallying their forces after the promulgation of their Metropolitan's Pastoral on August 8, 1915. Within five weeks they had elected two of their number to the episcopate. On September 26, the deposed Bishop of St Pancras, Frederic Samuel Willoughby, consecrated Bernard Edward Rupert Gauntlett and Robert King. This double consecration was intended as a gesture of defiance of Archbishop Mathew in view of what was held to be an unjustified exercise of authority. Both these clerics had been ordained by Mathew. The former, an ex-Irvingite, was Secretary of the Theosophical Society Order of Healers, and had already been given the rank of Canon. The latter was a consulting psychic, and advertized 'careful character delineation; aptitudes and other particulars from Birth Horoscopes; by a practitioner skilled in the true Placidian Method'. His charge for supplying such occult information was 10s. 6d. or $2.60.[2]

The real leader of this schism from the Mathew-founded Church was James Ingall Wedgwood, and it was mainly due to his remarkable personality that it finally extended its activities to every con-

---

[1] Between 1902 and 1913 Germany was the country where the Theosophical Society gained most members, due to the personality of Rudolph Steiner, who was its leader until he broke away and founded the Anthroposophical Society. Since 1889, when Edouard Schuré published his book *Les Grands Initiés* (translated into German in 1097), theosophical teachings had gained many adherents in France. Holland was another country where Oriental mysticism, as expounded by Mrs Besant and C. W. Leadbeater, became fashionable.

[2] Later on Bishop King helped to spread Theosophy in Scotland, and was largely instrumental in founding centres of the Liberal Catholic Church in Edinburgh, Glasgow, and Dundee. He died in 1954. Bishop Gauntlett resigned his episcopal status in 1924, and became a lecturer for the British Israel World Federation.

The Right Rev. Charles
Webster Leadbeater, Second
Presiding Bishop of the
Liberal Catholic Church,
Administrator-General in
Australia of the Universal Co-
Masonic Order, Protector of
the Order of the Star in the
East, Senior Knight of the
Round Table.

The Right Rev. James
Ingall Wedgwood,
First Presiding Bishop
of the Liberal Catholic
Church, Some-time Very
Illustrious Secretary of
the Supreme Council
of Universal Co-
Freemasonry for Great
Britain and its
Dependencies, General
Secretary of the
Theosophical Society
(English Section), and
Founder of the Temple
of the Rosy Cross.

tinent. He was born in 1883, and it has been said that his mother was a natural clairvoyant. As a youth he became an Anglo-Catholic, and was associated with the underground affairs of the moribund remnant of the Order of Corporate Reunion. He joined the Confraternity of the Blessed Sacrament, and most other Anglo-Catholic organizations of the same character. Having left school, he worked as an analytical chemist at York. Feeling convinced that he had a vocation to the priesthood, he lodged with the Rev. Patrick Shaw, the newly appointed rector of All Saints', North Street, York. This ancient church, with its famous late medieval stained glass, ornate ritual and ceremonial, satisfied all his religious and artistic instincts. In his spare time he took lessons from the organist of the Minster. A friend who knew Wedgwood about the age of twenty recalled him as 'a cultured and intelligent young man—dark-eyed, good-looking, and attractive in manner'.

One day Mrs Besant gave a lecture at York. Wedgwood was instantly converted to Theosophy by her convincing arguments. He informed Fr Shaw, who, though a most kindly man, was so horrified that he banished his lodger from the rectory. The Anglican Benedictine monks at Painsthorpe, fourteen miles east of York, were more tolerant, especially Abbot Aelred Carlyle, who throughout his long life took a keen interest in all forms of occultism, and never ceased to believe privately in the existence of the astral body. Wedgwood stayed at the monastery and lent the Abbot theosophical books and pamphlets. The latter, however, was critical of their fundamental content, and told his young friend that Catholic mysticism offered everything provided by Theosophy, but on sounder lines.

Mrs Besant's new convert bade farewell to the Anglican Benedictines and moved to London, where he became an active worker for the Theosophical Society. From 1911 to 1913 he acted as General Secretary of its English section.[1] In spite of his absorption in Theosophy, Wedgwood still regarded himself as an Anglo-Catholic, and had not ceased to yearn for the priesthood. Early in 1913 he wrote to Archbishop Mathew for details of his sect, which at that date was known as 'The Ancient Catholic Church of Great

---

[1] It was in 1912 that Wedgwood helped to found a cabalistic body known as 'The Temple of the Rosy Cross'. He also became 'The Very Illustrious Secretary' of the Supreme Council 33rd degree of International Co-Freemasonry British Federation. A photograph in the *Daily Mirror*, September 4, 1911, depicts him in masonic regalia at the foundation-stone laying of the new headquarters of the Theosophical Society in London.

Britain'.[1] He had been told that, unlike the Anglican and Roman Catholic Churches, the constitution of this new body made room for the free development of the individual conscience in relation to modern scientific discoveries and occult research, and that its worship retained all the traditional richness of the Western Church, to which he had been so attracted since boyhood. Having received a friendly reply from the Archbishop, he showed him a copy of Mrs Besant's *Theosophy* as representing his own beliefs. It appears that no difficulties were raised about his admission to Mathew's little flock. Wedgwood for his part had no scruples about signing the declaration by which he was 'formally united with the Ancient (Catholic) Church of England, Scotland, and Ireland'; thus professing his faith in 'the Decrees of the Seven Holy Ecumenical Councils as laid down, in precise terms, in the Niceno-Constantinopolitan Creed of the Universal Church, the Holy Sacrifice of the Mass, the Dogma of Transubstantiation, the Seven Sacraments, and the Decrees of the Synod of Jerusalem 1672'.[2]

Wedgwood was so elastic mentally that he managed to combine these traditional doctrines with Co-Masonry, Rosicrucianism, and Theosophy.

Mathew lost no time in giving him conditional baptism and confirmation. Then followed rapidly the four minor orders, subdiaconate and diaconate. Apparently his knowledge of theology needed no testing, for on July 22, 1913, he was raised to the priesthood. The Roman Rite was used at all the ceremonies. Before long the Secretary of the Supreme Council of Universal Co-Freemasonry in the British Empire was able to wear the robes of a canon beneath his regalia.[3] Three years elapsed, however, before Canon Wedgwood was raised to the high-priesthood of the now completely theosophical Old Roman Catholic Church. The function took place in the Co-Masonic Temple, 13 Bloomfield Road, Maida Vale, London, W. 9,because the public oratory, normally used for such ceremonies, would not have held the crowds expected.

In the imposing Latin *Instrumentum Consecrationis* it was stated that on February 23, the Sixth Sunday after Epiphany, 1916, 'the Most Illustrious and Most Reverend Lord Frederick Samuel

---

[1] In the spring of 1914 it had become 'The Catholic Church of England'. (See p. 192.)

[2] cf. *The Occult Review*, May 1918, p. 251.

[3] This is really the Rite of Mizraim and Memphis, set up in France in the early 1800s. It consisted of 96 degrees, but later on it became the so-called 'Primitive Rite of John Yarker', boiled down to 33 degrees. Mrs Besant had been initiated in 1902.

Churches of the Mathew Succession

Willoughby, M.A., of St Catharine's College, Cambridge, by the Grace of God Catholic Bishop, formerly Titular Bishop of St Pancras, assisted by the Most Illustrious Lords, Robert King and Bernard Edmund Gauntlett, Catholic Bishops of the Region of Britain, consecrated the Right Reverend Lord James Ingall Wedgwood, priest of the Catholic Church and Canon of the Metropolitan Cathedral'. Once more the Roman Rite, as adapted and translated in the 1909 *Old Catholic Missal and Ritual*, was followed. Affixed to the document were the signatures of the consecrator and co-consecrators, Canons Carter and Farrer, Fr Theodore Bell, and twenty-three layfolk, most of them well-known Theosophists.[1]

Leaving the psychic Bishop King in charge of the Old Roman Catholic Church, Bishop Wedgwood sailed for Australia, and on July 22, 1916, conferred the episcopate on Charles Webster Leadbeater at Sydney, New South Wales. Leadbeater's career had been full of strange adventures. His boyhood and youth were spent in South America, where on one occasion he was kidnapped and nearly murdered by savages. Returning to England, he was ordained deacon and priest at Farnham by Dr Harold Browne, Bishop of Winchester, in 1879. While serving a curacy at Bramshott, Hants, he met Madame Blavatsky, and was converted to Theosophy. From 1885 to 1893 he spent most of his time in Ceylon and India, absorbed in the study of Buddhism. He was a man of considerable learning in many subjects, and there is no doubt that he possessed unusual gifts as a clairvoyant. In 1906 Leadbeater was forced to resign the secretaryship of the Theosophical Society when charged with crimes of sexual perversion. He maintained that this was the ordeal he had to undergo as the symbolical crucifixion through which all candidates for the Arhat—the fourth stage in Theosophist initiation—must pass. The storm blew over by 1919, and he was invited by Mrs Besant to rejoin the Society. He went to Australia in 1913, and remained there for the rest of his life. He describes his consecration in a letter to Mrs Besant.

'Wedgwood has arrived and is in good health. His consecration to the Episcopate has had the unexpected result of putting him practically at the head of the Old Catholic movement so far as the British Empire is concerned, all his colleagues (except, I think, one) in it being Theosophists ready to work under his direction. This being so, he desires most earnestly to offer the movement to

[1] cf. Alban W. Cockerham, 'The Liberal Catholic Ministry III', in *The Liberal Catholic*, vol. XXXI, March 1958, pp. 16–17.

the World Teacher as one of the vehicles for His force, and a channel for the preparation of His Coming. I took him therefore to the LORD MAITREYA at the Festival (Asala, the occult festival), and He was graciously pleased to accept the offer, and to say that He thought the movement would fill a niche in the scheme, and would be useful to Him. From what He said I inferred that He Himself had so guided events as to produce this curious result, that a branch of the Catholic Church, having the Apostolic Succession in a form which cannot be questioned, should be entirely in the hands of the Theosophists, who are eager and willing to do exactly as He wishes . . . With His permission [the Lord Maitreya] Wedgwood has consecrated *me* as a Bishop, on the understanding that I am at perfect liberty to wear my ordinary dress, and am in no way bound to perform any ecclesiastical ceremonies or take any outward part in the work unless I see it useful to do so, but to act as an intermediary between the LORD and this branch of His Church.'[1]

Bishop Leadbeater also felt it worth while to tell Mrs Besant that his own 'Master' had come to him in the night and said to him:

'You thought you had given up all prospects of a bishopric when you left your Church thirty years ago to follow Upâsika [Madame Blavatsky] but I may tell you that it would have been in this very year that you would have reached it if you had remained in your original work, so you have lost nothing except the emoluments and the social position, and have gained enormously in other ways. No one ever loses by serving US!'

During the next thirteen years the Theosophists found more than enough omens and portents to convince them that the Old Roman Catholics in England had lost nothing by breaking away from Archbishop Mathew in order to serve the Lord Maitreya and the other Masters. On the contrary, they had gained both materially and spiritually. After Leadbeater's consecration, which was carried out according to the Roman rite, the two Bishops decided that a new Liturgy was needed. They agreed that it should conform to the traditional model of the Western Church as closely as possible. The work of revision took over three years.

Filled with zeal to serve the Lord Maitreya, Bishop Wedgwood left Australia for New Zealand, where he preached the Theosophical version of Old Catholicism. He made many converts and

[1] *Extracts from Letters of C. W. Leadbeater to Annie Besant, 1916–1923*, compiled by C. Jinarajasada (Theosophical Publishing House, Adyar, 1952).

ordained several priests. On his return to Sydney, assisted by Lead-beater, he consecrated the Jonkheer Julien Adrien Mazel, as Auxiliary Bishop for Australia, on the Feast of St John the Baptist, June 24, 1917.[1] This was the last occasion that Mathew's *Old Catholic Missal and Ritual* was used by the Theosophical branch of his Church.

It was in March 1917 that the editor of *Theosophy in Australasia* interviewed Bishop Leadbeater. In reply to a question about the 'World Teacher' (The Lord Maitreya) using the Old Catholic movement as the nucleus of 'His' new presentation of Christianity, Leadbeater said:

'At any rate, it is there for Him if He wishes to use it. There will be a great outrush of force when He comes, and many thousands will gather round Him. Among those there are sure to be some who love His older Church and its ritual, and the Old Catholic Church might well afford a convenient resting-place for them. Unhappily, it seems by no means certain that the great Churches of the present day will be prepared to recognize and receive Him; but at least this Branch will know Him and work for Him, putting itself wholly into His hands as an instrument to be used at His will.'

The reports of what was going on in Australia and New Zealand greatly worried Archbishop Mathew. On February 17, 1916, he had written to Canon Farrer, telling him that, like the rest of the Old Roman Catholic clergy, he had been 'a very naughty dis-obedient boy!' He said that if Mrs Besant wished 'to save her immortal soul' she must 'be obedient to the Voice of God's Church —and then ask Our Lord to give her a true vocation to a religious life, in which by the repression of her will and a life of obedience and self-annihilation, she would be able to expiate the sins of the past'. Mrs Besant might well have replied that she was already obeying the orders of the Lord Maitreya imparted to her on the astral plane.

Mathew had heard rumours that Wedgwood was going to Chicago to get re-consecrated by Vilatte, but he did not venture to express an opinion whether Mar Timotheos was 'a real Bishop'. He ended this long letter with the words: 'You are all very head-strong wayward young men, who believe very much in your own infallibility, though you cannot accept that of the Pope!'[2]

---

[1] In 1919 Mazel was appointed first Regionary Bishop for the Netherlands Indies, additionally for Holland. He died in 1928.

[2] T. F. Redfern, 'Bishop Mathew and his Theosophical Clergy', in *The Liberal Catholic*, July 1956.

Bishop Wedgwood then set off on a round-the-world tour, to prepare the way for the coming of the Lord Maitreya. Sailing from Australia, his voice was soon crying in the wildernesses of Los Angeles, Hollywood, Vancouver, Chicago, New York, and other large towns and cities of the United States and Canada. He made many converts and ordained several priests before arriving back in England in the late autumn of 1917. In December that same year he summoned an episcopal and clerical synod in London, where he was able to give glowing reports of his missionary labours. In view of the recent attacks made by the Dutch Old Catholics it was resolved to give the Theosophical section of the Church the official title of the 'Liberal Christian Church (Old Catholic)'. In the first months of 1918 Wedgwood gave his *imprimatur* to a small liturgical book containing a new version of the Roman Mass in the vernacular, also Vespers and Benediction. It was issued 'for use in the Churches of our Movement in the United Kingdom, Australia, New Zealand, and America'.

In North America Bishop Wedgwood was sure that the Lord Maitreya would find countless devoted disciples waiting to receive him when he chose to appear in the body of Krishnamurti. In 1918 the Rev. Charles Hampton had published at Hollywood a pamphlet in which he urged members of the Order of the Star in the East to support the Old Catholic Church.[1] He reminded his readers that the Old Catholic Church had been 'highly recommended by our great Protector, Mrs Besant, whose far-seeing eyes discern in it one of the Movements overshadowed by the Lord Maitreya to improve the religious development of the Western World'.[2]

Regarding himself as the twentieth-century St Paul, carrying a daily burden, the care of all the churches, but fortified by the knowledge that he was the chosen Messenger of the Lord Maitreya, Bishop Wedgwood, still only in his middle thirties, extremely handsome and always well dressed, made another voyage to Australia. He had to consult Leadbeater, who acted as the spokesman of the invisible Masters, who were in constant touch with him on the astral plane. Their approval had to be obtained for the final revision of the new Liturgy and other important matters. After

---

[1] On September 13, 1931, Hampton was consecrated as Regionary Bishop in the Liberal Catholic Church. Later on he separated from it and set up a neo-theosophical body of his own. (See p. 363.)

[2] *The Server*, vol. II, no. I, July 11, 1918) (Kotrona, California). Meanwhile Fr Hampton and his flock were sharing the same building at Kotrona with the Co-Masonic Order, the Order of the Star in the East, the Buddhist Church, and the Rosicrucian Order of the Red Cross, and in this esoteric setting he celebrated Mass on Sundays.

much discussion, and presumably having consulted the Lord Maitreya, the two Bishops agreed to adopt the name of 'The Liberal Catholic Church' for their schism from Mathew's original body. This title was recognized officially at a synod held in London on September 6, 1918, but with the addition of the words 'Old Catholic'. A complete edition of the new Rite was published on St Alban's Day, June 21, of that same year.

But over in North America there had been a double opposition to what Wedgwood and Leadbeater were planning. From her headquarters at Point Loma, California, a high priestess of the cult, Mrs Katherine Tingley, had continued to denounce the Old Catholic infiltration into Theosophy; every issue of *Divine Life*, published in Chicago, under the auspices of Mrs Tingley's bitter rival, Mrs Celestia Root-Lang, contained violent attacks of Madame Blavatsky's Society as being 'sold into Catholic bondage'.[1] Fr Hampton replied with a pamphlet entitled *The Occultism of the Mass and the Old Catholic Movement*, which appeared at Kotrona, California, in 1918.

Returning to Australia, Bishop Wedgwood used the revised version of the Roman Pontifical for the first time on July 13, 1919, when, with the assistance of Leadbeater, he consecrated Irving Steiger Cooper as Regionary Bishop for the U.S.A.[2]

The ever-increasing numbers of seekers after truth were informed that

'the Liberal Catholic Church exists to forward the work of her Master Christ in the world, and to feed His flock. . . . The Church draws the central inspiration of its work from an intense faith in the Living Christ, believing that the vitality of a Church gains in proportion as its members cease to think only of a Christ who lived two thousand years ago, and strive rather to serve as a vehicle for the Eternal Christ, who lives as a mighty spiritual Presence in the world, guiding and sustaining His peoples. "Lo I am with you alway, even unto the consummation of the age" "Before Abraham was I am".'[3]

[1] A series of tracts appeared, entitled: *The Incompatibility of Theosophy and the Teachings of the Old Catholic Church: Shall the American Section T.S. be sold into Catholic Bondage? Proof that the Old Catholic Church is the Roman Catholic Church; Why the Old Catholic Church should be ejected from the T.S.*

[2] A 'Regionary Bishop' in the Liberal Catholic Church has the rank of an Archbishop of a Province. A 'Suffragan' corresponds to a diocesan-bishop. An 'Auxiliary' is more or less equivalent to a bishop-suffragan in the Anglican Communion, or an assistant bishop in the Roman Catholic Church.

[3] *The Liturgy according to the use of the Liberal Catholic Church* (London, Los Angeles, Sydney, 1924), p. 5.

Theosophists have not always been in agreement about the historic Christ. Mrs Besant appears to have held the opinion that there was both an historical and a mystical 'Jesus'. The former, so she wrote in one of her books, was born in 105 B.C., became an Essene monk, studied Indian occultism, travelled in Egypt, and at the age of twenty-nine gave up his body to be a 'Buddha of Compassion', and who entered into the mystical body at Baptism. The man Jesus suffered in his body for the services rendered for it as the temporary 'home' of the Lord Maitreya. From this story grew up the belief of the Mystical Christ in the Logos, crucified, that is 'extended throughout matter, and also the divine spark in man'. All this, so she maintained, was revealed to her on the astral plane.[1]

Wedgwood and Leadbeater laid stress on the fact of the Liberal Catholic Church being

'an independent and self-governing body; neither Roman Catholic nor Protestant—but Catholic. This Church aims at combining the traditional sacramental form of Catholic worship—with its ritual, its deep mysticism, and its abiding witness to the reality of sacramental grace—with the widest measure of intellectual liberty and respect for the individual conscience.'

Here was none of the supposed hide-bound rigidity of Romanism. Liberal Catholics were permitted absolute 'freedom of interpretation of the Scriptures, the Creeds and the Liturgy. Regarding the mind as one of the great avenues to spiritual apprehension, it encourages among its adherents the freest play of scientific or philosophical thought.'[2]

Another feature of this all-embracing, comprehensive new Church was its welcome to its altars of 'all who reverently approach them, creating no barriers in the nature of standards of dogmatic belief'. Persons of any religion or none could receive communion at Mass, if they felt the urge. No priest had the right to refuse them. The broad-mindedness of Liberal Catholicism was shown by the statement that it had

'no wish to proselytise, in an aggressive sense, from among the adherents of any other Church, and as an earnest of this, welcome people to regular and full participation in its services without asking or expecting them to leave their original Church'.

Before all else it was a 'Modernist' Church in the sense that it maintained that

---

[1] cf. Annie Besant, *Esoteric Christianity* (1901), pp. 120 ff.
[2] ibid., p. 5.

'the form of religion should keep pace with human growth and enlightenment; "historic" in that it holds that the Church has handed down a very precious heritage from the Christ Himself'.[1]

Some years before this Liberal Catholic *Credo* was formulated, and about eighteen months before his death Archbishop Mathew wrote to Canon Farrer on June 4, 1918, deploring what he called Wedgwood's 'duplicity', and said:

'He distinctly gave me to understand that he was an orthodox Catholic in belief, that it was not necessary for any theosophist to agree with Mrs Besant, who was a Hindu, and that, in fact, he did not agree with her—excepting on the three objects of the T.S., which are so worded as to appear harmless. The cloven hoof only appeared when I required an explicit repudiation of heresies, which any bishop in authority has a right and indeed an obligation to do in such cases. I do not understand any of you and deplore the fact that you ever invaded my movement and played havoc with it. No doubt our Lord will take care of His own and of His own work and I leave you all in His Divine hands. . . .'[2]

After Mathew's death on December 20, 1919, the Liberal Catholic Church gained more and more adherents in Europe, Australia, New Zealand, the United States, and Canada. A Theosophical Congress took place at Ehrwald in the Tyrol in the summer of 1923. The Order of the Star in the East had already been presented by Baron von Pallant, a wealthy Dutch Theosophist, with Castle Eerde, near Arnhem. During the next few years several gatherings of the Liberal Catholic Church were held in this moated medieval castle hidden in the midst of a pine forest.[3]

On March 9, 1924, Bishop Leadbeater, assisted by Bishops Mazel and Cooper, consecrated, at Sydney, Frank Waters Pigott as Regionary Bishop for Great Britain and Ireland. Like his consecrator, the new prelate had formerly been a priest of the Church of England.

[1] ibid., p. 6.
[2] cf. T. H. Redfern, op. cit., pp. 84–85.
[3] In the early 1920s the British Province of the L.C.C. had centres in London, St Peter's-in-Thanet, Bradford, Bath, Plymouth, Crowhurst, Maidstone, Cardiff, Letchworth, Nottingham, Harrogate, Birmingham, Edinburgh, Glasgow, and Dundee. In the London area there were chapels in Upper Woburn Place, Lancaster Gate, and at Wimbledon. King and Gauntlett acted as Regionary Bishops for Britain. In the U.S.A. there were places of worship at Los Angeles, Chicago, Seattle, and Hollywood. The Church was already firmly established in Australia, New Zealand, and the Dutch East Indies, and was taking root in other countries.
After the L.C.C. was extended to Holland in the spring of 1920, and centres opened at the Hague, Amsterdam, Rotterdam, Blaricum, and Leiden, the Old Catholic Church of Utrecht was filled with indignation.

Churches of the Mathew Succession

The second edition of the Liberal Catholic *Liturgy* was published on the Feast of the Epiphany 1924, and bore the *imprimatur* '✠ Charles Webster Leadbeater, Presiding Bishop'. It appeared simultaneously at London, Los Angeles, and Sydney; a third edition appeared in 1942 with the *imprimatur* of Bishop F. W. Pigott. Leadbeater stated in the Preface that this new rite had been composed by Bishop Wedgwood, 'to whose wide erudition and indefatigable labours the Liberal Catholic Church owes a debt of the deepest gratitude'. The Roman rite of 1570 was chosen as the basis for the 'Celebration of the Holy Eucharist, commonly called the Mass', although some details were taken from the Liturgy of the Catholic Apostolic (Irvingite) Church. But 'all expressions involving fear of God, of His wrath, and the prospects of an everlasting hell were removed; also those expressive of servile cringing and self-abasement, abject appeals for mercy, even culminating in naïve attempts to bargain with the Almighty'. The new Liturgy contained 'no crude anthropomorphism'. Every trace of 'the jealous, angry, blood-thirsty Jehovah of Ezra, Nehemiah and the others—a god who needs propitiating and to whose mercy constant appeals must be made' had been deleted. Bishop Wedgwood explained that

'the knowledge of Eastern religions, and of the faiths of ancient Egypt and Babylon, that has increasingly become available in our times, has entirely dispelled the illusion that the Jews had any monopoly of divine truth, and proportionately lessens the value of the Old Testament as an integral basis of the Christian faith'.[1]

In the *Gloria in Excelsis* the phrase 'Lamb of God' was eliminated, with the explanation that 'such zoological characterization of our Lord does not impress the virgin mind with anything but a sense of the ridiculous'. This phrase, however, was retained in the Canon of the Mass because of its symbolical meaning.

This liturgical vade-mecum provided not only a vernacular adaptation of the Roman Mass, suitable for the 'modern mind', but also abbreviated forms of Prime, Vespers, and Compline. 'Benediction of the Most Holy Sacrament' featured a long Litany with twenty-two four-line verses, besides other non-Roman interpolations. The rites for Baptism, Confirmation, Confession, Matrimony, Holy Unction, and the Burial of the Dead could hardly have been more elaborate. The Liberal Catholic Church retained the four minor orders of the Latin Church, and the ritual for con-

[1] op. cit., p. 9.

ferring them (as well as those for the ordination of subdeacons, deacons, and priests, not to mention the consecration of bishops) contained most of the traditional Western ceremonial. Blessings were provided for many objects (including holy oils) and the consecration of a church.

Taking a hint from the simplification of the Benedictine Calendar, the number of saints' days to be observed was reduced to a bare minimum, for as it was explained, 'the whole system of such commemorations is an anachronism, which might be allowed for the most part to drop into abeyance without impairing our belief in the communion of saints. The Roman Calendar is overladen with saints, of whom few excite any real devotion at this distance of time, while others undoubtedly are mythical or transformed pagan deities'. It is worth mentioning, however, that Bishops Wedgwood and Leadbeater anticipated Pope John XXIII by thirty-six years by changing the Octave of the Epiphany to the Baptism of our Lord.

Another interesting feature is that the dialogue Mass was officially approved by the Liberal Catholic Church thirty-four years before the Sacred Congregation of Rites issued an Instruction of universal application on September 3, 1958, which was approved *speciali modo* by Pius XII shortly before his death. In his Preface to the Liturgy, Bishop Wedgwood writes:

'With the spread of education, the growth of intelligence, and the advantage of a vernacular liturgy, there is no reason at all why the laity should "assist" at the Holy Eucharist in the capacity of spectators only, or be debarred from following step by step what is taking place at the Altar. Liturgy means "public work or service", not merely in the sense of work done by the public, but also work for, on behalf of the public at large.'[1]

In a sense, the ethos of the Liberal Catholic Church was in keeping with the spirit of the 'twenties, when it reached the peak of its popularity, just another manifestation of the exotic attitude towards life which produced what Osbert Lancaster has called 'Curzon Street Baroque'.[2] Hence its appeal to the more mystical-minded 'Bright Young Things' of the nineteen-twenties, who got fed-up with dancing the Charleston and sought something more satisfying to the soul.

[1] ibid., p. 12. It should be mentioned, however, that there have been Theosophists strongly opposed to the use of the vernacular in public worship. They have maintained that there are proofs that ancient hieratic languages, such as Latin, produce great occult force, and more powerful astral vibrations.
[2] *Homes Sweet Homes* (1939), p. 64.

Churches of the Mathew Succession

The Liberal Catholic Church could claim with some justice that it had taken root in four continents. Already ensconced in Europe and America, the two chief spiritual centres of the cult were in India and Australia. At the headquarters of the Theosophical Society at Adyar, near Madras, Mrs Annie Besant expounded the mysteries to pilgrims from all countries who could afford to make the journey to sit at her feet. Born in 1847, this now white-haired old lady, who had married an Anglican clergyman, the Rev. Frank Besant, in 1867, from whom she separated six years later, becoming an agnostic Secularist, and propagandist for contraception, working with Charles Bradlaugh, was still a powerful personality, wielding a world-wide influence. Her numerous disciples regarded her as a saint.[1]

At Sydney, New South Wales, the venerable, tall, leonine long white-bearded Bishop Leadbeater ruled like a patriarch over a community of more than fifty persons of both sexes and many nationalities. Most of them were girls and boys, between the ages of nine and twenty-five. They were housed, not too comfortably, so it is related, in a big house, known as 'The Manor', situated at Mossman, a suburb of Sydney, on the north side of the harbour.[2] The majority of the young men and youths in the community had been ordained as doorkeepers, readers, exorcists, acolytes, sub-deacons, deacons, and even priests. One of the most important members of this strange confraternity was the Bishop's huge tortoiseshell cat, said to be in his last incarnation in the animal kingdom. Leadbeater, usually robed in a Roman purple cassock and cape, occupied a room lined from floor to ceiling with copper, beaten into weird and hideous shapes. He maintained that copper 'conserves magnetism', and that it is helpful for getting into touch with the Masters on the astral plane.

In the autumn of 1924 a very distinguished member of the Liberal Catholic Church, Lady Emily Lutyens, obtained her husband's consent to make the 10,296 miles voyage from London Tilbury Docks to Sydney, so that she and two of her daughters could benefit by the personal spiritual direction of Bishop Leadbeater.[3] They broke their pilgrimage in India, so that they could

---

[1] Cf.

[2] Leadbeater built a large open-air theatre overlooking the harbour, in readiness for the day when Krishnamurti would come walking over the waters between the Heads, and make a triumphal entry into Sydney. Unfortunately Krishnamurti never did this, so the theatre was not used for its original purpose, and later on was let out for secular entertainments.

[3] Emily Lutyens was the third daughter of the first Earl of Lytton, by his wife Edith Villiers, granddaughter of the first Earl of Clarendon. In 1897 Lady Emily

visit Mrs Besant at Adyar, and reached Sydney in the early spring of 1925.

Both Betty and Mary Lutyens were 'validly' re-baptized and confirmed within two days of their arrival. The former was also initiated as a Co-Mason—said to be a channel of access to the Masters—but for some reason or other this privilege was denied to her sister.[1]

We are told that every morning before breakfast Bishop Leadbeater descended from his copper-lined room to a basement chapel, where he celebrated Mass.[2] On Sundays the whole community crossed the harbour to Sydney for morning and evening services in St Alban's Liberal Catholic Church.[3] Very often the 'Service of Healing'—a feature of the official *Liturgy*—was carried out on Sunday afternoon, with the prescribed anointing with consecrated oils and the laying on of hands.

Mary Lutyens tells us that the patriarchal prelate insisted on regular attendance at Sunday worship, and used to explain to his spiritual children that 'if they could see the wonderful force going up in glowing colours through the church-roof and spreading over the whole city', they would 'realize the importance of this communal worship'. The boys and girls were reprimanded by him when the emanations through the roof were not sufficiently strong or beautifully coloured.[4]

---

married the well-known architect, Edwin Lutyens, who was knighted in 1918. She became a Theosophist in 1910, and took Krishnamurti and his brother, Nithyanda, under her wing when Mrs Besant brought them to England the following year. She seceded from the Church of England in 1917, when she was received into the Liberal Catholic Church. Full details of Lady Emily Lutyens's experiences as a Theosophist are given in her memoirs, entitled *Candles in the Sun* (1957). They are supplemented by those of her daughter, Mary Lutyens, in *To be Young—Some Chapters of Autobiography* (1957).

[1] During the 18th century there were androgynous Masonic Lodges in France which admitted women to the secrets of the Craft, and with separate governing bodies; one of them with a lady Grand Master. In 1882 a Lodge, formerly under the Supreme Council 33rd degree of France, initiated a woman, and was struck off the role. So the members set themselves up as a group of 'Maçonnerie Mixte', eventually with a Supreme Council. This body came to England in 1902, when Mrs Besant was initiated. It now has groups spread over the world, and additional bodies for the Higher Degrees.

[2] Leadbeater recommended Gothic Revival chasubles rather than those of Roman or Spanish shape, being convinced that the latter are 'distinctly less useful for the flow of the spiritual forces than the older plan of the Y cross'. He had discovered on the astral plane that 'a terrific torrent pours from the radiating disc on the back' of a typical Gothic Revival vestment. Sacristans and priests may be grateful for a word of warning. (cf. *The Science of the Sacraments*, p. 552, and diagram 17.)

[3] In some countries the L.C.C. adopted St Alban as its special patron, perhaps because of the legend that he formed in A.D. 287 the first Masonic Lodge in Britain. St Alban is one of the very few saints retained in the L.C.C. kalendar.

[4] *To be Young*, p. 170.

Churches of the Mathew Succession

The occult meaning of colours held a special place in Liberal Catholic worship, including the Roman colour sequence of the vestments worn. The faithful were told that 'violet, lying at the opposite end of the spectrum to red, produces vibrations which are cleansing, actinic, and piercing. The colour green holds the balance in the middle of the spectrum, and its vibrations help to produce sympathy and general goodwill'.[1]

Those who have time to peruse the 700 pages of Bishop Leadbeater's *The Science of the Sacraments* (2nd ed., Adyar, Madras, 1929) will find the fullest possible information about his strange theories of symbolism, magnetism, and much else. This mighty tome is illustrated with 21 diagrams and 27 plates, some of them in colour; and it is a complete exposition of and commentary on the worship of the Liberal Catholic Church.

It may surprise some priests to know that 'the value of a biretta is of the same character as that of a cork in a bottle—to prevent evaporation, and consequent waste. Such force as may be aroused with the Priest should be accommodated within him, and be discharged for the benefit of his people, and not allowed to escape fruitlessly into higher planes, as is the natural tendency' (p. 569). Bishops ought to know that 'the fanons of the mitre, which were originally merely strings to tie it in place, are now utilized to convey the force to the border of the cope or chasuble, and so out through these vestments to the people' (page 560). Abbots as well as bishops may not be aware that a pectoral cross 'acts as a prism for the forces which are always flowing through' these major prelates (page 573). The Liturgical Commission, if not the Sacred Congregation of Rites, will be glad to know about the mysterious forces that interplay in the host and chalice after consecration, the powerful 'magnetism' of holy water, and all the rays and sub-rays (including 'the 7th Ray, just now coming into operation').

Were he alive today, he would recognize an affinity between the new Catholic Cathedral at Liverpool and the coloured frontispiece of his *Science and the Sacraments*, and promise that when it is completed the 'forces' and 'vibrations' within this phallic-shaped building will be far more powerful than those in the Gothic Revival Anglican Cathedral in the same city; quite apart from the clergy of the former having a valid apostolic succession.

All sorts of strange things happened when Lady Emily and her two daughters were members of Leadbeater's mixed confraternity.

[1] cf. *The Liturgy* (1924 edition), p. 22.

One day the Bishop told her that the Masters had revealed to him that she was to propagate a new form of Mariolatry, and that he would get in touch 'on the astral' with Mahachohan (Buddha's favourite disciple), and find out if he approved. Lady Emily was advised to consult the Lord Maitreya, and the following morning she awoke with the certainty that He meant her to be a sort of Theosophist St Louis Mary Grignon de Montfort, and promote true devotion of our Blessed Lady by founding a World League of Motherhood.[1]

After these more awe-inspiring spiritual experiences, Lady Emily returned to Europe in June 1925, leaving her two daughters in Australia for the benefit of further mystical initiations by Leadbeater. But the Bishop insisted that they must be presented at Court the following year, because this would help 'to spread the Master's word in Society'.[2]

An international Theosophical Conference took place in Holland in August 1925. The programme included the consecration of George Sydney Arundale as Regionary Bishop for India.[3] Lady Emily, who was among the delegates, relates that up to the eve of the consecration no reply had been received from Leadbeater to the letter requesting him to confirm the election. So Arundale got through to Australia on the astral, and was able to assure Bishop Wedgwood that everything was in order.

The following morning, August 4, assisted by Bishops Mazel and Pigott, Wedgwood raised Arundale to the episcopate. On returning from the church there was a cable from Leadbeater 'couched in very disapproving forms'. Lady Emily recalls that it struck her that Mrs Besant 'looked very grave when she read it'.[4] This suggests that reception on the astral was subject to hazards, but the congregation were told that the Lord Maitreya and all the other Masters had been present at the consecration, invisible, of course, to mortal eyes. The previous day Bishop Wedgwood had distributed to the faithful crosses and swastikas which he had 'highly

---

[1] cf. *Candles in the Sun*, p. 123.
[2] *To be Young*, p. 172.
[3] Born in 1898, Arundale became a Theosophist at the age of seventeen. In 1909 he was appointed Principal of the Central Hindu College, Benares, but he resigned this post four years later to take on the duties of private tutor to Krishnamurti. In 1920 the Government of the Maharajah of Holkar nominated him Minister of Education. He had been one of the founders of the Order of the Star in the East, and devoted himself to spreading the cultus of his pupil, under the name of Alcyone. He resigned his office of Regionary Bishop for India in 1934, and became President of the Theosophical Society. He died in 1945.
[4] ibid., p. 131.

magnetized'. The astral vibrations at this castle in Holland appear to have been as powerful as those which Leadbeater had experienced in a village church in Sicily, about which he wrote at great length in *The Hidden Side of Things* (1913), relating how he first discovered what he called the 'Magic of the Mass'.

The Masters (who at that time were understood to be hidden in a remote spot in Hungary) were gracious enough to put over the air some very helpful messages.[1] For instance, the Lord Maitreya gave detailed rules on episcopal and sacerdotal fashions in clothing, and minute details of ritual and ceremonial. He laid down that henceforth silk underwear would be obligatory for clerics. Capes, and carefully designed crimson gowns, would have to form part of the trousseau of those in major orders. Hats were not permitted.[2] Frank W. Pigott, Regionary Bishop for Great Britain and Ireland, confided to Lady Emily that it would be difficult for him to obey these sartorial regulations, because he was not so rich as some of his episcopal brethren. Then, to add to the austerity of their rule of life, the bishops and the initiates were forbidden by the Masters to eat eggs or any foods containing eggs. As it was, most Theosophists were strict vegetarians, and some were even teetotallers.

On the evening of August 9, 1925, there was an open-air procession of the host, enclosed in a monstrance, around the chapel of the castle. The congregation wore their highly magnetized crosses and swastikas so that they could feel the astral vibrations radiating from them. Lady Emily tells us that Wedgwood had a vision of her being consecrated 'as a sort of Abbess'. The following day Arundale 'brought through the names of twelve apostles whom the Lord had chosen to walk with Him when He comes'. It must have been encouraging to be told that the two bishops present were 'direct pupils of Macachohan'.[3] What's more, Arundale had been selected as 'the Chief Staff of the Seventh Race', and he was now in his final incarnation. Henceforth he would be moved around the universe, 'and not attached to any planet'. A new sub-race would develop in California. Mrs Besant had an inspiring revelation that Wedgwood would be the Mahachohan of the Seventh Root-Race; that she was the Manu, and Leadbeater the Bodhisattva.[4]

Such was the situation in which Mathew's Ancient Catholic

---

[1] Bram Stoker in his hair-raising novel *Dracula* chose Hungary as the home of this horrible vampire.
[2] ibid., p. 132.
[3] ibid., p. 132.
[4] ibid., p. 136.

Church of Great Britain and Ireland found itself after ten years. Shortly after this Theosophical reunion in the Netherlands, Bishops Arundale and Wedgwood made a pilgrimage to Rome, where they appeared in the streets in Roman purple cassocks, displaying large pectoral crosses. Both prelates continued to have psychic revelations, often when saying Mass. Unfortunately, however, their visions of the future did not always agree; either because their respective Masters did not see eye to eye or because of interference on the astral.

On May 23, 1926, Leadbeater raised to the episcopate John Moynihan Tettemer, who the following year was appointed Suffragan Bishop for the U.S.A. Tettemer, born at St Louis, Missouri, in 1876, had been a Passionist priest, and had risen in 1914 to be Consultor-General of his Congregation. Then he fell ill, and while recuperating at Davos, lost his faith completely. Eventually he joined the Liberal Catholic Church, and resumed his priestly duties. He spent the last fifteen years of his life at Beverly Hills, California, where he married and had three children. The Bishop played the part of a priest in several films, including *Meet John Doe* and *Lost Horizon*. He died in 1949.[1]

There is sufficient evidence that Krishnamurti, otherwise Alcyone, who was still being exhibited as the New Messiah, had as little sympathy with Liberal Catholicism and Co-Masonry as with anything else that went with his cultus. On the other hand, thanks to Miss Mary Dodge, whom Lady Emily Lutyens had converted to Theosophy, he and his brother benefited from an income settled on them for life. So these two young Indians had no financial worries; and Mary Lutyens recalls that their slim figures were always exquisitely dressed. 'They went to the best boot-makers, tailors and shirt-makers; their neat brown shoes were always so beautifully polished, and their straight black hair, which was parted in the middle and smelt of some delicious unguent they both used, so sleek.'[2]

As time went on Krishna grew more and more weary of all this play-acting, and of being dragged around the world as the forthcoming re-incarnation of the Lord Maitreya. In 1929 he had the

---

[1] His autobiography, *I was a Monk* (1952), is a frank and moving account of his varied and tragic life, but makes no mention of his Liberal Catholic period. (See also 'A Bishop's Pilgrimage, an Autobiographical Sketch', in *The Liberal Catholic*, vol. VII, February 1929; and 'Rome and the Future' in the same magazine, November 1925.)

[2] *To be Young*, p. 45.

courage to dissolve the Order of the Star in the East, and retired into private life. This was a stunning blow to innumerable Theosophists. Most Liberal Catholics felt exactly as the early Christians would have felt if they had discovered that Jesus was merely a myth. Lady Emily was among those whose faith was shattered. But the Liberal Catholic Church, having recovered from the shock, managed to readjust itself to a new situation. In 1934 Pigott was elected Presiding Bishop in succession to Leadbeater, who had died that same year at the age of eighty-seven, having spent the last twenty-one years in Australia.[1]

During the past thirty years the Liberal Catholic Church has stressed that although many of its past members have been members of the Theosophical Society, the Church itself has never had any sort of administrative or official connection with the society, nor has there ever been the slightest attempt to limit Church membership to those who accept theosophical teachings. To quote from an official leaflet issued by the Province of Great Britain and Ireland:

'The aim has always been to have a Catholic Church in which everyone who seeks the sacraments of Christ in the spirit of befitting reverence may come and receive them, regardless of theosophical convictions or of their lack, regardless also of whether belonging to any other Church or not. . . . The clergy of the Liberal Catholic Church make no claim to temporal or spiritual domination over those people who adhere to the Church, nor do they seek to control the consciences of individuals. Auricular confession is entirely optional and voluntary, and is never required as a preliminary to the reception of Holy Communion. Almost all the clergy are unpaid, and it is expressly laid down that no fee may be exacted for administering the sacraments or for other spiritual work. Wherever practicable, the Church places the administration of its finances in the hands of the laity by means of elected representatives.'

Because few of the clergy ever receive stipends, they have to maintain themselves in the manner of the early Apostles, each by his own trade or profession. As a result, in the very mobile society of today, Liberal Catholic clergy move about a great deal. Wherever such a priest finds himself, he sets up an altar in his house, says

---

[1] In 1922 he made a conspicuous figure at the Eucharistic Congress held at Sydney, where, so it is related, he was convinced that he saw auras round the heads of several cardinals, archbishops, bishops, and priests, including that of Fr Martindale, S.J.

Mass as regularly and as frequently as his circumstances permit, and tries to reach out to any receptive souls in his vicinity. After a while he may be moved to some other part of the country, and he has to start all over again.[1] In their more settled parishes they sometimes draw quite cosmopolitan congregations of theosophically minded persons. In its own way the Liberal Catholic Church does appear to fill a need in the lives of a fair number of people who, for various reasons, cannot find themselves at home in Roman Catholic, Eastern Orthodox, Anglican, or Protestant Christianity.[2]

Few of the religious bodies dealt with in this book can claim that they were carried on for nearly thirty years without one or more schisms, but such was the case with the Liberal Catholic Church. During the Second World War, however, difficulties arose in the United States Province, due mainly to the independent line of action adopted by Charles Hampton, who had been consecrated in September 1931, as Auxiliary Bishop for the U.S.A. Most of the clergy appear to have sided with Hampton after he was formally deposed by the General Episcopal Synod of the Liberal Catholic Church on May 1, 1944. Some of them rallied under Ray M. Wardall, consecrated in October 1926 as Suffragan Bishop for the U.S.A. The confusion was increased when the Presiding Bishop of the Church, Frank W. Pigott, appointed John T. Elklund as Regionary Bishop *pro tem* for the U.S.A.[3] So there were now three groups of the Liberal Catholic Church in North America.

On June 8, 1947, Elklund raised to the episcopate as his Auxiliaries Newton A. Dahl and Walter J. Zollinger. On September 14 that same year Wardall consecrated Edward M. Matthews, the recently deposed Dean of the Liberal Catholic Cathedral at Los Angeles. The Presiding Bishop (Pigott) then stated that the Wardall-Matthews body had no further connection with the Liberal Catholic Church. Since then Pigott and Elklund have died, and so have Hampton and Wardall. After some years of litigation the Supreme Court of the State of California gave judgment on April 13, 1961, that the only legal Liberal Catholic

[1] This is also true of all the various religious bodies referred to in this book, and accounts largely for the lack of permanent churches and organizations.

[2] Since the Order of the Star in the East was dissolved in 1929 more than thirty bishops have been consecrated for work in different countries. A fairly complete list of them will be found in H. R. T. Brandreth's *Episcopi Vagantes and the Anglican Church* (2nd ed., 1961), pp. 31–34.

[3] Elklund was consecrated by Hampton on July 2, 1939.

Church in the U.S.A. was the group under Bishop Matthews.[1] Independently of these dissensions in North America, Johan Hubert Bonjer, consecrated by Wedgwood as Auxiliary Bishop for Holland on April 18, 1928, and who in 1948 became Regionary Bishop for South Africa, broke away from the Liberal Catholic Church. In 1959 he formed an independent body, which was incorporated in the Netherlands as *Broederschap van het Heilig Sacrament* (Brotherhood of the Blessed Sacrament). Its members claim to accept the whole of the Christian tradition, eastern as well as western, not confining themselves to one of the theosophic movements. After Bishop Bonjer had raised J. H. Dubbink to the episcopate he and his disciples decided to link up with the Mathews group of the Liberal Catholic Church in North America. Bonjer was appointed its Bishop-Commissary for Europe.[2]

Some time in 1957 Bishop Hampton of Los Angeles, long after he had been deposed by the Presiding Bishop of the Liberal Catholic Church, consecrated Hermann S. Spruit. This former Methodist minister was a Theosophist, who had formed a sect known as 'The Church Universal'. On June 23, 1959, there took place what was described as the 'consummation of the merger of the Church Universal and the United Episcopal Church—Christian Catholic'.[3]

The quarters of Archbishop Spruit's coat of arms blazon a swastika or cross gamma, certain masonic emblems, and a minoorah or seven-branch candlestick, together with a host *en soleil* and two keys crossed *per saltire*. This mixture of symbols suggests the eclectic element in the training given at the Saint Sophia Theological Seminary, and in the sermons preached at St Michael's Church, Downey, California, the headquarters of 'The Christian Catholic Church—Church Universal'. One detects a certain affinity between this heraldry with the Order of the Holy Wisdom

---

[1] The headquarters of this body are at 1041 North Argyle Avenue, Los Angeles, and it now has Suffragan Bishops resident in New York and Dundas, Ontario, Canada. In 1956 it claimed a total membership of 4,000, and eight ordained clergy.

[2] As the result of a meeting of the General Episcopal Synod on July 25, 1962, Bishop Mathews was dismissed from this branch of the Liberal Catholic Church in all his held capacities. On October 29, Bishop Francis Erwin of 7512 Clutter Street, North Burnaby, B.C., Canada, was elected by unanimous vote to succeed him as Presiding Bishop. Bishop Bonjer holds the office of Episcopal Commissary for Europe, with Mgr Dr J. H. Dubbink as his Vicar-General. It is stated that 'real progress is being made in negotiations for alliance with the Liberal Catholic group of Bishops Daw, Roberts, and Russell'. (November 1, 1962.)

[3] A Christian Catholic Church had been founded by John Alexander Dowie, who in 1899 bought land in Illinois on which Zion City arose. This Christian Catholic Church, still active and vigorous, protestant and apocalyptic in outlook, has spread all over the world. Its present membership is estimated at 7,000.

Churches of the Mathew Succession

(*Ekklesia Agiae Sophiae*), founded by Mar Basilius Abdullah III, Sovereign Prince Patriarch of Antioch, on the borders of Epping Forest, England, in 1943.[1]

At the time of writing the Presiding Bishop of the original Liberal Catholic Church is Adriaan G. Vreede, who was consecrated on August 15, 1926, by Wedgwood, assisted by Pigott, Hounsfield, Tettemer, and Bonjer, as Regionary Bishop for the Netherlands Indies. In Europe there are Regionary Bishops for the Dioceses of Austria, Germany, and the German-speaking parts of Switzerland; also for France, French Africa, and the French-speaking cantons of Switzerland. The Italian Diocese is directly subject to the Presiding Bishop. Belgium and Holland form a Province under a Regionary Bishop. The Scandinavian countries have a Regionary Bishop with the appropriate name of Otto Viking, with Assistant Bishops for Sweden and Finland. Australia and New Zealand, where Liberal Catholicism took root forty years ago, now form separate Provinces, divided in dioceses. The Regionary Bishop for the U.S.A. (Newton A. Dahl) has his headquarters at 3342 Oakland Avenue, Minneapolis 7, Minnesota, and he has three episcopal Assistants. More recently the Church has spread to Central and South America, where Provinces have been erected. In 1961 they were as follows: (1) Cuba—plus certain other countries; (2) Colombia and the surrounding countries; (3) Greater South America (Republics of Argentina, Brazil, Uruguay, Chile, Paraguay, and Bolivia). Great Britain and Ireland now have Sir Benjamin Hugh Sykes, a Baronet of the United Kingdom, as their Regionary Bishop, with Bishop J. B. S. Coates as his Auxiliary. His London Cathedral, dedicated to St Mary, is located in the 'holy land' of Islington, about a quarter of a mile from where in 1909 Bishop Mathew raised a former Congregationalist chapel to the status of an Old Catholic pro-cathedral.[2] Nearby, too, is Matilda Street, where in 1935 Mar Kwamin, Metropolitan of the Autonomous African Universal Church, consecrated Mar Frederic, founder of the Orthodox-Keltic Church of the British Commonwealth of Nations, in the tiny oratory dedicated to St Ignatius of Antioch.[3]

Standing on the triangle between Caledonian and Hillmarton Roads, a few yards north of Caledonian Road station on the Pic-

[1] See p. 237.
[2] See p. 178.
[3] See p. 279.

cadilly line, St Mary's Cathedral is a fairly typical specimen of mid-Victorian Gothic Revival English Nonconformist architecture, set back in a smoke-grimed garden. It must be admitted that it hardly attains to the richly symbolical ideal of a Liberal Catholic place of worship, depicted in some of the illustrations of Bishop Leadbeater's *Science of the Sacraments*. Nor is the well cared for galleried interior, evocative of an old-fashioned not very extreme Anglo-Catholic church, sufficiently inspiring to encourage trying to get in touch on the astral with the Lord Maitreya, Master Koot Hoomi, or any of the other Masters, who were venerated by pious Liberal Catholics in the 'good old days'. If Leadbeater were still alive, would he maintain that these stone walls in North London conserve magnetism quite as effectively as those of his copper-lined room at Sydney, New South Wales? If he were pontificating in Gothic Revival vestments—as perhaps he still does on the astral— at the Baroque high altar—would he see wonderful forces going up in colours through the roof? Very likely he would assure us that on Sunday evening the spire positively shimmers with rays and sub-rays as powerful vibrations flow from the host at Benediction. In fact, Dr Beeching may yet have to complain to the baronet Regionary Bishop that these vibrations disturb the Diesel engines hauling the 'Aberdonian' and other expresses on the main line north of King's Cross station as they emerge from the tunnel below the Cathedral. Possibly psychic passengers on the Piccadilly tube trains passing immediately beneath the building also perceive peculiar paranormal sensations.

It is a pity that Liberal Catholicism in London lacks a better advertisement than this little Gothic Revival Cathedral, for it fails to impress the fact that this body is still very much alive in many countries, judging from reports printed in *The Liberal Catholic* and *Ubique*.[1]

All the other bodies of which A. H. Mathew was the direct or indirect progenitor have been failures to a greater or lesser degree, but the Liberal Catholic Church, even if today it consists of two rival sections, has not only managed to keep going, but has spread over the greater part of the world.[2]

---

[1] The former is the English review of the Church, the headquarters of which are at Drayton House, 50 Gordon Street, London, W.C.1. The latter is published at 17 Cathedral Drive, Lakewood, New Jersey, U.S.A.

[2] *The Christian Community*, like the Liberal Catholic Church, is what might be called a by-product of the Theosophical Society. The two organizations have not a little in common. The former owes its inception and character to Rudolph Steiner (1861–1925), who appears to have been brought up a Roman Catholic. From 1902 until 1913

Churches of the Mathew Succession

he was the leader of the German section of the Theosophical Society. Having broken away from Annie Besant and G. W. Leadbeater, he founded his own neo-theosophical body, to which he gave the name of the Anthroposophical Society. Steiner's object was to develop the faculty of spiritual cognition inherent in ordinary people, and to put them in touch with the spiritual world from which materialism had long estranged them. It is somewhat doubtful if he found a place in his system for belief in God, as understood by orthodox Christians. The 'Gotheanum' at Dornach, near Basle, became the headquarters of the Society, whose membership increased rapidly.

In 1922 forty-five men and women who were among Steiner's disciples, felt that the time had come to form a religious body which would combine Anthroposophy with Christianity; in fact, a sort of inner circle of the Society. They consulted the Master and laid their plans before him, for they were convinced that they had been granted a vision of the Universe and Man in which the great Christian truths no longer appeared in conflict with the genuine understanding of modern thought and scientific discoveries. As was his custom, when faced with any important decision, Steiner went into 'the inner worlds', and returned to earth with a perfect scheme for expressing anthroposophical conceptions in a religious form. He visualized an absolutely free union of men and women seeking to live in true religion. They would not be asked to accept any creed. They could believe or not believe what they liked. There would be no need for them to give up their connections with other religious organizations, if they belonged to them. Catholics, Protestants, and members of any religion or none, would be welcomed. All this is very like the aims and ideals of the Liberal Catholic Church.

His esoteric circle of followers proceeded to work out what might be termed a system of 'natural catholicism'. There would be a 'natural priesthood' open to both men and women, who would spread the occult, mystical revelations which had been claimed by Steiner, who was believed to have been infused with extra-sensory perception. He was said to be able to see the real heart of things, including the Mind of God, and the mystic meaning of the New Testament. Since most of the founders of this new organization were at least nominal Lutherans, they did not feel the necessity of a 'valid' apostolic succession (in the material sense) for the 'Leaders', such being the name given to the male and female pastors, who are also called priests. Their inner consciousness would direct them in this 'natural priesthood'.

Notwithstanding this, it appears that the ministers of this body do undergo an ordination ceremony at the hands of persons who can trace their 'succession' from Steiner, who ordained the first 'Leaders'. Steiner himself claimed to be in the succession of the Black Templars who claim to trace themselves back to an early Johanite sect, ruled over by a mysterious Patriarch Theocratus. The military order of the Knights Templars was finally suppressed by Clement V in 1312, partly because of their cabalistic rites. The Christian Community, however, makes no claim to this medieval succession, and does not mention it in its publications.

The seven sacraments were retained. They were regarded as the 'true Festivals of Life', and, unlike those in the Catholic and Eastern Churches, were 'to be accessible to everyone'. An elaborate ritual was drawn up, with ceremonial including both incense and vestments. The chief act of worship, which is a vernacular adaptation of the Roman Mass, was given the name of 'The Act of Consecration of Man'.

According to one of its official publications, the Christian Community has for its chief aim 'to realize a living public worship and communal life founded on the basis of Christianity Universal, in which thinking people of today can take part in full sincerity. It is therefore, not a union of those who accept a common belief, but a union of those who experience together the working of the spirit'. The organization is directed by a circle of 'Leaders' who are supervised by an 'Arch-Leader'. Male and female Leaders are in charge of congregations in England, Scotland, Germany, Austria, Switzerland, Holland, Czechoslovakia, Norway, and Finland. Members of the Christian Community do not regard themselves as 'a new Church', rather as an elect body who are 'in the position of a man who has a tree in his garden which is quite unique'. They 'see hopes for the future uniting of all that is most precious in the ancient communions through the Living Acts of the Altar'. They are certain that it is their duty 'to bring healing and help in the form of free spiritual life in our modern age'. The Anthroposophists have been associated with the Iona Community since 1940, and one of their priests helped to distribute the Elements at the Oecumenical Communion service in the Abbey (on Whit sunday, 1963).

Churches of the Mathew Succession

(iv) *The Church Catholic*

After 'the Most Illustrious and Most Reverend Count Landaff of Thomastown in Ireland' had suspended the Right Rev. Frederick Samuel Willoughby, the 'Bishop of St Pancras', from the exercise of holy orders, and dismissed him from what was now called the Old Roman Catholic Church, six months after he had raised him to the episcopate in the banqueting hall of the Bell Hotel, Bromley, Kent, this ex-Anglican clergyman felt at liberty to make use of his powers according to his own conscience. Within four months he had consecrated Bernard Gauntlett and Robert King, both of them active members of the Theosophical Society.[1] The following year, on November 5, 1916, in the Theosophical Temple, Blomfield Road, Maida Vale, London, W.9, he found convincing reasons to raise to the episcopate another of Mathew's former priests, named Frederick James. The versatile new prelate, in the capacity of what would now be called a *prêtre ouvrier*, earned his living as a music teacher, a professor of elocution, and an actor.[2]

Monsignor James (to give him the title he preferred) opened a public oratory in St John's Wood and held services in other parts of London for the spiritual benefit of a handful of like-minded Theosophists. This apostolate was interrupted when he left England for the Far East to serve with the Y.M.C.A. as a war-worker with the Duke of Cornwall's Light Infantry. On returning to civil life, James resumed his episcopal status, and reorganized his disciples under the title of 'The Church Catholic'. He found a place of worship for them in a hall in Princess Street, Cavendish Square. Here the services continued until 1927, when he acquired premises at 23 Basil Street, Knightsbridge, behind Harrods, which he called 'The Sanctuary'. His 'palace' was a flat above the church, and before long he managed to gather round him a small but smart congregation. One of its most active members was the late Duke of Leeds.

The religion invented by Mgr James (like that of Rudolf Steiner's Christian Community) was encouragingly eclectic. It is surprising that it did not have a wider appeal, for he stated in one of his official publications that:

'The Creed of the Sanctuary is "I believe in God", and it reduces all ethics to one of non-injury. There is no belief in any

---

[1] See p. 344.

[2] In after years James used to maintain that his consecration had been performed by Mathew, probably because of Willoughby's unfortunate reputation.

special divine revelation, but revelation unfolds in the process of natural and spiritual evolution as the mind of man expands. . . . The teaching given at the Sanctuary is not dogmatic: it is to be accepted only in so far as it may strike a responsive chord within the soul. The aim should be to demonstrate in one's own life that the Divine Love, when understood and lived, leads to spiritual regeneration.'

Taken all round, the religion of the Church Catholic was a variant of Theosophy, much of it more or less identical with the official teaching of the Liberal Catholic Church. Converts were told that

'A Church that is Catholic, must include all sects, creeds, and religions. It should be a universal brotherhood, for the link joining all men is Divine Love. "Religion is Life", not a creed. The Eternal Principles were laid down by our Lord of Nazareth, and the other great World Teachers. If they be followed, the Divine Love, Divine Light, and Divine Life will be manifest in earthly life, and those of the Faith will become instruments of service to humanity.'

On November 21, 1932, the *Daily Express* described the Sanctuary as 'The Ballroom Church of all Creeds', telling its readers that the religion set forth by Mgr James embraced 'every Creed from Hinduism to Protestantism.' Attention was drawn to the images of Christ and Buddha on either side of the apse facing each other. The Sunday services featured Mass and Benediction.[1] The Church Catholic was in advance of the Roman Church, for at the back of Harrods an 'Evening Eucharist for Communion' was held every first Friday at 9.30 p.m. anticipating by nearly thirty years the permission for evening Masses granted by Pius XII. The ideal aimed at in these services was to 'establish communion with God in the Kingdom of Heaven that is *within*'. Mgr James was broadminded enough to borrow from Quakers as well as Buddhists. He explained that 'silent prayer and meditation take the place of the vocal prayers contained in the missals and liturgies'. The doors of the Sanctuary were closed ten minutes before the services started. Corporate participation in worship was far from encouraged, since absolute silence was obligatory. Consecrated oil was administered when desired. Incense was used generously to awaken the Theosophist Inner Self.

---

[1] The liturgy used was perhaps the shortest in the world, consisting only of the Invocation, Gloria in Excelsis, Veni Sanctificator, Preface, abbreviated Roman Canon, Pax, and a final Benediction.

There were rumours that the fully initiated members of this little flock off Knightsbridge indulged in occult ceremonies behind locked doors. Whether this was so or not, the idea of polarity was certainly there, for in his public services, Mgr James (like the priests of the Christian Community) was assisted by male and female acolytes, who were said to symbolize the positive and negative as expressed in sex. The Sanctuary closed its doors for the last time during the Second World War, when its founder retired into private life. He has now 'passed on'.[1]

(v) *Old Catholic Orthodox Church (Apostolic Service Church), originally the Independent Catholic Church*

Kelly's Handbook to the Titled, Landed, and Official Classes informs us that this most exclusive body of the Mathew succession was founded by the Most Rev. James Bartholomew Banks, P.G.M. K.V., P.G.M.S.E., P.G.M.C., G.B.C.E., G.B.I.C.N., P.G.C.K.T., K.G.C.S.F., K.G.C.S.B., K.G.C.S.M., K.D.O., D.D., LL.D., D.S.L., Ph. D. Born on August 15, 1894, he is the only son of Bartholomew Young Banks, of The Park, Sutton Bridge, Wisbech, and Thorney, Tydd St Mary, Cambs., J.P. for the Parts of Holland, Lincs (1928). His mother was Mary Adela, eldest daughter of James Tyler, of Gedney Marsh, Lincs. Educated at Woodbridge School, Suffolk, and Wells and Lichfield Theological Colleges, he served in the Artists' Rifles during the First World War. He was ordained priest in 1921, and to the episcopate by Bishop Willoughby on July 9, 1922.[2]

The new prelate opened a place of worship in Maiden Lane, off the Strand, London, called 'The Church of the Great Sacrifice'. In after years he stated that being the outcome of the 1914–1918 war,

---

[1] In the Foreword to her 'thriller' *Death in Ecstasy* (first published in 1936), Ngaio Marsh wrote: 'In case the House of the Sacred Flame might be thought to bear any superficial resemblance to any existing church or institution, I hasten to say that if any similarity exists it is purely fortuitous. The House of the Sacred Flame, its officials, and its congregation are all imaginary and exist only in Knocklatchers Row. None, so far as I am aware, has any prototype in any part of the world.'

Still, it is curious that 'the cul-de-sac leading off Chester Terrace and not far from Graham Street' described by this New Zealand novelist, in which the 'House of the Sacred Flame' was located, is not more than half a mile from Basil Street, where Bishop James's 'Sanctuary' was to be found. Moreover, the occult rites and ceremonies carried out by 'Father Jasper Garnette' had a close affinity with those said to have been performed in the place of worship off Knightsbridge. Perhaps their resemblance may have been due to telepathy or astral inspiration?

[2] This appears to have been the last consecration performed by the former titular Bishop of St Pancras, deposed by Mathew in 1915. Some time after this he retired into lay life, and is said to have been received into the Church of Rome before his death.

His Excellency the Most Rev. James Bartholomew Banks, LL.D., D.S.L., Ph.D., Universal Patriarch-Archbishop of the Old Catholic Orthodox Church (Apostolic Service Church); with the Rt. Rev. Sidney E. P. Needham, Rector of Farthinghoe, (Mar Theodorus, Bishop of Mercia), and his wife.

The Rt Rev. Bishop Geoffrey P. T. Paget King; The Most Rev. Mgr. Gerard G. Shelley, Archbishop of Caer-Glow and Primate of the Canonical Old Roman Catholic Church; and The Rt Rev. Bishop Willibrord (Hans Heuer).

this church existed as 'a LIVING MEMORIAL to our LOVED ONES who made the SUPREME SACRIFICE . . . believing it to be their command in going 'OVER THE TOP' to fearlessly teach the DIVINE TRUTHS free from all distortions'.[1] At the same time he gave his few followers the name of 'The Independent Catholic Church'.

On December 31, 1924, Mgr Banks announced his election as Patriarch of Windsor. Two years later he published the Constitution of what had now been renamed 'The Old Catholic Orthodox Church (Apostolic Service Church)'. The organization was described as 'a body of Old Catholics which came into a separate existence in 1925, and accepts the dogmatic decrees of the Holy Synod of Jerusalem 1672, held by the Greek Orthodox Church'. The objects of this new body were defined as follows:

'(*a*) the promotion of the Catholic Faith, by all legitimate means, as being the only form of Religion and Philosophy directly of Divine institution, and therefore most satisfactorily suited to deal with present-day problems, and in the development of this, the restatement of that faith in terms of its relation to modern thought; (*b*) the reunion, or absorbing of the various divisions now existing in Christendom.'

The Constitution set forth that the Sovereign Primate would be assisted by a Sacred Synod, composed of four Sovereign Primatial Chaplains (each a Bishop), a Chancellor, Episcopal Barrister, Prelates, Protonotary-Apostolic, and Nuncios-Apostolic. In addition to these officials there would be a Sovereign Primatial Bodyguard, enlisted from 'loyal Service and Ex-Service men in uniform'. These gentlemen would be entrusted with the military and ceremonial side of pontifical functions performed by the Patriarch. Provision was made also for 'Grand Magisteries of the Sovereign and Most Noble, Religious and Chivalrous Orders of the Saint Esprit, Keys and Vigil, and Sainte Couronne'. This showed that the Old Catholic Orthodox Church, with its patriarchal curia at Windsor, intended to rival the Most Noble Order of the Garter. The Sovereign-Primate also indicated that he had faculties to confer degrees in Arts, Divinity, Literature, Philosophy, Law, Sacred Law, Sacred Science, Music, and Divine Healing. It will be seen that his powers

---

[1] cf. *A Broad Statement of the Principles and Facts of the Old Catholic Orthodox Church, The Apostolic Service Church* (Revised edition, 1954).

The 'Great Sacrifice' alluded to was not the Sacrifice of Christ on Calvary, but the one made by the soldiers who fell in World War I, to whose memory Bishop Banks had a special devotion.

were far wider than those wielded by the Dean and Chapter of the Royal Chapel of St George within His Majesty's Castle of Windsor.

The clergy of the Old Catholic Orthodox Church would be formed, if possible, of men who had served or who were serving in some branch of the Fighting Forces, and whose vocation to the sacred ministry had been proved. Under no circumstances would the ordination of women be permitted. In this respect the Patriarch of Windsor was not so broad-minded as Mar Doreos, Archbishop of Caerleon; and he would have been the first to denounce the later Mariavite, and Old Holy Catholic custom of raising ladies to the episcopate.[1] In emulation of the Liberal Catholic Church, and the Ancient Catholic Church, he welcomed all baptized persons of any denomination whatsoever to receive communion.[2] Would-be catechumens were told that the Old Catholic Orthodox Church was 'a unique and real memorial, where Service and Ex-Service Men and others of ALL nationalities—friend and foe—may meet as BROTHERS in common REMEMBRANCE of THOSE who made the SUPREME SACRIFICE'.[3]

One of the special objects of this new Church would be to foster the great gift of Spiritual Healing, which, so it was stated, 'had been more or less ignored by other organizations of the Holy Catholic Church'. Special services would be held for this purpose, to which the sick and the suffering would be invited. Some of the doctrines set forth left no doubt that the Old Catholic Orthodox Church was striving hard to restate the Faith 'in terms of its relation to modern thought' as understood in the nineteen-twenties. For instance, 'The Father-Motherhood of God' was taught, and another belief (hardly in keeping with the Holy Synod of Jerusalem 1672, or the Greek Orthodox Church) was that it did not matter what creed the dear departed professed, 'or even none at all', because they could all 'be aided in their spiritual progress after transition by the thoughts and prayers of those remaining on earth'. Another doctrine, which may have surprised old-fashioned persons,

---

[1] See p. 295.

[2] See p. 352. Mgr Banks's Old Catholic Orthodox Church must not be confused with the body of the same name with which Mar Georgius and Bishop McFall were associated at one time. (See pp. 327, 342, 444.)

[3] It may well have been a sacrifice to soldiers who wished to become priests to shave off their moustaches 'to prevent sacrilege, or any suggestion of the same when partaking of the Precious Blood from the Chalice'. Laymen with either beards or moustaches were bidden to burn their handkerchiefs, or specially wash them, if used for rubbing their lips after drinking from the chalice.

who were not keeping abreast with modern thought, was that 'evolution or spiritual unfoldment of Man takes place under an inviolable law of cause and effect'.

As early as 1922 Mgr Banks had published the first edition of *The Holy Liturgy and Other Rites* for use in his Independent Catholic Church.[1] The later editions of this new liturgy, even more than the first, offered adherents a rich and elaborate form of worship. The Calendar—a veritable 'War Cry'—stressed the military and patriotic character of the Mgr Banks' Church. He had no sympathy with the pacifist ideals propagated by Mar Jacobus, Bishop of Mercia and Middlesex.[2] Among the collection of hymns printed was the following:

> *Their long way to Tipperary*
> *Was much shorter than we thought*
> *But they never feared that journey,*
> *Nor the anguish that it brought.*
> *May we ask Thee, then, Beloved,*
> *To unite with them and know*
> *That we're with them marching onward—*
> *And progressing as we go.*

Provision was made for solemn commemorations of dates associated with warfare. The new festivals to be observed included Zeebrugge Day (April 23), Anzac Day (April 25), Ireland's Remembrance Day (August 22), Trafalgar Day (October 21), and Armistice Day (November 11). The papally-imposed feast of Christ the King (1929) was adopted by the Lord Patriarch James I, who in emulation of Bishops Wedgwood and Leadbeater, also anticipated Pope John XXIII by changing the Octave of the Epiphany to the Baptism of Our Lord.[3] At the same time the faithful were taught how to readjust their faith in terms of modern thought, and were reminded that 'man is a link in the vast chain of lives leading from the Highest to the Lowest, as he helps those below him on the ladder of lives, receiving thus a free gift of grace'. Their Lord Patriarch proclaimed: 'We look through REINCARNATION, which is the only teaching concerning immortality consistent with a GOD OF

---

[1] Revised editions, with the *imprimatur* of '✠ James I, Universal Patriarch-Archbishop and Sovereign Primate' were issued in 1931 and 1948.
[2] See pp. 144, 145.
[3] See p. 355.

LOVE and JUSTICE, to the coming UNIVERSAL BROTHER-HOOD, for which we daily pray.' Did the more simple-minded and less educated feel that some of these doctrines were identical with those propagated by the Liberal Catholic Church, and wonder why it had been necessary to found a rival body?

In 1936, so it is stated in *Kelly's Handbook to the Titled, Landed, and Official Classes*, Mgr Banks became 'the first Universal Patriarch-archbishop of the Old Catholic Orthodox Church, on that Church being incorporated with the Independent Catholic Church, Ancient Catholic Church, and Apostolic Service Church'. He moved the headquarters of his united body from Windsor to East Molesey, Surrey, where he founded the Priory Church of St Michael and All Angels, adjacent to the patriarchal residence in Matham Road.

Here on the banks of the little River Mole, on the feast of St Augustine of Canterbury, May 28, 1940, His Excellency James I, Universal Patriarch-Archbishop of the Old Catholic Orthodox Church, pursuant to Letters Dismissory issued by Archbishop Daniel C. Hinton, Primate of the American Catholic Church, raised to the episcopate the Rev. Sidney Ernest Page Needham, since 1925 rector of Farthinghoe, in the Anglican Diocese of Peter-borough. The assistant consecrator was Mgr James Dominic Mary O'Gavigan, Archbishop of the Orthodox Catholic Province of Our Lady of England in Devon and Cornwall.[1] The new prelate, who was married, took the title of Mar Theodorus, Bishop of Mercia. He was able to retain Farthinghoe Rectory as his 'palace', and to benefit by the emoluments of the living, for the Canon Law of the Church of England makes no provision for the deprivation of priests who have obtained the episcopate elsewhere.

Archbishop Hinton, resident in Chicago, appointed him as the episcopal head of the University of Sulgrave. The Northampton-shire village of this name, about six miles south-west of Farthing-hoe, was the ancestral home of George Washington's family. The American Catholic Church had managed to obtain a charter for this University from the State Legislature of Delaware; and it followed much the same method of conferring degrees as the Lloyd-Sibley Intercollegiate University, whose goodwill it had inherited.[2] But it did not function for very long, because questions were soon asked about it in Parliament. Eventually both the *Spectator* and the *Cambridge Review* managed to ridicule this Anglo-American

[1] See p. 294, n.1.
[2] See p. 277.

University out of existence. To forestall action being taken by American universities, Sulgrave applied to the State of Delaware for the annulment of its charter.[1]

On January 4, 1945, Mar Theodorus exchanged consecrations with the already much consecrated Mar Georgius. The ceremony took place in the episcopal oratory of SS. Mary and John at Farthinghoe Rectory.[2] For a year Needham combined the duties of a priest of the Diocese of Peterborough in the Province of Canterbury with those of a bishop in the Eparchy of All the Britons within the Catholicate of the West. His diocese embraced the counties of Berks., Northants., and Oxon. Mar Theodorus retired from Farthinghoe in 1946, and his name continued to appear in *Crockford.* He died at his home near Newbury, Berks., on October 2, 1962.

In the spring of 1948, following conditional baptism, confirmations, and minor orders, the Universal Patriarch Banks re-ordained up to the priesthood, the Rev. J. E. Bazille-Corbin, rector of Runwell St Mary, Essex, who on April 3 that same year was raised to the episcopate by Mar Georgius.[3] It was in the Patriarchal Chapel at East Molesey that Mar Georgius re-ordained Mgr Van Ryswyk up to the priesthood on November 6, 1949.[4] Among later ordinations performed by the Universal Patriarch was that of Francis E. Glenn, who was consecrated by Bishop Schonbroodt in 1957, and who is now head of the Church and Order of the Servants of Christ.[5]

Although the Patriarch Banks had been leading a more or less hidden life for close on thirty years, attracting very little publicity, the *Daily Sketch* decided that he had news value. On February 9, 1955, this widely-read paper devoted an illustrated article to him. The now sixty-two-year-old prelate revealed to the reporter that he did not have to endure the poverty of Archbishop A. H. Mathew in his latter years, for he had been left £10,000 as the residue of his father's £120,000 estates at Tydd St Mary and Thorney, Cambridgeshire. His Excellency was described as 'thick-set, bespectacled, wearing riding breeches, Stetson-style hat, and water-

---

[1] cf. F. Brittain, 'Academia; or Old Friends with Old Faces', in *The Cambridge Review*, March 2, 1946.
[2] That same day Mar Theodorus reconsecrated conditionally Mar Basilius Abdullah III (Dr W. B. Crow). See pp. 236–238. It is said that he also raised an Anglican priest to the episcopate.
[3] See p. 466.
[4] See p. 470.
[5] See p. 486.

proof coat', with a jewelled ring on one of his fingers.[1] Outside the sixteen-roomed Priory at East Molesey where he resided was a small but dignified church. The Universal Patriarch-Archbishop's personal standard of fleurs-de-lys fluttered on a fifty-foot high flag-pole.[2]

Since then very little has been heard of the Old Catholic Orthodox Church. So far as is known, no recent statistics have been published; there have been no press releases from the Sacred Synod, and its four Sovereign Primatial Chaplains (each a Bishop). It would be surprising if the Sovereign Primatial Bodyguard were still able to attract recruits in sufficient numbers to add colour and dignity to pontifical functions in the Priory Church of St Michael and All Angels by their striking uniforms; and finally, as neither *Whitaker's Almanack* nor *Kelly's Handbook to the Titled, Landed, and Official Classes* includes the Orders of the Saint Esprit, Keys and Vigil, and Sainte Couronne among the Orders of Chivalry, it has been impossible to obtain particulars of their present knights companions.[3]

Apart from Archbishop W. H. Francis (consecrated in 1916), now reduced to the status of mitred-archpriest of the Russian Orthodox Catholic Church in America, the Universal Patriarch Banks (consecrated in 1922), is the oldest surviving bishop of the Mathew succession, and certainly the senior in date among them.

(vi) *The Old Catholic Evangelical Church of God and The Old Holy Catholic Church*

It is a matter of opinion whether the Old Catholic Evangelical Church of God and its offspring the Old Holy Catholic Church can be included with the churches of the Mathew succession. A recently published Statement of Tenets drawn up by the hierarchy of the Old Holy Catholic Church indicates that it has repudiated the Mathew succession, for it affirms: 'Our succession is Old Catholic (Church of Utrecht), and derived prior to such time as that Church fell under suspicion of heresy'. This takes the succes-

---

[1] Presumably to symbolize that his jurisdiction was co-extensive with, or even greater than the Pope's, because it embraced the whole Universe, he usually wore a white cassock. The white cassock now worn by the popes is said to derive from St Pius V's white Dominican habit.

[2] *Burke's Landed Gentry* gives the Banks Arms as follows: 'Sa. a pall or between three fleurs-de-lys arg. Crest—Upon a coronet composed of three crosses set upon a rim or, a stork ppr., holding in the beak a fleur-de-lys or.'

[3] *Kelly's Handbook* (1960), however, did give a hint of the multiform activities of the Universal Patriarchal Curia by the three telephone numbers—Molesey 1128, 1129, and 1130.

sion back nearly three hundred years, because accusations of Jansenism were first launched from Rome against the Dutch Catholics in 1697. If this statement is historically justified, then there must have been a link between the Old Holy Catholic Church and some unspecified Dutch bishop during the seventeenth century.[1] On the other hand, Archbishop Ignatius Carolus, Primate of the O.H.C.C., wrote in December 1962: 'Our Orders are direct through Patriarch Banks and Mar Georgius, the latter through Archbishop Nicholson and Archbishop Singer (Mar Philippus).' This raises further problems, because as was explained on page 370, the Patriarch Banks was raised to the episcopate by Bishop Willoughby in 1922, who had been consecrated by Archbishop A. H. Mathew in 1914. The last named derived his episcopate from Dr Gul, Old Catholic Archbishop of Utrecht, in 1908, and never claimed a pre-1697 line of succession. Again, it is not certain who it was who ordained priest and consecrated (apparently in 1924) Matthew Cooper, a second-hand furniture dealer at Greenwich, who was the founder of the Old Catholic Evangelical Church of God. Statements made from time to time, that it was the Patriarch Banks, have been strenuously denied by His Excellency, so the whole matter is shrouded in mystery.[2] Cooper adopted the style of 'Archbishop Matthew', but to save confusion with the *de jure* Earl of Landaff it is best to refer to him as Archbishop Cooper. Like his contemporary, Mgr Williams, Archbishop of Caer-Glow, he used to proclaim that his little sect (which had no connection with the Old Roman Catholic Church [Pro-Uniate Rite]) had been founded by St Willibrord and his eleven companions, who in the seventh century evangelized the Catti, Batavi, and Frisones. The Anglo-Saxon Rite they took from England to the Netherlands had managed to survive for thirteen hundred years, and had been transplanted to Greenwich in the second decade of the twentieth century. The members of this body, the aims and objects of which were not clearly defined, were never very numerous, during the thirty or so years that it existed. Their original headquarters were at 25

[1] The bishop who imparted this mysterious line of succession ought to be found in Pius Bonifatius Gams' *Series episcoporum ecclesiae catholicae* (Regensburg, 1873 with supplements Munich 1879, and Regensburg 1886; the whole work reprinted in 1931 and 1955). Reference should also be made to *Hierarchia catholica medii et recentioris aevi* (vols. iv, v, and vi; Padua, 1952–8). Unfortunately *The Handbook of British Chronology* (1961) makes no reference to the archbishops and bishops of the O.C.E.C.G. or the O.H.C.C.

[2] How the O.H.C.C. derived its second lines of successions from Archbishop Nicholson and Archbishop Singer, founder of the New Catholic and Free Church, will be found on p. 481.

Gloucester Circus, Greenwich, not far from the Roman Catholic Church of Our Lady Star of the Sea on Croom's Hill. If the Old Catholic Evangelical Church of God did nothing else, it provided a spiritual home for those who found the discipline of both Anglo and Roman Catholicism too rigid for their temperaments.

In September 1942, when the Archbishop was living at 64 Grove Road, Mitcham, Surrey, a clerical neighbour called to pay his respects, and found His Grace 'brilliantly arrayed in vestments, scarlet cap to match'. The sixty-year-old prelate explained that he was a widower, and that before he became an Old Catholic he had been keenly interested in all forms of philanthropic work—especially St Giles's Mission. There was a small oratory in his house, furnished complete with a throne, and filled with incense fumes. At that date he had six priests working under his jurisdiction, all of whom were engaged in secular jobs during the week, and received no payment for their ministrations. Although they used the Roman Missal in English, one of them expressed the opinion that their work was 'purely Evangelical'. Accordingly this tiny sect stood somewhat aloof from all other bodies claiming to be Old Catholic.

Archbishop Cooper informed his guest that he felt he had a special mission to those who belonged either to no religious persuasion or who had lost their faith. It was definitely not a refuge for extreme Anglo-Catholics who were averse to the Baroque and Rococo movement in their own churches, unless their souls thirsted for the Gospel Religion as preached by St Willibrord in the seventh century. Eventually the Old Catholic Evangelical Church of God had thirty-three priests and five bishops, but thirteen of these clerics deserted their Primate.

It must be admitted that 'the Old Man of Greenwich' (as his clergy referred to him) was sometimes hard to get on with. Apparently he accepted men for the ministry without making due investigation of their antecedents, and giving them adequate training for pastoral work. The result in the long run was that two of his priests obtained regrettable publicity in the national newspapers.

One of these, brought up an Anglican, failed to find a bishop to ordain him, and sought refuge in the Church of Rome. His experiences among Papists, however, were so shocking that he reverted to communion with Canterbury for a year or two, only to suffer further disillusionment. Having investigated all other religious bodies in Britain he decided to join the Old Catholic Evangelical Church of God, which seemed to offer the purest form of Christianity. The kind-hearted Archbishop Cooper had no doubt that this seeker after truth had a clear vocation for the sacred ministry, and lost no time in raising him to the priesthood. But so strong was the convert's nostalgia for dignified Anglican ritual and ceremonial that it was lucky that four or five bishops accepted his orders as genuine Old Catholic; apparently not realizing that the little sect to which he belonged was not in communion with the Church of England. Meanwhile, wishing to ensure an absolutely valid apostolic succession, he had himself re-ordained by another free-lance prelate. After this fairly long Anglican interlude— much enjoyed while it lasted—he received Archbishop Cooper's blessing on the proposed foundation of an Old Catholic Evangelical theological college, which, like Kelham and Mirfield, would be directed by a religious community, and the following advertisement was inserted in the personal columns of a certain Sunday newspaper:

'Gentlemen wanted for ordination in ancient foundation and as members of a community Catholic (not R.C.). All details from the Rev Superior . . .'

More than thirty gentlemen (including two clergymen already ordained) sought information. Literature was sent them, describing the observances of this venerable Community of St Willibrord and its spacious buildings. But it was not long before another newspaper discovered that the community existed only in the vivid imagination of its would-be founder. The eventual result was that he abandoned Archbishop Cooper and found a prelate of a rival church of the Mathew family to give him conditional re-ordination up to the priesthood. As is related elsewhere in this book, the foundation of religious communities which never materialized is a not uncommon phenomenon in the autocephalous churches of the past hundred years.

The Old Holy Catholic Church evolved out of the Old Catholic Evangelical Church of God in 1955. Little has been recorded about the early life of its founder, Charles Brearley, but it appears that from boyhood—like the cleric just mentioned—he was convinced that God was calling him to serve the Lord and to save sinners. Brearley is said to have earned his living in manual occupations, and later on to have engaged in evangelistic work with the Church Army. Stories that he tried to persuade several bishops of different denominations to ordain him have been strenuously denied; also that in the early thirties he had found secular employment in Sheffield. No matter, eventually he became the lay-minister of a small independent Protestant mission chapel at Heeley, a southern suburb of the city. Having no narrow sectarian scruples, he appealed to Archbishop Cooper, who on Sunday, January 31, 1954, laid hands on him in a rented room at Sheffield. The new prelate was placed in charge of the Northern Province of the Old Catholic Evangelical Church of God, which had very few adherents in Yorkshire at that date. So far as is known, the name of the bishop who raised Brearley to minor and major orders up to the priesthood has never been published. Archbishop Cooper returned to London after a week-end in Sheffield, and it was not long before he broke off relations with his Northern Metropolitan. The reason given was that both Bishop Brearley and Dr Pitt-Kethley, then acting as Archdeacon, wished for what was described as 'a more democratic way of Church Government, to which the Archbishop was opposed'.[1]

Finding himself definitely a bishop at large in Yorkshire, subject to no higher authority but God, and apparently not content with the Old Catholic succession believed to have been derived from Cooper, Brearley welcomed an invitation from Mar Philippus (P.C.S. Singer) to be re-consecrated at his hands. It was a tempting offer, because it guaranteed the eighteen or more lines of succession understood to have been imparted to Mar Philippus by Mar Joannes, Archbishop of Karim, by way of Mar Georgius, Patriarch of Glastonbury.[2] So he went to London and called on Mar Philippus, who had recently assumed the primacy of a tiny sect known as 'The New Catholic and Free Church' of which he was the founder. On Sunday, November 14, 1954, the two bishops exchanged conse-

---

[1] On June 18, 1960, Pitt-Kethley was raised to the episcopate by Bishop Julien Erni, assisted by Bishop W. H. Turner. He held the offices of Administrator for Great Britain of the Reformed Catholic Church (Utrecht Confession), and British Representative of the Universal Life Foundation and International Academy of Burnaby, B.C., Canada. He now holds among other offices those of British Representative of the United Old Catholic Patriarchate of the World, and belongs to the Sacred Synod of the *Église catholique apostolique primitive d'Antioche orthodoxe et de tradition Syro-Byzantine.* Bishop Pitt-Kethley is also said to be a Fellow of the Evangelical Preachers Association.

[2] Singer had been raised to the episcopate as titular Bishop of Hebron by H. P. Nicholson on April 14, 1952, but he soon broke off relations with the Ancient Catholic Church and its Cathedral in Chelsea (see p. 481), and founded a new body. At the time of writing, having apparently dropped the title of Hebron, Archbishop Singer conducts services for a handful of disciples (known as the Catholic Apostolic Church, though having no connection with either the Irvingites or with Mar Georgius' church of the same name) in an upstairs room at Sudbury, Middlesex.

crations in a room of a house at 5 Bramshill Road, N.10, which served Mar Philippus as a Pro-Cathedral. It seems to have been on this occasion that Brearley met for the first time Mr Leslie Pearse and his wife Maureen, both Theosophists and members of the Liberal Catholic Church; a meeting that was to have unforseen influence on his future career.[1] By way of trial and error the former Church Army evangelist and independent Protestant minister was gradually finding his way towards a species of Catholicism which, so it must be admitted, has always remained somewhat fluid in doctrine and discipline so far as outsiders can make out.

Bishop Brearley soon acquired news value in South Yorkshire, and with good reason, for he could now proclaim that he was the 137th in line from St Peter the Apostle as first Bishop of Antioch. On February 21, 1955, the *Sheffield Telegraph* published a full-length photograph of him in cope and mitre taken outside St Peter's Mission Chapel at Heeley. Towards the end of that same year the twice consecrated prelate was obliged to resign his charge, and to close the Ministerial Training College he had opened in this suburb of Sheffield.

Mrs Pearse then invited him to become her resident chaplain at Cusworth Hall, near Doncaster.[2] Hitherto the chapel had been served by a priest of the Liberal Catholic Church, but the first thing Bishop Brearley did was to expunge any reference to Theosophy in the liturgical books used. By this time he had severed all associations with both the Old Catholic Evangelical Church of God and the New Catholic and Free Church. It is understood that he disapproved of Mar Philippus' alleged dabbling in Spiritism, and his conferring 'valid' orders on Nonconformist ministers. Bishop Brearley remained at Cusworth from December 1955 to July 1956.

Several impressive pontifical functions took place in the sumptuous Baroque chapel, dating from 1740. One of the first was the ordination of a deacon and priest at which Archbishop Mattheus Viktor Schonbroodt assisted, as well by the titular Abbess of Bethany (Mrs Pearse).[3] December 15, 1955, appears to have been

---

[1] Mrs Pearse, born in 1890, is the only daughter of William H. Battie-Wrightson, J.P., of Cusworth Hall, near Doncaster, and a great-niece of the 3rd Marquess of Exeter.

[2] She had been blessed as Abbess of Bethany by Archbishop Nicholson of Karim, and it has been stated that in July 1954 she was raised to the diaconate and priesthood by Archbishop Mattheus Viktor Schonbroodt of the Free Catholic Church in Germany (see p. 483). It appears that immediately after this she was consecrated a bishopess.

[3] A photograph taken some years later depicts Archbishop Brearley, also Bishops Boyer and Turner, each in full pontificals; together with Mrs Pearse wearing a mitre and wielding a crozier. Mrs Brearley is vested in biretta, cassock, clerical collar, lace-trimmed cotta, deacon's stole and cope.

the date when Brearley (who about this time assumed the title of Archbishop of Danum—the ancient name of Doncaster), raised to the episcopate George William Boyer as Bishop of Boston.[1]

Possibly anxious to hold his own with the two rival Metropolitans Dr Garbett, Archbishop of York, and Mgr Godfrey, Archbishop of Liverpool, the Archbishop of Danum added to his hierarchy on May 20, 1956, by consecrating Henry (Francis) Angold.[2]

Unfortunately some people did not grasp the spiritual significance of the ceremonies performed in the private chapel of this South Yorkshire mansion. The eventual result was nation-wide publicity in more than one newspaper, including a photograph of His Grace, vested in cope and mitre, conferring a university degree. Although the Archbishop complained that most of the statements printed were lies, he was forced to become inactive for a time, so the Liberal Catholic Lady Abbess lost the services of her chaplain, but he maintains that at no period of his career has he ever countenanced Theosophy or similar heresies.

The persecuted prelate received no further publicity for nearly a year. Meanwhile Archbishop Cooper had resigned the Primacy of the Old Catholic Evangelical Church of God on account of his age and failing health, and was living in retirement. The autocephalous church he had founded at Greenwich in 1924 faded out, and little more was heard of it.[3]

The storm having blown over, the Archbishop of Danum felt able to rally his forces and to revive the body for which he had been originally consecrated, but on more up-to-date lines as a 'New Age Ecumenical Institution'. He renamed it 'The Old Holy Catholic Church'. One of his clerics persuaded him to adopt the names Ignatius Carolus, in spite of his own dislike of flamboyant titles, and with the prefix 'His Grace Most Reverend'. A wide range of erudition was suggested by the degrees of M.A., D.D., Litt.D. and D.C.L. An organization called 'The Union of Churches' is said to have appointed him Primate. The headquarters of the new body were set up in a housing estate in the Manor District of Sheffield. Although His Grace's Anglican *vis-à-vis*, Bishop Hunter, could add M.A., D.C.L., D.D., and LL.D. to his name, he may have

---

[1] Later on Boyer was reconsecrated by Richard, Duc de Palatine, and became one of the mystic hierarchy of the Pre-Nicene Gnostic Catholic Church (see p. 494, n.3).

[2] Angold, like Boyer, eventually broke off communion with Brearley, and found new fields for his apostolic labours.

[3] There is a report that he laid hands of a certain Francis Gill as his canonical successor. At the time of writing the Archbishop is still alive, but has long since ceased to perform any episcopal functions.

envied the magnificent heraldic blazon displayed in a circle one-and-a-half inches in diameter displayed in a circle on the primatial writing-paper. It was the future Bishop Turner, so Archbishop Brearley relates, who devised the coat of arms, and persuaded his Primate to have it printed. The shield was superimposed on a patriarchal cross, crozier, and one key; surmounted by a heraldic archiepiscopal hat; with the words *Ignatius Carolus dei Gra. Archiepus. Vet. Ecc. Sanct. Catholicae* within the circle. The motto chosen was *Fides Spes Caritas*.

An impressive statement was issued in 1957 explaining the nature, scope, and origins of this New Age Institution with its Roots in Apostolic Tradition. The remote Founder, so it appeared, was St Willibrord, the seventh-century Northumbrian monk who evangelized the Netherlands. 'We are proud to acknowledge him as one of our earlier prelates', the Primate asserted. Thanks to Arnold Harris Mathew, consecrated as Regional Old Catholic Bishop for Britain in 1908, the Willibrordian line of apostolic succession had passed on to the Old Holy Catholic Church, which also claimed to have acquired the Antiochian, Assyrian, and other lines. This New Age Institution should have appealed especially to the female sex, because it acknowledged the Sacred Ministry of women, claimed to have full Biblical support. The lady bishops, priests and deacons were known as abbesses, prioresses and deaconesses. As in the case of male ordinands, they were given minor orders before being raised to the priesthood or episcopate. Both ladies and gentlemen were warned that admission to the Sacred Ministry would not be easy, since a high standard of spiritual experience was demanded. There was no room for persons of either sex who just wished to have clerical status, because the object of this new Church, both in the Realm of Britain and overseas, was 'to bring the people of all nations into a dynamic touch with the Lord Jesus Christ, whom to know is Life Eternal'. The training would be long and hard, with no prospect of large stipends. That the Old Holy Catholic Church was not just another little nonconformist sect was made clear in another brochure, which stated:

'Our Primate is THE MOST REVEREND IGNATIUS CAROLUS, D.D., D.C.L., who has been honoured by many European and American Universities and is by appointment from the Sovereign head of the House of Deols in Italy, PRINCE OF VILLIERS. We know him as Father Charles.'

It should be explained that both during and after the second world war, various claimants to the throne of the Byzantine Empire were generous in bestowing titles and degrees on almost anybody who sought them. Alessandro Licastro de la Chastre Grimaldi-Lascaris, the Sovereign head of the House of Deols in Italy, was only one of the gentlemen who coveted imperial rank. Among his rivals was a youth whose followers addressed him as 'His Imperial Majesty Marziano II Lavarello Lascaris', and who in November 1956, was crowned and consecrated in Rome as Emperor of Constantinople and all the Christian East.[1] Then there was also the *de jure* Emperor Eugenius, whose son, Prince Theodore Lascaris-Commenus was President of the Imperial Byzantine University at Madrid.[2] The Prince de Deols was consecrated at Milan by Archbishop Ignatius Carolus on June 15, 1957, needless to add, without the assistance of Cardinal Montini, who became Archbishop of Milan in 1954, and was elected Pope in 1963, with the title of Paul VI.[3]

The statement continued: 'The LADY ABBESS SUPERIOR is Head of the Women's work throughout the world, and is The Most Rev. Mary Francis, O.S.H., D.D., etc. Marquise de Saulney.

'In the South we have the Right Rev. Bishop William Turner, M.A., D.D., and in France two Bishops work with us: The Most Rev. Roger Regnier of Colombes; and the Right Rev. Henry Engel Plantagenet in Paris.'[4]

'Italy has as its Primate, The Most Rev. Alex Licastro de la Chastre, Prince de Deols, and he lives in Rome. In Bari there is another great scholar allied to us, Prince Amoroso d'Aragona, and in Cuba the Most Rev. Fernandez Jane, D.D., while in America Dr Meeks, Dr Voultros, and Dr Parker are representing us.[1] In Germany we have Dr The Right Rev. Hans Heuer of Nuremburg, so you see we are world-wide in scope.[5]

[1] See p. 314

[2] Mar Marcus Valerius, titular Bishop of Selsey (The Rev. J. M. Bazille-Corbin, rector of Runwell St Mary, Essex) was given the titles of Duca di San Giacomo and Marquis de Beuval by the *de jure* Emperor Eugenius, and made a Doctor Laureatus of the Imperial Byzantine University by Prince Theodore Lascaris-Commenus, some time after 1948 (see p. 467).

[3] It has been stated that Mgr Alessandro Licastro de la Chastre was re-consecrated in 1958 by Mgr Sgroi-Marchese, Mariavite Bishop for Italy, but the former has denied it, so Archbishop Ignatius Carolus writes.

[4] Archbishop Regnier is believed to have been consecrated by Archbishop Ignatius Carolus on June 20, 1957, as Primate of the *Sainte Eglise Apostolique*. It appears that Bishop Plantagenet was consecrated as his Suffragan the same day. The handful of clergy of this small sect are militant Gallicans, specializing in faith-healing and occultism (see p. 315). A report that Archbishop Ignatius Carolus was re-consecrated by these two French prelates has been denied by His Grace.

[5] Prince Amoroso d'Aragona (Academia 'Phoenix e Minerva') was also one of the eighteen illustrious patrons of Bishop-Primus Boltwood's unsectarian Ecumenical

'Now for its scope: we are anxious to extend this Scope outside our present boundaries, and in the past twelve months we have been able to penetrate into Prisons, Poor Houses and Hospitals with a message of Cheer and Blessing. There is NO LIMIT to our Scope, and it must be pointed out that the Church consists of MEMBERS—men and women, boys and girls, filled with a love of God and willing to spend and be spent for His Service.'

The published statements conveyed the idea that within two years of its foundation the O.H.C.C. had spread so rapidly that it had branches in Italy, France, Germany, Cuba, North America, Poland and Malaya. There were rumours that groups were being formed in Ireland and Ceylon. Strange to say, Dr Visser't Hooft had not seen his way to admit this apparently world-wide body to membership of the World Council of Churches, in spite of the fact that its object was said to be 'the promotion of THE TRUE CATHOLIC DOCTRINE and to unite the Christian Churches into One Body wherever this is possible'. Two of his hierarchy having broken off relations, the Archbishop-Primate consecrated William Handsworth Turner on December 15, 1957, as Bishop for London and the South of England.[1] The new prelate urged his Primate to adopt the style of Patriarch, and so did Archbishop Regnier, pointing out that he could well claim to be the Supreme Pontiff of an embryo Universal Church, but he told them that he had no use for pretentious titles, and that he much preferred being addressed as 'Father Charles'.

Considering the apparent international character of Old Holy Catholicism, and its rapid growth, it is not surprising that the Archbishop soon found that his tireless efforts to establish 'a TRUE Catholic Church' in Britain and overseas were meeting with fierce

---

Church Foundation at South Tottenham, N.15 (see p. 247). No information is forthcoming about Archbishop Jane in Cuba, or of the three other representatives in North America. Hans Heuer, a former Lutheran (otherwise known as 'Bishop Willibrord'), was one of the five prelates recognized in August 1957 by Mgr Shelley, Archbishop of Caer-Glow, in his encyclical letter addressed from Rome to the bishops and clergy of the Canonical Old Roman Catholic Church throughout the world. (See p. 437.)

[1] Turner had previously been associated with the Ancient Catholic Church. Soon after his consecration he was released by Archbishop Ignatius Carolus, and founded the Church and Order of Christian Unity within the One, Holy, Catholic and Apostolic Church. On June 17, 1960, he was re-consecrated by Bishop Erni, and thus obtained the Mariavite and a few more lines of apostolic succession. With the title of Mar Guillimus, he is with Mar Rupertus (Pitt-Kethley) of Ealing Common, one of the fifteen prelates forming the Sacred Synod of the *Église catholique apostolique primitive d'Antioche orthodoxe et de tradition Syro-Byzantine* (see p. 314, n.3). His curia is located in Armadale Road, Fulham, S.W.6.

opposition from the leaders of other Christian bodies, not only the Churches of England and Rome, but even of the Liberal Catholic Church. One of its priests, so His Grace became aware, had been harassing him for three years. Eventually the long-suffering Prince-Primate felt obliged to protest to the Baronet Regionary Bishop of the L.C.C., Sir Benjamin Hugh Sykes.

By this time the official liturgy of the New Age Institution with its Roots in Apostolic Tradition was Bishop A. H. Mathew's *Old Catholic Missal and Ritual,* first published in 1909, but long since out of print. Mimeographed copies of the Common were distributed to the clergy, who had to make up the rest of the rite as best they could, with the help of either the *Book of Common Prayer* or vernacular Roman Missals. An *Order of Compline and Administration of Holy Communion with the Reserved Sacrament* was issued about the same time, and based on the Ancient Catholic office, as carried out in 'The Miracle Cathedral' in Chelsea.[1] Compline, followed by solemn Benediction with the monstrance formed the normal evening service in the oratories of the Old Holy Catholic Church.

Far more in keeping, however, with the spirit of this new Church, which as Abbess Mary Francis explained, had 'come into being as an answer to the inarticulate cry of the millions groping for Spiritual Light, without being stifled by Dogmas which they can neither understand nor accept', was *The Liturgy of St Hubert and The Church of the One Life,* published at Hastings by Her Ladyship. The purpose of this profoundly occult and mystical rite (intended mainly for use in the chapel at Cusworth Hall) was 'to guide Christianity again to a knowledge of those spiritual Truths which will place its teaching and worship upon a Foundation Rock of Natural Laws, a foundation which is not undermined but strengthened by the experimental research of the Physicist, the Archeologist, the Geologist, and the Astronomer'. The long outdated Nicene Creed was replaced by a new formula of belief suggesting Theosophical inspiration, and which could be recited by persons of almost any religion without conscientious scruples. It contained the words: 'We hold the Fatherhood of God, the brotherhood of man with all life, above and below Him on the endless ladder which all in turn ascend.' At the end of the liturgy there were special intercessions for Animal Welfare, since it was vitally important to make all Christians realize that the Animal Creation (of every species) have 'their Rightful Place as our younger Brethren who shall all share our Home and who need our love and Care'.

[1] See p. 477.

Churches of the Mathew Succession

The Liturgy of St Hubert had been issued without a *nihil obstat* and *imprimatur* by the Archbishop-Primate. He was profoundly shocked by its heretical tendencies, and forbade its use, but as the chapel at Cusworth Hall was a sort of ecclesiastical 'peculiar' under the immediate jurisdiction of the Lady Abbess, it seems that she did not feel obliged to obey his orders. Although *de facto* a member of the O.H.C.C., she remained loyal to her Liberal Catholic beliefs. *Ubi libertas ibi Ecclesia.*

Meanwhile Cusworth Hall had become the spiritual power-house of the Old Holy Catholic Church, where Lady Abbess Mary Francis, Marquise de Saulney, directed the 'Subsidiary Orders', among which was the Most Sacred Order of St Hubert, whose members, male and female, pledged themselves at their initiation to combat the evils of every kind of cruelty to animals. Also housed in this South Yorkshire mansion was the Ministerial Training College (known as 'The Collegium'), moved here from Sheffield. Another sphere of activity was an interdenominational Bible Study Circle.[1]

The Lady Abbess was left a widow on October 5, 1960.[2] It has been stated that the Archbishop of Danum gave her a second episcopal consecration in 1959. He never became a permanent resident at Cusworth Hall after he ceased to be Chaplain in June 1956. Eventually the property passed into the hands of the Doncaster Corporation. This had involved the loss of the eighteenth-century chapel, so an adjacent stable was refurnished as a place of worship, where, so it was hoped, men and women would find peace and take away an upliftment of soul, and where the 'Sacredness of Life' in the animal kingdom would be taught. Everybody, regardless of creed, would be welcomed to receive the sacraments if they wished. The titular Abbess of Jerusalem (Mrs Jessie Dove) was placed in charge of this shrine on the borders of the South Yorkshire coal-mines.

In recent years Dr Brearley's encyclopedic erudition which, so it was stated, had already been honoured by many European and American universities, though apparently not by any of the twenty-one degree-giving seats of learning in Great Britain, has been recog-

[1] *The Cusworth Courier and St Hubert Chronicle* (the official organ of the O.H.C.C.) was devoted to Christian Thought, Devotional Aspiration, and Animal Welfare. 'A Message from our Beloved Lady Abbess' was a regular feature, and so were Women's Guild and Young Folks' pages.
[2] Her husband had been President of the Hastings' branch of the Theosophical Society, and it was fitting that his requiem Mass and burial service should take place in the Liberal Catholic Cathedral, Caledonian Road ,London.

nized by the Athenian Order, consisting of an *élite* of *Literati* and *Illuminati*, who claim that their Order was founded in 1580 by Francis Bacon, first Viscount St Albans.[1] It is composed of three Triads of thirty-three persons, all British subjects leal to the Sovereign, ruled over by the Grand Matre, Dr Mabel Atkinson, D.D., Litt.D., S.S.D., F.M.T.C., O.S.J., from her *'Sanctum'* (Wesley House), hidden in the heart of the Pennines on the borders of Westmorland and Yorkshire.[2] Not only can Archbishop Ignatius Carolus style himself both Paladin of the Athenian Order and Prince de Villiers, he can now be addressed also as Grand Master of the Order of the Holy Cross of Jerusalem. Since this Order of Chivalry is not mentioned in either *Whitaker's Almanack* or any *Peerage* known to the author, it is not possible to give any information about its history. It may be a British non-papal revival of the military order of the same name founded in Bohemia during the thirteenth century; if so, then Archbishop Ignatius Carolus could claim the right to embroider a red six-pointed star on his cloak of state, as authorized by Pope Innocent IV in 1250.[3]

In spite of defamation and molestation by countless enemies— Anglo-Catholic, Roman Catholic and Liberal Catholic—the Grand-Master-Paladin-Prince-Primate of the Old Holy Catholic Church sees signs in the heavens that a second spring is nigh, and that his

---

[1] Strange to say, none of Dr Brearley's publications appear in the printed catalogues of the British Museum and the Library of Congress, Washington, D.C.

[2] The Grand Matre also signs herself Lady Grand Cross of the Sovereign Order of St John of Jerusalem, Knight of Malta, and Grand Commander of the Order of the Holy Cross of Jerusalem. Among her more illustrious honorary foreign associates are Dr Verhank Pistorius, Grand Master of the Rosicrucian Order of Holland; and Mr P. MacDonnell, Private Secretary to H.R.H. Prince Donogh of Thomond (a medieval principality in Eire), who represents him and the Royal Dalcassian Order in the Athenian Order. In 1936 a certain Raymond Moulton O'Brien claimed the precedence and right to the ancient dignities of the Earldom of Thomond and the Barony of Ibrackan in the Peerage of Ireland. By 1949 O'Brien had assumed the title of Prince of Thomond, and had appointed Count Howard D'Angerville (living on Canvey Island, Essex) as Minister Plenipotentiary and Envoy Extraordinary to the Court of St James. To complete the trappings of royalty, the Prince (already in possession of the insignia of some twenty Orders of Chivalry), founded the Most Honourable Dalcassian Order of the Princely House of Thomond. By 1952 he had a 'Dalcassian Legation' in Dublin. (Cf. Cyril Hankinson, *My Forty Years with Debrett* (1963), pp. 147–50).

[3] The Chancellor of the Order is the Very Rev. Dr George Pullin, Ph.D., Litt.D., D.D., of Barry, Glamorganshire. Miss Lilian Parsons, F.M.T.C., is Master of the Keys; and Dr Louis Canivet, Ph.D., F.M.T.C. of Thionville (Moselle), France, acts as General Director and Chancellor of Honour. He is now one of the hierarchy of the Old Holy Catholic Church.

It should be explained that neither the Rosicrucian Athenian Order nor the Order of the Holy Cross of Jerusalem have *official* connection with the O.H.C.C. The Archbishop wishes it to be stated that it just happens that he is personally connected with these and other Orders, such as the Sovereign Military Order of Templars.

New Age Ecumenical Institution is progressing, even if still weak financially, and obliged to worship in the catacombs, so to say. On July 3, 1960, he consecrated Ronald Marwood Watson, at one time associated with the Anglican Society of St Francis at Cerne Abbas, as Bishop for Yorkshire, giving him the style of Mar Gregorius Ebor.[1] The ordination of a deacon followed in July 1962, and then Archbishop Ignatius Carolus had the consolation of receiving into fellowship a brother prelate—Dr William Charles Cato-Symonds, Bishop of Elmham (Norfolk), who resides at Staines, Middlesex. After eighteen years as an Anglican clergyman, Mr Cato-Symonds joined the Free Protestant Episcopal Church, in which he was raised to the episcopate by Bishop Primus Boltwood at Easter 1962, but three months later came the call to secede to the Old Holy Catholic Church.[2] Dr Brearley at the time had two Archdeacons working under him in the south of England, claimed communion with about a dozen autocephalous churches on the Continent, and was about to go to France to consecrate two bishops (one of them an ex-Roman Catholic priest).

In August 1962 the Rev. R. Dominic Bruce, M.A., who in the course of a long career had belonged to several religious bodies, and who since 1958 had been laying the foundations of the first parish 'over the Border' of the Old Roman Catholic Church (English Rite), decided to transfer his allegiance from Mgr W. A. Barrington-Evans, Archbishop of Verulam, to Archbishop Ignatius Carolus. The latter immediately raised the seventy-five year old convert to the rank of Very Reverend Canon, awarded him the degree of Doctor of Divinity, and appointed him Examining Chaplain for Scottish Ordinands. Convinced that God had called Canon Bruce to the episcopate, His Grace consecrated him as first Old Catholic Bishop of Scotia and the Isles on February 19, 1963. The function took place in the Canon's presbytery at Auchterarder, Perthshire. That same day the English Primate erected a Scottish Province of the O.H.C.C., although there were as yet no dioceses territorially contiguous to

---

[1] It has been reported that Mar Gregorius Ebor was re-consecrated conditionally in 1962, and that he has now ceased to be one of the hierarchy of the O.H.C.C.

[2] See p. 249. Dr Cato-Symonds acted as Registrar of the Society for Proclaiming Britain in Israel. With some unnamed tutors he conducted Correspondence Courses on 'The Life, Teaching and Works of Our Lord', 'Anthropology and Eugenics', 'Celto-Anglo-Saxon Studies', and 'The Migration of Israel'. The 1962 Report of the Society included the names of Archbishop Brearley and the Very Rev. C. Brearley, jun., S.T.D. among the speakers at meetings for promoting the theory that the British people is ultimately descended from the last Ten Tribes of Israel. In 1963 the Archbishop's son, who held the office of Archdeacon, seceded to the Old Roman Catholic Church (English Rite). (See *The People*, Dec. 1, 1963, 'Four out of seven are Jailbirds'.)

justify the formation of such an ecclesiastical unit. Neither had the aged Metropolitan any minor or major clerics to assist him in his Missionary labours; nor were there any places of worship other than his domestic oratory. It was a curious coincidence that Auchterarder should have been chosen as the birth-place of the Scottish Province of this English autocephalous church, because it has been world-famous since 1839 as the scene of the contest which led to the Disruption of 1843, and the formation of the Free Church of Scotland.

Dr Bruce pointed out in the March 1963 number of *Diocesan Notes: Perth and Kinross*: 'Bishops are anathema to the Scots. Mention such a person to any Scot, and at once he ceases to operate. This is where we have a great deal to overcome in this new Province. The people must be trained in the acceptance of Bishops as quite ordinary workers in the good cause or religion.' The Bishop of Scotia and the Isles also informed his readers (said to number nearly 2,000) that before long there will be no congregations left in the Established Church of Scotland, because few of its ministers pay any attention to the rising generation; hence the 'Sacred Duty' of the O.H.C.C. to come to their rescue by means of evangelistic missions.

In addition to the spiritual oversight of the whole of Scotland and its many islands, Bishop Bruce also holds the offices of Vicar General of the Fraternity of St Willibrord, and Superior of the Order of St Dominic. The former, so he explained, was founded in 1945 'with the object of campaigning against the evils of this wicked world and all the sinful lusts of the flesh'. The latter is not an Order in the Catholic meaning of the word, i.e. an institute whose members profess solemn vows, but a Correspondence Course 'for men interested in the Ministry of the Church which is an unpaid one'. *Diocesan Notes* drew attention to Universal Churchcraft (of Auchterarder and Leven); a firm under the direction of Bishop Bruce which supplies the clergy with vestments and all church requisites; its special line being Mother's Union banners for Anglican parishes.

The Constitutions and Rules of the Old Holy Catholic Church (as revised in 1962) still found a place for women clergy, with the titles of Abbess, Prioress and Deaconess, but with the stipulation that they would never take precedence over male clergy of the same rank, although the authority of both were equal, and all were ordained with the same rite. The Most Rev. Mary Francis still retained episcopal rank and authority.[1] It was stated that the O.H.C.C. recognized the validity of orders and sacraments of unspecified Churches in France, Italy, Cuba, California, Pennsylvania, Poland, Malaya and Canada; striving to work and worship in communion with them.

It appears that the Realm of Britain is now divided into four Provinces—Northern, Midland, Southern and Scottish. The hierarchy at the time of writing consists of the Primate, Bishops Bruce and Cato-Symonds, with Bishops André Enos and Louis Canivet on the continent of Europe. Each Province, so it is stated, is divided into Districts, under the oversight of an Archdeacon, or Abbess. No statistics, however, are forthcoming of the number of priests and parishes, or the estimated total of communicants. The headquarters of this still almost unknown body, claiming continuity with the supposedly non-Roman Catholic Church founded by St Willibrord in the Netherlands more than twelve hundred years ago, remain at 49 Ravencarr Road, Sheffield, 2. 'We seek no grandeur, but intend to propagate the Catholic Faith and Purity' was the message sent out by the Primate in December, 1962. Meanwhile His Grace (still insisting how he dislikes flamboyant titles and much prefers to be addressed as 'Father Charles') awaits 'offers of service from any Cause to proclaim the Uplifting of the Lord Jesus Christ', for this is 'all his Heart's Desire'.[2]

(vii) *The Free Anglo-Catholic Church and The Order of Llanthony Brothers*

In December 1940 most of the independent Old Catholic clergy in England received a printed paper which read as follows:

'As I have only recently returned to this country after an absence of close on thirty years, my name will not be known to many of you. I must then introduce myself.

'I was the first person to be consecrated Bishop by the late Archbishop Mathew, and my consecration took place in the Old

[1] A more recent *Short Statement of our Tenets* implies that priestesses and bishopesses have been abolished, since only 'the diaconate of women' is recognized. A new claim made is that the orders of the O.H.C.C. 'are derived prior to such times as the Old Catholic (Church of Utrecht) fell under suspicion and heresy'. The Primate ends this pastoral statement: 'We admit to novel doctrines; we have nothing to commend us to those whose religion is vague or whose standards are "of this world".'

[2] *Rhymes of a Happy Christian* (Barry, Glam., n.d.). Owing to the often confused and sometimes contradictory statements made about the O.H.C.C. since its foundation in 1955, it cannot be guaranteed that all the dates and details in this section are correct.

Churches of the Mathew Succession

Meeting House, Birmingham, on June 8, 1910.[1] You will see from the Chart on the other side that this makes me the senior Old Catholic Bishop in the United Kingdom.

'I am appalled and bewildered by the vast number of Bishops of the Mathew line now existing, the majority of whom are making no effort whatever to carry on the genuine and original Old Catholic body and all in schism one from another. As there is no central authority to which all are subject, my seniority of consecration entitles me to the headship of British Old Catholicism, and I am here to claim my rights.

'All Bishops, Priests and other Clergy in Old Catholic orders are reminded of their duty of canonical obedience, and must submit themselves to my jurisdiction. The Laity also must fall into line. I do not want to make anyone's position difficult, and although I know that many consecrations have been contrary to the canons, I am willing to recognize all Bishops whose names appear on the Chart, and all claiming orders by them, and waive all enquiries as to the circumstances of their consecration or ordination, as their subjection to my lawful authority will regularize their status.

'I have consecrated one Bishop, Ernest Odell Cope, and this was to revive Fr Ignatius's Llanthony Foundation; and he is in communion with me.

'It is true that I am an old man and that the task before me is hard, but I will persevere to the end, and if I am able to heal some of the wounds in the Old Catholic body, I shall be satisfied, and will hand on my torch to a younger successor, who will be better able to finish the work.

'Yours in His service,
'RALPH WHITMAN ✠
'Old Catholic Bishop, Gloucester.

'Advent Sunday, 1940.'

The recipients of this leaflet were utterly mystified, for none of them (not even the Archbishop of Caer-Glow, who lived within five miles of Gloucester) had even heard of this Bishop Ralph Whitman. No evidence of the consecration of a person named Whitman has ever been found among the documents of the first Regionary Old Catholic Bishop in England. Whitman's consecra-

---

[1] This is a Unitarian place of worship. Its minister in 1910 was the Rev. J. M. Lloyd Thomas, President of the Society of Free Catholics, and friend of Vernon Herford, Bishop of Mercia and Middlesex. (See p. 145.)

tion was denied by all the other Mathew bishops who were alive in 1940. His name does not appear in either of Mathew's Registers which have been preserved. Lastly, there is no certainty that such a person as Ralph Whitman actually existed.

On the other hand, we have Cope's testimony, for what it is worth, written on August 21, 1945. This letter, whose phraseology reveals a lack of education, reads as follows:

'Ralph Whitman is described as a Congregationalist minister, trained for the Wesleyan ministry. Went to Canada and worked on Canadian Pacific Railway. Returned to England was Ordained and then Consecrated by Archbishop Mathews [*sic*]. Returned to Canada and set up a small community of men. Failed; Helped in Canadian Church. Returned home before last war. Did war work for Church Army Hut, near "Pop". Lived at Gloucester for some years. And now too old, his relations have placed him in some Home. The Document I sent you he personally made out himself, and was conveyed to me very mysteriously, it having been posted to me during one of the Blitzes from Paddington. And bearing all the marks of rough usage. The wax seal was smashed and the soiled appearance was very suggestive of being handled grimly. It was accompanied by a soiled card with a regimental crest upon it, of the Burma Command. And written upon it was, "I found this amongst my Uncle's papers, I believe they belong to you. I.W." There was no address and I cannot trace anyone who sent it to me. It was evidently intended for me. And evidently made out since my Consecration, 1940.'[1]

So Cope's consecration and consecrator, remain one more unsolved mystery of the by-ways of English Church history.

Ernest Odell Cope was born in 1883, and spent the greater part of his life at Burton-on-Trent. As a youth he was greatly attracted by Fr Ignatius of Llanthony; and shortly after the latter's death on October 16, 1908, he became a novice in the community now reduced to four monks, with two nuns, and several extern sisters.

In the autumn of 1909 Cope was one of the three brethren who accompanied the Superior, Fr Asaph Harris, to Caldey Island, where they were allowed by Abbot Aelred Carlyle to test their vocations to his form of Anglican Benedictine life 'as simple laymen'. A fortnight was enough for him: Cope went home to Burton-on-Trent, where he was employed in one of the larger breweries. Soon after this he married and a son was born. Having

---

[1] Letter from Cope to the Rev. H. R. T. Brandreth.

served in the Army during the First World War, his evangelistic zeal found an outlet in the Stapenhill district of Burton, first in a small room over a garage, and then in the little wooden church, dedicated to St John, which had been erected by Mar Jacobus, Bishop of Mercia and Middlesex, as a Midland outpost of his Evangelical Catholic Communion.[1]

Ernest Cope and his companion, Henry Cotton, were both laymen, but they were authorized by Bishop Herford to conduct morning and evening services, for which they used the Book of Common Prayer. At intervals, Dr Oakden, one of Herford's priests, came from Glasgow to celebrate the eucharist and to renew the reserved sacrament. He generally used Herford's vernacular version of the Liturgy of St Serapion.[2] In 1936 Cope had a disagreement with Herford, and the following year he resigned from the Evangelical Catholic Communion. By January 1939 his imagination was at work on a plan to revive what he called 'The Llanthony Abbey Tradition'. But the outbreak of Second World War prevented anything being done until the summer of 1940, when, according to his own statement, he was secretly raised to the episcopate in a private chapel at Repton, Derbyshire, on July 19. He did not reveal this, even to his closest friends, until June 1945. Even then he persistently refused to divulge the name of his consecrator.[3] Cope merely hinted that his consecrator had been assisted by two ex-Colonial Anglican Bishops, whose names must not be divulged until he had permission to do so.

There are indications that Cope embellished his first account of this mysterious function, suggesting that he realized the necessity of justifying an incredible story. There was also a tale that his previous ordination to the priesthood had taken place on 'the lawn of the house' where Whitman was staying at the time, but he never mentioned when or where he was raised to the diaconate. What is suspicious about the whole business is that the writing of the alleged instrument of consecration bears a strong resemblance to Cope's own handwriting, especially the signature of 'Ralph Whitman ⳨'.[4]

It is quite possible that Cope's fertile brain concocted the whole business in satisfaction of his intense desire to be at the *head* of a

[1] See p. 151.
[2] See p. 144.
[3] Whitman claimed to have performed the ceremony in the printed leaflet sent out in Advent 1940.
[4] One wonders why, if he consecrated Whitman at Birmingham on June 8, 1910, Mathew did not obtain his assistance to consecrate Beale and Howarth at Corby, Lincs, on June 13—only five days later.

new religious movement. He may even have concocted, or got somebody else to write, the circular letter signed 'Ralph Whitman ✠. Old Catholic Bishop'. The Rev. Alban Cockerham, who knew Cope intimately, writes:

'I still believe that Cope was no rogue, but an earnest and simple enthusiast, with a fertile imagination and little education. The wording and spelling of the documents are very like Cope, and the practice of appending the cross after the signature is characteristic of him. The peculiar phraseology is characteristic of Cope, who was entirely Prayer Book in outlook and practice. Yet that strange meeting of Cope and Whitman in the Church Army Hut at Poperinghe, Flanders, just before the Armistice in 1918 (mentioned in one of his letters), set going a whole train of events, and the whole affair sounds so circumstantial that it leaves a vague sort of feeling that it *might* be true.'

Here is an example of Cope's peculiar phraseology—a letter from him dated August 7, 1945, explaining the reasons for his secret consecration:

'After the years of lying in obeyance, and the dispersal of the monks of Llanthony, We do regret the persecution which the late Fr Ignatius suffered at the hands of His own Churchmen, And the absence of ministerial necessities, denied by the Church of His Baptism. We do agree that this Consecration shall give a stand Apostolically to create and supply the spiritual ministrations for Ever. And at the present moment We desire that the name of the consecrator shall be held secret until such times we gather it is a seasonable moment to disclose Our action made this day.'

Just what is meant by this rigmarole (with its invariable use of a capital letter at each reference to himself or Fr Ignatius) is not clear. No matter: on August 2, 1942, Cope found reasons for raising to the episcopate (in the utmost secrecy) James York Batley, originally one of Bishop Herford's priests, and who acted as his Vicar-General for a time.[1]

'The Bishop of the Order of Llanthony Brothers'—a community which as yet existed only in his imagination—had certainly inherited Fr Ignatius's indifference to ecclesiastical jurisdiction. Nothing mattered so long as it was for 'JESUS ONLY'—the Llanthony war-cry or slogan. On June 18, 1944, Cope performed another secret consecration, when he laid his hands on John Syer, giving him the title of 'Bishop of Llanthony'. Why three bishops

[1] See p. 152.

should have been thought necessary for a non-existent flock is difficult to grasp. Neither is it easy to find reasons for Syer's consecration of Frank Ernest Langhelt as 'Bishop of Minster' on July 23, 1944.[1]

The episcopal brewery worker at Burton-on-Trent was absolutely convinced that he must found a community of some sort in the Vale of Ewyas, as close as possible to Llanthony. But as he had a wife and family to support, he could hardly desert them to become the actual founder of the brotherhood. Then one day he came across a man who showed what Father Ignatius would have held to be clear signs of a monastic vocation, and who appeared to be eager to dedicate his life, in the words of the Llanthony motto, to 'JESUS ONLY'. This was a certain William Albert Corke, who had received the four minor orders from Mar Georgius on November 18, 1947, but who had lost no time in persuading Mar Doreos, Bishop of Caerleon, of the Jesuene or Free Orthodox Catholic Church, to raise him to the priesthood.[2] Cope, always easy-going, had no scruples about promoting Corke to abbatial status, and never bothered about any sort of novitiate. Not satisfied with this, he consecrated him as bishop on January 1, 1948.[3]

The ceremony took place in a room at 'St David's', a bungalow at Capel-y-Ffin, just below Llanthony Abbey, which belonged to two nieces of Fr Ignatius—Hilda and Irene Ewens.[4] These kindhearted spinsters, who managed to combine Anglo-Catholic principles with membership of the Salvation Army, offered the use of their retreat to the embryo community until either a real Abbey could be built, or until Eric Gill's widow be prepared to sell Ignatius's monastery to the new Order.[5]

[1] As stated already, Minster Abbey, Kent, became the property of Roman Catholic Benedictine nuns from Eichstatt, Bavaria, in 1937.

Langhelt, as 'Presiding Bishop of the Old Catholic Church in England', was one of the five prelates who consecrated W. J. E. Jeffrey as titular Bishop of St Marylebone on May 20, 1945. (See p. 453.) For many years Langhelt was closely associated with Mar Georgius and the Catholicate of the West. Some years ago the former Bishop of Minster was reconciled with the Church of Rome.

[2] Subsequently Corke claimed to have received ordination to the priesthood in the Liberal Catholic Church. When applying for help to an Anglican Church society he produced 'Letters of Orders' signed by F. W. Pigott (Presiding Bishop of the L.C.C. from 1934 to his death in 1955). In the place for Deacon's orders was written "*in Eccl. Ang.*".

[3] On January 10, 1948, Bishop-Abbot Corke was one of the seven clerics (including three bishops and three priests) excommunicated by Mar Georgius for various alleged crimes and offences. (See p. 463, n. 2.)

[4] cf. A. Calder-Marshall, *The Enthusiast* (1962), p. 290.

[5] The Benedictines of Caldey, with the consent of Dom Asaph Harris, who was still the legal owner, had sold the Llanthony property to Eric Gill in 1924. The never completed abbey church was more or less a ruin by 1948.

Hopeful of attracting vocations, a prospectus was printed by 'The Order of Llanthony Brothers', containing the information that the 'Presiding Bishop' was 'The Right Rev. E. O. Cope (known as Ignatius, O.S.B.)'. Other dignitaries were 'The Assistant-Bishop, the Rt. Rev. J. Y. Batley; the Bishop-Abbot, the Rt. Rev. William Corke, O.S.B., and the Prior, the Very Rev. Charles Hastler, O.S.B.'[1]

The public were informed that the objects of the new Order were:

(1) To re-establish the Monastic Vocation, with the spirit of the former Llanthony Abbey, a Community of Men under the late Abbot Ignatius, O.S.B.; (2) To provide possibilities of study, prayer, and evangelistic priests and ordinands to the Ministry of the Church of Jesus Christ, with the Anglical [*sic*] and Catholic system.

There would be 'a Simple Rule of Life', and no great austerities. The Brothers would wear a picturesque costume consisting of 'a Black Sermon [*sic*] Cassock, a Hooded Scapular, and a Blue Girdle'. All Christian young men were given a cordial welcome, 'no matter to what denomination' they belonged. Like his beloved Fr Ignatius, the Rt. Rev. Bishop Cope, O.S.B., wanted to fraternize with Methodists, Baptists, Plymouth Brethren, Roman Catholics, the Salvation Army—in fact, any persons who could prove to him that they were 'saved'. But in emulation of the Universal Patriarch Banks of East Molesey, the Llanthony Brothers would give special preference to ex-Service men. Not only had the Presiding Bishop, who lived with his wife at Burton-on-Trent, founded a new religious community, he had also created (at least on paper) a new religious denomination, which he called 'The Free Anglo-Catholic Church'.[2] He guaranteed that its orders were genuine 'British Old Catholic'.

The Right Rev. William Corke, O.S.B., only managed to rule over his little community in the Black Mountains for three months. In April 1948 he was bound over for two years at the Old Bailey, having pleaded guilty to solemnizing marriages at a place other than a church or licensed chapel, and to performing an irregular

---

[1] Hastler was another of the seven clerics excommunicated by Mar Georgius on January 10, 1948. His alleged offences were 'a breach of agreement, and behaving schismatically, libel, etc.'.

[2] Not to be confused with the 'Free Catholic Church' founded in 1930. (See pp. 227–231.) It was in May 1949 that its founder, V. A. P. Hayman, Archbishop of Waltham, was sentenced to two years' imprisonment.

burial service. His 'Elevation', which was due to have taken place during Pontifical High Mass in the bungalow at Capel-y-Ffin on September 26 had to be postponed indefinitely.

Such was the end of the last attempt to revive monastic life at Llanthony. Yet it perpetuated the Ignatian tradition, as is disclosed in his Register, in which so many postulants and novices failed to persevere. Corke's next well-meant effort was to found a sect called 'The Orthodox Ecclesia'. Since 1958 he has been leading an almost eremitical life, with none of the worries which would have faced him had he remained Lord Abbot of Llanthony.[1]

'The Right Rev. Bishop Ignatius, O.S.B.', otherwise Ernest Odell Cope, must have been heart-broken that his well-meant effort to 'create and supply spiritual ministrations for Ever' to the Order of Llanthony Brothers proved a failure. After the death of his wife he lived with an adopted daughter at Burton-on-Trent, where he died on November 9, 1957. His episcopal adventure was not exactly a happy one.

(viii) *Old Roman Catholic Church* (*English Rite*)

This posthumous offspring of the Mathew family came into the world on September 22, 1950, the Feast of St Thomas of Villanova, after Fr Wilfrid Barrington-Evans and three other priests had repudiated the authority of Mgr Williams, Archbishop of Caer-Glow.[2] Today this handful of clergy and laity proclaim that their object is to 'preach the Faith in an English Manner' (in opposition to the alien manner propagated by the 'New' Roman Catholic Church). At the same time, however, they have insisted that of all the Churches in the world they are the nearest to Rome, and because of this, declined to enter into any sort of relations with any bodies calling themselves 'Old Catholic'.

The founder and his followers justified their schism by explaining in the first issue of *Onward!* (January, 1951) that this was felt to be 'the only way to preserve the Movement, and to make progress'. The public were informed that this new Church had been

---

[1] The Bishop-Abbot was released from gaol in August, 1963. Under the name of 'The Reverend Brother Rodney Lance Lynn-Walls', he immediately appealed all over Britain for £15,000 to enable him to found what he called 'Pope John's Rehabilitation Hostel for Ex-Borstal Boys and Ex-Young Prisoners' .He visualized this establishment as 'a sort of monastery for ex-convicts of all races and creeds', with himself as Abbot. An impressive photograph of Rev. Brother Rodney, robed in full pontifical vestments, mitre and all, was published in *The People* (September 22, 1963).

[2] See p. 336.

formally inaugurated four months previously, when a Declaration was signed, and a revised Constitution adopted. Fr Barrington-Evans, being the senior priest, was appointed Administrator. Under his jurisdiction were missions at West Drayton (Middlesex), Vauxhall, S.W. 11, Gillingham (Kent), Newton Abbot (Devonshire), and Birmingham. Their reasons for breaking away from the prelate whom they had hitherto regarded as the canonical successor of Mgr Mathew, first Regionary Old Catholic Bishop for Great Britain and Ireland, were summed up as follows:

'It cannot be denied that in renouncing membership of the Old Roman Catholic body to which they had formerly belonged, the first members of the Church have involved themselves in a schismatic act. But neither can it be denied that had they not acted as they did, the Old Roman Catholic Movement in England most likely would have come to an early end, and it seemed better to them to continue the work, at whatever cost, rather than to allow it to be extinguished. . . . They are confident, therefore, that, eventually the result of their work will outweigh the initial disadvantages of being separated from the main stream of the Movement, represented by Mgr Mary Bernard Williams, and will more than justify the means taken.'

The tone of the editorial in the April 1951 issue of the official organ of the new Church could not have been more hopeful of a glorious future, for it stated:

'Among the letters received was one from Father Carlo Miglioli, who was ordained by Mgr Mathew as long ago as 1915, and who with Mgr B. M. Williams, must be the only survivors of his clergy.[1] Fr Miglioli, now resident in Italy, not only sent us his greetings, but expressed great concern at the cleavage of the Movement, and makes a suggestion towards ending it. . . . Letters have reached us also from several other countries, notably from Holland, Austria, Germany, and Hungary. In three of these places we are now in friendly correspondence with the Bishops presiding over autocephalous Churches, and we are specially pleased to learn that in Holland, under the direction of Monsignor Tollenaar, Bishop of Arnhem, a Church with very similar aims to ourselves has been set up. We have always deplored the lapse into heresy of the Church of Utrecht, and it is very consoling to know

---

[1] Miglioli, having failed to find a Catholic bishop on the Continent to raise him to the priesthood, came to England, where he joined Mathew's Old Catholic Church. Later on he went to the U.S.A., and threw in his lot with Carfora's Old Roman Catholic Church. (See pp. 434, 435.)

that a move is on foot to bring some at least of the people of the Netherlands back to the true Faith, and the One Fold, through the organization of a Uniate Church. In Hungary, Archbishop Fehervary, of the Old Catholic Church, has given a warm welcome to us, and friendly relations between the respective Churches are fast being established.'

Where ignorance is bliss, 'tis folly to be wise. Perhaps it was a good thing that the newly appointed Administrator of the schismatic branch of the Old Roman Catholic Church in England had not taken the trouble to study the nature and origins of some of these autocephalous Churches on the Continent with which such friendly relations were being formed. For instance, Archbishop Fehervary and his followers in Hungary were not only in schism from the Old Catholic Churches, but were associated with the extremely heretical Mariavites in Poland. Fehervary himself had been raised to the episcopate by Prochiewski, who was one of Michael Kowalski's hierarchy, which included several female bishops.[1]

Again, it is somewhat doubtful if Mgr Tollenaar was trying to bring back the Dutch Old Catholics into communion with the Holy See, granted that he had vague ecumenical visions. In his earlier days he had been a priest of the Liberal Catholic Church. Apparently having rejected Theosophy, and broken away from this church of the Mathew succession, he formed a small sect of his own at Arnhem. About 1942 he got into touch with the Swiss Society of Deacons (*Schweizerische Diakonierverein*), which had started a mission at Opende in Friesland. Two or three Brothers were trying to link up Christians of all denominations (except Roman Catholics) and enrol them in the Lutheran Brotherhood of the Common Life at Rüschlikon in Switzerland, directed by Bishop Gothilf Haug.[2] In 1946 Tollenaar was re-ordained in France by Mgr Giraud, the ex-Trappist monk, who, as Primate of the *Église catholique française*, was trying to revive Gnosticism, and who had made a name for himself as an occultist and faith healer, being regarded as an authority on magic. On his return to Arnhem, Tollenaar assumed the title of Apostolic Vicar of the Netherlands. Feeling that he was called to the episcopate, and unable to find any prelate on the Continent to consecrate him, he decided that he

---

[1] See p. 518.

[2] Haug had been raised to the episcopate some time in 1930 by Mgr Giraud, the neo-Gnostic Patriarch of the Gallican Church (*Église catholique française*), who styled himself Archbishop of Almyra. (See pp. 306–310.)

might do worse than make use of Charles Saul, the ex-Mar Leofric, Archbishop of Suthronia (Catholicate of the West), now head of the English Episcopal Church.[1] So this obliging Bishop travelled from Acton to Arnhem, where, on January 8, 1950, in the Kapel van Onze Lievre Vroue, he laid hands on Tollenaar. Considering his otherwise militant Protestantism, it is surprising that he felt able to interpolate certain ceremonies from the Roman Rite into the 1662 Prayer Book Form of Consecrating a Bishop. The new prelate gave himself the title of 'Old Roman Catholic Bishop of Arnhem'.[2] Neither he nor his few followers were recognized by the Church of Utrecht, or by the Liberal Catholic Church in the Netherlands. They were merely a little sect of Theosophical, Lutheran, French Gnostic, and English Evangelical origins, with their Bishop in the Protestant Chechemian line of succession.[3] His Pro-Cathedral was an attic in his house, said to be rather stuffy, owing to a generous use of incense. It was reported that the congregation sometimes consisted of Mrs Tollenaar, but this may have been malicious gossip on the part of the genuine Old Catholics in Arnhem.

The clergy of the new dissident body, having elected Fr Barrington-Evans as their first bishop, had to find a prelate to consecrate him, and this was not easy, in spite of so many autocephalous Continental Churches now being in friendly relationship.[4] An offer, however, came from Bishop Radavan Jost, one of the hierarchy of Marko Kalogjera's schismatic Old Catholic Church in Yugoslavia, founded in 1933.[5] The bishop-elect may not have felt it worth while to investigate the antecedents of this liberal-minded prelate far away beyond the Adriatic, but, having decided to accept

---

[1] See pp. 232–234.

[2] No doubt he felt he had received many valuable lines of succession, because they had been imparted to Saul by Mar Georgius, when on September 9, 1945, he reconsecrated him as Leofric Archbishop of Suthronia in the Catholicate of the West, from which he broke away in 1947, having cast off all his Patriarchate of Glastonbury trimmings. (See p. 234.)

[3] See p. 234.

[4] It would appear that this schismatic branch of the O.R.C.C., remembering no doubt that the founder, A. H. Mathew, had a wife and three children at the time of his consecration in 1908, had decided not to enforce celibacy on its bishops. So there existed no canonical objection to a married priest being raised to the episcopate, although this would have been impossible in any Church in communion with the Holy See or in any of the Eastern Churches not in communion with Rome, except on the condition that the bishop (if married) lived apart from his wife.

[5] Kalogjera had been denounced at the Old Catholic Bishops' Conference at Munich in 1933, because he allowed divorced persons to remarry, for a fee, and have their marriages declared null. He consecrated Radavan Jost on December 21, 1947. (See p. 537.)

his offer, arranged to make the long journey with his domestic chaplain. It was a bitter blow when, at the last moment, the Yugoslav Embassy in London refused to give them visas.

An SOS was dispatched to Holland, and Bishop Tollenaar replied that he would be delighted to provide the schismatic Old Roman Catholics with a primate. He came to England, and on August 5, 1951, consecrated Fr Barrington-Evans at Iver, Bucks. The new prelate, enriched with the Syrian-Antiochene, Armenian-Uniate, Order of Corporate Reunion, Old Catholic, Syrian-Malabar, Chaldean-Uniate, Syro-Chaldean, Roman Catholic, Old Catholic (Senior Line), Syrian-Gallican, Anglican, Nonjuring, Irvingite and other lines of apostolic succession, believed to have been obtained from Tollenaar by way of Saul, and Mar Georgius (Patriarch of Glastonbury and Prince-Catholicos of the West), assumed the title of Bishop of Verulam and started to organize his followers.

Mgr Williams was horrified when the news reached him a few days later, and wrote: 'I have no idea who Tollenaar may be, or anything of his claims to be a bishop, but if they were real, and would stand inspection, I have no doubt that we should have been loudly informed of them.'[1] A few days later he wrote:

'These "bishops" increase like plague germs, so that it is impossible to keep up sides with them. . . . Some of them, hitherto unheard of by me, have *quite privately* written to me expressing sympathy, and informing me of their refusal to act. From this I judge that the person who in the end did act must be someone of particularly poor standing. In the notice of the "consecration" issued by Mr Evans, giving particulars of the times of the various functions, the name of the "consecrator" is not mentioned. I thought this rather significant.'[2]

All that the Archbishop of Caer-Glow could do was to insist that the new schismatic body was renamed 'The Old Roman Catholic Church (English Rite)'. Five months before his consecration Barrington-Evans had approached his former Metropolitan, hoping that he would reconsider his attitude about 'closing down' the Pro-Uniate Rite, but in vain. After the latter's death in June 1952,

---

[1] The source of this episcopate was definitely neither Old Catholic nor Old Roman Catholic, for Tollenaar could trace his line of succession no further back than Stevens and Richardson, who in 1890 appear to have laid their hands on the lapsed Uniate Armenian *vartapet*, Chechemian, who shortly afterwards became one of the co-founders of the Free Protestant Episcopal Church of England. (See pp. 217–224.)

[2] Letters to the Rev. W. H. de Voil.

the way was made clear to go ahead with the conversion of England to Old Roman Catholicism by means of vernacular liturgy.

Everything looked most hopeful. Two or three quasi-Franciscan Tertiaries were a proof that the new Church already had members prepared to lead a life of Holy Poverty.[1] Their leader was a certain Fr Anselm Harris, a convert from the Latin rite. It was said that he had already tested his religious vocation with both the Canons Regular of the Lateran and the Capuchin Friars Minor. Garbed in brown habits, these twentieth-century *fratacelli* preached in the Bull Ring at Birmingham, and appear to have extended their apostolate to holiday resorts on the South Coast. Mgr Masterson, the 'New' Roman Catholic Archbishop of Birmingham, grew alarmed, and felt it his duty to issue a warning against proselytism by men who might be mistaken for the Capuchins from Olton. He gave orders that it was to be read in all churches of his diocese. Unfortunately Fr Anselm had to be suspended for a while by the Bishop of Verulam, but he was soon restored to favour.

Several more priests were ordained, but two or three of them, however, were unable to resist the temptation to submit to either Rome or Canterbury. One of them even sought preferment in the Church of Scotland, but having been turned down by both the General Assembly and a Presbytery, returned like a lost sheep to the fold of Verulam. Another did worse in the opinion of the Bishop of Verulam, for he transferred his allegiance to Mgr Shelley, Archbishop of Caer-Glow, whose followers, according to Mgr Barrington-Evans, are 'not the Old Roman Catholic Church at all, but a group of people who persist in using our name though any connection with the Church is of the slightest. In fact, of course, they are connected with the heretical and excommunicated North American Old Roman Catholic Church headed by Richard Marchenna of New York, a body with which we are not and have no desire to be associated'.[2]

In the autumn of 1955 the Bishop of Verulam and two of his priests went to Germany, in the hope of effecting a merger between the Old Roman Catholic Church (English Rite) and the microscopic sects ruled over by Mgr Tollenaar of Arnhem and Mgr Labs of Dusseldorf, but nothing came of this project.[3] Still there was no

---

[1] No autocephalous Church on the Continent could claim any religious orders or congregations, except the Polish Mariavites.

[2] *Onward!* (May 1962), p. 4. For Marchenna, see pp. 434–436.

[3] It appears that Labs was originally raised to the episcopate by Schonbroodt (see p. 483), and then linked up with Nicholson's Ancient Catholic Church.

reason to be downhearted: the Bishop was able to boast of seven parishes and Mass centres in England. Once £200 had been raised; he planned to open a Franciscan Friary and a House of Studies for ordination candidates.

The most active parish at this time was that of the Sacred Heart of Jesus, at Westbourne Park, London, W.11, where, so the Bishop stated, many West Indians were living, and quite a number of lapsed Irish Catholics. Here was 'a vast field of work', but the clergy were fully occupied with their own parishes or missions elsewhere, so His Lordship had no choice but to act as rector for the time being.

In September 1956, at the invitation of his friend and spiritual adviser, Abbot Wilfrid Upson, the Bishop of Verulam took part in the community retreat at Prinknash Abbey. The result of a week's prayer and meditation was a generous decision to offer the services of himself and his priests to the Holy See. A petition was drawn up, which Mgr O'Hara, Apostolic Delegate to Great Britain, forwarded to the Congregation of the Holy Office. It contained the words:

'We wish to state that the following suggestions are made in all humility, and with the desire, not to obtain any advantage for ourselves, but because we believe that they will be of benefit to the Church and our fellow countrymen. If in his wisdom, the Holy Father rejects these proposals, our plea that we should be reconciled with him still stands, and we will gladly accept integration to the Latin Rite here, for we do not feel that we can do any further good by remaining in our present state of separation. But we would humbly and sincerely ask that His Holiness will graciously accept us as we are, that is as Priests of the Holy Catholic Church, and be pleased to allow us to continue our priestly labours in some way.'

In preparation for the integration of the 'New' and the Old Roman Catholic Churches, the Pro-Cathedral at Westbourne Park was closed. In May 1957 the Bishop wrote:

'We have entered upon a period of waiting, during which it is not advisable for us to attempt anything more than keep things going on a reduced scale; in the meantime preserving silence on the future prospects of our Rite, which, of course, depend almost entirely now on the goodwill of the Holy Father.'[1]

It should be explained that 'our Rite' then consisted of six priests and eighteen layfolk, of whom four were the wives of priests, and

[1] *Onward!* (April May, 1957).

seven their children, including the Metropolitan's own offspring. In spite of this total membership of twenty-four males and females being an almost invisible grain of sand amid the estimated Catholic population of 3,401,276 of England and Wales at that date, Mgr Barrington-Evans seems to have believed that it would be greatly to the advantage of the Roman Church were he to be granted the status of head of a handful of the faithful in communion with the Holy See, whose priests would celebrate Mass in English instead of in Latin, and who would not be obliged to observe celibacy. His position would be more or less the same as that of the Bishop-Auxiliary for Ukrainians in England and Wales, with the Cardinal Archbishop of Westminster as his Exarch; or that of the episcopal Vicar Delegate of the Polish priests serving in Great Britain.

So it was a bitter disappointment to the Bishop of Verulam and his six priests that the Congregation of the Holy Office decided it would not benefit the Western Patriarchate to be integrated with the Old Roman Catholic Church (English Rite). They had hoped that Pius XII would agree to accept them as they were, and allow them to continue their ministrations under the immediate jurisdiction of the Catholic hierarchy of England and Wales. Not only did the Holy Office shelve the petition, even worse, the Pope ignored all letters addressed to him by the Bishop of Verulam.

The doors of the Vatican having been slammed in his face, His Lordship saw clearly that nothing more could be done meantime, and raised himself to the rank of Archbishop *ad personam*, though not yet having any suffragan bishops under his jurisdiction. A new Constitution for the Church was drawn up, which, so it was hoped, would be approved by the Holy See sooner or later. The position of the clergy and laity of this minute would-be Uniate body was thus summed up by its Metropolitan in the August 1961 issue of *Onward!*:

'We should like to make it clear that our policy . . . is the same as that of Mgr Williams, who declined to enter into any sort of relations with any of those [Old Catholic] bodies. We are poles apart, our history, our aims, and above all our Faith, are very different, and it is not thought that any good could be expected from contacts with them. The only body which we have any desire to be united with is our Holy Mother the Church of Rome, and that we shall strive for. Until the day comes when our desire is fulfilled we are content to go on as we are—alone, friendless, persecuted. We neither recognize nor seek recognition from any Bishop save that of our Holy Father the Pope.'

Mgr Barrington-Evans had travelled a long way on the road to Rome in ten years. In April 1951 he was so proud of the 'friendly relations' which had been established between his newly founded schismatic sect and 'the Bishops presiding over autocephalous Churches in Holland, Austria, Germany, and Hungary', some of whom were heretical, and all bitterly opposed to the Church of Rome.[1] At that date he was eager to have closer contacts with these anti-papal prelates. The pendulum had swung round very quickly.

In 1961 Archbishop and Mrs Barrington-Evans moved from Iver, Bucks, to a half-timbered residence in Hurst Road, which was renamed 'Bishop's Lodge'. Still employed as a bank official on weekdays, in addition to three or four priests in England, he also had under his jurisdiction a mission-priest in Scotland. It was stated that he was laying the foundations of the Church's first parish over the Border well and truly. Unfortunately this cleric, who throughout his life has always been a spiritual pilgrim, repudiated the authority of the English Metropolitan in the summer of 1962, and was granted the rank of Canon in another schismatic body claiming the Mathew succession.

So far the Old Roman Catholic Church (English Rite) has not been able to build a cathedral, rivalling either Coventry or Guildford, let alone fulfilling Archbishop Mathew's dream of erecting in London a granite replica of the Votivkirche in Vienna.[2] Its less than half a dozen places of worship are rooms in private houses, which (as is pointed out) 'whilst quite in accord with the practice of the Early Church, means that we are unable to advertise our Services and invite all and sundry to them'.[3] The Archbishop's Domestic Chapel of St Aidan at Twyford, Berks, has to make do as a pro-cathedral; and is also the focus of a parish of Our Lady of Ransom and St Andrew, which it is hoped to form at Reading sooner or later.

In spite of the fact that this otherwise aggressively papalist autocephalous church has never enforced celibacy on its deacons, priests and bishops, thus casting overboard the ruling of the Council of Trent and earlier legislation, it has not gained many adherents since its foundation in 1950. Even today it has no more

---

[1] See p. 399.
[2] See p. 193.
[3] *The Diocesan Chronicle* (December 1962).

than half a dozen priests in Britain, and it is virtually unknown to the general public. Until fairly recently its members seemed rather proud of their exclusive isolation.

More recent events, however, suggest that the Archbishop of Verulam has been moderating his hitherto intransigent papalism, since he attained the status of Supreme Pontiff of an International Church. On February 2, 1963, His Grace assumed jurisdiction over an American Province, consisting of ten small parishes in the States of Illinois, Indiana and Wisconsin, thus adding another 554 persons to his flock. Apparently without reference to either Mgr Egidio Vagnozzi, Apostolic Delegate to the United States, or to Cardinal Meyer, Archbishop of Chicago, Bishop Robert Burns, who had broken off relations with Archbishop Marchenna of the Canonical Old Roman Catholic Church, was given the title of Archbishop of Chicago and the rank of Metropolitan.[1] It is expected that before long Mgr Barrington-Evans will extend his supreme primatial jurisdiction over California and Texas, because in both States there are prelates seeking communion with Verulam.

There are signs that the Old Roman Catholic Church (English Rite) is fast becoming more ecumenical in its outlook than was the case a few years ago when the Metropolitan refused to enter into any sort of relation with any non-papal autocephalous church. For instance, on December 9, 1962, its Lay Secretary had his infant daughter baptized by the Vicar of the Anglican parish in which he resided, and in the presence of his O.R.C. Mission Rector. Not long after this a party of clergy and lay helpers took part in the opening Rally of the 'Croydon for Christ Campaign'. On March 17, 1963, His Grace of Verulam dedicated St Bonaventure's Chapel, situated in what used to be the booking hall of Crystal Palace Station. Assisting at the pontifical Mass were the Chairman of the Penge Urban District Council and the Mayor and Mayoress of Lambeth. Two months later, Mar Gulielmus (W. Turner), Primate of the Church and Order of Christian Unity, preached at the Crystal Palace on the occasion of the Annual Festival of the Confraternity of St Pancras for English Rite acolytes. Attended by his Chaplain, Fr Matthew of Mitcham, robed as an archimandrite, His Grace blessed the congregation with Lourdes water. On the Feast of SS Cyril and Methodius, July 7, 1963, this same prelate, who is also one of the fifteen bishops of many nations forming the Sacred Synod of the Catholic Apostolic Primitive Orthodox Church

[1] See p. 340.

of Antioch of the Syro-Byzantine Tradition, welcomed the interdenominational Confraternity of the Precious Blood at the Chapel of St Stephen, 8 Armadale Road, Fulham, for their Annual Festival. This is indeed an interesting alliance, indicating that Mgr Barrington-Evans (who is Warden of the Confraternity) is now more catholic in outlook than he was in 1957–8, when the only prelates in the world he would consort with were those in communion with Pope Pius XII.

The O.R.C.C. (English Rite) is quite active in the Anglican and Catholic Dioceses of Southwark. In addition to St Bonaventure's Chapel at the Crystal Palace, S.E.19, there are oratories dedicated to St Benedict at 4 Windermere Road, S.W.16, and to St Philip Neri at 110 Auckland Road, S.E.19. Within the boundaries of the Anglican Diocese of Chelmsford and the Catholic Diocese of Brentwood is the Chapel of St Camillus of Lellis at 35 Chingford Road, E.17. On the other hand, the presentation of the Faith in an English manner in the Oratory located at Edgbaston, Birmingham, does not appear to have proved so attractive so far as the activities of the near-by Oratory Church of the Immaculate Conception, where public worship is conducted in Latin and with an Italianate setting.

Among other recent spiritual and social activities which have been reported are: a Guy Fawkes night bonfire for the boy acolytes at the Crystal Palace; a football match; a Quiet Day conducted by the Primate; a visit to the Zoo on the Sunday after the Feast of St Willibrord; open-air preaching on Streatham Common; public lectures at Lambeth Town Hall; a Pentecostal pilgrimage to the grave of Archbishop Mathew at South Mymms; and the formation of an Old Roman Catholic Cemetery Company Limited.[1]

OVERSEAS CHURCHES OF THE MATHEW SUCCESSION

(ix) *Église catholique évangélique*

This dissident French body can be included as one of 'Lord Landaff's' spiritual grandchildren, because its founder was raised to the episcopate by a bishop of his succession.

Louis Charles Winnaert was born at Dunkirk in 1880. Having completed his studies at the Catholic University of Lille, he was

---

[1] Publicity was given to the Archbishop and his clergy by *The People* (October 28 and December 1, 1963). The two articles were entitled: 'How dare these two men run a boys' club?', and 'Four out of seven are jailbirds'.

ordained priest in 1905. After his appointment as *vicaire* at Aniche, he devoted himself enthusiastically to the various activities then carried on by Marc Sangier's organization known as '*Le Sillon*' (the Furrow). He gradually found himself drawn more and more towards the *mystique* of Modernism, under the influence of Tyrrell, von Hügel, and Laberthonnière. The decrees against Modernism, culminating in Pius X's *moto proprio* of 1910, imposing on all clerics an anti-Modernist oath, finally drove Winnaert out of the Roman Church in 1916. Some of his disciples followed his example He was one of those men whose temperament rebels instinctively against any form of 'red tape'.

Dr Bury, then Bishop of the Anglican Diocese of Northern and Central Europe, feeling sorry for this obviously sincere suspended priest, about whom there was not a breath of scandal, allowed him to celebrate Mass in the Church of St George, rue Auguste Vacquerie, Paris. It has been said that Winnaert toyed with the idea of joining the Church of England. Then he got in touch with the Dutch Old Catholics, and for a time, officiated at both St George's and the Old Catholic church in the Boulevard Blaqui, Paris. He had now drifted further into Modernism, and appears to have held no definite religious opinions. Eventually he opened an independent place of worship in the Rue de Sèvres, where he expounded his own elusive version of Catholicism.

His little flock, rather like the congregation of the King's Weigh House, London, under Dr Orchard, was extremely eclectic.[1] Some of them were Theosophists, and through them Winnaert first heard of the Liberal Catholic Church. In that *naïveté*, which was typical of him throughout his life, he presumed that it was merely an English branch of the Old Catholic Church in communion with Utrecht.

Having read some of its literature, he felt that here was a Church that would suit him—Catholic yet liberal, and profoundly spiritual. Not realizing the full implications of Theosophy, he went to London, where Bishop Wedgwood, then Presiding Bishop of the Liberal Catholic Church, raised him to the episcopate. But Winnaert was never regarded as one of the hierarchy of this body. Having secured the Mathew succession, he gave to his followers the name of *Église catholique libre*, in emulation of the now international Theosophical body. After a year or two he broke off all relations with the Liberal Catholics and renamed his sect the *Église catholique*

[1] See p. 145.

évangélique. By 1930 it consisted of small groups in Paris, Rouen, Brussels, Arnhem (Holland), and even in Rome.

During the nineteen-twenties this priest who had broken from the unity of the Church did his best to bring about reunion. At Pentecost he used to organize interdenominational conferences. At one of these gatherings he managed to collect a very mixed bag, which included Mgr Kibarian, Archbishop of the Armenian Church; Metropolitan Eulogius of the Russian Orthodox Church; Hieromonk Lev Gillet; Archimandrite Gerasimos Goulan; Pastor Marc Boegner (President of the French Protestant Federation); and Louis Appia, who represented the Lutherans in Paris.

In some ways Winnaert had much in common with Vernon Herford. He was another impractical visionary, full of admirable intentions for the benefit of mankind, believing, like Herford, that he had at last found the way to reunite all the broken fragments of Christendom.[1]

But he was not satisfied with his isolated status as the head of a small French schismatic body, in communion with none of the historic churches. Fifteen years after he had ceased to be a priest of the Latin rite, he consulted the Metropolitan Eulogius (Georgievsky) about the possibilities of being received into the Orthodox Church. Approaches were made on his behalf to the Oecumenical Patriarch, who, after a long delay, replied to the effect that Winnaert and his flock could be received into Orthodoxy only on the acceptance of the Byzantine rite and the Julian Kalendar. Like Overbeck in the eighteen-seventies, Winnaert felt that it was possible to become Eastern without ceasing to be Western. He wanted to join the Eastern Church and at the same time revive the Western.[2] Unwilling to accept the conditions imposed, he appealed to the Metropolitan Sergius (Starogrodsky), the *locum tenens* of the Patriarchate of Moscow, who proved more understanding. It almost looked as if Overbeck's dream of a Western Orthodox Catholic Church was going to materialize after nearly seventy years.

By a decree of June 16, 1936, the Metropolitan Sergius agreed to admit the *Église catholique évangélique* into communion with the Patriarchate of Moscow. But Winnaert's episcopate was not

---

[1] Père Gard, who was one of Winnaert's priests, formed in 1937 'La Ligue Internationale pour l'Unité des Chrétiens', out of which evolved Julien Erni's 'Ligue oecuménique pour l'Unité Chrétienne'. (cf. J. Erni, *Je Crois la Sainte Église Universelle* (n.d.), pp. 44–45.)
[2] See p. 149.

accepted, not because of its doubtful validity, but because of his *naïveté* which had led him to take a wife after ordination. Here again he found himself in the same unfortunate position as Overbeck, but Winnaert had better luck; he was allowed to exercise his priesthood, though refused the status of a bishop. After being received into communion with Moscow on December 26, 1936, he was given the rank of hieromonk in January the following year. Having taken the religious name of Irenée, he was blessed as archimandrite.

The founder of the *Église catholique évangélique* was now so frail that he had to be carried to the throne of his chapel on February 7, 1937, so that he could assist at the reception of his flock into union with the Russian Orthodox Church. He died on March 3, and was buried by the Metropolitan Eleutherius of Lithuania, Exarch for Western Europe, who was deputed to this task by the Metropolitan Sergius.

While he was still head of his little schismatic body, Winnaert consecrated two bishops for the National Church of Czechoslovakia—Dr Proharska (Patriarch-elect), and Dr Stejikal (Bishop of Olomuc, and Secretary of the Czech National Synod). Hitherto this National Church had been Presbyterian in polity and methods of ordination. Winnaert insisted that both bishops should ordain on episcopal lines, but public opinion proved too strong. Before long they had to revert to the custom of the laity joining in the laying on of hands.[1]

Lucien Chambault succeeded Winnaert as administrator of this curious autocephalous church eventually linked up with the Patriarchate of Moscow. By this time it consisted of three groups in Paris. In one of them the Roman rite was celebrated in French with certain modifications; in another a revised form of the liturgy of the *Église catholique évangélique*; there was a third group following the Oriental Rite, for Chambault's ideals were more Eastern than Western. He had studied monastic life in Paris under the Archimandrite Athanasius, and eventually he founded a small quasi-Benedictine monastery at 26 rue d'Allcray, Paris, 15e, dedicated to St Denis and St Seraphim of Sarof. Taking the religious name of Denis, he made his monastic profession on March 5, 1944. For some reason or other this hybrid form of monasticism made little appeal to young Frenchmen. For several years the

---

[1] cf. letter from A. Frank-Duquesne (a former priest of the *Église catholique évangélique*) in *The Church Times*, September 9, 1949.

community consisted of two monks; Père Denis, whose charismatic gifts as a healer were much sought after, and an Englishman who eventually found his way into communion with Moscow after two interludes with Canterbury and one with Rome. The latter has since joined a small community of Russian monks in France, and at the time of writing, the former leads a more or less solitary life in the Parisian *Kathismata*. Loosely associated with Winnaert's Church after 1947 was a quasi-Benedictine brotherhood on the Isle of Jersey, whose founder, Frère Timothée, had two or three young men living with him on his own property, where he fitted up one of the rooms as a private oratory. He had been professed as a monk and ordained priest at the Paris monastery. He was drowned in 1957, and this was the end of what was always a somewhat unconventional fraternity.

One of the attractions of this tiny Occidental-Oriental autocephalous church is that its priests (following the practice of a growing number of Latin priests with due authority) are allowed to celebrate the Eucharist with either Eastern or Western rites, but the vestments proper to each must be worn.[1] This French schismatic church does not appear to have progressed much since it was linked up with the Patriarchate of Moscow in 1937.

The Mathew succession was first transplanted to North America by Mgr Bacon, titular Bishop of Durham, who retired to Canada shortly before the Theosophists managed to gain control of the Old Roman Catholic Church in England. On December 2, 1914, without the knowledge of Archbishop Mathew, whose jurisdiction he had repudiated, he consecrated Thomas J. Bensley. Some time in 1915 the latter prelate raised Arthur W. Henzell, one of Mathew's priests, to the episcopate.[2] The Mathew succession was passed on by Henzell to Walter P. Crossman, whom he consecrated on March 1, 1946.[3]

The real founder of the trans-Atlantic Old Roman Catholic Church, and its schismatic groups, was Prince-Bishop de Landas

---

[1] In this respect there is greater rigidity than that observed by Mar Jacobus, Bishop of Mercia and Middlesex, whose custom it was to celebrate the fourth-century Egyptian Liturgy of St Serapion, wearing either a paenula (which is fondly believed to be the old Roman shape) or a chasuble of Gothic Revival cut. (See p. 151.)

[2] Later on Henzell joined the Protestant Episcopal Church, was re-ordained in the Diocese of Pennsylvania, and died in 1946. Bensley also ended his career as an Episcopalian pastor, and died in 1944.

[3] Crossman, formerly a priest of the Episcopal Church, is said to have become the founder of a sect known as 'The Independent Episcopal Church in the United States and Canada'.

Churches of the Mathew Succession

Berges et de Rache, who, as related in chapter six, fled from England in the autumn of 1914 to escape arrest and probable internment as an enemy-alien after the outbreak of the First World War.[1] It has usually been stated that the Prince promised 'Lord Landaff' that he would not perform any episcopal functions so long as he was obliged to remain in the United States, but there appears to be no proof that he actually made this promise.[2] Before de Landas was reconciled with the Roman Church in 1919 he consecrated two bishops who passed on the Mathew succession in two distinct lines, and in independent churches, both of which produced schisms.

(x) *The Old Catholic Church in America; known later as The Catholic Church of North America, and The Orthodox Old Catholic Church in America*

The founder of this variously named body, the remnant of which was received into union with the Exarchate of the Russian Orthodox Catholic Church in America on April 6, 1962, has had a long and adventurous career, during which he has run after many a will o' the wisp, and been lured by more than one *fata morgana*. He started life as William Henry Francis, but added his mother's name of Brothers later on. It has been said that he was brought up in England as a Roman Catholic, and that his parents took him to North America at an early age. They settled at Waukegan on Lake Michigan, a busy industrial centre forty miles north of Chicago.

William seems to have heard the call of the cloister at an early age. There were many monasteries waiting to welcome him, including the twenty or more flourishing abbeys and priories of the American-Cassinese and the Swiss-American Benedictine Congregations, and three Trappist communities, if the observances of the former were not strict enough for him. Within a few hours' journey of his home-town were two Benedictine houses: St Procopius Abbey, Chicago, founded in 1885; and St Peter's Priory, also in the State of Illinois, but which was transferred to Saskatchewan in 1930. Did he, even more than half a century ago, dream of becoming the Abbot-General of a Benedictine Congregation not in communion with the Holy See, subject to no bothersome higher superior? Had he been prepared to become an Anglican monk, he could have thrown in his lot with Dom Aelred Carlyle, Lord Abbot

[1] See p. 194.
[2] On January 12, 1915, de Landas was a co-consecrator of Dr Hiram R. Hulse, as Bishop of Cuba, a Missionary District of the Protestant Episcopal Church in the U.S.A. Had Mathew known of this, he would have probably excommunicated him forthwith.

of Painsthorpe, who in the late autumn of 1904 arrived in the Middle West of the United States, with a view to the foundation of a Benedictine community in Wisconsin. During this six weeks' tour, when the Abbot and his companion stopped at twenty-seven places, they got widespread publicity. Their shaven heads, tonsures, and romantic black and white monastic motley, were a splendid advertisment for the strictly enclosed and purely contemplative life. It is probable that they passed through Waukegan on their way from Chicago to Fond du Lac by way of Milwaukee. With the permission of Dr Maclagan, Archbishop of York, Bishop Grafton ordained the Abbot deacon on November 12, 1904, and three days later raised him to the priesthood at Ripon, Wisconsin.[1]

On his return to England, in the canonical state of a 'Clergyman in Colonial Orders', Abbot Aelred's visions of an American foundation grew brighter. He saw 'every possibility of two or three postulants' arriving at his Yorkshire abbey to be trained in the purely contemplative life. A few aspirants from the U.S.A. did find their way to Painsthorpe, but none of them persevered, and William H. F. Brothers was not among them. He had already decided to form his own community at Waukegan, and the influence stemmed mainly from Dom Augustine de Angelis, at one time a Benedictine monk of the Cassinese Congregation of the Primitive Observance, who had thrown off the yoke of Rome, and who was a close friend of the Old Catholic, Mgr J. F. Tichy, of whom more later on.

None of the original members of this brotherhood established in 1908 were Protestant Episcopalians, save a Brother Cyril. The founder took the religious name of Francis and acted as Prior. As indicated by a photograph, he clothed the brethren in the black and white Cistercian habit adopted by Aelred Carlyle for his community in 1899.[2] Towards the end of the same year the Waukegan fraternity received into its fold the Rev. Herbert Parrish. This Episcopalian clergyman had developed monastic ideals after he became rector of the Church of the Advent, San Francisco, in 1898. Having tested his vocation with The Companions of the Holy Saviour at Philadelphia, he founded in 1906 a brotherhood on Benedictine lines with the blessing of Bishop Grafton. This more or less ruled out Abbot Aelred Carlyle's projected American foundation, about which the latter had quite forgotten. The amalgamated

---

[1] cf. P. F. Anson, *Abbot Extraordinary* (1958), pp. 85–86.
[2] ibid., p. 63.

brotherhood, consisting of five members, moved from Waukegan to Fond du Lac in 1909, where Bishop Grafton gave them a large ramshackle building as a home, which was renamed 'St Dunstan's Abbey'. Some time after this he had this Old Catholic community legally incorporated as 'The American Congregation of the Order of St Benedict'.[1] Fr Parrish soon realized he had no vocation for this sort of Benedictine life, left Fond du Lac, and eventually became a very Broad Church pastor in New Jersey. Bishop Grafton appointed himself non-resident Abbot of the community, and Dom Francis continued as Prior.

Ever since Antoni Stanislas Kozlowski, who was an assistant priest at St Jadwiga's Polish Roman Catholic Church in Chicago, had formed a schismatic congregation in January 1895. Bishop Grafton had been trying to achieve intercommunion between the Protestant Episcopal Church and the widely scattered groups of Polish Old Catholics in the United States. On November 13, 1897, Kozlowski was raised to the episcopate at Berne by Bishop Herzog, with Archbishop Gul of Utrecht and Bishop Weber of Bonn as co-consecrators. On his return to North America he was welcomed at Fond du Lac, and made much of by its Bishop.[2] Kozlowski called his loosely organized flock 'The Polish Old Catholic Church'. In 1904 he attended the Old Catholic Synod at Olten, Switzerland, accompanied by a priest named Jan Francis Tichy, where the latter was nominated his Vicar-General, apparently with the full approval of Mgr Gul, Archbishop of Utrecht.[3] Some time after this Kozlowski introduced Tichy as Bishop at the annual Old Catholic Convention in Chicago.[4] The former's death on January 14, 1907, upset Grafton's hopes of an eventual union between the Episcopalians and the Polish Old Catholics, because most of the latter, starting with those in the Chicago area, decided to link up with the congregations of the Polish National Catholic Church, of which Francis Hodur was elected the first Bishop on August 7 that same year. The Old Catholic hierarchy in Europe did not see their way to confirm Tichy as Kozlowski's successor; and on September 29,

[1] In 1905 Abbot Aelred had given his little community the title of 'The English Congregation of the Strict Observance of the Holy Rule of St Benedict', but, unlike Bishop Grafton, did not have it constituted by either civil or ecclesiastical procedure.
[2] cf. C. C. Grafton, *A Journey Godward* (Milwaukee, 1910), especially chapter XIII.
[3] cf. *Report of the Anglican and Foreign Churches Society* (1905), p. 43; also *The Orthodox Catholic Review* (March 1927), pp. 116–17.
[4] Letter from the Rev. Dom Horton, O.S.B., to the Rev. W. H. de Voil, August 22, 1936.

in St Gertrude's Church, Utrecht, Hodur was raised to the episcopate by Mgr Gul, assisted by the Bishops of Haarlem and Deventer.[1]

Mgr Tichy now found himself the lonely leader of a small group of Polish Old Catholics who had not accepted Bishop Hodur's authority, and he was still supported by Bishop Grafton. It has been stated that Grafton sent several men to Tichy for ordination to the priesthood; that Bishop Weller (Grafton's coadjutor and successor) knew of this, because he, too, was a friend of Tichy.[2] The result was that on October 3, 1911, 'The American Congregation of the Order of St Benedict' at Fond du Lac was formally received into union with Tichy's group of Old Catholics. Its few members retained possession of St Dunstan's Abbey, with Bishop Grafton as non-resident Titular Abbot. So eager was the Bishop to attract postulants that he wrote a small booklet entitled *A Commentary on the Rule of the Benedictine Abbey of St Dunstan*, which was published early in 1912.[3]

On July 24, 1912, Abbot Aelred Carlyle, having heard from Prior Francis that the Bishop was recovering from a long illness, wrote to find out if it would be possible to have two of his senior monks, Dom Samson and Brother Wilfrid, ordained 'for community purposes' in the Chapel of St Dunstan's Abbey, subject to the approval of Dr Davidson, Archbishop of Canterbury. Grafton replied on August 5, saying that his heart had been gladdened by the news that the Caldey Benedictines had resisted the temptation to 'go over to Rome' the previous Easter, and went on to say:

'Our little Monastery of St Dunstan is the baby Monastery of Christendom. We have been blessed financially. I have been able to have the Monastery well fitted up and with a beautiful Chapel to the Order, which I have had incorporated. Spiritually, we have had many trials, as is usual in new beginnings. For five months I have been confined to my house and under the care of professional nurses. It has been a long and painful illness, and prevented me paying my half-weekly visits to the Monastery, as I had begun to do. We began with five members, and some aspirants, but I was obliged to reduce the number, for various causes, till we are, at

---

[1] See p. 525. It is stated by Theodore Andrews in *The Polish National Catholic Church in America and Poland* (1953, p. 19) that Kozlowski did not consecrate any bishops in the U.S.A., so it is not certain who raised Tichy to the episcopate, though it may have been Kozlowski.

[2] Letter to the author from Archbishop W. H. Francis, July 29, 1957.

[3] A proof that the community was not recognized by the Protestant Episcopal Church is to be found in its ceasing to appear in *The Living Church Annual* after 1909.

the present moment, only two. . . . Our great Father Benedict's work was tested in the same way. If the work is of God, as I believe it is, it will in time grow. I have no fear of it. I only earnestly pray that in time to come the Abbey may be known as "The Holy Abbey of St Dunstan".'[1]

Bishop Grafton's sudden death a few weeks later prevented Dom Samson and Brother Wilfrid from being ordained in the Chapel of the monastery under the jurisdiction of a free-lance Old Catholic bishop, but with a Protestant Episcopalian bishop as its titular abbot. About the same time Mgr Tichy gave up his duties on account of ill health, and placed his followers under the charge of Prior Francis, whom they elected bishop.[2] Tichy remains an elusive figure, whose history has never been cleared up, so far as can be discovered. Mgr Rinkel, appointed Old Catholic Archbishop of Utrecht in 1937, must have forgotten or been ignorant of the 1904, 1905 and 1907 *Reports of The Anglican and Foreign Churches Society*, which all contain brief references to Bishop Tichy, when he wrote:

'Never was this man known to us, never was he acknowledged as a bishop by us, nor—this is not the least—was he appointed to some mission by Mgr Gul, the predecessor of my predecessor. We know nothing of these Benedictine monks professing Old Catholic principles.'[3]

Due to the constant interference of the Protestant Episcopalian clergy, who disapproved of this Old Catholic community in their midst, Prior Francis decided to transfer 'The American Congregation of the Order of St Benedict' to Waukegan, where he acquired a house, renamed 'St Dunstan's Abbey'. He had now assumed the rank of Abbot, and wanted to be ordained priest, being the bishop-elect of a remnant of Kozlowski's Polish Old Catholic Church. Unable to find any other prelate to oblige, he emulated Father Ignatius of Llanthony, and availed himself of the services of Archbishop Vilatte. After the ordination in Chicago, Mar Timotheos and Abbot Francis soon parted company, which is not surprising. Not being prepared to join Bishop Hodur's Polish National Catholic Church, which issued a somewhat heterodox Confession of Faith in 1913, and being unrecognized by the Old Catholics in Europe, Abbot Francis hardly knew what to do, and he had to wait

[1] *A Correspondence between Abbot Aelred Carlyle and the Anglican Bishops* (Caldey Abbey, 1913).
[2] Letter to the author from Archbishop W. H. Francis, July 29, 1957.
[3] cf. H. R. T. Brandreth, op. cit. (2nd ed., 1961), p. 26, n.2.

nearly three years before he found a bishop prepared to consecrate him. This was the Prince de Landas Berghes et de Rache, who eventually took up his residence at St Dunstan's Abbey, Waukegan. It was in its chapel on October 3, 1916, that he raised Abbot Francis to the episcopate.[1] The following day the new prelate assisted de Landas at the re-consecration *sub conditione* of Carmel Henry Carfora.

It can be understood that Vilatte resented the formation of a rival schismatic body in North America. He had been keeping an eye on Carfora, whom he had described in the May 1915 issue of *The American Catholic* as 'an Italian ex-Roman priest who is masquerading as one of our Bishops. His alleged consecrator denies having ever consecrated this man Carfora bishop'. Some of the Episcopalian periodicals, remembering the Old Catholic Bishop-Abbot's previous associations with the Diocese of Fond du Lac, were even more indignant. One of their editors issued the following warning:

'Caution is suggested with a man styling himself as "Bishop Gregorios", otherwise "Dom Francis", or "Rev. Willy Brothers", who claims to be a Bishop consecrated by Archbishop Vilatte and the Armenian Archbishop Serapion.[2] Archbishop Vilatte states that he ordained Brothers a priest, and afterwards deposed him for a cause. . . . There is likewise a man in our country just now styling himself "Prince de Landas Berghes et de Rache, Old Catholic Bishop". As this man says he "comes to this country at the suggestion of the Protestant Archbishop of Canterbury, and was licensed to serve in a Protestant Episcopal Diocese after his arrival", it seems rather indecent of him, while acting as a Protestant Episcopal minister, still to style himself "Old Catholic Bishop". It is to be distinctly understood that no man is to be received as an Old Catholic priest unless he can show faculties from the Archbishop dated 1915.'

According to his own story, 'Bishop Gregorios, otherwise "Dom Francis" or "Rev. Willy Brothers",' was elected Archbishop and Metropolitan of the Old Catholic Church in America on January 8, 1917. Whatever may have happened, both de Landas and Carfora soon parted company with him (or vice versa), just as Vilatte is said to have done. It has been asserted that de Landas

---

[1] See p. 428. This consecration imparted to Abbot Francis the Old Catholic line of succession, obtained by A. H. Mathew at Utrecht in 1908.

[2] The Armenians started to settle in North America after the massacres of 1895–6, and eventually had an archbishop in New York City, with widespread jurisdiction.

cabled Mathew not to recognize Brothers as a bishop. The Arch-bishop-Abbot, however, paid no attention to these attacks made on him by the Austrian Prince-Bishop and the former Italian Catholic priest. He drew up an impressive Constitution for his little body, fixing the Metropolitan See at New York, in spite of the fact that there was already a Catholic archbishop there in the person of Patrick Hayes—not yet a cardinal. The hierarchy of this particular Old Catholic Church in America would meantime be limited to the mystic number of seven. One of them would be styled Archbishop, the others Bishops-Coadjutor.

On May 13, 1917, three children at Fatima in Portugal had the first of five visions of Our Lady. The following year the Archbishop heard a call bidding him extend his jurisdiction to this country, now a republic, where the Roman Catholic Church had been disestablished since 1911. In June 1918 he consecrated Antonio Rodriguez as his Bishop-Auxiliary, but for some reason or other the American Old Catholic Church failed to take root in Portugal, even with the support of the anti-clerical government.[1]

Archbishop Brothers must have felt that he had got even with Vilatte on March 9, 1924, when he raised to the episcopate one of his former priests, Albert E. Selcer. On October 2 that same year Charles Marzena was added to the hierarchy, but he soon abandoned his consecrator, and reverted to Protestantism. To make up for this loss the Archbishop had the consolation of receiving Bishop Joseph Zielonko into his little flock. This somewhat unstable prelate appears to have been consecrated by Miraglia Gulotti, Bishop of Piacenza, the founder of the Vilatte-succession, short-lived Italian National Episcopal Church.[2]

Zielonko, who was acting as American Administrator of the Polish Mariavites, assisted Brothers early in 1925 to consecrate William Montgomery Brown as Auxiliary Bishop in succession to Stanislas Mickiewicz.[3]

Brown was a brilliant but heterodox character. He had resigned the see of Arkansas in the Protestant Episcopal Church in 1912, and was deposed for heresy by the House of Bishops in 1925. His associations with the Old Catholic Church in America were some-

[1] For the Lusitanian Church, founded in 1880, see pp. 528, 529.
[2] See p. 120.
[3] Mickiewicz, formerly a priest of Hodur's Polish National Catholic Church in America, had been raised to the episcopate by de Landas in 1917. Not long after this he was deposed by both his consecrator and by Carfora, and transferred his allegiance to Brothers. He died in 1925.

what elusive, for he was more at home with Communists. Having been converted to the doctrines of Karl Marx, he proudly accepted the title bestowed on him by some of his friends—*Episcopus in partibus Bolshevikium et infidelium*. Later on he returned to the comprehensive fold of the Protestant Episcopal Church as a layman, and attended Christ Church, Galion, Ohio, but remained a militant Communist until his death in 1957.[1]

Another bishop consecrated by Brothers in 1936 was Albert D. Bell, who claimed to have received a previous consecration by the Old Catholic Bishop Kreutzer of Bonn, and who had worked under Carfora for a time.

Two years after the consecration of the Bolshevik Bishop, the Episcopal Synod of the Polish Mariavite Church showed its confidence in Archbishop Brothers by entrusting him in 1927 with the oversight of its now widely scattered groups outside Poland. After the First World War the new republican Government of Poland had expelled the first Primate, Jean Marie Kowalski, for certain offences against Catholic order, including the ordination of women. Two of his priests and seventy nuns followed him into exile. In 1924, Mgr Kenninck, Archbishop of Utrecht, broke off the communion with the Mariavite Church and the Old Catholics which had existed since 1909.[2] Rather later the dictator, Joseph Pilsudski, imprisoned Kowalski for both moral anarchy and sedition. An Episcopalian rector recalls one of several visits to Archbishop Brothers, 'who was always the soul of graciousness'. That day he was entertaining a group of Mariavite monks and nuns, whose joint-convent had been at Plock in Poland. Most of them were married, and the nuns priestesses. They wore beautiful white woollen habits, with golden monstrances embroidered on the front of their scapulars.

Meanwhile Archbishop Brothers had not forgotten his Benedictine first-love, and it seems that he usually had a few young men around him leading what may have been a somewhat unconventional sort of monastic life; certainly different to that of either the American-Cassinese or the Swiss-American Congregations. In the early thirties he found a home for them at Cos Cob, Connecticut, about half-way between Greenwich and Stamford, on Long Island Sound. A prospectus was issued stating that 'the abbey demesne'

---

[1] cf. W. C. Heitz, 'Bishop Brown of Galion' in *Bulletin of Bexley Hall* (Divinity School of Kenyon College, Ohio), December 1961.

[2] See p. 517.

covered 100 acres. St Dunstan's Abbey was advertised as 'the Mother-Community from which in time a nation-wide group of similar houses' would be founded. The teaching given to the postulants and novices suggested Theosophical influence, with references to 'the great Teachers of mankind'; and the assertion that 'God has revealed himself progressively to the World, through the ages, in all religions'. The public were informed that the monks were laying the foundations of a social polity of self-supporting industry, in which all the useful crafts were represented. For the moment, however, 'the plan was still in its infancy'. But the Archbishop-Metropolitan-Abbot felt able to write that before long 'the industrial arts will be practised and developed; science will be taught and applied; and schools for the training of students in all useful learning as well as the fine arts will be progressively established and co-ordinated in the Benedictine Renaissance which is the ideal of the Brotherhood'.

An Episcopalian clergymen, who visited Cos Cob Abbey on several occasions, recalls that the community usually consisted of the Archbishop-Abbot, his wife, and one lay-brother. For it should be explained that Brothers, perhaps because of the abolition of clerical celibacy in all the European Old Catholic Churches after 1922, when Holland fell into line with Germany and Switzerland, appear to have had no scruples about taking a wife.[1]

This must have helped him to feel in much closer unity with the Mariavites, who had recognized married monks and nuns for several years. Archbishop-Abbot Brothers, however, was not quite so emancipated as Archbishop Kowalski, who on March 29, 1929, had raised Sister Isabella Wilucka to the episcopate. The following year she consecrated eleven bishopesses.[2]

The Archbishop-Abbot and his wife were nothing if not 'catholic' in their circle of friends, and saw no reason why they should not enter into close contact with militant Communists as well as with married monks and nuns. Having linked up his Old Catholic Church in America with the Mariavites in Poland, he managed to unite it with the so-called 'Soviet Living Church', which had been set up in North America by Bishop John Kedrovsky, who claimed to be the official religious representative of the U.S.S.R. in the United

---

[1] It may be that Brothers found valid reasons for contracting matrimony from the fact that St Benedict in his Rule nowhere states specifically that a monk is to observe chastity—only to 'love it' (ch. IV, 'What are the Instruments of Good Works', no. 63).

[2] See p. 518.

States. It was then that Brothers assumed the title of 'Archbishop Francis'.[1]

No effort was spared to promote culture in the Cos Cob community, and the Archbishop-Abbot composed a letter to well-known authors, asking their co-operation by presenting copies of their books, so that a library of general reference could be formed to assist the Fathers in their own literary labours. He ended this appeal as follows:

'Your benefaction will be recorded and remembered. Should we ever achieve—as we hope to do—the reproduction of that fragrant essence for which our brethren were famous in the past— the Benedictine Liqueur—we would assure you that our donors will be the first to receive a gift in kind. Until then, your reward will be in a less material token of the Benedictine spirit.'

Neither the great library of standard literature, nor the monks to make use of the books, nor the distillery for the manufacture of a liqueur, ever materialized at Cos Cob, but the Founder never lost hope (just as Bishop Grafton had done in the past) that in time to come it would be known throughout the world as 'The Holy Abbey of St Dunstan'.

On September 18, 1932, he issued a statement in which he explained that he and his followers, now legally incorporated as 'The Catholic Church of North America', and resisting the Papal Claims to Infallibility, had come to the conclusion that 'Truth is progressive and that accepted truth must be liable to re-verification and re-interpretation in course of time'. The Cos Cob Benedictines were convinced that 'spiritual Truth and the truths of Science can never be in conflict; hence increase of knowledge in all branches of science and philosophy is desired'. Moreover, the hierarchy of the Catholic Church of North America had for a long time past been 'keeping a careful watch upon the developments of psychic science throughout both hemispheres'. It appeared that 'the time had now come for active participation in the work of bringing to light the truths concerning the Survival of Human Personality and the possibilities of intercommunion between the living and the dead'.

The hierarchy, which at that date had been reduced to two members, had been greatly impressed by the work and writings of the distinguished English ecclesiastical author and architect, Frederick Bligh Bond, F.R.I.B.A., who from 1908 to 1921 had been

---

[1] Kedrovsky's death in 1934 helped to kill this schism, which was subsequently repudiated by the U.S.S.R.

Director of Excavations at Glastonbury Abbey, and who was the first to apply psychical methods to archeological work.[1]

This document, signed on behalf of the Chapter of the Catholic Church of North America by '✠ Wm. H. Francis, Arcphiepüs', and duly sealed, stated that Mr Bond, although still for a while remaining as Editor of *The Journal of the American Society for Psychic Research*, had accepted ordination at the hands of the Metropolitan-Archbishop on Trinity Sunday last [1932]. Since then he had entered the Benedictine Order, and would shortly be appointed Prior of St Dunstan's Abbey. In addition to this office he would also act as Vicar-General 'of the English-speaking congregations on the North American continent'. The public were informed that:

'This office will imply episcopal rank and the ceremony of his consecration is due to take place some time in October next. The act will be symbolic of the Communion of the Eastern and Western Catholic world, and of the friendship that subsists between us and the Anglican Church; since an Eastern (Greek Orthodox) Bishop and another Bishop formerly of the Protestant Episcopal Church and now Old Catholic will be present as witnesses of the Act of Consecration. In the enrolment of a professed psychic researcher as a member of the Apostolic Hierarchy may be seen the intention that the ancient Church now recognizes its responsibility in regard to the custody and teaching of all that pertains to the Science of the Soul and the cultivation and dispensation of the spiritual Gifts and the Inspiration of seer and prophet.'

The psychic English archeologist was dispensed from the usual twelve months' canonical novitiate, perhaps because it had been revealed that he had been a professed monk in a previous incarnation. After his consecration he became known as 'The Right Rev. Monsignor Bond, O.S.B.'[2] From 1933 to 1937 his unmonastic

---

[1] It was in 1908 that Bligh Bond claimed to have discovered the long-forgotten foundations of the Edgar Chapel and the site of the problematic Chapel of Our Lady of Loretto at Glastonbury by means of automatic writing. He also claimed to have found the bones of the martyred last abbot, Richard Whyting (beatified by the Holy See in 1895), through messages given by a medieval monk at spiritist séances held in Gloucester. In 1910 he presented these bones to Abbot Aelred Carlyle, who enshrined them in the church of the then Anglican Benedictine community on Caldey Island (cf. P. F. Anson, *Abbot Extraordinary* (1958), pp. 137-9). The Abbot's first cousin was among those who believed that they had found the Holy Grail at Glastonbury by similar psychic methods.

[2] His books were widely advertised. Specially recommended was *The Secret of Immortality*, 'derived from an intimate experience of psychical research covering upwards of thirty years'. Its 'philosophy, both ideal and practical' would be found 'extraordinarily attractive and intuitively convincing'; proving conclusively 'the continuity of life after the death of the body'.

address was Hyslop House, 15 Lexington Avenue, New York. After this the Vicar-General broke off relations with his Metropolitan, and returned to England, where he failed to get any Anglican bishop to recognize his orders. By 1938 he had dropped the prefix 'Reverend', and moved from Wimbledon to North Wales in 1942. The one-time Right Rev. Monsignor Bond, O.S.B., died in 1945.

By 1934 the community had left Cos Cob, and moved to a small rented farmhouse at Bedford Village, near Mount Kisco, New York. It was advertised that this new St Dunstan's Abbey was 'The Mother Community of the Old Catholic Benedictines in North America', conveying the idea that they were a rival to the approximately 1,890 professed members of the two Roman Catholic Benedictine Congregations in the United States, whereas the truth was that the Bedford Village community seldom mustered more than half a dozen monks, few of whom ever reached profession. Nevertheless the Archbishop-Abbot wrote that his Abbey

'provided for the welcoming of all who in the outer world desire retreat for meditation or for intercourse with congenial minds as a rest from their secular vocations. . . . With the co-operation of the laity it will give expression of a new ideal and a larger interpretation of the term "catholic"; a word no longer narrowed to the sense of religious opinion, but embracing every activity in constructive and creative effort, to the end of universal well-being and spiritual contentment. . . . A letter of a confidential nature will receive sympathetic attention. . . .'[1]

But few persons availed themselves of the invitation given them by '✠ W. H. Francis, Archbishop', and his dreams and visions failed to materialize, though he renamed his followers 'The Orthodox Old Catholic Church in America'. He was fighting a losing battle all the time, for the Roman Catholic Benedictines were ranged against his little community in ever-increasing numbers. By 1934 the American-Cassinese Congregation had sixteen houses and over 1,400 professed members; the Swiss American Congregation five houses and about 500 professed religious. In 1924 and 1926 the English Congregation had invaded the United States with priories at Washington, D.C., and Portsmouth, Rhode Island. There was really little or no demand for Orthodox Old Catholic monastic life.

[1] *St Dunstan's Manuals*, No. 1 (New York, 1934).

Churches of the Mathew Succession

After struggling along at Bedford Village for some years, the Archbishop-Abbot made a final move to Woodstock, an artists' colony and summer resort in the Catskill Mountains. Here the monastery was burned to the ground in 1948, and the community, such as it was, dispersed. Four years before this, on October 19, 1944, Mgr Williams, Archbishop of Caer-Glow, Metropolitan of the Old Roman Catholic Church (Pro-Uniate Rite) had solemnly excommunicated Archbishop Francis, together with all the other bishops and clergy of rival Old Roman Catholic Churches in North America.

Not that this made any difference, however, and after the death of Mgr Williams in 1952, with only two of his priests remaining loyal to him, Archbishop Brothers could claim that his Old Catholic Church was 'the American representative of the Old Catholic Church of Poland (the Catholic Church of the Mariavites), and the Old Catholic Church in Czechoslovakia, Yugoslavia, France, and Morocco'. Its membership in the U.S.A. was estimated at about 6,000, with twenty-two churches, under the charge of eighteen priests. Since the death of Bishop Marc Fatome in 1951, the French Mariavites had been under the immediate jurisdiction of Bishop Robert J. Bonnet, who also directed the Mission in Morocco.[1] The Archdiocesan Chancery was located at Box 433, Woodstock, New York, with the Right Rev. John Augustine Whitfield, O.S.B., holding the rank of Chancellor.[2] Considering his international responsibilities it was fitting that Archbishop Francis should have a richly embossed paper on which to write his official letters. His name and address were printed in black gothic script. The multi-coloured coat of arms included a red, white, blue, and gold shield superimposed on a gold primatial cross and crozier; also a green and gold mitre. Surmounting the shield was a green heraldic archiepiscopal hat with two cords and twelve tassels.

'But there had been trouble at home as far back as 1940, when Bishop Zielonko repudiated the jurisdiction of his Metropolitan after being subject to him for fifteen years. He set up a rival body, which was incorporated as 'The Old Catholic Archdiocese for the Americas and Europe', with its curial offices at 216 East 183rd Street, Bronx 58, New York. Then news reached Archbishop Francis that a Ukrainian priest, Peter Zurawetsky, said to have been in communion with the Holy See at one time, had been

[1] See p. 521.
[2] cf. *Yearbook of American Churches 1958.*

consecrated by Bishop Joseph Klimovich, of Springfield, Mass.[1] Zielonko died in 1961, whereupon Archbishop Francis issued a statement to the effect that the said Zurawetsky had no claim whatsoever to be regarded as Zielonko's canonical successor, or as Archbishop of New York. The schismatic body was dismissed as bogus.[2]

None of this mixed bunch of dissident Albanian and Russian bishops dispersed in North America paid any attention to the pastoral letters, encyclicals, etc., issued by the official representative of the Polish Mariavite Church, and the Old Catholic Churches in Czechoslovakia, Yugoslavia, France, and Morocco, from his Chancery at Woodstock, New York. All that he could do under the circumstances was to publish a special *Newsletter*, which ended with the words: 'The whole unfortunate escapade just goes to show one how men pretend to tamper with Godly things for their own selfish ambitions and vanity.'

William Henry Francis Brothers has played many parts in his time, with some curious exits and entrances during the past sixty years. Nobody can tell if he has now played the last scene of all at the end of his strange eventful history, but this is the latest available news up to the time of writing, as printed in the May–June 1962 issue of *One Church*:

'A new chapter in Orthodox history has been written with the inauguration of Western Rite parishes with the Exarchate of the Russian Orthodox Catholic Church in America. On 21 March 1962, a petition from the clergy of the Old Catholic Church in America (a formerly independent religious body) was received by Bishop Dositheus, for unity with the Orthodox Church; and on April 6 the first contingent of these clerics (including their superior, Right Rev. William H. Francis) received Chrismation, followed by Ordination. Others of the group include Hieromonk Augustine Whitfield, Father Stephen Marion, and Deacon James Hroblak. At the midnight Liturgy on Pascha, the new clergy concelebrated in St Nicholas Cathedral, New York, with our Bishop.

[1] Klimovich had been raised to the episcopate by Archbishop van Stylian Noli, of the independent Albanian Orthodox Diocese in America. He was the head of a few dissident Russian Orthodox congregations, which formed a remnant of Kedrovsky's Soviet Living Church. (See p. 422.) Various shadowy prelates were associated with it, among them Nikolas Climowitch, who came from Bessarabia, and who was said to have a following of about 80,000 around Ottawa, Canada, and whom some people were bold enough to call 'The new Rasputin'.

[2] For some reason or another in 1954 Archbishop Sherwood, Primate of the American Orthodox Catholic Apostolic Eastern Church (affiliated with the Orthodox Catholic Patriarchate of America)—see pp. 263–264—had deposed and excommunicated Zurawetsky.

'It is hoped that a Western Rite parish can soon be established in new York City, ministered by some of the new Priests. Meanwhile some of them are assigned to the Cathedral staff. Father Francis has returned to his parish in Woodstock, New York.'[1]

Having enjoyed the status of Archbishop and Metropolitan for nearly forty-six years, W. H. F. Brothers had no alternative but to accept re-ordination to secure union with this group of Russian Orthodox in North America, whose Acting Exarch, Bishop Dositheus Ivanchenko, granted him the rank of Mitred-Archpriest. He still has around him at Woodstock, New York, a few monks, whose habit is now dark grey, similar to that of the Roman Catholic Benedictines at Mount St Saviour's Monastery, Elmira, New York.[2]

(xi) *North American Old Roman Catholic Church, Old Catholic Church in North America, and other bodies in the United States claiming the Mathew succession*

This section overlaps the previous one, as well as the pages telling the complex story of the Churches of the Vilatte succession in North America.[3] Again and again the same characters meet, often disagreeing, and if they are prelates, invariably excommunicating each other. In these three sections most of the earlier events happened between the gaudy and chaotic periods between the two world wars. As Isabel Leighton expresses it:

'The United States of the twenties and thirties appears, in retrospect, as a strange, uncharted, and enchanted land; so many of the personalities and events that challenged our imagination during that time now seem almost to have been part of a spell . . . hectic, frenzied, not always beneficial . . . cast over the entire country. We seem to have fluctuated between headaches; sometimes induced by prohibition, more frequently by the fevered pace of the times. During these throbbing years we searched in vain for a cure-all, coming no closer to it than the aspirin bottle. . . .'[4]

Archbishops Lloyd, Brothers, Carfora, and most of the bishops they consecrated, were typical of that 'strange and almost somnambulistic time when America was much younger in spirit than it ever

---

[1] op. cit., p. 142.
[2] The Russian Orthodox Church in North America is now divided into three main jurisdictions: (1) *The Russian Orthodox Greek Church of America*—the largest and oldest body; (2) *The Russian Orthodox Church outside Russia*; and (3) *The Russian Orthodox Catholic Church*—the smallest of the three groups.
[3] Chapter eight, pp. 252–264.
[4] Editor's Preface to *The Aspirin Age 1919–1941* (1950).

can be again . . . years of high tragedy and low comedy, of truth
and delusion, of complacency and hysteria. Sacco and Vanzetti died
in this period, and so did prohibition.'[1]

As related already, it was on the Feast of St Francis of Assisi,
October 4, 1916, that Prince-Bishop de Landas Berghes et de
Rache reconsecrated Carmel Henry Carfora, assisted by Bishop-
Abbot Francis Brothers. The imposing Latin *instrumentum con-
secrationis* stated that Carfora was a priest of the Old Roman
Catholic Church of America, that he had been elected bishop by the
episcopal synod of this Church, that the *Pontificale Romanum* had
been used, and that he had been given the title of Archbishop of
Canada. The ceremony took place in the chapel of St Dunstan's
Abbey, Waukegan, Illinois, where de Landas was then living.

Carfora was born in Italy, and claimed to be a Doctor of Philosophy of the University of Naples, and also a Doctor of Theology of
the Theological Institute in the same city. Having been ordained
priest, he was sent to North America for mission work among
Italian immigrants. It seems that he became unpopular with his
Bishop, and was reprimanded by Mgr Falconio, who was Apostolic
Delegate to the United States between 1902 and 1911. Some time
after this Carfora broke away from the jurisdiction of the Holy See,
and opened an independent Old Catholic mission for his Italian
flock in West Virginia. Later on he formed at least three schismatic
parishes.[2]

Carfora did not remain under the jurisdiction of de Landas for
more than three years. After the latter's resignation, the former
assumed the status of Archbishop of the North American Catholic
Church. De Landas then retired to an Augustinian monastery at
Villanova, Pennsylvania, where he was reconciled with the Holy
See, and where he died on November 17, 1920. Chicago became
Carfora's headquarters, but he failed to make many converts from
the more than four hundred Catholic parishes which were under
the jurisdiction of Archbishop (later Cardinal) Mundelein from
1915 to 1939. Both Bishop Anderson, who ruled over the Protestant
Episcopal Diocese of Chicago from 1905 to 1930, and his successor,
Bishop Stewart (1930–40), found this schismatic Italian prelate
much more of a menace to their smaller flock. Carfora's followers

[1] ibid.
[2] Very little has been recorded about Carfora's earlier career, but there is a report
that he was associated with Vilatte's activities in Europe between 1907 and 1908, and
that the latter raised him to the episcopate, or that it was one of Vilatte's bishops who
consecrated him.

The Most Illustrious Lord, Carmel
Henry Carfora, Supreme Primate of
the North American Old Roman
Catholic Church.

(Left to right) The Most Rev. Sister Mary Francis,
O.S.H., D.D., Marquise de Saulney, Lady Abbess of
Bethany (with mitre and crozier); The Rev. Sister
Marie Philips (in white veil with cape); The Right
Rev. Abbess Dorcas (in biretta, cotta and cope); The
Most Rev. Ignatius Carolus Brearley, D.D., D.C.L.,
Archbishop and Primate of the Old Holy Catholic
Church; The Right Rev. George W. Boyer, Bishop of
Boston; The Right Rev. William H. Turner, Bishop
for London and the South of England; and others at
Cusworth Hall, Doncaster.

consisted of widely scattered groups of quasi-Old Catholics, mainly Italians, Poles, Lithuanians; together with some lapsed Episcopalians and Roman Catholics of British origin. There was virtually no unity between them, other than their opposition to the papacy. It would have needed a St Charles Borromeo or a St Francis de Sales to keep the peace between these wrangling factions. Carfora lacked the virtues of these two archbishops, whatever his qualifications in other directions—above all his remarkable gift for deposing bishops he had consecrated.

For instance, Roman W. Slocinski, who was raised to the episcopate on May 30, 1921, was later deposed, restored again, and deposed again within five years. This must surely be a record? On June that same year Carfora consecrated Samuel Durlin Benedict, but he had to be deposed on January 24, 1927.[1] The next man to be raised to the episcopate was an ex-Episcopalian, Edwin Wallace Hunter, who on February 11, 1924, became Regionary Bishop for the United States and Canada. But he got bored playing second fiddle, and in 1929 assumed the title of Archbishop in a new sect which he called 'The Holy Catholic Church of the Apostles in the Diocese of Louisiana'. This body faded out after the death of its founder in 1942.

Prohibition had been enforced in the United States on January 16, 1920, resulting in 'rum ships prowling off the coasts, illicit breweries and distilleries, bootleggers and speakeasies, the corruption of police and judiciary, hijackers and their machine-guns, the multi-millionaire booze barons, the national breakdown of morals and manners, and all the rest of the long train of evils that sprang from the Eighteenth Amendment'.[2]

Carfora gave himself the title and style of 'Most Illustrious Lord, the Supreme Primate of the North American Old Roman Catholic Church'. A *General Constitution and Bye-Laws* was drawn up in 1923, in which it was stated that 'The Supreme Primate is recognized as the Spiritual Head of the Church. All doctrinal laws or new articles of faith shall be considered final when he speaks *ex*

---

[1] Benedict in revenge set up a rival body, known as 'The Evangelical Catholic Church of New York', which seems to have collapsed before his death in 1945. On May 7, 1925, he had consecrated George D. Quinn (apparently without Carfora's approval), and in January 1927 he raised George A. Newmark to the episcopate. The latter repudiated Benedict's jurisdiction, and founded what he called 'The American Old Catholic Church', most of whose members, said to number about 1,000 at one time, were in Louisiana. Since Newmark's death in 1940 they seem to have been dispersed.

[2] ibid., p. 34.

cathedra. . . . . He shall have full and exclusive jurisdiction over the whole Church in all matters ecclesiastical, civil, and temporal.'[1] The wonder is that the Knights of the Ku Klux Klan, who on July 4 that same year staged a spectacular 'Konklave' at Kokomo in central Indiana, resulting in a nation-wide crusade against Roman Catholics and negroes, did not lynch the Italian Old Roman Catholic 'Pope' in Chicago. But very few of the Supreme Pontiff's clergy and laity were prepared to accept his infallibility, which exceeded that of Pius XI, as defined by the first Vatican Council in 1870.

It was hardly to be expected that a self-appointed infallible pontiff would be satisfied with his body being linked up with the Vilatte-Lloyd American Catholic Church, which took place at a conference in Chicago in August 1925, when it was agreed to adopt a joint title of 'The Holy Catholic Church in America'. By 1926 Carfora was at blows again with Lloyd, and regained his complete freedom. As Supreme Primate he added a few more bishops to his hierarchy, yet sooner or later he quarrelled with most of them. There was, for instance, Charles Alphonse Blanchard, who was raised to the episcopate as Bishop of Portland on September 21, 1926. A month later, on October 17, Carfora helped to launch the schismatic *Iglesia Ortodoxa Catolica Mexicana* by consecrating José Joachin Pérez y Budar in the Cathedral of Our Lady of Grace, Chicago, giving him the title of 'Archbishop-Primate-Metropolitan of Mexico City'.[2] Five months before the Wall Street stock exchange crash William S. Hammond was made a bishop on May 29, 1929, but he was deposed by his consecrator within two years.[3] Neither was the choice of a former Roman Catholic priest, named Pamphile Cyril Depew, more fortunate. Carfora consecrated him on December 15, 1929, but he was reconciled with the Holy See the following year. That same day Henry Frederick Van Trump was raised to the episcopate by the Supreme Primate but he, too, was expelled from the North American Old Roman Catholic Church, and after a not very creditable career, died in the late nineteen-thirties.

Archbishop Davidson of Canterbury described Archbishop Mathew as a 'fomenter of schisms', who had 'played fast and loose with the great questions of Church Order, and thus set going, in

[1] op. cit., p. 7.
[2] See p. 439.
[3] Hammond formed a little sect of his own with its headquarters at Detroit, Michigan, with a mission at Windsor, Ontario, but after his death it faded out.

many different ways and in different lands, schisms which it may take many years to heal'.[1] But the apostate Italian priest in America could beat the apostate English priest when it came to rending the garment of the Bride of Christ, yet after all, Carfora was no worse than Vilatte. Having failed to unite the North American Old Roman Catholic Church, he did his next best to smash up the Catholic Church in Mexico. His deposed bishops set up yet more splinter churches, such as the Protestant Orthodox Church, the Evangelical Catholic Church, the Apostolic Polish Catholic Church of Canada, and the Holy Catholic Church in the Diocese of Louisiana—just to mention a few of them.

On March 19, 1931, when Fr Coughlin, a Roman Catholic priest at Royal Oak, Michigan, was becoming notorious all over North America as a radio speaker, attacking Communism, and raking in thousands of dollars for his Shrine of the Little Flower; maintaining that economics must transcend denominationalism, Carfora sponsored yet another schismatic body. That day he consecrated James Christian Crummey, who had organized what was known as 'The Universal Episcopal Communion'. Its aim was to reform and bring into order the scattered sects in North America and in other continents, all claiming to be Old Catholic. Crummey —like Coughlin—soared above denominations, but he did not denounce Communists, or manage to obtain the support of Protestants and Jews. His interests were narrower: he visualized merely the formation of 'a conciliar body of bishops'; and he got as far as creating a species of episcopal council, to which he gave the name of 'The Universal Christian Communion'. He hoped that it would link-up the now numerous small independent Old Catholic bodies in the United States and in other countries.[2]

Crummey held the title of both bodies until 1944, when he broke away from Carfora. 'The Corporate Headquarters for the Universal Episcopal Communion and the Universal Christian Communion' were at St Willibrord Old Catholic Church House, 6955 South Perry Avenue, Chicago 21, where the founder went on dreaming that the day might not be far off when 'All would be One'. He had two bishops associated with his movement: Mather W. Sherwood (consecrated with him by Carfora in 1931), and Murray L. Bennett, whom he raised to the episcopate on May 11, 1941.

---

[1] See p. 211.
[2] In a sense it was a prototype of Julien Erni's Oecumenical League for Christian Unity, founded in Switzerland in 1937. (See pp. 519–520.)

After Crummey's death in 1949, his two organizations collapsed.

From his bungalow on the Cotswolds in England the papalist-minded Mgr Williams, Archbishop of Caer-Glow, looked with ever-increasing alarm at Carfora's irresponsible behaviour across the Atlantic. In the early nineteen-forties he wrote to the Rev. H. R. T. Brandreth:

'Carfora appears to have consecrated a multitude of strange people, so many, so strange, that a few years ago I refused to have anything more to do with any of them.'

In another letter to the same Anglican correspondent he explained what had hitherto been his policy in regard to the North American Old Roman Catholic Church, saying:

'It is true that Carfora was recognized by Bacon when the latter was acting for me in my sickness.[1] But I do not wish to take shelter behind Bacon. I also thought it the best course, because I had some hope of exercising a restraining influence over Carfora. I continued to recognize Carfora until Bacon resigned [in October 1920], still in that vain hope, until I saw from their publications that I simply dared not continue to do so, if I had any intention of continuing to save my soul.'

Among Carfora's multitude of bishops and priests were Ukrainians, Poles, Lithuanians, West Indian negroes, mulattoes, ex-Roman Catholic priests, lapsed Episcopalian pastors, several Mexicans, and other men whose past history did not always bear close examination. Yet nobody could say that his Church was not 'catholic', for it was largely made up of the flotsam and jetsam of the ecclesiastical underworld of North America, and offered a refuge for almost any cleric of any denomination who was homeless. The state of affairs reached by the early nineteen-forties has been summed up as follows:

'In North America, for many decades, the picture presented of the Old Roman Catholic Church has been one of the greatest possible confusion. The confusion existed, because of the many who used the name to achieve in many instances improper gains to further their own venial ambitions. From the very first, the Church began its existence in a state of formal schism, a state which was permitted to exist for nearly fifty years.'[2]

Carfora was growing old, but his energy when it came to ordain-

---

[1] See p. 324.
[2] *The Old Roman Catholic Church in North America* (Archives of the Metropolitan Secretariat).

ing priests and consecrating bishops was unquenched.[1] Hubert Augustine Rogers, a West Indian negro, originally a bishop in a section of the African Orthodox Church (Vilatte succession), to whom Carfora had given conditional re-consecration on July 30, 1942, and appointed Archbishop of New York (possibly to show that he was quite indifferent to Archbishop Spellman's jurisdiction), became his Coadjutor with right of succession. But as might have been expected, there was a quarrel, and the aged hot-headed Neapolitan Primate found another negro, Cyrus A. Starkey, whom he had raised to the episcopate in 1944 for work among coloured people in New York City, and made him Coadjutor.

Carfora's consecration of Earl Anglin James as Bishop of Toronto on June 17, 1945, led to the birth of two more posthumous sects of the Mathew succession.[2] Five years later this prelate raised to the episcopate Grant Timothy Billett, who called himself Patriarch of the Old Catholic Church in America—as if there were not enough bodies with this name already. After this it is difficult to disentangle the threads of the story, but in 1957 Billett consecrated Christopher C. J. Stanley, who on November 12, 1960, gave the Gnostic Catholic Church its first bishop in the person of Michael Augustine Itkin.[3] This esoteric fraternity was also known as 'The Old Catholic Orthodox Western Primitive Rite Synod of the One Holy Catholic and Apostolic Church'. These American neo-Gnostics obtained another bishop from Itkin a fortnight later— Armand Constantine Whitehead. That same day (November 20, 1960) they repudiated the authority of Bishops Billett and Stanley. The reasons given were their 'lack of stress on the social gospel, lack of freedom on interpretation for the individuals of the doctrinal symbols of the faith, lack therefore of the channels to most fully develop the individual in the current era, and due also to the lack of recognition of the unquestionably valid Apostolic Succession of the

---

[1] Among those he raised to the episcopate after March 1931 were: Basil Drapak (Founder and Archbishop of the Ukrainian Orthodox Church, November 29, 1931); John R. Weld (December 8, 1940); Richard A. Marchenna (April 16, 1941); Hubert A. Rogers (July 30, 1942); Frederick L. Pyman (first bishop of 'The Protestant Orthodox Western Church', August 15, 1943); Alfred T. B. Haines (December 9, 1943); Cyrus A. Starkey (1944); Sigismund K. Vipartas (a Lithuanian bishop, 1944); Paul A. R. Markiewicz and Francis Mazur (April 20, 1945); Earl A. L. James ('Bishop of Toronto', June 17, 1945); Charles G. Vestle (November 3, 1946). During this same period Carfora consecrated two bishops for the Mexican National Catholic Church. (See pp. 440–441.)

[2] For further details of Earl Anglin James, see pp. 245, 246, 458.

[3] H. E. the Most Rev. Christopher C. J. Stanley, D.D., S.T.D., is now the Ecumenical Patriarch of the United Old Catholic Patriarchate of the World, with Bishop Pitt-Kethley of Ealing Common (Mar Rupertus) as its British Representative.

Church of England and the Anglican Communion'. It is understood that since this pronouncement Whitehead and Itkin have taken separate roads to heaven.

Having survived the Second World War, Carfora died on January 11, 1958. Starkey, who was growing old, felt unable to take on the burdens of Supreme-Primate, and persuaded another coloured bishop, Richard Arthur Marchenna, to accept the office.[1] This led to the formation of two independent bodies: *The North American Old Roman Catholic Church* (with Hubert A. Rogers as Primate); and *The Old Roman Catholic Church in North America* (with Gerard George Shelley as Primate).[2]

There had been yet another split in the ranks of the North American Old Roman Catholic Church about seven years before Carfora's death, the complex history of which it is difficult to explicate. A certain Fr Joseph Kelly had built a pro-cathedral at Niagara Falls, New York, dedicated to the Holy Saviour. This was not the seat of a bishopric, but it may be presumed that Kelly intended it to become one as soon as he could obtain consecration. His past history had been rather out of the ordinary. It appears that he was ordained deacon in the Church of Rome, but in the late nineteen-thirties he was raised to the priesthood by some Eastern Orthodox prelate. Soon after this he was received in the A.O.R.C.C., and according to the story, having been re-ordained conditionally by Carfora, was consecrated bishop by Hubert A. Rogers. After his lapse from the fold, he was excommunicated and deposed by the Supreme-Primate. He retaliated by deposing and excommunicating all the bishops who had been responsible for this sentence.

The source of all this trouble seems to have been that about 1950 Kelly had obtained the backing of the Mexican Archbishop, Stephen Corradi.[3] Shortly after this he reported that the Vatican had agreed to consider a project for granting Uniate status to all Old Catholic bodies which were prepared to enrol themselves under his jurisdiction. In support of this Kelly procured a document, dated August 15, 1950, from the Rev. Carlo Miglioli, of Cremona, Italy, who described himself as 'Delegate at Large to carry on the Work of Union with the Vatican'.[4]

---

[1] Carfora had suspended Marchenna at least twice after raising him to the episcopate on April 16, 1941.

[2] Shelley had been ordained priest in England by Archbishop A. H. Mathew, and was consecrated in the U.S.A. by Bishop Marchenna on March 25, 1950.

[3] See p. 535.

[4] Miglioli, who had been ordained priest by Mathew in 1913, was one of the

Churches of the Mathew Succession

This now elderly free-lance Old Catholic priest at Cremona seems to have believed that he held a sort of ambassadorial status between the Holy See and the Old Catholic Churches. It appears that in 1915, when Mathew tried to open up negotiations with Rome, he gave a document to Miglioli, authorizing him to act on his behalf. Thirty-five years later he was trying to use this personal commission to suggest that he was still the accredited Delegate for the purpose of setting up a Uniate Church. On the strength of this a number of schismatic bodies—or 'autocephalous Churches', as they preferred to call themselves—petitioned to be admitted to Uniate status, only to discover, later on, that the whole thing was an illusion.

When he found that there was nothing doing in Rome, the self-appointed Regent of the Diocese-Vicariate of Niagara Falls turned to the Rhineland for support. He had better luck: the elusive prelate Joseph Maria Thiesen, otherwise known as Mar Justinos, proved to be far more obliging.[1]

On the Feast of the Holy Rosary, October 7, 1952, Mar Justinos (styling himself Archbishop of the Old Roman Catholic Church of Germany), issued a 'Bull' in which he accepted into full communion the said Diocese-Vicariate of Niagara Falls, New York, as being the *only true and legitimate* Old Roman Catholic Church in the U.S.A. and Canada. In ultra-pontifical, though admittedly somewhat crude, language, he proclaimed:

'We have condemned the spurious sect known as the North American Old Roman Catholic Church, and the persons named— Rogers, Smith, Marchenna, Davis, Kleinschmidt, and G. Shelley. . . . All honest and decent clergy are asked to have nothing to do with any of the "N.Y.C. Clique or Bunch", and to ignore completely the malicious and filthy propaganda which comes from a sick man, Mr Richard A. Marchenna. . . . We declare, here and now, that Shelley is not a "bishop" and where is his cathedral, parishes and clergy? Shelley, a bishop, as many claim him to be, first sought "consecration" from a *fraud*, Willy Brothers, and to justify himself, he sought another "consecration" or "reconditioning" from Mr R. A. Marchenna, who was reduced to the state of the laity on September 22, 1948. Let's preserve the priceless

---

Continental ecclesiastics who had written letters of support and encouragement to Barrington-Evans, after he and his followers broke away from the jurisdiction of Mgr Williams, Archbishop of Caer-Glow in 1940. (See p. 399.)

[1] See p. 320.

heritage of the Old Roman Catholic Rite of England, and let's not ruin it with G. Shelley.'

It is not clear how Mar Justinos claimed to be one of the Old Roman Catholic hierarchy. He belonged to the Vilatte line of bishops, having been consecrated on April 17, 1949, by Aloysius Stumpfl, who called himself Mar Timotheos, thus perpetuating Vilatte's designation.[1] But this did not worry Mgr Joseph Kelly, who, having received this pontifical pronouncement from Western Germany, appointed Bishop John Barker as his British Representative.[2] He himself assumed the title of 'His Excellency the Regent', and managed to persuade Stephen Corradi, a free-lance Bishop in Mexico, associated with Duarte Costa's Brazilian Catholic Apostolic Church, to agree to raise him to the episcopate. Unfortunately this prelate found himself unable to leave Mexico.

The situation had now become far more chaotic than when there were two Popes, each claiming to be the Vicar of Jesus Christ, during the Great Schism of 1378–1447. Without taking the trouble to disclaim the accusation made by Mar Justinos that his first and second consecrations by Brothers and Marchenna were irregular, Mgr Shelley, the Jansenist Archbishop of Caer-Glow, rushed into the fray. From his headquarters in Rome, he issued a Pastoral Letter on August 12, 1957, in which he declared that Archbishop Marchenna was 'the only regular, lawful and canonical representative of the historic Old Roman Catholic Church in the United States of America'. He requested the faithful to append their signatures to 'this canonical Letter of Communion', so that God's blessing might accompany his effort to promote Unity. A month later His Grace dispatched—'*Urbi et Orbi*'—a Letter *ad clerum* to those who were to take part in a Synod at Lancing, Michigan; assuring them that he was confident that at long last it was the dawn of a new day, and that 'the holy remnant' would restore the broken unity of this American church of the Mathew succession, representing the Anglo-Saxon Rite taken to the Netherlands in the seventh century by St Willibrord and his fellow monks, and transplanted to America by Prince-Bishop de Landas Berghes et de Rache in the twentieth century.

It was recommended that Benediction of the Blessed Sacrament

[1] As Stumpfl had been re-consecrated by Mar Georgius in 1947, perhaps Thiesen felt he obtained the Mathew succession from this source.

[2] For John Barker, Head of the Christian Mission in England: later Bishop of Beulah in the Free Catholic Church, and subsequently Archbishop of Waltham, see pp. 229–231.

should be given once a month 'for all misguided souls', that they might 'be converted from the error of their ways, and be restored to the unity of the Church'. He warned his children in North America that there were still 'many wild and arrogant spirits stalking around seeking whom they could devour'. Finally, His Grace, writing more or less under the shadow of the Vatican, confirmed Archbishop Marchenna as his Metropolitan for the U.S.A. The Letter ended with the warning that the only bishops recognized by ✠ Gerard George Caer-Glow as being in communion with himself were Zigismund Vipartas (U.S.A.), José P. Ortiz (Mexico), and Willibrord (Germany).[1] This ruled out the rest of the Mathew succession of bishops, not only in North America but in other countries as well.

By 1960 this section of the Old Roman Catholic Church in North America had its headquarters at Newark, New Jersey, and it was in full communion with a handful of priests and layfolk in England, which claimed to be the canonical body in direct succession to the late Mgr Williams.[2]

Archbishop Shelley, still holding the office of Primate, had also acquired the rank of Grand Prior of a branch of the Sovereign Order of St John of Jerusalem, which had founded a Priory at Shickshinny, Pennsylvania, as long ago as 1906.[3] The Primate is likewise associated with the *Ordo Militiae Crucis Templi*, said to have Imperial Austrian origin, of which until recently Felix Graf von Luckner was Grand Master, and Archduke Franz Josef, the Knight Prior. How this would have met with the approval of that militant Legitimist, Mgr Bernard Mary Williams![4]

But this is not the end of the story. The *Yearbook of American*

---

[1] Vipartas, originally a Friar Minor and priest of the Latin rite, having given up communion with the Holy See, had been raised to the episcopate by Carfora in 1944. Later on he returned to the Rogers group. Ortiz was consecrated by Carfora in 1935 as Primate of the Mexican Old Roman Catholic Church. Willibrord (otherwise Hans Heuer, formerly a Lutheran) had been made a bishop by George F. Davis in 1952, by mandate from Carfora.

[2] See p. 339. On January 1, 1963, Archbishop Marchenna and his followers in North America ceased to be in communion with the Primatial See of Caer-Glow. In the autumn of 1962, Bishop Robert A. Burns, consecrated by Archbishop Marchenna, assisted by his Chancellor, Bishop Fairfield, on October 9, 1961, sought affiliation with Archbishop Barrington-Evans and his Old Roman Catholic Church (English Rite).

[3] This Order claims to have been formed by some of the descendants of the hereditary Knights created by Czar Paul, who was murdered in 1801. It appears that they were driven out of Russia in 1815, and settled in North America. The late Baroness d'Uxkull and Madame Olga Novikoff, as ardent Pan-Slavists, would have been glad had they known that Archbishop Mathew's successor has acquired these links with Russia. (See p. 185.)

[4] See p. 333.

Churches (1961) stated that the Primate-Metropolitan of the North American Old Roman Catholic Church (The North American Catholic Church) was the Most Rev. Archbishop Hubert A. Rogers, whose three assistant bishops were James H. Rogers, Z. K. Vipartas, and Joseph Kelly, resident respectively in New York; Westville, Illinois; and Niagara Falls.[1] We were informed that 'this body is identical with the Roman Catholic Church in worship, faith, etc., but differs from it in discipline', also that 'it was received into union with the Eastern Orthodox Church by the Archbishop of Beirut on August 5, 1911; and by the Orthodox Patriarch of Alexandria on February 26, 1912'.[2] The headquarters of the N.A.O.R.C.C. were at 954 Gates Avenue, Brooklyn 21, the residence of the Metropolitan.[3] Yet another rent was made in the already much torn garment of the Old Roman Catholic Church in North America in 1962, when Bishop Robert Burns broke off relations with Archbishop Marchenna, and sought affiliation with the English Rite branch of this body ruled over by Mgr W. A. Barrington-Evans, Archbishop of Verulam.[4] The formal erection of a United States Province took place on February 2, 1963. Mgr Burns, now holding the titles of Archbishop of Chicago and Metropolitan of America, has ten small parishes under his jurisdiction; three within Chicago, two in other parts of Illinois, three in Indiana, and two in Wisconsin. The present estimated number of his flock is 554.[5] Two other bishops, the one in California, the other in Texas, have applied for intercommunion. It is stated that they 'hope to re-establish the O.R.C.C. in America as it used to be when the late Archbishop Carfora was in good health and at the helm of the ship'.[6]

It would indeed need the wisdom of Solomon to decide which of the sects in North America is the canonical successor of the schismatic Church launched by Prince de Landas Berghes in 1916, all of

---

[1] Kelly and Rogers were finally reconciled, and it seems that in December 1959 the former was consecrated by the latter, and so brought back into full communion with this branch of the N.A.O.R.C.C.

[2] It is not so certain that the present Patriarchs of Antioch and Alexandria accept the N.A.O.C.C. as being in union with them.

[3] In March 1960 a 'newly consecrated' Bishop Bernardino Sandonato appointed a certain Rev. W. W. Hains-Howard as assistant priest of the Old Roman Catholic Cathedral of the Holy Saviour, Niagara Falls, New York, 'until it is possible to establish a congregation of the O.R.C.C. in Toronto'. (*Toronto Globe & Mail*, March 12, 1960.)

[4] See p. 407.

[5] The present population of the Catholic Archdiocese of Chicago, comprising 2 of the 102 counties of Illinois, is 2,118,831.

[6] *O.R.C. Chronicle*, May 1963.

which regard as their progenitor the *de jure* fourth Earl of Landaff, of Thomastown, Co. Tipperary.[1]

(xii) *Iglesia Ortodoxa Catolica Apostolica Méxicana (Mexican Old Roman Catholic Church)*

In the minds of the Mexican people, taken as a whole, the Catholic Church as an organization had become associated with the power of Spain, which was finally overthrown in 1821, when the republic was set up. From time to time attempts were made with the support of Protestant bodies in the U.S.A., and by Freemasons at home, to form a National Church independent of Rome, but none of them succeeded, including one sponsored by Vilatte during the first decade of the present century.[2] In 1911, after the overthrow of President Porfirio Diaz, the anti-religious laws were enforced, and the Catholic Church was subjected to fierce persecution. Priests could minister lawfully only if licensed by the civil authority. After 1917 all property used in any way for religious purposes was seized by the Government. A large number of cathedrals and churches were closed. Others remained open, but there were no priests to serve them. An estimated 2,500 priests went about in disguise, celebrating Mass in secret. Religious vows were forbidden. Monasteries and convents were suppressed; the communities dispersed; Christian teaching in schools was forbidden. Between 1924 and 1938 roughly 1,400 priests were expelled from Mexico, and an unestimated number put to death.

By 1926 the time seemed ripe to set up a National Church. A leader was forthcoming in the person of a priest called José Joaquin Peréz y Budar, who had the support of the Government; even more important, that of President Plutarco Elias Calles. It must have gladdened the heart of Archbishop Carfora to be invited to put a spoke in the Roman wheels by raising this apostate priest to the episcopate. The function took place in Chicago on October 17 that same year, when Antonio Benicio López Sierra and Macario López Valdes were also consecrated. The former was appointed Coadjutor to Peréz, the latter Bishop of Puebla de Zaragoza.

---

[1] It is almost impossible to keep up with the 'births, marriages, divorces, and deaths' in the schismatic churches in North America, or to be sure if any of them are in communion with other bodies. For instance, in July 1953 letters patent were issued constituting Archibald Patrick Mahoney, Bishop, and Nelson Dudley Hillyer and William Melville Gourlay, all of the city of Toronto, together with other clerics mentioned by name, as 'The Old Catholic Church of Canada', with its head office at Hamilton, Ontario.

[2] See p. 124.

Churches of the Mathew Succession

On their return to Mexico, Peréz assumed the title of Patriarch, and lost no time in forming a schismatic hierarchy by consecrating Eleuterio Benigno Goméz Ruvalcaba as Bishop of Hidalgo; José Emetorio Valdés as Bishop of Veracruz; José Augustin Mojica as Bishop of Puebla; and Francisco Aguilera Nobles, whose see is not recorded. Carfora took a keen interest in the sect he had helped to create, and on December 24, 1929, he provided it with another bishop named Hieronymus Maria. This was to infiltrate the schism into Texas, and the new prelate was given the title of Bishop of San Antonio, a Catholic diocese since 1874, and raised to archiepiscopal rank in 1926.

The state of religion in Mexico was becoming chaotic, as the persecution of Catholics was intensified. People accepted the ministrations of the schismatic priests and bishops, because there was no other way to receive the sacraments. To make matters worse, there was no unity among the clergy of the National Church. The Primate, now in his seventies, had grown too frail to enforce discipline. In 1931, shortly before his death, he was reconciled with the Holy See.

One of the most fanatical leaders of the Nationalist movement was a young priest, Eduardo Dávila-Garcia, who had been ordained deacon and priest at the age of eighteen. Shortly after this he was initiated as a Mason. It is asserted that he was secretly consecrated bishop in May 1931, and a few months later he took the title of *primer papa de México*, with the style of *Eduardo Primero*. But it was a case of plot and counterplot, and it would be impossible to try to disentangle the threads of the sordid events of this period. Meanwhile the Archbishop of Morelia, the Apostolic Delegate to Mexico, was forcibly deported from his own country, and obliged to seek refuge in the United States. Dávila also had to flee from Mexico in August 1936, and managed to get over the border into Texas.

At this point Carfora rushed into the ecclesiastical civil war, showing his support for the National Church by consecrating on June 26, 1932, Armín von Monte de Honor (a foreign-born Mexican citizen), and Vincente José Liman. The ceremony took place in the Church of St Anthony of Padua, Chicago, with Bishops Mather W. Sherwood and James C. Crummey, both of the Universal Episcopal Communion, as assistants.[1] Carfora gave yet another proof of his hatred of the papacy on February 26, 1933, when he

[1] See p. 431.

raised to the episcopate Francisco José Duran de la Vega as Bishop of the State of Veracruz. After this there seemed every hope that the foundations of the Mathew succession Church in Mexico had been well and truly laid. Never again, so it looked, would Rome regain its hold over the Republic, or interfere with its spiritual and temporal affairs.

But Liman soon severed relations with his brother bishops, and retired to Texas, where he was safe from persecution. Dávila managed to return to his own country, and until 1938 he led a most adventurous life as Patriarch and Primate of the schismatic body. His opinion of his own importance was almost as exalted as that held by Carfora, because he styled himself '*Sua Santidad y Sumo Pontífice, Eduardo I*'. Then he suddenly disappeared.

'The Most Illustrious Lord, the Supreme Primate of the North American Old Roman Catholic Church' performed his last episcopal act on behalf of the Mexican schismatics by giving them a new Primate on June 29, 1933, in the person of Joseph Petrus Ortiz.

There was no great excitement in the summer of 1961 when Armín Monte de Honor, who succeeded Ortiz as Primate in 1958, announced his intention to consecrate José E. Xavier Cortés as his Coadjutor. At the present time the *Iglesia Ortodoxa Catolica Apostolica Méxicana* is in full communion with the branch of the Old Roman Catholic Church which has its headquarters at Steenoven House, Highbury, London, N.5, of which Mgr Gerard G. Shelley, Archbishop of Caer Glow, was the Primate until 1963.[1] As such, its few priests, so one presumes, are obliged to conform to the revised Constitutions authorized by the unanimous decision of the Synod of the Primatial See on February 23, 1962.[2]

During the past quarter of a century this schismatic body, in spite of having the recognition of the Republican Government, has declined steadily, and today it is a power no longer. It still has a Cathedral in Mexico City, but the activities of its bishops and other clergy attract little or no attention. A nominal connection with the State is still maintained, in so far as its name has not yet been removed from official registers. But the tide has turned, and now it is the National Church which is being persecuted by the Mexican people, as if in revenge for the way

[1] See p. 339.
[2] See p. 340.

441

in which its bishops and priests helped the anti-clerical Government to persecute Catholics in the twenties and thirties.[1]

If Arnold Harris Mathew, one-time priest of the Holy and Catholic Apostolic Roman Church, who tried and failed to get reconciled with *Ecclesia Romana* and *Ecclesia Anglicana,* and died out of communion with both, were alive today and looked around the world at the bishops, clergy, and layfolk who claim him as their spiritual ancestor, he might feel inclined to mutter to himself the words of the Prophet Jeremias:

'Alas, for my wounding, for the grievous hurt is mine! . . . all my citizens have deserted me, and are no more to be found. . . . And the cause of it? Unskilful shepherds that would have no recourse to the Lord; see how their art has failed them, and all the flock is scattered far and wide! A sound comes to me that brings tidings with it, a great stir from the north country; all Juda is to become a desert, a lair for serpents now.

'Lord, I know it well enough, it is not for man to choose his lot; not human wisdom guides our steps aright. Chasten me, Lord, but with due measure kept; not as thy anger demands, or thou wilt grind me to dust. . . .'[2]

[1] Some of Graham Greene's books, e.g. *The Lawless Roads: A Mexican Journey* (1939) and *The Power and the Glory* (1940), give a vivid idea of the sufferings of Mexican priests during the years of persecution. Detailed historical information about the National Church will be found in Arnulfo Murtado's *El Cisma Méxicano* (Mexico City, 1956).

[2] Many still-living prelates claim that they are Mathew's canonical successor as head of the Old Catholic Church set up in 1908, e.g. Mar Georgius, Patriarch of Glastonbury and Catholicos of the West; the Universal Patriarch Banks of East Molesey; Archbishop G. G. Shelley of Caer-Glow; Archbishop W. A. Barrington-Evans of Verulam. It is probable that the heads of other schismatic churches of the Mathew succession would maintain that they have priority over the above, e.g. Bishop A. G. Vreede (Presiding-Bishop of the Liberal Catholic Church), Archbishop H. A. Rogers (Old Roman Catholic Church in North America); Archbishop R. Wardall (Liberal Catholic Church in North America); Archbishops E. M. Matthews and Erwin (2nd schism, Liberal Catholic Church in North America); Archbishop G. T. Billett (Old Catholic Church in America); and Archbishop Ignatius Carolus (Old Holy Catholic Church).

CHAPTER X

The Catholicate of the West (Catholic Apostolic Church), otherwise known as The United Orthodox Catholic Rite and The Celtic Catholic Church.

Churches which have been associated with the Catholicate at one time or another:

(a) *Ancient British Church—British Orthodox Catholic Church—United Armenian Catholic Church in the British Isles—Syro-Chaldean Metropolitan See of India, Ceylon, Socotra and Messina.*

(b) *African Orthodox Church—Orthodox Catholic Church in England—Evangelical Church of India—Evangelical Apostolic Church of England—Free Catholic Church—Ancient Christian Fellowship—Free Orthodox Catholic Church.*

(c) *Église Catholique du Rite Dominicain—Apostolic Church of St Peter—New Pentecostal Church of Christ—Ancient Catholic Church—New Catholic and Free Church—Indian Episcopal Church—English Episcopal Church—Coptic Orthodox Church Apostolic Incorporated—Ancient Apostolic Catholic Church—Universal Apostolic Church of Life (Universal Life Foundation)—Church and Order of the Servants of Christ (Catholic Episcopal Church)—Ancient Catholic Church in France—United Hierarchy of the Ancient Catholic Church—Pre-Nicene Gnostic Catholic Church—Ecumenical Church Foundation.*

In previous chapters frequent reference has been made to Mar Georgius and his Catholicate of the West, so it is necessary to give an account of the origins and history of this elaborate organization which has been the progenitor of a number of small sects, and closely associated with many more since 1944. Although this unique body was originally founded by Mar Jacobus (Heard), Patriarch of the Ancient British Church, its development is due entirely to the vivid imagination and enthusiasm of the man who eventually rose to the status of Mar Georgius I, Patriarch of Glastonbury, Caertroia, and Mylapore; Successor of St Thomas; Apostolic-Pontiff of Celtica and of the Indies; Prince Catholicos of the West, and of the United Orthodox Catholic Rite.[1]

Hugh George de Willmott Newman, M.A., D.D., D.C.L., LL.D., Ph.D., D. Litt., was born at Forest Gate, London, E.7, on January 17, 1905, and was baptized in the Catholic Apostolic (Irvingite) Church, Mare Street, Hackney, E.8. Both his father and grandfather had been deacons in the Irvingite Church. He himself performed the duties of an acolyte in this body from the age of seven until he was thirty, so he was well grounded in their elaborate ritual and ceremonial. In 1937 he was married in the Catholic Apostolic Church in Maida Hill, N.W.8, to Lola Ina del Carpio Barnardo, great-niece of the Founder of Dr Barnardo's Homes for Orphan Boys. The ex-acolyte was then acting as General Manager and Secretary of the National Association of Cycle Traders, an employers' trade association. He also edited the Cycle Traders' magazine, *The National Journal*.

De Wilmott Newman's interest in Old Catholic churches and kindred bodies resulted from a meeting with the Lord Patriarch Banks of Windsor in 1924. By 1938 he was convinced of a clear call to the priesthood. It would have been impossible for him to have been ordained in the Catholic Apostolic Church, for Henry Woodhouse, the last of its twelve Apostles, had died in 1901, so it must have been difficult for him to decide which bishop to approach. In the summer of 1938 he wrote to James McFall, who styled himself Regionary Old Catholic Bishop for Ireland, offering himself as a candidate for holy orders.[2] This erratic prelate replied that he would be delighted to oblige, and it was arranged that he and one of his grandsons named Malachy should visit the Newmans at South Harrow. Accordingly Bishop McFall came over from Belfast, administered baptism *sub conditione*, confirmation, the four minor orders, the subdiaconate and diaconate to this former acolyte of the Catholic Apostolic Church, and raised him to the priesthood on October 23, 1938, using Mathew's *Old Catholic Missal and Ritual* for the ceremonies. At that date McFall was dreaming of

[1] For some of his additional titles, see p. 468. His Beatitude relates that in the early days of his pontificate his followers used to refer to him as 'Bo-Peep', in allusion to the shape of his crozier, but this has long since given place to the sobriquet 'The M.G.', by which he is known among the faithful. According to Thomas Coryate (1577?–1617) the ancient name of London was Troynovan—hence Caertroia.
[2] For McFall, see pp. 340–342.

His Sacred Beatitude Mar Georgius I (Hugh George de Willmott Newman), D.D., D.C.L., Patriarch of Glastonbury, Caertroia and Mylapore; Successor of St Thomas; Apostolic Pontiff of Celtica and of the Indies; Prince-Catholicos of the West, and of the United Orthodox Catholic Rite; Prince de Mardin; Exarch of the Order of Antioch for Britain; Ruling Prelate of the Order of Corporate Reunion; Grand Master of the Orders of St Thomas Acon, St Gregory of Sarkis, and the Spiritual Christian Nation; Prelat Commandeur of the Order of the Crown of Thorns; Chevalier Grand Officier of the Order of the Lion and Black Cross; Doctor Christiantissimus; Prince of Saxe-Noricum, etc., etc.

reviving the Liturgy of the 'Illustrious Church of Sarum', for no other rite was rich enough to satisfy his passion for ornate ceremonial. He told Fr de Willmott Newman that he must turn one of the rooms in his house into an oratory, and gave detailed instructions about its furnishings. Only the Sarum colour sequence would be permitted. Before departing the Bishop presented a relic of the fourth-century martyr, St Vincent, to be enshrined in the oratory; otherwise all the ornaments would have to be paid for by the newly ordained priest. The Irish would-be Metropolitan of this new Sarum Rite Old Catholic Church, which as yet was only at the planning stage, promised to send plans for its organization once he returned to Ulster. But nothing ever materialized—not even faculties. McFall wrote that they were not necessary, and explained politely that it would be better to release this English priest from his jurisdiction![1]

De Willmott Newman now found himself in the position of a free-lance priest belonging to no Church, and subject to no ecclesiastical superior. Early in 1939 he heard of the existence of the so-called Old Catholic Orthodox Church, which consisted of a few layfolk who had broken away from Mgr Williams in 1925 after the latter had made Papal Infallibility an article of faith in the Old Roman Catholic Church (Pro-Uniate Rite).[2] They had lost the services of a priest of the Vilatte-Lloyd American Catholic Church who had ministered to them at Hounslow, Middlesex, for a few years, and had nobody to say Mass for them. So it was arranged that the little groups at South Harrow and Hounslow should be linked up under de Willmott Newman, who did his best to look after both.

Then he tried to find a shepherd to take over this amalgamated flock. An effort to contact Archbishop Sibley, Primate of the Orthodox Catholic Church in England, led to the discovery that he was dead. His successor, Archbishop J. S. M. Ward, of the Confraternity of the Kingdom of Christ, did not reply to the letters addressed to him. Fr William Jeffrey (the future Bishop of St Marylebone), then trustee of Bishop Vernon Herford's Evangelical Catholic Communion, showed no interest in the idea.

Soon after the outbreak of the Second World War Fr de Willmott Newman had to close his oratory at South Harrow, his civilian

---

[1] cf. Mar Georgius, *A Twig on the Tree of Life* (Glastonbury, 1950), p. 5. See also p. 342; and *Silver Jubilee Souvenir* (Glastonbury, 1963), p. 7.
[2] See p. 327.

avocation requiring him to move to Northampton, where he opened a chapel in his house for the benefit of a few followers. In spite of his frequent journeys around England in the interests of the cycle trade, he managed to find time to fulfil his priestly duties. At the same time he kept up the quest for a bishop, but met with no success. Letters sent to Mar Frederic, Primate of the Orthodox Keltic Church of the British Commonwealth of Nations, were returned 'address unknown'. Early in 1941 an appeal was made to Bishop Howarth, the excommunicated Domestic Prelate to Pope Leo XIII, who had been consecrated by Archbishop Mathew in 1910. We are told that he was most indignant at being approached and was 'downright rude'![1]

Having tried almost every free-lance prelate in Britain and Ireland, Fr de Willmott Newman turned to the U.S.A., but he got no reply to the letter addressed to Archbishop Carfora, Primate of the North American Old Roman Catholic Church. Finally, on August 16, 1941, he besought the help of Arthur Wolfort Brooks, otherwise known as Mar John Emmanuel, Titular Bishop of Sardis, who ruled over a body in New York, called the Apostolic Episcopal Church (Holy Eastern Catholic and Apostolic Orthodox Church).[2] This prelate claimed that his orders were derived from the Uniate Patriarchate of Babylon in far-off Chaldea.

A month later Mar John Emmanuel cabled that he was prepared to accept the office of Presiding Bishop of the Old Orthodox Catholic Church in England. This was confirmed in a document dated October 8, 1941. By a Brief issued on October 26, the Titular Bishop of Sardis constituted Fr de Willmott Newman as Abbot Nullius of St Albans, in the Order of Corporate Reunion. His jurisdiction would be limited to a radius of five miles of St Albans, but extended to the whole of Great Britain and Northern Ireland in the cases of members of the O.C.R. Four days later the Abbot-Nullius was appointed Archpriest and Vicar-General of the Old Catholic Orthodox Church in Europe with unlimited jurisdiction. Many an abbot has kept a mistress, beginning with a solitary in the Egyptian desert during the fourth century, right through the Middle Ages down to the eighteenth century, when the Benedictine Abbot of Fiecht in the Austrian Tyrol eventually married his lady love, but she died a penitent widow. So far as is known, this was the first occasion that a lawfully married priest in England had

[1] *A Twig on the Tree of Life*, p. 8.
[2] See pp. 508–512.

ever been raised to the status of Abbot-Nullius.[1] He relates: 'I do not know whether Mar John Emmanuel thought I was likely to have thousands of converts, and thousands of sick people within a short period, but for some months I received from him consignments of Holy Chrism, Oil of Catechesis, and Oil for the Sick almost every month! It will be understood, of course, that I was not empowered to consecrate the Holy Oils myself, and that in administering Confirmation, I was bound to use Chrism blessed by a Bishop.'[2]

In the spring of 1943 the Abbot-Nullius of St Albans and Vicar-General of the Old Catholic Orthodox Church in Europe, took up the duties of Secretary and Registrar of the Incorporated Institute of Cycle Traders and Repairers. Now that he had the designation of 'Right Reverend' he felt it consistent with the custom of the Western Church that his printed notepaper should carry a mitre on the coat of arms. By this time the Abbot and his wife had left Northampton for Enfield Lock, Middlesex, where the curia of the Old Catholic Orthodox Church was set up.

His knowledge of the ramifications of the ecclesiastical world was increasing. He met Dr W. B. Crow, who on June 13, 1943, had been raised to the episcopate by Mar Jacobus II, fifth British Patriarch, as Bishop of Santa Sophia.[3] Then he had the privilege of being introduced to Mar Jacobus, who explained that although the history of the Ancient British Church 'had got somewhat entangled in the past', he had been successful in unravelling the tangle. He convinced Abbot Hugh that he was the true successor of St Aristobulus, first Archbishop of the Britons. The fifth Patriarch of this revived Church, who was also Chancellor of the International Orthodox Catholic University, granted the Abbot a Doctorate in Divinity on the presentation of two theses.

As European representative of Mar John Emmanuel and his Apostolic Episcopal Church in America, Abbot Hugh was among the minor and major prelates who faced the perils of a war-time journey to Palmers Green on October 17, 1943, to take part in the Council of London, when Mar Ignatius Ephrem I, Jacobite Patriarch of Antioch, was deposed for reason of the 'mendacious docu-

---

[1] It may be presumed that Mar John Emmanuel did not know that the English Benedictine Congregation has the privilege of perpetuating as titular dignities the greater pre-Reformation English abbeys, and nine cathedral-priories once served by Benedictine monks.

[2] ibid., p. 11.

[3] See pp. 236–238.

ment' he had put out in 1938, repudiating the orders of the Vilatte succession.[1] As has been related in chapter seven, Dr W. B. Crow, Bishop of Santa Sophia, was elected as his successor, with jurisdiction over the so-called 'extensions' of the Patriarchate in Western Europe, and given the title of Mar Basilius Abdullah III.[2] Shortly before the Council of London, Mar John Emmanuel had decided that it was high time that the Old Catholic Orthodox Church in Europe had a bishop of its own, even if its members were hardly more than a dozen all told. A Pro-Synod of the Clergy and Laity met on October 8, 1943, at which the titular Abbot of St Albans was elected to the episcopate, under the title of Archbishop and Metropolitan of Glastonbury. The election was confirmed in New York on December 20. Since this tiny body claimed historic continuity with the ancient Gallican Church in which the celibacy of the clergy was not clearly defined, no doubt precedent was found for the bishop-elect having a wife. Mar John Emmanuel authorized Mar Basilius Abdullah to perform Abbot Hugh's consecration, as war-time conditions made it impossible to him to travel to England. At that time mails took a long time to cross the Atlantic and go through the censor's hands, so his mandate did not reach the interested parties until nearly three months later. During the interval the bishop-elect, having been forced in conscience to accept the fact that the Ancient British Church was the true indigenous Orthodox Church in England, and that its venerable Patriarch was the twentieth-century successor of both St Joseph of Arimathea and St Aristobulus, decided that the Old Catholic Orthodox Church was both schismatic and redundant, and that it ought to be absorbed into the body under the jurisdiction of Mar Jacobus II. As already related, the O.C.O.C. was one of the four bodies which on March 23, 1944, while Allied bombers were laying waste the Abbey of Monte Cassino, were united and merged together in a new ecclesiastical organization known as 'The Catholicate of the West'.[3]

There had been no time to buy or rent a suitable building as a pro-cathedral for the new Antiochene Patriarchate set up in England. As none of the dissident Eastern Churches represented in this country had seen their way to enter into communion with the Occidental-Oriental organization, it was hardly likely that any of

[1] See p. 239.
[2] See p. 241.
[3] See p. 242.

them would have been willing to lend a church for the consecration of the Titular Abbot of St Albans. So Mar Basilius Abdullah III had to avail himself of the hospitality of the Free Protestant Episcopal Church of England, which had a church situated between the Hackney Marshes and the Harringay Stadium, within a small triangle of streets leading into Seven Sisters Road, and Stamford Hill Road.

The modern pilgrim to this forgotten shrine, who hopes to find a Byzantine church evocative of an Eastern Patriarchate, or even a replica of the Little Metropole at Athens—the smallest building in the world dignified by the name of cathedral—will be disappointed. For the edifice which confronts him at the corner of Highweek and Stonebridge Roads is merely an uninspired red-brick, vaguely Gothic Revival nonconformist conventicle, even lacking a cross to indicate that it is a Christian place of worship.[1] Nevertheless it has the supreme merit of being perfectly in harmony with the surrounding brown-yellow brick two-storied houses, most of which have known better days. The notice-board states that it is 'The Collegiate Church of St Andrew', in communion with the Free Protestant Episcopal Church of England, founded in 1897. The doors are usually locked, but on one of them are the names of several organizations which have their offices here, including the Ecumenical Church Foundation, and St Andrew's Collegiate College.[2] The only service advertised is an eleven o'clock Communion on Sundays. A side door gives access to a hidden 'Manse'.

No time was wasted, and within less than three weeks of the foundation of the Western Orthodox Catholic Church on March 23, 1944, and its constitution as the Catholicate of the West, the former Methodist chapel had been thoroughly made ready for what some of the Free Protestant Episcopalians may have regarded as idolatrous and superstitious rites and ceremonies. On the morning of Easter Monday, April 10, St Andrew's Collegiate Church was the setting of a colourful function unique in the ecclesiastical annals of Britain. At the same time the U.S.A. bombers were hitting

[1] Originally a Methodist chapel, it became redundant in 1932, when the Wesleyan Methodists, Primitive Methodists, and United Methodists were amalgamated as 'The Methodist Church'. William Hall, who was Chaplain at Abney Park Cemetery, had lost his church in Retreat Place, Hackney, owing to site demolition, and induced a patron to provide a deposit and a mortgage so that he could run the Stonebridge Road chapel as a place of worship of the Free Protestant Episcopal Church of England (see p. 244). He did so until he disposed of it to Dr Boltwood's Ecumenical Church Foundation. (See p. 244.)
[2] The absence of any collegiate buildings is due to these organizations being conducted by post. (See p. 244.)

targets in Poland and the Soviet forces were advancing into the Crimea.

As this was a Bank Holiday, His Beatitude, Mar Basilius Abdullah III, the Senior Lecturer in Biology in the South-West Essex Technical College at Walthamstow, was free from his tutorial duties; and came over to South Tottenham from his residence at Woodford Green. Assuming his style and title of Sovereign Prince Patriarch of the God-Protected City of Antioch and of all the Domain of the Apostolic Throne in the East and the West, he raised Fr Hugh George de Willmott Newman, D.D., D.C.L., LL.D., Ph.D., Lord Abbot Titular of St Albans, to the holy office of Bishop, giving him the name and style of 'Mar Georgius, Archbishop and Metropolitan of the Holy Metropolis of Glastonbury, the Occidental Jerusalem, and Catholicos of the West'. The consecrator conferred on the consecrand the Sacred Pallium and the Primatial Cross.[1] Vernacular versions of the *Missale Romanum* and *Pontificale Romanum* were used during the functions instead of the Syrian-Jacobite liturgical books, *Kthobo Dkourobo* (The Book of the Sacrifice), etc. So it was that Abbot Hugh received the reputedly Antiochene line of succession, imparted by a Patriarch who also believed that he had access to the divine wisdom of Theosophy, embodied in the symbols of all nations, not excluding the Christian religions.[2]

An exotic Oriental note was introduced into the tiny sanctuary —normally used for the austere ritual of the Free Protestant Episcopal Church—by the uniform of William Francis Liberty, Captain of the Patriarchal Bodyguard—baggy trousers, white spats, zouave tunic, and tasselled tarboosh. Fr Langhelt, Registrar-General and Protonotary Apostolic (not yet raised to the episcopate as Mar Francis, Bishop of Minster), made a sombre contrast in his black gown and biretta, set off by white bands, which showed up the white and gold vestments worn by the two prelates. Fr Figg (of Archbishop Hayman's Free Catholic Church) acted as Deacon, and Fr Banning as Subdeacon. Fr Emery directed the elaborate function as *caeremonarius*. Little Fred Saunders, vested in cassock and abbreviated cotta, acted as acolyte, and swung a thurible when required. It was regrettable that the Jesuits did not offer to lend their nearby church on Stamford Hill for the occasion;

[1] Presumably the Pallium was not woven from the wool of a sheep raised in Rome, blessed by the Pope, and kept in the niche over St Peter's Tomb?
[2] See p. 237.

its spacious sanctuary is ideal for patriarchal ceremonial. When all was over, a lengthy and involved *instrumentum consecrationis* was duly signed and witnessed by some of those present, including the new Patriarch's wife.[1] As they made their way back to their suburban homes that Easter Monday, looking forward to their lunch, the various participants may well have been repeating to themselves the words of that Bank Holiday Gradual: 'This is the day which the Lord has made; let us be glad and rejoice in it.'

The only cloud in the sky was the absence of any official delegates; either Catholic, representing the Patriarch of all the West; or Orthodox, representing the four Patriarchates who divide the ancient East; even the Primate of All England was not represented. Even now none of these has as yet seen his way to recognize Mar Georgius as Archbishop and Metropolitan of the Holy Metropolis of Glastonbury, the Occidental Jerusalem, and Catholicos of the West.

Having been raised to the episcopate and patriarchate, the General Manager and Secretary of the National Association of Cycle Traders and Repairers was convinced that his first duty was to establish and secure a legitimate and validly ordained ministry in the full Catholic sense. To achieve this he naturally felt it vital for him to receive in his own person as many lines of succession as possible. By this method it ought to have been possible to create an episcopate whose validity could not be questioned by either Latin or Eastern theologians, and to form a Bridge Church between the East and the West; a sacred viaduct linking Canterbury, Constantinople, and Rome with Glastonbury. People who did not belong to any organized religious denomination would at least be able to receive valid sacraments on the very long bridge, with the option of eventually crossing it into communion with the really ancient Churches of the East and the West. Of course, it was hardly a new idea, for Ferrette, Overbeck, Herford, and indeed many other pioneers had been granted the same vision of this particular Grail in the past seventy years, but none of them could compete with Mar Georgius in thoroughness. Within the next decade he managed to add to his enviable collection twenty-three lines of apostolic succession, stated to have been 'derived from every part of the One Holy Catholic and Apostolic Church', and he maintains that this idea of an Oecumenical Succession was originally Anglican; that is, derives from Resolution 9 of *An Appeal to All Christian*

[1] cf. *Successio Apostolica* (Glastonbury, 1959), Appendix B, pp. 50–52.

451

The Catholicate of the West

People, no. VIII, issued by the 1920 Lambeth Conference.[1] It is improbable that any bishop during the past nineteen centuries has been re-consecrated so many times as Hugh George de Willmott Newman. He is convinced that this 'Oecumenical Apostolic Succession is now an established fact, and the Orders and Sacraments of THE CATHOLIC APOSTOLIC CHURCH (Catholicate of the West) are thus placed beyond all shadow of dispute'. Here is the winning list of the first eighteen lines of succession received by Mar Georgius at ten re-consecrations, and so generously handed on by him to other prelates.

(1) *Syrian-Antiochene, Armenian-Uniate, Order of Corporate Reunion* (Consecrator: William B. Crow), April 10, 1944.

(2) *Old Catholic, Syrian-Antiochene, Syrian-Malabar* (Consecrator: S.E.P. Needham), January 4, 1945.

(3) *Chaldean-Uniate* (Consecrator: Charles W. Keller), April 29, 1945.

(4) *Syro-Chaldean, Roman Catholic* (Consecrator: H. C. Bartlett), May 20, 1945.

(5) *Syrian-Malabar* (Consecrator: J. S. M. Ward), August 25, 1945.

(6) *Old Catholic* (Senior Line) (Consecrator: W. D. de O. Maxey), June 6, 1946.

(7) *Syrian-Gallican* (Consecrator: Charles L. Saul), July 14, 1947.

(8) *Coptic-Orthodox* (Consecrator: D. Q. Arthur), November 19, 1951.

(9) *Mariavite* (Consecrator: C. A. S. Marchese), September 18, 1954.

(10) *Greek-Melkite, Russian Orthodox, Russo-Syriac, Old Catholic* (Junior Line), *Liberal Catholic* (Consecrator: O. A. Barry), July 17, 1955.

The other five lines of succession were acquired from various sources: *Anglican, Nonjuring, Celtic, Welsh*, and the *Restored Apostolic* (better known as 'Irvingite)'.[2]

[1] cf. *Successio Apostolica* (Glastonbury, 1959), pp. 9, 48–49.

[2] Full details of how, when, and where all these twenty-three 'lines' were obtained will be found in *Successio Apostolica*. Mar Georgius has published a table showing that he has derived his Non-juring succession in a very roundabout way from Marco Antonio de Dominis, Archbishop of Spalato, who on December 14, 1617, consecrated George Monteigne, Bishop of Lincoln, afterwards Bishop of London; one of the last three links in the chain was William Montgomery Brown, the Protestant Episcopalian Bishop of Arkansas, who was deposed for heresy in 1925, and became notorious for his militant Communist opinions. (See p. 419.)

The Catholicate of the West

The Irvingite succession, believed to have come directly from the Holy Ghost, was obtained from Leofric, Archbishop of Suthronia (Charles Leslie Saul) at the same time as (7) above on July 14, 1947. This prelate, subsequently the founder of English Church Episcopal, derived his succession in an indirect way through Mar Timotheos, Metropolitan of Aquileia (Aloysius Stumpfl) from Francis Valentine Woodhouse, who was one of those appointed to the twelvefold Apostleship commissioned in 1835, and who died at a great age in 1901. So it was that Mar Leofric raised the Patriarch of the Occidental Jerusalem to the lofty status of Angel and Bishop, using the Irvingite rite.[1]

Between September 1944 and November 1946 Mar Georgius consecrated two bishops, assisted at the consecration of a third, and conferred 'additional lines of apostolic succession' on thirteen prelates.[2] He has pointed out that this was 'a procedure advocated by the Anglican Bishops at the Lambeth Conference of 1920 (Resolution VIII), but which they have never had the humility or courage to adopt in practice'.[3]

The only two bishops he consecrated *ab initio* during this period were designated for special purposes. He helped to give the Evangelical Catholic Communion a new episcopal leader in succession to the late Bishop Vernon Herford, in the person of the Rev. W. J. E. Jeffrey (one of the ministers at the Congregationalist King's Weigh House), on May 20, 1945. The new prelate took the title and style of Mar Johannes, Titular Bishop of St Marylebone, an Auxiliary of the Patriarchal Throne of Glastonbury, and General Moderator of the Evangelical Catholic Communion. The imposing ceremony took place in the twelfth-century Chapel of St John, Pembridge Castle, Monmouthshire. The co-consecrators were Mar Hedley, Bishop of Siluria; Mar Francis, Bishop of Minster; Mar John, Bishop of Verulam; and Mar Adrianus, Bishop of Deira, Abbot of the Order of Rievaulx, and Protosynkellos of the Catholicate of the West. It was claimed that these prelates represented nine independent lines of succession. We are told that

---

[1] The Irvingite formula of commission was 'Receive the Holy Ghost for the office and work of an Angel or Bishop in the Church of God'. Mar Georgius regards himself as having, in addition to his other numerous ecclesiastical obligations, 'the duty of perpetuating the Irvingite tradition within the historic Church'.
[2] An interesting *Casus Moralis* might be made out of the problem whether Mar Georgius could pass on all the fifteen lines at once with a single sitting and laying on of hands, or whether he should perform the operation fifteen times. And if the latter, how distinct should each go be? A week's rest between each fifteen? Or just fifteen appropriate touches in rapid succession?
[3] *Orthodox Catholic Review*, June 1947, p. 21.

'prior to the main ceremony, all five bishops formally merged their respective orders and successions by means of reciprocal consecration *sub conditione*, so as to form one re-united line in the interests of Christian reunion'.[1] Mr Jeffrey's consecration was carried out according to a vernacular version of the East Syrian or Chaldean Rite, which may have enabled the congregation at the King's Weigh House, Mayfair, to feel that they had thus acquired undisputable links with the Persian Church and the Indian Branch of the Syro-Chaldean Church, said to have been founded by St Thomas the Apostle.

On April 22, 1946, Mar Georgius raised to the episcopate Richard Kenneth Hurgon, feeling that it would benefit the inter-denominational Christian organization known as 'The Order of Christ our Most Holy Redeemer and Heavenly King' to be ruled over by a major prelate. The purpose of this Order was to bind men and women together in one Universal Christian Fellowship, very much on the same lines as those of Vernon Herford's Evangelical Catholic Communion.[2] Hurgon was given the name and style of Mar Benignus, titular Bishop of Mere.[3] Both Mar Johannes of St Marylebone and Mar Benignus of Mere were made Auxiliaries of the Patriarchal Throne of Glastonbury, and must have been highly honoured.

For the admirable purpose, however quixotic, of 'establishing the Oecumenical Succession in the interests of Christian Unity', fifteen bishops were re-consecrated by the Patriarch of Glastonbury, with the object of 'conferring as many additional commissions as possible in other lines of Apostolic Succession.'[4] Mar Georgius also assisted at the consecration of Mar Gregory, Titular Bishop

---

[1] ibid., May 1945.

[2] See p. 137.

[3] Mar Benignus twice broke off relations with Mar Georgius, and was excommunicated. The first split appears to have arisen because of his opposition to Archbishop Hayman, who was then in favour with Mar Georgius. The second is said to have resulted from his refusal to comply with a request to assist at very short notice in the consecration of a man he did not know.

[4] Dorian Herbert, Bishop of Caerleon, founder of the Jesuene (Free-Orthodox Catholic Church) December 3, 1944; Mar Carolus, titular Bishop of Amesbury (Charles W. Keller), April 29, 1945; Mar Hedley, Bishop of Siluria (Hedley C. Bartlett), May 20, 1945; Mar John, Bishop of Verulam (John Syer), May 20, 1945; Mar Adrianus, Bishop of Deira (G. H. Brook), May 20, 1945; Mar John, Archbishop of Olivet (J. S. M. Ward), August 25, 1945; Mar James, Archbishop of India and Exarch (J. C. Ryan), August 25, 1945; Mar Leofric, Archbishop of Suthronia (C. L. Saul), September 9, 1945; Mar David, Bishop of Repton (F. D. Bacon), January 12, 1946; Mar David, Patriarch of Malaga (W. D. de Ortega Maxey), June 6, 1946; Mar Theodorus, Bishop of Mercia (S. E. P. Needham), November 28, 1946; Mar Philippus, Bishop of Amersfoort (H. P. Abbinga), November 28, 1946.

of Bethany (C.M. Chamberlain), performed by Mar John, Archbishop of Olivet, in the Abbey Church of Christ the King, New Barnet, on June 6, 1946.[1]

The editor of *The Orthodox Catholic Review*, in its issue of June 1946, hailed with joy the commissioning of Wallace David de Ortega Maxey, as Mar David I, Patriarch of Malaga, and Supreme Hierarch of the Catholicate in the Americas. This was 'yet another step forward in the work of unifying the independent Episcopal Churches throughout the world upon the basis of Apostolic Catholicism and Orthodoxy'. He was confident that Mar David's 'patriarchal throne in California would become a centre of unity to which all clergy and laity interested in the development and extension of a truly Oecumenical work, free of all the mistakes, controversies, and heresies of the past, have now the opportunity to rally and engage in active participation'.[2]

Perhaps it was a good thing that the Patriarch of Malaga did not find it convenient to extend the active work of the Catholicate to the Iberian Peninsula, since he would have been overlapping two other and rival Patriarchs: the one in Spain and the other in Portugal.[3]

Developments had also been taking place in Britain. On July 14, 1945, it was mutually agreed 'in perfect friendship', that the Patriarch Basilius Abdullah III should neither have nor possess any jurisdiction over Mar Georgius. It was decreed that the Catholicate of the West was an autocephalous and autonomous Church or Rite under its own Catholicos, and subject to no other jurisdiction. This meant that the Patriarch of Glastonbury could regard himself as having equal status to that of all the historic Eastern Patriarchs,

---

[1] See p. 289. Archbishop Ward and the Orthodox Catholic Church in England were received into full communion with the Catholicate of the West on August 25, 1945, but the body itself was expelled from it on August 21, 1951. (See pp. 290–291.) Later consecrations performed by Mar Georgius, or at which he assisted, are mentioned further on in this chapter.

[2] Shortly after his return to California, Mar David I consecrated in St James's Church, Santa Monica, Matthew N. Nelson on March 16, 1947, giving him the title and style of Mar Matthew, Bishop of Hawaii. This indicated that the Supreme Hierarch regarded his jurisdiction as extending not only over the Iberian Peninsula, North and Central America, but also over the Pacific Ocean.

[3] Resident at Madrid was Archbishop Elijo y Garay, Patriarch of the West Indies, created in 1540. Lisbon was the headquarters of the Patriarch Cardinal Manuel Gonçalves Cerejeira, whose dignity dated from 1716. Since the Apostolic Eparchy of all the Iberians (one of the twelve established by the Catholicate of the West) embraced both Spanish and Portuguese overseas possessions, Mar David I might have found relations with the Patriarch of the East Indies, resident at Goa, somewhat delicate. Finally, the Patriarch of the West (in the person of Pope Pius XI) might have been forced to issue a *motu proprio* denouncing the Patriarch of Glastonbury and his Catholicate of the West.

not to mention the Bishop of Rome, in his wider capacity of Patriarch of the West. On August 25 that same year the Orthodox Catholic Church in England and the Evangelical Church of England were formally received into union with the Catholicate. Nothing could have been more impressive on paper than the United Hierarchy in communion with the Catholicate of the West as given in June 1943.[1]

As she looked around the world, the Patriarch's wife, Lola Ina del Carpio Barnardo, must have felt that their large family of spiritual children more than rivalled the orphan boys adopted and cared for by her great-uncle, Dr Thomas Barnardo, the Irish philanthropist. It has been said that 'Her Beatitude' was a shrewd judge of character, and often warned her too kind-hearted patriarchal husband to be on his guard against some of their miscellaneous episcopal and sacerdotal progeny. Indeed, Mar Georgius found himself at times in much the same position as Old Mother Hubbard.

On September 1, 1945, yet another burden was laid on His Beatitude's shoulders, because the aged Mar Jacobus II relinquished the important office of Grand Master of the Order of the Spiritual Nation, and conferred it upon Mar Georgius. He added to it the dignity of Prince-Religious in the said Order.[2]

But there had been storms brewing, and in the autumn of 1946,

[1] APOSTOLIC PRIMATES: (1) *Of All the Britons:* His Beatitude Mar Georgius, Patriarch of Glastonbury, Catholicos of the West; (2) *Of All the Iberians:* His Beatitude Mar David I, Patriarch of Malaga, Supreme Hierarch of the Catholicate in the Americas.

OTHER PRIMATES: (3) *Of The African Orthodox Catholic Church:* His Beatitude Mar Kwamin I, Prince-Patriarch of Apam; (4) *Of The Apostolic Episcopal Church:* His Grace Mar John Emmanuel, Titular Archbishop of Ebbsfleet; (5) *Of The Orthodox Catholic Church in England:* His Grace John, Archbishop of Olivet; (6) *Of the Evangelical Church of India:* His Grace James, Archbishop of India, Vicar Apostolic of the Indies; (7) *Of The Evangelical Apostolic Church of England:* His Grace Leofric, Archbishop of Suthronia; (8) *Of The Free Catholic Church:* His Grace, Victor, Archbishop of Waltham. ARCHBISHOP: (9) His Grace, Mar Jacobus, Archbishop of Selsey. BISHOPS: (10) The Rt Rev. Hedley, Bishop of Siluria; (11) The Rt Rev. Mar Carolus, Titular Bishop of Amesbury; (12) The Rt Rev. Mar David, Bishop of Repton; (13) The Rt Rev. John Bishop of Verulam;. (14) The Rt Rev. Francis, Bishop of Minster; (15) The Rt Rev. Mar Adrianus, Bishop of Deira; (16) The Rt Rev. Mar Joannus, Titular Bishop of Saint Marylebone; (17) The Rt Rev. Benignus, Titular Bishop of Mere; (18) The Rt Rev. Gregory, Titular Bishop of Bethany. *The Ancient Christian Fellowship:* The Rt Rev. Matthew Nicholas Nelson D.D., Titular Bishop-Elect of Hawaii.

[2] As befitted his illustrious status the Metropolitan of the Holy Metropolis of Glastonbury had already acquired the following degrees: M.A. (Apostolic Academy of St Peter at Antioch); D.D. (International Orthodox University); D.C.L.· (Apostolic Academy of St Peter at Antioch); LL.D. (Université Philotechnique Internationale); Ph. D. (Apostolic Academy of St Peter at Antioch); and D. Litt. (The Keltic University).

The Catholicate of the West

so it was stated in *The Orthodox Catholic Review*, 'certain ill-disposed persons in the U.S.A., and possibly in England, not having the fear of God before their eyes, and being seduced by the instigation of the Devil, had seen fit to constitute themselves enemies of the Catholicate of the West'. They had been making 'bitter attacks on the Patriarch Mar Basilius Abdullah III, Mar David, Patriarch of Malaga, and Mar John Emmanuel, Titular Archbishop of Ebbsfleet'. They had even gone to the length of describing these three prelates as 'phoney'. The editor stated that it would be 'incongruous to indulge in vulgar controversy', and that the only line to adopt was to pray for these enemies of 'The Bride of Christ'.

In England the *Spectator*, the *Cambridge Review*, and the *News Review* had now started to attack the University of St John and the Western Orthodox Academy, both of which were under the jurisdiction of the Catholicos of the West, now as anxious as ever to foster true learning and culture. These journals insinuated that the academic degrees conferred by these bodies, though possibly legal, were worthless.

The Western Orthodox Academy, afterwards raised to the rank of a University, had been founded on August 1, 1945, to perpetuate the defunct University of Sulgrave.[1] According to its *Handbook of Information and Faculty Regulations*, published by the Authority of the Senate, this little-known Academy was 'Autocephalous and Autonomous'. The public were informed that it had been 'granted University Status for the promotion of learning and the encouragement of study with a view to Graduation'. It conferred degrees in Arts, Theology, Literature, Philosophy, Law, and Music. These degrees were 'available for all persons of twenty-one years and upwards, without discrimination as to sex, race, or creed'. The power to impart degrees in this international and interdenominational educational establishment rests on a charter granted Mar Georgius 'in virtue of the plenary authority vested in him by the Constitutions and Canon Law of the Western Orthodox Catholic Church'. A Doctorate of Divinity could be obtained for £15 15s.; a Mastership of Arts for £10 10s. Full particulars of the most attractive Faculty Gowns, Hoods, Caps, and Bands could be obtained from the Registrar. This official was Mar Theodorus, Bishop of Mercia, who also held the office of Chancellor.[2] It was lucky for this prelate of the Old Catholic Orthodox Church (Apostolic Service Church)

[1] See p. 374.
[2] See p. 375.

457

that both the Church of England and the Catholicate of the West were able to make use of him. He still remained in charge of his Northamptonshire parish, as he had done when head of the University of Sulgrave under the direction of the Primate of the American Catholic Church.[1]

In the meantime the curial offices of the Catholicate were transferred to 3 Ruskin Avenue, Kew Gardens, Surrey. A mission chapel, dedicated to St Michael, had been opened at 45a Winchester Road, Twickenham. Mar Georgius felt himself constrained to ordain more priests for the spiritual benefit of his would-be worldwide flock.

On November 24, 1946, he enthroned in the Patriarchal Domestic Chapel of St Aristobulus, Kew, Bishop Earl Anglin Lawrence James, D.D., LL.D., but only *in absentia*. This prelate was represented by his Proxy, Mar Leofric, Archbishop of Suthronia.[2] It was pointed out that no better choice for an Exarch of the Canadas could have been found than Bishop Earl James, for there was a North American Indian strain in his ancestry. The absentee prelate, who had been consecrated by Archbishop Carfora, Supreme Primate of the North American Old Roman Catholic Church, on June 17, 1945, was given the style of 'His Eminence Mar Laurentius, Archbishop and Metropolitan of Acadia, and Exarch of the Catholicate of the West in the Canadas'.[3]

On January 17, 1947, the Holy Governing Synod issued a decree that the *Filioque* clause in the Nicene Creed had been dropped, in conformity with the usage of the Orthodox Eastern Churches. Meanwhile all sorts of important events were taking place. Archbishop Ryan had flown from India to Britain to confer with the Catholicos. On the Feast of St Antony the Abbot, January 17, Archbishop Swain and his American Episcopal Church (said to number some 160,000 members) had been united with the Catholicate of the West as an autocephalous affiliated rite. It was also on January 17, 1947, that a union was effected between Mar Timotheos Stumpfl and his so-called 'Orthodox Catholic Missions' in Austria with Mar Georgius, but on January 10, 1948, the Patriarch of Glastonbury found reasons solemnly to excommunicate him.[4] Meanwhile the Vicariate of the Catholicate of the

[1] See p. 375. The Vice-Chancellor was the Rev. Isaac Harthill, LL.D., B. Phil.; and the Senior Proctor, Dr Sidney Linfoot, Ph. D., D.D. Mar Georgius acted as Supreme Head of the Academy.
[2] Charles L. Saul, later head of the English Episcopal Church. (See pp. 233.)
[3] For further details of Mar Laurentius, see pp. 245, 246.
[4] See p. 320.

His Sacred Beatitude Mar David I (William David de Ortega Maxey), Patriarch of Malaga, Apostolic Primate of All the Iberians, and Supreme Hierarch of the Catholicate of the West in the Americas. Behind him are the Rev. C. W. Powell, D.D.; the Very Rev. Fr Mgr Bartholomew; and the Rev. Matthew N. Nelson, D.D., later titular Bishop of Hawaii. Among the five white-gowned Deaconesses is the Rev. Mother-General Marie Hunt, D.D. The photograph was taken at Los Angeles, California, April 28, 1946.

West in the Indies had been raised to an Exarchate under Archbishop Ryan, who was given the title of Mar James. A Missionary District had been constituted in Eire, under the Rev. Maurice J. Keenan of Dublin. There was no doubt that it would not be very long before the Anglican Communion, the dissident Eastern Churches, and the Roman Catholic Church would be forced to realize that the Catholicate of the West must be taken seriously.

The March 1947 issue of *The Orthodox Catholic Review* explained that the Apostolic Primacy of All the Britons, which was coterminous with the Patriarchate of Glastonbury, covered the whole of the British Empire, but for the convenience of organization, and to relieve the curial staff at Kew Gardens, British possessions in the Americas had been attached to the Patriarchate of Malaga.[1]

Although there were now eight dioceses in England and Wales, none of them, with the exception of Glastonbury, had so much as a pro-cathedral, and the Patriarch himself had to make do with a small domestic oratory at Kew, not having the hospitality of either St Margaret's Roman Catholic Church in Pope's Grove or any of the nearby Anglican churches. Still, as more and more men were being raised to minor and major orders it would not be long before the new hierarchy had sufficient clergy to minister to the faithful when they materialized.

Mar Georgius himself had no doubt that the Catholicate of the West would make a strong appeal to 'many modern-thinking people whose hearts respond to the Message of Our Divine Lord and Saviour Jesus Christ'. He was sure that thousands were 'repelled by the coldness and formality of the average Christian Church, and the narrowness of outlook' which pervaded both clergy and people in the nineteen-forties. In Anglican churches of the 'Catholic' type they found 'fussiness' and aloofness; in those of Moderate Anglicanism they detected 'a civil-service atmosphere of drab respectability; whilst in the Low Churches and Protestant chapels they felt repelled by what seems to be sanctimonious

---

[1] The Patriarchate of Glastonbury had now been divided as follows: (1) *Patriarchal Archdiocese of Glastonbury* (Counties of Somerset, Wilts, Dorset, Hants, Surrey, London, and Middlesex), Mar Georgius, with assistants; Mar Joannes, Titular Bishop of St Marylebone; and Mar Benignus, Titular Bishop of Mere; (2) *Diocese of Selsey* (Sussex), Mar Jacobus II; (3) *Diocese of Siluria* (Principality of Wales and County of Monmouth), Mar Hedley; (4) *Diocese of Mercia* (Berks and Oxon), Mar Theodorus; (5) *Diocese of Repton* (Counties of Derby, Stafford, Cheshire, and Lancashire), Mar David; (6) *Diocese of Minster* (Kent and Essex), Mar Francis; (7) *Diocese of Deira* (County of York), Mar Adrianus; (8) *Diocese of Verulam* (Hertfordshire), Mar John. All the rest of the British Isles remained under the personal jurisdiction of Mar Georgius, pending the erection of more dioceses.

unctuousness, or else by a form of lifeless intellectualism'.[1]

Intensive propaganda was carried on with the hope that people who had drifted away from both Anglo and Roman Catholicism would find a happy spiritual home in what was now called the Catholic Apostolic Church, which was no new sect, and which offered to all Christians exactly those conditions and privileges for which thirsty souls were yearning. In all its services, so it was stated, 'beauty, love, joy, and uplift are in evidence, and the ornate ritual is not just put together for the sake of effect, but each act has a highly symbolic meaning'. Seekers after truth were told that 'the preaching and instruction is practical and helpful, and is full of beautiful philosophy, and we present to the people also a full system of Biblical prophecy in relation to the events which are going on around us, throwing much light upon those things which are obscure to the conventional churches'. Nine spiritual gifts of the Holy Spirit were recognized. Those possessing these gifts or *charismata* were permitted to exercise them to the help and edification of the people. Even more important:

'The Bishops of the Church are in close touch with the parochial clergy, make frequent episcopal visitations, and like to get to know the people, so that they can bring them Christ's love and blessing in that great fullness which particularly attaches to the Bishops as the successors of the Apostles. The Priests and other Clergy are not afflicted with "professionalism", but delight to be real fathers of their flocks, giving to all love, sympathy, understanding, blessing and help.'

Remembering that all the eight bishops of the Glastonbury Patriarchate had to earn their livings in secular employment, including the Patriarch himself, it is much to their credit that they found time to make occasional visitations of their respective dioceses. After reading the following message, it is indeed surprising that so few people were attracted to the Catholic Apostolic Church.

'There is nothing cold, sanctimonious, unctuous, condemnatory, or "puritanical" in our midst; the most spiritual people are usully the most natural. We hold that natural pleasures were given us by God to enjoy, and the people are encouraged not only to have fellowship together in public worship and works of mercy and love, but as members of the same Family of God to enjoy their social

[1] Maranatha Pamphlets. No. 2. *The Catholic Apostolic Church Catholicate of the West* (Glastonbury, 1947).

pleasures together also. We do not teach total abstinence from the good things of life, and our people are free to go to theatres, cinemas, dances, and so forth, and to take liquor and to smoke, just as they desire; although we do inculcate moderation in all things. The "killjoy" attitude is emphatically condemned by us, for it is really Manicheeism, an ancient heresy against which the early Church strenuously contended.'

In conclusion, the people of Britain were urged to remember that

'THE CATHOLIC APOSTOLIC CHURCH (Catholicate of the West) is no new church or sect, but a living branch of the Church established of old by Our Lord Jesus Christ, restored to the pristine purity and joy of Apostolic times and fully equipped to meet the needs of our times—THE OLD CHURCH FOR THE NEW AGE. The keynote of the whole movement is love. *"Let that mind be in you which was also in Christ Jesus"*. Our churches are veritable storehouses for the pouring out in great volume of God's life and power. By so doing we make ready the way of the Lord, for the day of His Return draws near. "Even so, come Lord Jesus".'[1]

It was a pity that this edifying leaflet did not give a list of the churches in England, Wales, and Scotland which were 'veritable storehouses for the pouring out in great volume of God's love and power', but the truth was they existed for the moment only in the vivid imagination of the author.

No matter, there was every prospect of a great forward movement being initiated a Catholic Apostolic Crusade covering every continent. On April 14, 1947, Mar James, Archbishop of India, boarded a plane at Heathrow Airport, bound for La Guardia Airport, New York. He had been nominated 'Catholicatial Legate' to America, with a special mission to contact Mar Shimum Jesse, Patriarch of Seleucia-Ctesiphon, Nestorian Catholicos of the East, then staying in Chicago. Nothing came of this meeting, and before the end of the year His Eminence Mar James had severed his relations with Mar Georgius and the Catholicate of the West.[2] Another rent in its garment took place in 1947 when Mar Leofric, Archbishop of Suthronia, withdrew and founded a new body, known eventually as 'The English Episcopal Church', with its headquarters at Acton, W.3.[3]

[1] ibid.
[2] See p. 235.
[3] See p. 234.

More prayers were obviously needed to prevent further schisms, so Mar Georgius appointed an official Anthem to be sung at patriarchal ceremonies and visitations. It ran:

God bless our Patriarch, whose Holy See,
Shines as a centre of true unity;
Strengthen his hands with Apostolic power,
That on Thy people, he Thy love may shower.

Anoint his lips with heavenly doctrine rare,
That Apostolic truth he may declare;
Grant him discernment 'twixt the dark and light;
Evil and falsehood may he put to flight.

May he prepare the way of Christ the King,
And cause Thy praise throughout the world to ring,
And at the last present his flock to Thee,
In holy love and spotless unity.

It was suggested that these inspired verses should be sung to the tune of 'Saviour again to Thy dear Name we raise'.

It really did look as if the Patriarch's hands were being filled with apostolic power, for by a Bull dated July 27, 1947, he formally erected a small group of ex-Latin Catholics in Belgium into an autocephalous Rite under his own jurisdiction. This new body was given the name of *L'Église Catholique du Rite Dominicain*. The founder, Robert Gustave Marie Lutgen, had been introduced to Mar Georgius by Bishop Friedrich Heiler of the Vilatte succession.[1] Mgr Lutgen was appointed Vicar-General, and a vernacular version of the liturgical books of the Dominican Order was made obligatory.[2]

In the 1947 edition of *Crockford's Clerical Directory* some sarcastic remarks were made by the writer of the Preface about the Western Orthodox University, which, as stated already, Mar Georgius had chartered. The Preface to the 1948 edition contained further comments concerning the Patriarch of Glastonbury, ending with the words:

'The only recent activity on the part of this prelate of which we

---

[1] See p. 491.
[2] cf. *Ni Romains, ni Protestants . . . mais Catholiques Apostoliques* (Hove Anvers, n.d.) On February 22, 1953, Mar Georgius consecrated Lutgen as Archbishop of Antwerp.

have any knowledge is the holding of an ordination during April 1945 at a church in London. If he should try to assert himself at any time in any way in the neighbourhood of Glastonbury, we imagine that whoever may be responsible for the ruins of the Abbey there is accustomed to dealing with cranks (harmless or otherwise) and obscene birds of every kind.'[1]

This was really going too far, and Mar Georgius instituted legal proceedings, and when his Statement of Claim was delivered, he naturally obtained an apology and damages from the Oxford University Press and Geoffrey Cumberlege, the publishers of *Crockford*. Owing to some legal difficulty, however, the anonymous writer of the Preface got off scot-free.

Realising that it was his duty to put to flight both evil and falsehood, Mar Georgius started the New Year of 1948 with the excommunication of three bishops, three priests, and one exorcist.[2]

Yet in spite of internal disagreements, the Catholicate appeared to be expanding, for on November 12, 1947, a new Apostolic Eparchy of All the Frisians was erected. Its Patriarchal Throne was fixed at Amersfoort, whose Bishop, Mar Philippus (H.P. Abbinga), became Primate.[3]

The now world-wide Church, claiming to be both Catholic and Orthodox, had already been organized on paper under twelve Apostolic Primates (only three of whom existed in human form), ruling as mass Eparchies, representing the twelve tribes of the Spiritual Israel, which were constituted on a general basis of the origins, races, and languages of Europe and Asia Minor in the days of the Undivided Church. Territories since discovered were regarded as 'suburbs' of the nations mainly responsible for their development.[4]

---

[1] Preface, p. xv.

[2] Mar Timotheos, Metropolitan of Aquileia (Aloysius Stumpfl), 'for sacrilege, superstition, etc.'; Mar David, Bishop of Repton (F. D. Bacon), 'for breach of his oath of Canonical Obedience, etc.'; Mar Benignus, Bishop of Mere (R. K. Hurgon), 'for breach of his Oath of Canonical Obedience, etc'.; Rev. Hubert G. Knowles, 'for slander and malicious gossip'; Rev. Charles Hastler, 'for breach of agreement, libel, etc.'; Rev. William A. Corke, 'for behaving schismatically, libel, etc.'; Rev. William Mellor, 'for entering into a relationship with a Bishop other than his Ordinary without due authority and sanction'. (*The Orthodox Catholic Review*, February, 1948.) Corke and Hastler were the Abbot and Prior of the Order of Llanthony Brothers. (See p. 396.)

[3] See p. 509. He had formerly been a Liberal Catholic priest, and was consecrated on October 13, 1946, by Mar John Emmanuel (A. W. Brooks). Later on Abbinga was styled 'Vicar Apostolic of the Catholicate of the West in the Netherlands and Dutch East Indies'. He severed all relations with Mar Georgius in January 1952.

[4] These Eparchies had been organized as follows: (1) *Of All the Britons*—the British Isles, and all British possessions, other than those situated in the Americas (Patriarchate of Glastonbury); (2) *Of All the Iberians*—Spain, Portugal, Portuguese

463

The Catholicate of the West

To ensure the proper organization of these twelve Eparchies (not to mention the eight dioceses of the Glastonbury Patriarchate), five Church Courts were set up at the 'phanar' half-a-mile from the eighteenth-century Chinese Pagoda in Kew Gardens: Diocesan, Provincial, Exarchal, Patriarchal, and a Supreme Ecclesiastical Tribunal for the Catholicate of the West. Had they ever got working on a world-wide scale, their officials might have been even more numerous by 1963 than those listed in the 1736 page *Annuario Pontificio*.

Not satisfied with any of the ancient or modern rites of either Eastern or Western Christendom, Mar Georgius felt constrained to compile a new liturgy. The object was to make it the most elaborate (but not necessarily the most liturgical) rite in the world, even richer than that of the Catholic Apostolic Church, which required a team of sixty-four ministers to conduct properly the angelical version of the Holy Eucharist. Having been an Irvingite acolyte for more than a quarter of a century, there was little that Mar Georgius did not know about the minutiae of ritual; and now, at last, he had the chance to put his encyclopedic knowledge to some practical use. He borrowed a good deal from *The Liturgy and other Divine Offices of the* (Irvingite) *Church*, but interpolated extracts from other liturgies into his Glastonbury Rite.

Most important was the design of the Patriarchal Tiara; it was laid down that it must bear the words 'Holiness to the Lord', and be adorned with floral emblems, crosses, etc., and with a double-ended patriarchal cross. As no doubt, the Catholicate of the West would soon be blessed with religious orders, so the ceremonial vesture of a deaconess must be settled. Having consulted ancient Pontificals, Mar Georgius decided that a *tunica* was indicated, with an *orarium* pendent over the left shoulder, together with a *maphora* or veil. He thought that a Protodeaconess might be allowed a cross

---

overseas possessions, Republic of Andorra, and the Americas (Patriarchate of Malaga); (3) *Of All the Frisians*—Netherlands, and Indonesia (Patriarchate of Amersfoort); (4) *Of All the Helvetians*—Switzerland, and the Principality of Lichtenstein; (5) *Of All the Latins*—Italy, Italian overseas possessions, Vatican City State, and the Republic of San Marino; (6) *Of All the Franks*—France, French overseas possessions, Belgium, and its overseas possessions, and the Principality of Monaco; (7) *Of All the Teutons*—Germany, and the Free City of Danzig; (8) *Of All the Pannonians*—Austria and Czechoslovakia; (9) *Of All the Slavs*—Russia, Poland, and the Baltic States; (10) *Of All the Turanians*—Hungary, Finland, and Turkey; (11) *Of All the Scandinavians*—Denmark, Norway, Sweden, Iceland, and Greenland; (12) *Of All the Levantines*—Greece, Albania, Balkan States, Asia Minor, and Egypt.

In recent years the term 'Apostolikes' has been used instead of 'Eparchies'.

suspended on a golden cord, to show that she had the status of a Lady Abbess.

The Glastonbury Rite was provided with its first Protodeaconess in February 1948, when the rare and impressive ceremony of a Consecration of a Virgin was carried out in the Cathedral and Abbey Church of Christ the King, New Barnet.[1] It is recorded that Sister Mary was then elevated to the 'protodiaconisate', and invested with a pectoral cross; and that 'with sweet, holy, and modest demeanour she looked as though she had walked right out of the Acts of the Apostles into the twentieth-century'.[2]

Having been robed by His Beatitude, Sister Mary was given the kiss of peace upon her forehead, after which she made her threefold vow of poverty, chastity, and obedience. We are told that 'the air was vibrant with power' as the choir sang the hymn 'Love that will not let me go'. The Protodeaconess was then anointed with chrism, invested with a ring and wreath, and handed a breviary. After this Mar Georgius led her to a throne on the epistle side of the sanctuary, where she was inducted, installed and enthroned by the name, title, style, and jurisdiction of 'The Venerable Mother in Christ, Mary, Titular Abbess of Wirral'. Finally, her name was inserted into the Diptychs of the Loving in the Canon of the Glastonbury Rite—'especially Mary our Abbess'.[3] More ordinations of deacons, deaconesses and priests were held in September 1948, but for the moment the Catholicate of the West did not have any monks or friars.[4]

Much more important, however, were the Prophetic, Evangelical, Pastoral, and Diaconal Colleges. They formed junior departments of the Apostolic College, evocative of the Irvingite College of Apostles, which held its first Council in 1835. But the Catholicate of the West never managed to find a rich banker to erect collegiate buildings, or even a modest Cathedral, as Henry Drummond (1786–1860) did for the Irvingites at Albury, Surrey. So there was no Apostles' Chapel in which the Plenary Episcopal Council could meet. The Council was composed of all Bishops with jurisdiction of, or affiliated to, the Catholicate, and was stated to be

[1] See p. 284. The tithe-barn chapel of the Confraternity of the Kingdom of Christ had now superseded St Aristobulus's Oratory, Kew, as Mar Georgius's cathedral.
[2] Unfortunately St Paul does not record if 'our sister Phoebe, who devoted her service to the church at Cenchrae', wore a pectoral cross on a golden cord. (cf. Romans 16, 1.)
[3] cf. *Hieratika*, January–September 1948.
[4] The male members of the Confraternity of Christ the King had the nominal status of Canons Regular. (See p. 288.)

'the nearest equivalent of a General Council which it is possible to hold in an organization which does not in itself comprise the whole Universal Church'.

Like the Irvingites in the eighteen-thirties, the newly constituted Catholic Apostolic Church of the nineteen-forties did not claim to be the *whole* Church; merely a part thereof. It acknowledged the legal canonical status of all properly constituted Episcopal Churches possessing Apostolic Succession in unbroken lines; and accepted all validly baptized Christians, irrespective of sect, to be members as individuals of that One, Holy, Catholic and Apostolic Church. Its system of organization was, therefore, put before all Christian peoples as a sign and test—'Gracious the sight, and full of comfort, when brethren dwell together united.'[1] The pity was that, unlike the Irvingite hierarchy of apostles, prophets, evangelists, pastors, teachers, angels, deacons, and deaconesses, the disciples of Mar Georgius found it quite impossible to live together in peace and unity for very long. The balm poured down on the heads of the bishops, reaching to the very skirts of their albs, like the dews of Hermon falling on the hill of Sion, did not grant much benediction or life everlasting.[2]

All the same, one or two quite distinguished converts were made. Possibly having formed the opinion that the Anglican Communion was on the decline, and tending to disintegration by reason of her association with the interdenominational Church of South India; and not feeling drawn to the Old Roman Catholic (Pro Uniate Rite), ruled over by the Archbishop of Caer-Glow in the Cotswolds, the Rev. John Edward Bazille-Corbin, Barrister-at-Law (Lincoln's Inn), and since 1923 rector of Runwell St Mary, near Wickford, Essex, decided to apply for *sub conditione* validation of his Anglican Orders to the Catholicate of the West. This he received, and on April 3, 1948, following conditional baptism, confirmation, and the bestowal of minor and major orders up to the priesthood by the Universal Patriarch Banks of the Old Catholic Orthodox Church, he was raised to the episcopate by Mar Georgius. The Roman Pontifical was used for all the ceremonies. The new prelate was given the name and style of Mar Marcus Valerius, titular Bishop of Selsey, and appointed Chancellor of the Glastonbury Patriarchate and Western Catholicate.[3] He was also made

[1] Psalm 132 (133), 1.
[2] cf. Psalm 132, 1–3.
[3] Marcus Valerius Corvinus was a well-known writer and a personal friend of the poet Horace. Believing that he was directly descended from a Norman nobleman named

The Catholicate of the West

Rector-Provincial for Canterbury in the Order of Corporate Re-union.[1] Two years later His Lordship added to his Oxford M.A. and M.R.S.T., the degree of D.D. (Western Orthodox University). In 1957 Prince Theodore Lescaris Commenus (son of one of the claimants to the throne of the Byzantine Empire), as President of that chartered international institution, granted him the degree of Doctor Laureatus in the Imperial Philo-Byzantine University (Madrid). The would-be Emperor Flavius Eugenius conferred upon him the Order of St Eugene of Trebizond (Knight Commander). From the same imperial source were received the Grand Collar of the Order of Santa Agata di Paterno, and the title of Duca di San Giacomo. The French claimant to the thrones of Aragon, etc., the Balearic Isles, etc., and would-be *de jure* King of the Two Sicilies, made the Essex clergyman a member of the Order of Saint Michel, with the title of Marquis de Beuvel.[2]

The titular Archbishop of Selsey retained his living in the Diocese of Chelmsford until he retired on September 30, 1961. During his incumbency of the parish, Mar Marcus Valerius, with the knowledge of the Anglican Local Ordinary, though without his authorization, used a vernacular version of the ancient Sarum Rite instead of the Book of Common Prayer. As a liturgist he held it to be more appropriate to an ancient parish church than the somewhat exotic Glastonbury Rite, authorized elsewhere in the Eparchy of All the Britons.[3] As the county of Essex formed part of the wide-spread Diocese of Minster in the Patriarchal Province of Glaston-bury, ruled over by Mar Francis (Langhelt), Mar Marcus Valerius claimed to wield no territorial jurisdiction beyond the boundaries of his parish, of which he was the patron. During the tenure of his office as Rector it presumably constituted what is called an ecclesiastical 'peculiar'.[4]

Corbino, who appears among the followers of the Conqueror in the Battle Abbey Rolls, and feeling that Marcus Valerius Corvinus may have been one of his remote ancestors, Mr Bazille-Corbin decided to adopt his two first names for his designation as a prelate, even if Marcus Valerius were a pagan.

[1] In 1958 he received the status of Archbishop *ad personam*.

[2] By the summer of 1947 the number of persons with exotic titles had grown to such an extent, that the editor of *Debrett* was constantly being called up on the telephone to answer questions about them. (Cf. Cyril Hankinson, *My Forty Years with Debrett* (1963), p. 144).

[3] He is the author of *Toward a Uniate Rite, being the text of the Sarum Ordinary and Canon, closely rendered into English* (1951).

[4] Among the many titles and distinctions held by this prelate are the following: Chairman National Clergy Association (Chelmsford Branch), 1943–53; Warden-founder of the Monarchist League; Fellow of the American International Academy, 1954; Chancellor of the Order of the Crown of Stuart, 1955; Médaille d'Or de la

467

The Catholicate of the West

As the Supreme Pontiff of a Universal Church, and the spiritual head of twelve Apostolic Eparchies (most of them still only *in petto*) it was fitting that His Sacred Beatitude Mar Georgius should be able to add a few more ranks, titles, decorations, and academic qualifications to those he had acquired already. By December 1949 the editor of *Christocracy* was able to confirm that in addition to being Patriarch of Glastonbury, Apostolic Primate of All the Britons, and Catholicos of the West, Hugh George de Willmott Newman was also Prince de Mardin in the Principality and Patriarchate of Antioch. Moreover, he could claim the offices of Exarch of the Order of Antioch for Britain, Ruling Prelate of the Order of Corporate Reunion, and Chancellor of the International University, which was virtually universal. On ceremonial occasions he could add to his patriarchal robes the imposing insignia of Grand Master of the Orders of St Thomas Acon, SS. Gregory and Sarkis, and the Spiritual Christian Nation; as well as those of Prelat Commandeur of the Order of the Crown of Thorns, and Chevalier Grand Officier of the Order of the Lion and Black Cross. He held the rare distinction of Doctor Christiantissimus; and had also acquired the rank of His Serene Highness Prince of Saxe-Noricum.[1]

The Catholicate of the West was very much in the limelight during the Congress of Healing, organized by one of its priests, Fr John Beswarwick, Ph.D., which was held at the Kingsway Hall, London, on July 24, 1948. It was reported that some 1,750 people were present, including many Roman Catholic, Anglican, and Orthodox clergy, besides Free Church ministers. Mar Georgius presided and gave his patriarchal blessing to the healers. It was claimed that some remarkable cures were effected at this Congress, the first of its kind ever to be held in Britain. It was stated that Mar Georgius (with similar ideals to those of the late Miss Dorothy Kerin), 'anxious to do all things according to the ancient customs and traditions of the Church', had revived the ancient Guild of the Parabolani, said to have been founded at Alexandria by a decree of the Emperor Theodosius II, dated September 28, A.D. 416. The Patriarch of Glastonbury wrote that the new Guild had been placed

---

Renaissance Française, 1956; Le Mérite National Français (Croix de Commandeur), 1959; and Fellow of the International Lunar Society.

[1] Mardin, over which Mar Georgius ruled as Prince *in absentia*, is a city in Kurdistan. Apparently his other princedom was in the former Roman province of Noricum, south of the Danube, comprising the modern Lower and South Austria, and the greater part of Carinthia, Styria and Salzburg. Unfortunately no estates went with these titles, so he did not benefit by them financially.

under the jurisdiction of the successor of St Cyril of Alexandria. It consisted of three grades: (1) *Clerical Healers*—Priests, Deacons, Subdeacons, Acolytes, Exorcists, and Deaconesses; (2) *Charismatic Healers*—gifted persons holding the Bishop's Licence; (3) *Professional Healers*—Physicians, Surgeons, Osteopaths, Naturopaths, Masseurs, Nurses, and the like, enrolled by the Bishop in the Guild. No fee or reward of any kind might be demanded or accepted by anybody engaged in 'Divine Healing'.[1]

By this time a hitherto unknown prelate, Mgr John James Van Ryswyk, who claimed far more ranks, titles, and decorations than Mar Georgius, was being much talked about in London. It appeared that he was a widely travelled British-naturalized Dutchman, reported to have served in the Netherlands navy, and also to have been engaged in secret political activities in the Near East. He had founded what was called the Apostolic Church of St Peter in 1935. There were rumours that he had been raised to the episcopate in Rome by a bishop (whose name could not be revealed) so that he could assist the Vatican in its fight against international Communism.

About a month before the Cominform, a new international Communist organization was set up at Belgrade on October 6, 1947, Bishop Van Ryswyk had presided over a cosmopolitan Congress held at Paris, where sun-worshippers, alchemists, Rosicrucians, 'Friends of Edgar Allan Poe', and representatives of hundreds of esoteric sects planned the salvation of the human race on psychic principles. One of their objects was to set up a 'World Spiritual Parliament' somewhere in Africa. The U.S.A. delegates represented 2,200 groups; those from India formed a group of mystics; and Catholic France provided 300 delegates from fifty-two neo-Gnostic bodies. Conspicuous among them was American-born Raymond Duncan, robed in a toga, who taught occultism, dancing, and made sandals. Another striking feature was the silver-haired Brother Michael, Bulgarian-born superior of the White Brotherhood, whose members got up before dawn to do mystical gymnastics as the sun rose.[2]

In the opinion of his apparently vast circle of cultured and deeply spiritually-minded friends, Bishop Van Ryswyk might yet turn out to be the saviour of humanity. Not only had he founded the Apostolic Church of St Peter; he was also Supreme Master of the

[1] See Information Bulletin, No. 11, *Divine Healing*, 1948.
[2] cf. *Huddersfield Daily Examiner*, September 18, 1947.

Temple of Service, claiming about 16,000,000 members, though, naturally enough, few people in Britain could be expected so far to have come across any of them. His Lordship likewise held the office of Founder-President of the Avatar Defenders of Civilization, who were among the bodies which had assembled in Paris.[1]

The headquarters of the Bishop's multiform world-wide apostolate was a mansion at 52 Victoria Road, Kensington, W.8. One of its larger rooms had been furnished at great expense as the 'Sanctum of the Vigil', and served as a pro-cathedral for the Apostolic Church of St Peter. Mgr Van Ryswyk having decided that it would benefit him to acquire some more lines of apostolic succession, it was the privilege of Mar Georgius to re-ordain him up to the priesthood on November 6, 1949. The function took place in the domestic chapel of the Lord Patriarch Banks at East Molesey, who acted as server to His Beatitude. An even more impressive ceremony, however, was performed in the Sanctum of the Vigil on November 20, when the Supreme Master of the Temple of Service and Founder President of the Avatar Defenders of Civilization was reconsecrated by the Catholicos of the West, using a vernacular version of the Byzantine Rite. His assistant was Mar Francis, Bishop of Minster. Here is a description of the consecration printed in the official organ of the Apostolic Church of St Peter:

'After the opening voluntary, *Ave Verum*, the procession entered to the music of the Creed, rendered by the choir of the Russian Orthodox Church of Paris. The Lord Patriarch was attired in robes of cloth of gold, Bishop Langhelt and Fr Sandys-Pemberton in white dalmatic and tunicle respectively, and Mgr Van Ryswyk in white and gold, in sharp contrast to which stood out the black and

---

[1] The Order of Avatar, so it was stated, was an organization of people of all races, believing in the fundamental spiritual basis of life, as opposed to present-day materialism—in this sense a 'Spiritual Kingdom'. The members regarded themselves as the defenders of true civilization. It was advertised that knighthoods in this esoteric Order could be bought for the sum of £5 5s. The annual subscription fee was £3 3s., but it naturally cost a little extra to get the rank of 'Prince of the Faith'. *Avatar* is said to be 'a sanskrit word which, freely translated, means "bringer of light"', or the highest good, and has the advantage that it may be spoken by any tongue'. It is stated that 'the primary object of the Avatar Plans are decentralization of political power and the independence of all peoples and nations in Autonomous States, which may be federated into cultural and ethical groups, provided this is done with the consent of the peoples concerned.' The *Avatar Imperium Internum* is described as 'a Universal Order working for a new way of life based upon the sacredness of The Individual and the Spiritual Foundations of human existence'. In Hindu philosophy the highest avatara is a man on earth in human form of the Second Aspect of the Trinity, i.e. Vishnu. There are alleged to be ten avatars of Vishnu, including Krishna. They are subject no longer to the laws of Karma and Reincarnation, but voluntarily return to earth to help on the spiritual evolution of humanity.

white bands of the Solicitor (Mr E. F. Power-Green). It is interesting to note that the *epigonation* worn by Mgr Van Ryswyk was presented to him by Bey Sulik Acarli, President of the Turkish Social Democratic Party, and Secretary of the Red Crescent (the Islamic equivalent of the Red Cross Society, whose wife had beautifully embroidered it.)[1]

'After the long function Mgr Van Ryswyk was solemnly enthroned by the Patriarch by the name, style, and jurisdiction of Mar Joannes, Lord Bishop of Ryswyk, and Imperator of the Order Equestris Militaris Avatar. . . . Before the recessional His Beatitude conferred upon Brigadier L. M. Poole, D.S.O., the Knighthood of the Order of St Gregory and Sarkis, and upon the Bishop of Ryswyk, the grade of Grand Knight Cross with the title of Duke de Richelieu-Ryswyk in the Order of the Spiritual Christian Nation, these honours having been awarded for the services which the gentlemen concerned had rendered to religion.'[2]

For some reason or other the Apostolic Church of St Peter did not make many converts from the nobility and landed gentry in the next sixteen years, although this might have been expected when one recalls the ranks, titles, distinctions and degrees claimed by its founder. The World Spiritual Parliament, planned at Paris during the esoteric gathering in September 1947, was never set up in Africa, so the salvation of the human race on psychic principles hung fire. There may have been political reasons why the inter-

---

[1] The *epigonation* is a lozenge of stiffened material worn by Byzantine bishops. It is suspended at the right side from the girdle by a ribbon, and reaches the knee.

[2] *Christocracy*, December 1949, p. 149. It is improbable that any prelate, Eastern or Western, could boast of so much 'blue blood', or claim so many ranks, titles, distinctions and degrees as Mgr James John Van Ryswyk, with the exception of Mgr William Franklin Wolsey. (See pp. 484–5.) It has been stated that Van Ryswyk was a Hereditary Count of the Holy Roman Empire; Knight of the Order of the Golden Fleece; Duke de Valmahon; Prince de Usipiae; Marquis de Casaldorato; Baron, Imperator, Pontifex-Avatur Imperium Internum; Grand Master of the Ordo Equestris Militaris Avatar; Prior (Great Britain) of the Order of St John of Jerusalem (Malta); Knight Grand Cross of the Order of Charles III; Knight Grand Collar of the Order of Charles VII; Knight Guardian and Councillor of the Order of the Iron Crown; and Knight Grand Cross of the Order of St Mary of Bethlehem. His Lordship also held (*honoris causa*) the degrees of D.D., D. Phil., and D. Sc. of unspecified universities. In addition to the above titles he could display the insignia of the Grand Collar of the Ordine Dinastico di S. Agate dei Paterno (Two Sicilies); Grand Collar of Ordine dei Cavalieri del Concordia (Spain); Grand Collar of the Ordo Capitularis Stellae Argentae Cruciatae (Rome), and the Grand Cross of Justice of the Ordre Militaire de la Liberté (Principality of Liechtenstein). It is understood that Mgr Van Ryswyk had reason to believe that he was a re-incarnation of both Cardinal Richelieu and of St Peter the Apostle: the interesting corollary to this which suggests that Richelieu was the re-incarnation of St Peter has not been confirmed—the alternative hypothesis (that the Monsignor re-incarnated two separate people) is subject to the observations made in *Cosmos* (November–March 1962).

471

national Temple of Service and the Avatar Defenders of Civilization had to lie low, and never got press, radio, or TV publicity.

Mar Joannes, Duke de Richelieu-Ryswyk, continued to reside in the fading red-brick Gothic Revival mansion (formerly the vicarage of Christ Church, Kensington) at the corner of Eldon and Victoria Roads, but no notice boards beside either the front or back doors informed passers-by what services were held behind the leaded lights of the upstairs Sanctum of the Vigil.[1] The Imperator of the Order of Equestris Militaris Avatar appears to have led a more or less enclosed life in this retreat until he 'moved over' on February 24, 1963, in his sixty-fourth year. After a Requiem Mass had been celebrated in the Kensington Sanctum, his body was cremated at Golders Green. Whether the Apostolic Church of St Peter will survive him for long remains to be seen.

*   *   *   *   *

Much to the disgust of those who had chosen to constitute themselves its enemies, the Catholicate of the West kept its flag flying, and the work of reorganization and consolidation went forward with rapid strides, so the public were informed. On February 20, 1950, the Catholicate was incorporated in India under Act XXI of 1860 with the following Constituent Corporations: (1) *The Catholic Apostolic Church* (Catholicate of the West); (2) *The Western Orthodox University;* and (3) *The International College of Arms and Noblesse.*[2]

Unfortunately not all the hierarchy were loyal to the Prince Patriarch. Mar Benignus (Hurgon), Titular Bishop of Mere, who had been solemnly excommunicated in January 1948, but reconciled with His Beatitude on April 5, 1950, defied his authority again on June 24. Without apostolic mandate, in the Cathedral of the Good Shepherd, Chelsea, he laid hands on the Rev. A. St Denis Fry, a priest of the Evangelical Church of England, then acting as chaplain

---

[1] Van Ryswyk composed a special liturgy, called *The Most Holy Sacrament of the Presence*, best described as an interesting mixture of Anglican, Roman Catholic, and Eastern elements. The Canon appears to be based on the Gelasian Canon, but before the *Unde et memores* is inserted the following verse:

Thy hidden Splendour we adore
Let all creation now be still
And hail Thy glorious Presence here
And bow itself before Thy Will.

[2] So far the Patents of Arms granted by the last-named body have not been recognized by either the English College of Arms (Heralds' College) founded in 1483, or by the Court of the Lord Lyon, which is the equivalent for Scotland.

of St Nicolas School, Clevedon, Somerset, which was under the direction of Dr Pinder, Primate of this Protestant body. Mr Fry was given the elusive rank of prelate in the Order of Christ our Most Holy Redeemer, an interdenominational organization which was neither a church nor a sect, and he made no claim to the episcopate. Mar Georgius, having heard of this, and other irregular episcopal actions performed by the Titular Mar of Mere, who was Assistant to the Patriarchal Throne of Glastonbury, promptly excommunicated him for the second time.

After this painful exercise of his authority, it must have been a consolation to Mar Georgius on the Sunday within the Octave of Corpus Christi to carry the monstrance in procession through the streets of Chelsea, to give solemn Benediction in Sloane Square, and afterwards from the high altar of the Cathedral of the Good Shepherd.[1] The Catholic Apostolic Church of the Dominican Rite in Belgium appeared to be prospering under its Vicar-General, Mgr T. M. Lutgen. The Acting Vicar-General in Bermuda reported a constant round of activity. Far away in California, both the Patriarch of Malaga and the Bishop of Hawaii were said to be engaged in a strenuous apostolate. Mar Petrus, Exarch and Primate of the Apostolic Church in the Indies, wrote of the consoling work being done among Buddhist labourers in Ceylon, and the culture fostered at St John's University at Ambur, Madras Province.[2] In spite of severe handicaps, His Eminence Mar Laurentius, Exarch of Canada, was making progress with the bridge church, which would eventually link up the Atlantic, the Pacific, and the Arctic Oceans.[3]

Looking back over the year 1950, Mar Georgius wrote:

'But there are still very difficult days ahead, and the prophetic eye can discern still further attacks from without, not to mention "perils among false brethren" within. But this is a work of God, we know that God is with us, and one man with God on his side is in a majority. Those who expect very spectacular moves forward during the coming year will be doomed to disappointment. for the time is not yet.'

*   *   *   *   *

To go back three years before the consecration of the Duke de Richelieu-Ryswyk on October 13, 1946, at the Church of the Good

[1] See pp. 474–475.
[2] See p. 536.
[3] *Orthodox Catholic Review*, December 1950.

Shepherd, Wallington, Surrey, Mar Georgius, assisted by Mar Benignus, ordained to the priesthood Harold Percival Nicholson and John Beswarwick.[1] Both these men were reputed to possess remarkable charismatic gifts, and were put in charge of the Catholicate's department of spiritual healing.[2] Fr Nicholson soon made such a name for himself by his allegedly miraculous cures that it is not surprising he heard a call to found a new religious body, more likely to suit a weary post-war world than any of the existing churches in Britain. He gave it the inspiring name of 'The New Pentecostal Church of Christ'. His increasing number of disciples were indeed being filled with what appeared to be the Holy Spirit, beginning to speak in strange languages, as the Spirit gave utterance to each; even if the more mundane minded said mockingly: 'They have had their fill of new wine.'[3] Having acquired the blitzed neo-Byzantine-Romanesque Baptist Chapel in Lower Sloane Street, London, S.W.3, he restored and refurnished it in a super Anglo-Catholic manner. *The Orthodox Catholic Review* in its September-October 1948 issue reported the opening of the Church of the Good Shepherd, and published a photograph of Mar Georgius and Fr Nicholson. The former was depicted in the convocation robes of an Anglican bishop—rochet, chimere, and lawn sleeves, the latter in a gown and academic hood.

Not long after this Fr Nicholson broke off relations with the Glastonbury Patriarchate, and was released from the jurisdiction of Mar Georgius on April 13, 1949. It was obvious that the New Pentecostal Church of Christ needed a Primate, so in September that same year the rector of the Church of the Good Shepherd was raised to the episcopate by Mar David (Forster), Bishop of Devonia, Patriarch of the English Orthodox Church, who came over to Chelsea from Battersea to perform the ceremony.[4] By this time there were rumours that Bishop Nicholson was associated with Spiritualists, preached the doctrine of Reincarnation, accepted the Theosophical belief in 'The Masters', allowed services to be conducted by unordained persons, and read at some of his rites

[1] For the latter, see pp. 243, 244.
[2] See p. 268.
[3] Acts of the Apostles 2, 13.
[4] Forster had been ordained by Mar Georgius, but after severing his relations with the Catholicate of the West, got himself consecrated on July 17, 1949, by P. E. O'D. Cheshire, who had been raised to the episcopate on April 18, 1948, by Archbishop Hayman of Waltham, who fortunately at that particular moment was out of prison. (See p. 228.)

extracts from the apocryphal book called *The Aquarian Gospel of Jesus the Christ*.[1]

Of course, all this may have been scurrilous gossip and slander, but there was no doubt that young men were seeing visions and old men dreaming dreams in the converted Baptist Chapel between Sloane Square and Pimlico Road. Moreover, before long a smart eclectic congregation filled the newly erected Cathedral, among them Lady Munnings, wife of the famous horse-painter (President of the Royal Academy, 1944). For various reasons Bishop Nicholson decided that it might be to his advantage to rejoin the Catholicate of the West, and to have a further consecration *sub conditione* by Mar Georgius. This took place in his Chelsea Cathedral on the Vigil of Pentecost, May 27, 1950, when his body was re-named 'The Ancient Catholic Church'.

It was impressively reported in the Press that this function was heralded by a peal of bells. A splendid procession entered the building to the strains of 'Ye watchers and ye holy ones', sung by the male choristers in black cassocks and white surplices; the ladies of the *schola cantorum* looked fetching in their red gowns and caps. Mgr Nicholson, every inch a prelate, conveyed the impression of having been born to the crozier. His vestments and mitre were, of course, very properly of cloth of gold. The Lord Patriarch's vestments were of red and white silk, and gold tissue. The mixed choir gave a rendering of Blake's 'Jerusalem', as well as of the Patriarchal Anthem.[2] During the course of the long ceremonies Mgr Nicholson was invested by the Patriarch with the title of Mar Joannes, Archbishop of Karim, and granted the degrees of D.D. (Glastonbury), and Doctor of Spiritual Therapeutics in the International University. At the same time degrees were conferred on the co-consecrator, Benignus, the titular Mar of Mere. Having been vested with the Sacred Pallium and enthroned, the Archbishop of Karim listened to the choristers singing 'Crown him with many crowns'. The final procession wended its way around the Cathedral to the chanting of 'For all the Saints, who from their labours rest', as ✠ Joannes Karim graciously distributed his blessings to right and left.

During the afternoon there was a *thé dansant* and variety show in the crypt, when, so we are told, 'the congregation enjoyed them-

---

[1] The Aquarians were an early Christian sect which, for ascetic or other reasons, used water instead of wine in the Eucharist.
[2] See p. 462.

selves in a convivial atmosphere of love and brotherhood'.[1] It was also stated that

'those colourful ceremonies performed in the beautiful surroundings of a Cathedral Church, built up by the devoted labours of Archbishop Nicholson over a period of years, are very seldom to be witnessed in England, and that those present felt very happy to be privileged to attend. The Church is well renowned for the wonderful work of Divine Healing carried on there, for which the Archbishop trains his own workers, and has received world-wide publicity for the innumerable cures effected through the laying on of hands.'

Mar Joannes, however, was able to attract even bigger crowds to his animal services, one of which was reported by the *Daily Mail* on September 4, 1950. Readers were told how dogs barked and rabbits squealed. The choir boys and choir girls carried up to the sanctuary steps cats, rabbits, tortoises, and dogs of all breeds. There were mongrels as well as thoroughbred Alsatians; not forgetting 'Chou-chou', the shaven French poodle belonging to Mrs Vera Miderigh. Seated on his throne, the Archbishop blessed each animal, sprinkled it with holy water, and gave it a few whiffs of incense from the thurible. 'All doggies go to heaven,' he informed the reporter: 'Children must not cry when their doggies die, because they have a greater life hereafter. I would like to have had horses and cows here.'[2]

'*The Seven Principles governing Divine-Human Relations*', promulgated by Mar Joannes of Karim in 1950, provided a simple *Credo* for members of the Ancient Catholic Church, indicating that it was one of the most 'catholic' religious bodies in the world, able to offer a spiritual home for any man or woman, regardless of race or colour. So long as a catechumen was prepared to accept (1) The Fatherhood of God; (2) The Brotherhood of Man; (3) The Communion of Saints and the Ministry of Angels; (4) The continual existence of the human soul; (5) Personal responsibility; (6) Compensation and retribution hereafter for all the good and evil done on earth; and (7) Eternal progress open to every human soul, nothing else mattered. Archbishop Nicholson went even further than Mrs Mary Baker Eddy, who proclaimed in her *Science*

---

[1] *Orthodox Catholic Review*, June 1950.

[2] It seems a pity that the Catholic Study Circle for Animal Welfare never got Cardinal Griffin to hold a similar service in Westminster Cathedral; or that the Royal Society for the Prevention of Cruelty to Animals never persuaded Dr Wand, Bishop of London, to hold a national Blessing of Animals in St Paul's Cathedral.

The Most Rev. Mar Lukos (Davison Quartey Arthur),
Archbishop of the West Indies (Coptic Orthodox
Church Apostolic Incorporated), with the Mayor and
Mayoress of Deptford, at a Boys' Brigade inspection
(April 1957).

(By permission of the *Kentish Mercury*)

The Most Rev. Harold P. Nicholson, M.A., D.D.,
Archbishop of Karim, blessing Pet Dogs in the Ancient
Catholic Cathedral of the Good Shepherd, Chelsea,
London.

(*Photo: News Chronicle*)

and Health (1875) that suffering and death are merely the effects of false thinking, which consists in a mistaken belief in the existence of matter, i.e. the illusions of 'Mortal Mind'. He was bold enough to announce that there is no such thing as Death. Ancient Catholics were forbidden to believe in it. His Grace explained to readers of the *Daily Mail*: 'We believe that every religion has a grain of truth. I specialize in Divine Healing. I can cure people of almost any disease. I do not make money out of it. You should see the bills which have to be paid.' His Grace confided to the reporter that he had been a waiter in a well-known West End restaurant, that he was now married, and the father of children.

The Divine Healing carried on in Chelsea was widely advertised, not only in English, but in foreign newspapers. Sometimes letters containing offerings in money were delivered by mistake at the nearby Roman Catholic presbytery of St Mary's, Cadogan Street. This caused some embarrassment, for neither the titular Bishop of Lamus (made titular Archbishop of Beroea in 1951) nor any of his curates could claim to perform miracles like the Archbishop of Karim did. On the other hand, the clergy of the Anglo-Catholic Church of St Mary, Bourne Street, were highly amused by their rival's ritual and ceremonial attractions in 'The Miracle Cathedral', which after 1950 claimed to be 'affiliated as an Autocephalous Tropus to the Catholicate of the West'.

On the Vigil of Pentecost 1950 (the same day as his reconsecration) ✠ Joannes, Titular Archbishop of Karim, gave his imprimatur to a booklet entitled *Services of Love and Blessing* for the use of the Ancient Catholic Church; stated to have been 'compiled from Eastern and Western sources, both ancient and modern'. Here were to be found the four services most frequently held in 'The Miracle Cathedral'—The Holy Eucharist, Solemn Benediction, Complin, and Healing Service. It was explained that 'although fully Catholic, all these services are essentially bright and modern in outlook, embracing as they do the great truth of survival, and the nearness of those who are able to aid us from a higher life'. Complin [*sic*) must have been most helpful and devotional, because it ended with the popular hymn 'Bless this house', instead of the traditional Antiphons of Our Lady. And what more perfect finale to Benediction could have been found than the hymn 'Closed is the solemn hour', borrowed from the L.C.C. (Liberal Catholic Church —not London County Council) Liturgy?

Harold Percival Nicholson was a superb spiritual showman, who kept the merry-go-rounds of religion going almost night and day, but he was never quite in the same class as, e.g., Aimee Semple McPherson. London, however, was not so hungry and thirsty for an evangel of joyousness as was Los Angeles; there were more people who were quite satisfied by Christianity as served up to them by the larger religious denominations in Britain. It was different in Southern California, where 'in most instances, new-comers could not find the church of their childhood; or, if they did, there was something about the impishly impious sunlight of the region that undermined their interest in "the old-style religion". Migration severs allegiances and weakens old loyalties. It creates the social fluidity out of which new cults grow and flourish.'[1] In spite of the crowds that did flock to 'The Miracle Cathedral' in the fifties, and the 'miracles' which were performed there, its novel publicity stunts never attracted the millions who filled the Angelus Temple. The different results may have been due to the fact that Nicholson claimed that *he* performed the miracles, whereas 'Sister never contended that she was a miracle woman or that she could actually heal the sick. 'I am not a healer,' she once said: 'Jesus is the healer. I am only the little office girl who opens the door and says, "Come in." '[2]

It was in the winter of 1950–1 that the negro cleric named Denison Quartey Arthur arrived in Chelsea. He styled himself Mar Lukos, Bishop of Lagos, Accra, and Trinidad. He related that he had been brought up in Ethiopia and that later on he had found his way to North America, where on May 27, 1947, he had been consecrated by Archbishop St John-the-Divine Hickersayon, said to belong to the Coptic Orthodox Church, and in charge of its Foreign Missions.

It is rather unlikely that there were two bishops in the U.S.A. during the nineteen-forties both called 'St John-the-Divine', so it is a reasonable conclusion that Hickersayon was the same person as Hickerson, an American negro who worked as an evangelist in Baltimore in 1908, with Samuel Morris and George Baker. Rather later Baker acquired a world-wide notoriety as 'Father Divine', and claimed that 20,000,000 people called him God. By 1915 Hickerson had assumed the title of Bishop St John-the-Divine, and he was run-ning an unconventional place of worship on 41st Street, New York

---

[1] Carey McWilliams, 'Aimee Semple McPherson: Sunlight in My Soul', in *The Aspirin Age* (1950), p. 59.
[2] ibid., p. 57.

City, known as 'The Church of the Living God'. Sara Harris writes:
'He must have been an impressive figure, for even today he is
still imposing. Tall, ascetic, he looks like the old masters' painting
of Jesus, except for his tan complexion and advanced age. He was a
born preacher with an electrifying style when the spirit was in him.
He would begin preaching in a low quiet tone, all the while walking
slowly about. As his voice grew louder, and his words faster, he
would break into a lope, and suddenly he would leap straight into
the air and land shouting.'[1]

The negro prelate—it is not certain who ordained or consecrated
him—appears to have regarded himself more or less as God. He
gathered round him lesser divinities (known as 'The Temples of
God'). We are told that they 'wore crowns festooned with gold and
silver, and they shouted: "God in you. God in me. Everybody he
God. God lives in this Temple, and Ah'm so glad. Can't never
die." '

Unfortunately St John-the-Divine got into trouble with the
police. Some of the 'Temples of God' went berserk, even stabbing
the ungodly. The result was that the Bishop had to disband his
organization. It is not clear what were his subsequent activities
until 1942, when he had chartered in the Borough of Manhattan,
New York, a new sect called 'The Coptic Orthodox Church Apostolic Incorporated'.[2]

Mar Georgius states that when he first met Mar Lukos and
heard about his Coptic Orthodox Succession, he was filled with
scepticism; but the documents Mar Lukos produced made it clear
that he was no impostor. Mar Georgius felt sure that the seals
could not have been forged by a Harlem negro, and that they
appeared to be genuine Coptic. The result was that on February 19,
1951, a fraternal exchange of lines of succession took place in
Chelsea. Mar Joannes, Archbishop of Karim, re-consecrated *sub
conditione* Mar Lukos, while the latter kindly handed on what was
believed to be the Coptic-Orthodox line of succession to both Mar
Joannes and Mar Georgius.[3] It is related that pontifical High Mass

---

[1] *The Incredible Father Divine* (1954), p. 20.

[2] Its official address in 1947 was 2032 Fifth Avenue, New York City. It is not
mentioned in the 1961 *Yearbook of American Churches.*

[3] It is easy to understand why the Ancient Catholic Church and the Patriarchate of
Glastonbury were so eager to obtain the alleged Coptic line of apostolic succession,
even by way of Harlem. By so doing they felt that a link had been forged between them
and the colony of Copts who settled at Lerins; some of whom found their way to
Ireland, and possibly thence to Glastonbury. (cf. F. L. Warren, *Liturgy and Ritual in
the Celtic Church* (1881), p. 56; *Irish Litanies* (Henry Bradshaw Society), Vol. II,
pp. 64–65.)

was celebrated according to an English adaptation of the Coptic *Korban*—quite a change from the bright and breezy Liturgy of the Ancient Catholic Church. The long ceremony, which was reported on March 2 in the *West London Press*, a weekly newspaper published in Chelsea, would have been even more dramatic had the Chelsea congregation been entertained with traditional Ethiopic church music—bells, rattles, and big drums throbbing in double-quick time. It would have been awe-inspiring had the *schola cantorum* been taught to emit wild howls (expressive of joy), and mastered the weird melodies which are a feature of the ancient Coptic rite. Lastly, to create the correct African atmosphere, the bishops and clergy ought to have danced before the ark, as did King David.

Some time after this Mar Lukos was raised to archiepiscopal status by Mar Joannes of Karim, and was given the title of Archbishop of the West Indies. During a visitation of his Caribbean flock his position became difficult and he has since remained on this side of the Atlantic. In 1952 he visited Ethiopia, where he was received by the Emperor Haile Selassie in the Imperial Palace at Addis Ababa. But it seems that he was not recognized as a bishop by the katholikos-patriarch of the Ethiopian Church. So far as is known Mar Lukos has never been accepted by 'His All-holiness, the Pope and Patriarch of the Great City of Alexandria, of Libya, the Pentapolis and Ethiopia, and of All the Land of Egypt'—as the head of the Orthodox Coptic Church is called. Lastly, it does not appear that any of the Coptic bodies in America (Orthodox and Monophysite) regard the Archbishop of the West Indies as being in communion with them.

Not much has been heard of Mar Lukos in recent years, though he appeared at Deptford in April 1957, where he was photographed in a striking version of the garb of an Anglican bishop—gaiters, apron, frock-coat, pectoral crucifix, ring, white bands, and his white-bearded ebony face surmounted by a sort of Cranmer square cap with a pom-pom on top. He was snapped while inspecting a Boys' Brigade in company with the Mayor and Mayoress.[1]

A month after Mar Lukos had exchanged consecrations at the

[1] *Kentish Mercury*, April 12, 1957. Mar Lukos is now one of the fifteen prelates (representing Ghana) of the Sacred Synod of the Primitive Catholic Apostolic Orthodox Church of Antioch of the Syro-Byzantine Tradition. (See p. 314.) He is sometimes confused with Bishop John Luker, of whom an impressive photograph appeared in *Weekend* (December 15–17, 1961). He was shown in magnificent robes, assisting at the Convocation of the Imperial Order of St George. He was raised to the episcopate by Van Ryswyk.

The Catholicate of the West

Chelsea Cathedral, both the Patriarch of Glastonbury and the Archbishop of Karim got into the headlines, because the latter had sued a Spiritualist newspaper for libel. The case was heard at Manchester Assizes in March 1951, when Mr Justice Ormerod awarded Nicholson £150 damages and costs, but at the same time made some uncharitable remarks on the activities of the Catholicate of the West, maintaining that the plaintiff had no 'reasonable grounds for complaint'.[1] The Archbishop of Karim had explained that parents had stopped their sons going to his youth clubs, and that only two members remained in the Chelsea Cathedral Ladies' Guild. He also stated that the Ancient Catholic Church had about 5,000 adherents in Britain, with five churches and a number of chapels.

No matter: the persecuted prelates continued to keep alive interest in 'The Miracle Cathedral' by more impeccable functions staged there, as when on the Feast of the Nativity of Our Lady, September 8, 1951, Mar Joannes, assisted by Mar Georgius, raised to the episcopate one of the clergy—Fr Cecil Valentine Wainwright, M.A., D.D. Among the assistants in the sanctuary were Rev. Mother Mary, titular Abbess of Magdala, and Mother Prioress Gertrude E. Enticknap (L. Th., Western Orthodox University). The new prelate was given the style of Mar Valentine, titular Archbishop of Mount Carmel, and Primate of the Ancient Catholic Church.[2] By this time the Chelsea Cathedral staff included six canonesses, and even a mitred abbess, the Right Rev. Mother Truda. This galaxy of male and female minor and major clerics quite put into the shade the Metropolitan Cathedral Chapter of Westminster, which merely consisted of Canons, Honorary Canons, and a College of Chaplains.

About a year after his Roman Catholic neighbour Mgr Myers at St Mary's, Cadogan Street, had been made titular Archbishop of Beroea, the Archbishop of Karim, on April 14, 1952, consecrated Charles Stuart Singer (L. Th., Western Orthodox University), and Melville Peregrine Knill-Samuel (Mus. Bac., Western Orthodox University), the son of a former priest of the Church in Wales, The former took the title of Mar Philippus, titular Bishop of Hebron, and the latter became Mar Peter, titular Bishop of Naim.[3]

---

[1] cf. *Manchester Guardian*, March 20, 1951.

[2] He soon fell into schism, and assumed the primacy of a new body which he called 'The Ancient Apostolic Catholic Church'.

[3] In November 1954, Mar Philippus exchanged consecrations with Bishop Charles Brearley (later Archbishop Ignatius Carolus of the Old Holy Catholic Church), having already assumed the title of Archbishop-Primate of the New Catholic and Free Church —yet another schism from the Catholicate of the West. (See p. 380.)

The Catholicate of the West

Crowds still attended 'The Divine Healing Service (with Holy Unction)' which, for preference, was held in a dim religious light. It is related that the faithful came up to the altar rails, where the Archbishop of Karim anointed them with the holy oils. The miraculous cures were far more numerous than those registered by either the Medical Office at Lourdes or the Church of Christ Scientist off Sloane Square. The ritual and ceremonial of the Ancient Catholic Church—described as 'bright and modern in outlook'—became more than Gallican in daring display, but basically Celtic in the happy-go-lucky mingling of all the little bits and pieces that with the right touch make religion seem so helpful and devotional.

If the number of candles on a high altar is an index of 'Catholicity', then the Chelsea Cathedral was definitely the most 'Catholic' church in London. A ruby light flickered before the tabernacle and exposition throne, as a symbol of the Divine Presence. The *tout ensemble*, so some visitors felt, was evocative of an overcrowded 'Catholic Repository', for there was a glut of statues, shrines, and pictures.

The *West London Press* reported on June 27, 1952, that Sir Alfred and Lady Munnings had presented the Cathedral with an oil painting of the Virgin Mary, as an *ex voto* for the spiritual benefits received from the Archbishop of Karim. Lady Munnings was specially grateful for help afforded to her favourite dog, 'Black Knight', and to her other dog, 'Toby', in his last illness. The same journal also stated that at a recent animal service, filmed for television, over 300 people with their pets made their way to the Cathedral through dense fog.

On one of the walls of the Cathedral was hung a reproduction of the well-known painting, 'The Presence', representing the interior of St Mary's Episcopal Cathedral, Edinburgh, at a celebration of the Holy Communion. It may have inspired one of the priests, Fr John Brabazon Brabazon-Lowther, of Shrigley Park, Cheshire, to found 'The Order of the Cloister of the Holy Presence'.[1] In one of the leaflets issued it was stated that it was 'an impersonal Order, which nevertheless unites in common purpose the Companions in individual endeavour to live in the understanding of the Eternal NOW of the Kingdom of Heaven'. Quite in keeping with the

---

[1] Brabazon-Lowther, born in 1883, belonged to a younger branch of the very ancient Yorkshire family of Lowther, raised to the peerage in 1696 under the title of Lonsdale. He had transferred his allegiance from Canterbury to Karim.

undenominational character of the Ancient Catholic Church was the fact that the Order was open to non-Christians as well as Christians. The Rules laid down that the Lord Abbot should always wear a pectoral cross—openly or concealed according to his discretion. The Companions, if they desired, might wear a cassock or habit in private, but were bidden to remember that they should be known by their Fruits rather than by their Apparel. It was soon realized that this new Order (like the Order of Llanthony Brothers) needed an episcopal major superior, so on November 8, 1952, the Archbishop of Karim consecrated Fr Brabazon-Lowther, giving him the title of Bishop Francis Huntingford.[1] Later on this aristocratic prelate was granted archiepiscopal status *ad personam*. A vegetarian, non-smoker, and animal-welfare enthusiast, His Grace, now crippled with rheumatoid arthritis, is obliged to direct his Order by post. It is understood that vocations have never been very numerous in the past twenty years.

Mar Joannes of Karim, like John Wesley, regarded all the world as his parish, and never bothered much about jurisdiction. He was prepared to give minor or major orders to almost anybody who turned up in Chelsea. On August 8, 1952 took place the consecration of Anselmus Theodor Labs of Dusseldorf, as titular Bishop of Ekron in Palestine. On July 18, 1954, he raised to the episcopate Mattheus Viktor Schonbroodt, a priest associated with Mar Justinos of Cologne, who now assumed the style of Archbishop of the Free Catholic Church in Germany. Schonbroodt also held the title of Abbot-General of the Order of the Good Shepherd.[2] Four days later this new prelate ordained deaconess and priestess, Mrs Maureen Pearse, a Theosophist who belonged to the Liberal Catholic Church, and who had already been blessed as Abbess of Bethany.[3]

It was in keeping with this recognition of the Ministry of women that the Ancient Catholic Church should welcome Mgr Clemente Alfio Sgroi Marchese, the Mariavite Bishop for Sicily, on his arrival in London during the summer of 1954.[4] On September 18 he re-consecrated both Mar Georgius and Mar Joannes, thus increasing their lines of apostolic succession to eighteen.[5]

[1] One of his ancestors was a niece of Dr George Isaac Huntingford, appointed Bishop of Gloucester in 1802, and translated to Hereford in 1815. (cf. *Burke's Landed Gentry*).

[2] See pp. 381, 486.

[3] For Mrs Pearse's re-ordination and consecration by Bishop Brearley, see p. 387.

[4] See pp. 523.

[5] Marchese traced his line of succession back to Mgr Gul, Archbishop of Utrecht, via Kowalski, Fatome, Maas, and Fusi. Some of the later consecrations probably had female assistants.

The Catholicate of the West

The most sensational of all the spectacles staged at the Chelsea Cathedral was the consecration of Mgr William Franklin Wolsey, which was performed by Mar Georgius, assisted by Mar Joannes, on the Fourth Sunday in Lent, March 20, 1955. This new prelate held the office of Patron and President of the International Academy, described as 'a World Fraternity of Learned and Reverend People Chartered and Sponsored for Humanitarian Purposes'. It was stated that this Academy (of which few persons in England can have heard) had been founded at Toulouse, France, in 1880 by Chevalier Jules Ferez. It was indeed a privilege for the Patriarch of Glastonbury to raise Wolsey to the episcopate, for the consecrand claimed to hold nearly a hundred 'Ranks, Titles, Decorations, and Academic Qualifications'. They started off with Duca Wolsey di Oberwintz, Marquis de Diaz et Vivar (Cid Campeador), and Count of Salvador with the Franco-Bolivian Cross of Friendship. A list of the Bishop's ranks, titles, decorations, and other qualifications fills up nearly five pages of his pamphlet entitled *A United World*. It ends with nine or ten Doctorates, and also includes many Scientific, Philosophical, Dramatic, Operatic, and Theatrical Societies of which he was a member. He was in addition a Knight Commander or Knight of about ten Military Orders, and the Sovereign Grand General Inspector of the 33rd Degree of Freemasonry of the Spiritual Center of S.O.M.A.L. of Egypt and Italy. It has been said that he also regarded himself as a reincarnation of Cardinal Wolsey.

At this hyper-aristocratic function Wolsey took the title of Archbishop John I of Vancouver, of the Universal Apostolic Church of Life. His ducal seal was described as 'the Old and Glorified Double Eagled Byzantinian Seal of the House of Constantine the Great', which, so he said, had been conferred upon him personally by 'the present direct descendant of this early Christian Emperor of Rome'.[1] The versatile and illustrious Archbishop John I now has his headquarters at 4835 East Grandview-Douglas Highway, North Burnaby 2, British Columbia, where he directs the world-wide operations of the Universal Life Foundation (*Sedis Universalis Apostolica*).[2] The spirit of this organization has much in common with that of the Ancient Catholic Church, because 'ALL People' are 'recognized as Brothers and Sisters'. There are 'no Barriers, no Denominationalisms, no Sectarianisms, or Creeds'. In a 1958

[1] op. cit., n.d. or p., p. 15.
[2] Strange to say, this establishment is not included among the thirty-four universities and 246 other institutions of higher education in Canada.

The Catholicate of the West

report, a West German government official who was investigating international operations of 'degree mills' described this one as 'a far-flung organization for the sale of doctor diplomas with branches in London, New York, Paris, Rome, Geneva, The Hague, Athens, Brussels and Vancouver. . . . This is a big business.'[1]

Presuming that the more liturgical-minded of the congregation at 'The Miracle Cathedral' were familiar with either the Book of Common Prayer or the Roman Missal, it must have struck them, that Fourth Sunday in Lent 1955, how the words of the Epistle were being fulfilled under their very eyes. Like Jerusalem, the Ancient Catholic Church was indeed 'free and the mother of all' when it came to providing bishops. Not only did the Mar Georgius and Mar Joannes consecrate an Archbishop for the Universal Apostolic Church of Life, the latter (assisted by Mar Peter, Bishop of Naim), also re-consecrated Mgr Jean-Marie Blom Van Assendelft-Altland, who had been raised to the episcopate at Cologne on January 25, 1953, by Mar Justinos Thiesen of the Vilatte succession.[2] Enriched with many more lines of apostolic succession, he assumed the title of Archbishop of France, hopeful of planting a branch of the Ancient Catholic Church across the Channel, in full communion with the Chelsea Cathedral and its Archbishop. Hitherto Mgr Van Assendelft-Altland had been in charge of an independent Old Catholic chapel in Paris.[3]

In September 1955 the Archbishop of Karim was reported to have made a triumphal tour of West Germany. He stated that he 'was given an official reception at Cologne R.C. Cathedral, with full Archiepiscopal honours, including a detachment of the famous Swiss Guards, of which much was made in the German Press, and reference also in the English Press'.[4]

---

[1] Cf. Barbara Moon, 'The Heyday of the Degree Mills', in *Maclean's Magazine* (Toronto, April 6, 1963). On July 11, 1956, Archbishop Wolsey of Vancouver re-consecrated Bishop Erni, of Bienne, Switzerland, who acted as General Secretary of this international fraternity. (See pp 519, 520.) The British Representative was the Rev. Rupert Pitt-Kethley, of Ealing Common, later raised to the episcopate. (See p. 380, note 1.) Mexico the Foundation was directed by Mgr J. P. Ortiz-Rodriguez, who had been Primate of the Mexican Old Roman Catholic Church since 1933. (See p. 441.)

[2] See p. 313.

[3] See p. 313. His present title is Mar Joannes, Prince-Patriarch of the *Église Catholique Apostolique Primitive d'Antioche Orthodoxe et de Tradition Syro-Byzantine*, with an international Sacred Synod composed of fifteen 'Mars'.

[4] Cf. 'Our History', in *The Cathedral of the Good Shepherd* (n.d.), p. 5. In 1962 the Archbishop of Karim consecrated the Rev. Bryan Peers (Founder, Secretary and Archivist of the London Appreciation Society), whom he had raised to the priesthood in 1955, as Titular Bishop of Samaria. His Grace is one of the thirty-three distinguished Vice-Presidents of the Society, which include Lord Brabazon of Tara, Somerset Maugham, Dame Sybil Thorndyke and Dame Myra Hess.

485

The Ancient Catholic Church has been responsible, directly or indirectly, for the consecration of yet more free-lance prelates. One of these is Francis Everden Glenn, whose pilgrim's progress had led him along many a by-way of the ecclesiastical border land. Having been a novice in the Society of St Francis, he gave up communion with Canterbury for that of Caer-Glow. After being associated with the Jansenist group of the Old Roman Catholic Church for a few years, he passed on to the Old Catholic Orthodox Church, ruled over by the Lord Patriarch Banks of East Molesey, who raised him to the priesthood. Then he became the Superior of a society of layfolk, whose members pledged themselves to a way of life based on the Evangelical Counsels. On September 13, 1957, Fr Glenn was consecrated at München-Gladbach in the Rhineland by Bishop Schonbroodt, after which he assumed the title of Provincial of the English Province of the Order of the Good Shepherd, but still continued to earn his living in secular employment in London. A house was acquired at 78 Bolingbroke Grove, Wandsworth Common, S.W.11, where one of the rooms was furnished as a chapel dedicated to St Michael and All Angels. The following year, Schonbroodt, having been convinced that both prelacy and popery are perversions of primitive Christianity, resigned his offices, and joined the respectably Protestant body known as 'The Disciples of Christ'.[1]

So it was that Bishop Glenn found himself at the head of Schonbroodt's followers in Western Germany as well as of his own handful of disciples in England. He renamed them 'The Church of the Servants of Christ', and the Order of the Good Shepherd adopted the same designation. Having grave doubts about the validity of the episcopate received from Schonbroodt, Mgr Glenn had himself re-consecrated by Mar Georgius on May 18, 1959, who was now able to guarantee imparting more than twenty lines of apostolic succession.

This little 'autocephalous, or self-governing Church, within the wider context of the One, Holy, Catholic and Apostolic Church', faces the world and Wandsworth Common from within half a mile of Clapham Junction. The founder feels sure that it offers the ideal

[1] Organized in the U.S.A. by Alexander Campbell in 1811 as a group within Presbyterianism, and formed into a separate body in 1827. The object of this now almost world-wide organization is the reunion of Christians on the basis of a return to the polity of the New Testament. It is congregational in government. The world-headquarters are at Indianopolis, Indiana, and the present inclusive membership is given at 1,801,414.

spiritual home for those sincere Christians who seek 'a Catholicism that is neither Ultramontane and encumbered with modern doctrinal innovations that have no root in Holy Writ, nor yet a State Church riddled with Erastianism'. The Servants of Christ explain that although their religion is 'based on the Old Catholic Tradition', they 'make no claim to be linked with, or in Communion with the Utrecht Union of Old Catholics, or with any other Church of the same tradition'. Such being the case, it is easy to understand why this exclusive body has not sought fellowship with the World Council of Churches, or with any of the other autocephalous churches dealt with in this book.

On the feast of Pentecost, 1960, Mgr Glenn ordained priest a certain Brother Paulos to minister to Schonbroodt's faithful remnant in the Rhineland, who had resisted the temptation to become Roman, Liberal, or Old Catholics. He was given the status of Vicar-General for Western Germany and the Netherlands. At the same time permission was granted to him to celebrate the Holy Eucharist 'according to Eastern practice', with the use of 'Orthodox vestments'.[1] In the spring of 1963 Mgr Glenn gave his disciples the subsidiary name of 'The Catholic Episcopal Church'. An Anglican layman at Bournemouth, Mr Harry S. Groome, was then appointed Chancellor of the Church, and is now compiling a Code of Canon Law and Constitutions for the benefit of the four priests and other clerics who may be added to their number in the future. On July 6, 1963, a former Welsh Congregationalist chapel on Battersea Rise, S.W. 11, was solemnly dedicated to Christ the King. The service used was said to be a blending of the Gallican and Latin Rites, adapted to needs and limitations. After the function the faithful and their friends made their way to the nearby department store of Arding and Hobbs for an afternoon *agape*.

After seven years, during which the 'Miracle Cathedral' had attracted crowds to Chelsea, the property was sold and the Karim *cathedra* translated to Clapton. The Ancient Catholic Church had arranged to rent from the Trustees of the Agapemonite body, a small though imposing Gothic Revival edifice (complete with a lofty spire), known as 'The Ark of the Covenant'.[2] Among its

[1] The headquarters of this body are still at 78 Bolingbroke Grove, Wandsworth Common, S.W. 11.

[2] In 1902 the Rev. John Hugh Smyth-Pigott, an eccentric Anglican clergyman, became the second founder of the *Agapemone*, otherwise known as 'The Abode of Love'. This body had been founded in 1859 by another Church of England incumbent, the Rev. J. H. Prince, who proclaimed himself 'The Beloved', and took spiritual wives who bore real children to him. Smyth-Pigott was unfrocked in Wells Cathedral,

ornate external decorations are the four beasts of the Apocalypse, carved in bronze, full of eyes, and each with six wings.

This pretty little Cathedral in Rookwood Road (*vis-à-vis* a somewhat larger Synagogue), within a stone's throw of Clapton Common, is an almost forgotten shrine. Unfortunately its doors are not always left open for private prayer and meditation, so it is impossible to keep up either Perpetual Adoration or a Living Rosary in its Animal Chapel on behalf of all God's dear dumb creatures. A notice-board states that both Animal and Healing Services are held, just as they were in Chelsea, but if some of the local inhabitants are telling the truth, only a few persons attend them. So far Ancient Catholicism does not appear to have caught on in this far-off corner of North East London; nevertheless the Archbishop of Karim has not abandoned hope of making converts, for he still proclaims:

'We do not mind whether a man is a Roman Catholic, Eastern Orthodox, Anglo-Catholic, Evangelical, Free-Church, Spiritualist, or even a Moslem, Buddhist, or Hindoo, or, for that matter, an Atheist or Agnostic. All alike are the Children of God, and as such, our brothers and sisters, and are fully entitled to all our love and help.'[1]

If one thinks of it, what are the above words but an echo of the immortal message of Miss Ella Wheeler Wilcox (1855–1919)?

> *So many gods, so many creeds.*
> *So many paths that wind and wind,*
> *While just the art of being kind*
> *Is all the sad world needs.*[2]

In spite of the fact that the Ancient Catholic Church has for twenty years opened its arms wide to embrace all creation (including animals, birds, fish, and reptiles), irrespective of colour, creed, or race, it seems to have faded out as a new world-religion.[3]

---

and emulated his predecessor's example by propagating a species of free love. Sister Ruth, the chief of the mystic brides, died in 1955. Until 1962 a remnant of the community still carried on at Spaxton, Somerset, awaiting the return to earth of 'The Messiah', i.e. Mr Smyth-Pigott.

[1] ibid., p. 5.

[2] *The World's Need.*

[3] Having been an 'autocephalous tropus' of the Catholicate of the West from 1950 to 1953, it became an independent body. Later on it linked up with the remnant of Hayman's Free Catholic Church. (See p. 228.) More recently it has been united with the American branch of the Old Roman Catholic Church, of which Archbishop Barker of Waltham is the British Representative. (See p. 436.) Today it forms part of the 'United Hierarchy of the Ancient Catholic Church', presided over by the Archbishop of Karim. Various other small bodies in Europe and North America are said to be affiliated with this United Hierarchy.

Cathedral Church of the Good
Shepherd (Ancient Catholic
Church), Clapton, London, N.16,
formerly the Ark of the Covenant
of the Agapemone.

The Catholicate of the West

To return to the affairs of the Catholicate of the West as an international organization: a cloud was mushrooming over the Pacific after April 7, 1951, when Mar David I had resigned his status as Patriarch of Malaga. Apparently on his own authority, he appointed as his successor Archbishop Lowell P. Wadle of the Vilatte succession, allegedly a Theosophist, and already calling himself Primate of the American Catholic Apostolic Church of Long Beach.[1] After this the ex-Patriarch and Supreme Hierarch took on the duties of pastor at the First Universalist Church at Los Angeles.[2] During the first twelve months following its incorporation in India, the Western Orthodox University, with an accommodation address in England, had granted degrees to twenty-three persons in its Faculties of Theology, Laws, Arts, Philosophy, Letters, Science, and Music—an indication that the Catholicate was promoting culture.[3]

Looking back over the year, Mar Georgius felt able to write that the work of reorganization had progressed slowly but surely. Much of this work had been of necessity 'behind the scenes' of the patriarchal curia in London, and those who looked for spectacular developments would have been disappointed. While it was impossible for His Beatitude to give details of affairs which were more or less *sub judice*, this much could be said, that when all this work had been accomplished the Catholicate would emerge purified and strengthened in every way. But he ended his message to the faithful with this warning:

'At its inception in 1944, it made one very big mistake, in that it adopted the policy of attempting to unify *all* the so-called *episcopi vagantes*. Experience has proved this to be not only impossible, but undesirable, for oil and water cannot mix. Many Bishops do not desire to be part of a disciplined Hierarchy, but prefer to adhere to the schismatic policy of so-called 'independence', a position utterly unknown to the Church of God. Others again do not accept the Catholic Faith, and the Catholicate has suffered much loss of reputation through being (though wrongly) identified in the public mind

[1] See p. 261.
[2] The Universalist Church of America describes itself as 'a democratic religious body believing in the worthiness of man and his ability to create the good life (Kingdom of God) for all men in this world'. Each member of the body has 'the right to formulate his own philosophy of religion and the universal religious truths found in all of the great religions'. The inclusive membership in 1958 was given as 66,949. The headquarters are at Boston, Mass.
[3] In spite of having been incorporated in India, the Western Orthodox University never managed to obtain official recognition as one of the universities of the British Commonwealth, of which there were thirty-seven in India in 1960.

with the aberrations of such folk. Therefore, the changes which are in process of formulation will be very drastic indeed.'[1]

Reference must be made to the literary output of Mar Georgius —far greater than that of any other prelate mentioned in these pages.[2] Since 1944 he has issued many pastoral letters and encyclicals. His nine booklets of an historical nature are indispensable to a student of the subject. So, too, are the volumes of *The Orthodox Catholic Review*, starting in 1944.[3] While one may admire the labour which went into the compilation of the eight liturgical volumes of *The Glastonbury Rite*, one cannot help wondering if the result of the labour was worth it, considering how few clergy there have been to adopt the rite, or the laity to assist at it. Similar reactions are almost inevitable when perusing any of Mar Georgius's (mostly mimeographed) published writings of a doctrinal or controversial nature, such as *The Charter and Organic Constitution* (a vernacular *codex juris canonici* for the clergy and laity of the Western Catholicate), the nine *Orthodox Catholic Leaflets*, and the fourteen *Information Bulletins* issued between 1944 and 1951. These make this the best-documented side-line of church history in the past quarter of a century. It seems a real shame that all these data and all the intentions which lie behind them, and all the labour for the Lord which it represents, should have been lavished for so few— *cui bono?* The Catholicate of the West seems to have achieved little so far in the ecumenical sphere of Christian Reunion.

'The best laid schemes o' mice an' men gang aft agley', as the poet Burns reminds us, but when this has been made to Mar Georgius, his reply is optimistic: he says that it is unreasonable to expect his Catholicate to have achieved Reunion in eighteen years while Rome has not achieved it in the whole fifteen centuries since the Nestorians detached themselves from the rest of Christendom.

On June 1, 1952, His Beatitude promulgated from the Occidental Jerusalem a Dogmatic Constitution for his Catholic Apostolic Church, known as *The Glastonbury Confession*, which became binding on the few bishops and clergy who still recognized his jurisdiction. In his own estimation he added to their number after the death of Mgr Williams, Archbishop of Caer-Glow, on June 19, when he proclaimed that he was the legitimate successor of Archbishop

---

[1] *Orthodox Catholic Review*, December 1951.

[2] See bibliography on pp. 566–569. The total number of his books, pamphlets, etc., up to 1960 was thirty-four, exclusive of many leaflets now out of print.

[3] More recent periodicals edited by him are *Hieratika* and *Maranatha*.

Mathew as head of the Old Roman Catholic Church in England.[1] Not one of its branches, unfortunately, was prepared to accept him as their ecclesiastical superior.

After this Mar Georgius retired to Belgium, where for the greater part of the year 1953 he remained in retirement. There had been severe losses to his flock; on August 21, 1951, the Orthodox Catholic Church in England had been expelled from the Catholicate.[2] Since then both the Ancient Catholic Church and the Indian Orthodox Church had fallen away. But he had the consolation of merging the little Belgian Catholic Apostolic Church of the Dominican Rite with the main body of the Catholicate, and for its benefit decided to revive the see of Antwerp, which had been suppressed by Pius VII by the Bull *Qui Christi Dominici vices*, on November 29, 1801. So it was that Robert Marie Gustave Lutgen was raised to the episcopate in London on February 22, 1953, with the title of Archbishop of Antwerp, thus becoming the schismatic successor of Bishop Cornelius Nelis, who died in 1798. His Metropolitan Pro-Cathedral Chapel was at 41 rue James-Watt, Schaerbeek-Brussels, and it was here on March 1, 1953, that he ordained priest for the second time the French hieromonk, Clodoald Danyel, the future Tugdual I, Archbishop of Dol, and Founder of the *Sainte Église celtique de Bretagne*, who doubted the validity of his Mariavite Orders.[3]

Mar Georgius's next step was to hold a Synod of Glastonbury, when the Catholicate of the West was declared dissolved. By this time it had shrunk to three Provinces: (1) Britain, (2) Belgium, Holland, and Luxembourg, (3) Germany, and a French Mission. A new organization was created, known as the United Orthodox Catholicate. This was considered necessary for the State Law of India to give effect to the dissolution of the old incorporated body, which was then struck off the Register. Later on, in 1959, the old title, Catholicate of the West, was re-adopted by what was then called the United Orthodox Catholic Church. The object of these puzzling manoeuvres was to bring to an end the unsatisfactory system of so-called 'autocephalous tropoi', which could be done legally only by dissolving the corporation and starting *de novo*.

Meanwhile a cleric had turned up in London whose origins appeared to be almost as illustrious as those of the Duke de

[1] See p. 338.
[2] See p. 291.
[3] See p. 316.

491

The Catholicate of the West

Richelieu-Ryswyk, founder of the Apostolic Church of St Peter, the Temple of Service, and the Avatar Defenders of Civilization.[1] This was Count Richard Jean Chrétien de Palatine, M.A., Ph.D., D.D., who also held the rank of Lord Abbot, and who resided at 38 Kensington Place, W.8. It was understood that he claimed descent from the Counts Palatine who in the fourteenth century became Electors of the Holy Roman Empire in Germany. There were reports that he had been educated in Australia at the Melbourne College and University, also at the Western Orthodox University (Antioch and India), and that he was one of the truly illuminated and inspired exponents of occult philosophy and spiritual training in the world today. The honours bestowed on him were certainly impressive. With the name of Ronald Powell, he had been raised to the priesthood of the Liberal Catholic Church in Australia, where he had made a profound study of Theosophy. On November 14, 1952, Count Pedro de Costa-Malatesta, the Archon of 'The Ancient Mystic Order of the Fratres Lucis (Italy)', which he had founded at Florence in 1948, transmitted the office of Archon to Powell—now known as Richard, Duc de Palatine. About the same time he felt constrained to found a new religious body, which he called 'The Pre-Nicene Catholic Church'. Its doctrines suggested the influence of Madame Blavatsky and other Theosophists. De Palatine had already gone to the trouble of compiling a Liturgy for its members; and he explained in the Foreword: 'The Mass is designed to enable all the people to take part in this act of service to God and to release the spiritual outpourings upon the world as a whole. This will cause the participants to be uplifted and receive spiritual refreshment.' The rite contained both Eastern and Western elements, allowed for a generous use of bells and thuribles, and, so far as could be interpreted, the rubrics permitted communion in one kind.

Mar Georgius, ready as ever to help along any new spiritual organization, agreed to provide a bishop for the Pre-Nicene Catholic Church. On October 25, 1953, he consecrated Richard, Duc de Palatine, in the Juvenile Courtroom, Denison House, Vauxhall Bridge Road, a few yards from Vanpoulles Ltd, the well-known church furnishers. It is understood that no attempt was made to revive pre-Nicene ritual and ceremonial at this unique function performed by His Beatitude the Patriarch of Glastonbury. Neither did His Eminence Cardinal Griffin, Archbishop of Westminster,

[1] See p. 469.

nor his Bishop-Auxiliary assist in the improvised sanctuary.[1] On October 3, 1954, the *Sunday Chronicle* published an article in which it was stated that Richard, Duc de Palatine, was connected with the Université Philotechnique Internationale, which had been granted a charter by Mar Georgius.[2] In keeping with the Bishop's social status, its accommodation address was 11 Old Bond Street, W.1. Here for the sum of £38 students could obtain degrees in Arts, Divinity, Philosophy, Literature, Psychology, and Metaphysics; also diplomas for Divine Healing, and for the training for Ordination in the Church—'either Catholic, Free Church, or Spiritualist'. This modish West End rendezvous also served as the house-of-call or enquiry office for the International Headquarters of the Order of St Raphael, of which Richard, Duc de Palatine, was the Lord Abbot.

The Bond Street Université Philotechnique, which had not managed so far to obtain recognition as one of the degree-giving universities in Britain, or to obtain grants from the University Grants Committee, was reported to run a branch at Wessex College, 26 Florence Road, Bristol, 6, where Divine Healing was taught. The Registrar, Dr Dennis C. Green, Ph.D., well known as a metaphysician and psychologist, conducted a course of studies entitled 'Yoga of Christ' at ten shillings a time. He had been raised to the priesthood by Mar Georgius.[3]

Nothing could have been more inspiring than the objects of the Order of St Raphael, which were 'to establish a co-operative movement made up of all people who are interested in TRUTH, irrespective of race, colour, creed, or sect; based upon the pattern of the United Nations Organization, for the interchange of ideas and co-operation of all people to make the ideal of Universal Brotherhood a living reality'.[4] This cosmopolitan interdenominational Order had much in common with Archbishop Wolsey's International Academy, which he claimed had been founded in 1880 as a 'World Fraternity of Learned and Reverend People Chartered and Sponsored for Humanitarian Purposes'.[5] It also had a certain affinity

---

[1] De Palatine never held episcopal status within the Catholicate of the West, nor was he ever in communion with it.

[2] In his later years Archbishop Heard, fifth Patriarch of the Ancient British Church, was Chancellor of this University which existed only on paper. (See p. 226.)

[3] Dr Green is now Dean of the Catholicate of the West Collegiate Church of the Epiphany, Ashley Down, Bristol 6. (See p. 499.)

[4] The United Nations Organization, the successor of the League of Nations, was set up at San Francisco in 1945.

[5] See p. 484.

with the Duke de Richelieu-Ryswyk's Temple of Service and Avatar Defenders of Civilization, which also wanted to organize people of all races and religions.[1] The 'Religious Section' of the Order of St Raphael—like the Theosophical Society—encouraged the study of beliefs held by Catholics, Protestants, 'and especially adherents of non-Christian religions', all of whom were welcomed as members. There was also the 'Secular Service' to teach 'the Ancient Wisdom to our peoples without any name or tag' and 'to expound the best in every system of philosophy'. Members of both nonconformist and episcopal Churches were specially invited to join in the work of healing and religious endeavour carried out at 'The St Raphael Presbytery of the Free and Evangelical Church'. It was stated that the Order had representatives in Australia, New Zealand, and Africa, although its 'Grand Superior' for America had recently resigned, suggesting that life vows were not taken.

Some time later Richard, Duc de Palatine, whose religious opinions had become even more esoteric, changed the name of his cryptic organization to Pre-Gnostic Catholic Church.[2] With a private address (B.C.M./Consortium, London, W.C.1), which ensures that its cabalistic rites and ceremonies are not disturbed by the uninitiated, the Sovereign Imperium of the Mysteries (registered in India under the Mysore Societies Registration Act No. III of 1904) carries on a World Healing Campaign, helping people to achieve Self-Realization and to master the Art of Illumination.[3] Then there is the international Brotherhood of the Pleroma, which claims that it can draw people closer together and combine their efforts in prayer, meditation and the living of the Life of the Spirit, thus helping the Lords of Light to hold back the march of Darkness upon the world. Here an *élite* will find 'the so-called "AGELESS WISDOM RELIGION—THE GNOSIS"', so often neglected and yet so needed'. Christians, Buddhists, and members of all great world religions or none will realize after initiation into the Brotherhood

---

[1] Perhaps a remote ancestor was the *Université Éliaque*, alleged to have been founded in England in 1859 by Pierre Vintras, who in 1848 proclaimed that the High Priest Christ had consecrated him *Pontife Adorateur, Pontife d'Amour*, and *Pontife Provincial*; and who later on consecrated so many *pontifes divins*. (See p. 303.)

[2] The Pre-Nicene Gnostic Catholic Church publishes *The Lucis Magazine*. Its object is to 'co-ordinate the Masonic, Theosophical, Rosicrucian, Hermetic, Spiritualist, Alchemist, New Thought, Healing, Mysticism, Gnostic, and Esoteric Christianity, the underlying truths in the present Christian Religion and their relationship to the Eternal Truths of God'. Then there is a leaflet entitled *Who will help us to hold back the forces of darkness? Introductory Letter to Those who seek.*

[3] The Perpetual Healing Group is directed by Bishop G. W. Boyer, formerly a prelate of the Old Holy Catholic Church. (See p. 382.)

of the Pleroma 'that all forms of knowledge are simply stepping-stones to the ABSOLUTE TRUTH which is within yourself: let them be banded together to hasten this final realization'.[1] Richard, Duc de Palatine, being convinced that the Christian Church was originally Gnostic, founded his Brotherhood of the Pleroma (formerly the Brotherhood of the Illuminati) to 'restore the Gnostic teachings as held by the Sages, Mystics and Fathers of the Christian Church up to and including 325 A.D.; and to our present day by the Secret Brotherhoods of Light'. He also sponsors the Ancient and Universal Pan-Sophic Rite of Freemasonry, transmitted to him by Mar Georgius in 1955, and which was incorporated in both the Order of the Illuminati and the Hermetic Brotherhood of Light in 1959.[2]

Unfortunately the reorganization of the Catholicate of the West as the United Orthodox Catholicate in 1953–4 did not lead to a real forward movement. One by one cracks started to appear in its never sound walls resting on weak foundations. An attempt to shore them up was made by admitting Bishop Boltwood to the Eparchy of All the Britons. He had been raised to the episcopate of the Free Protestant Episcopal Church of England by Bishop-Primus Hall on Palm Sunday 1952, and was the legal owner of St Andrew's Collegiate Church, South Tottenham, where Mar Georgius received the first of his many consecrations on Easter Monday, 1944.[3] On July 6, 1956, Boltwood was re-consecrated *sub conditione* by the Patriarch of Glastonbury as titular Bishop of Thorney, and the

[1] Among de Palatine's publications are: *The Great Parable, Christ of Jesus? The Christian Mysteries, You and Reincarnation, God-Man, The Mystery Beyond the Veil,* and *The Inner Meaning of the Mystery Schools.* We are told that they 'constitute a most valuable contribution to the study of the Divine Mysteries since H. P. Blavatsky published her *Isis Unveiled* and the *Secret Doctrine.* But now they are even more monumental, in that they set forth an entirely new concept of religion and philosophy, wherein the ancient Gnostic teachings are adapted to the needs of the present age, in a manner both revolutionary and scientific.'

[2] The Duke warns the faithful against all the existing so-called Rosicrucian bodies, since he has it 'on the highest authority of the Society of Jesus that it was they who manufactured the commonly known legend of the "Rosicrucians" in order to steer the minds of its adherents away from the True Source'. (*Illuminism,* p. 30.) The Brotherhood of the Pleroma (said to be linked indirectly with the original pre-Jesuit 'Fraternity of the Rosy Cross', founded in the fourteenth century) is stated to have been formed in Bavaria in 1776. We are told that its teachings were based 'upon those held by the Mysteries of Antiquity and the Secret Assemblies in Europe, who sought to advance the intellectual and spiritual life of mankind by the principles of Liberty, Equality and Fraternity'. De Palatine's booklet *Illuminism* expresses gratitude to 'the British Museum, the Bodleian and Ashmole Libraries, the Archives of the Grand Orient of France, of the Masonic Rites of Memphis and Misraim, of the Ancient and Primitive Rite of John Yarker Jnr', and others. Another publication is *Lux,* which is a general account of the Hermetic Brotherhood of Light.

[3] See pp. 448–451.

The Catholicate of the West

Patriarch's Auxiliary for London north of the Thames. Free use of the Collegiate Church was allowed to the Prince-Catholicos for the next four years. Since the Orthodox Catholic Church in England had been cast out of the Catholicate in August 1951, Mar Georgius had ceased to have the use of the Abbey of Christ the King, New Barnet, as a pro-cathedral, and most of his ordinations and consecrations had taken place in the Ancient Catholic Cathedral in Chelsea, by the permission of the Archbishop of Karim. Whenever possible on Sundays between 1956 and 1960 one of Mar Georgius's priests celebrated the Glastonbury Rite in the ex-Methodist Chapel in South Tottenham. The evening service, conducted by Bishop Boltwood, with the help of presbyters, deacons, and deaconesses, was usually a sort of Protestant 'Gospel Meeting', with spiritualist elements, so it is recalled.[1]

After the death of the ninety-three-year-old Mar Hedley (Bartlett), Bishop of Suthronia, in June 1956, Mar Georgius assumed the additional title of Archbishop of the Metropolitan See of India, Ceylon, Mylapore, Socotra, and Messina, believing that he was now the canonical successor of Bishop Vernon Herford, who, in 1903, found himself the head of a handful of neo-Nestorians in South India after the death of his consecrator, Mar Basilius Soares.[2] This gave the Patriarch of Glastonbury an undefined jurisdiction over an unestimated flock in the Far East, the remnant of those who had thrown off the yoke of Rome in the eighteen-sixties, and obtained the protection of the Nestorian Patriarch of Seleucia-Ctesiphon. Unfortunately his many commitments in Europe, which included the oversight of the British cycle trade, made it impossible to conduct a Visitation of his spiritual children in Asia, whose position had become even more difficult after 1950 when India was declared a Republic. They were still in constant danger of perversion by Papist missionaries, as well as by Syro-Malabar infiltration into their ranks.

But Mar Georgius did manage to find time to slip over to Belgium, for it had become obvious that the Église Catholique

---

[1] For further details of Bishop Boltwood and his Ecumenical Church Foundation, etc., see pp. 244–250.

[2] See p. 138 . Mar Georgius explains that the Messina in question is not the city in Sicily; and that the word Messina, Massina, Masina (it enjoys all these varieties of spelling) is a Europeanization of the Indian word 'Mahacina', meaning literally 'Great China', derived through the contraction 'Macin'. Mahacina is said to have been in use down to the thirteenth century. At one time the Syro-Chaldean Archbishop of India had two suffragans, one for Socotra (an island in Indian Ocean, south of Arabia), and the other for Mahacina.

Apostolique du Rite Dominicain needed the nucleus of a hierarchy to counteract the influence of the Roman Catholic clergy of the Archdiocese of Malines, and the Dioceses of Bruges, Ghent, Liége, Namur, and Tournai. As there was no chance of borrowing the former Cathedral at Antwerp, the interdenominational chapel of the Young Men's Christian Association in that city had to serve for the dual consecration ceremony, which took place on September 1, 1956. His Beatitude was assisted by Archbishop Lutgen and Bishop Boltwood. Nestor Emile Antoine Frippiat was raised to the episcopate as titular Bishop of Tongeren, and Walter Josef Henrik Van Den Berghe as titular Bishop of Ypres, with the name of Willibrordus Clemens. But peace and unity among the Belgian bishops did not last long, for on May 18, 1957, the Patriarch of Glastonbury issued a Bull by which he excommunicated the Bishop of Ypres for 'heresy, schism, participation in magical practices and breach of his oath of canonical obedience'.[1] By this time the Catholic Apostolic Church of the Dominican Rite had a rival in Belgium with a branch of the *Église orthodoxe gallicane autocéphale*, whose Vicar-Apostolic since 1953 had been a married Olivetan Benedictine monk, Gaston Seghers.[2]

The reputed canonical successor of St Joseph of Arimathea and St Aristobulus, as well as of the first Regionary Old Catholic Bishop for England, and of the first English Metropolitan of the Syro-Chaldean Church in the Far East, could not forget that he also had responsibilities towards the Free Protestant Episcopal Church. In 1958 he entrusted his Auxiliary, Bishop Boltwood, with an Apostolic Mandate to perform ordinations and consecrations in North America. During this tour the titular Bishop of Thorney raised three ministers to the episcopate of the Free Protestant Episcopal Church, for service in Canada, the U.S.A., and Liberia.[3] Boltwood, who held among his other offices that of Protosynkellos of the Catholicate of the West, appears to have laid hands on a certain Benjamin Millard, who, for a time had the oversight of a few Free Protestant Episcopalians in East Anglia.

As St Peter remarked to those who dwelt at Jerusalem: 'Your young men shall see visions, and your old men shall dream dreams.'[4] By October 1959 the dreams indulged in by Mar

---

[1] Recently Bishop Frippiat was nominated Coadjutor with right of succession to Mgr Lutgen, Archbishop of Antwerp.
[2] See p. 312.
[3] See p. 248.
[4] Acts of the Apostles 2, 17.

Georgius fifteen years earlier had grown very dim. There were only two bishops left in Britain who recognized his jurisdiction: Mar Marcus Valerius (the Rev. J. E. Bazille-Corbin, rector of Runwell St Mary, Essex), and the titular Bishop of Thorney (the Right Rev. C. D. Boltwood). Over in Belgium, Archbishop Lutgen and his Coadjutor, Bishop Frippiat, still remained in full canonical relationship with the Catholicate of the West, as did Bishop Enochs in California.[1] Otherwise the world was strewn with blighted hopes. Of the twelve Eparchies of the Britons, Iberians, Frisians, Helvetians, Latins, Franks, Teutons, Pannonians, Slavs, Turanians, Scandinavians, and Levantines, erected in 1948, little more than half-forgotten memories. In spite of the intensive course of spiritual education, advertised as carried on at St Andrew's Collegiate College, South Tottenham, no male or female Free Protestant Episcopalian missionaries, with degrees conferred by the College of Science off Seven Sisters Road, went to minister to the neo-Nestorian faithful of the vast Archdiocese of India, Ceylon, Mylapore, Socotra, and Messina, of which Mar Georgius was still the Metropolitan. Yet he was determined to fight on, for, as he said, 'the defeats of yesterday may become the victories of tomorrow'.

A cataclysmic blow was inflicted on the Catholicate in 1960, when Bishop Boltwood heard what he felt to be a clear call to revert to the somewhat nebulous Protestantism of his youth; explaining that his 'Early Christian upbringing could never be erased'. As related in chapter seven, he repudiated the authority of the Patriarch of Glastonbury, and reorganized the Free Protestant Episcopal Church on lines which would have been approved by John Kensit and his Wycliffe Preachers.[2] This involved for the Glastonbury Patriarchate the loss of St Andrew's Collegiate Church.

The Prince-Catholicos rallied his now much reduced forces, and on August 15, being the Feast of the Dormition of the Holy Theotokos, reissued the *Chapter and Organic Constitution*, first adopted in 1955. Article VI stated that

'This Rite is not autogenic, but is . . . the direct spiritual heir of the Ancient Celtic Church, established at Glastonbury in A.D. 37. immediately after the Passion of Christ by St Joseph of Arimathea,

---

[1] Enochs, resident at Los Angeles, has since become the head of the Free Protestant Episcopal Church of the Ecumenical Church Foundation in the U.S.A.
[2] See pp. 248–250.

and afterwards extended into the Celtic and other lands of Western Christendom, and restored in 1866 upon the authority of the Syrian-Orthodox Patriarchate of Antioch; and in the East represents the remnant of the Syro-Chaldean Christians of St Thomas, derived from the preaching of the blessed Apostle St Thomas in the first century, and reorganized in 1862 upon the authority of the Syro-Chaldean Patriarchal See of Seleucia-Ctesiphon. This Rite is also the Repository of the mission conferred upon the late Archbishop Arnold Harris Mathew in 1908 by the Old Catholic Archiepiscopal See of Utrecht. By virtue of its threefold continuity and mission aforesaid, this Rite is not a sect or a schism, but a lawful and canonical Rite within the Church Universal.'[1]

Accordingly on January 6, 1961, the administrative headquarters of 'The United Syrian Orthodox and Old Catholic Missions of the West, and of the Syro-Chaldean Christians of the East, holding the Orthodox Catholic and Apostolic Faith of Undivided Christendom under the jurisdiction of and in communion with the United Patriarchate of Glastonbury, Caertroia, and Mylapore, within the One Holy Catholic and Apostolic Church', were transferred to a modest dwelling-house at 12 Ashley Hill, Ashley Down, Bristol, 6. One of its larger rooms was furnished as a pro-cathedral for the Supreme Hierarch, the Prince-Catholicos, and his patriarchal throne translated here from South Tottenham. The oratory was given the title of 'The Collegiate Church of the Epiphany and the Three Magi', and made a Chapel of Ease of the *Ecclesia Vetusta* at Glastonbury.[2]

The Dean of the Chapter, the Very Rev. Dr Dennis C. Green, Ph.D., is stated to be a Yogic philosopher and a consecrated Priest of the Catholic Templars. It is reasonably certain that neither Mgr Thomas J. Hughes, V.G., Administrator of the Pro-Cathedral of the Apostles, Clifton, nor the Very Rev. Douglas E. W. Harrison, Dean of Bristol Cathedral, has as yet published such stimulating lessons as Dean Green has done by the authority of the Ecclesiastical Chapter of the Catholicate of the West. His brochure surmounted with the badge of the Ancient Arcane Order of the Great Pyramid (*ex Aegypto*)—containing Lesson Two—explains how visualizing Arjuna as the Aspiration of oneself, careful study of the writings of the great thinker Dandemis, and daily meditation on

---

[1] op. cit., p. 5.
[2] cf. *Souvenir Guide*, published by Authority of the Dean and Chapter (Glastonbury, 1961).

the Bhagaved Gita, combined with relaxation and stretching of all parts of the body, will soon lead towards perfect Devitalization. The enlightened Archpriest also recommends initiation into the Orders of St Raphael and the True Rosy Cross, since both, in his opinion, are continually contributing to the welfare of mankind by creating 'an avenue of Brotherhood of All Nations and All Creeds'.

The staff of the Collegiate Church of the Epiphany and the Three Magi at the time of writing consists of the Dean, one priest, one subdeacon, one acolyte, and a deaconess. Between them they carry out the elaborate Glastonbury Rite, and recite regular portions of the Divine Office on Sundays and weekdays. The Dean himself is much resorted to as a spiritual healer by members of many denominations, so it is stated. The mystic teachings of the Yoga of Christianity, including 'the alpha rhythm of the brain, the blood tide, the lympth tide, the air tide and the muscle tonus tide, are all imparted on Ashley Down.

According to one of its latest official publications, the Catholicate of the West 'has no connections whatsoever with Old Roman Catholicism, Anglicanism, or with any psychic cult, in any shape or form, but it is in all respects Catholic, Apostolic, and Orthodox, having valid Orders, Mission and Jurisdiction as an Autocephalous Rite within THE ONE HOLY CATHOLIC AND APOSTOLIC CHURCH'.[1] It is not certain if the Catholic Apostolic Church (Catholicate of the West), otherwise known as The United Orthodox Catholic Rite and The Celtic Catholic Church, has now got any more places of worship in Britain other than the Collegiate Church at Bristol.[2]

So far the Catholicate has neither been offered membership of the World Council of Churches, nor has the Prince-Catholicos ever applied for it. The Glastonbury Patriarchate still awaits recognition by its fellow Patriarchates of Constantinople, Alexandria, Antioch, Jerusalem, and Moscow. The Patriarch of the West, His Holiness Pope John XXIII, did not even invite the Patriarch of the Occidental Jerusalem to take part in the sessions of the Second Vatican Council as an observer.

If the truth must be told, the Catholicate of the West has never

---

[1] *Maranatha*, Quadragesima, 1961.
[2] On June 1, 1961, the Patriarch decided that ordination candidates must have a period of six years' training preceding ordination to the priesthood in normal cases, and that ordinands would be required to pursue their studies in a Diocesan Seminary. It was not stated, however, if such seminaries had been founded, or if Anglican or Roman Catholic theological colleges would suffice.

been much more than an unsubstantial pageant, a fascinating castle in the air, with cloud-capped 'autocephalous tropoi' conjured up by the versatile patriarchal Secretary and Registrar of the Incorporated Cycle Traders and Repairers. Mar Georgius is the magician to whom the credit must be given for having kept it alive on paper for the past nineteen years; always hoping that by some stroke of his Prospero's wand its twelve world-wide Eparchies would materialize.[1]

But who has ever understood the Lord's thoughts, or been his counsellor? Who can tell that the day may not yet dawn when all the Eastern Patriarchates are reduced to dust and ashes? Who knows if even the Western Patriarchate, as represented by Rome, may be a forgotten memory? Quite likely the Prince-Catholicos has been granted a vision (like that of St John the Divine on the Isle of Patmos), and knows that one day the sun will rise on the Vale of Avalon and disclose an all glorious Occidental Jerusalem— 'that city which is the new Jerusalem, being sent down by God from heaven, all clothed in readiness, like a bride who has adorned herself to meet her husband.[2]

[1] Much interesting information will be found in Mar Georgius's latest pamphlet *Episcopi in Ecclesia Dei and Father Brandreth* (Glastonbury, 1962). It is dedicated to 'The Most Pious and God-beloved Hierarchs, Our Fathers in Christ, Julius, Bishop Ferrette; Joseph René, Archbishop Vilatte; and Arnold Harris, Archbishop Mathew'. Following the dedication is the quotation: '*Blessed are ye, when men shall revile you, and persecute you, and shall say all manner of evil against you falsely for My sake. Rejoice and be exceeding glad; for great is your reward in heaven; for so persecuted they the prophets which were before you.*' (Matthew 5, 11–12.) It should be mentioned that the Patriarch of Glastonbury, in addition to the burdens involved by being Duke of Saxe-Noricum, Prince of the Holy Roman Empire, Supreme Head of The Western Orthodox University, and Fellow of divers Learned Societies, has recently taken on the duties of Prior-General of The Order of St Gilbert of Sempringham of the Modified Observance. Many interesting details of his career will be found in the *Silver Jubilee Souvenir* (Glastonbury, 1963).

[2] Apocalypse 20, 2.

CHAPTER XI

Miscellaneous Churches Claiming to be 'Apostolic', 'Catholic' and 'Orthodox'

This final chapter deals with miscellaneous bodies, some of which have an infinitesimal membership, and whose origins cannot be traced directly to the lines of succession recorded already. It is difficult to decide how to classify them. As the majority are to be found in North America, the simplest way might have been to treat them geographically, but instead they have been arranged in two sections: those claiming Eastern origin, and those whose founders broke away from the Roman Church, though even this scheme is not altogether satisfactory, as in some instances the roots overlap.

(A) CHURCHES CLAIMING EASTERN ORIGINS

    (i) *American Orthodox Church*
    (ii) *Holy Orthodox Church in America (Eastern Catholic and Apostolic)*
    (iii) *Apostolic Episcopal Church*
    (iv) *Greek Oriental Hungarian Orthodox Church*
    (v) *Byzantine American Church*
    (vi) *Eastern Orthodox Catholic Church in America*
    (vii) *Episcopal Orthodox Church (Greek Communion)*

(i) *American Orthodox Church*

The A.O.C. states that it consists of a small group of American converts to Orthodoxy, established in 1940 by an act of the New York State Legislature. Its origins can be traced back as early as the Russian revolution of 1917. The founder, Aftimios Ofiesh, was a monk who had been ordained priest by a Bishop of the Orthodox Patriarchate of Antioch. Shortly before the Bolshevists were bombarding the Kremlin, the Holy Synod of Moscow, with Tikhon Belavin as first patriarch of a new line, elected Aftimios a bishop.

Miscellaneous Churches

He was consecrated by Archbishop Evokim on May 11, 1917. The revolution of 1917 led to the migration to North America of large numbers of Russians. Arrangements for their spiritual welfare were complicated by the fact of the hierarchical changes and internal divisions of the widely scattered Russian Church in Europe. It is possible that the Patriarch Tikhon, who had been bishop in the United States before he returned to Russia, may have authorized Aftimios to form an independent American Orthodox Church, either during his imprisonment by the Soviet Government, or shortly before his death in 1925. What is certain, however, is that in 1927 the Metropolitan Platon Rojdestversky, with the approval of the Metran Sergius Stargrodsky, then in charge of the 'official' Russian Patriarchate, did give his consent to the formation of a group of Orthodox bishops in North America. Aftimios was appointed President of this projected organization, with the title of Archbishop of Brooklyn.

He issued a 'Letter of Peace' to all the autocephalous Eastern Churches in the United States and Canada, but none of them was prepared to recognize his authority. The Oecumenical Patriarch consequently denounced him as schismatic; the Russian bishops then withdrew their support, and Aftimios found himself a prelate on his own.

Cast thus adrift, all he could do was to act on his own judgment without reference to any authority but the now repudiated commission received in 1927. On September 29, 1932, assisted by Bishop Joseph A. Zuk, a Ukrainian whom he appears to have raised to the episcopate the previous year, and a certain Bishop Sophronios, Aftimios consecrated the Rev. William Albert Nichols.[1] The fact that this clergyman was married shows that Aftimios had rejected the traditional rule in all Eastern Churches that bishops must be celibate. The following year he took a wife himself, and retired to Pennsylvania. After this he was deposed by the Metropolitan Sergius in a decree promulgated in the United States by the Archbishop-Exarch Benjamin. His followers split up into several groups.

It was Nichols, under the title of Ignatius, Archbishop of Washington, D.C., who managed to save Aftimios's Holy Orthodox Church in America. Born in 1867, he had had a most varied career. Trained as a journalist, he was ordained priest in the

[1] According to Mgr de la Thibauderie (op. cit., pp. 106, 123), Nichols was first consecrated in 1929 by Bishop A. E. Leighton (Vilatte succession).

Protestant Episcopal Church, and worked for a time in Arkansas. During World War One he served in the U. S. Navy, but resumed journalism after he was demobilized. In 1926 he became religious editor of the *New York Sun*, and later of the *New York Telegram*, a post he held until he retired in 1943.

Nichols was well acquainted with the ecclesiastical underworld of North America. Before he became a bishop in the American Orthodox Church he had sampled one or two of the Vilatte sub-schisms. It is said that he received his first consecration from Bishop Arthur E. Leighton, who set up a sect of his own, propagating a mixture of Old Catholicism and Spiritualism. Later on Nichols got himself re-ordained *sub conditione* by Bishop Gregory Lines, who walked out of the American Catholic Church twice, and formed an independent body in California.[1] Nichols was a 'broad churchman' in every sense. He acted as chaplain of the Long Island American Legion Post, and at one time was local chaplain of the Maritime Brigade. After his death a friend wrote:

'When I knew Nichols in 1934 he was a sporty old dog. He wore his clericals in the newspaper office in New York, and when we got to the ferry boat to go to his home on Staten Island, I followed him down the length of the dock, while he greeted everyone he knew cordially with a word and the sign of the cross in blessing. Picturesque is no word for him. He had a dollar up on the horses every afternoon, and in a very warm and human way was very much of the bohemian world of newspaperdom.'[2]

On May 8, 1934, the 'sporty old dog' New York journalist Archbishop of Washington consecrated George W. Plummer, at one time a Roman Catholic priest, who had assumed the headship of a body known as the Anglican Universal Church. He claimed 'valid' orders from a certain Manuel Ferrando of Puerto Rico— another lapsed Catholic—but who does not appear to have been a bishop. Plummer took the title of Archbishop Georgius, and formed a sect of his own—The Holy Orthodox Church in America. One of his first actions was to re-consecrate three of his former bishops—Harry Van Arsdale Persell, Adrian Grover, and Marcus Allen Grover.[3]

Some very unconventional characters found a home in the American Orthodox Church. Their religious opinions were not

---

[1] See pp. 254–257.
[2] cf. Brandreth, op. cit. (2nd ed., 1961), p. 96, note 2.
[3] See p. 507.

always 'orthodox' in the accepted usage of the word. For instance, there was Alexander Tyler Turner, formerly pastor of a Liberal Catholic place of worship at Rochester, New York. In 1931 he founded a quasi-religious community, known as 'The Clerks Secular of St Basil', of which Archbishop Ignatius Nichols became the first superior. It was advertised as being composed of 'American Orthodox laity, who wish to assume its obligations, of which the chief is the daily recitation of the Divine Office in spiritual unity with the other members. Full membership is preceded by a year's noviciate.'[1]

On March 16, 1936, the New York State Legislature formally incorporated the parishes and churches of the Holy Orthodox Church in America, thus giving the body formed by Aftimios Ofiesh a legal status, with Archbishop Ignatius as Administrator of properties, etc. On November 12, that same year, he consecrated Turner, giving him the title of Archbishop Alexander, and the style of Provincial of the Clerks Secular of St Basil.[2]

With a zest for life, and filled with boundless energy, Archbishop Ignatius went on ordaining priests and consecrating bishops until his death in December 1946.[3] He saw nothing unorthodox in consecrating Frank Dyer in the early nineteen-forties. The consecrator and consecrand were kindred spirits, for the latter had been ordained priest by Archbishop Lloyd, and he still remained, as Bishop, what he had been, a Congregational minister. It was very much like Vernon Herford, Bishop of Mercia and Middlesex, ordaining Dr Orchard of the King's Weigh House, London.[4]

In 1942 Dyer, in his turn, laid hands on the Rev. Robert A. Jardine, who, feeling that it was an injustice that H.R.H. the Duke of Windsor should not be allowed a religious marriage with Mrs Wallis Simpson, offered to perform the ceremony. It took place on June 3, 1937 (the birthday of King George V), before an improvised altar in the music-room of the Chateau Candé in Touraine, lent by the French-American, Charles Bedaux. Having achieved world-wide fame, Mr Jardine retired to America, where five years

---

[1] A. T. Turner, *An Orthodox Primer*, p. 26.

[2] The Society, whose headquarters are now at Mount Vernon, N.Y., published from 1938 to 1952 an illustrated quarterly, *The Basilian*, usually containing scholarly articles dealing with ecclesiastical history or liturgy. It was continued under the title of *Orthodoxy*, which retains the quality of its predecessor.

[3] cf. *William Albert Nichols, Archbishop Ignatius: A Tribute to the twentieth Anniversary of his Consecration* (Mount Vernon, N.Y., n.d.).

[4] See p. 145. Sometime after Lloyd's death in 1933, Dyer joined forces with the schismatic Bishop Gregory Lines in California, and at the request of his Co-adjutor, Howard E. Mather, was raised to the episcopate again.

later he was raised to the episcopate. About 1948 he returned to Britain, and threw in his lot with Bishop C. L. Saul's English Episcopal Church. Then this buccaneering parson (vicar of St Paul's, Darlington, from 1927 to 1937) went to South Africa, and assumed the headship of a small and rigidly Protestant body. Many years before he had been honoured by appearing in Mr Kensit's 'Gallery of Protestant Stalwarts'. He died in the early 1950s.

Bishop Dyer early in 1948 raised to the episcopate another Congregational minister, J. Morrison Thomas; also a Unitarian minister at Chicago, by name Preston Bradley—probably the best-known Unitarian in the Middle West, with a large radio audience. That same year Bishop Thomas, doubting the validity of his orders, was re-consecrated by Bishop Timothy Mather (of the Vilatte succession through Lines). He, too, earned his living as a Congregational minister, and styled himself in after years 'Archbishop and Exarch of the Order of Antioch'.

For the next fifteen years the American Orthodox Church carried on as an independent body, with its headquarters at 52 Kingsbridge Road West, Mount Vernon, New York. In Holy Week, 1961, acting on a directive of His Beatitude Alexander III, after an eight years' period of probation, Archbishop-Metropolitan Antony Bashir received the three parishes with their clergy into the Syrian Antiochian Orthodox Archdiocese of New York. He authorized them to continue the use of the Latin Rite, but 'purified of its heterodox elements'. Archbishop Alexander Turner was given the rank of 'Mitred Archpriest', and the status of Vicar-General. Archbishop Bashir set up a commission to aid and assist the clergy and laity with changes in the rite and other matters.[1]

(ii) *Holy Orthodox Church in America (Eastern Catholic and Apostolic)*

As related in the previous section, the founder of this little body, George Winslow Plummer, had wandered in many strange paths after he ceased to be a priest in communion with the Holy See. It is said that he managed to combine the headship of his Anglican Universal Church with that of Supreme Magnus of the *Societas Rosicruciana* in America, but this may be a legend. Having been consecrated (or re-consecrated) by Archbishop Ignatius Nichols in May 1934, he assumed the style of Archbishop Georgius and

[1] cf. *Orthodoxy* (Summer, 1961); also *American Review of Eastern Orthodoxy* (November, 1961).

reconsecrated three of his bishops, to whom he gave the episcopal names of Irenaeus, Patricius, and Marcus respectively. That same year he legally incorporated his followers as 'The Holy Orthodox Church in America (Eastern Catholic and Apostolic). The objects of this new sect were said to be the presentation in the English language of the Eastern Liturgies and primitive Christianity, and the maintenance of the Eastern Orthodox Faith and Rite for all men indiscriminately. The public were informed that the H.O.C.I.A. (E.C. & A.) recognized no head but the head of the Christian Faith, Jesus Christ our Lord; and that its members were inseparably joined in faith with the great Church of Constantinople, and with every other orthodox eastern church of the same profession. What was not mentioned, however, was that none of these Eastern Churches recognized this new American body.

The Metropolitan Georgius took good care that its few congregations were well supplied with bishops. Although presumably Irenaeas (Henry Parsell), Patricius (Adrian Grover), and Marcus (Allen Grover) were still functioning, he added to their number on November 12, 1936, by consecrating Stanislaus Witowski, with the assistance of Archbishop Ignatius of the American Orthodox Church. Witowski took the episcopal name of Theodotus, and seized the opportunity to change his Polish-sounding surname to De Witow. In 1957 Theodotus assumed the Primacy in place of Georgius. By this time the hierarchy had dwindled to an Auxiliary, i.e. Irenaeus (Persell). Still, two bishops were quite enough to supervise four priests and four places of worship.[1]

In the long run it is quality not quantity that counts, as is made clear in a recent official leaflet, where we are told that 'the work of the Holy Orthodox Church in America is to elevate the interpretation and administration of the Holy Mysteries from the more popular appeal of conventional religious practice to the more serious and spiritual level of supplying the means for the development and unfolding of individual spiritual consciousness. . . . It does not attempt to proselytise those who are happy in their Church affiliations. It seeks to reach those who have no Church affiliations, in the conviction that they would welcome a return to Christianity in its original apostolic form, interpreted in the light of highest reason and understanding. . . . Great stress is laid by this Church upon the truth and necessity of spiritual healing.'

[1] cf. *Yearbook of American Churches, 1958,* p. 47. Two years later there were only three ordained clergy having charges, and total membership of the Church had sunk to 213.

So persons of refined tastes, who are repelled by the popular presentation of religion offered, e.g., at St Patrick's Cathedral, or at the Cathedral of St John the Divine, and who strive towards a more serious and spiritual level of the Christian religion for the development and unfolding of their inner consciousness, may be glad to sample what Archbishop Theodotus can offer in his Cathedral Chapel of St Joseph of Arimathea, 321 West 101st Street, New York 25. Here the Divine Mysteries are celebrated on Sunday according to the Holy Orthodox American version. Services of intercession for the sick and suffering are special extra-liturgical devotions for this exclusive body, the members of which like to feel that they are joined in faith, if not in the canons, with all Eastern Orthodox Churches.[1]

(iii) *Apostolic Episcopal Church*

Contradictory legends have been handed down regarding the origins of this American sect. Consequently it is quite possible that some of the dates and details given in this section are incorrect. The following are the chief facts of the story as told after the death of the founder, Arthur Wolfort Brooks, on July 7, 1948. In his younger days he was a priest of the Protestant Episcopal Church, and served this body in and around New York. It has been said that he was 'loaned' to the Greek Orthodox Seminary in New York, and there came into contact with the clergy of various Eastern Churches in North America. Then comes the statement that on May 4, 1925, he was raised to the episcopate by Mar Antonio Lebferne, assisted by Archpresbyter James and Archdeacon Evodius, so that he could look after some of the various Chaldean groups which had sought refuge in the U.S.A. after the First World War.[2] Another version is that Brooks was 'received into the Eastern Church by the titular Bishop of Iconium and the titular Bishop of Tarsus', whoever they were. Furthermore, we are told that a new body was instituted 'by canonical authority, by representation and delegation from the Patriarch of the Chaldean Church'.[3] But it is not stated who was this unspecified Patriarch, or over what groups of Chaldeans he ruled. Thus it is not clear whether or not Brooks found he had to adopt the

---

[1] The monthly magazine, *The Messenger of Holy Wisdom*, is edited by Archbishop Theodotus.

[2] Mar Antonio is said to have been consecrated in 1917 by Mar Emmanuel Thomas II, Patriarch of Babylon of the Chaldean Uniates.

[3] See Brandreth, op. cit. (2nd ed., 1961), pp. 112–13.

Nestorian doctrine of the two Persons in the Incarnate Christ. The two traditions combine to state that on June 23, 1926, at what is described as 'a business session of the First Annual Convocation of the Metropolitan Synod of the Anglican Universal Church', Brooks was duly elected as Titular Bishop of Sardis. But by 1932 he had broken away from his body, which appears to have been the nucleus of the Holy Orthodox Church in America.[1] Then, he assumed the style of 'Right Reverend' and formed a new sect, known as the Apostolic Episcopal Church. Its headquarters were at Christ's Church-by-the-Sea, at Broad Channel, Long Island, N.Y. On June 22, Archbishop George W. Plummer, still Primate and Presiding Bishop of the Anglican Universal Church, issued a statement alleging that Brooks's pretensions to associations with the Chaldeans were 'utterly without merit or basis in fact—utterly worthless and absolute fabrications'. Surprisingly, Brooks then turned for consecration to this free-lance prelate, who gave him the Russian Orthodox succession (derived from Aftimios Ofiesh by way of the journalist Archbishop of Washington, Ignatius William Albert Nichols) and the title of Mar John Emmanuel.

Shortly after this, as head of the new Apostolic Episcopal Church, Mar John Emmanuel consecrated two bishops on September 16, 1934—Charles W. Keller, and Harold F. Jarvis.[2] It is related that an American version of the Chaldean Uniate Rite was used at this ceremony. In August 1941, Mar John Emmanuel, having consulted Archbishop Athenagoras Spyron, then head of the Greek Orthodox Church in North and South America, agreed to become Presiding Bishop of the so-called Old Catholic Orthodox Church in England, and appointed Hugh George de Willmott Newman (the future Mar Georgius) as his Vicar-General in Europe, with the style of Abbot-Nullius of St Albans in the Order of Corporate Reunion.[3]

Judging from Mar Georgius's recollections, Mar John Emmanuel must have been a kindly but somewhat eccentric prelate, with very broad views on ecclesiastical jurisdiction. Later on he was granted the style of Titular Archbishop of Ebbsfleet in the Catholicate of the West. On October 13, 1946, he consecrated at New York a former Liberal Catholic priest named Hermann F.

[1] See previous section.
[2] Later on Keller became known as Mar Carolus, Titular Bishop of Amesbury in the Catholicate of the West.
[3] See p. 446. In 1948 His All-Holiness Archbishop Athenagoras was elected Oecumenical Patriarch of Constantinople.

Abbinga, who became known as Mar Philippus, Bishop of Amersfoort, of the Eastern Apostolic Episcopal Church, 'First Missionary Bishop for Holland and Indonesia, attached to the Catholicate of the West (H.Q. London).'

He issued a leaflet in which he explained that his sect was 'a perfectly regular but independent Western branch of the Eastern One Holy Catholic and Apostolic Church'. This little body, with its headquarters in the Netherlands, was said to have evolved from the American Apostolic Episcopal Church, which could trace its roots to 'the first independent branch (fourth century) of the ancient Church in Chaldea'. He stated that

'The E.A.E.C. strives as much as possible to approach to the original Christendom, without losing sight of the demands of modern culture and science, and adapts itself according to Eastern custom to national needs and circumstances. . . . Its chief aim is nobility of soul through the mystical living out of the Mysteries and the bearing of them out into the outer world. The charismatic gifts of the Holy Ghost are highly esteemed, especially the gift of healing. It stands for World Peace, and commemorates (also individually) the dead, and especially the souls of those who cruelly lost their bodies in the last war turmoil.'[1]

Moreover, Mar Philippus could snap his fingers at Mgr Rinkel, Archbishop of Utrecht, and the rest of the Old Catholic hierarchy in Holland, also Mgr Vreede, the Dutch Presiding Bishop of the Liberal Catholic Church, for none of them could claim that their 'Apostolic Plenipotentiary Powers' had been given them by 'the Apostles Peter and Paul, Thomas and Bartholomew, through the Syrian-Chaldean, the Syrian-Malabar, the Syrian-Antiochene, and the Armenian Channels of Apostolic Succession'—right down through the 126 Patriarchs of Antioch known to history. Mar Philippus was convinced that his little body, for the moment concentrated within the Utrecht province, would soon become 'a refuge for all who in post-war Holland and Indonesia have orientated themselves religiously, but who for church historical right, show friendship to Islam, as the Eastern Patriarchs, during more than a two-thousand-years-long Mohammedan overlordship set the example and often lived on good terms with the califfs'.

But few persons in Holland, and still less in Indonesia after it

---

[1] In this respect the Eastern Apostolic Episcopal Church perpetuated the spirit of the Universal Patriarch Banks's Apostolic Service Church, founded in 1922 as a Living Memorial to our Loved Ones, who 'had "gone over the top" to fearlessly teach the Divine Truths free from all distortions'. (See p. 371.)

became a Republic in 1950, were greatly interested in the
E.A.E.C., and not many applied for membership by writing to
its headquarters at Anna Paulownalaan 5, Amersfoort.[1]

Mar John Emmanuel, Titular Archbishop of Ebbsfleet (Isle of
Thanet, Kent), living on Long Island (New York), was granted
the status of Exarch of the Catholicate of the West in the United
States. From reasons which are not clear, his Apostolic Christian
Fellowship of Los Angeles, California, which remained under
Archbishop de Ortega Maxey, Mar David I, Patriarch of Malaga,
until he joined the Universalist Church of America in 1951.[2] The
united body retained the name of Apostolic Episcopal Church,
adding 'Province of the West', but the union does not appear to
have lasted very long.

According to Mar Georgius, Mar John Emmanuel 'was a man
of great sympathy and understanding, and very learned in the
ancient customs of the Eastern Churches'.[3] This erudition evidently
enabled the Exarch to find canonical reasons for having a wife. His
widow, Mrs Jane Naglo Brooks, and his daughter, Miss Margaret
Ellon Brooks, both survived his death on July 7, 1948.

Mar John Emmanuel had always regarded his jurisdiction as
cosmic, in which respect his only rival on earth was the Universal
Patriarch Banks of East Molesey, England.[4] After his death the
three virtually independent groups of the Apostolic Episcopal
Church became independent in fact, because they could not agree on
a Primate. On July 24, 1948, Mar Matthew, Titular Bishop of
Hawaii, Auxiliary to the Patriarchal Throne of Malaga, wrote
from California, to notify Dr Fisher, Primate of All England, that
Mar David I, Archbishop of the West and Patriarch of Malaga,
would be solemnly enthroned as Presiding-Bishop of the Apostolic
Episcopal Church at the coming Synod, and to ask remembrance in
his prayers. Mar David I resigned both his patriarchal and primatial status three years later, and as stated already, took on the less
onerous duties of pastor at the First Universalist Church in Los
Angeles. He was succeeded as Primate by Bishop Jarvis.[5]

---

[1] Perhaps Abbinga was over optimistic in thinking that there was room in Holland
for another autocephalous church. The Liberal Catholic Church had maintained a
Regionary Bishop since 1919; and in 1946 a priest, D. L. T. Tollenaar, having rejected
Theosophy, formed a little sect of his own, and assumed the title of Apostolic Vicar of
the Netherlands. After his consecration by Bishop Saul of the English Episcopal Church
in 1950, he called himself Old Catholic Bishop of Arnhem. (See p. 401.)

[2] See p. 489.

[3] *Hieratika*, September 1948.

[4] See p. 376, note 1.

[5] See p. 509.

Mar Philippus (Abbinga) took over the duties of Primate of Europe, and still holds this status. On May 31, 1953, he consecrated P. H. Cedarholm in Oslo, giving him the title and rank of 'Mar Nikolaus, Bishop for Scandinavia, in the Chaldean-Oecumenical Succession'. It is stated that the Province of the Apostolic Episcopal Church (Eastern) in Western Europe has congregations in Holland, Norway, Sweden, France, and Hungary, but no statistics of their numbers are forthcoming.[1]

(iv) *Greek Oriental Hungarian Orthodox Church*

About 1925 the Archbishop of Ipek, Metropolitan of Belgrade and Karlovtsy, the Serbian Patriarch, announced his intention to extend his jurisdiction to Hungary, and to send a bishop to Bucharest. The Orthodox Hungarians protested and, backed up by the Government, appealed to the Patriarch of Constantinople, but he was unwilling to interfere. About nine years later a priest named Stephen Nemeth had obtained the support of a sufficient number of clergy and laity to enable him to form an independent Hungarian Orthodox Church. He went to Syria, and on September 23, 1934, was consecrated by the Jacobite Patriarch, Mar Ignatius Ephrem I.[2] The result of this irregular consecration was that Nemeth was excommunicated by both Belgrade and Constantinople.

Some of his never very numerous followers emigrated to North America. At the time of writing, a former priest of the American Catholic Church (Vilatte succession), one Stefan Boros, styles himself a bishop of the Hungarian Greek Catholic Church in New York. Another independent Hungarian prelate, Imre Joseph Fekete, with the style of 'Titular Bishop of Munkacs, Acting Supreme Pontiff of the Hungarian Eastern Church in Exile', turned up in England some years ago, begging alms on behalf of his fellow countrymen in exile, but his origins remain uncertain.

(v) *Byzantine American Church*

Early in the present century a Catholic Melkite priest, named Antony Aneed, was acting as secretary to Archbishop Sawaya of Beirut.[3] He was sent to the United States, where he worked in one

---

[1] The last statistics of the Apostolic Episcopal Church in the U.S.A. appear to be those issued in 1947, when the inclusive membership was given as 7,086, with forty-six places of worship. (*Yearbook of American Churches, 1961*, p. 43.)

[2] The same prelate who was deposed at the Council of London in 1943, when Dr W. B. Crow was elected as his successor. (See p. 240.)

[3] The Melkites are the survivors of the Patriarchate of Antioch, part of which fell into heresy in 451, and the rest into schism about 1060. A patriarchal line in communion with the Holy See was definitely restored in 1724. The supreme head of the

of the Melkite parishes in New York.[1] In 1911 Archbishop Sawaya decided to visit his co-religionists in North America, but Pius X refused him permission. In spite of this the Archbishop sailed for New York, where he stayed with his former secretary. In after years Aneed produced documentary evidence that Swaya had consecrated him as his Auxiliary Bishop; and also nominated him as Exarch for the Melkites in North America. If this is true, then the act would be highly irregular, not to say schismatic, having been performed without either episcopal witnesses or papal permission.

However, it was not until about 1942, after Aneed had broken off all relations with the Holy See, and after the death of Sawaya, that he put forward his claim to be a bishop. He formed what he called 'The Byzantine American Church', which he described as an autocephalous body, had it incorporated in California in 1944, and styled himself 'Patriarch-President, Federated Independent Catholic and Orthodox Churches' in the United States. His flock consisted mainly of groups of Syrians in and around San Francisco.

By this time Aneed had succumbed to the predominating ethos of the independent bishops in California, and had become a very broad-minded churchman. In 1945, with the assistance of Bishops Kleefisch, Wadle, and Verostek (all of them alleged to be Theosophists), he consecrated an occultist named Frank B. Robinson, who ran a 'Psychiana Society' at Moscow, Idaho. Next followed the consecration on January 1, 1946, of Edmund Walker-Baxter as Lord Abbot of San-Luigi. On July 29 that same year, assisted by Bishops Kleefisch and Hampton, the Patriarch President raised to the episcopate Odo Acheson Barry (later Mar Columba) as first Primate of the Canadian Catholic Church.[2] On December 8, 1949, Aneed handed on the Melkite succession to Nicolas Urbanovitch at San Francisco, more lines being supplied by Bishop Kleefisch, who assisted at the function.[3]

The Byzantine American Church has now ceased to appear in the

---

Catholic Melkites holds the title of Patriarch of Antioch and of All the East, and resides at Ain-Traz in Lebanon.

[1] In 1960 the Catholic Melkites had twenty-six parishes, thirty priests, and about 50,000 faithful in the U.S.A.

[2] See p. 535. Barry was re-consecrated by L. P. Wadle, Primate of the American Catholic (Vilatte Succession) Apostolic Church of Long Beach, on October 3, 1948.

[3] Urbanovitch claimed that he had been a history professor at the University of Krakow, and was a Ph.D. of the University of Prague. In 1938 he had been ordained priest of the Orthodox Ukrainian Church in the United States, under the jurisdiction of Bishop Bogden Shpilta. His headquarters were at Winnipeg, Canada. On May 7, 1955, Urbanovitch, assisted by Mgr Efrem Fusi, Mariavite Bishop for Italy, consecrated Eugenius de Batchinsky at Florence.

Miscellaneous Churches

Yearbook of American Churches, so it is not certain if it still functions.

(vi) *Eastern Orthodox Catholic Church in America*

All that the *Yearbook of American Churches* tells us in its 1961 edition is that this sect was 'organized in 1927, in New York, as an independent body; membership dispersed, in 1959, among other Orthodox churches'.[1] But the 1958 issue was more informative: 'the foundation of this body stems from the authority and wishes of the Patriarch Tikhon of the Russian Orthodox Church, and the acts of his successors, to propagate the Orthodox Faith among the English-speaking people in America. In 1927 the Holy Eastern Orthodox Catholic and Apostolic Church in America was created'.[2] This statement suggests that his body may have been an offshoot of the American Orthodox Church, founded by Aftimios Ofiesh, after the Russian bishops had withdrawn their support in 1927.[3] Until 1959 the Ruling Bishop was John M. More Moreno, whose headquarters were at the Cathedral of Our Saviour, 251 West 69th Street, New York City 23.

It has been stated that Moreno was raised to the episcopate on November 20, 1943, by a prelate named J. T. Beckles, known as Mar Thomas Theophilus, Archbishop-Primate-Metropolitan and Patriarch of the Evangelical Orthodox Church. His Beatitude Beckles claimed to have been consecrated in 1927, but where and by whom is not certain. This body must have been the smallest orthodox church in the world, for in 1958 it had only one place of worship, only one ordained clergyman, and a total membership of thirty-nine.

(vii) *Episcopal Orthodox Church (Greek Communion)*

The yearning among negro Christians in North America to be in communion with one or other of the Eastern Churches is one of the things which suggests the Roman Church might succeed more in Africa if she introduced Oriental Rites. This particular body, however, did not last more than twenty-five years. The Episcopal Orthodox Church appears to have been founded at San Fernando, Trinidad; it was incorporated in Cuba in 1921, and in the New York State in 1939. The founder, 'His Eminence' E. N. Jack, gave himself the title of 'The International Exalted Archbishop in Charge', and by 1945 had fixed his headquarters at St McGinley

[1] op. cit., p. 44.
[2] op. cit., p. 46.
[3] See p. 503.

514

the Martyr's Orthodox Cathedral, Bridgetown, Barbados. Also located here was St Mcginley's Greek Orthodox Seminary, where were taught Pitman's Shorthand, Book-Keeping, Touch Typewriting, Theology, and General Instruction.[1] Quite a large staff was attached to the Cathedral, including several Deaconesses and Sub-Deaconesses, a Canon and a Curate, and a couple of lady Missionaries.

It appears that His Eminence was raised to the episcopate by Bishop Grant Barrow of the African Orthodox Church (Vilatte succession), who had lapsed into schism from the main group under Patriarch McGuire.[2] The International Exalted Archbishop's sheep were all black, most of them negroes in Barbados and Trinidad. He claimed that his Church really dated from A.D. 33, when it was founded in Greece by a certain Kokorakis, and acknowledged by Paul the Apostle at Athens in A.D. 54. He reckoned that there were 5,000 persons under his jurisdiction. Moreover, it was 'the oldest Catholic Church in Europe'—apparently because it 'taught congregational singing by the Plag Tone of Kyrie Eleison', whatever this meant.

This outpost of the Eastern Orthodox Church in the West Indies must have been a fascinating body, and interestingly heterodox in its beliefs. Among the obligatory subjects in the curriculum to be studied by its clergy was Rosicrucian Philosophy; Greek, Spanish, and Instrumental Music were only recommended. They had no choice but to be 'worker priests', and the trades suggested would have been quite in keeping with Mission de France—tailor, watch and clock repairer, shoemaker, printer, or bookbinder. The International Exalted Archbishop died in 1954, and no recent information about the Orthodox Diocese of the West Indies and British Guiana is forthcoming.[3]

(B) CHURCHES OF LATIN ORIGIN

(i) *Polish Mariavite Church*
(ii) *Polish National Catholic Church*

[1] cf. *The Annual Synopsis . . . for the 22nd Year, 1945.*
[2] See p. 265.
[3] Although outside the scope of this book, reference should be made to the adoption of innumerable Roman Catholic rites and ceremonies into the Voodoo or spirit worship in Dahomey, Cuba, Haiti, and Guadeloupe; a subject which would need a volume to itself. (cf. Major Louis Maximilian, *Le Voudoo haïtien* (Port-au-Prince, n.d.); Jacques Roumain, *Le Sacrifice du Tambour-Assoto (Rada)* (Port-au-Prince, 1943); Milo Marcelin, *Mythologie Voudou (Rita Aroda)*, vol. I (Port-au-Prince, 1949); 'Les Grand Dieux du Voudoo haïtien' (*Journal de la Société des Américanistes*, n.s., vol. 36, 51–135); Harold Courlander, *Haiti Singing* (University of California, 1939); Patrick Leigh Fermor, *The Traveller's Tree* (London, 1956).

Miscellaneous Churches

(iii) *Spanish Reformed Episcopal Church*
(iv) *Lusitanian Church, Catholic, Apostolic, Evangelical*
(v) *Philippine Independent Church*
(vi) *Brazilian Catholic Apostolic Church*
(vii) *Canadian Catholic Church*
(viii) *Old Catholic Church of Yugoslavia*
(ix) *Reformed Catholic Church (Utrecht Confession)*

(i) Polish Mariavite Church

The origins of this schismatic body are to be found in Poland, where in 1883–4 the Rev. Kasimir Przjemski formed a group of priests who observed the Rule of the Third Order of St Francis. About three years later a poor seamstress, Maria Franciska Kozlowska, founded a community of Franciscan Tertiaries, who were directed by the former body. On August 2, 1893, Maria—now known as Sister Felicya—claimed to have had a vision of the Blessed Virgin, and a divine command to establish a mixed Order of men and women dedicated to Our Lady. The Tertiaries were united as The Mariavite Union. The Mother House was established at Felicianov, near Plock, about fifty-five miles north-west of Warsaw. Sister Felicya soon had a large following, mainly drawn from the peasant classes, who called her *Mateczka*, or Little Mother. She continued to have revelations, with the result that she began to be venerated as a saint.

The Mariavites were united by a strong belief in Polish Messianism; convinced that through the sufferings and ultimate resurrection of the Polish nation great benefits would result to the Catholic Church and to all mankind. The double-monasteries of friars and sisters maintained homes for the aged, ran dispensaries, and sponsored co-operative societies. Although much good work was being done by these people, they had many enemies. The Polish bishops finally decided to make an inquiry into the irregularities of faith and morals which were suspected, and a report was submitted to Rome. The authorities came to the conclusion that Sister Felicya's visions were merely hallucinations, and ordered the suppression of the Mariavites.

They refused to obey, and were excommunicated by a Bull of Pius X, dated April 5, 1906. By this time there were about fifty priests and some twenty parishes. The total number of the schismatics was estimated at 500,000, but by 1907 they had dropped to about 60,000. Meanwhile the Russian Government had given its approval to the Mariavites, in spite of strong protests by the Polish Catholic hierarchy. General Alexei Kiréef, the well-known Russian layman who was always ready to back any movement which he thought would weaken the political power of the Papacy, managed to win the support of the Old Catholic bishops in Holland.[1] The Mariavites were admitted into communion with the Church of Utrecht, and on October 5, 1909, Archbishop Gerardus Gul, with Bishop A. H. Mathew as one of the co-consecrators, raised Jean-Marie (Michael) Kowalski to the episcopate, under the title of Archbishop of Felicianov, Primate of the Old Catholic Church of the Mariavites. The new prelate had under his jurisdiction about forty priests, twenty-two parishes, and an estimated 20,000 layfolk. Most of them were in central Poland.

The Russian Duma gave official recognition to the Mariavite Church in 1911. At first there was little or nothing heterodox about its fundamental doctrinal opinions, but the ritual and ceremonial tended to be exotic. Mass was always celebrated before the Blessed Sacrament exposed, and in the vernacular. It was not long, however, before clerical celibacy was abolished. During the First World War an unhealthy development towards near 'Mariolatry' led to permission being granted for the ordination of women. Archbishop Kowalski eventually came to the conclusion that he was more or less infallible and impeccable.

He took one of his Franciscan Sisters, Maria Isabella Wilucka, as his spiritual directress. Before long 'mystical marriages' between the priests and alleged holy women became common, and it is said that some of these associations were akin to those which existed among the members of 'The Abode of Love' in England.[2] Sister Isabella managed to gain great power over the Archbishop, and became known as the *Episcopal Sister* or the *High Priestess*. In 1921 Benedict XV had established the feast of Mary, Mediatrix of all Graces, stressing the doctrine of Mary's maternal solicitude for the human race, closely connected with her Son's redemptive mission, so that it is an integral part of it, and extends to all graces won for us by Christ. Having already opened up the ranks of the priesthood to women, Kowalski felt that devotion to Our Lady could not be perfect without lady bishops. On March 29, 1929, he

---

[1] His sister, Madame Olga Novikoff, in 1910, tried to use her brother's influence with the Holy Synod of Moscow for the union of A. H. Mathew's *English Catholic Church* (as it was then called) with the Russian Patriarchate. (See p. 185.)
[2] See p. 487, note 2.

consecrated the Episcopal Sister, who acted as his coadjutrix, and the mediatrix of all graces. Good use was made of her charismata. As Superioress-General of the Mariavite Sisters, she ordained many priestesses (some of them still alive), and also consecrated eleven bishopesses between April 5 and June 4, 1931.

Michael Kowalski loved making bishops, among whom were Andrezj Golebiowski (1910), Jakub Prochniewski (1910), Franszej Roztoworowski (1924), Barthelemey Pryzysiecki (1929), Philip Feldmann (1929), Simon Bucholz (1933), and Titus Siedlecki (1935).[1] Not content with ordaining Polish priests (of both sexes), Kowalski further consecrated a Lithuanian, Felix Tulaba (1939), and a Frenchman, Marc-Marie-Paul Fatome. The latter—a lapsed Roman Catholic and student at the seminary of Coutances—was raised to the episcopate on September 4, 1938, as Regionary Bishop for France.[2] After this he called himself 'Père Marc', and adorned the door of his chapel at Nantes with a monstrance as a symbol of being in mystical union with the Mariavites. On April 5, 1949, he consecrated Gaston Perrier as his coadjutor; and on October 9, that same year, Paulus Helmut Norbert Maas as Regionary Bishop for Germany. Fatome died at Nantes on August 28, 1951.[3]

Soon after Fatome's death Perrier broke away from the Mariavites, and formed what he called the *Église catholique de France*.[4] Maas, having returned to Germany, on May 24, 1953, consecrated Ephrem Maria Mauro Fusi to win over the Italians to Mariavitism. Perrier having deserted the Mariavites, Maas gave them another bishop in the person of Jean-André Prevost on August 9, 1953. Feeling that there was a good chance of converting the Sicilians to Sister Felicya's version of Catholicism, Fusi consecrated Clemente Alfio Sgroi-Marchese on May 26, 1954.

There is no doubt that the Mariavites have a great sense of mission, and they were generous either in providing bishops for autocephalous churches, or adding a few more lines of apostolic

---

[1] Prockniewski became Archbishop of Plock, and eventually leader of a reformed group of Mariavites. Feldmann, his auxiliary, although deported to Germany by the Nazis, remained head of the Polish Mariavites for many years. Subsequently he was reconciled with the Old Catholics, and ended his days as a parish priest in the Rhineland.

[2] He had been ordained priest by the Old Catholic Archbishop of Utrecht, and ran an independent chapel at Nantes.

[3] In July 1951 Fatome gave the French Oriental monk, Jean-Pierre Danyel, the first of his ordinations to the priesthood. In 1957 Danyel was raised to the episcopate as Tugdual I, first Primate of the *Sainte Église Celtique en Bretagne*. (See pp. 315–318.)

[4] It is possible that before this he raised Robert Bonnet to the episcopate.

succession to prelates already consecrated. Archbishop Prochniew-ski, for instance, gave the Old Catholics of Hungary their first bishop in the person of Thomas Csernohorsky-Fehervary on November 11, 1945. Mgr Fusi, although holding the title of Bishop of Milan and Rome, did not regard his jurisdiction as confined to Italy, and on April 14, 1955, gave to Julien Erni, pastor of a Free Protestant parish at Bienne, Switzerland, what in the event proved to be the first of several consecrations.

Erni had been brought up in France by pious Catholic parents, had spent some years in the Seminary of St Nicholas de Chardonnet, Paris, but lost his faith during the First World War. By 1917 he had regained a vague belief in a sort of non-institutional Christianity. Having studied at Geneva, he worked for several years with the *Église Chrétienne Belge*, mostly among the poorer classes in rural districts. Contacts with Frank Duquesne, a priest in Brussels, who belonged to Winnaert's *Église Catholique Évangelique*, helped him to realize that Calvinism could not create the Universal Church about which he was now dreaming. Eventually Erni accepted a call to become the pastor of an '*église libre* at Bienne in the Berne canton of Switzerland.[1] He was such a liberal and modernist in his opinions that it would have been difficult for him to find a niche in any organized religious body. His main interest was the promotion of an all-inclusive Christian Church. With this end in view he founded the *Ligue Oecuménique pour l'unité chrétienne*, inspired by a similar organization planned by Père Gard, who belonged to Winnaert's little body.[2]

Having contacted several of the neo-Gnostic French bishops, Erni became dissatisfied with the status of what he called a *pasteur oecuménique*, and yearned for the episcopate. He tried to induce Bishop Küry of the Swiss Christian Catholic Church to consecrate him, but this prelate did not see his way to oblige, no doubt because Erni was now associated with all sorts of heterodox bodies on which the respectable Swiss Old Catholics looked with disapproval. In the end Erni had to be satisfied with the Mariavites. The consecration by Fusi made him feel that he had

---

[1] cf. Julien Erni, *Seminariste Romain, Pasteur Protestant, Pasteur Oecuménique* (Bienne, n.d.).
[2] Associated with Erni were Mgr Giraud, Patriarch of the *Église Gallicane*; Mgr Vigue, first Consulter of the Episcopal College of the *Églises Catholiques Apostoliques Orthodoxes d'Occident*; Mgr Haug, Archbishop of the *Église Catholique Apostolique*, and Superior of the Institut des Frères at Rüschlikon, Switzerland; Mgr Laemner, Bishop of the *Église Catholique Primitive* (Paris); and Mgr Lescouzères, Bishop of the *Église Gallicane*, and Coadjutor to its Patriarch.

greater authority to go ahead with planning his Universal Church. But Erni wanted more lines of apostolic succession, so on July 11, 1956, he got Archbishop John I of Vancouver (W. F. Wolsey), head of the Canadian Temple of the More Abundant Life and President of the Universal Life Foundation, to re-consecrate him.[1] The ecumenical visions grew larger and brighter, and Erni was eager to share his multiform apostolic succession with almost anybody, and ready to entrol any sect in his League for Christian Unity. He could claim that it had countless distinguished members, lay and clerical, in Switzerland, France, Germany, Austria, Italy, Holland, Norway, Belgium, Great Britain, the U.S.A., Mexico, Brazil, North and South Africa, and India. They came mostly from some of the less-known bodies which have not been admitted to the World Council of Churches. In the U.S.A., especially, these autocephalous bodies were very eclectic in their affiliations, and included the Reformed Catholic Church, American Catholic Church, Old Catholic Church in America, First Methodist Church, Universal Spiritualist Church, Evangelical Church, Church of Simon of Cyrene, Church of the Merciful Saviour, Church of the New Jerusalem (Swedenborgian), Church of the Order of Antioch, and the Christian Ecumenical Church of Truth. In Europe Mariavites, Gnostics, Reformed Orthodox, and numerous tiny sects (most calling themselves Old Catholic) were all on more or less friendly terms.[2]

A few years ago Bishop Erni retired from Bienne to Aire-Geneva, where he continues to propagate his Ecumenical League for Christian Unity with tireless zeal. He has stated that several bishops of autocephalous churches are hoping to form what is called a *Siège Ecclésial Oecuménique*, without creating a new or *Super Church*.[3] It remains to be seen what will come of this 'true crusade of the twentieth century', and if, as its promoters hope, it will 'create a One Church, Holy, Universal and Apostolic, in which Unity would reign in diversity'.[4]

In the land of its birth, the Mariavite Church has certainly not

[1] See p. 484.
[2] After his second consecration by Wolsey, Erni reconsecrated Charles-Borromée d'Eschevannes on May 2, 1957 (see p. 317); and William Handsworth Turner on June 17, 1960 (see p. 385, note 1).
[3] There are said to be at last forty bishops in the League—Old Catholic, Mariavite, Ukrainian, 'Reformed Orthodox', National Polish Catholic, American Methodist, etc. etc. There are rumours that some of these prelates have ordained Protestant ministers to ensure that their orders are 'valid', thus emulating the Order of Corporate Reunion.
[4] cf. Julien Erni, *Les Sacraments de l'Église Universelle* (Lausanne, 1948); and *Je crois la Sainte Église Universelle* (Bienne, 1945).

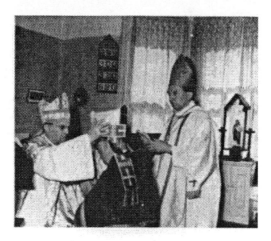

Consecration of the Rt Rev. Rupert Singleton Ian Angus Pitt-Kethley (British Representative of the Universal Life Foundation and International Academy, and Administrator for Great Britain of the Reformed Catholic Church, Utrecht Confession), by Mgr Julien Erni, assisted by the Rt Rev. William Handsworth Turner (Primate of the Church and Order of Christian Unity, within the One Holy, Catholic and Apostolic Church).

Consecration of the Most Rev. John Van Ryswyk, Primate of the Apostolic Church of St Peter, Baron, Imperator-Pontifex-Avatar Imperium Internum, Grand Master Ordo Equestris Militaris Avatar, Hereditary Knight of the Holy Roman Empire, Duc de Ryswyk, Duc de Valmahon, Prince de Usipiae, Marquis de Casaldorato, etc., etc., by Mar Georgius, Patriarch of Glastonbury.

shown an ecumenical character. It has been torn by internal dissensions ever since it was founded half a century ago. Bishop Feldmann gained more and more followers, and finally managed to depose Archbishop Kowalski, who was shut up in a monastery by the Government, the only alternative to confinement in a mental hospital. Bishopess Isabella Wilucka, together with all the other lady priests and prelates, withdrew from public activity, but managed to continue ministering secretly in several parishes. By 1946 the numbers of the Mariavites were greatly reduced, and they linked up with the so-called 'Old Catholic Church of Poland', a body not recognized by the Utrecht Union. It was decreed that each group would retain its own organization, respective beliefs, and modes of worship. The first Primate of the united church was Barthelemey Pryzysiecki (consecrated by Kowalski in 1929), but who had helped to form the Polish Old Catholic Church. Bishop Faron acted as his assistant, and a second assistant was Zygmunt Szypold (consecrated by Prochniewski in 1947). Three years later, Faron, weary of the wranglings of heretics and schismatics, submitted to the Holy See. Under Przysiecki's leadership the Old Catholic section sought affiliation with Carfora's North American Old Roman Catholic Church, having abolished the ordination of women.

Another group of Mariavites who emigrated to North America placed themselves in 1927 under the jurisdiction of Archbishop-Abbot Brothers of St Dunstan's Abbey, Cos Cob, Connecticut.[1] Later on he claimed to be the American Representative of the Mariavite Church, not only in North America, but also in Czechoslovakia, Yugoslavia, France, and Morocco. He was still promoting Mariavitism as late as 1950, and boasted of a Jew—'a most splendid young fellow—a fine example of what a Mariavite can and should be'. The Archbishop-Abbot (himself married like a good Mariavite) was planning to find a sphere for this Brother Bernard in California, the breeding ground of so many strange cults. On May 5, 1956, Mgr Prevost, the Mariavite Bishop for France, raised Robert Bonnet to the episcopate as Regionary Bishop for Morocco, and he was also in full communion with Archbishop-Abbot Brothers in North America. On January 20, 1957, Mgr Prevost gave a Mariavite bishop to Belgium in the person of Jacques Niset.

Mariavitism, with its apocalyptic mysticism, glamorous ritual

[1] See pp. 420, 421, 425.

and ceremonial, had much the same appeal for a small esoteric circle of Anglo-Catholics as the Order of Corporate Reunion had for an earlier generation. Such persons—most of them romantic young men—were usually Jacobites, Polish Messianism could be linked up with the Stewart dynasty, because Bonnie Prince Charlie's mother was Maria Clementina Sobieska, a member of the de-throned royal house of Poland. During the nineteen-thirties there were several cryptic clerics in England who confided that they were Mariavites—secret agents of what ordinary folk regarded as a lost cause. One of them, a former Anglican clergyman, called himself 'Augustyn, Polish Old Catholic Priest'.

The best known of the English Mariavites was Walter Wilman, who as a youth worked in the cloth trade at Bradford. In 1913 he was licensed as a lay reader by Dr Drury, Bishop of Ripon. Having served in the Royal Artillery on the Western Front during the First World War, Wilman became a lay missionary in South Yorkshire. On May 2, 1934, he was ordained priest by Basil M. Stannard, Bishop of Walsingham, and founder of the Catholic Christian Church.[1]

This short-lived body was already associated with some of the lesser-known so-called 'Old Catholic' churches on the Continent, so Fr Wilman went to Poland with another like-minded young man, hoping to link-up with the Mariavites. It is said that the Government (possibly the dictator Pilsudski himself) prevented Archbishop Kowalski from consecrating Wilman. After staying with the Mariavite monks and nuns at Plock, he returned to Eng-land invested with the bizarre white habit worn by this mixed community, most of whom were married. In July 1935 he was notified from Plock that he had been elected Bishop. Later he received from Kowalski (now in enforced confinement) a document purporting to appoint him to the episcopate by post. About 1943, Fr Pat Shaw, who had been rector of All Saints', York, for thirty years, made this Catholic Christian priest and Mariavite bishop his parish clerk, and installed him in the medieval anchorhold adjoining this famous Anglo-Catholic church. There is a legend that on the written authorization to perform episcopal acts, said to have been received from Archbishop Kowalski (who died in Dachau concen-tration camp in 1942), Wilman 'consecrated' one bishop, Anthony (King) Wilson, known as 'Bishop Anthony of Leeds', but actually he merely installed him as the superior of an independent Christian

[1] See p. 275.

Mission in that city.[1] On November 1, 1950, the Minister-General of the Mariavites appointed Wilman as Minister-Provincial of the Mariavite Order in England, with jurisdiction over all others claiming to belong to this Church. Some tried to supplant him, but without success. Eventually the bishop-hermit's health broke down, and he had to leave his cold damp cell and was taken to the old people's home at Brackenhill, York. He died in the York City Hospital in September 1962, aged seventy-five, and was buried with Anglican rites in the family grave in his native Bradford. The Mariavite anchorite is recalled as a genial little man, with a fund of racy clerical stories.

It is not known what were his reactions as Minister-General of the Mariavite Order in England when on September 18, 1954, Mgr Sgroi-Marchese, Mariavite Bishop for Sicily, re-consecrated both Mar Georgius, Patriarch of Glastonbury, and Mar Joannes, Archbishop of Karim, or if he was invited to the function in the Ancient Catholic Cathedral of the Good Shepherd, Chelsea.[2] Did he regard himself as being in loose communion with Archbishop Ignatius Carolus, Primate of the Old Holy Catholic Church, who in 1957 appears to have consecrated Mgr Alexander Licastro de la Chastre Grimaldi-Lascaris, Prince de Deols; who was said to have been reconsecrated by Mgr Marchese, Maraviate Bishop for Italy? During the past half-century the Mariavites have mothered such a numerous and hybrid offspring that it is difficult for a student of the by-ways of church history to catalogue them correctly.

(ii) *Polish National Catholic Church*

It would be true enough to say that the visions seen by Sister Felicya Kozlowska resulted in almost as much disunity as those of Joachim di Flora in the twelfth century. The Congregation of the Holy Office may not have been far wrong in deciding that this nineteenth-century Franciscan Tertiary was a victim of hallucinations. Poles who wanted to throw off the yoke of Rome had to wait until Francis Hodur came along a few years later before they managed to lay the foundations of an independent church, purged as they believed of papalist corruptions, and immune, as they hoped, from the Mariavite ones.

Some of the Polish emigrants in North America strongly resented being under the jurisdiction of either German or Irish

---

[1] See p. 229.
[2] See p. 483.

bishops, and to having non-Polish pastors appointed to almost exclusively Polish parishes.[1] By the eighteen-eighties most large cities in the U.S.A. contained groups of Poles living apart from other Catholics, and having no wish to be integrated with them. These aliens had their own traditions of church administration, and naturally saw no reason why things should be different from what they had been accustomed to at home. The majority of these expatriate Poles were poor and ignorant, and accepted their priests as almost infallible. The first schismatic Polish congregation was formed at Chicago by Fr Antoni Koslowski in 1895. On November 17, 1897, he was raised to the episcopate at Berne by Bishop Herzog, assisted by Archbishop Gul of Utrecht and Bishop Weber of Bonn. Within the next ten years he had organized twenty-three schismatic parishes from New Jersey in the East to Manitoba in the West. Koslowski called his followers the Polish Old Catholic Church.

Another schism was started at Buffalo in 1895 under the leadership of Fr Stanislas Kaminski, who, as stated already, was consecrated by Vilatte in 1898.[2] There was another and larger group of nationalistic-minded Poles in Pennsylvania, mostly in and around Scranton. Their leader, Fr Francis Hodur, had been born near Cracow of peasant stock in 1866. After his ordination in 1893, he came to the United States, and within four years found himself in opposition to his Irish bishop, Mgr William O'Hara.

We are told that 'Hodur was full of the spirit of Polish Messianism as expounded by Mickiewicz, an author whom he greatly admired; he was also touched by the poetry of Maria Konopnicka, who in her writings had shown great sympathy for the Polish poor; he was, besides, a voluminous reader in the fields of philosophy, comparative religion, and Church history. His whole background and experience disposed him to sympathize with these people; so, after hearing their story and pondering in silence for a while, he said: 'Let all those who are dissatisfied and feel wronged in this affair set about organizing and building a new church, which shall remain in possession of the people themselves. After that, we shall decide what further steps are necessary." '[3]

The church was built, and the Poles refused to hand it over to Bishop O'Hara. Fr Hodur went to Rome, hoping to gain support

[1] See p. 113.
[2] See p. 113.
[3] Theodore Andrews, *The Polish National Catholic Church in America and Poland* (1953), p. 27.

for his people, but got no satisfaction. All that resulted was his own excommunication on October 22, 1898. He burned the document before his congregation, and declared that he no longer recognized the authority of the Holy See. He started to celebrate Mass in Polish, and by 1904 his separatist movement had gained about 16,000 adherents. He was elected bishop, but it was not until September 29, 1907, that he managed to get consecrated at Utrecht by three Old Catholic prelates.

Bishop Koslowski died that same year, and eventually Hodur managed to incorporate most of his Old Catholic parishes into what was now known as the Polish National Catholic Church.

The independence of Hodur's mentality may be gauged by his statement:

'The leaders of the P.N.C.C. are of the opinion that before God and before America all beliefs, all sects, are equal. If God did not wish a certain sect to exist, He would not give it the necessary powers to exist and to develop.'[1]

In the course of time he changed not only the government of his Church, but the doctrines as well. An official Confession of Faith was drawn up and adopted in 1913. Six years before this Hodur had raised the Word of God—read, expounded, or listened to—to the status of the great sacrament of a Christian, National Church. In order to retain the traditional number of seven he reckoned Baptism and Confirmation as one sacrament. Adults were not obliged to make use of the sacrament of Penance, which was only obligatory on persons to the age of twenty. The doctrine of eternal punishment was rejected—an emotional reaction against some of the then popular hell-fire sermonizing of Roman Catholic, especially Irish, mission preaching. Hodur's teaching, without denying the Divinity of Christ, and like Arians and Unitarians, gave the impression that Jesus is primarily a lofty human example rather than the second Person of the Holy Trinity. Only a few changes were made in the structure of the Roman rite, and more in the internal form of the prayers. Although Hodur retained the kalendar of the Roman Missal, he instituted several new feasts of a popular and nationalistic character.[2] Then there were also solemn com-

---

[1] ibid., p. 45.
[2] Feast of the Poor Shepherds (first Sunday after Christmas); Feast of the Polish National Catholic Church (second Sunday in March); Feast of the Remembrance of the Dear Polish Fatherland (second Sunday in May); Feast of Brotherly Love (second Sunday in September); and Feast of the Christian Family (second Sunday in October).

memorations of religious reformers and Polish patriots, several of whom had been openly opposed to the papacy.[1]

Four more bishops were consecrated at Scranton in 1924, including a coadjutor, Leon Grochkowski. Hodur appointed one bishop for the eastern diocese, one for the western, one for Poland, and one for the Lithuanians. He had already helped to form a Lithuanian National Catholic Church for North America in 1914. Clerical celibacy was abolished in 1921, and most of the priests took advantage of this, though Hodur himself remained a bachelor.

Between 1926 and 1936 the National Church increased its membership from 61,874 to 186,000. A seminary for training priests was opened at Scranton, and dedicated to Girolamo Savonarola, the fifteenth-century Dominican who was hanged as a heretic at Florence after his excommunication by Alexander VI. Hodur venerated this Italian reformer and felt that the students could not have a better example to imitate. The founder of the P.N.C.C. died at the age of eighty-six on February 16, 1952, and was succeeded as Prime-Bishop by his married coadjutor, Leon Grochkowski.

The attempt to organize a rival schismatic church to the Mariavites in Poland did not have the success expected. In 1930 Hodur had consecrated Wladislaw Faron for Poland, but deposed him within a year.[2] Joseph Padewski was raised to the episcopate in 1936 in the hope of keeping the Church afloat.[3] At the time of writing it is said to number about 50,000 members, but even with the support of the Communist Government it has not made much progress.

In North America, the P.N.C.C. claimed an inclusive membership of 271,316 in 1958; with 147 ordained clergy having charge of 157 places of worship. Its headquarters are at 529 East Locust Street, Scranton 3, Pennsylvania.[4] Leon Grochkowski still holds the office of Prime-Bishop, and combines this with the care of the

---

[1] Adam Mickiewicz (November 28), Julius Slawacki (April 3), Zygmunt Krasinski (February 23), John Hus (July 6), Jerome Savonarola (May 23), and Peter Waldo (June 26).

[2] Faron then joined the independent Old Catholic Church of Poland, which was united with the Mariavites in 1946. Three years later he was reconciled with the Church of Rome. (See p. 521.)

[3] He died in a Nazi prison camp.

[4] In 1962, among the twenty-four Catholic churches in the city of Scranton, there were two Polish, one Magyar, one Slovak, one Syro-Melkite, one Syro-Maronite, three Italian, two Lithuanian, and two German places of worship. The present Auxiliary Bishop of Scranton, Mgr H. T. Klonowski, is of Polish origin.

Central Diocese. There are three other dioceses: Eastern, Western, and Buffalo-Pittsburgh.

Since 1946 the P.N.C.C. has been in full communion with the Protestant Episcopal Church. About thirty Episcopalian bishops have had as their co-consecrators prelates of the schismatic Polish Church. This enables them to claim the Old Catholic line of succession, derived from the Church of Utrecht. In 1948 the P.N.C.C. was admitted to the World Council of Churches, having already joined the National Council of Churches (U.S.A.).

Rather surprisingly, this hitherto exclusively Polish church has now begun to co-operate actively with the Puerto Rican National Catholic Church, which, so it is stated, is a growing body under the ecclesiastical jurisdiction of the Rev. Fr Hector Gonzalez. On November 5, 1961, Bishop Grochkowski confirmed 273 schismatic Latin Catholics. It appears that Fr Gonzalez is optimistic of breaking down the power of the Papists, who at the moment are estimated to form 92.6 per cent of the total population of this West Indian island. He has established a radio network over five stations to spread the Christian Faith. So before long the two bishops in Puerto Rico who are in communion with the Holy See may find out that more and more of their flocks are being brought into communion with Canterbury, Scranton, and Utrecht.

Had there been more sympathy and understanding on both sides sixty years ago, it is doubtful if the Polish Americans would have felt it worth while to set up a National Church. Today, with the almost complete integration of the Poles into normal American life, there is not even the original language bond, so it is hard to find convincing reasons for maintaining a state of schism, unless the modern disciples of Koslowski and Hodur are convinced that in cutting themselves adrift from the Papacy they have found a purer form of Catholicism.

(iii) *Spanish Reformed Episcopal Church (Iglesia Española Reformada Episcopal)*

The rigid religious laws have always made it difficult for any religious body not in communion with the Holy See to exist in Spain. An independent church on Protestant lines was formed in 1871, and in 1894 Lord Plunket, Archbishop of Dublin, laid hands on a Señor Cabrera so that this body, which had much in common with the Church of Ireland, could have a bishop, able to counteract idolatry and superstition among the Iberians.[1] Three years later, Bishop Maaers, who had been consecrated in London on Guy Fawkes Day, 1897, by Leon Chechemian (who then combined the duties of Primate of the Free Protestant Episcopal Church of England with those of Metropolitan of both the Ancient British Church and the United Armenian Catholic Church in the British Isles), was sent to Spain to assist Bishop Cabrera.[2] The last named died in 1916, after which the Protestant body did not have a Spanish bishop until April 29, 1956, when Santos M. Molina was consecrated in Madrid by Dr James McCann, the Bishop of Meath, assisted by the Bishops of Minnesota and Northern Indiana.[3] The Spanish Reformed Church in recent years has become much more liturgical in its modes of worship, and it has been said that if you want to attend the Mozarabic Rite, 'you must go to the Cathedral of Christ the Redeemer, Madrid', where an Anglican-American version of it is carried out with much greater 'decency and dignity' than in the Mozarabic Chapel at Toledo Cathedral.[4] Archbishop Lord Plunket, were he alive today, would be shocked to hear that Bishop Molina wears eucharistic vestments, based on ancient Spanish models, when celebrating the vernacular version of the Mozarabic Rite. Although toleration for non-Roman Catholic Christianity became effective in 1910, the position of minorities in Spain is still far from easy, and non-Roman Catholic services cannot be advertised; but as has been pointed out, 'a Spain that could treat her religious minorities as her critics would wish, would cease to be Spain'.[5]

(iv) *Lusitanian Church, Catholic, Apostolic, Evangelical (Igreja Lusitana, Catolica Apostolica Evangelica)*

In 1880 a few scattered congregations of lapsed Latin Catholics in Portugal, whose priests had been influenced by the Old Catholic movement after the definition of Papal Infallibility at the First

---

[1] Lord Halifax, as the leader of the Anglo-Catholic party, wrote to the Cardinal-Archbishop of Toledo, recording 'the profound distress which has been caused by the recent action of the Archbishop of Dublin in having presumed without the sanction of your Eminence . . . to consecrate a certain schismatic'. Cardinal Vaughan felt it necessary to explain 'that this nobleman is not . . . a Catholic but the chief of one of the sects of the Anglican Protestant Church subject to the civil power'.

[2] See p. 222.

[3] cf. *The Lambeth Conference, 1958* (1958), p. 2.56.

[4] cf. C. Gray-Stack, 'Lusitanian Liturgy and Spanish Services', in *Parish and People* (Michaelmas 1962), p. 7.

[5] Ronald Baron, 'Religious Liberty in Spain', in *Faith and Unity* (January 1963), p. 17. cf. *Libertas Religiosa en España*, by Eustaquio Guerrero, S. J., and Joaquin Ma. Alonson, O.F.M. (Madrid, 1962).

Miscellaneous Churches

Vatican Council, formed themselves into the *Igreja Lusitana Catolica Apostolica Evangelica*. It was stated in the first Prayer Book published in 1882: 'We do not desire to found a new religion but simply to cleanse the Christian Religion from the corruption of ages, and to recover the ancient liberties of the early Lusitanian Church—so long subjected to the foreign yoke of Rome—and to spread through all this country a doctrine, which shall be Catholic and Apostolic, in a Church that shall be Portuguese and not Roman.' The Roman Catholic Church was disestablished in 1911, and it was not until 1918 that diplomatic relations with the Vatican were resumed. The National Church remained a small and almost unknown body, and it was not until June 22, 1958, that the Rev. António Ferreira Fiandor was raised to the episcopate by Dr Plinio L. Simões, the Protestant Episcopal Bishop of South-Western Brazil, assisted by Dr James McCann, Bishop of Meath (Premier Bishop of the Church of Ireland), and Dr Norman B. Nash, Bishop in Charge of Protestant Episcopal European Churches. Bishop Finador has been succeeded by Dr Luis César Rodriguez Pereira, who was consecrated on June 24, 1962, by Bishop Stephen Bayne, Executive Officer of the Anglican Communion, assisted by the retired Lusitanian Bishop, and the Old Catholic Archbishop of Utrecht and Bishop of Deventer. The worship of the Lusitanian Church (based as far as possible on the Rite of Braga) is being developed so as to bring it into conformity with the modern Liturgical Movement, with midnight Eucharists at the greater festivals, the observance of the Easter Vigil, and the wearing of eucharistic vestments by the bishop. It is hoped that this indigenous and autonomous episcopal Church may soon have the same relationships to the Churches of the Anglican Communion as have the Old Catholic Churches of the Utrecht Union. Relations with the Roman Catholic hierarchy in Portugal appear to be friendly. During the week of prayer for Christian Unity in 1961, Dr Pereira (not yet a bishop) was invited to address the students of a seminary.

(v) *Philippine Independent Church (Iglesià Filipina Independiente)*

If the size of membership is taken as a criterion, then this church, the *Iglesia Filipina Independiente*, is by far the most important we have dealt with in this book.[1] Spanish and Catholic influ-

[1] In 1960 the total membership was given as between 1,000,000 and 2,500,000. The population of the Philippine Islands was 23,703,788; the total number of Catholics, 19,523,124 (82·4 per cent).

ence only began in the Philippine Islands in 1521, nearly two centuries after the coming of Islam. By 1600 most of the archipelago had been peacefully reduced to a colony of Spain. During the three centuries that elapsed before the first beginning of a national church in 1890, at least five interconnected situations arose all of which bear some responsibility for the schism.

The Spanish colonists (never more than 5,000 at any one time) did little and perhaps less than elsewhere, to prepare themselves or the natives (Indios is the official pre-independence name for Filipinos) for ecclesiastical or political independence. Even Castilian which might have forged a bond between the archipelago and Spain was little taught outside Manila, and only one Philippine-born priest, a *mestico*, was raised to the episcopate.[1]

The political as well as the ecclesiastical control of the islands was consolidated in the hands of the bishops and clergy, who were nearly all Spanish friars.[2] Augustinians, Friars Minor, Dominicans, and Franciscan Recollects, who with the Jesuits, contested successfully every attempt by Spain to replace them with secular clergy. On the other hand, the Spaniards were not to be blamed more than others for the state of affairs; there were wheels within wheels all the time.

The balance of social life between the native Indios, the Spanish colonists, the Filipinos (local-born Spaniards) and the mesticos (half-breeds); either Philippine-Spanish, or Philippine-Chinese— the Chinese, not numerous but influential, being the nearest civilized nation—was upset by the fact that these same friars were among the major landowners on the islands. It must not be forgotten, on the other hand, that their peaceful conquest obviated the presence of Spanish troops till 1822. In 1869 the opening of Napoleon III's Suez Canal by his Spanish-born Empress Eugénie opened Europe and its liberalism to native Philippine youth; the resulting anti-Spanish rebellion which was prevented at Manila, and openly repressed in 1872, ended in wholesale imprisonments and the execution for complicity of (among others) three secular

---

[1] The refusal to teach Spanish was deliberately to preserve the eighteen dialects of the native population.

[2] The Augustinians arrived in 1565; and by 1896 numbered 310, ran 242 towns with population of 2,000,000; Franciscans came in 1577; by 1896 ran 153 towns with population of 1,000,000; Dominicans came in 1587, and by 1896 ran 69 towns with population of 700,000; with Recollects and the Jesuits. The result was that by 1896 1,330 religious looked after a Catholic population of over 5,000,000, out of a total population of about 8,000,000 (62·5 per cent).

priests, Gómez, Zamora, and Burgos. This it was which more than anything consolidated the Young Philippino Party and ruined permanently whatever ease had grown up between imperialists and colonials.

In 1890, at Paniqui, Isabelo de los Reyes, and a thirty-year-old priest, Gregorio Aglipay (ex-houseboy at the Augustinian friary in Manila), who had been ordained the previous year, and several other secular clergy, organized an anti-Spanish church which they put under the immediate protection of the Vatican, thus by-passing the local Spanish hierarchy. Less than twelve months later José P. Rizal y Mercado began his preparations for political independence by founding the Liga Filipina; the revolt itself broke out in 1896; many Filipinos lost their lives—but independence was proclaimed on June 12, 1898.

During the Spanish-American (and short ensuing American-Philippine) War (February 1898 to the end of 1899), and only four months after the Declaration of Independence, the President of the new Republic, General Aguinaldo, on October 20, 1898, appointed his friend Aglipay to be his military Vicar-General. For eight years Rome, for whatever reason, had allowed the Philippine question to remain unsettled, and had taken no steps against either the Archbishop of Manila or Aglipay. Now, in spite of the cause pending at Rome, the former peremptorily excommunicated the latter for accepting the military appointment without the permission of his Spanish ordinary.

Following the Spanish-American War (the Spanish by treaty evacuated Cuba and for $20,000,000 sold the Philippines to the U.S.A.), after three years of military government, the U.S.A. appointed Judge Taft as Civil Governor (1901–4). His task was difficult—it was made more difficult by the power and the 'Spanishness' in thought of the Church. On the one hand, after negotiating with the curia of Leo XIII, he paid St Pius X $8,000,000 for 400,000 acres of land belonging to the friars, and secured the replacement of the Spanish bishops with an American hierarchy. On the other hand, further to weaken Spanish clerical influence, he strongly supported the *Iglesia Filipina Independiente*, and it was under his governorship. On August 3, 1902, this body, still orthodox, went officially into schism, and broke off relations with the Vatican. Aglipay, declared *Pontifex Maximus*, proclaimed: 'I solemnly declare that today we definitely secede from the Church of Rome, and renounce our allegiance to the Vatican, and proclaim ourselves a Christian, Catholic, and Independent Church'.[1]

Soon after this Aglipay became the Supreme Bishop of the schismatic body, but he had to be satisfied with a laying on of hands by some of his priests. He explained that, since a layman can baptize in an emergency, so, when no prelates are available, a priest can make a bishop, as is the law in the Finnish Lutheran Church. By 1904 he had about 200,000 followers (mostly in the North) out of a total population of 7,000,000. He was on good terms with the Freemasons, and received their support. Not long after this Pius X attempted a rapprochement with the other 'supreme pontiff', sending a conciliatory message by the Maltese Benedictine Archbishop of Palmyra, Dom Ambrose Agius, monk of Ramsgate, who had been appointed Apostolic Nuncio to the Philippines. The belated kindly offer was rejected.

The *Pontifex Maximus* in his *Fundamental Epistles* remained orthodox by at least keeping to the Great Creeds, and insisting on the use of the *Missale Romanum*, but in 1906 the U.S.A. handed back to the Catholic hierarchy properties which the schismatics had acquired by 'peaceable possession'—in other words, by having had control of the church-door and cemetery-gate keys at the crucial juncture. In the same year Aglipay introduced his new Prayer Book, *Officio Divino*, and Gospel Harmony, the latter with a distinct Marcionite tinge: the deity was reduced from a trinity of persons to a trinity of attributes. Aglipay was initiated as a Mason in 1914.

Having lost so many church-keys, he was in danger of losing all control and power; in vain he tried to negotiate with Protestants, Anglicans, and Old Catholics. He approached Bishop Brent, who had been appointed to the Protestant Episcopal missionary district of the Philippines, and he approached the Swiss Old Catholics. But Bishop Herzog had become alarmed at the reported unitarianism of the two founders and leaders, Aglipay and Isabelo de los Reyes Sr. These two turned more and more to American Unitarianism, and fostered the growth of contacts with the International Association for Liberal Christianity and Religious Freedom: they were not followed by many others, priests or intellectuals. Isabelo de los Reyes Sr. was the real founder of the Church and wrote all the theological statements of the new religion. He was reconciled with the Roman Church two years before his death.

[1] cf. Wm. J. Whalen, 'The Philippine Independent Church', in *The Priest* (December 1961), p. 1030, see also his *Faiths for the Few* (Milwaukee, 1963), pp. 132–145.

The Unitarians in the U.S.A. encouraged Aglipay's approaches, and arranged for him and two other bishops to attend the Unitarian Convention at Boston, Mass. A year or so afterwards he took part in the Convention of the Association for Liberal Christianity and Religious Freedom at Copenhagen. He died on September 1, 1940. He had lived in concubinage for many years, but latterly he was married by a Unitarian minister. He asked for a priest during his last illness, but his followers took care that he was not reconciled with the Roman Church, and he died in a maternity home.

Aglipay was succeeded by Santiago Fonacier, who, after being deposed six years later by the more orthodox members of the *Iglesia Filipina Independiente*, set up a second and rival schismatic church called the Independent Church of Filipino Christians; in effect a small unitarian sect.[1] For a few months after 1946, Gerardo Bayaca acted as *Pontifex Maximus*, and was succeeded by the founder's son, Isabelo de los Reyes Jr., married, aged twenty-five, already the father of several children, and a lapsed Catholic, on whom Aglipay and four other bishops had laid hands. Though he had little real theological training, his experiences in the Army and Navy had shown him to be a leader of men. In 1946 he led his bishops and clergy to: (1) renounce unitarianism; (2) declare acceptance of the theology of the Protestant Episcopal Church; and (3) issue a 'Declaration of the Faith and Articles of Religion' (all in perfect conformity with Nicaea). Next he petitioned the Protestant Episcopal Church for Anglican orders. On April 7, 1948, Isabelo de los Reyes Jr., and two other bishops were consecrated by Norman S. Binstead, the American Episcopalian Bishop of the Missionary District of the Philippines, assisted by his suffragan bishop, Robert F. Wilner, and by Harry S. Kennedy, Bishop of Honolulu. The three Philippine prelates then consecrated all other bishops, and ordained deacons and priests according to the Anglican rite.

Some time after this the Philippine Independent Church was admitted to the National Council of the Churches of Christ in the U.S.A.[2] By 1957 it had obtained membership of the World Council of Churches. In 1960 the Supreme Council voted for full commu-

---

[1] Fonacier has been dissociated from the Aglipayan movement since 1952, and no longer heads a sect of his own.
[2] Composed of Baptists, the Brethren, Eastern Churches, Evangelical United Brethren, Friends, Lutherans, Methodists, Moravians, Polish National Catholics, Presbyterians, Protestant Episcopalians, Reformed Hungarians, and the United Church of Christ.

nion with the Protestant Episcopal Church, which was achieved the following year. This also resulted in communion with the Utrecht Union of Old Catholic Churches.

The liturgy now in use is a vernacular adaptation of the Roman rite, with interpolations from the American version of the Book of Common Prayer. Most of the priests and bishops are married; nearly all are Masons; but Bishop Isabelo de Los Reyes Jr. (the father of a large family) is not a Mason. This National Church works side by side with the Protestant Episcopal Church in the Philippines, as what A. H. Mathew had described to Dr Davidson, Archbishop of Canterbury, as *une église amie*.[1] In fact, the *Iglesia Filipina Independiente* is in very much the relationship to the Anglican Communion that Mathew had hoped for his Old Catholic Church in 1908. In the opinion of Lewis Bliss Whittemore, retired Bishop of Western Michigan, 'the friendship and co-operation of both Churches offer the best hope that the Philippines, independent politically, will have that religious freedom which is essential for a democracy'.[2] On the other hand, it is reported that the influence and membership of this schismatic body are declining slowly but steadily.[3] Still Bishop Whittemore is optimistic that the witness of a powerful Reformation Church offers an alternative to Roman Catholicism to a catholic-minded people, and thus redresses the balance which is lacking. Whether this is true, time alone will prove.

(vi) *Brazilian Catholic Apostolic Church* (*Igreja Católica Apostolica Brasileira*)

Brazil, a Portuguese colony from 1532, became a kingdom in 1815, a republic in 1889. The first serious attempt to set up a national church appears to have been made after June 1945, when Mgr Carlos Duarte Costa (1888–1961), formerly Bishop of Botucatú, was excommunicated by the Holy See because of his attacks against the papacy.[4] This led to the formation at Belo Horizonte (Minas Gerais State) of a schismatic body known as the *Igreja Católica Apostolica Brasileira*.

[1] See p. 167.
[2] *Struggle for Freedom: History of the Philippine Independent Church* (Greenwich, Conn., 1961), p. 218.
[3] A third schismatic body was formed in the Philippines during the 1930s by a certain Raymundo O'Donnell; which was known as *Iglesia Independiente de la Santisima Trinidad de Filipinos*. This reference to the Holy Trinity must have been a protest against the unitarian beliefs held by most of Aglipay's clergy. Today there are about eight schismatic Aglipayan sects with a total membership of between 2,000 and 4,000.
[4] He had retired from the see of Botucatu in 1937, and was given the style of Titular Bishop of Maura.

There was another but less successful effort in the same direction in 1936, when a priest named Salomão Ferraz organized his followers as the *Igreja Católica Livre no Brasil*. He was elected bishop, and arranged with Mgr Faron, formerly of the Polish National Catholic Church, to consecrate him, but Faron found it impossible to go to Brazil. Finally on August 15, 1945, Ferraz was raised to the episcopate by Duarte Costa.

Brazil is still a predominantly Catholic nation, although Church and State have been separated since 1891, and Duarte Costa and Ferraz did not succeed in making many Catholics join their schismatic bodies. The former consecrated Paulo Castillo-Mendez, who on January 23, 1949, raised Stephen Corradi to the episcopate as an independent bishop for Mexico.[1] Corradi, who made his headquarters in Panama, consecrated Albert A. Steer on November 6, 1949, who appears to have received a previous consecration from Archbishop W. F. Francis of Woodstock, New York (Old Catholic Church in America), on July 13, 1947.[2]

Meanwhile Duarte Costa had introduced a vernacular Portuguese liturgy for his followers. He also abolished the Sacrament of Penance, and repudiated clerical celibacy. He died in 1961, and was succeeded by José Aires da Cruz as Primate of the *Igreja Católica Brasileira*.

(vii) *Canadian Catholic Church*

This little-known body with such a comprehensive title claims to possess the Greek-Melkite, Russian Orthodox, Russo-Syrian, Old Catholic (Junior), and Liberal Catholic lines of succession, thanks to the prelates who laid hands on its founder, Odo Acheson Barry. His first consecration appears to have been on July 29, 1946, when Antony Aneed, who styled himself Exarch of the Greek Melkite Rite in the U.S.A., assisted by Harry J. Kleefisch, who claimed of the Russian Orthodox succession, raised Barry to the episcopate.[3] The third assistant prelate was Charles Hampton, who, having been Regionary Bishop for the U.S.A. in the Liberal Catholic Church since 1935, had lapsed into schism.[4] On October 3,

---

[1] For Corradi's associations with Mgr Kelly of Niagara Falls, N.Y., see p. 436.
[2] See pp. 413–427.
[3] For Aneed, see pp. 512, 513. Kleefisch appears to have been a lawyer at San Francisco, who propagated 'The Truth Movement' as a form of free-lance Theosophy. He claimed to have been consecrated at Harbin by Sergius Starogrodsky, Metropolitan of Novgorod, some time in 1918.
[4] See pp. 364, 365.

Miscellaneous Churches

1948, Barry was re-consecrated *sub conditione* by Lowell Paul Wadle, another Theosophist, who since 1942 has used the title of 'Primate of the American Catholic (Vilatte Succession) Apostolic Church of Long Beach'[1]

The Canadian Catholic Archbishop, shortly after his consecration, went to New Zealand, where he remained six or seven years. Then he moved to Ceylon. On September 10, 1953, having no scruples about jurisdiction, he consecrated J. G. Peters at the Y.M.C.A. in Colombo. This was to make sure that a previous consecration by an unnamed Anglican clergyman, said to have been raised to the episcopate by Vilatte, was not deficient. Nobody appears to have heard of this prelate until Peters produced him as his first consecrator. The Patriarch of Glastonbury appointed Bishop Peters as Exarch of the Catholicate of the West for the Indies, with the title of Mar Petros. Not long afterwards he was deposed from this exalted status.[2] He also held the offices of President and Chancellor of St John's University at Ambur in the Madras Province. He issued an official brochure, stating that he had been granted ancient plenary powers to confer degrees in virtue of being Primate of the Apostolic Church of the Indies; also that he possessed 'the right and authority to confer Academic Degrees, University, and other Titles, by several charters granted him by the British, American, Swiss, French, and other Patriarchs of the Church of Christ from every country in the world'. Mar Petros died in 1954, so not many persons were able to benefit from the unique advantages he offered them.

Mar Columba—to give Barry his new title—arrived in England from Ceylon in 1954. On July 17, the following year, he bestowed on Mar Georgius what were claimed to be the Greek-Melkite, Russian-Orthodox, Russo-Syriac, Old Catholic (Junior), and Liberal Catholic lines of succession, thus increasing the Patriarch of Glastonbury's apostolic succession to fifteen lines.[3] After remaining in England some years he returned to Canada about 1960. His long absence from the Dominion had prevented him from developing the Canadian Catholic Church, which seems to have remained a sort of independent branch of the so-called 'American Catholic (Vilatte Succession) Apostolic Church of Long Beach', of which Archbishop Wadle was the founder-primate.[4]

[1] See pp. 256, 489.
[2] See p. 473.
[3] See p. 452.
[4] See p. 489.

(viii) *Old Catholic Church of Yugoslavia*

After the Vatican Council of 1870 several congregations in what was until 1918 the Empire of Austria-Hungary prepared the way for an Old Catholic Church by falling into schism. There were two main groups: one in the north in what was then Bohemia and Moravia, the other in the south in and around Vienna. Not till 1924, however, did the former, that is the Old Catholics in what had been the Czechoslovakian Republic since 1918, manage to obtain their first bishop, Alois Pachcek (Pasek), who was consecrated by Archbishop Kenninck of Utrecht. The Viennese Old Catholics obtained their first bishop, Adalbert Schindelaar, in 1925, when he was consecrated at Berne by Bishop Küry on September 1, 1925.

By this time an Old Catholic body had been formed among the Croats and Slovenes of Yugoslavia. Marko Kalogjera, a canon of Split (Spalato) Cathedral, was elected bishop, and was consecrated at Utrecht on February 25, 1924. Kalogjera got into trouble in 1933, having been accused of accepting payment for granting faculties of nullity to divorced persons who wished to remarry. On hearing of this, the Old Catholic Bishops, at their Conference at Munich in March 1933, broke off relations with the Yugoslav prelate. He managed to make the Government realize that he was the innocent victim of a Pan-German persecution, on the plea that all the Old Catholic bishops, except the Dutch, were German speaking.

The result was a schism among the Old Catholics of Yugoslavia. One group elected a bishop named Ivan Cerovski, who was never consecrated. This body remained in communion with Utrecht. The other group remained loyal to Kalogjera, who was supported by the Government. On December 21, 1947, Kalogjera consecrated Radavan Jost.[1] The former was growing old, and realized that he must find a successor. His death took place before he managed to consecrate Grgur Cengíc. Eventually it was arranged for him to be raised to the episcopate by Bishop Milan Reiching of the Liberal Catholic Church, permission having been obtained from its Presiding Bishop, Adriaan Vreede. The ceremony took place on February 24, 1957, when Reiching was assisted by J. B. S. Coates, Auxiliary Bishop for Great Britain.[2]

---

[1] In 1951 Jost offered to raise Wilfrid A. Barrington-Evans to the episcopate, as first bishop of the Old Roman Catholic Church (English Rite). (See p. 401.)

[2] Aloysius Stumpfl, who called himself 'Mar Timotheos, Orthodox Missionsbichof', and who was consecrated by Vigué (Vilatte succession in France) in 1924, acted as a

Miscellaneous Churches

(ix) Reformed Catholic Church (Utrecht Confession)

Just how, when, and where this body, claiming to have active episcopates in Great Britain, France, and Germany, came into being is not certain. According to its own statement it is one of the world-wide group of reformed Catholic Churches, holding valid orders derived from former Roman and Eastern Catholic sources, from the inception of the Church in the seventeenth century. Doctrine is based on the Nicene Creed and the teaching of the Ecumenical Councils prior to the Great Schism.[1]

The Province of North America is ruled over by Archbishop W. W. Flynn, whose address is given as P.O. Box 1421, Los Angeles 28, California. It has not been possible to find out who consecrated this prelate, but in 1957 he claimed twenty churches and eighteen priests under his jurisdiction. The total membership of the Reformed Catholic Church was given as 2,217. It is not certain if the Province of France, which in 1955 was under the jurisdiction of Bishop Louis Paul Mailley, resident in Paris, still functions.

Its British Representative, Bishop Rupert Pitt-Kethley of Ealing Common, who, as Mar Rupertus, forms one of the fourteen prelates of the Sacred Synod of the *Église Catholique Apostolique Primitive d'Antioche Orthodoxe et de Tradition Syro-Byzantine*, under Prince-Patriarch Mar Joannes Maria Van Assendelft Altland, also acts as the British Representative of the United Old Catholic Patriarchate of the World. This international organization has H.E. The Most Rev. Christopher C. J. Stanley, D.D., S.T.D., as its Ecumenical Patriarch.[2]

It would appear that the Reformed Catholic Church (Utrecht Confession)—if this is still its official designation—is one of the comprehensive collection of denominations about which Bishop Erni spoke so enthusiastically in a conference entitled *L'Unité en Marche dans l'Oecuménisme*: churches now associated with his *Siège Ecclésial Oecuménique*. He visualizes it as a vast international

---

free-lance Old Catholic bishop in Austria. He was associated with Mar Georgius and the Catholicate of the West. (See pp. 319, 320, 463, note 2.)

[1] *Yearbook of American Churches, 1961*, p. 34.

[2] Bishop Stanley until recently was associated with the Patriarch G. T. Billett of the Old Catholic Church in North America, who claimed consecration from Earl Anglin James, at one time Mar Laurentius, Archbishop and Metropolitan of Acadia, and Exarch of the Catholicate of the West in the Canadas. (See pp. 245, 246.) Later on Archbishop James acted as head of the International Synod of the Ecumenical Church Foundation of the Free Protestant Episcopal Church. (See p. 245.)

Miscellaneous Churches

combine of every Christian body, except the Catholic and Roman Church.[1]

An even more unlikely caricature of Catholicism has recently arisen in South Viet-Nam (Cochin China).[2] It is known as Caodaism, and embodies a hierarchy of pope, cardinals, and bishops, said to reflect the organization of Roman Catholicism.[3] Among its lesser divinities are Victor Hugo and Sun Yat Sen. We are told that the towered Temple at Tay Ninh is the spiritual centre of Caodaism. Here God speaks through the medium of a moving pencil. Near the altar are images of Jesus, Confucius, Buddha, and Lao-tse. The Caodaists call the Temple site their Holy Land.[4] This strange sect was founded about 1925, and is reputed to have at least 2,000,000 members. An American in Saigon related how he had lunched with Cardinal Truong Van Trang and an Archbishopess at Tay Ninh, who explained that they called the creator Cao Dai; and that they did not represent a *new* religion, for there are too many already. All that the founder had done was to take the best of Confucianism, Taoism, Buddhism, and Christianity, and fuse them into one religion. The Cardinal said: 'We honour Victor Hugo as an Apostle because he wrote with Holy Compassion for mankind. We receive messages from him and from great spirits of the past and from the Creator. It doesn't matter *how* the message comes, what it says matters.' At the midnight Mass on the feast of Tet or New Year's Day, at which the female worshippers wore white hoods, the Acting Superior gave a sermon and spoke about 'spiritual cleanliness', and urged people not to be afraid to be poor and to be kind to each other. There were rumours that Winston Churchill and Danny Kaye would soon be beatified and canonized, but the Caodaist Cardinal denied this.

A less exotic prelate than the Caodaist Cardinal Truong Van Trang was James Fitzgerald Crawford, who at an earlier period of his career had been a minister of the Reformed Presbyterian Church in Ireland. About 1946 he joined the English Episcopal Church, and Bishop C. L. Saul appointed him Archdeacon of Cornwall, but soon found reasons to dismiss him. Later on Crawford

---

[1] The Constitutions have been drawn up, and any Church can be enrolled by signing the mimeographed slip at the end of the brochure, clipping it, and mailing it to the address given—all quite simple!

[2] cf. P. T. White and W. E. Garrett, 'Suiet Nam fights the Red Tide', in *National Geographic Magazine* (Washington, D.C.), October 1961.

[3] op. cit., p. 466.

[4] p. 467.

took the title of Bishop of Anglia, and proclaimed that he was the head of the Lutheran Episcopal Church of England. He gave out that this new body was associated with the Lutheran World Federation. For various reasons, however, Bishop Crawford found it necessary in 1956 to give up the conversion of England to this form of German Protestantism, and it is not known if he has been able to resume his episcopal activities.

It is uncertain if the so-called 'Free Holy Catholic Church of England (Diocese of Mercia)' still exists. In February 1952, a certain Bishop A. F. Baker circulated letters appealing for money to build a Cathedral Church on the borders of Worcestershire and Warwickshire. Those who subscribed would have their names on permanent display within the Cathedral, with the promise that 'this continual acknowledgement will bring its return benefits through keeping your name in the public mind'. This elusive prelate also described his chimerical sect as 'The Free Protestant-Catholic Communion', and stated that 'this Cathedral may, in the event of a Third War, be the Sole Survivor among English Cathedrals and in that case it would become as the Nerve Centre for the continuation of the Christian Religion of ALL DENOMINA-TIONS'. It seems that not many people responded to the appeal for 'Generous Help and Assistance to provide this Need to ensure that a Future Christian and Civilized Way of Life will be secured and by the building of this Cathedral for this Present Generation and for Generations yet to come, it will stand as a Guardian to withstand the Savageries of Civilization'. Eleven years have come and gone, and the Midlands are still without this 'Free Holy Catholic' Cathedral.

There are more free-lance bishops and odder little churches than those mentioned in these pages, some of which appear to exist only in the brains of their founders, and still they go on being planned. Some of these prelates are eager for publicity, others prefer to lead a secluded existence.

For instance, in 1915 a certain Archbishop Basilius Kujlowski appeared in England, claiming to be a Melkite. There were rumours that in December that year he consecrated a gentleman who called himself Jean-Marie, Comte de San Severi, but this reputed Melkite prelate vanished after this and nothing more was heard of him. Even more exciting, especially to those who met him, was the arrival in 1932 of Mar Silwa, Archbishop of Nineveh, who, so it appears, found few friends and benefactors in Britain. About ten years later the Rt Rev. Peter J. G. Grazeola, S.T.D., Ph.D., who had the title of Primatial Legate of the American National Catholic Church, and who described himself as Apostolic Administrator of the Diocese of New Jersey, N.Y., wrote that there are no barriers of jurisdiction or otherwise in the pursuance of the precepts and ideals of true Catholicism. All men are brethren in Christ—Greek, Roman, and 'Old' Catholicism are limbs of the same tree. He felt it deplorable that the mundane should be permitted to obscure this obvious fact, and as the result, human frailty is kept apart in hardly ethical or justifiable or altruistic *status quo*.[1]

Straying off the beaten track into the ecclesiastical forest, the harder it is to distinguish the wood for the trees, even more to memorize the names of its galaxy of fauna and flora.[2] In the end one almost despairs of disentangling the infinite ramifications of splinter-churches during the past century, for they are legion. So we will leave these autocephalous bodies, their prelates, priests, and peoples.

I have tried hard not to pass judgment on any of them, but to depict each church as it made itself known in order to gain adherents. It is for my readers to decide which of these bodies on or over the border of historical Christendom can be regarded as what St Peter called 'a chosen race, a royal priesthood, a consecrated nation, a people God means to have for himself'.[3] It is a matter of opinion whether God called some of the pioneers out of darkness into his marvellous light. Can we regard the behaviour of their disciples as honourable, and praise God for them? Were the founders of these schismatic churches, before they broke away from authority, really no more than sheep going astray? Did the liberty they enjoyed after gaining their independence become a

[1] Letter to the Rev. H. R. T. Brandreth, August 26, 1949.
[2] Students of the bypaths of recent church history may feel it worth while to investigate the origins of some of the following churches and their founders: M. Akpan, Bishop of the Militant Universal Christian Church of Mercy (Universal Christ Army) in Nigeria; Abed-Negro Bambara, Bishop of the African-Negro Mission of Haiti; D. P. Cockeye, Archbishop of the Spiritual Holiness Church of Cameroon; Etuk Bwa, Bishop of the Confederation of Nigerian Churches; Joannes Khor, Primate of the Essene Church in the Hashemite Kingdom of Jordan; Napoleon G. M. Mensah, Bishop of the Africa Church of Ghana; T. Rolland, Archbishop of the Universal Gnostic Church of France; N. E. Udoh, Bishop of the Universal Church of the Holy Spirit in Nigeria; Stephanus Uebelhoer (a free-lance prelate in Austria); and Mgr D. F. Whiteley-Wilkin, C.M.P., Ph.D., D.P., F.Ps. (Gt. Brit.), F.C.S.P.F., Mis.M. of Nigel, Transvaal.
[3] I Peter 2, 8.

pretext for wrongdoing, or was it used in God's service?[1] Have the disciples been submissive to their masters, not only those who were kind and considerate, but to those who were hard to please?[2]

Another way to form an opinion on any group of Christians is to investigate how it has performed the corporal and spiritual works of mercy during the course of its history. So take any of the bodies dealt with in this book and decide if its members have fed the hungry; given drink to the thirsty; clothed the naked; harboured the stranger; visited the sick; ministered to prisoners; and buried the dead.

Having studied its external activities, what about the spiritual life of this or that autocephalous church? Have its clergy and laity shown zeal in converting sinners; instructing the ignorant; counselling the doubtful; comforting the sorrowful; bearing wrongs patiently; forgiving enemies; praying for the living and the dead?

Let us look closer, bearing in mind the words of Christ: 'Be on your guard against false prophets, men who come to you in sheep's clothing, but are ravenous wolves within. You will know them by their fruits.'[3] What fruits *have* these independent Christian bodies yielded in the past hundred years? Have they made any definite contribution to scholarship or spirituality? Reference to the printed catalogues of the British Museum, National Library of Congress, or the Bibliothèque Nationale, will supply the answer. It will be seen from such sources that neither the clergy nor the laity of these bodies have made names for themselves as authors, apart from two or three exceptions; but, of course, it may have been that they were far too busy trying to save souls to be able to give the time to literary work. Will the fairly large output of controversial pamphlets, brochures and tracts, the authors and titles of which are given in the bibliographies, find a permanent place in reference libraries? Time alone will show if the various vernacular liturgies composed by some of the founders will be classed with the historic Eastern and Western rites of Christendom. So far none of these bodies have managed to erect churches which symbolize their zeal for corporate worship, but perhaps it is too soon to expect an architectural renaissance led by autocephalous churches and their *tropoi*, marked by a bold 'modernist' outlook? It is impossible to say if either the Eastern or Western Churches will eventually make use of the

[1] ibid., 2, 16.
[2] ibid., 2, 18.
[3] Matthew 7, 15–16.

expositions of canon law, ritual, and ceremonial which have been drawn up for bodies often existing largely in the imagination of their founders. Dare we prophesy that the few works of a spiritual character published by members of these over-the-border churches will be ranked with the classics of mystical theology?

How can we account for the fact that none of these bodies have prospered? Why is it that not one has led a peaceful existence since it was formed? What are the reasons for most of them splitting up into rival litigious groups; each off-shoot excommunicating the other sooner or later? Why has this process of spawning continued with slight variations of detail for more than a century? How is it that when some of these tiny churches have tried incorporation or intercommunion in the hope of survival, there has seldom been any lasting result?

Christ indeed said: 'There are many places in my father's house'. Was he picturing what can only be called the unsubstantial collection of spiritual 'places' described in these pages? It must be confessed that most of them convey the impression of being built on sand, even if quite a number offer themselves as desirable residences, with every modern convenience. Yet which of the founders whose lives have been recorded could be singled out as a wise man who built his house on rock? It would be hard to decide if anything has been gained in the long run by erecting between one and two hundred detached or semi-detached autocephalous churches, comparable to villas and bungalows, and so transforming the City of God into a nondescript caravan camp.

If any of my readers are dissatisfied with the Holy, Catholic, Apostolic Roman Church, any of the Eastern Churches either in or not in communion with the Bishop of Rome, the Anglican Communion, or the nearly two hundred constituent bodies which make up the World Council of Churches, then they can take their choice of the substitutes offered them in these pages, of which there is indeed an *embarras de richesse*—enough to satisfy almost every taste. Having given this invitation, I will end this book by quoting a parable which seems applicable to the subject-matter:

'Here is the sower gone out to sow. And as he sowed, there were grains that fell beside the path, so that all the birds came and ate them up. And others fell on the rocky land, where the soil was shallow; they sprang up all at once, because they had not sunk deep in the ground; but as soon as the sun rose they were parched; they had taken no root, and so they withered away. Some fell among briars, so the briars grew up, and smothered them. But others fell where the soil was good, and these yielded a harvest, some a hundredfold, some sixtyfold, some thirtyfold. Listen, you that have ears to hear with.'[1]

[1] Matthew 13, 3–9.

BIBLIOGRAPHY

General

(1) Old Catholic Churches

Evangelisches Kirchenlexikon (Göttingen, 1955 ff.), I, 91 ff.

Lexikon für Theologie und Kirche (Freiburg, 1930–38), I, 398 ff.

Oxford Dictionary of the Christian Church (1957), p. 980.

Realencyclopädie für protestantische Theologie und Kirche (21 vols., 1898–1908), I, 415 ff.

Die Religion in Geschichte und Gegenvart (5 vols., 1927–31), I, 295 ff.

Weltkirchenlexikon (Stuttgart, 1960, 37 ff.)

Algermissen, K., *Konfessionskunde* (Celle, 1957), 705 ff.

Molland, E., *The Christian Churches Throughout the World, etc.* (1961), 127 ff.

Mulert, H., *Konfessionskunde* (Berlin, 1956), 389 ff.

Kirchliches Jahrbuch für die Alt Katholiken (1962).

Collinon, M., 'Qu'est ce que les Eglises Vielles-Catholique?', in *Ecclesia* (Paris), n. 131, February 1960.

Gauthier, L., *Le Vieux-Catholicisme* (Geneva, n.d.).

de Voil, W. H., *The Origin and Development of the Old Catholic Group of Churches* (Edinburgh University Ph.D. thesis 1937).

Kok, M., *The Old Catholic Church of the Netherlands* (Utrecht, 1948).

Lagerwey, E., *De Oud-katholicke Kerk van Nederland, haar leer en leven* (Amsterdam, 1951).

Moss, C. B., *The Old Catholic Movement, its Origins and History* (1948).

Neale, J. M., *History of the So-called Jansenist Church of Holland* (1853).

Siegmund-Schultze, F., *Die altkatholische Kirche*, in the series *Ekklesia* (Gotha, 1955).

Gschwind, Paulin, *Geschichte der Entstehung der christskatholischen Kirche der Schweiz* (2 vols., Berne, 1904–1910).

Zelinka, E. K., *Der Altkatholizmus* (5th ed. Freiburg, 1924).

Bibliography

*Rinkel, A., *Interkommunion, ihre Grundlagen, ihr Inhalf und ihre Folgerungen* (Schönweid, 1954).
Dimmel, J. J., *Hirtenbrief uber das hl. Abendmahl* (1956) *Was ist Alt-Katholish?* (1958).
(Periodicals)
Alt-Katholische Kirchenzeitung (Bonn, monthly).
Christkatholisches Kirchenblatt (Bern, monthly).
Christkatholischer Hauskalender (Bern, annual).
De Oud-Katholiek (Rotterdam, weekly).
Le Sillon (Geneva, monthly).
Internationale Kirchliche Zeitschrift (Bern, three-monthly).
Alt-Katholisches Jahrbuch (Bonn).
(Worship)
Kirchliche Ordungen und Satzungen fur die deutschen Alt-Katholiken (1938).
Das Rituale für Kasualien und Verwaltung der Sakramente.
Gebet und Gesangbuch für did Alt-Katholiken in Deutschland (1952).
Die Messliturgie, ed. by A. Küry (Bern, 1945).
Old Catholic Worship in the Netherlands (Amersfoort, 1961).

(2) *Autocephalous churches and bishops at large*

Brandreth, H. R. T., *Episcopi Vagantes and the Anglican Church* (1st ed. 1947; 2nd ed. 1961).
de la Thibauderie, Ivan, *Eglises et Evèques Catholiques non Romains* (Paris, 1962).
The Lambeth Conference 1958: *The Encyclical Letter from the Bishops together with the Resolutions and Reports* (1958).
Micklewright, F. H. Amphlett, articles in *The Pilot*: 'Ecclesia in Partibus' (Summer 1951); Editorial (Autumn 1951); 'A Chapter of Vagrant Episcopacy' (Autumn 1951); Correspondence (Winter 1951); 'The Vilatte Succession' (Winter 1951); 'Episcopacy and Reunion' (Summer 1952); 'Vagrants Still' (Spring 1955); 'Some Orders of Corporate Reunion' (Summer 1955 and Spring 1954—A Rejoinder). (See also 'Bishop Morris, South India or elsewhere' (Spring 1956).)

Chapter I

JULIUS FERRETTE, BISHOP OF IONA

Attwater, D., *The Christian Churches of the East*, vol. II, *Churches not in Communion with Rome* (new ed., 1961), pp. 204–10.

Bibliography

Brandreth, op. cit. (2nd ed., 1961), pp. 70–89.
—*Dr Lee of Lambeth* (1951), pp. 111–12, 120.
Bristol Daily Post, The, October 1, 1866.
Church Monitor, The, October 1866.
Church Times, The, December 15, 1866.
Etheridge, John Wesley, *The Syrian Churches* (1846).
Ferrette, Jules, *Euchologion: The Eastern Liturgy adapted for Use in the West* (London and Oxford, 1866).
—*The Eastern Liturgy of the Holy Orthodox Church Simplified* (1866).
—*Les Rites Essentiels du Christianisme* (Geneva, 1903).
Fortescue, A., *The Lesser Eastern Churches* (1913), ch. X, 'The Jacobites'.
Georgius, Mar, *The Man from Antioch, being an Account of Mar Julius, Bishop of Iona, and of his Successors, the British Patriarchs, from 1866 to 1944* (Glastonbury, 1958).
Lammens, H., *La Syrie, précis historique,* 2 vols (Beirut, 1921).
Morgan, Richard Williams, *Liturgy* (1874).
—*St Paul in Britain* (1861).
—*History of Britain from the Flood to A.D. 700* (new ed., 1933).
Parry, O. H., *Six Months in a Syrian Monastery* (1895).
Church Review, The, December 8, 1866; December 22, 1866; March 17, 1882.

Chapter II

J. JOSEPH OVERBECK AND S. G. HATHERLY

Belanos, A., 'Archbishop A. Lykourgos', in *Theologia* (vol. I, 1923), pp. 180–94.
Hatherly, S. G., *A Lecture delivered in the Greek Syllogus, Manchester, October 2nd (14th), 1874* (Cardiff, 1877).
Neill S. G., and Rouse, R., *History of the Ecumenical Movement 1517–1948,* pp. 205–7. (1954).
Novikoff, Olga, *Le général Alexandre Kiréef et l'ancienne catholicisme* (Berne, 1911).
—*Quelques lettres du général Alexandre Kiréef au professeur Michaud sur l'ancienne catholicisme* (Neuchâtel, 1913, new ed. 1914).
Overbeck, J. Joseph, *Libellus invitatorius ad Clerum Laicosque Romanos-Catholicos* (Halle, 1871).
—*Catholic Orthodoxy and Anglo-Catholicism* (1866).
—*Liturgia Missae Orthodoxi-Catholicae Occidentalis* (n.p. 1871).

547

Bibliography

—*Die Bonner Unionsconferenzen oder Altkatholizismus und Anglikanismus in ihrem Verhältnis zur Orthodoxie* (Halle, 1876).
—(ed.) *The Orthodox Catholic Review* (1867–85).
Shann, G. V., *Manual of Prayers* (1879).
—*Euchology, A Manual of Prayers of the Holy Orthodox Church, Done into English by* . . . (Kidderminster, 1891).
—*Book of Needs of the Holy Orthodox Church, Done into English by* . . . (1894, n.p.).
Tolstoy, Dmitry A., *Romanism in Russia* (Eng. ed. with Preface by Dr Eden, Bishop of Moray and Ross, 2 vols. (1874).
Williams, G., *The Orthodox Church of the East in the eighteenth century* (1868).
—*A Collection of Documents relating chiefly to the visit of Alexander, Archbishop of Syros and Tenos to England in 1870* (1876).

Chapter III

AMBROSE PHILLIPPS DE LISLE
AND THE ORDER OF CORPORATE REUNION

Brandreth, H. R. T., op. cit. (2nd ed. 1961), pp. 105–7.
—*Dr Lee of Lambeth* (1951).
—*The Oecumenical Ideals of the Oxford Movement* (1947).
Church Review, The, 'Catholic Churchmen and the O.C.R.' (March 17, 1882).
Anglo-Catholic, The, 'The Order of Corporate Reunion' (Detroit, May 1880).
Civiltà Cattolica (Rome), April 20, 1878, (article by English correspondent).
Clarke, R. F., *Dr Lee and the Order of Corporate Reunion* (1881).
Crehan, Joseph, S. J., 'Black Market in Episcopal Orders', in *The Month* (June, 1953).
Embry, J., *The Catholic Movement and the Society of the Holy Cross* (1931).
Grant, W., *Is the Order of Corporate Reunion Schismatical?* (1878).
Lee, F. G., (ed.) *Essays on the Reunion of Christendom* (1867).
—'The Order of Corporate Reunion', in *The Nineteenth Century* (November 1881).
—*Order Out of Chaos* (1881).
—*The Life of Cardinal Pole, with* . . . *a Practical Epilogue* (on the O.C.R.) (1888).

Bibliography

'The O.C.R. and its Work', in *The Nineteenth Century* (November, 1898).

Leslie, Shane, *Henry Edward Manning, His Life and Labours* (1921).

Livius, T., C.SS.R., *The Order of Corporate Reunion* (Dublin, 1882).

Mathew, A. H., *The Catholic Church of England, its Constitution, Faith, Episcopal Succession, etc.* (1914).

Middleton, R. D., *Newman and Bloxam, An Oxford Friendship* (Oxford, 1947).

Morris, J., 'Dr Lee and Corporate Reunion', in *The Month* (January, 1888).

Mossman, T. W., *The Keys of the Kingdom of Heaven* (Sermon on O.C.R.) (1879).

—*A History of the Catholic Church of Jesus Christ from the death of St John to the middle of the second century, etc.* (1873).

Pastoral Letter by the Rector, Provincials, and Provosts of the Order of Corporate Reunion (1877).

Purcell, E. S., *Life and Letters of Ambrose Phillipps de Lisle* (2 vols., 1900).

Reunion Magazine, The (4 nos. only) (1877–79).

Saturday Review, The, 'The Order of Corporate Reunion' (November 5, 1881).

Slosser, G. J., *Christian Unity, Its History and Challenge* (1920).

Statement, A, By the Society of the Holy Cross concerning the Order of Corporate Reunion (1878, rev. ed. 1879).

Stevens, T. P., 'Dr Lee of Lambeth', in *Southwark Diocesan Gazette* (Michaelmas, 1937).

Tablet, The, 'The Order of Corporate Reunion' (November 12, 1881).

—'The Church of England: A Clergyman's View' (November 4, 1898).

—Long correspondence on O.C.R., 1908–19.

Unità Cattolica, 'Ritorno dell Chiese schismatiche all' Unità cattolica' (January 19, 1898).

Walsh, W., *The Secret History of the Oxford Movement* (1897), ch. V.

Williams, B. M., *A Pastoral Letter for Advent 1920* (Stroud, Glos.).

Wright, Thos., *The Life of Walter Pater* (2 vols., 1907).

Dictionary of National Biography, The, articles on 'Lee, F. G.' and 'Mossman, T. W '

Bibliography

Chapter IV

JOSEPH RENE VILATTE, MAR TIMOTHEOS

Acolyte, The, 'Wildcat Bishops', November 25, 1933.
American Catholic Quarterly (Chicago, December 1915).
American Ecclesiastical Review (Washington, D.C., July 1899).
Annals of St Joseph (West De Pere, Wisconsin, September 1925).
Attwater, Donald, *Father Ignatius of Llanthony* (1931).
Aubault de la Haulte-Chambre, *J. K. Huysmans, souvenirs* (Paris, 1942).
Baldrick, Robert, *The Life of J. K. Huysmans* (Oxford, 1955).
Bayerischer Kurier, July 1925 (Letter from Mgr Ceretti, relative to Vilatte's ordination and consecration).
Bartoszek, D. S., *Episcopi Vagantes, Old Catholics and their recent Counterparts in the U.S.A.* (MS thesis lent by Mgr Marx of Green Bay, Wis.).
Bricaud, Jean, *Notice sur le Sacerdoce et l'Episcopat de Monseigneur Vilatte* (Lyon, 1927).
Brown, L. W., *The Indian Christians of St Thomas* (Cambridge, 1956).
Calder-Marshall, A., *The Enthusiast* (1962).
Catholic Citizen, March 2, 1907.
Catholic Quarterly Review, July 1889.
Clark, Elmer Talmage, *The Small Sects of America* (Nashville, 1937, rev. ed. 1949).
Cleveland Plain Dealer, August 20, 1894.
Curtis, Alonzo, *History of the Diocese of Fond du Lac* (Fond du Lac, 1925).
de Angelis, A., *A friendly Correction of the Rev. A. Parker Curtiss' Statements about Father Vilatte in the Holy Cross Magazine for August 1920* (Chicago, 1920).
de Bertouch, Baroness, *The Life of Father Ignatius, O.S.B.* (1904).
Fortescue, Adrian, *The Lesser Eastern Churches* (1913), p. 372.
Grafton, Charles C., *A Journey Godward* (Milwaukee, 1910).
—letter in *The Church Times* (October, 1898).
Green Bay Advocate, March 28, 1898.
Holy Cross Magazine (West Park, N.Y.) August 1920.
Holand, H. R., *Wisconsin's Belgian Community* (Sturgeon Bay, Wis., 1933).
[Iltud Mary of the Epiphany, O.S.B.] *The Recent Ordinations of*

Bibliography

Father Ignatius at Llanthony Abbot (Llanthony Tracts, no. 17, 1898).

Marx, Joseph A., 'The Old Catholics in America'; 'Vilatte and the Catholic Church', in *Salesianum* (October 1941, and February 1942).

Milwaukee Sentinel, April 9, 1899.

Parisot, Jean, *Mgr Vilatte: foundateur de l'Eglise Vielle-Catholique aux Etats-Unis d'Amérique* (Tours et Mayenne, 1899).

Schaff-Herzog, *Encyclopedia of Religious Knowledge*, vol. XII 'Vilatte, J. R.'.

Tisserant, E., *Eastern Christianity in India* (1957).

Vilatte, Joseph R., *Catechisme Catholique* (Green Bay, Wis., 1886).

—*A Sketch of the Belief of the Old Catholics* (Green Bay, Wis., 1889).

—*The Old Catholic* (a few issues only) (Green Bay, Wis., 1892).

—*The Independent Catholic Movement in France* (London, 1907).

—*My Relations with the Protestant Episcopal Church*, ed. with Introduction and Footnotes by H.S.B. Mar Georgius I, Patriarch of Glastonbury (Glastonbury, 1960).

—*Mode of Receiving the Profession of the Old Catholic Faith from one newly converted* (Chicago, 1919).

William, Bro., O.S.B., *The Genesis of Old Catholicism in America* (Buffalo, 1898).

Schurhammer, G., *The Malabar Church and Rome* (Trichinopoly, 1934).

Worcester Sunday Times, October 1, 1892.

Chapter V

ULRIC VERNON HERFORD, BISHOP OF MERCIA AND MIDDLESEX

Attwater, D., *The Christian Churches of the East, Vol. II Churches not in Communion with Rome* (new ed. 1961), ch. IX.

Badger, G. P., *The Nestorians and their Rituals* (2 vols., 1852).

Brandreth, H. R. T., op. cit., (2nd ed. 1961), pp. 14, 46n, 90–94.

Fortescue, A., *The Lesser Eastern Churches* (1913), ch. V 'The Present Nestorian Churches'.

Georgius, Mar, (ed.) *A Voyage into the Orient, being Extracts from the Diary of the Rt Rev. Vernon Herford*, with Introduction, Footnotes and Appendices (Antwerp 1954).

Herford, Vernon, (ed.) *The Christian Churchman: The Monthly*

Bibliography

Paper of the Order of the Christian Faith (Oxford, February 1900, ff.).

—*Christianity and Theism: a sermon* (Oxford, 1902).

—*Pastoral Letter . . . to the Syro-Chaldeans of the Metropolitan See of India, Milapur, Ceylon, etc.* (Oxford, 1903).

—*The Holy Sacrifice and Communion of the Lord's Supper or Eucharist* (Oxford, 1905); rev. ed. *The Lord's Supper or Mass* (Oxford, 1920).

—*An Open Letter to Lord—from one who sympathizes with the aspirations of the Working Classes* (n.d.).

—'For the Nestorian Church', in *Oxford Times*, March 7, 1914.

—*Christian Unity, a Practical Step* (6th imp. Oxford ,1918).

—'Open Letter to the Archbishop of Canterbury', in *The Times*, January 1921.

—*A Free Catholic Guide to Daily Devotions* (Oxford, 1925).

—*The Liturgy of St Serapion* (2nd ed. Oxford, 1927).

—(ed.) *Church and Chapel, Parish Magazine* (Oxford, 1929 ff.).

—*Catechism of Evangelical Catholic Doctrine for those who refuse any real division in the One great Church of Jessu Christ* (Oxford, 1931).

—'The Modern Value of Franciscanism', in *Reconciliation* November, 1934.

—*A Collection of Prayers for the Welfare and Protection of Animals* (1939).

—(ed.) *Evangelical Catholic Communion Leaflets, I–X* (Oxford, n.d.).

Jones, W. Rowland, *Diary of a Misfit Priest* (1960).

Light-Bearer, The :Quarterly of the Evangelical Catholic Communion (1952 ff.).

Orchard, W. E., *From Faith to Faith* (1933).

Peck, W. G., *From Chaos to Catholicism* (1920).

Sewell, Brocard, O. Carm., 'The Clerk without a Benefice' in *Corvo 1860–1960*, ed. by Cecil Woolf and Brocard Sewell (Aylesford, 1961).

Tisserant, F., *Eastern Christianity in India* (1957).

Tull, G. F., *Vernon Herford, Apostle of Unity* (Bradford, 1958).

Guardian, The, September 9, 1938 (obituary notice).

Chapter VI

ARNOLD HARRIS MATHEW, 'DE JURE' EARL OF LANDAFF

Angus, George, 'A New Old Catholic Bishop', in *The Tablet*, May 18, 1908.

Bibliography

Bell, G. K. A., *Randall Davidson* (Oxford, 1935), ch. lxiii.

Brandreth, H. R. T., op. cit., (2nd ed. 1961), pp. 5–7, 16–46, 75, 92.

Complete Peerage, The (rev. ed. vol. VII, 1929), 'Landaff and Landaff of Thomastown'.

Debrett's Peerage 1912, 'Landaff, Earldom of (Mathew)'.

de la Thibauderie, Ivan, *Église et Évêques Catholiques non Romain* (Paris, 1962), pp. 60, 85, 87, 99.

Georgius, Mar, *In the Shadow of Utrecht: Being an Account of the late Most Rev. Arnold Harris Mathew, D.D., and the Old Catholic Movement in the British Isles* (Antwerp, 1954).

Guardian, The, 'Bishop Mathew's Declaration of Autonomy and Independence', January 6, 1911.

—'An Episcopal Odyssey' (Letter from the Rev. J. V. Macmillan, Chaplain to the Archbishop of Canterbury, with a memorandum thereon), May 19, 1915.

Inquirer, The, July 13 and July 17, 1889.

Mathew, A. H., *The Old Catholic Missal and Ritual* (1909).

—*Are Anglican Orders Valid?* (1910).

—(ed.) *Catholic Standard, The*, (Bromley, Kent, 1911). Only a few issues.

—(ed.) *Torch, The, A Monthly Review advocating the Reconstruction of the Church in the West and Reunion with the Holy Orthodox Church of the East.* (Acton, 1912). A few issues only.

—(ed.) *Union Review, The*, (Bromley, 1913). Three issues only.

—*Catechism of Christian Doctrine* (Bromley, 1914).

—*Articles of Belief of the Old Catholics of Great Britain and Ireland, of the Western Orthodox Church* (Bromley, 1911).

—*The Ancient Catholic Church of Great Britain and Ireland* (n.p. or d.).

—*Pastoral Letter on Membership in the Theosophical Society and in the Order of the Star in the East* (1915).

—*An Episcopal Odyssey* (Kingsdown, Kent, 1915).

Morison, Stanley, *Some Fruits of Theosophy: The Origins and Purpose of the so-called Old Catholic Church* (1919).

Moss, C. B., *The Old Catholic Movement* (1948), pp. 298–304, 325.

Petre, Maude, *The Life of George Tyrrell* (2 vols., 1912).

Redfern, T. H., 'Bishop Mathew and his Theosophical Clergy' in *The Liberal Catholic* (July, 1956).

Réveil Catholique, Le: Organe de l'Église catholique française (Paris, 1914). One issue only.

Bibliography

Tablet, The, January 8, 1916 (Act of submission to the Holy See by A. H. Mathew).

Times Law Reports, The, 'Mathew v. The Times Publishing Co. Ltd' (May 2, 1913).

Thurston, H., S.J., 'The Scandal of the Theosophist Bishops', and 'The Origins of the Theosophical Priesthood', in The Month, July 1919 and September 1918.

Tracts on Reunion:

(1) Union with the Anglican Church: An Open Letter to the Most Rev. Jean-Marie Kowalski. From Arnold Harris Mathew.

(2) The Conversion of Great Britain. What can the Ancient Catholic Church of England do? By A. H. Mathew and F. S. Willoughby.

(3) The Ancient Catholic Church of England: Her Authority, Her Mission, Her Work, Her Appeal, etc. By F. S. Willoughby. (All issued at Twickenham, n.d., but 1914).

Williams, B. M., Pastoral Letter for Advent 1920 (n.p. 1920).

—The History and Purpose of the Old Roman Catholic (Pro-Uniate) Rite in Great Britain (Gloucester, 1939).

—Open Letter to the Archbishop of Canterbury (Painswick, 1947).

—The Archbishop of Canterbury and Bishop Mathew (n.p. or d.).

—Supplement to the Diocesan Chronicle (West Drayton, May 1949.

Chapter VII

CHURCHES CLAIMING THE FERRETTE SUCCESSION

LEON CHECHEMIAN

[Boltwood, C. D.], Origin, Orders, Organization, etc., of the Free Protestant Episcopal Church (n.d.).

Brandreth, H. R. T., op. cit. pp. 71–72, 79, 84.

Chechemian, Leon, An Eastern's Steps from Darkness to Light (1888).

Bulwark, The, or Reformation Journal, 'Notes from Dr Leon Chechemian, an Armenian Ex-Priest', Vol. XVI, October-December, 1887; 'Report of the Annual Meeting of the Scottish Reformation Society', ibid., April 1887.

Crockford's Clerical Directory, 1893, 'Chechemian, Leon'.

Dowling, T. E., The Armenian Church (1910).

Bibliography

Fortescue, A., *The Lesser Eastern Churches* (1913), pp. 419–20.
Georgius, Mar, *The Man from Antioch, being an Account of Mar Julius, Bishop of Iona, and of his successors, the British Patriarchs, from 1866 to 1914* (Glastonbury, 1958).
Intuitive Interpreter, The, (Free Protestant Episcopal Church of the Ecumenical Foundation, Igsoff).
Tournebize, F., *Histoire politique et religieuse de l'Arménie* (Paris, 1910).

VICTOR A. PALMER-HAYMAN
Free Catholic, The, occasional issues from 1948.
Hayman, V. S. P., *Catholic Freedom: A Brief Summary of the Position and Outlook of the Free Catholic Church* (1930).

GEORGE FORSTER
Forster, G., *Notes in Refutation of the Rev. Brandreth's Book 'Episcopi Vagantes'* (Battersea, 1952).
—*Ecclesia, The: Official Organ of the English Orthodox Church* (Battersea, 1951–2).
Orthodox Church News, The, (Battersea, 1952).
English Orthodox Church, The, (Battersea, 1951–2).

WILLIAM HALL
Hall, W., *The Origin, Orders, Organization, etc., of the Free Protestant Episcopal Church* (Wimbledon, n.d.) (Virtually the same as Bishop Boltwood's pamphlet with the same title).

CHARLES L. SAUL
Saul, C. L., *Episcopacy*, (n.d.).
—*The Task of our Church* (n.d.).
—*The Origin and Organization of the Evangelical Church of England* (n.d.).
Scott-Montagu, P., *Reunion?* (n.p. or d.).
Monthly Recorder, The: Official Organ of the Evangelical Church of England (Preston, 1943–8).

WILLIAM B. CROW
Brandreth, H. R. T., op. cit. pp. 74–76. 80.
Crow, W. B., *Order of the Holy Wisdom, Ekklesia agiae Sophiae, Ancient Universal (Orthodox Catholic) Church, Ancient and Universal Rite of Cosmic Architecture, Universal Spiritual Kingdom, Institute of Cosmic Studies* (n.d.).
A detailed list of Dr Crow's publications is given in *Who's Who*

Bibliography

1930–44, and a list also appears in *The Author's and Writer's Who's Who* (4th ed. 1960).

Georgius, Mar, *The Catholicate of the West: Historical Notes concerning the Western Orthodox Church* (Orthodox Church Leaflets, No. 2) (n.d.).

Chapter VIII

CHURCHES OF THE VILATTE SUCCESSION

Brandreth, H. R. T., op. cit. pp. 54–69.

AMERICAN CATHOLIC CHURCH

American Churchman, The: Official Publication of the American Catholic Church (Chicago, 1928 ff.).

American Liturgy and Missal, The. Prepared by Ernest Leopold (Peterson), Bishop-Auxiliary, with Imprimatur of Archbishop Lloyd (Chicago, 1928).

Lines, G., *The American Catholic Church: What it is; Where it comes from; What it stands for.* (Los Angeles, n.d.).

Liturgy, The, according to the Use of the American Catholic Church (Western-Orthodox) in the Province of the Pacific (n.p. or d.).

Wynne-Bennett, H. D., *The Status of the American Catholic Church* (n.p. or d.).

AFRICAN ORTHODOX CHURCH, ETC.

African Orthodox Churchman, The, (Beaconsfield, S. Africa, 1932, ff.).

Alexander, D. W., *The African Orthodox Church: its Declaration of Faith, Constitution, and Canons, and Episcopate, with Summary of Proceedings of first General Synod* (Beaconsfield, 1942).

—*The Onward Movement in Preparation for the Tenth Annual Synod* (Beaconsfield, 1934).

—*Synopsis of Proceedings of the twentieth Synod: Province of South and Central Africa and Rhodesia* (Beaconsfield, 1949).

—*The African Orthodox Church: What it stands for* (Beaconsfield, 1949).

—*An Appeal in Commemoration of the 25th Anniversary of the Organization of the African Orthodox Church, Province of South and Central Africa and Rhodesia* (Beaconsfield, 1949).

American Review of Eastern Orthodoxy (November, 1961).

Negro Churchman, The, Published in the Interest of the African Orthodox Church (New York, 1923 ff.).

Bibliography

Terry-Thompson, A. C., *The History of the African Orthodox Church* '(New York, 1956).

Welbourn, F. B., *East African Rebels: A Study of Some Independent Churches* (1961), with full bibliography of unpublished and published sources.

VILATTE SUCCESSION IN ENGLAND

Brittain, F., 'Academia: or Old Friends with Old Faces', in *The Cambridge Review* (March 2, 1946).

Catholic Apostolic Church Information Bulletin No. XIV: *The Succession of the Orthodox Catholic Church in England from the Catholicate of the West, being a Report of a Synod Meeting and various Happenings thereat.* (London and Glastonbury, 1951).

Bournemouth Daily Echo, The, August 11, 1953 (Bishop Dorian Herbert).

Catholic Christian, The, A Magazine of the Catholic Christian Church (Bournemouth, 1934). One issue only.

Georgius, Mar, *Varied Reflections* (Antwerp, 1954).

Harrington, F. C. A., *The Apostolic Succession of the One, Holy, Orthodox-Catholic Church* (1938).

—*The Orthodox-Keltic Rite of the Ordination of Deacons and Priests* (1939).

—*The Christian Doctrine of the Theandric Final Life* (n.p. or d.).

Herbert, Dorian, *The Jesuene Church* (Abergavenny, 1937).

—*The Free Orthodox Catholic Succession* (n.p. or d.).

—*Women Priesthood* (Abergavenny, 1943).

—*Agnostic Christianity: The Credentials of the Creeds* (Newport, Mon., 1962).

Hornsey Journal, The, September 13, 1935. (Mar Kwamin).

Intercollegian, The, (1930 ff.). (Archbishop Sibley).

John Bull, March 7, 1931, and October 12, 1931. (Archbishop Sibley).

Lucas, E. V., 'An Educational Abbey' (A Wanderer's Note Book), in *The Sunday Times*, September 9, 1934.

'*Ignatius Redivivus*': *Llanthony Atmosphere at Abergavenny*. Reprinted from *The Abergavenny Chronicle*, May 1, 1942 (Abergavenny, 1942).

Marsh-Edwards, H. M., *Pastoral Letter on the appalling Advance of Rationalism in the Church of England* (1903). (Written by H. B. Ventham).

Old Catholics and the Vicar of Branksome (Parkstone, 1918).

Bibliography

Orthodox Catholic Church Pamphlets: (1) *Table of Succession of the Patriarchate of Antioch showing its Western Extension;* (2) *The Orthodox Catholic Church;* (3) *The Orthodox Catholic Church and its Contribution to the Cause of Christian Unity* (n.p. or d.).

Picturesque Ceremony at Abergavenny, A Consecration of a Bishop (F. D. Bacon) (Abergavenny, n.d.).

Sibley, C., *The Syrian Rite of the Holy Eucharist abridged* (1929).

Stannard, B. W., *Statement of the primary Doctrines and Principles of the Catholic Christian Church* (Bournemouth 1933).

—*Statement concerning the Church, Sacraments and Worship of the Catholic Christian Church* (Bournemouth, 1933).

Whitebrook, W., *The Independent Catholics of Great Britain* (n.d.).

Ward, J. S. M., *The Confraternity of the Kingdom of Christ: What it stands for and how it came into existence* (n.p. or d.).

—*The Orthodox Catholic Church in England* (New Barnet, 1936).

—*The Liturgy of the Orthodox Catholic Church in England* (New Barnet, 1938).

—*Hymns of the Abbey of Christ the King* (New Barnet, n.d.).

—*A Brief Guide to the Abbey Folk Park and Museum* (New Barnet, 1935).

Who's Who, 1926–43, 'Ward, (Father), John Sebastian Marlow'. (With list of publications).

Langhelt, Francis Ernest, (ed.), *A Chapter of Secret History* (Being an account of some little-known bishops in the nineteenth century in England), *reprinted by kind permission from The Church Times from the issue of 28 April, 1922,* page 445, *with sundry Notes not forming part of the original Article* (Glastonbury, 1945). (2nd ed., with Introduction and notes by His Sacred Beatitude Mar Georgius I, Patriarch of Glastonbury, Glastonbury, 1960). Also refers to incidents in chapter VII.

CHURCHES OF THE VILATTE SUCCESSION AND GNOSTIC BODIES IN FRANCE, ETC.

(1) *The Constitutional Church and the Templars*

Amberlain, R., *Templiers et Rose-Croix* (Paris, 1955).

Dermenghem, E., *Joseph de Maistre, mystique* (Paris, 1946).

de la Thibauderie, Ivan, *Églises et Évêques Catholique non Romains* (Paris, 1962), pp. 39–48.

Joly, A., *Un mystique lyonnais* (Lyons, 1938).

Bibliography

Maillard de Chambure, C. H., *Règles et statuts secrets des Templiers, précédés de l'histoire de l'établissement de la destruction et de la continuation moderne de l'Ordre du Temple* (Paris, 1840).

Mauviel, *Annales de la Religion*: VI, 44–46; XI, 423; XII, 24–31; XIII, 139; XIV, XV, XVI: Correspondence.

Fabre-Pelaprat: Abbé Roche: *Sciences historiques des prétendus reformateurs* (Paris, 1834).

(cf. *Ami de la Religion*, 30 juin, 1831; 26 avril 1832; 9 aout 1833; 3 mars, 1838).

Pierre l'Ermite (Mgr Loutil), in *Contemporains*, 14 avril 1894.

(2) *Mgr Chatel and L'Église Catholique Française*
de la Thibauderie, Ivan, op. cit., pp. 49–51.

Martin, A., *Chatel ed l'Église Française* (Paris, 1904).

Pérot, F., *L'abbé Chatel* (Paris, n.d.).

Rougeron, G., 'Mgr Chatel et les libertés gallicanes', in *L'Étincelle* (December, 1960).

(3) *L'Église Gnostique Universelle*
Amadou, Robert, *L. C. de Saint Martin et le Martinisme* (Paris, 1946).

Ambelain, R., *Le Martinisme* (Paris, 1946).

—*Le Martinisme contemporain et ses véritables origines* (Paris, 1948).

Bois, Jules, *Les petites religions de Paris* (Paris, 1894).

Boudet, Ch. L., *Le rite ancien et primitif Memphis-Misraim (Les documents maconiques, mai 1944*).

Bricaud, J., *Notes historiques sur le Martinisme (Les Annales Initiatiques*, Lyon, 1934).

—*Notes historiques sur le rite ancient et primitif de Memphis-Misraim (Les Ann. Init.*, Lyon, 1938).

Chevillon, C., *Jean II Bricaud, sa vie, ses idées (Les Ann. Init. nos. 56, 57*, janvier-juin, 1934).

Gascoin, E., *Les religions inconnues* (Paris, 1928).

Grant, R. M., *Gnosticism and Early Christianity* (New York, 1959).

L'Initiation (about 1911), 'L'Église Gnostique Universelle'.

(4) *Pierre Vintras* and his *Oeuvre de la Miséricorde*
Amann, E., 'Vintras (Michel)', in *Dictionnaire de Théologie Catholique* (1903–50).

Bricaud, J., *L'abbé Bouillan: sa vie, ses doctrines, et ses pratiques magiques* (Lyon, 1927).

Garfon, Maurice, *Vintras, herésiaque et prophète* (Paris, 1928).

Bibliography

Barrès, Maurice, *La colline inspirée* (novel based on Vintras) (Paris, 1913).

Mangenot, E., *La colline inspirée . . . à propos d'un roman* (Paris, 1913).

—MSS on Vintras and Baillard in Library of Seminary at Nancy.

(5) Gallican churches

Appolis, E., *Une petite secte d'aujourd'hui : l'Église Catholique Apostolique et Gallicane* (Paris, 1952).

—*Le Vieux Catholicisme en France* (Paris, 1956).

Catéchisme National à l'Usage des Catholiques-Français (n.d.).

Catholique français, Le; Bulletin mensuel de la Tradition gallicane (Bordeaux and Paris, 1951 ff.).

Chery, O. P., H. Ch., *L,Offensive des Sectes* (Paris, 1960).

Gallican, Le, bulletin de l'Égliase gallicane (1921–47).

'Julio, abbé' (Mgr Houssaye), *Prières liturgiques, etc.* (Paris, n.d.).

—*Le Livre secret des Grands Exorcismes et Bénédictions, etc., etc.,* (Paris, 3rd ed. 1920).

L'Étincelle (ed. abbé Julio (Mgr Houssaye)) 1887–1912.

L'Étincelle (Le Catholique Français). n.s. (Romainville, Seine).

Notre Joie (Hol Levenez): Bulletin trimestriel d'Information chrétienne et d'édification spirituelle à l'Usage des Celtes (Saint-Dolay, 1957 ff.).

Liturgie de la Messe, rite gallican (n.d. or p.).

Profession de Foi d'Église Catholique, Apostolique et Gallicane (Pessac, Gironde, 1945). ed. by Mgr Lescouzères.

de la Thibauderie, Ivan, *Le Réveil Gallican au XXe siècle et l'Église Catholique Française* (Paris, 1960).

—*Le secret du bonheur et de la guérison* (Paris, 1962).

Rituel du Sacre de sa Majesté Impériale Marziano II (Rome, 1957).

(6) Offshoots of the Vilatte succession in other European countries

Brandreth, H. R. T., op. cit. (2nd ed. 1961) pp. 59–62.

Heiler, F., *Der Katholisimus* (1923).

—*Evangelische Katholizität* (1926).

Chapter IX

CHURCHES OF THE MATHEW SUCCESSION

(1) OLD ROMAN CATHOLIC CHURCH (PRO-UNIATE RITE)

British Uniate Rite, A. By an Old Roman Catholic Priest (Stroud, n.d.).

Bibliography

Old Catholic Almanack and Guide, The, (Stroud, 1926 ff.).

Williams, B. M., *What is an Old Roman Catholic?* (n.p. 1920).

—*A Pastoral Letter for Advent, 1920* (n.p. 1920).

—*A Summary of the History, Faith, Discipline and Aims of the Old Roman Catholic Church in Britain* (Stroud, 1924).

—*The English Text of the Ordinary of the Mass for Use in the Old Roman Catholic Church in Great Britain* (Stroud, 1924).

—*The History and Purpose of the Old Roman Catholic (Pro-Uniate) Rite in Great Britain* (Gloucester, 1939).

—*The Diocesan Chronicle* (West Drayton, 1947–51).

(2) OLD ROMAN CATHOLIC CHURCH IN GREAT BRITAIN, NOW KNOWN AS THE OLD ROMAN CATHOLIC CHURCH IN COMMUNION WITH THE PRIMATIAL SEE OF CAER-GLOW

—*Open Letter to the Archbishop of Canterbury* (Painswick, 1947).

The Old Roman Catholic Church: Its History and Purpose (London, n.d.).

What is an Old Roman Catholic? (London, n.d.).

O.R.C. Notes. Bi-monthly (London, 1951–4).

One Faith: The magazine of the Old Roman Catholic Church (Quarterly, 1954 ff.).

St Ambrose Bulletin (1960 ff.).

The Shrine of Our Lady of Islington (1959).

Shelley, G. G., *The Spirit of Port Royal: Poems* (New York, n.d.).

(3) OLD CATHOLIC CHURCH IN IRELAND

Georgius, Mar, *Varied Reflections* (Antwerp, 1954).

A Twig on the Tree of Life (Glastonbury, 1960).

(4) LIBERAL CATHOLIC CHURCH

Besant, Annie, *Esoteric Christianity* (London and Benares, 1901).

—and Leadbeater, C. W., *Man, Whence, How, and Whither?* (Adyar, 1913). The works of Annie Besant occupy nearly ten double column pages in the British Museum Catalogue.

Bulletin Saint-Alban, (Paris, 1945 ff.).

Catholique Libéral, Le. (Bordeaux, 1950).

Cockerham, A. W., 'The Liberal Catholic Ministry', in *The Liberal Catholic* (January and September, 1957; March and June, 1959).

Gauntlett, Rupert, *Health and the Soul* (1916).

Hampton, C., *The Old Catholic Movement in Great Britain* (Hollywood, Calif., 1918).

Bibliography

Hull, E. R., *Theosophy and Christianity* (C.T.S. London, 1903).

King, Robert, *Varieties of Psychism*, with an Introduction by Mrs Besant (1914).

Liberal Catholic, The, (London, 1922 ff.). Six times a year.

Leadbeater, C. W., *The Christian Creed* (1904).

—*The Other Side of Death* (Adyar, 1904).

—*The Hidden Side of Things* (Adyar, 1913).

—*The Science of the Sacraments* (1920, new ed. 1929).

—*Healing Forces and Healing Angels* (1925).

—*The World Mother as Symbol and Fact* (Adyar, 1929).

—*The Hidden Side of Christian Festivals* (Adyar, 1920).

—*The Inner Life* (Adyar, 1910).

—*Invisible Helpers* (Adyar, 1901).

—*Extracts from Letters of C. W. Leadbeater to Annie Besant 1916–23*, compiled by C. Jinarasada (Adyar, 1952).

Liberal Catholic Church, The, *Code of Canons* (revised ed. London, 1959).

—*The General Constitutions* (1959).

—*Statement of Principles, Summary of Doctrine and Table of Apostolic Succession* (new ed. 1959).

Liturgy, The, according to the Use of the Liberal Catholic Church (London, Sydney, Los Angeles, 1924; revised ed. 1942).

Lutyens, Lady Emily, *Candles in the Sun* (1957).

Lutyens, Mary, *To be Young—Some Chapters of Autobiography* (1957).

Martindale, C. C., *Theosophy* (C.T.S., London, 1917).

Morison, S., *Some Fruits of Theosophy: The Origins and Purpose of the so-called Old Catholic Church* (1919).

Occult Review, The, May 1918. (Letter from Bishop Wedgwood).

Pigott, F. W., *The Parting of the Ways: The Teaching of the Liberal Catholic Church compared and contrasted with traditional Catholic Teachings* (1927).

—*Religion for Beginners* (1932).

—*Catholicism—Past and Future* (1926).

—*A Summary of the Proceedings of the American Debate* (1944).

—*The Liberal Catholic Church: What is it?* (1954).

Redfern, T. H., 'Bishop Mathew and his Theosophical Clergy', in *The Liberal Catholic* (July, 1956).

Stokes, H. N., *The Ass in the Lion's Skin: the Relation of the Old Catholic Church to the Theosophical Society* (Washington, D.C., 1918).

Bibliography

Tettemer, J., *I was a Monk: The Autobiography of John Tettemer* (1952).

Thurston, H., 'The Latest Split among the Theosophists', in *The Month*, March, 1916; 'The Scandal of the Theosophist Bishops', ibid., July 1918; 'The Origins of the Theosophist Priesthood', ibid., September, 1918.

Ubique, published quarterly (Lakewood, New Jersey).

Wedgwood, J. I., *The Liberal Catholic Church and the Theosophical Society: Where they agree and where they differ* (Los Angeles, London, Sydney, 1919).

—*The Facts regarding the Episcopal Succession in the Liberal Catholic Church* (Sydney, 1920).

—'Some Reminiscences of Mr Leadbeater' in *Union Lodge T.S. Transactions* (February 26, 1918).

—'Twilight to Dawn' in *Theosophy in New Zealand* (December, 1916).

—*Meditation for Beginners* (3rd ed., Adyar, 1918).

—*The Lambeth Conference and the Validity of Archbishop Mathew's Orders.* An Open Letter to the Archbishop of Canterbury (Sydney, 1921).

—*The Distinctive Contribution of Theosophy to Christian Thought* (1926).

—*The Larger Meaning of Religion* (1929).

—'History of the Liberal Catholic Church' in *The Liberal Catholic* (January, February, and June, 1938).

—*The Presence of Christ in the Holy Communion* (1928).

—*The Place of Ceremonies in the Spiritual Life* (1928).

Woods, Charlotte E., *Christianity Reborn* (1930).

(5) OLD CATHOLIC ORTHODOX CHURCH (APOSTOLIC SERVICE CHURCH)

Banks, J. B., *The Independent Catholic Church: Its Constitution, etc.* By James, Patriarch of Windsor (Sutton Bridge, 1922).

—*The Pontifical of the Independent Catholic Church* (Sutton Bridge, 1922).

—*A Broad Statement of the Principles and Facts of the Independent Catholic Church* (privately printed, 1924).

—*The Service Church: Its Constitution, etc.* (1925).

—*The Holy Liturgy and other Rites, authorized for Use in the Old Catholic Orthodox Church, the Apostolic Service Church* (n.p., 1948).

Bibliograhpy

—*The Old Catholic Orthodox Church (The Apostolic Service Church): Its Constitutions, etc.* (n.p., 1954).

—*A Broad Statement of the Principles and Facts of the Old Catholic Orthodox Church: The Apostolic Service Church* (n.p., 1954).

Brittain, F., 'Academia; or Old Friends with Old Faces', in *The Cambridge Review* (March 2, 1946).

Daily Sketch (February 9, 1955).

(6) THE OLD CATHOLIC EVANGELICAL CHURCH OF GOD

Sunday Pictorial (February 5, 1955; and June 17, 1956).

Brandreth, H. R. T., op. cit., pp. 36–37.

(7) OLD HOLY CATHOLIC CHURCH (CHURCH OF THE ONE LIFE)

Ignatius Carolus, Archbishop (C. Brearley), *The Service of the Holy Eucharist and The Benediction of the Most Holy Sacrament* (n.d. or p.).

—*The Admission of Deacons, The Ordination of Priests, The Consecration of Bishops* (n.d. or p.).

—*The Old Holy Catholic Church: A Clarification of Our Position and Right to Existence as a Church.* (n.d. or p.).

—*Constitutions and Rules of the Old Holy Catholic Church* (rev. ed. 1962).

—*A Short Statement of Our Tenets* (n.p. 1962).

—(ed.) *The Cusworth Courier and St Hubert Chronicle* (1960 ff.).

Mary Francis, Rt Rev. Lady Abbess, *News Letters* (Cusworth Hall, 1957 ff.).

—*Meditations* (1957 ff.).

—*The Liturgy of St Hubert and The Church of the One Life* (Hastings n.d.).

The Bruce Magazine (Auchterarder, Perthshire, 1961 ff.).

[ed. R. Dominic Bruce] *Diocesan Notes: Perth and Kinross* (Auchterarder, March, 1963).

(8) ORDER OF LLANTHONY BROTHERS (FREE ANGLO-CATHOLIC CHURCH)

Whitman, R., *An Open Letter to British Old Catholics* (Gloucester, 1940).

(Corke, W.), *Llanthony Abbey Brothers* (n.p. or d.).

The People, Sept. 22, 1963, 'The Nerve of this old lag!'

(9) OLD ROMAN CATHOLIC CHURCH (ENGLISH RITE)

Brandreth, H. R. T., op. cit., pp. 45–46.

Bibliography

Barrington-Evans, W. A., *A Brief History of the Old Roman Catholic Church* (Twyford, Berks, 1961).

Onward!: The Quarterly Paper of the Independent Old Roman Catholic Church (Iver, Bucks, 1951 ff.—now issued at Twyford, Berks).

The Constitutions of the Old Roman Catholic Church (Iver, 1959).

Pastoral Letters from the Archbishop, 1951–9.

Priest Workmen (Twyford, 1961).

Questions and Answers (Twyford, 1961).

The Road to Rome: details of the unsuccessful negotiations in 1957 between the Church and the Holy See for our reconciliation, and the cause of their failure (Twyford, 1962).

[Harding, J. W. ed.] *St Bonaventure Bulletin* (London, 1962 ff.).

The People (October 28, 1963) 'How dare these two men run a boys' club?'; and (December 1, 1963) 'Four out of seven are jailbirds'.

(10) OLD CATHOLIC CHURCH IN AMERICA

Articles of Belief of the Old Catholic Church in America (Woodstock, N.Y., 1955).

Brandreth, H. R. T., op. cit. p. 26 note 2, 38 f. etc.

Marzena, C., *The Bishop finds Christ* (New York, n.d.).

Pax: the Old Catholic Magazine (Ocassional, Woodstock, N.Y.).

Principles of the Old Catholic Church (Woodstock, N.Y., 1955).

Story of the Old Catholic Church in America, The (Cos Cob, Conn., n.d.).

Why the Old Catholic Church? (Woodstock, N.Y., 1955).

Seitz, W. C., 'Bishop Brown of Galion', in *Bulletin of Bexley Hall* (Divinity School of Kenyon College), December, 1961.

(11) NORTH AMERICAN OLD ROMAN CATHOLIC CHURCH

American National Catholic, The: Official Quarterly Bulletin of the North American Old Roman Catholic Church (Chicago, 1944 ff.).

Augustinian, The, (Chicago, 1946 ff.).

Brandreth, H. R. T., op. cit., pp. 40–44.

Brief Life of the Most Rev. Carmel Henry Carfora (n.p. or d.).

[Carfora, C. H.] *General Constitution and By-Laws of the North American Old Roman Catholic Church* (New York, n.d.).

Catholic American, The: Official Publication of the Holy Catholic Church in America (ed. by Carfora and Lloyd). One issue only, Chicago, 1925.

Official Directory of the Old Roman Catholic Church 1960–1. Ed. by Bp. Marchenna. (Newark, N.J., 1960).

Bibliography

[Marchenna, R.] *One Church: Organ of the Old Roman Catholic Church in North America* (n.p., 1960 ff.).

Vanderfil, H. J., *Explanation of the present Position of Old Catholics in the World* (Chicago, 1919).

(12) UNIVERSAL EPISCOPAL COMMUNION

(J. C. Crummey) *Old Catholic Quarterly, The*, (Chicago, 1943 ff.).

(13) IGLESIA ORTODOXA CATOLICA APOSTOLICA MEXICANA

Hurtado, Arnulfo, *El Cisma Mexicano* (Mexico City, 1956).

Y Torres, Leopoldo Lara, *Conflicto Religioso por un obispo católico mexicano* (n.p. or d.).

García Gutierrez, Cango. Jesús, *Acción Anticatólica en Mexico* (n.p. or d.).

—*Apuntamientos de Historia Eclesiastica Mexicana.*

Ramírez, Cabañas J., *Las Relaciones entre México y el Vaticano* (n.p. or d.).

(14) ÉGLISE CATHOLIQUE ÉVANGELIQUE

(ed.) *L'Unité Spirituelle Revue Mensuelle* (1924 ff.).

Winnaert, L. C., *Le Problème de l'Unité chrétienne* (Paris, 1924).

—*Quelques Mots sur l'Orthodoxie adressés à des Occidentaux* (Paris, 1944).

—*Vers un Libre Catholicisme* (Paris, 1919).

Nash, Evans, 'The Paris Benedictines' in *The Basilian* (New York, August, 1948).

Chapter X

CATHOLICATE OF THE WEST

Moon, Barbara, 'The heyday of Degree Mills', in *Maclean's Magazine* (Toronto, April 6, 1963); and 'The Prince of Degree Merchants' (*ibid.*).

Newman, H. G. de Willmott (Mar Georgius).

Pastoral Letter of His Beatitude Mar Georgius on the occasion of his Consecration (1944).

Pastoral Letter of His Beatitude Mar Georgius for Advent, 1945 (1945).

Encyclical Letter from the Holy Governing Synod addressed to the Members of the Lambeth Conference (1948).

Encyclical Letter of His Sacred Beatitude Mar Georgius I, Patriarch of Glastonbury, Prince-Catholicos of the West, concerning the Dissolution of the Catholicate of the West (Glastonbury, 1953).

Bibliography

Encyclical Letter of His Sacred Beatitude Mar Georgius I, Patriarch of Glastonbury, Prince-Catholicos of the West, regarding the Re-Adoption of the Title Catholicate of the West by the Catholic Apostolic Church (United Orthodox Catholicate), (Bristol, 1959).

Encyclical Letter of His Sacred Beatitude Mar Georgius I, Patriarch of Glastonbury, Prince-Catholicos of the West concerning the conferring of Sacred Orders upon Anglican Clergymen (1959).

Encyclical Letter of His Sacred Beatitude Mar Georgius I, Patriarch of Glastonbury, Prince-Catholicos of the West, for Advent, 1959. (1959).

Historical

Orthodox Catholic Leaflets:

(i) *Table of Apostolic Succession in the Western Orthodox Catholic Church.*

(ii) *Historical Notes concerning the Western Orthodox Catholic Church.*

(iii) *The Restoration of Apostolic Catholicism.*

(iv) *Table of Apostolic Succession (Armenian Uniate Line).*

(v) *Table of Apostolic Succession (Old Catholic Line from America).*

(vi) *Table of Apostolic Succession (Nonjuring Line).*

(vii) *Table of Apostolic Succession (Anglican Line).*

(viii) *Table of Apostolic Succession (English Old Catholic Line).*

(ix) *Table of Apostolic Succession (Syro-Chaldean Line).* (Glastonbury and London, 1944–7.)

Information Bulletins:

(i) *The Functions of the Diaconissate and Regulations concerning Admission thereto.*

(ii) *Conditional Consecration considered in the Light of the Restoration of the Oecumenical Apostolic Tradition.*

(iii) *The Chrismatic Gifts of the Holy Spirit and their Exercise in the Body of Christ.*

(iv) *A Memorandum for the Use of prospective Ordinands.*

(v) *The Organization of the Catholicate.*

(vi) *The Lord's Work in these latter Days.*

(vii) *The Calendar according to the Glastonbury Rite.*

(viii) *The Structure of the Divine Liturgy of the Holy Eucharist or Mass.*

(ix) *Memorandum on local Organization and Activities.*

Bibliography

(x) *Memorandum on Church Membership.*
(xi) *Divine Healing.*
(xii) *A Brief Summary of Doctrine.*
(xiii) *The Table of Commemoration of Saints, observed throughout the Year according to the Glastonbury Rite.*
(xiv) *The Secession of the Orthodox Catholic Church in England from the Catholicate of the West, being a Report of a Synod Meeting and various Happenings thereat.* (London and Glastonbury, 1947–51).

Doctrinal
The Glastonbury Confession (Confessio Glastoniensis) being the Dogmatic Constitution of the Catholic Apostolic Church (Catholicate of the West) (Glastonbury, 1952; 2nd ed. 1960).
Statement of Principles of the Catholic Apostolic Church (Catholicate of the West) (Glastonbury, 1953).
The Orthodox Catholic Catechism (Glastonbury, 1960).

Controversial
A Brief Glossary of Terms in Common Use among Anglican Controversialists.

Canon Law
A Brief Directory of the Orders, Offices, and Ministries of Christ's Holy Church (Glastonbury, 1960).
The Charter and Organic Constitution of the Catholic Apostolic Church (Glastonbury, 1960).

Liturgical
Low Mass according to the Glastonbury Rite (Shorter Form).
Low Mass (Missa Cantata).
The Glastonbury Service Book: A Selection of Services in most frequent Use from the Sacred Liturgy and other Divine Offices, Rites and Ceremonies of the Church, according to the Glastonbury Rite (Antwerp, 1954).
The Order for the Consecration of a Bishop according to the Glastonbury Rite (Glastonbury, 1958).
The Order for the Setting Apart of a Deaconess.
The Sacred Liturgy and Other Divine Offices, Rites, and Ceremonies of the Church, according to the Glastonbury Rite, being the Use of the Patriarchal and Catholicatial See of the Venerable Churches of Glastonbury, Caertroia, and Mylapore within the Catholic Apostolic Church (Catholicate of the West), otherwise known as The

Bibliography

United Orthodox Rite: Liber IV, The Rituale or Manuale (prepared for the use of English-speaking Congregations) Glastonbury, (1959).

Miscellaneous

Select documents relating to the enoblement (sic) of his Serene Highness the Duke of Saxe-Noricum (1930).
Lectures on Religion, given at the Catholic Apostolic Church, Wood Green (1924–29).
History of the Bicycle (1938).
Cycle Traders Unite (1939).
Ten Years of Conservatism in New Southgate (1939).
The Catholic Apostolic Church: A Statement for candid Enquirers (Glastonbury, 1946).
Consolidated Ordination Regulations (Glastonbury, 1961).
Varied Reflections (Antwerp, 1954).
Episcopi in Ecclesia Dei and Father Brandreth (Glastonbury, 1962).
Souvenir Guide to the Collegiate Church of the Epiphany and of the Three Magi, Bristol (Glastonbury, 1961).

Periodicals

The Orthodox Catholic Review (Enfield Lock—Kew—London—Bristol, 1944 ff.).
Hieratika, or The Voice of the Hierarchy, Published for the Clergy only (1947 ff.).
Maranatha, The Journal of the Prophetic College of the Catholic Apostolic Church (Catholicate of the West); devoted to the Study of Biblical Prophecy, Christian Mysticism, and the Charismata (Bristol, 1960 ff.).
(ed. by W. D. de O. Maxey), The Ancient Christian Fellowship Review (Los Angeles, 1946 ff.).
Encyclical Letter of the Holy Governing Synod of the Catholicate of the West concerning the Extension of the Catholicate to the Americas (n.p. 1946).
Langhelt, F. E., (ed.) A Chapter of Secret History (Glastonbury, 1945; 2nd ed. with introduction and notes by Mar Georgius, 1960).
Scott-Montague, P., The Catholic Apostolic Church: the East-West Bridge (Glastonbury, 1950).
[Green, Dennis C.] Lessons on Yoga (Bristol, n.d.).
Ni Romains ni Protestants . . . mais Catholiques Apostoliques (Antwerp, n.d.).

Bibliography

ANCIENT CATHOLIC CHURCH

Nicholson, H. P., (Archbishop of Karim). *Validation of the Orders of the Ancient Catholic Church* (London, n.d.).

—*Services of Love and Blessing, compiled from Eastern and Western Sources, both ancient and modern, for use in the Ancient Catholic Church* (1950).

—*The Cathedral Church of the Good Shepherd* (London, n.d.).

APOSTOLIC CHURCH OF ST PETER

Van Ryswyk, John, (ed.) *Christocracy, Official Organ of the Temple of Service (Apostolic Church of St Peter)*, monthly (London, 1947 ff.).

PRE-NICENE GNOSTIC CATHOLIC CHURCH

de Palatine, Richard, *The Holy Eucharist* (1953).

—*The Order of St Raphael* (n.d.).

—*Christ or Jesus?* (2nd ed., 1955).

—*The Christian Mysteries* (2nd ed., 1958).

—*Monographs, 1–22 of The Brotherhood of the Illuminati* (n.d.).

—*The Pre-Nicene Catholic Church* (n.d.).

—'*Lux*', *The Brotherhood of the Pleroma, etc., A Message from Richard, Duc de Palatine* (n.d.).

—*Illuminism, Who and What are the Illuminati?* (n.d.).

—*A Call to Arms issued by The Sovereign Imperium of the Mysteries* (n.d.).

—(ed.) *The Lucis Magazine* (1960 ff.).

CHURCH AND ORDER OF THE SERVANTS OF CHRIST

Glenn, Francis E., *What? Why? Whither? of the Church and Order of the Servants of Christ* (n.d.).

—(ed.) *Oblatum* (quarterly 1960 ff.).

Chapter XI

MISCELLANEOUS CHURCHES

(General) *Year Book of American Churches* (New York).

AMERICAN ORTHODOX CHURCH

The Basilian Quarterly. (Mount Vernon, N.Y., 1938–52). Continued as *Orthodoxy* (Mount Vernon, N.Y., 1952 ff.).

William Albert Nichols, *Archbishop Ignatius: A Tribute to the twentieth Anniversary of his Consecration* (Mount Vernon, N.Y., n.d.).

Bibliography

The Western Calendar for Orthodox Catholics (Mount Vernon, N.Y., n.d.).

Orthodoxy: General Information (Society of St Basil, New York, n.d.).

The Missal for the Use of Orthodox (Mount Vernon, N.Y., 1952).

An Orthodox Primer (Mount Vernon, N.Y., 1955).

Brandreth, H. R. T., op. cit., pp. 95–98.

HOLY ORTHODOX CHURCH IN AMERICA (EASTERN
CATHOLIC AND APOSTOLIC)

The Liturgy of the Holy Orthodox Church in America: The Divine Liturgy of St John Chrysostom abridged and arranged for the use of the Faithful (New York, 1952).

The Holy Orthodox Church in America (New York, n.d.).

Messenger of the Holy Wisdom. Monthly, (New York).

POLISH MARIAVITE CHURCH

Moss, C. B., *The Old Catholic Movement; Its Origins and History* (1948), pp. 307–8.

Gajowski, K., *Mariavitensekte* (Cracow, 1911).

Rhode, A., *Bei den Mariaviten* (1911).

Janin, R., 'Les Mariavites et l'orthodoxie' in *Echos d'Orient* XXX (1927), pp. 216–20.

Niwinski, M., 'Les Mariavites de Pologne' in *Revue apologétique*, liv. (1932), pp. 570–80.

Neuhaus, C., 'Mariaviten' in *Die Religion in Geschicte und Gegenwart*, ed. 2 by H. Gunkel and L. Zscharnack, iii (1929), cols. 2,000–4.

LIGUE OECUMÉNIQUE POUR L'UNITÉ CHRÉTIENNE

Erni, Julien, *Je crois la Sainte Église universelle* (Bienne, 1945).

—*Les Sacraments de l'Église universelle* (Lausanne, 1948).

—*Seminariste romain, Pasteur protestant, Pasteur oecuménique* (Bienne, 1949).

—(ed.) *Bulletin de la Ligue oecuménique pour l'unité chrétienne* (Bienne and Aire-Geneva, 1960 ff.).

POLISH NATIONAL CATHOLIC CHURCH

Andrews, Theodore, *The Polish National Catholic Church in America and Poland* (1955). With full bibliography.

Bibliography

APOSTOLIC EPISCOPAL CHURCH

Abbinga, P, (Mar Philippus), *De Liturgie der Helige Offerende* (Doorn, 1951).

—*Irenische en Oecumenische Beschovwingen* (Doorn, 1955).

Brooks, A. W., *Apostolic Episcopal Church* (New York, 1950).

PHILIPPINE INDEPENDENT CHURCH

Lopez, Santiago, *Mons. Aglipay y la religion del Porvenir* (Manila, 1936).

Whittamore, Lewis B., *Struggle for Freedom, History of the Philippine Independent Church* (Greenwich, Conn., 1960).

Whalen, W. J., 'The Philippine Independent Church', in *The Priest* (Huntington, Indiana), December, 1961.

—*Faiths for the Few* (Milwaukee, 1963). This book also deals with Old Catholicism, Theosophy and the Liberal Catholic Church, Rosicrucianism, etc.

INDEX

(1) Churches and Organizations

Index

Index

Index

Index

INDEX

Index of Persons

Index of Persons

Index of Persons

Finch-Styles, F., 327
Fisher, Abp, 332
Flavius Eugenius, Emperor, 467
Fleming, D., 118, 119
Flynn, W. W., 538
Forbes, Bp, 60
Fornacier, S., 533
Forster, G., 229, 474
Fournié, J.-M., 310, 311
Franciscus, Mar, 314, n.3
Francis, Mar, see Langhelt, F. E.
Frederic, Mar, see Harrington, F. C. A.,
Freemantle, Dean, 114
Frere, Bp W. H., 285
Frippiat, N. J. E. A. (Bishop of Tongeren), 497, 498
Fry, A., St D., 233, 472
Fryxell, A. Z., 254, 258, 277, n.1
Furse, Bp M., 285, 286
Fusi, E. M. M., 317 n.3, 483 n.5, 513 n.3, 518

Galton, A., 175
Gamble, R. H., 163
Garvey, M., 264
Gauntlett, B. E. R., 202, 344, 347, 368
Gauthier, Fr, 98, 101, 112
Geikie-Cobb, W. F., 343
Geniotis, S., 262
Georgius, Mar, 41, 44, 45, 47, 227, 232, 235, 238, 243, 246, 247, 260, 279, 287 n.1, 288, 289, 291, 295, 319, 320, 337, 338, 375, 380, 402, 442 n.2, 444–501, 509, 586
Geyer, A. R., 319
Gibbons, Cardinal, 113
Giebner, M., 321
Gill, E., 396
Gill, F., 382 n.3
Giraud, L. F., 123, 126, 191 n.3, 306, 308, 309, 311, 315, 318, 319, 321, 400, 519 n.2
Glenn, F. E., 375, 486, 487
Glintz, G. A., 321
Golebiswski, A., 518
Gobat, Bp, 34
Gonzalez, H., 527
Grafton, C. C., 98, 99, 100, 101, 102, 104, 107, 109, 117–18, 124, 414, 415
Grant, W., 75
Graziola, P. J. G., 541
Green, D. C., 493, 499
Greenland, T., 220 n.1
Grégoire, abbé, 299

Gregorios, Mar G., 107
Gregory XVI, 59, 302
Griffiths, B., 332
Grimaldi-Lascaris, A. L. de la C., 523
Grissel, H. de la G., 75
Grochowski, L., 526, 527
Groome, H. S., 487
Grover, A., 504, 508
Grover, M. A., 504, 508
Gul, Abp G., 170, 172, 175, 377, 415, 417, 483 n.5, 524
Gulielmus, Mar (W. H. Turner), 314 n.3

Haas, G., 244
Haile Selassie, Emperor, 480
Haines, A. T. B., 433 n.1
Haines-Howard, W. W., 438 n.3
Hakimi, Abdulla A. E., 298
Halifax, Lord, 61
Hall, W., 46, 223, 224, 231, 235, 243, 244, 449 n.1
Hamilton, Duchess of, 149
Hamilton, Duke of, 189 n.1, 192 n.1
Hammond, W. S., 430
Hampton, C., 350, 351, 363, 364, 513, 535
Harding, A., 104, 105
Harmer, Bp, 166
Harrington, F. C. A. (Mar Frederic Archbishop of the Diocese of St George), 231, 236, 239, 278 n.1, 279, 280–2, 292, 446
Harris, Anselm, 403
Harris, Asaph, 193, 393, 396 n.5
Harris, B. C., 224, 231, 232
Hastler, C., 397, 463 n.2
Hatherly, S. G., 52–56
Haug, G., 400, 519 n.2
Hay, A., 89, 193, 206, 207, 209, 214
Hayman, V. A. P. (Archbishop of Waltham), 227–30, 397 n.2, 456 n.1, 474 n.4, 488 n.3, 552 n.2
Heard, H. J. M. (Mar Jacobus II), 224–6, 227, 235, 238, 240, 243, 282, 443, 448
Hedley, Bp, 184
Hedley, Mar, see Bartlett, H. C.
Heiler, F., 321, 322, 462
Henzell, A. W., 412
Herbert, D. (Mar Doreos, Bishop of Caerleon), 294–8, 324, 396, 454 n.4
Herford, A. U. V., (Bishop of Mercia and Middlesex), 121, 130–55, 212, 292, 305, 319, 394, 453, 496

581

Index of Persons

Héry, abbé, 303
Herzog, Bp, 95, 97, 98, 100, 101, 102, 127, 166, 170, 171, 304, 309, 319, 415, 524, 532
Herzog, K. E., 319
Heuer, H. (Bishop Willibrord), 339, 384, 385 n.1, 437
Heykamp, Abp, 99, 100, 101
Hickersayon, St J. the D., 478
Hinton, C. F. (Bishop of Hereford), 180, 182, 201, 258, 259
Hinton, D. C., 256, 260, 374
Hinkson, G. D., 266 n.2
Hodur, F., 123, 262, 415, 416, 417, 523-7
Howard, E., 33
Howarth, A. W., 168, 169, 180, 181, 201, 394 n.4, 446
Hroklak, J., 426
Hulse, H. R., 197
Hunter, E. W., 429
Huntingford, Bishop Francis, see Brabazon-Lowder, J. B.
Hurgon, R. K. (Mar Benignus, Bishop of Mere), 233 n.5, 454, 472, 475
Hussaye, J., 141, 191 n.5, 306, 308, 315
Huysman, J. K., 119, 308 n.5

Ignatius Carolus, Abp, see Breasley, C.
Ignatius Ephrem I, 239, 240, 241, 256, 282, 447, 512
Ignatius of Llanthony, Fr, 75, 114–17, 121, 217, 269, 272, 285 n.3, 294, 298, 392, 395, 417
Ignatius Peter II, 35
Ignatius Peter III (Mar Bedros), 35, 36, 44, 45, 105, 107, 242, 250, 256
Iltud-Mary, Fr, 115
Inge, W. R., 343
Itkin, M. A., 433, 434

Jack, E. N., 514, 515
Jackson, R. A., 86 n.1
Jackson, R. C., 86, 87, 90
Jacobus I, Mar, see Martin, J.
Jacobus, II, Mar, see Heard, H. J. M.
Jalbert-Ville, B. I., 309, 310, 311, 312
James, E. A. L. (Metropolitan of Acadia, Exarch of the Canadas), 233, 245–6, 247, 433, 458, 473, 538 n.2
James, F., 369–70
James-Franciscus, Mar, 314 n.3
James, Mar, see Ryan, J. C.
Jandel, Père, 33, 34

Jardine, R. A., 505
Jarvis, H. F., 509, 511
Jeffrey, W. J. E. (Mar Johannes, Bishop of St Marylebone), 154, 235, 288, 292, 396 n.1, 445, 452
Joannes-Maria, Mar, see Van Assendelft-Altland, J. M. B.
Joannes, Mar, see Jeffrey, W. J. E.
Joannes, Mar, see Nicholson, H. P.
John Emmanuel, Mar, see Brooks, W. A.
John, Mar, see Syer, J.
John, Mar, see Ward, J. S. M.
Jones, Spencer, 173, 177
Jones, W. R., 146–9, 152
Jost, R., 401, 537
Julius, Mar, see Alvarez, A. F. X.
Justinos, Mar, see Thiesen, J. M.

Kalogjera, M., 401, 537
Kaminski, S., 113, 524
Kanski, F., 256 n.1, 258, 259
Katzer, Mgr, 94, 100, 101, 110, 119
Kaufmann, abbé, 287
Kedrovsky, J., 421
Keenan, M. J., 459
Keller, C. W. (Mar Carolus, Bishop of Amesbury), 452, 454 n.4, 509
Kelly, J., 230, 434–6, 438
Kennedy, H. S., 533
Kenninck, Abp, 420, 537
Khor, J., 541 n.2
Kibarian, Abp, 410
Kilburn, Fr, 89
King (Wilson), A., 195, 220, 522
King, R., 202, 344, 347, 368
Kiréef, A., 55, 185, 517
Kleefisch, H. J., 513, 535
Klimowich, J., 426
Knight, W. S. McB., 150
Knill-Samuel, M. P. (Mar Peter, Bishop of Naim), 313, 481
Knosrov, P. M., 276
Koerner, G. T., 339
Kolazewski, Fr, 113
Kowalski, J. M., 179, 295, 400, 417, 421, 517, 518, 521, 522
Kozlowska, M. F., 516, 517, 523
Kozlowski, A. S., 102, 113, 179, 420
Krautbauer, Mgr, 94
Kreutzer, Bp, 420
Krishnamurti, J., 196, 361
Kujlowski, B., 540
Küry, Bp, 519, 537
Kwamin, Mar, see Anderson, E. J.

Index of Persons

Index of Persons

Mazel, J. A., 349, 353, 359
Mazur, F., 433 n.1
Mbina, I. W., 269
Mead, G. R. S., 309
Meindaerts, P. J., 172
Merry del Val, Cardinal, 138, 183, 184, 201, 204
Messera, Abp G., 194, 209
Messmer, Bp, 111, 112, 119
Metaxakis, M., 268
Miraglia-Gulotti, P. M. (Bishop of Piacenza), 84, 120, 124, 125, 141, 191 n.3, 306, 419
Moffay, C. K. S., 248
Mojica, J. A., 440
Morgan, R. W. (Mar Pelagius I), 43–47, 219, 250, 296, 316
Mortimer, A. J., 331 n.1
Mosley, Sir O., 228
Moss, C. B., 334
Mossman, T. W. (Bishop of Selby), 54, 75, 77, 78, 82, 83, 84
Motsepe, S. L., 269
Moule, Bp, 194, 209
Munnings, Lady, 475, 482
Munnings, Sir Alfred, 475, 482

Nash, N. B., 529
Neale, J. M., 32, 86
Needham, S. E. P. (Mar Theodorus, Bishop of Mercia), 236 n.4, 294 n.1, 374, 375, 452, 457, 454 n.4
Nelson, M. N. (Mar Matthew, Bishop of Hawaii), 455 n.2
Nemeth, S., 512
Newman, J. H., 59
Newmark, G. A., 429 n.1
Newton, W., 331
Nicolas, Mar, 314 n.3
Nichols, I. W. A., 503–6, 506, 509
Nicholson, H. P. (Mar Joannes, Archbishop of Karim), 229, 230, 313, 314, 380, n.2, 381 n.2, 474–88
Niset, J., 521
Noble, J. B., 249
Nobles, F. A., 440
Noli, van S., 426 n.1
Novikoff, O., 185, 187, 189, 437 n.2, 517 n.a
Nugee, G., 37, 38, 51, 67, 86, 272
Nurse, G. St C., 266 n.2
Nybladh, C., 254

Oakden, Dr, 394

O'Donnell, R., 534 n.3
Ofiesh, A., 501, 503, 509, 514
O'Gavigan, J. D., 236, 292–4, 295 n.2, 374
O'Halloran, R., 167, 168–70, 174, 175, 272
O'Hara, Mgr, 404
O'Hara, W., 524
Omand, D., 233 n.5
Orchard, W. E., 145, 146, 409
Ortiz, J. P., 339, 437, 441, 485 n.1
Overbeck, J. J., 48–52, 410
Overs, D., 231
Ozouf, abbé, 300

Pachcek, A., 537
Padewski, J., 526
Paget, Bp F., 138
Paget King, G. P. T., 230, 331 n.1, 336, 338, 339, 340
Palmer, W., 32
Palumbo, E. don A., 247
Panelli, Mgr, 185 n.1
Papus, 308
Parrish, H., 414, 415
Parsall, H. van A., 504, 508
Parsons, L. M., 297
Patrick, père, 311
Paul Athanasiu, Mar, 107
Paulos, Br, 487
Peabody, P. R. (Mrs Lloyd), 258
Pearse, Mrs M. (Marquise de Saulney, Abbess of Bethany), 381, 382, 386, 387, 390, 483
Peers, B. (Bishop of Samaria), 485 n.4
Pelagius, Mar, see Morgan, R. W.
Pennings, Fr, 110
Pereira, R., 529
Perez y Budar, J. J., 430, 439, 440
Perrier, G., 518
Peter, Mar, see Knill-Samuel, M. P.
Peters, J. G. (Mar Petros, Exarch of the Indies), 473, 536
Peter, W., 86
Petros, Mar, see Peters, J. G.
Philippus, Mar, see Abbenga, H. P.
Philippus, see Singer, P. C. S.
Photios, Patriarch of Alexandria, 187, 268
Pigott, F. W., 353, 354, 359, 360, 362, 363, 365, 396 n.2
Pillai, J. C., see Ryan, J. C.
Pinder, G., 231, 233 n.5, 234, 473
Pinto, L., 106, 108

584

Index of Persons

Index of Persons

Index of Persons

587

INDEX

(3) *Places*

Index of Places

Index of Places

Hooton Pagnell, Yorks., 193
Hounslow, Middlesex, 445
Hull, Yorks., 174
Hungary, 400, 512

India, 235, 458, 496
Indiana, 438
Iona, Scotland, 36, 37
Ireland, 219, 221, 340–2, 385
Iver, Bucks, 406

Jersey, Isle of, 412
Jerusalem, 34, 243

Kingsdown, Kent, 203, 206, 208
Kokomo, Indiana, 430
Kotrona, Calif., 350 n.2
Krakow, Poland, 573 n.3

Laguna Beach, Calif., 259, 261
Lancing, Michigan, 436
La Vendée, France, 300
Leeds, Yorks., 229
Leicester, England, 275, 276
Leiden, Holland, 353 n.3
Lepton, Huddersfield, Yorks., 295
Letchworth, Herts., 353 n.3
Liberia, 248, 250, 314, 497
Ligugé Abbey, France, 119, 120
Little Sturgeon, Wis., 97, 98, 101
Liverpool, 297, 358
Llanthony Abbey, Mon., 75, 114–17, 121, 123, 272, 275, 296, 298

London:

Abney Park Cemetery, Stamford Hill, N.15, 243, 449 n.1
All Saints', Knightsbridge, S.W.7, 343
All Saints', Lambeth, S.E.1, 71, 74, 80, 81, 274
All Saints', Margaret Street, W.1, 332
All Saints', Mile End New Town, E.2, 327
Ancient British Patriarchate, 271 Green Lanes, Palmers Green, N.13, 240, 447
Apostolic Church of St Peter (Sanctum of the Vigil), Kensington, W.8, 470–2
Armenian Church, Kensington, 56 n.1, 276
Bishop Bacon's Oratory, Bedford Park, W.4, 85, 182
British Museum, 37

Cathedral of the Good Shepherd (Ancient Catholic Church), Chelsea, S.W.3, 229, 338 n.5, 312, 313, 472, 473, 474–87, 496, 523
Cathedral of the Good Shepherd, Clapton, E.5, 488
Catholic Apostolic (Irvingite) Church, Camberwell, S.E.5, 87 n.2
Catholic Apostolic (Irvingite) Church, Hackney, E.8, 444
Catholic Apostolic (Irvingite) Church, Maida Hill, N.W.8, 444
Christ the King (Church of the Servants of Christ), Battersea Rise, S.W.11, 487
Church of the Great Sacrifice (Apostolic Service Church), Maiden Lane, W.C.1, 370
Co-Masonic Temple, Maida Vale, N.W.8, 346, 357, 368
Crystal Palace, 221
Dennison House, Vauxhall Bridge Road, S.W.1, 492
Deptford, S.E.8, 480
Devonshire Lodge, Marylebone Road, N.W.1, 330, 331
Greek Orthodox Church, Bayswater, W.2, 53, 56 n.1
Holy Trinity, Sloane Street, S.W.3, 161–3
Hornsey, N.8, 279, 280, 281, 282
Intercollegiate University, 22 Ferndale Road, S.W.3, 276, 277
Kensington Cemetery, 226
King's Weigh House, W.1, 145, 146, 147, 149, 150, 153, 154, 409
Lambeth Palace, 71
Liberal Catholic Cathedral, Caledonian Road, N.1, 30 n.2, 365, 366, 387 n.2
Mare Street, Hackney, E.8, 219, 223
Monastery of St James, 600 Green Lanes, Stoke Newington, N.16, 225
Nazarene College, Kent House Road, Sydenham, 221
New Catholic and Free 'Pro-Cathedral', 5 Bramshill Road, N.10, 381
Oratory of St Ignatius of Antioch, 9 Matilda Street, Islington, N.1, 280, 293, 365
Our Lady of the Rosary, Marylebone, N.W.1, 382
Pre-Nicene Gnostic Catholic Church, 38 Kensington Place, W.8, 492, 494

Index of Places

Index of Places

Mitcham, Surrey, 378
Mochave, Montgoms., 44
Monteil, France, 312
Montepellier (Hérault), 156
Montreal, 92, 108, 110
Morocco, 521
Moscow, Idaho, 513
Mosul, Iraq, 34, 243
Mount Lebanon, Syria, 34
Mount St Bernard's Abbey, Leics., 63, 66, 68
Mount Vernon, N.Y., 506
München-Gladbach, Rhine Province, 406

Namur, Belgium, 92
Nantes, France, 316, 518
Nashotah, Wis., 95
Newark, N. J., 437
New Barnet, Herts (Abbey of Christ the King), 233, 235, 284–90, 320, 465, 496
Newport, Mon., 296, 298
Newton Abbot, Devon, 294, 399
New York, N.Y., 113, 124, 235, 262, 266, 350, 419, 425, 426 (St Nicholas Russian Orthodox Cathedral), 461, 485, 508 (Holy Orthodox Church in America), 512, 513, 514 (Eastern Orthodox Catholic Church in America)
New Zealand, 348, 349, 350, 353
Niagara Falls, N.Y., 434, 435, 438
Nigeria, 250, 314, 541 n.2
Nineveh, Assyria, 540
Northampton, England, 446, 447
North Burnaby, B.C., 364 n.2, 484
Norway, 512
Nottingham, England, 174, 180 n.3, 353 n.3
Nuremburg, Germany, 384

Offord d'Arcy, Hunts., 46
Orpington, Kent, 174
Outwood, Yorks., 232
Oxford, 58, 130, 131, 134, 139, 142, 143, 144, 147, 148, 153, 154, 155

Painswick, Glos., 326
Painthorpe Abbey, Yorks, 340, 345, 414
Palithamen, South India, 135
Panama, 535
Paraguay, 365
Paris, 91, 191, 303, 304, 305, 306, 315, 384, 409, 411, 485

Parkstone, Dorset, 270
Pennsylvania, 391, 503
Perth, Scotland, 271
Pevensey, Kent, 47
Philippines, 529–34
Piacenza, Italy, 120
Plymouth, Devon, 158, 353 n.3
Point Loma, Calif., 351
Poland, 385, 391, 400, 516–23, 526
Pont Colbert Abbey, France, 126, 127
Portugal, 419, 528, 529
Preston, Lancs., 232 n.5
Prinknash Abbey, Glos., 328, 336, 342, 404
Puebla, Mexico, 440
Puerto Rico, 504, 527

Reading, Berks., 406
Redruth, Cornwall, 151
Repton, Diocese of, 459 n.1
Ripon, Wis., 414
Rochester, N.Y., 505
Rodbourne Cheney, Wilts., 152
Romainville (Seine), 312
Rome, 33, 118, 119, 314, 361, 384, 451, 485
Rotterdam, 353 n.3
Rouen, 410
Runwell St Mary, Essex, 375, 466, 467, 498
Ruschklikon, Switzerland, 310, 400
Russia, 32, 53, 118

San Antonio, Texas, 440
San Fernando, Trinidad, 514
San Francisco, Calif., 100, 103, 414
Saint-Dolay, Brittany, 316
Sainte-Amande, Roche-Savine, France, 308
St Albans, Herts., 446, 447
St Joseph's Island, Ont., 120, 121
St Peter's-in-Thanet, Kent, 353 n.3
Scandinavia, 364, 512, 572
Scranton, Pa., 264, 524, 526
Seattle, Wash., 353 n.3
Selby, Yorks., 75, 76
Selsey, Diocese of, 459 n.1
Schaerbeik–Brussels, 491
Sheffield, Yorks, 380, 382, 391
Shickshinny, Pa., 437
Siluria, Diocese of, 459 n.1
Sion, Lorraine, 303
Smyrna, 55
Solesmes Abbey, France, 309

592

Index of Places

South Africa, 222, 314
South Creake, Norfolk, 273, 274
South Harrow, Middlesex, 44, 445
South Mymms, Herts., 89, 214, 215, 324, 408
South Viet-Nam, 539
Spain, 222 n.1, 527, 528
Spaxton, Somerset, 488 n.1
Springfield, Mass., 426
Staines, Middlesex, 389
Stapenhall, Staffs., 151, 394
Stockton-on-Tees, Co. Durham, 193
Stuttgart, 157
Sudbury, Middlesex, 380 n.2
Sulgrave, Northants., 374, 375, 457
Sweden, 365, 512
Switzerland, 365
Sydney, N.S.W., 347, 349, 353, 354, 356, 357, 366

Terrington St Clement, Norfolk, 42
Texas, 407, 438, 441
Thaxted, Essex, 272 n.4
Thomastown, Co. Tipperary, 157, 209, 212
Thorney, Cambs., 375
Toledo, Ohio, 113
Tonbridge, Kent, 339
Toronto, Ont., 245, 246, 439 n.1
Toulouse, 311
Tregynon, Montgoms., 43
Trichur, South India, 132
Trowbridge, Wilts, 159
Tunbridge Wells, Kent, 224
Twyford, Berks., 406
Tydd St Mary, Cambs., 375

Uganda, 269

Uppsala, Sweden, 321
Uruguay, 365
Utrecht, 172, 416

Vancouver, B.C., 350, 485
Veracruz, Mexico, 440, 441
Verulam, Diocese of, 459 n.1

Walhain, Wis., 110
Wallington, Surrey, 474
Walmer, Kent, 210
Warwickshire, 540
Waukegan, Ill., 111, 124, 413, 414, 415, 417, 418, 428
West Africa, 314
West Bridgford, Notts., 369
West Drayton, Middlesex, 331, 332, 399
West Malling Abbey, Kent, 183, 272, 326
West Torrington, Lincs., 54, 75 n.1, 82, 83, 84
Westville, Ill., 438
Windsor, Berks., 371, 372
Winnipeg, Manitoba, 123
Wisconsin, 438
Wolverhampton, 54, 56 n.1
Woodchester Priory, Glos., 158
Woodford Green, Essex, 236
Woodstock, N.Y., 415, 426, 427
Woolwich, Kent, 49
Worcestershire, 540
Worksop, Notts., 159

Yeddingham, Yorks., 44
York, England, 345, 513, 522
Yugoslavia, 337, 401, 521

Zion City, Ill., 364 n.3